T0330914

The Routledge Handbook of Maritime Management

'This handbook can be used as an excellent reference for undergraduates and postgraduates in maritime studies.'

— *Professor Jin Wang, Liverpool John Moores University, UK*

This handbook provides a wide-ranging, coherent, and systematic analysis of maritime management, policy, and strategy development. It undertakes a comprehensive examination of the fields of management and policy-making in shipping by bringing together chapters on key topics of seminal scientific and practical importance.

Within 21 original chapters, authoritative experts describe and analyze concepts at the cutting edge of knowledge in shipping. Themes include maritime management and policy, ship finance, port and maritime economics, and maritime logistics. A study examines the determinants of ship management fees. Aspects of corporate governance in the shipping industry are reviewed and there is a critical review of the ship investment literature. Other topics featured include the organization and management of tanker and dry bulk shipping companies, environmental management in shipping with reference to energy-efficient ship operation, a study of the BIMCO Shipping KPI standard, utilizing the Bunker Adjustment Factor as a strategic decision-making instrument, and slow steaming in the maritime industry. All chapters are written to provide implications for further advancement in professional practice and research.

The Routledge Handbook of Maritime Management will be of great interest to relevant students, researchers, academics, and professionals alike. It provides abundant opportunities to guide further research in the areas covered but will also initiate and inspire effective maritime management.

Photis M. Panayides is Professor at the Department of Commerce, Finance, and Shipping, Cyprus University of Technology, Cyprus.

The Routledge Handbook of Maritime Management

Edited by Photis M. Panayides

LONDON AND NEW YORK

First published 2019 by Routledge

2 Park Square, Milton Park, Abingdon, Oxon, OX14 4RN

605 Third Avenue, New York, NY 10017

Routledge is an imprint of the Taylor & Francis Group, an informa business

First issued in paperback 2020

British Library Cataloguing-in-Publication Data
A catalogue record for this book is available from the British Library

Library of Congress Cataloging-in-Publication Data
Names: Panayides, Photis M., author.
Title: The Routledge handbook of maritime management/edited by Photis M. Panayides.
Description: First Edition. | New York: Routledge, 2019. |
Series: Routledge international handbooks | Includes index.
Identifiers: LCCN 2018057251| ISBN 9781138671249 (hbk) |
ISBN 9781315617138 (ebk)
Subjects: LCSH: Shipping–Management. | Ships–Management. |
Merchant marine–Management. | International cooperation.
Classification: LCC HE571 .P276 2019 | DDC 387.5068–dc23
LC record available at https://lccn.loc.gov/2018057251

ISBN: 978-1-138-67124-9 (hbk)
ISBN: 978-0-367-72991-2 (pbk)

Typeset in Bembo
by Deanta Global Publishing Services, Chennai, India

Contents

Contents

Preface

The Handbook of Maritime Management represents a compilation of chapters from academics and researchers in the fields of shipping, maritime management, ship finance, port and maritime economics, and maritime logistics. What makes this book different is that the contributors were provided with general guidelines as to the academic and quality criteria for publishing a chapter in the book but had the freedom to choose the topic. This approach provides added value as it ensures that contributors worked on a topic of direct interest to their research agenda and expertise whilst at the same time highlighting contemporary areas at the cutting edge of research in maritime management.

Management entails the organization of resources and coordination of activities of companies or organizations to achieve defined objectives. Management is important for achieving competitive advantage whereas managerial ability is central to the formulation and implementation of corporate policy guidelines and strategies that affect long-term business viability.

In an environment of competitive intensity, market uncertainty, volatility and market, financial, and environmental risk, such as those prevailing in the shipping industry, the ability to plan and implement effective policies and innovative strategies as well as the art of managing are especially important.

The aim of this volume is to compile a set of relevant papers that focus on topics identified by the contributors as of seminal scientific and practical importance, written by authoritative experts, and describing and analyzing concepts at the cutting edge of knowledge. It is envisaged that the approach to the selection and compilation of the volume will lead to further research and empirical investigation in the field of maritime management.

In this context, the volume contains topics on policy, company management, maritime financial management, port management, and maritime logistics. From a policy perspective, contributions include the development of European Union and international maritime shipping policies and an analysis of policies for the development of a ship finance centre such as Singapore. In the context of shipping company management, the first chapter provides a comprehensive overview of maritime management which includes managerial characteristics and management functions, organizational structures, and performance measurement and management. Other relevant contributions deal with the organization and management of tanker and dry bulk shipping companies, environmental management in shipping with reference to energy-efficient ship operation, a study of the BIMCO Shipping KPI Standard for performance measurement in maritime companies to ensure sustainability, using the Bunker Adjustment Factor as a strategic decision-making instrument, and slow steaming in the maritime industry. In addition, a study examines the determinants of ship management fees, representing an innovative approach to the field of third-party ship management. Aspects of corporate governance in the shipping industry are reviewed, and the book also includes a critical review of the ship investment literature, highlighting opportunities for further research. Other relevant topics in the ship finance context include the ownership structure of US listed shipping companies, and potential research contributions are made by the chapters examining the appraisal of shipping investment projects using real options, freight risk management, and derivatives and shipping credit risk analysis, measurement, and management.

Finally, relevant contributions are made in the area of maritime logistics and ports through contributions that deal with an overview of contemporary maritime logistics and supply chain management decision areas, investments, and financial instruments in port management, inter-organizational relationships of European port management entities, private sector participation, port efficiency and economic development, and the impact of climate change on port organization.

Contributors

Roar Adland, Norwegian School of Economics

Christoforos Andreou, Cyprus University of Technology

Panayiotis C. Andreou, Cyprus University of Technology

Diego Artuso, Pricewaterhouse Coopers, Italy

Yari Borbon-Galvez, University of Antwerp, Belgium

Tobias Buer, University of Bremen, Germany

Pierre Cariou, KEDGE Business School, Bordeaux, France

Evangelos F. Darousos, World Maritime University, Sweden

Janos Ferencz, Panteia, The Netherlands

Claudio Ferrari, University of Genoa, Italy

Hans-Dietrich Haasis, University of Bremen, Germany

Yile He, University of Manitoba, Canada

Stavros Karamperidis, Plymouth Business School, UK

Isabella Karasamani, Cyprus University of Technology

Manolis G. Kavussanos, Athens University of Economics and Business, Greece

Aseem Kinra, Copenhagen Business School, Denmark

Paraskevi Kladaki, University of the Aegean, Greece

Herbert Kotzab, University of Bremen, Germany

Contributors

Neophytos Lambertides, Cyprus University of Technology

Menno Langeveld, Panteia, The Netherlands

Yui-yip Lau, The Hong Kong Polytechnic University

D. V. Lyridis, National Technical University of Athens, Greece

Hilde Meersman, University of Antwerp, Belgium

Maximo Q. Mejia Jr., World Maritime University, Sweden

Konstantinos D. Melas, University of Central Lancashire Cyprus

Antonis A. Michis, Central Bank of Cyprus

Enrico Musso, University of Genoa, Italy

Adolf K.Y. Ng, University of Manitoba, Canada

Erland Østensen, Norwegian School of Economics

Athanasios A. Pallis, University of the Aegean, Greece

Photis M. Panayides, Cyprus University of Technology

C. Papaleonidas, National Technical University of Athens, Greece

Francesco Parola, University of Genoa, Italy

Yasmine Rashed, Arab Academy for Science, Technology & Maritime Transport, Egypt

Satya Sahoo, World Maritime University, Sweden

Giovanni Satta, University of Genoa, Italy

Jasmine Siu Lee Lam, Nanyang Technological University, Singapore

Christa Sys, University of Antwerp, Belgium

Alessio Tei, Newcastle University, UK

Ioannis Theotokas, University of Piraeus, Greece

Kristoffer Thomassen, Norwegian School of Economics

Jose L. Tongzon, Inha University in Tashkent, Uzbekistan

Dimitris A. Tsouknidis, Cyprus University of Technology

Thierry Vanelslander, University of Antwerp, Belgium

Ilias D. Visvikis, American University of Sharjah, UAE

Eddy Van de Voorde, University of Antwerp, Belgium

Sun Xi, Nanyang Technological University, Singapore

Barry Zondag, Significance b.v., The Netherlands

1

Principles of maritime business management

Photis M. Panayides

1.1 Introduction

Although management is more of an art rather than a science and management achievements may depend to a large extent on individual managerial characteristics and traits (e.g. Malmendier et al., 2011), managerial decision-making and other management practices can benefit from the knowledge created through scientific inquiry. Management in the shipping industry is even more challenging, bearing in mind the specific external environmental circumstances that maritime companies face in the pursuit of their short-term and long-term strategic goals. Shipping is a highly capital-intensive industry and financing and other management decisions are made within a highly risky economic, physical and financial environment. The highly volatile freight rates (see Kavussanos, 1996) dictate, to a large extent, various managerial decisions in operational ship deployment (e.g. time vs spot market decisions), whereas the consequent impact on ship prices influences ship sale, purchasing, newbuilding and scrapping decisions. At the same time, the volatile market environment may present shipowners and other maritime decision makers with an array of opportunities that effective managers and entrepreneurs may be able to spot and take advantage of (see Harlaftis and Theotokas, 2013). For example, in the late 90s, low freight-rate levels forced Norwegian investors to sell off their K/S shares at distress prices allowing a quick-thinking entrepreneur to establish majority shareholdings in K/S companies and later on force the sale of assets at higher prices. Based on this business acumen, the entrepreneur went on to establish one of the biggest and most successful maritime enterprises, General Maritime Corporation. It is also part of the shipping folklore literature how Aristotle Onassis, John Fredriksen, Stavros Niarchos and other shipping entrepreneurs managed, through shipping business acumen and shrewd managerial decisions, to establish successful enterprises and amassed fortunes in a highly competitive business environment.

The aim of this chapter is to provide readers with a comprehensive overview of management concepts with relevant applications to the business of shipping. After the introduction, Section 1.2 defines management indicating the key management goals and associated functions of management. Management takes place at different levels within the organization including at higher strategic level and at a lower operational level. Section 1.3 discusses the relation between management and strategy, highlighting the distinction between corporate strategy and business strategy. The key functions of management, such as planning, organizing, staffing, leading, coordinating, and controlling are discussed in Section 1.4, which also explains the significant role of delegation and decentralization in management. One of the key management functions is to develop effective organizational structures that will facilitate efficient organizational processes. Organizational structures and departmentalization in shipping companies are discussed in Section 1.5, whereas Section 1.6 describes the key organizational processes that take place in a shipping company. Section 1.7 focuses on the management aspect of control by discussing key concepts in the measurement and management of performance in shipping. Particular reference is given to the analysis of key performance indicators that can be used to measure shipping company performance in the context of financial, customer, and internal processes and innovation and growth objectives. The chapter considers how advances in information technology and shipping-related innovations can have a significant impact on the shipping industry and in using data to make more informed decisions. The chapter concludes by highlighting areas where further research will potentially provide significant contributions to the maritime management literature.

1.2 Management defined

One of the leading gurus of management, Peter Drucker, once said that every achievement of management is the achievement of a manager, and every failure is the failure of a manager. The vision, dedication and integrity of managers determine whether there is management or mismanagement (Drucker, 2004).

Management is the process of reaching organizational goals through the deployment of organizational resources (human, technological, etc.) and development of internal and external inter-organizational relationships. Management is a never-ending process or series of continuing and related activities. Management is a continuous process that evolves over time and entails activities that are fundamental to the operation of the business. Hence, even if goals are achieved, it is the task of management to develop new goals and plans for achieving them (Lussier, 2018).

On this basis, management focuses on the achievement of organizational goals within specified timeframes. The ultimate responsibility and accountability for achieving the organization's goals lies with the managers. One of the fundamental tasks of managers is to accumulate a resource base for the organization that will be allocated efficiently among competing internal users. One of the major resources is people and managers need to work with people, organizing them into departments and teams, or through people via delegation and decentralization to achieve earmarked organizational objectives that relate to customer and business performance. With respect to the external activities, one of the main tasks of managers is the development of business value propositions to which the market place will respond in accordance to a predefined strategy. Managers in the shipping industry should then seek to determine what really creates value for customers. For instance, customers in liner shipping may value freight cost, shipping punctuality and reliability. In ship operations, oil majors may focus on safety, the environment, image and reputation. Shipowners may be looking for asset preservation, maximization of earning period and operational reliability from their ship managers. Time chartering is about punctuality in delivery and re-delivery and minimization of off-hires.

Management entails the performance of certain management tasks and functions. However, integral in the performance of functions such as planning, organizing, leading, staffing, coordination, and controlling is that these functions need to be undertaken by managers in the context of achieving corporate and business strategy goals.

1.3 Management and strategy

Strategy entails an assessment of where the company is, a statement of where it plans to be at a finite point in the future, and a plan of how to get there. Companies in the shipping industry have various strategies at both corporate and business level.

Corporate level strategy involves decisions at a higher managerial level that affect the organization's corporate direction and existence (Puranam and Vanneste, 2016). One critical corporate strategy decision is the identification of the business or set of businesses that the company should be in. If the decision is to invest in a number of strategic business units, then corporate strategists need to decide how to coordinate effectively and efficiently resource flows across the corporate portfolio. Typical corporate level strategies in shipping are decisions of merger and acquisition (Alexandridis and Singh, 2016; Fusillo, 2009), strategic alliance or joint venture formation (Panayides and Wiedmer, 2011; Rau and Spinler, 2017), diversification and divestiture, and mode of exit (Lorange, 2005).

Business strategy on the other hand involves strategic decisions and strategies that aim at achieving and maintaining a competitive advantage in product-market domains. It entails decisions pertaining to which markets to serve and which customer segments to target, the adoption of a positioning strategy that will differentiate the company from competitors, the distribution channels to reach customers as well as the communication channels to reach the markets, and the scope and scale of the activities to be performed (Brooks, 1993; Casaca and Marlow, 2005).

Setting strategy requires companies to develop a vision and mission statement and strategic intent in the context of internal and external strategic challenges (environmental, regulatory), and to define the areas of competitive advantage.

Vision does not entail any measurable goals or timeframes and merely represents a general future aspiration. A mission statement is more focused and addresses the perspective of who the organization serves (e.g. a tanker owner will be focusing on oil majors), what value the company is willing to deliver to the customer (e.g. quality, safe transportation of oil), and how the organization plans to deliver that (e.g. by harnessing employee competencies). In this context a mission is specific yet succinct and can be refined and changed based on changing economic or environmental circumstances.

1.4 Management functions

The primary challenge for managers is to be able to tackle daily problems in a creative manner. To address the challenge, management has been classified into the undertaking of major functions, namely planning, organizing, staffing, leading coordinating, and controlling (Lamond, 2004; Mintzberg, 1973). The functions are highly integrated when carried out in the day-to-day realities of running an organization.

According to Koontz and O'Donell (1968), planning is deciding in advance what to do, how to do it and who is to do it, and bridges the gap between where we are and where we want to go. Planning is concerned with the success of the organization in the short term as well as in the long term. Typically, planning involves flexibility, as the planner must coordinate with all levels of management and leadership in the organization. Planning also involves knowledge of the company's resources and the future objectives of the business. In the shipping business there are several areas where planning is of the essence, not least finding the best adaptation and deployment of the fleet (short-term versus long-term charters) (e.g. Panayides, 2018) relative to the volatile market conditions, or planning for liner ship deployment under chartering-in options (Meng et al., 2012). In this context, one of the most critical areas that requires careful planning is the fleet renewal decision, which consists of deciding how many and which types of ships to add to the fleet and which available ships to dispose of (Alvarez et al., 2011; Pantuso et al., 2014). Planning permeates many other areas of maritime business management. Maritime business managers need to plan for the sourcing of seafarers amidst supply constraints (Mitroussi, 2008). Human resources then need to be appropriately deployed, which requires careful planning from the crewing department (Anastasiou, 2017). Planning is of the essence for the maintenance programme of the ships and for dry docking, for ship inspections (Furnival and Crispe, 2017), for the purchasing of spare parts and consumables, and for the training and development of the workforce.

Organizing is used to create a mechanism to put plans into action and for that reason managers need to develop an appropriate organizational structure, the chain of command within the company, and relevant job descriptions. The organizing function of leadership controls the overall organizational structure of the company. The structure is usually represented by an organization chart, which provides a graphic representation of the chain of command, and delineates lines of communication, authority, responsibility, and accountability. Organizing involves designating tasks and responsibilities to subordinates that have the specific set of skills to undertake and complete the tasks. People within the organization are given work assignments that contribute to the company's goals. Tasks are organized so that the output of each individual contributes to the success of departments, which, in turn, contributes to the success of divisions, which ultimately contributes to the success of the organization (see also Pastra et al., 2017).

The staffing function of management controls all recruitment and personnel needs of the organization. It is especially important in shipping, since it deals with the recruitment and management of shore-based staff as well as personnel on board ships. Staffing involves more than just recruitment; it also encompasses training and development, performance appraisals, promotions and transfers. In the context of crew recruitment, the relevant manager needs to undertake appropriate assessments of the needs and source competent and qualified seafarers through programmes of collaboration with crew agencies and marine academies. In addition, the manager needs to make decisions on the appropriate training, programmes of motivation, and policies for dealing with seafarer behaviour on board.

Leading can be defined as guiding the activities of organization members in the direction that helps the organization move towards the fulfilment of the goals. It includes decision-making, communicating, motivating, selecting, and developing people. Managers may be distinguished and classified into leaders or administrators (Northhouse, 2018). Leaders are relationship-oriented and focus on transformational-type activities. On the other hand, administrators are task-oriented and focus on transaction-type activities. Leaders develop relationships internally and externally; they motivate and inspire the workforce in accomplishing organizational objectives. They are also actively involved in developing external business relationships with a particular focus on growing the business. On the other hand, administrators are managers characterized by order and compliance, by setting tasks and measuring results and performance. Managers with a focus on administrative duties are more concerned with maintenance of the status quo, monitoring and controlling staff, spreading the organizational culture, planning and budgeting, problem solving, efficiency, and staying on the right path.

On the other hand, leaders have different traits and characteristics. They focus on the future by delineating a vision and providing inspiration and a sense of purpose and direction for followers. They deal with change and the effects of change, trying to develop the business via innovation to achieve growth and organizational objectives. Successful leaders deflect attention away from themselves and encourage others to voice their opinions. They are great communicators, especially with respect to performance expectations, indicating the organization's core values and mission and also ensuring that their vision is translated into actionable objectives that are appropriately executed. They are shrewd decision makers that lead by example and challenge people to think, having a good understanding of the capabilities of people in the organization. Great leaders are particularly focused on business performance; they measure organizational performance and provide rewards as motivation to successful and consistent high performers. They provide continuous feedback and properly allocate and deploy the organizational human skills and capabilities. They are great problem solvers, yet they are always on the lookout to learn new things and are receptive to ideas internally and externally. They are committed to making themselves better through the wisdom of others while creating a positive and inspiring workplace culture. Successful leaders expand their domain by investing in mutually beneficial relationships and genuinely enjoy their leadership responsibilities. Leadership characteristics are essential in the context of maritime management where leadership charisma and team orientation are particularly important traits (Fjaerli et al., 2015).

Key to managerial decisions within the contexts of leading and organizing is the implementation of the management techniques of delegation and decentralization (Agrell and Bogetoft, 2017; Dobrajska et al., 2015). Delegation is the process of transferring authority and creating responsibility between a manager and subordinates. Delegation can take place without decentralization and is confined to managers and subordinates. The purpose of delegation is to ease the burden on managers of having to fulfil too many tasks while at the same time fulfilling all required responsibilities in terms of executing particular tasks and operations. The responsibility still lies with the manager, as authority is delegated but not responsibility, hence control remains with the delegator who can also withdraw authority at any time. Delegation is an important part of the management process.

Decentralization on the other hand is both delegation and dispersion of authority, between top-level management and departments or units of the enterprise (as opposed to between manager and subordinate). In this context, both authority and responsibility are transferred from the top manager to lower-level managers who are now free to make decisions and exercise authority on the decision-making process as well as responsible and accountable for the results. Withdrawal of authority is not a simple, straightforward act like in the case of delegation, as this concept is a philosophy of management that permeates the organization. Decentralization is not possible without delegation.

The coordinating function of management controls all organizing, planning, and personnel-related activities, and ensures that activities are well integrated. Fundamental to this is that all departments share organizational goals and objectives are totally aligned to the strategy of the organization. On this basis, coordinating involves communication, supervision, and direction by management.

Controlling is an ongoing process and involves establishing performance standards and monitoring the output of organizational processes and routines to ensure that targets are met, and includes monitoring of employee performance. It entails the development of performance standards, measuring, evaluating, and correcting performance (see Otley, 1999). Managers need to gather information that measures performance; to compare present performance to pre-established performance norms, and to determine the next action plan and modifications for meeting the desired performance parameters.

1.5 Organizational structures and departmentalization

In terms of developing the appropriate organizational structure, traditionally, in the shipping industry, companies had a hierarchical structure that would entail the managing director at the top of the hierarchy and the different departments organized in parallel to each other and further sub-divided hierarchically into fleets. However, organizations may also adopt a flatter organizational structure. Organizational structures are very important because they determine responsibilities, accountabilities, and how leadership is disseminated throughout the organization, whilst at the same time indicating the method of information flow (Pastra et al., 2017).

A flat organizational structure has few or no levels of management between management and other employees at a lower level. This means that employees are not under direct supervision as in a formal hierarchical organization and may also have, as a result, increased involvement in making decisions or in the decision-making process. A hierarchical organization, on the other hand, follows a pyramidal layout where every employee in the organization, except the CEO, is subordinate to someone else. There are multiple entities in the organizational structure that eventually descend into the base of staff-level employees, who sit at the bottom of the pyramid. A flat organizational structure has certain advantages emanating from the fewer levels of rank and hierarchy, which make such organizations leaner and less bureaucratic. The latter aspect may be encountered in a hierarchical structure since the different levels of hierarchy will need to be at least informed if not to examine and provide approval in the decision-making process. In a flat structure, employees are encouraged to expand their expertise, take risks, and work together, enabling a process of rotation as opposed to climbing a hierarchical ladder. Managers might regularly report progress to the CEO, and get insight from the CEO, but the CEO isn't micromanaging every daily detail.

Maritime companies tend to move away from the traditional pure vertical hierarchy into a more process-based structure. This has been manifested by the development of the so-called fleet teams, which are smaller groups consisting of people from a variety of backgrounds who are entrusted with the management and organization of a given number of ships. For example, in a fleet team there would be one person from operations, technical, purchasing, crewing, and accounts who would have the ultimate responsibility to liaise with the captains of their allocated ships and make decisions regarding the operations of the vessels. The structure reduces interfaces between the different departments and makes the management process much more efficient. At the same time, each fleet team has clear ownership of the ship management process and is responsible and thus accountable for the results. The performance and appraisal process is also more efficient as each team can be given specific targets and performance indicators facilitating further improvements where necessary.

1.5.1 Shipping company departments

Shipping companies are organized into several departments, each responsible for undertaking responsibility for particular tasks and achieving specific objectives. The main departments include operations, technical, crewing, marine and safety, chartering (or commercial department), sale and purchase, purchasing, insurance and claims, and support departments such as accounting and information technology (IT).

The operations department is responsible for the day-to-day running of the vessels and in particular the monitoring of the vessels' performance during time and voyage charters with respect to the cargo and its safe transportation, crew, safety, environment, and other matters of a technical and financial/accounting nature (see also Visvikis and Panayides, 2017). Operations are responsible for the evaluation and appointment of shipbrokers and port agents, and are always in close liaison with the masters and agents for the issue of voyage instructions and other operational matters during a voyage charter. Operations also undertake post-fixture work, which includes the remittance of disbursements and payments, including the invoicing for freight and hire, checking and defense of off-hires as well as the calculation of laytime and invoicing for demurrage. The operations department is in close cooperation with other departments such as marine and safety and the technical department, particularly in relation to the supply of navigational aids for the ships as well as the arrangement of vetting inspections.

The responsibilities of the technical department include the maintenance of the seaworthiness and cargoworthiness of vessels in accordance to national and international laws and regulations and the requirements of port states, flag states, classification societies, and those of the charterers themselves (Furnival and Crispe, 2017). The technical department is staffed by people with engineering knowledge and ship technical expertise who are able to closely monitor the day-to-day performance of the vessel through frequent visits, and develop and implement plans for maintenance, repairs, and upgrading of the vessel's systems.

Crew departments in maritime companies are principally engaged in the recruitment and management of crew personnel on board ships. In terms of crew recruitment, the departments aim to obtain high-quality crew (qualified, skilled and medically fit) quickly at the least possible cost and, for that reason, they have a number of cooperation initiatives with marine agencies and maritime academies. It is also possible to sub-contract with crew managers for hiring shipboard personnel. The department needs to monitor the manning levels and forecast the manning needs (determination of required qualifications and skills) for the fleet of vessels (Anastasiou, 2017). In terms of crew management, the department is responsible for the training, promotion, and retention of the crew in the company's database. The performance of the seafarers needs to be consistently evaluated and updated records are kept. The annual crew budgets are also set and controlled by the department.

The marine and safety department is one of the most critical in a maritime organization, not least because the fulfilment of its objectives is directly related to safety, operational reliability, and ultimately charters and revenue. The department coordinates with charterers, especially long-term customers such as in the oil trades, arranging for vetting inspections, providing guidance to masters, officer and crew as to safety matters, and updating on regulations and safety processes; it also follows up on certification and the ISM Code, and liaises with classification societies to ensure the continuous certification of the organization and its ships. The marine and safety department may also undertake the conduct of training seminars for seafarers, deal with the investigation of accidents, and develop safety and other operational processes.

Purchasing is responsible for supplying the vessels with necessary deck and engine stores and consumables including bunkers, lubricants, engine and deck spare parts, chemicals, and paints, using a documented purchasing process. The purchasing department needs to fulfil its processes efficiently but at the same time obtain high-quality products at competitive prices.

The commercial or chartering department is responsible for the utilization of the company's assets (ships) to ensure their deployment on beneficial chartering terms, be it voyage, time, or long-term charters such as bareboat charters and contracts of affreightment (Assimenos, 2017; Panayides, 2018). The department should have an established network of brokers to ensure the collection and dissemination of relevant information that would lead to rapid deployment of assets. It is the task of management to develop efficient interface and internal processes to accomplish the above tasks. It is also imperative that this department pursues and develops close business relationships with reputable clients and established charterers.

The insurance and claims department is responsible for negotiating and taking out insurance for H&M, P&I, war risks, loss of hire, and freight, demurrage, and defense insurance (FD&D), or other types of insurance that may be required, as well as deal with claims prevention and claims negotiation and settlement.

The sale and purchase department oversees the processes that will ultimately lead to the fulfilment of the company's S&P strategy, fleet disposal and renewal via newbuilding and second-hand projects, and fleet development strategy. To do so, it needs to have good long-lasting relationship with major broking houses so as to identify sellers and buyers of ships and to keep accurate data on prices and trends, bidding levels, and construction projects. The sale and purchase department (S&P) normally works in close cooperation with the chartering department as the employment strategy and employment prospects of ships are critical in ship investment appraisal.

The accounts and finance department is a key support department that is made up of competent and qualified personnel with specific expertise in book-keeping and the preparation of accounts. The task of the department is to control all aspects of debit and credit, to ensure suppliers' payment, and to produce balance sheets and profit and loss accounts as well as other relevant financial reports as required by management.

The department is also responsible for preparing the yearly master budget that will be critical in the decision-making processes of management. Key aspects of the tasks of the finance and accounts department include controlling the cash flow of the business, investment appraisal and feasibility studies, negotiations with financial institutions, overseeing investments, and honoring of debts of the company.

Information technology is a support department but has the all-important role of ensuring that the company's communication, data dissemination, and electronic storage systems are fully operational.

1.6 Organizational processes and routines

Internal organizational processes and routines focus on analysing, designing, and developing workflows to improve customer service and optimize and/or reduce operational costs. For this reason, organizations may require re-structuring and re-organization. According to Davenport and Short (1990), a business process is a set of logically related tasks performed to achieve a defined business outcome.

In this context, business process re-engineering (e.g. Champy, 1995), emphasized a holistic focus on business objectives and how processes related to them, encouraging full-scale recreation of processes rather than iterative optimization of sub-processes.

Of fundamental importance in maritime management is the development of organizational processes and routines that will safeguard the efficiency of the daily operations of the company. Managers need to develop organizational process protocols where specific processes are defined in a structured process flow chart. The processes need to be followed by the employees undertaking the specific activity and relevant key performance indicators recording process performance will also be developed. According to Pastra et al. (2017), organizational processes in maritime companies need to be developed in crewing (crew recruitment, crew management, and crew training); in purchasing (selection and contracting with suppliers, ordering, order processing, and invoicing); marine and safety (monitoring and maintaining safety and pollution prevention on board ships); bunkering (selection and purchase of bunkers when needed, at the right quality and minimum possible costs); a wide range of financial and accounting processes including treatment of revenue from spot and time charters post-fixture work; overseeing bank accounts, and capital market monitoring. They must also have processes for the preparation of financial statements and other financial reports and for payroll, ship financing (second-hand and newbuilding vessel acquisition, method of financing and vessel sales), dry docking, insurance and claims, port agency, and IT processes.

In addition to the above processes, other value-added processes may be developed depending on the type of shipping operation. In the context of liner shipping for instance, Lu (2007) identified seven capability dimensions for liner shipping companies. These are purchasing, operation, human resource management, customer service, information integration, pricing, and financial management. The findings suggested that the operation capability is perceived as the most important dimension, followed by customer service, human resource management, information integration, pricing, purchasing, and financial management.

Management in shipping companies needs to clearly identify the business processes and establish procedures that each department will implement so that business objectives are achieved.

1.7 Measuring and managing performance

Performance is the ability to carry out a task or fulfil some promise or claim. Performance measurement is the process of collecting, analyzing and/or reporting information regarding the performance of an organization. It can involve studying processes/strategies within organizations to see whether the output is in line with what was intended or should have been achieved. Performance measurement is one of the fundamental cornerstones of modern management, manifested in the well known maxim that if you cannot measure a business task, then you cannot control it, and if you cannot control it you can neither manage it nor improve it (Harrington, 1991). Performance management (PM) includes activities which ensure that goals are consistently being met in an effective and efficient manner. Performance management can focus on the performance of an organization or a department, and includes the processes to conceive, test, develop, and market a product or service, as well as many other areas including the performance of human resources.

Performance management encompasses a process by which organizations align their resources, systems, and employees to strategic objectives and priorities. Strategic alignment entails the development of an organizational structure and deployment of resources, capabilities, and technological systems with a view towards achieving strategic goals, and leads to higher performance by optimizing the contributions of people, processes, and inputs into the realization of measurable objectives (Henderson and Venkatraman, 1999). Strategic alignment may lead to higher business performance by optimizing the contributions of people, processes, and inputs into the realization of measurable objectives (Venkatraman et al., 1993). Through strategic alignment, resources are directed towards intended purposes and waste is minimized.

An effective performance measurement system can provide management with relevant information for planning and control. Planning determines courses of organizational action, whereas the purpose of control is to ensure that there is progress towards objectives defined in the plan.

In implementing performance management, it is important to develop a thorough understanding of what must be measured and managed. Performance management aims at performance improvement and metrics and key performance indicators (KPIs) are not developed for the sake of having a performance management system but in the context of measuring specific goals of the organization which drive its strategy.

On this basis, a top-down approach is adopted considering the strategy of the company as a basis for developing the performance management system. On the other hand, a bottom-up approach is one that many companies seem to have been adopting, particularly in the shipping industry whereby the concept of performance is narrowly viewed to mean operational performance resulting in the adoption of many operational KPIs without having a particular framework to work with. However, there is a distinct difference between strategy and operational excellence (see Porter, 1996). Whilst both are important for achieving better performance, operational excellence focuses on doing things better (e.g. efficiency-oriented), whereas strategy is about finding ways to do things differently from competitors.

Once strategies and plans have been determined, they must be implemented. To evaluate and control strategy performance, standards of control must also be established. Since strategies and plans are formulated to achieve objectives (profit, market share, sales), these same objectives can be used to establish standards against which performance can be measured. The company's historical trends can also be used to establish objective targets in these areas. Evaluation and control methods make it possible to better determine the impact of current activities on costs, revenues, and profits, but also to respond more quickly to opportunities and threats.

Control is the complement of planning, and neither element is useful without the other. The fundamental step in control is the measurement of deviation from goals and standards which have been set during the planning activity. Control is being exercised when operations of the enterprise follow the guidelines in the plans adopted, are held within limits of tolerance in the face of varying conditions or are returned to an acceptable state after deviations are located.

To enable planning and control, companies need to determine strategy and implement a top-down approach towards performance management. Shipping companies have different strategies; therefore, performance management needs to be multi-dimensional in order to gauge the variation and variety of company goals and objectives. Performance and KPI systems of maritime companies need to accurately and adequately reflect the link between strategy and performance and not be merely focused on operations and performance. Systems which promote and develop universal KPIs may work at operational level but are insufficient at strategic and business level. Companies may be able to benchmark operational KPIs against each other, but it would be insufficient to aim to benchmark strategic KPIs. Companies must recognize that KPIs should reflect and measure their strategies and strategic goals. This is accomplished by focusing on the alignment of strategies, business activities, and metrics with business goals. In maritime companies, a performance management system utilizing KPIs should not be focused on operational, environmental, and safety measures, but should focus on measuring, managing, and analyzing performance to maximize effectiveness and optimize return on investment. Hence, consideration of the different performance levels in maritime management is essential.

Performance measurement permeates across the organization and includes strategic performance at the top management levels down to operational performance at the ship level. In this context, the balanced scorecard framework is an appropriate conceptualization to develop a system for measuring business performance. The balanced scorecard is a concept developed by Kaplan and Norton (1992) and has been widely adopted in business and industry. The system has undergone many iterations and considerable refinements and improvements though its widespread use, so that it is now considered one of the most successful concepts for measuring performance and has been adopted by global companies, including Fortune 500 firms as well as smaller institutions.

At a top management and shareholder level, financial performance would be of particular relevance, and includes but is not limited to goals such as sales revenue, revenue growth, cost, profit margin, cash flow, leverage, shareholder returns, equity risk, credit rating, and cost of capital. Risk management performance, which refers to a company's ability to confront opportunities and threats in its environment, may also be measured. At a customer level, relevant performance goals include, perceived quality, reputation, satisfaction, loyalty, customer retention and customer acquisition. At an operational level, issues like safety, quality, ship performance and environmental performance are of the essence.

According to the balanced scorecard perspective, organizations need to develop a strategy map in order to document their key strategic goals (Kaplan and Norton, 1996). Strategy maps, according to Kaplan and Norton (1996) should have an underlying framework of horizontal perspectives, typically the financial/shareholder perspective, the customer perspective, the internal process perspective, and the learning and growth perspective. Each perspective contains the objectives/goals of the organization (derived from critical success factors, vision, mission, and strategy). Objectives may be linked (causal effects) both within the perspective and across perspectives. Vertical sets of linked objectives are called strategic themes. The themes represent propositions as to how strategy will influence the performance of the organization. Strategy maps are developed for the corporate level and for the organization's departments. To measure performance, each goal in the corporate and department strategy maps is measured by appropriate key performance indicators that the organization develops.

1.8 Managing with key performance indicators

Managers need to continuously analyze and improve the efficiency and effectiveness of their activities and strategies. This is accomplished by focusing on the alignment of strategies and goals with metrics of performance. A key performance indicator (KPI) is a measure of a critical success goal. KPIs represent a set of concise measures focusing on those aspects of performance that are critical for the achievement of the company's strategy, and in extension the fulfilment of organizational goals (Parmenter, 2015). The measures provide insight into whether the company is achieving its objectives, foster accountability for results, and ensure that it maintains the course of strategy implementation.

The diverse and multiple objectives and goals associated with maritime companies and organizations suggest that different aspects of management, production, and operations need to be measured. Given the complexity and multi-facet characteristics of maritime operations, multiple indicators should be used. A goal may have more than one dimension, so for each goal you need one or more KPIs. In addition, at different managerial levels the indicators should be different. This means that there should be different objectives and different measures of performance at strategic, departmental, and lower operational/team level. The responsibility for attaining the targets for each KPI rests with an individual who is considered to be the owner of the KPI set.

Most shipping companies and maritime organizations have recognized the importance of KPIs and many of them have embarked on the development of KPIs and their application and use. However, certain limitations have been recognized. The first is that the KPIs used by many maritime organizations are over-reliant on accounting performance metrics, for example profit/loss and balance sheet measures. Such measures are historical in nature and are known as lag performance measures. Their limitation is that they measure past performance but do not accurately reflect, or even better, drive, future performance. Another limitation is that, because the concept of performance management originated from the need to gauge operation or shipboard performance, measures are mostly of an operational and not business nature (e.g. accidents, near misses, lost time, injury frequency, emissions, etc.). In this context, an additional limitation arises from either the use of unbalanced performance metrics in those important areas of business performance or the fact that drivers of future performance are being overlooked. The third limitation concerns the system that is adopted for measuring management performance, which needs to be both systematic and comprehensive.

KPIs are quantitative indicators that can be of several types, and their effectiveness hinges to a large extent on the use of the appropriate KPI for the measurement of a specific goal.

Input indicators are those that measure the amount of resources that are used during the production process. In maritime management, they may include the amount invested in US$, the number of ships (assets) utilized, the ships' capacity, equipment deployed, and labour hours. Output indicators reflect the results of the production process, i.e. they represent a measure of yield. This may include number of containers handled, amount of cargo carried, number of routes served. Outcome indicators represent the resulting effect from the use of the output, such as customer satisfaction with the transportation process.

There are certain rules that, if followed, will lead to a selection of an appropriate set of KPIs. In choosing KPIs, managers should not overcomplicate the measurement decision. New and missing measures are valuable; however, many times the most obvious measure that comes to mind is also the most appropriate. Measures must be a mix of lead and lag indicators. Individual indicators need to be quantifiable, i.e. precisely measurable and verifiable by arithmetic means. At the same time, they must be practical in the sense that data must be easily retrievable at a low cost. KPIs must be based on accurate and reliable data, i.e. they must be credible. In addition, KPIs must be timely, i.e. data must be collected and reported within a timeframe that is relevant for the decision-making process. Such data must be also be relevant over time, as KPIs are used to make comparisons with other data over time. Finally, KPIs must be easy to calculate and understand. KPIs in shipping companies will not necessarily reflect new measures and new data. Most of the data already exist so it is a matter of collecting the data and using them as practical indicators that interface with existing company processes. At the same time, indicators must be used to evaluate whether or not an organization is getting better, and should also be actionable, i.e. they can be used by management to control and effect change.

KPIs are rarely new to the organization. Many maritime companies have developed and use KPIs. However, persistent questions that relate to the adoption of KPIs in maritime organizations include whether they form part of a comprehensive system to measure business and strategic performance, whether the KPIs are updated, and whether the KPI set is balanced and complete.

Table 1.1 presents relevant KPIs that can be used for measuring performance in maritime management in accordance to the four balanced scorecard perspectives.

1.9 The impact of technology on maritime management

Decision makers in the shipping industry need better, faster, more accurate data upon which to base their decisions. It is imperative that managers have access to data about markets, customers, and processes which are hard for competitors to duplicate and can lead to a competitive advantage. Technology can be used for the collection of data remotely (ship to shore) and facilitate knowledge flows across business units.

In the last few years, shipping companies have embraced the concept of big data analytics as a means for creating value. Value is created by acting on insights that are derived from the analysis of high-volume, high-velocity and high-variety sets of dynamic data, what has been referred to as "big data", i.e. data that exceed the processing capabilities of traditional data management approaches (Russom, 2011; Chen and Zhang, 2014). As more and more data are collected, stored and analyzed, shipping companies should aim to utilize the value of the data in order to make informed decisions at tactical, operational, and strategic levels.

Big data analytics can assist companies by improving their strategy and enhancing operations efficiency, and through value creation to improve their financial performance. This can be achieved through a deeper understanding of business dynamics, intensifying customer engagement, optimizing daily operations, and capitalizing on new sources of revenue (Russom, 2011).

Table 1.1 Strategic Goals and KPIs for Maritime Management

Strategic Goals	Examples of Key Performance Indicators
Financial/shareholder perspective: This perspective focuses on the goals that an organization may set in its pursuit of creating shareholder value, namely by focusing on financial goals that are typically part of the organization's financial statements.	
Revenue, Profit margin, Costs reduction, Return on investment, Return on equity, Return on capital, Risk management, Cost-benefit, Market-share position, Communication effectiveness, Raise awareness of brand/company, Loyalty, Reduce customer attrition.	ROI, Net profit to net sales (profit margin), Net profit to total assets, Return in net worth (equity), Current ratio (current assets to current liabilities), Revenue growth, % cost reduction, Operating income as a percent of sales, Cash conversion cycle, EBITDA, Net revenue, Revenue growth, Return on net assets, Operating income growth, Growth in cost, Increase in investment, Reduction in cost/income ratio, Cost vs budget, Ship's operating costs vs budget, Net sales to total assets (market share), % awareness of brand/company/campaign, Brand/corporate perceptions by customers/non-customers, Duration of customer relationships, Customer retention rate, Percentage of total category spending.
Customer Perspective The perspective focuses on how the customer should view the company, if the company was to be successful in terms of creating customer value.	
Customer satisfaction, Delivering and fulfilling customer needs, Customer attraction, Customer retention, Cost, Price, Operational reliability.	Customer growth rate (increase in number of customers relative to previous period), growth through old customers (percentage of turnover from old customers >3 years/increased turnover), growth through new customers (percentage of turnover from new customers <3 years/increased turnover), Improvement in customer satisfaction index, Customer retention rate, Customer attraction rate (increase in the number of customers of less and more than three years respectively), Budget deviation (purchasing, operation, M&R, crewing, costs vs budgets), days off-hire.
Internal Process Perspective The ability to determine how well the business is running and whether or not the services and operations meet the needs of the customers and are aligned to company objectives. It addresses the internal organizational processes and routines that are essential for the seamless operations of the company in terms of creating and delivering value to its stakeholders.	
Decrease internal process time, Decrease cycle time (internal process for production), Improve business processes (safety, quality, purchasing), Reduce cost of processes, Improve planning and quality, Improve effectiveness of project management.	Number of new products launched, Average time to resolve a customer inquiry, Frequency of customer contact by customer service, Number of safety failures, Number of unscheduled maintenance calls, Production time lost because of maintenance problems, Order fulfilment cycle time (OFCT), Average actual cycle time to fulfil customer orders, Time from order receipt to customer acceptance of the order (source + make + deliver cycle time), Average cycle time, Price per unit (measures ability to reduce prices of supplies), Cost of order fulfilment as a % of revenue, Observations per audit, No. of observations (measured against tolerance values), No. of non-conformities, No. of % incidents reduction, No. of incidents, No. of near accidents, No. of customer complaints and corrective action, Process waste level (waste is any activity that does not add value, e.g. inventory waste: materials WIP or FGI in excess), No. of project completed on time, on budget.

(Continued)

Table 1.1 Continued

Strategic Goals	Examples of Key Performance Indicators

Learning and Growth Perspective
This perspective focuses on the organizational resources that are essential for implementing strategy. The main resource of an organization is its people and their development. In addition, in an era of rapidly changing technological advancements, technology is essential and forms a critical part of this perspective. Focus is placed on how to allocate financial resources that are becoming increasingly scarce.

Staff satisfaction, Staff training, Personnel experience, Innovation capability, Innovation.	Staff satisfaction index, Personnel turnover, Revenue per employee, Personnel training hours, Training hours per employee per period, Turnover rate, Investment in new technology, US$ investment per year/per period.

In the context of shipping, ship management, or ship operations, big data business analytics can help create value and achieve management objectives in several areas as follows:

1 **fuel consumption:** significant cost reduction can be achieved by understanding the conditions for fuel consumption optimisation of a ship at a given level of speed performance through the collection of data from the appropriate sensors and the application of optimization techniques;

2 **route and supply-chain optimization:** big data analytics and optimization techniques can be applied on the data related to the ship routes. This will lead to the development of an optimal route strategy including the order of port calls on the route;

3 **operational efficiency:** value can be created through efficient management of time and identification of areas for cost savings in operations such as port visits, route details, and operational ship data;

4 **maintenance prediction:** data and predictive analytics can be used to identify the areas of the ship that need priority in terms of maintenance. This will ensure that maintenance is considered at the optimum moment, preventing delays, increasing efficiency, and reducing maintenance and off-hire time;

5 **cargo tracking:** added value by providing to customer real-time cargo-tracking information and cost savings by tracking containers that have been lost;

6 **regulatory compliance:** ship ownership and registration data can be used to determine whether the ship poses any safety, legal, or financial risk. The same checks can be carried out for companies;

7 **procurement:** analysis of organizational spend profiles, procurement processes, and future demand to ensure optimal sourcing strategies and supplier selection, optimal bid processes, cost modelling, and supply-chain risk assessment;

8 **market size and competition:** understand the world fleet, ship, and ship ownership information, as well as new markets.

In recent years, there has been heightened consideration related to the potential application of blockchain technology in business management context (Deloitte, 2016; Froystad and Holm,

2015; Goldman Sachs, 2016). In this context, there are various opportunities for the implementation of blockchain technology in maritime management, as follows:

1 **digital records of maritime data/assets/ships:** in shipping, the lifecycle of the asset (ship) can be digitalized and transferred on a blockchain. Blockchains have the ability to create a system where every ship has its own digital passport with all relevant characteristics of the ship and idiosyncratic information including ownership, registration/flag, history of sale and purchase with price-related data, transaction dates and owners, charter party contracts, loans, maintenance records and dry-docking/repairs data, and even the origin of the building materials and their condition recorded digitally;

2 **re-design of maritime management processes:** if maritime data including assets-related data are stored digitally on the blockchain, transactions could be handled on a blockchain in a similar way to how payments between parties are handled using digital currencies. Blockchains enable the development of a fully secure, verifiable system, so that two parties can conduct a transaction immediately, without the need for a trusted third party to verify the transaction. Because the history is easily audited, all parties have confidence in the data being shared, and the time needed to close a transaction can be much shorter;

3 **transparent markets:** by creating a public ledger of transactions, the shipping market becomes more transparent and new platforms may arise. Platforms that provide, for instance, orders, positions, and fixtures will improve transparency, which is bound to increase the performance of the actors in the chartering process thanks to the transparency and the immutable results recorded in the ledger. The immutable track record of performance that is stored in the blockchain may lead to a possible new rating system. An increase of transparency will also allow regulators and agencies such as classification societies and mutual insurance clubs to get a better understanding of the risks affiliated with maritime business;

4 **payment systems:** another point which is argued by literature is using cryptocurrencies in, for instance, lease payments, or as deposits for rental agreements. The advantage is that cryptocurrency can be programmed to escrow and distribute itself. However, as long as digital currencies suffer volatile price fluctuations, it is unlikely that they can be used in a maritime ecosystem;

5 **smart contracts:** smart contracts are inherent to the development of blockchain-based applications. The technology enables self-executing contracts, which can automatize several processes in maritime management.

1.10 Conclusion

This chapter reviewed fundamental principles and core concepts in the management of maritime companies, including organizational design structures, managerial functions, business processes, measuring and managing performance using KPIs, and the potential impact of innovation and new technology in maritime management. It has been recognized that there is a relative lack of relevant papers on these key areas in maritime management, and although many generic concepts would apply, it is also necessary to carry out shipping- and maritime-related research. This book represents an attempt to address conceptually and empirically specific aspects of maritime management. Yet, further research is needed to address issues such as organizational structures, management control, delegation, and decentralization in maritime companies in relation to the impact on business operational process efficiency. In the context of the maritime industry, there are numerous examples of leaders that inspired their organizations to unprecedented success. Yet, research in the area is characterized with relative paucity, providing opportunities for new researchers. In this contemporary era, where research output success hinges on multi-disciplinary approaches, there is scope for investigating the relationship between managerial characteristics and business success in the maritime industry. In addition, recognizing the fundamental difference between operational excellence and strategic excellence, there is ample opportunity to examine the relationship between the two as well as to explore the determinants of operational and strategic performance excellence in shipping, ship operation, and ship management. Finally, there are great opportunities for investigating the application of technology in the maritime management context. This includes the adoption and implementation of big data analysis and the adoption of smart contracts in areas such as ship management and chartering.

References

Agrell, P.J. and Bogetoft, P. (2017) Decentralization policies for supply chain investments under asymmetric information, *Managerial and Decision Economics*, 38(3), 394–408.

Alexandridis, G. and Singh, M. (2016) Mergers and acquisitions in shipping, In Kavussanos, M.G. and Visvikis, I.D. *The International Handbook of Shipping Finance: Theory and Practice*, pp. 371–413.

Alvarez, J.F., P. Tsilingiris, E.S. Engebrethsen, N.M.P. Kakalis (2011) Robust fleet sizing and deployment for industrial and independent bulk ocean shipping companies, *INFOR: Information Systems and Operational Research*, 49(2), 93–107.

Anastasiou, J. (2017) Crew operations management, in Visvikis, I.D. and Panayides, P.M. (eds) *Shipping Operations Management*, WMU Studies in Maritime Affairs 4, Switzerland: Springer International Publishing, pp. 73–97.

Assimenos, N. (2017) Commercial operations management, in Visvikis, I.D. and Panayides, P.M. (eds) *Shipping Operations Management*, WMU Studies in Maritime Affairs 4, Switzerland: Springer International Publishing, pp. 47–72.

Brooks, M.R. (1993) International competitiveness – assessing and exploring competitive advantage by ocean container carriers, *Logistics and Transportation Review*, 29(3): 275.

Casaca, A.C.P. and Marlow, P.B. (2005) The competitiveness of short sea shipping in multimodal logistics supply chains: service attributes, *Maritime Policy and Management*, 32(4), 363–382.

Champy, J. (1995) *Reengineering Management*, New York: Harper Business Books.

Chen, C.L. Philip and Zhang, C-Y. (2014) Data intensive applications, challenges, techniques and technologies: A survey on big data, *Information Sciences*, 275, 314–347.

Davenport, Th. and Short, J. (1990) The new industrial engineering: Information technology and business process redesign, *Sloan Management Review*, 31(4), 11–27.

Deloitte UK (2016) *Blockchain: Enigma, Paradox, Opportunity*. London: Deloitte LLP.

Dobrajska, M., Billinger, S. and Karim, S. (2015) Delegation within hierarchies: How information processing and knowledge characteristics influence the allocation of formal and real decision authority, *Organisation Science*, 26(3), 687–704.

Drucker, P.F. (2004) What makes and effective executive, *Harvard Business Review*, 82(6), 58–63.

Fjaerli, B.A.B., Øvergård, K.I., Westerberg, T.V. (2015) Maritime managers of the future – What do they think is good leadership?, *TransNav: International Journal on Marine Navigation and Safety of Sea Transportation*, 9(1), 107–111.

Froystad, P. and Holm, J. (2015) *Blockchain: Powering the Internet of Value*, Fornebu, Norway: Evry Financial Services.

Furnival, D. and Crispe, J. (2017) Technical operations management, in Visvikis, I.D. and Panayides, P.M. (2017) (eds) *Shipping Operations Management*, WMU Studies in Maritime Affairs 4, Switzerland: Springer International Publishing, pp. 99–128.

Fusillo, M. (2009) Structural factors underlying mergers and acquisitions in *Liner Shipping*, 11(2), 209–226.

Goldman Sachs Global Investment Research (2016) *Profiles in Innovation – Blockchain: Putting Theory into Practice*. New York: The Goldman Sachs Group Inc.

Halraftis, G. and Theotokas, I. (2013) Maritime business during the 20th Century: Continuity and change, in Grammenos, C. Th., (ed) *The Handbook of Maritime Economics and Business*, London: Lloyd's List, pp. 3–34.

Harrington, H. J. (1991) *Business process improvement: The breakthrough strategy for total quality, productivity, and competitiveness* (Vol. 1), New York: McGraw-Hill.

Henderson, J., Venkatraman, N. (1999) Strategic alignment: Leveraging information technology for transforming organizations. *IBM Systems Journal* 38(2/3): 472–484.

Kaplan, R.S. and Norton, D.P. (1992) The balanced scorecard: Measures that drive performance, *Harvard Business Review*, 70(1), 71–79.

Kaplan, R.S. and Norton, D.P. (1996) *The Balanced Scorecard, Translating Strategy into Action*, Boston: Harvard Business Press.

Kavussanos, M.G. (1996) Comparisons of volatility in the dry cargo ship sector: Spot versus time charters and smaller versus larger vessels, *Journal of Transport Economics and Policy*, 30(1), 67–82.

Koontz, H. and O'Donnell, C. (1968) *Principles of Management: An Analysis of Managerial Functions*, 4th ed., McGraw-Hill, New York.

Lamond, D. (2004) A matter of style: Reconciling Henri and Henry, *Management Decision*, 42(2), 330–356.

Lorange, P. (2005) *Shipping Company Strategies: Global Management under Turbulent Conditions*, Oxford: Elsevier.

Lu, C-S. (2007) Evaluating key resources and capabilities for liner shipping services, *Transport Reviews*, 27(3), 285–310.

Lussier, R. N. (2018) *Management Fundamentals: Concepts, Applications, and Skill Development*, 8th ed., Springfield College: Sage.

Malmendier, U., Tate, G. and Yan, J. (2011) Overconfidence and early-life experiences: The effect of managerial traits on corporate financial policies, *Journal of Finance*, 66(5), 1687–1733.

Meng, Q., Wang, T.S. and Wang, S. (2012) Short-term liner fleet planning with container transshipment and uncertain container shipment demand, *European Journal of Operational Research*, 223(1), 96–105.

Mintzberg, H. (1973) *The Nature of Managerial Work*. New York: Harper & Row.

Mitroussi, K. (2008) Employment of seafarers in the EU context: Challenges and opportunities, *Marine Policy*, 32(6), 1043–1049.

Northhouse, P.G. (2018) *Leadership: Theory and Practice*, 8th ed., Western Michigan University: Sage.

Otley, D. (1999) Performance management: a framework for management control systems research, *Management Accounting Research*, 10(4), 363–382.

Panayides, Ph.M. (2018) Principles of Chartering, 3rd ed., New York: Create Space Publications.

Panayides, Ph. M. and Wiedmer, R. (2011) Strategic alliances in container liner shipping, *Research in Transportation Economics*, 32(1), 25–38.

Pantuso, G., Fagerholt, K. and Hvattum, L.M. (2014) A survey on maritime fleet size and mix problems, *European Journal of Operational Research*, 235(2), 341–349.

Parmenter, D. (2015) *Key Performance Indicators: Developing, Implementing and Using Winning KPIs*, 3rd ed., New York: Wiley.

Pastra, A., Gkliatis, I., Koufopoulos, D.N. (2017) Organisational Behaviour in Shipping, in Visvikis, I.D. and Panayides, P.M. (eds) *Shipping Operations Management*, WMU Studies in Maritime Affairs 4, Switzerland: Springer International Publishing, pp. 25–46.

Porter, M. E. (1996) What is Strategy, in Mazzucato, M. *Strategy for Business: A Reader*, London: Sage Publications, pp. 10–32.

Puranam, P. and Vanneste, B. (2016) *Corporate Strategy: Tools for Analysis and Decision Making*, Cambridge: Cambridge University Press.

Rau, P. and Spinler, S. (2017) Alliance formation in a cooperative container shipping game: Performance of a real options investment approach, *Transportation Research Part E: Logistics and Transportation Review*, 101(3), 155–17.

Russom, P. (2011) *Big Data Analytics*, Renton. Washington: The Data Warehousing Institute.

Venkatraman, N., Henderson J.C., and Oldach, S. (1993) Continuous strategic alignment: Exploiting information technology capabilities for competitive success, *European Management Journal*, 11(2), 139–149.

Visvikis, I.D. and Panayides, P.M. (2017) (eds) *Shipping Operations Management*, WMU Studies in Maritime Affairs 4, Switzerland: Springer International Publishing.

2

Evolution of the EU and international maritime shipping

Drivers, challenges, and scenarios

Diego Artuso, Yari Borbon-Galvez, Janos Ferencz, Menno Langeveld, Christa Sys, Thierry Vanelslander, and Barry Zondag

2.1 Introduction

The Athens Declaration of the EU Member States acknowledges that 75% of the EU imports and exports depend on maritime transport. The importance of the EU shipping industry is reflected in economic values published by Oxford Economics (2015), whereby it is estimated that the EU shipping industry has a total impact on the EU GDP of 147 billion Euro, and on the labour market with 2.2 million jobs. The EU-controlled fleet represents 40% of the world tonnage and grew by 70% from 2005 to 2014 (Oxford Economics, 2015).

The maritime transport sector is part of a global market that has developed a global governance system based on the historical background of the "Mare Liberum" principle (International Labour Organization – ILO; International Maritime Organization – IMO). On issues such as market access and market conditions, however, ship operators still rely mostly on bilateral agreements between individual states. Besides this, the EU concluded Free Trade Agreements (FTAs) and Partnership and Cooperation Agreements (PCAs) containing provisions relevant for the maritime industry with a number of countries. In the future, more agreements may be concluded with other countries.

A basic condition for an effective EU maritime policy would be to have European ships sailing the flags of the Member States, thus applying EU legislation to these ships. However, the global nature of international shipping makes EU policy-making in this field very challenging, as many EU-owned ships are registered outside the EU. Hence, it is important to know and understand the development of the EU-flagged fleet, and see whether non-EU shipping registries develop and why.

All the above-mentioned challenges require a more comprehensive treatment of the status and future of EU shipping, taking into account developments in other jurisdictions and strategies deployed by players from such jurisdictions. The aim of this chapter is, therefore, to provide the required comprehensive treatment of the topic so as to give recommendations as to the evolution of EU shipping.

Section 2.2 outlines the approach taken to obtain the findings from this chapter. Section 2.3 starts with an analysis of economic and business elements, and therefore consecutively explores the macro drivers and challenges of EU global maritime trade, the meso trends of shipping company performance, the market conditions of competition at trade lane level, and micro analysis of the cost structure of EU international shipping trips. Subsequently, the section also deals with technological, environmental, labour, and regulatory challenges (maritime agreements). The above-mentioned drivers and challenges are, in Section 2.4, combined into future scenarios for EU shipping, including outlooks and policy options for each scenario. Consequences for these sectors are qualitatively indicated, supported where possible by calculations, and the specific impacts at macro-economic, social welfare, and micro-economic levels are shown. Finally, Section 2.5 summarizes the impact of the trends under the various scenarios and gives recommendations as to policy reactions for mitigating or strengthening effects.

2.2 Approach of the analysis

The approach of this chapter consists of conducting a literature review of the scientific and relevant sector literature, discussions with sector representatives, and a comprehensive survey among sector associations and companies doing own model runs and scenario building.

A total of 120 sources turned out to be of immediate relevance. The literature was complemented with interviews with relevant business actors among shippers, shipping companies, and terminal operating companies, as well as related cluster segments such as shipbuilding, towage and offshoring, and sector and trading associations. In total, 40 interviews were conducted, with players active around the globe, and covering the various sub-segments of maritime shipping: containers, dry bulk, liquid bulk, general cargo, and ro/ro. Furthermore, own models were applied to estimate, among others, the impact of policy measures on the generalized transport chain cost structures and the degree of competitiveness within the shipping sector.

Subsequently, scenarios over the future evolution of the shipping business need to be drawn, contributing to developing a framework within which decisions can be taken.

To do so, it is essential to understand the needs of the European shipping industry. This study therefore assessed these needs using a survey amongst shipowners and by conducting interviews with other relevant stakeholders. The outcome of the survey was combined with basic trading models as developed by the Organization for Economic Co-operation and Development (OECD), and both were used to build scenarios of future trade developments and make the translation to shipping, port, and the mentioned clusters.

2.3 EU and international shipping industry trends

This section reviews the current state of the shipping market and business. It consecutively deals with macro, meso, market, and micro issues, and furthermore also analyzes the impact of side constraints, namely the technological, environmental, and labour playing field, and the established maritime agreements.

2.3.1 Macro analysis: demand and supply developments

The shipping industry, globally, depends heavily on world economic growth. From 1980 to 2014, the world GDP grew by 3.5% yearly. The bi-polar world of the 1980s, consisting of North America and Europe, has been changing to a world with three growth poles: North America, Europe, and Asia. Given that trade grows approximately twice as much as the GDP (UNCTAD, 2014; Bussiere et al., 2011), the world trade has been growing by 7% yearly, and in South Asia at a faster pace than in the rest of the world, by 12% yearly approximately. The developments in seaborne trade from 1980 to 2013 show that container transport grows yearly by 42%, major bulk (iron ore, grain, coal, bauxite/alumina, and phosphate) trades by 12%, and oil and gas by 2% (UNCTAD, 2014).

The trends in fleet development show shifts in volumes and country of registry (Artuso et al., 2015). Container vessel gross tonnage grew by a factor 14 from the year 1980 to 2014, and that of bulk vessels by a factor 4. This growth has been the result of increasing the number of ships, but more important during recent years has been the increased size of the vessels (IHS Global Limited, 2015). It should be noted that the system of open registry has become very popular and nowadays more than 40% of the worldwide share in flagging is concentrated in three specialized countries: Panama, Liberia, and the Marshall Islands. The growth in EU flagging is lower than the growth in EU fleet ownership. The faster growth in EU ownership than in EU flagging is related to the use of flags of open registries or local flags when ships are engaged in trade outside EU waters.

Potential explanations for the increased use of open registries, besides lower labour costs, are favourable tax policies (tonnage tax, tax exemptions), the economic advantage of lowered environmental, labour, and safety standards, the quality of services, and the ease of registration. Over the years, the differences between the open registries and the EU flags state registries have diminished as a substantial number of EU countries have introduced the tonnage taxation system, and most open registries comply with minimum international regulations. Regarding environmental, safety, and labour standards, De Sombre (2006), on flagging standards, concludes that in practice, the economic advantage of lowered standards is offset by collective action by international organizations and states. De Sombre notes that overall, open registries are pressured to raise their standards while traditional maritime states lower their standards somewhat (DeSombre, 2006). The principles of this framework are confirmed through recent data of the yearly shipping industry flag state performance table for 2014 (ISF/ICS, 2014). In this overview, the main open registries, such as the Marshall Islands, Panama, Liberia, and Singapore, all have a positive score for their performance on port state control indicators, as well as on the ratification of conventions. The latter is confirmed by Mitroussi and Arghyrou (2016), who conclude that flagging out is determined mainly by a country's tax system, the ease of starting a new business, and the country's corruption/transparency level. These authors also find that a high level of transparency and of institutional performance and friendliness to business allows a country to maintain nationally owned ships and attract foreign-owned ships under the national flag.

Labour standards of registries differ in their requirements regarding nationalities of officers and crew, and for certification requirements (Hill Dickinson, 2013). For the registries of Panama, Liberia, the Marshall Islands, Malta, and the UK, there are no requirements with regard to the nationality at all. Several EU Member States have requirements regarding the nationality of the master of the ship or a minimum percentage requirement for the nationalities of the crew. The limitations in choice of crew nationality have an impact on the manning costs of a vessel following wage differences between European and non-EU Member States. Besides the nationality requirements, labour regulations and inspections of the flag state also seem important, and representatives from the industry indicate that inspections by European flag states are considered to be more cumbersome than from open registries.

Tax reductions in many EU Member States seem to be an important factor by which EU Member States have not lost a larger share of their flags. However, to remain competitive, further pressure on taxation levels seems likely and without international minimum standards, EU Member States will need to follow this trend. This "race to the bottom" implies that worldwide maritime nations are likely to lower their taxes by reducing tax rates, increasing the number of tax exemptions, or expanding the definition of the maritime cluster.

2.3.2 Market analysis: competition and concentration

One might expect that the port and maritime industry is a highly competitive sector due to the many different players, large volumes transported, and long distances covered because of the considerable spatial separation of production and consumption. However, the nature of this competition has changed in recent years. Nowadays, ports and the shipping industry compete as part of the (maritime) supply chains to which they belong.

The forms of control of the maritime industry and ports are likely to become increasingly flexible as, in addition to mergers, recent developments in particular in the container business include alliances as well as joint ventures and dedicated handling activities. Alliances typically are less structural and less permanent than mergers or acquisitions, so it is much easier to abandon them, witness the shifts of the last years among the world's large container alliances. Cooperation may involve carriers, terminal operating companies, port authorities, hinterland operators, and hinterland terminal operators (Meersman et al., 2015; Van de Voorde & Vanelslander, 2014).

The driving forces of integration in container liner shipping include: increasing control over costs, pricing, entry and exit behaviour, access to technology and knowledge, reduced uncertainties, supply assurance, and reduced complexities. Developments in the maritime industry require paying attention to shifting competitive balances and market power. Anti-trust enforcement revolves around the identification and measurement of market power. In fact, following a methodology developed to assess the container shipping industry's market power by trade lane (Sys, 2010), it is clear that the market changed. Before the 2008 global economic and financial crisis, there was a situation with highly competitive trade lanes, where some were more heavily concentrated while others were much less to not at all. This provided potentially new or smaller carriers with the option to enter some of the markets (see Figure 2.1). This has shifted after the crisis due to a situation where the market became more highly concentrated and stable. This implies that market competitiveness is a point of attention for public governments and regulators, especially European ones, as Europe depends to a high extent on international shipping trade, and as a growing number of large container operators are non-European.

2.3.3 Meso analysis: economic performance of the shipping industry

This section presents a benchmark analysis of the economic performance of shipping companies in all shipping markets[1]. It compares European shipping lines' performance with that of companies from Asia and worldwide and by transport segment: container; dry bulk; tanker; and miscellaneous (Avention, 2014; PwC, 2014).

A first observation is that average cost per employee in all shipping segments is higher in Europe than in Asia. The widest gaps are found in the container liner shipping and miscellaneous sectors with European shipping companies facing average costs per employee that are two times higher than their Asian counterparts. Several studies have reported on the different labour regimes and the economic convenience coming from cheaper East Asian labour force in particular. According to our findings, not only the wages, but also labour taxes and social security costs tend to be higher for the employees of European companies.

In this context, several European shipping companies have mitigated their costs for onboard personnel by having their fleet or part of their fleet under open registry (see also Section 2.3.1). Shipping companies using open registries may avoid the strict regulations of developed countries and benefit from several advantages including the reduction of operating expenses as the labour costs involved in ship operation. Other advantages include the easy registration of maritime vessels, lower taxes, and freedom of control by the country of registry. Several of the companies selected

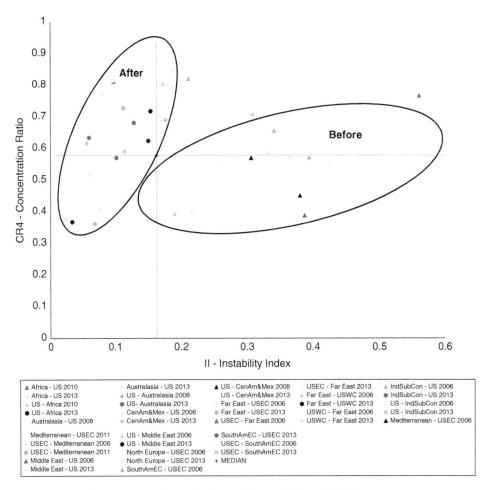

Figure 2.1 Market structure dynamics by trade lane (2006 and 2013).
Source: Artuso et al., 2015.

for the analysis have their fleet fully or partially flying an open registry flag. This actually applies to more than 80% of European shipping companies in the sample. Unfortunately, this practice has a detrimental effect on the employment opportunities for European ratings and seafarers.

On the other hand, the productivity of European labour is higher than in Asia, measured by the sales per employee. Yet, the higher productivity does not offset the higher cost of labour in the EU shipping industry (Avention, 2014; PwC, 2014). It is relevant to note that only a small part of the overall costs faced by shipping companies are related to labour. Indeed, other operative and financial costs might have a greater influence in this respect. Moreover, the labour productivity is impacted on, among other things, by different labour conditions and laws (i.e. across countries, sectors, etc.), the labour intensity of the shipping sector, the level of training of employees, the quality of equipment employed, optimal planning, and organization. In that respect, European shipping companies also perform better. Sales can also vary as companies are restructured, or lease vessels, to respond to a peak in demand. The same is true for European seaports: Chang and Thai (2016) show that higher port security and service quality reflect in higher customer satisfaction and loyalty.

2.3.4 Micro analysis: loop level cost structures

This section examines the cost structure at route level. The most recent development at the micro level is the increasing importance given to the full supply chain visibility and coordination (Arshinder et al., 2008; Klievink, 2014). The main intention is to reduce not only the operational risks, but also the operational costs through enhanced end-to-end supply chain efficiency. This is the end result of port competition (Álvarez-SanJaime et al., 2015). A methodology that allows assessing the competitive position of EU ports in the container segment was developed by van Hassel et al. (2014). It captures the total costs of the chain (hinterland, port, and sea costs) of moving cargo door to door and the differences based on the selection of ports. The analysis shows that the nearest port is not (Table 2.1) always the one minimizing the total chain costs.

An important factor explaining the selection of a port of origin is the hinterland costs (by rail or by road) of moving cargo to distant ports. Note that this has implications for the selection of the shipping company, as each shipping company may call at different ports. Common sense might point shippers in Milan to use the Port of Marseille, for instance, to move cargo to the Far East. However, the simulation shows the best option in this setting is the Port of Antwerp, after taking into account the total chain costs.

Port capacity plays an increasingly important role. For instance, the case of Antwerp versus Marseille ports, where cargo moved in larger ships enjoys economies of scale that drive down the per-container chain costs. The port capacity of Antwerp seems to be a reason for such advantages vis-à-vis Marseille for cargo originating from Milan, as cargo can be loaded in larger ships, substantially reducing the generalised costs at the port and of sea transport.

On the other hand, the restriction of the port capacity not only prevails at the origin port but also at the destination port. For instance, most US East Coast ports do not allow vessels larger than 7,200 TEUs for draught reasons. In such case, the economies of scale of Antwerp versus Marseille for a shipper located in Milan lose ground.

A port such as Lisbon shows a negative correlation between the length of the sea transportation distance and port competitiveness, which is mainly due to the lack of capacity to handle ultra-large container vessels in Lisbon.

2.3.5 Technological, environmental, and labour developments

Next, to the micro, meso, and macro environment, the impact of side constraints on the development of international shipping is examined. This section, therefore, deals with three issues which are considered side conditions for the way international shipping can develop: technological, environmental, and labour developments and regulation. They constrain the shipping playing field and come out of the survey and literature analysis as the key extra-sectoral drivers and challenges of shipping, influencing Europe's competitiveness as a shipping and port-of-call centre. That influence comes through impacts on fleet requirements, market structures, shipping company performance, and trip costs, which were the topics of Sections 2.3.1 to 2.3.4. They are therefore consecutively analyzed in the next sub-sections.

2.3.5.1 Technological playing field

Technological developments taken up by the shipping and maritime industry respond to a number of priorities, such as: efficient and reduced power used on board vessels; improved hydrodynamics and performance and reduced vessel impact at sea; safer, secure, and efficient maritime transport; improved overall vessel performance; efficient and environment-friendly vessel powering; and new concepts for innovative services (Sames, 2015). Furthermore, the growth in the world

Table 2.1 Total Chain Costs by Origin, Departure and Destination Port

EU Region	Trip			Port Capacity Limitation		Total Chain Costs		
	Origin	Departure Port	Destination Port	Max Ship Size (TEU)	Port Limiting Ship Size	Generalised Costs at EU Ports and International Sea (A)	Hinterland Cost (B)	Total (A+B)
Northern Europe to Far East	Brussels	Bremerhaven	Shanghai[1]	17000		606	420	1,026
	Paris						599	1,205
	Berlin						356	962
	Milan						749	1,356
	Madrid						1,619	2,225
	Brussels	Antwerp				573	164	737
	Paris						352	925
	Berlin						522	1,095
	Milan						631	1,204
	Madrid						1,291	1,864
	Brussels	Le Havre				584	387	972
	Paris						245	829
	Berlin						733	1,318
	Milan						693	1,277
	Madrid						1,070	1,655
Southern Europe to Far East	Brussels	Marseille	Shanghai[1]	7200	Marseille	788	686	1,474
	Paris						672	1,460
	Berlin						994	1,781
	Milan						561	1,348
	Madrid						862	1,650
	Brussels	Lisbon			Lisbon	741	1,623	2,364
	Paris						1,396	2,137
	Berlin						2,189	2,931
	Milan						1,695	2,436
	Madrid						557	1,298

	City	Port	Norfolk[2]	7200	USA ports		
Northern Europe to US East Coast	Brussels	Bremerhaven			448	420	868
	Paris					599	1,047
	Berlin					356	804
	Milan					749	1,198
	Madrid					1,619	2,067
	Brussels	Antwerp			419	164	584
	Paris					352	771
	Berlin					522	941
	Milan					631	1,050
	Madrid					1,291	1,710
	Brussels	Le Havre			426	387	813
	Paris					245	671
	Berlin					733	1,159
	Milan					693	1,119
	Madrid					1,070	1,496

	City	Port	Norfolk[2]	7200	US & EU ports		
Southern Europe to US East Coast	Brussels	Marseille			480	686	1,166
	Paris					672	1,152
	Berlin					994	1,474
	Milan					561	1,041
	Madrid					862	1,342
	Brussels	Lisbon			404	1,623	2,028
	Paris					1,396	1,801
	Berlin					2,189	2,594
	Milan					1,695	2,099
	Madrid					579	984

economy and trade has a corresponding effect on maritime freight. However, shippers and consumers increasingly require maritime freight to be more reliable and cost-competitive (Carbone & Martino, 2003). The response of the shipping industry has been to increase capacity with the same number of vessels, which allows control and reliability (Tran & Haasis, 2015). However, the net effect is a reduced number of companies able to provide the services. Ship size has to be coupled with port capacity developments to provide competitive and efficient services (Sys et al., 2008).

Further important developments are the unmanned vessels, which still require remote monitoring and controls, leading to substantial re-skilling needs of maritime labour (Porathe, 2014; Rødseth & Burmeister, 2012).

Reliability, capacity and vessels' increasing technological contents tend to require the corresponding development and uptake of Port Community Systems (Bichou & Gray, 2004; Long, 2009). Such systems allow for efficient and reliable information exchange among all willing stakeholders in the port system (Posti, Häkkinen, & Tapaninen, 2011), contributing to a synchronization of the end-to-end supply chains, as shippers and consumers request (CORE Project, 2014). Further technological developments include alternative methods of propulsion, and new environment-friendly developments such as retrofitting, alternative fuels, automation, and others (European Maritime Safety Agency, 2017; DNV, 2012; Futurenautics, 2014; Skaarup Shipping Corporation, 2011).

Environmental regulations and standards are traditionally key drivers of vessel design and business strategies in the shipping industry. Since the SOLAS Convention 1974, double hull designs are required in all passenger ships. After the Exxon Valdez accident, the USA required the double hull design on oil tankers with the Oil Pollution Act 1990. The IMO followed with the creation of the MARPOL convention in 1992 for tankers' oil spills prevention. Finally, the EU accelerated the phasing in of double hull design requirements for oil tankers in its Regulation EC 417/2002.

2.3.5.2 Environmental playing field

Environmental regulations emerging up to the year 2020 driving the developments of the shipping industry are listed in Table 2.2. Each of them impacts to a large extent on fleets, markets, company competitiveness, and trip costs.

2.3.5.3 Labour playing field

Crew sizes have become smaller due to technological changes, greater efficiencies (larger ships), and a push from shipowners to save labour costs. The skills required by maritime professionals have become more complex due to technological developments and the increasing emphasis on multi-modal supply chains. In the last decade, security tasks have been added above the usual working tasks of crews in order to comply with the ISPS code (International Ship and Port Facility Code, as part of the International Convention for the Safety of Life at Sea SOLAS, 1974), as well as additional security tasks to address piracy threats. The effect that larger ships have on saving labour costs is also interesting to note, as the same number of crew handles larger and larger ships. At the same time, minimum numbers of crew members, balanced watch schedules, equitable distribution of competencies within gangs, etc. are required to safely operate ships, as shown by Alapetite and Kozine (2017).

2.3.6 Maritime agreements

Maritime agreements include a number of themes, notably commitments on maritime freedoms: access to international maritime transport, cargo-sharing, cabotage operations, access to port services and maritime auxiliary services, commercial presence, feedering and relay, offshore

Table 2.2 Environmental Regulations and Standards Due for the Maritime Industry

←	2015	2016	2017	2018	2019	2020	→
SEEMP	0.1% ECA sulphur limit	NOx III	Cargo liquefaction (IMSBC Code amendment)	EU CO_2 monitoring, reporting, and verification (MRV)	Future ECAS	EEDI II	Global SOx limit
US BW requirement	EEDI I	Ballast Water Convention	Polar Code	Low sulphur availability review		0.5% Global SOx limit	EEDI III
EEDI 0	EU Recycling Regulation, EC CO_2 Monitoring, and Reporting Verification (MVR)					Operational requirement on CO2. Energy Efficiency Operational Index (EEOI)	

Elaborated based on: IMO, and DNV, 2012; Stevens et al., 2014 services, and movement of empty containers. This section analyzes the state-of-play for each of the above types of agreements for the ten countries which are judged strategically most relevant to the EU from a shipping perspective: Russia, USA, Brazil, Singapore, China, Turkey, Republic of Korea, Japan, India, and Panama.

In general, the analysis shows that the number and range of cargo-sharing arrangements have declined in the agreements between the EU and its Member States, and this appears to be consistent with the international trend. The reason for this decline is the emergence of the principle of freedom of maritime transport and the intensification of "de-flagging" (i.e. the process of removing a vessel from a national registry and registering it in another country) due to the spread of open ship registries.

Cabotage operations have been largely excluded from any liberalization effort at the international level, partly due to their politically sensitive nature in many countries. This general trend to exclude cabotage is well reflected in the agreements. In the USA, the Jones Act provides a stricter regime since ships must also be built in the USA in order to be allowed to operate. Yet, coastwise trade represents only a limited share of the total waterborne transport, amounting to 6.8%, whereas foreign trade amounts to 62.5%. Accordingly, the strict regime of the Jones Act is mitigated by the limited share of the cabotage operations in the total USA waterborne transport. Consideration should be given also to the Chinese cabotage regime due to the overall relevance of this region for maritime transport. Through the Shanghai Free Trade Zone, China has recently permitted cabotage for Chinese-owned but foreign-flagged vessels. The cabotage scheme in India also deserves attention. Pursuant to domestic legislation, foreign-flagged vessels may be chartered and granted a special periodic license if no suitable Indian-flagged vessel operates on the route in question. With regard to feedering[2] and relay[3], the former takes a higher share of overall traffic than the latter, approximately at a ratio of 85% to 15% of the total transshipment traffic. This means that in economic terms and at a global scale, feedering operations are much more relevant than relay operations. Figures on global regions indicate that feedering operations are particularly relevant in China, and the South East Asia region. South Korea is also relevant due to the large transshipment traffic that is carried through its ports as a result of feedering and relay restrictions in China. In the USA, feedering and relay are also problematic due to the stringent requirements imposed under the Jones Act. However, the problem is considered moderate due to the limited share of feedering and relay, which represented merely 1.5% (in 2012) of the overall USA waterborne transport. Moreover, feedering operations within China are more important than relay operations, as close to 25% of all traffic represents feedering while only about 4% are relay operations. Most maritime agreements of the EU and its Member States do not address feedering and relay of international cargo. Those that do mention it (e.g. the EU–China agreement) merely permit access to it, but prohibit the supply of such services by EU operators. Furthermore, both of these services form part of cabotage operations when the transport of international cargo happens between ports of the same country. Therefore, these services are generally prohibited for EU shipping companies.

Access to port services is generally liberalized in the agreements. Nonetheless, the examination of the agreements and other available studies has not revealed any prominent difficulty for EU operators to have access to the ports of the ten selected countries. The same applies to maritime auxiliary services. Consideration should be given to port areas in Brazil where, as a result of recent liberalizing trends, the activities of EU shipping companies in ports are mainly carried out under leasing contracts. This gives them the long-term benefit of securing port facilities in a more cost-efficient way.

Almost all agreements of the EU and its Member States provide for the possibility for EU shipping companies to establish some form of commercial presence in the ten partner countries.

The permitted forms range from representative offices to branches and subsidiaries. A few countries must be highlighted in this regard as being problematic. The effectiveness of having a commercial presence in the USA is hindered by the fact that the operation of a vessel is contingent on the vessel being wholly owned by USA citizens, where a company qualifies under this title when it meets a set of stringent administrative requirements. China has a 49% threshold on maximum foreign equity shares permitted in local companies, which means that control of the company will remain at the hands of locals.

The coverage of social, environmental, and safety clauses is limited in the maritime agreements and is focused on reiterating the applicable international regulations. Our desk research has not revealed any significant country that should be marked for attention. Some stakeholders, however, did raise safety issues that they face in the day-to-day operations in the USA and China.

The movement of empty containers accounts for 15% of the operational costs related to container assets, representing a cost factor of €15 billion per year for the shipping companies (Rodrigue, Comtois, & Slack, 2013). Although most agreements do not address the movement of empty containers, some agreements do. For instance, the EU–China agreement permits the repositioning of empty containers between Chinese ports as an exception to cabotage restrictions. Where the agreements do not regulate the movement of containers, local regulations will be applicable. Accordingly, in the USA, only containers owned or leased by the owner of the vessel can be moved. In other countries, such as South Korea and India, movement of empty containers is restricted due to cabotage limitations. With regard to the other non-EU countries, no relevant information was found on this aspect.

With regard to offshore services, our analysis revealed that this segment is of growing importance for the EU shipping industry. The EU's offshore sector grew by more than 150% in GT between 2005 and 2014. This means that the EU's share of global offshore fleet grew from 28% in 2005 to 37% in 2014 (in GT terms). The EU industry faces great competition in this segment from Asian competitors especially because of lower costs. However, EU operators seems to have identified a way to keep a competitive advantage. They do so by specializing in smaller segments, especially in building offshore support vessels and in educating highly qualified offshore service personnel.

Changes at macro, market, micro, or meso level materialize, most likely strongly influenced by the identified technological, environmental, labour, and regulatory drivers and challenges, may drive the EU shipping into a better or worse competitive position. The following analysis presents the results of a scenario approach, whereby conventional, sustainable, or fragmented growth takes place, and the outcome for the EU shipping industry is checked, as well as the potential policy options for the EU.

2.4 Scenarios

A scenario exploration channels the uncertainties in future developments. The future challenges for the European maritime sector are discussed for three scenarios (see Artuso et al., 2015). These future challenges are scenario-dependent and the three scenarios differ on macro-economic and maritime drivers and are labelled as below:

- the *Sustainability Scenario* describes a world that is making good progress towards sustainability and combines an open, globalised economy with relatively rapid technological change. International cooperation results in a more global playing field regarding environmental, safety, and labour regulations;
- the *Fragmented World Scenario* describes a world separated into regional blocks of countries with little coordination between them. The world has de-globalized and international trade

is restricted. International coordination is not functioning, even existing regulations and conventions are ignored or poorly enforced, and a wide variety of region- or country-specific regulations exists, affecting the level playing field;

- the *Conventional Growth Scenario* is oriented towards economic growth and, in this high-growth scenario, fossil fuels play a dominant role resulting in high GHG emissions. The world has increasingly globalised and the economic centre of the world is in Asia with dominant South-South trade flows. International cooperation is well functioning in this scenario, creating a rather equal level playing field for the industry.

These are long-term scenarios and address possible fundamental changes in the global economy, maritime sector, or international cooperation. They describe transitions in the period up to 2050 and their intermediate results for 2030. In this section, the scenario insights are enriched with the perception of stakeholders on challenges for their sector, so as to verify the outcome and perspectives for the EU shipping sector. In general, the time horizon of stakeholders is more focused on short- or medium-term issues rather than on long-term issues. The challenges raised by the stakeholders are included as part of the scenario where this issue is assumed to be the most important. The focus of the discussion in this section is on the ten countries selected in Section 2.3. Additional countries are included in the discussion specifically when it becomes relevant. Specific attention is given to future conditions where the playing field is not even due to trade barriers, market competitiveness, or abusive incentives or regulation.

The outcomes are grouped into four main fields, which are consecutively presented in this section: fleet, competition, new routes and ports, and incentives and support.

2.4.1 Fleet registry competitors

The challenges regarding the competitiveness of the European registries differ for the three scenarios. First, in the Sustainability Scenario, international conventions set higher standards for environment, safety, and labour conditions. On top of the international standards, regulations by the EU are not needed in this scenario, and a level playing field exists for the European flag states on this aspect. The aspect of fiscal competition is still unsolved and this is a remaining issue for European flag states in the competition with Singapore, China, Panama, and other open registries such as Liberia and the Marshall Islands. The Conventional Growth Scenario has much in common with the Sustainability Scenario except for the lack of attention for environmental regulations. Under both scenarios, quality of services of the registries is considered, besides fiscal conditions, as an important competitive aspect.

The importance of a high-quality registry service is emphasized by industry stakeholders, in particular to avoid cumbersome inspections. In their view, open registries, such as Panama, score well on service aspects and minimize the number of cumbersome inspections. Additional administrative requirements and inspections seem not to be necessary to score well on Port State Control indicators. For instance, the Tokyo MoU on Port State Control[4], which includes China, Japan, Korea, Russia, Singapore, and other Asia-Pacific countries, has the three main open registries, Panama, Liberia, and Marshall Islands on its white list. Most European flags are on the white list as well, but some European flags, such as Belgium, Sweden, and Luxemburg are positioned on the grey list. Open registries seem to remain on white lists for lower costs and less administrative burden. It is, therefore, a challenge for European flags to improve their performance to move up to the white list, for instance through better information and reducing processing times and costs.

Regarding the mentioned cumbersome inspections, one needs to be careful in our view as a dedicated balance needs to be considered between the costs of inspections and need to perform them. For example, on the sulphur regulations in the North Sea and Baltic Sea, in the Conventional Growth Scenario, the stakeholders complain about the lack of enforcement and a competitive advantage of free riders not complying with the regulation. In the Sustainable Growth Scenario, stakeholders are confident to comply, as regulations are well enforced and the likelihood of free riding remains limited.

Under the Fragmented World Scenario, the level playing field is affected by the lack of new developments in international conventions on the environment, safety, and labour, and a weak compliance with the existing international agreements. Different regulations between EU and competing registries, such as China, Singapore, and Panama, are a challenge for the competitive position of European flag states. Increasing protectionism under this scenario is a concern for the EU. Stakeholders point out that protectionism might force a flagging-out process to non-EU flags in order to access regionalized and protectionist markets. Operating under another flag is attractive in regions where market access is restricted or other flags can operate more beneficially, for example by applying lower labour and environmental standards. As international conventions setting global standards are less relevant and often not enforced in this scenario, different regional blocks set their own labour, safety, and environmental standards the fleet needs to comply with in order to access the market in their region. As European flags states are likely to use stricter regulations, it is more attractive for European shipowners to operate in these markets under non-European flags, either open registries or local flags.

2.4.2 Market competitiveness

Regarding market competitiveness, in the Sustainability Scenario, international conventions on employment, safety, security, environment, and market access set good standards to ensure market competitiveness. In this scenario, market access is liberalized and the European shipping industry can compete in most countries under comparable market conditions. In some countries and regions, such as Russia, Brazil, and West Africa, market protectionism remains an issue but, as a result of the open international political climate, it is less severe than under the other scenarios. Market conditions in China remain a high priority, mainly due to the high relevance that this market represents for the EU and its central position in global supply chains. For example, inefficiencies in Chinese ports have large domino effects on delays of supply chains serviced by ultra-large container vessels.

In the Fragmented World Scenario, market competitiveness is a high priority issue for the European maritime industry in many countries including the USA and China. The USA is highly important due to the size of its economy, and visa requirements, cabotage restrictions, and discriminatory treatment are reinforced under the Fragmented World Scenario. The shipping industry is under economic pressure to improve margins, the market shifts from low concentration and high competition to more concentration and less competition. Reduced margins are the norm, except in highly specialized or diversified segments.

If the market is not liberalized and is likely to become more severe under the Fragmented World Scenario, it is less severe, but still an issue, under the Conventional Growth Scenario; in such situation, substantial market disruption exists which prevents, for example, shippers from benefiting from lower oil prices. In a highly concentrated market, with little competition, carriers are reluctant to transfer the benefits of lower oil prices in the form of lower freight rates. Another example of market disruption is related to the increasing practice of operating in alliances including various shipping lines offering different quality levels. In this situation, the shipper can pay for services to a shipping line that has high schedule reliability and on-time arrivals, but the service is executed by another shipping line as part of the alliance, which has lower reliability and on-time arrivals. These practices, which can only exist under non- or low-competitive conditions, have a negative impact on the competitiveness of the European maritime industry and the European economy as they increase transport costs. Stakeholders stress their fear for market concentration and call for mechanisms to strengthen competition in the long term, and to reduce market concentration. Such mechanisms should balance the improved margins of the shipping industry with the interest of consumers to benefit from competition.

Under the Conventional Growth Scenario, international conventions are functioning well and overall competitive conditions are better than in the Fragmented World Scenario. But as is the current case, there are still a variety of challenges, such as unreliable customs brokerage, lengthy security checks, cargo handling delays, and lack of sufficient repair and maintenance services that hinder the EU maritime industry. Table 2.3 presents the challenges as mentioned by the stakeholders. This addresses today's situation, but many challenges are likely to remain issues at least in the short and medium future, for all scenarios, and for the Fragmented World Scenario and Conventional Growth Scenario also in the long run.

2.4.3 New routes and ports

Regarding new international routes, the Sustainability Scenario specifies the potential for the Eurasia land bridge between Europe and China. In the long term, depending on political change in North Korea, this route can be potentially extended to South Korea. For a successful operation of this line, active coordination and partnership is needed between European countries, Russia, and China. Alternative routes exist for the Eurasia land bridge and, depending on

Table 2.3 Challenges that Hinder Competitiveness of the EU Maritime Industry

Main challenges hindering competitiveness to the EU shipping industry	China	USA	Russia	Brazil	India	Turkey	Other:_ West Africa, Australia, Egypt, Mexico
Transshipment				X			
Nationality/residency/visa	X	X					X
Cabotage restrictions	X	X	X	X	X		X
Security checks		X					X
Cargo-handling		X		X			
Pilotage	X		X				
Towage	X		X				
Port dues and charges				X		X	
Dishonest use of power and bribery	X		X	X	X		X
Customs brokerage	X	X					
Taxations issues	X			X			
Repair/maintenance services		X	X				
Offshore services	X		X				
Discriminatory treatment		X					X
Unreliable port information	X						
Temporary import			X				X

the routing, Mongolia and or Kazakhstan are important partners as well. For the Northern Sea Route, considered under the Conventional Growth Scenario, international cooperation with Russia and Asian countries, such as the Republic of Korea, Japan, and China, seems crucial for an efficient operation of this route, next to external factors such as navigational feasibility linked to icing conditions, and commercial feasibility linked to sufficient trade flows (Meng et al., 2017; Pruyn, 2016).

In the Sustainability Scenario, a switch towards more sustainable fuels has been undertaken by the European and international shipping industry. An EU-wide LNG network is an important element for the future competitiveness of EU ports. At the moment, North-European ports seem more active in developing LNG facilities and this might reinforce their leading position under this scenario compared to South-European ports. Stakeholders state that incentives to set up LNG facilities favour the North-European ports where there is a longer tradition of clean energy and environmental regulations. It is advisable that the EU focuses on a balanced approach including the South-European ports from the start. For ports with a strong position in handling energy carriers, such as coal or oil, or ports with a large petrochemical processing industry, a substantial transition is needed for them to maintain their competitive positions. Alternative energy carriers, such as biofuels, might be part of new activities in the ports, replacing loading, unloading, storage, and processing activities for conventional energy carriers.

In the Fragmented World Scenario, port capacity needs are more modest than in the other two scenarios and Europe might apply port state control instruments more frequently as a substitute for the lack of international conventions to preserve Europe's interests. Under this scenario, the increase in ship size and associated infrastructure needs are also more modest. A low economic growth in combination with trade barriers reduces freight volumes in this scenario and associated demand for vessel volumes. Furthermore, a higher share of regional flows, instead of global flows, makes an increase in vessel size less attractive. For larger vessels, the trade-off between lower sailing cost and higher transshipment cost is more advantageous for global flows than for regional flows.

In the Conventional Growth Scenario, port capacity demand increases very quickly and an increasing average ship size results in higher peak loads. Stakeholders emphasize that there is especially a need in South-European ports to upgrade their operational capacity to handle larger ship sizes and increased transshipment services. Furthermore, in this scenario, substantial port and hinterland infrastructure investments are needed for serving the European economy efficiently.

2.4.4 Incentives and support

In the Sustainability Scenario, international conventions set worldwide applicable standards for an equal level playing field, but these standards do not cover taxation levels. Hence, fiscal competition will remain with countries, such as Singapore, offering advantageous tax conditions for the maritime industry. The scope of incentives can cover maritime transport activities or wider definitions of the maritime cluster, for example including offshore or on-land activities. The EU's relations with West-African countries are, in this scenario, similar to the other two scenarios, a high priority. From the shipping industry, there is a call of attention for trade, ports, and infrastructure capacity building support from the EU to West- and other African countries.

As international conventions are rather generally implemented under the Sustainability Scenario, which sets an equal level playing field regarding labour, environmental, safety and security regulations, competition between companies will focus on quality and price as all other conditions are rather similar. Countries can support their own industry by offering high-quality and efficient services, for example, flag registration or compliance with conventions, at low costs and a reduced administrative burden for the maritime industry. Economies of scale play an important role in offering high-quality services at low cost, and the ongoing worldwide concentration of market shares in few specialized registries is likely to continue. It is questionable whether the large number of European registries can all play an important role under these conditions. Most likely, market forces will result in a further concentration of registry activities within Europe, or else European countries will need to be willing to increase support for their relatively small registries.

In the Fragmented World Scenario, the world is divided into various regional blocks, and countries support their industry with supportive measures and hinder the entrance of competitors with protectionist regulations. In this scenario, the EU faces unfair competition with almost all countries outside their economic partnership. Equally then, the EU has to rely on bilateral agreements to improve competitive conditions. This process will result in a variety of agreements and regulations for the maritime industry to comply with. From an economic perspective, this variety in regulations, compared to global regulations, is inefficient and results in increasing costs related to trading goods. Park et al. (2016) show how South-Korean firms apply the potential benefits of multi-Free Trade Agreements for achieving their global supply chain management strategic priorities and goals.

In this scenario, local governments support their own industry by setting advantageous standards for it, and international competitors are required to meet these standards as well. Local governments also provide direct transfers to their own maritime industry and other supportive measures such as tax exemptions, beneficiary access to capital, and privileged conditions for port-related services. Some of these actions might violate existing agreements, but under this scenario, international conventions and their implementation play a marginal role.

In the Conventional Growth Scenario, international cooperation and conventions are functioning relatively well, ensuring a level playing field. In this scenario, due to high growth rates, dominance of the Asian countries (East Asia is by far the largest economic region in the world) should be avoided and specific attention is needed for the relationships with Asian countries, such as China and Singapore. International cooperation, within the EU and between the EU and other partners, will be needed to negotiate effectively with these dominant Asian economies. Furthermore, in this liberalized world, Asian registries and open worldwide registries have a strong market position. Many aspects under this scenario, like focus of competition on taxation levels and quality of services, are similar to the Sustainability Scenario. The biggest difference is the lack of international attention for environmental issues and increased importance of Asia.

2.5 Conclusions, implications and recommendations

This chapter described the key drivers in the international and EU shipping market, as well as the main challenges of the EU shipping access to key non-EU markets. The analysis concludes with a number of key trends, implications, and recommendations regarding possible steps to reiterate at EU and non-EU forums the need for framing a global level playing field.

2.5.1 Market conditions: trends and possible next steps

In terms of *trade developments*, the trends show EU trade relationships and maritime flows with fast-growing and developing countries benefit from their industrial progress, population growth, and higher income levels. Fast-growing and developing countries increase the share of imported processed and industrialized goods, benefitting the EU exports, and balancing trade more. There is an uncertain scenario for large maritime flows of oil, coal, and gas, as a consequence of the growing importance of renewable resources and geopolitical concerns for self-sufficiency. The possible next steps, both for European governments, through facilitation, and for European shipping and port companies in their target strategies, could be to reinforce and sustain trade developments with fast-growing and developing countries, and to face the uncertainties for the EU supply of maritime transport services and port infrastructure and facilities for global energy flows.

Regarding *fleet registry competitors,* the trend is that the EU shipping risks flagging out if it stays at disadvantage as a result of an uneven global playing field on fiscal competition. There is lack of harmonized implementation of international conventions on environment, safety (IMO), and labour (ILO); on the quality of the registry services; on the inspection and enforcement standards of Port State Controls; and on the use of competitive registries to access otherwise protectionist markets. Possible next steps for European governments could be to foster a level playing field on fleet registry competition. It is important to follow developments at global level on fiscal regimes and make efforts for harmonization; to develop and harmonize enforcement of environmental, safety, and labour standards through international organizations, and to promote efficiency among registries and maritime authorities, taking into account the market access to provision of services by the entire EU maritime industry. European shipping and port companies should then also specifically target the markets to which such access is facilitated.

The *market competitiveness* tends to be higher and facing tight economic performance. Low margins have been the norm, except in very highly specialized or in highly diversified segments. In between the specialized and diversified segments, container liner industry markets had to change dynamics to improve their margins, from low concentration and high competition, to more concentration and less competition. The EU maritime industry margins have been also hindered by non-competitive challenges. Possible next steps could be to balance out improved margins in the shipping industry and reduced market concentration, to allow shippers and consumers to benefit from competition, and to reduce the likelihood of shipping companies to engage in collusive behaviour. Especially with Asian shipping companies gaining importance and engaging into alliance-building, European port operators and shippers should welcome such moves.

The importance of *new routes* varies according to the scenario. A Sustainability Scenario specifies the potential for the Eurasia land bridge between Europe and China; whilst the Conventional Growth Scenario specifies the potential of the Northern Sea Route. Possibly, a successful operation of the Sustainability Scenario requires an active coordination and partnership between the European countries, Russia, and China. For a successful operation of the Conventional Scenario, international cooperation with Russia and Asian countries, such as the Republic of Korea, Japan, and China, seems crucial for an efficient operation of this route. Companies will be followers rather than decision makers in such geopolitics games, but it is important for European policymakers and industry to be united, as a similar united stance can be expected from Asian, Russian, and increasingly also USA players.

The trends in *ports in the EU* are also scenario-dependent. The challenges are the development of a balanced EU-wide LNG network supportive of the future competitiveness of EU ports; preparing the transition of conventional fuels towards more sustainable sources of energy; and the increased ship sizes leading to high growth in peak flows to be managed by ports and hinterland infrastructure. A possible next step could be to balance the LNG network development to include South-European ports from the start. For ports with a strong position in handling energy carriers, such as coal or oil, or ports with a large petrochemical processing industry, a substantial transition is needed for them to retain their competitive positions.

Alternative energy carriers, such as biofuels, might be part of this transition of port activities. The operational capacity of ports and hinterland infrastructure in Europe needs to be upgraded to handle larger ship sizes and increased transshipment services. These actions involve transport infrastructure as well as management solutions, including ICT solutions, further automation of flows, and logistics concepts better differentiating between high-speed urgent flows and less urgent flows. In that respect, European shipping companies and port operators should ensure they are at the forefront of technological development, and prepared knowledge-wise, organizationally, and financially, to step into the right types of investment at the right moment.

The trend in incentives for the maritime industry is to ease one or more of the following burdens from stakeholders: operational, financial, and regulatory. Alternatively, incentives contribute to building up their operational, scale, or scope capabilities. The presence of incentives in a country favours its position to be selected as the country flag. Possible steps could be at three levels. First, sustaining favourable taxation schemes and creating mechanisms to strengthen the corporate culture and structure of EU shipping companies. Second, setting up mechanisms to attract and sustain companies to maritime clusters; facilitating bank finance; and sustaining mechanisms for competence and skills building and development for the shipping industry. And third, trade facilitation by removing trade limits through diplomatic means with protectionist country/region/trade lane; reducing red tape in the EU; and supporting favourable unionization to the maritime industry industrial relations.

Labour is one of the few cost items which shipowners can directly act upon to reduce transport costs. As a consequence, there has been an ongoing process during several decades to reduce labour costs through technological developments, increasing ship size, and replacing expensive with cheaper labour. Combined with additional security, related workload for existing crews in piracy-affected areas has led to situations where fatigue of crew members is more often the standard than the exception. The whole process has also worsened shipping's reputation for attracting new employees, and has limited possibilities for including new labour and training of new labour. Although the trend of reducing labour costs will be difficult to stop independently, there are a few areas where improvements can be made. For instance, as a result of an increasing average ship size and further automation of activities on board, the share of labour costs of the overall shipping costs is likely to decrease. Research is being pursued into schemes to make a maritime career more attractive for EU citizens and support the position of the EU as frontrunner in maritime technology in practice, e.g. R&D support measures, enabling the testing of new technologies, such as unmanned ships.

2.5.2 Maritime agreements

Many of the older bilateral maritime agreements, while still in force, appear to have gained a "dormant" status as the contracting parties seldom invoke them. In general, all countries exclude foreign operators from cabotage.

Feedering and relay operations are not addressed in most maritime agreements of the EU and its Member States. Due to the increasing ship sizes, feedering is becoming more and more important. Relay operations are an important component in making maritime traffic more cost-efficient through optimal routing. Feedering also presents additional operational costs due to the necessity to outsource these operations to domestic shippers. Possible steps could be to consider more carefully feedering and relay operations and services in maritime agreements.

The *offshore* market is particularly important in Brazil, the USA, and Russia, but EU shipowners face restrictions in gaining access to this segment due to the need of using domestic flag vessels and abide by additional domestic rules. In the case of the EU, it may be necessary to research into clarifying the eligibility requirements under the Maritime State Aid Guidelines to extend also to vessels providing offshore services. It is particularly important for companies in this segment to be able to maintain and even reinforce their built-up skills and frontrunning role at global level.

Acknowledgements

The authors first of all thank the European Commission for the funding that enabled this research. Furthermore, the research strongly benefitted from the discussions with various sector stakeholders and associations, as well as from the survey contributors.

Notes

1 See Artuso et al. (2015) for more extensive detail of the analysis.
2 Feedering operation is defined as the pre- and onward transportation of international cargoes by sea, notably containerized, between ports located in a country.
3 Relay of international cargo is defined as the practice of one company carrying cargo from one country to an overseas destination on its own vessel, transferring the cargo from one vessel to another operated by the same company in another port of that country.
4 See http://www.tokyo-mou.org/.

References

Alapetite, A., & Kozine, I. (2017). Safe manning of merchant ships: an approach and computer tool. *Maritime Policy & Management, 44*(3), 323–335.
Álvarez-SanJaime, Ó., Cantos-Sánchez, P., Moner-Colonques, R., & Sempere-Monerris, J. J. (2015). The impact on port competition of the integration of port and inland transport services. *Transportation Research Part B: Methodological, 80*, 291–302.
Arshinder, S., Kanda, A., & Deshmukh, S. G. (2008). Supply chain coordination: Perspectives, empirical studies and research directions. *International Journal of Production Economics, 115*(2), 316–335. doi:10.1016/j.ijpe.2008.05.011
Artuso, D., Borbon, Y., Ferencz, J., Langeveld, M., Sys, C., Vanelslander, T., & Zondag, B. (2015). Study on the analysis and evolution of international and EU shipping. Brussels: European Commission.
Avention. (2014). *Avention Database*. Retrieved from: http://www.avention.com/
Bichou, K., & Gray, R. (2004). A logistics and supply chain management approach to port performance measurement. *Maritime Policy & Management, 31*(1), 47–67.
Bussiere, M., Callegari, G., Ghironi, F., Sestieri, G., & Yamano, N. (2011). Estimating trade elasticities: Demand composition and the trade collapse of 2008–09. Retrieved from faculty.washington.edu/ghiro/BussiereCallegariGhiroSestieriYamanoAEJMacro13.pdf
Carbone, V., & Martino, M. D. (2003). The changing role of ports in supply-chain management: an empirical analysis. *Maritime Policy & Management, 30*(4), 305–320.
Chang, C-H, & Thai, V. (2016). Do port security quality and service quality influence customer satisfaction and loyalty?, *Maritime Policy & Management, 43*(6), 720–736.
CORE Project. (2014). Consistently optimised resilient secure global supply-chains. Retrieved from http://www.coreproject.eu/
DeSombre, E. R. (2006). Flagging standards: globalization and environmental, safety, and labor regulations at sea. *MIT Press Books, 1.*
DNV. (2012). *Shipping 2020*. Retrieved from http://www.dnv.nl/binaries/shipping%202020%20-%20final%20report_tcm141-530559.pdf
European Maritime Safety Agency. (2017). EMSA study on the use of fuel cells in shipping. Retrieved from http://www.emsa.europa.eu/emsa-homepage/2-news-a-press-centre/news/2921-emsa-study-on-the-use-of-fuel-cells-in-shipping.html
Futurenautics. (2014). Shipping 3.0. The speculation is over. *Futurenautics. The maritime future*. Retrieved from https://issuu.com/futurenautics/docs/futurenautics_issue5_october14

Hill Dickinson. [1974](2013). International Ship Registration Requirements. *Shipping at a Glance – Guide 7*. Liverpool, UK: International Convention for the Safety of Life at Sea.

ISF/ICS. (2014). *Shipping Industry Flag State Performance Table – 2013–2014*. Retrieved from http://www.libramar.net/news/shipping_industry_flag_state_performance_table_2013_2014/2015-01-03-1876

Klievink, A. (2014). Cassandra-D7. 3-final report: dissemination results. Retrieved online from https://repository.tudelft.nl/islandora/object/uuid:28b06365-c977-48b0-8d06-9c41f95e3614?collection=research

Long, A. (2009). Port community systems. *World Customs Journal*, *3*(1), 63–67.

Meersman, H., Sys, C., Van de Voorde, E., & Vanelslander, T. (2015). L'histoire se répète? Current competition issues in container liner shipping – OECD working party no. 2 on competition and regulation – n°5. Retrieved from http://www.oecd.org/daf/competition/competition-issues-in-liner-shipping.htm

Meng, Q., Zhang, Y., & Xu, M. (2017). Viability of transarctic shipping routes: a literature review from the navigational and commercial perspectives. *Maritime Policy & Management*, *44*(1), 16–41.

Mitroussi, K., & Arghyrou, M. (2016). Institutional performance and ship registration. *Transportation Research Part E: Logistics and Transportation Review*, *85*, 90–106.

Oxford Economics. (2015). The economic value of the EU shipping industry – update. Retrieved from http://www.ecsa.eu/images/Studies/150220%20European%20Shipping%20Update.pdf

Park, Y., Hong, P., & Li, S. (2016). Free trade agreements and maritime supply chain costs: Competitiveness of Korean firms. *Maritime Economics & Logistics*, *18*(1), 3–18.

Porathe, T. (2014). Remote monitoring and control of unmanned vessels – The MUNIN Shore Control Centre. Paper presented at the Proceedings of the 13th International Conference on Computer Applications and Information Technology in the Maritime Industries (COMPIT '14).

Posti, A., Häkkinen, J., & Tapaninen, U. (2011). Promoting information exchange with a port community system–case Finland. *International Supply Chain Management and Collaboration Practices*, *4*, 455–473.

Pruyn, J. (2016). Will the Northern Sea route ever be a viable alternative? *Maritime Policy & Management*, *43*(6), 661–675.

PwC. (2014). PwC Global Shipping benchmark database.

Rodrigue, J.-P., Comtois, C., & Slack, B. (2013). *The Geography of Transport Systems*: Routledge.

Rødseth, Ø. J., & Burmeister, H.-C. (2012). Developments toward the unmanned ship. Paper presented at the Proceedings of International Symposium Information on Ships–ISIS.

Sames, P. (2015). Vision 2050: European vessels for the future initiative. Paper presented at the European Shipping Week 2015. 2015-03-02, Radisson Hotel, Room Schuman 1+2+3.

Skaarup Shipping Corporation (Producer). (2011). Skaarup Shipping Corporation self-u technology. Retrieved online from https://www.youtube.com/watch?v=cZgw_sxAM1k.

Stevens, L., Sys, C., Vanelslander, T., & van Hassel, E. (2014). Is new emission legislation stimulating the implementation of sustainable (retrofitting) maritime technologies? Conference proceedings International Forum on Shipping, Ports and Airports (ISFPA) 2014.

Sys, C. (2010). *Inside the Box: Assessing the Competitive Conditions, the Concentration and the Market Structure of the Container Liner Shipping Industry*. Ghent: Ghent University.

Sys, C., Blauwens, G., Omey, E., Van De Voorde, E., & Witlox, F. (2008). In search of the link between ship size and operations. *Transportation Planning and Technology*, *31*(4), 435–463.

Tran, N. K., & Haasis, H.-D. (2015). An empirical study of fleet expansion and growth of ship size in container liner shipping. *International Journal of Production Economics*, *159*, 241–253.

UNCTAD. (2014). *Review of Maritime Transport*. Retrieved online from https://unctad.org/en/pages/PublicationWebflyer.aspx?publicationid=1068

Van de Voorde, E., & Vanelslander, T. (2014). Trends in the maritime logistics chain: vertical port co-operation: strategies and relationships. In T. Vanelslander & C. Sys (Eds.), *Port business: Market challenges and management actions* (pp. 119–140). Antwerp: Antwerp University Press.

Van Hassel, E., Meersman, H., Van de Voorde, E., & Vanelslander, T. (2014). Impact of scale increase of container ships on the generalised chain cost. Paper presented at the IAME Annual Conference, International Association of Maritime Economists, Norfolk, 16-18/07/2014.

Organization and management of dry bulk shipping companies[1]

Ioannis Theotokas

3.1 Introduction

In this chapter, the analysis centres on the organization and management of dry bulk shipping companies. Organizing is defined as the management function that deals with the assignment of tasks, the grouping of activities into departments, and the allocation of resources to the departments, while management refers to the attainment of organizational goals in an effective and efficient manner through the functions of planning, leading, and controlling (Daft, 2010). The need for a separate examination of the organizational and management approaches adopted by dry bulk shipping companies has to do with the characteristics of the environment in which they operate. As a rule, these are companies which are active in the world shipping market, derive their factors of production on a world-wide basis, and provide their services all over the world. In parallel, they are not subject to geographical limitations either as to the basic factors of production (capital-labour-institutional framework of operation of ships and offices), or as to the offer of their services.

Dry bulk shipping companies produce transportation services to meet derived demand, a characteristic which leads to major fluctuations in freight rates, and, at the same time, to fluctuations in the prices of ships. The strategy they implement determines their degree of flexibility. Thus, they are able to implement strategies which lead to immediate yields, either through the buying and selling of ships, or in the form of chartering of the vessels; at the same time, they are able to remain flexible in dealing with conditions in the freight markets in which they are active, by increasing or reducing their fleet accordingly.

All the above characteristics have a reciprocal influence with the organization of the companies. In the first part of the chapter an account is given of the processes and departments of bulk shipping companies. This provides the basis for understanding the tasks of the shipping companies and the way they are allocated in departments. In the second part, basic principles of the organization of these enterprises are analyzed, which provides a better understanding of structural and contextual factors that affect the structure of organization. The third part of the chapter highlights the structuring of the enterprises including their organizational structure and departmentalization, and the last part discusses issues relating to the human resources on board the ships of dry bulk shipping companies.

3.2 The processes and departments of dry bulk shipping companies

The processes of the shipping enterprise, though in their basic form they do not differ from the processes of other enterprises, nevertheless manifest themselves as complex, since the productive units are constantly on the move and may be thousands of miles away from their headquarters – that is, the administrative centre, where the company is established and manages its fleet. Naturally, a shipping company may have branches in different geographical areas, depending upon the strategy and the range of its activities. The reference to the place of operation of the shipping company is connected to the fact that the conditions which shape the institutional framework, the availability of the factors of production, and a series of other factors pre-eminently affect the manner of organization and operation of its infrastructures on land.

In the case of a shipping company, the groups of processes and the systems of support resources and control can be analyzed by means of the core processes and systems approach (Miller, 1998). However, the individual processes which make up each group differ from one another, since the object of the activity of the enterprises gives rise to special needs which are expressed both in the definition of each process, and in the procedures and activities of which it is composed. The groups of processes and systems of the shipping enterprise include processes relating to the development of the service, those relating to the creation and management of demand, and those relating to the satisfaction of demand, support systems, and control systems (Exhibit 3.1).

3.2.1 Process for developing the maritime transport service

The process which is related to the development of the maritime transportation service is the selection and acquisition of a vessel. This is a basic strategic decision which has to do with the aims, the strategy for their realization, the sourcing of the necessary resources, and the development of the corresponding capabilities. The process includes decisions in connection with the composition

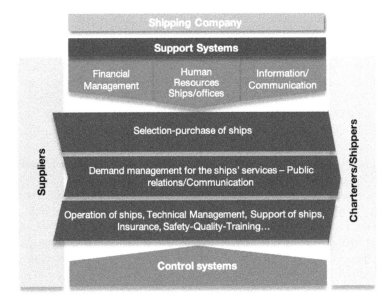

Exhibit 3.1 The processes and systems of a shipping company.
Source: I. Theotokas (2018: Figure 3.2), based on Miller, 1998: Figure 4.7).

of the company's fleet (and therefore the freight markets in which it will be active with its ships) and the purchase of new ships (by means of shipbuilding) or second-hand ships, as well as the time of implementation of the decision. In the context of this process, decisions for the sale of managed ships either for further trading or for scrap are taken. The type and individual characteristics of the ship will determine the freight markets in which it will take part and the service which it will provide. They will also define its earning potential because volatility in the dry bulk freight markets is different for different-sized ships (Kavussanos, 1996). The larger the ship the more drastic are the responses of profitability to unexpected changes in the market (Alizadeh and Nomikos, 2010). In the case of liner shipping or passenger shipping, this process is more complex and includes the planning of the routes or the lines on which the enterprise's vessels will be active. In bulk shipping, the development of the service involves the choice of the type of vessel and of the geographical region in which it will be active.

The need for capital for financing the acquisition of high-value assets is very high. Bulk shipping companies enter the international markets to gain access to the capital they need. Thus, like any other resource they employ, capital also comes from the international market. In most cases, the amount of capital needed defines the source as well as the number of institutions which provide it. Fund-raising in shipping is based on financing instruments and tools which are sophisticated, innovative, and complex. These instruments can be distinguished in equity finance (public fundings, seasoned equity offerings, retained earnings, and private equity funding), debt finance (bank lending, corporate bond issues, specialized financial institutions, shipyard finance, private debt finance) and alternative finance (lease, mezzanine finance, securitization, hybrid finance) (Syriopoulos, 2007). The most important source of capital for shipping are still the shipping banks. They provide capital after a credit risk analysis which is based on character and capacity of the head of the shipping company and the management team, on capital, on company, on conditions, on collateral, and on cash flow analysis (Grammenos, 2010). Several factors related to limitations faced by the financial institutions, as well as the need for risk sharing, lead shipping companies to choose a combination of methods for raising the needed funds. For example, the NYSE-listed Star Bulk Carriers, to which the private equity fund Oaktree Capital Management made a placement (Star Bulk, 2017b), states in its website as a core element of its business strategy the support of 15 international banks and two prominent leasing companies (Star Bulk, 2017a).

3.2.2 Chartering process for demand management

This process has to do with the creation of demand for the maritime transportation services of the company, that is, in essence, with making available the company's vessels in the charter markets and the ensuring of employment for the vessels. It is, then, a process which is carried out by the specialized chartering department. Chartering personnel have duties similar to those of ship brokers and also possess, as a rule, apart from information on the market, the required specialist skills and knowledge (information, technical knowledge, knowledge of the legislation, negotiating skills, etc.) to negotiate the terms of the charter party. The choice of the form of the charter, that is voyage charter, time charter, or bareboat charter, as well as the decision to participate in commercial pool, is a process of strategic character, as it is connected with the approach of the company towards the risk created by the fluctuations in the chartering markets. An accurate analysis of market data and the choice of the appropriate form of charter by a creditworthy charterer are necessary conditions for the survival and development of the enterprise.

Market volatility forces companies operating fleets of medium and large size to adopt a balanced chartering strategy, i.e. a portfolio of voyage and time charters. This allows them to make effective use of the prevailing conditions and reduces the risks which may result from a sudden fall in the demand for transportation services. Eagle Bulk Shipping, for example, who operates a fleet of more than 40 bulk carriers, focuses on voyage chartering; however, it monitors the dry bulk shipping market and considers taking advantage of long-term time charters when the market conditions favour this choice. At the end of 2019, 23 ships were time-chartered, 17 ships were voyage-chartered, and one ship was linked to a commercial pool (Eagle Bulk, 2017). To further reduce the risk caused by fluctuations in the freights markets, many shipping companies engage in forward agreements, such as forward freight agreements, i.e. agreements between two parties on the determination of a freight rate to be applied to a specific quantity of cargo or type of vessel, for one or a combination of the major shipping routes in the dry-bulk or the tanker markets at a certain date in the future (Kavussanos and Visvikis, 2006; Nomikos and Alizadeh, 2010). Companies implementing freight options are able to hedge if the market moves against their forecast and to take advantage of favourable conditions if their forecast proves to be true (Nomikos and Alizadeh, 2010). The type of charter it employs for the ships affects the flexibility of the company in the short term. The choice of voyage charter provides flexibility for the geographical or market positioning of a ship as well as for the selling of the ship when conditions in the charter market favour this choice.

For the optimal implementation of this process, the company must develop and manage in a suitable way communication with potential clients and, overall, with the stakeholders, that is, with all the groups of individuals with an interest in the course followed by the company (suppliers, state authorities, etc.).

3.2.3 Operations, technical, and supply processes to satisfy demand

When the chartering of the vessel has been secured, the enterprise must now ensure the provision of the maritime transportation services to the clients/charterers at the appropriate time, with the quality required by them and with safety for human life and for the environment. In practical terms, this means that the vessel which has been chartered must be ready to load, to carry, and to discharge the cargo at the destination port on the basis of the scheduling in the charter party; it must be properly maintained and observe the terms of the regulations; the crew must have at its disposal all the means necessary for the operation of the vessel, while the ship itself, as a means of production, must be insured against risks, and, finally, the operation of the ship and the crew must be supported by systems which ensure their quality and safety. The above processes are carried out by specialist departments of the enterprise, which have the responsibility for the operational and technical management of the vessel, support for its operation by the provision of spare parts, of catering for the crew, etc., for the insurance cover and handling of the claims for compensation which are generated, and for the management of the safety, quality, and training of the workforce.

The activities which relate to the day-to-day operation of the vessel are carried out by the ship operators, who are members of the personnel of the **operations department**. This department in many companies serves as the basic link between the administration, the rest of the enterprise's departments, the vessels which it manages, the charterers, the suppliers, and other individuals or organizations. The activities of the operations department can be divided into the following areas (Goulielmos, 1996: 290):

- external processes, that is, relations with the ship's agents, the suppliers of fuel, the charterers, and others having dealings with the vessel;
- the ships, the movements of which it follows closely and supports;
- internal processes, that is, the relations it maintains with other departments of the enterprise and the information which it supplies to or receives from them.

The operator is usually a captain, who possesses first-class knowledge of the individual characteristics of the vessel, of the terms of the charter party which the ship is fulfilling, and of the conditions which its crew is likely to encounter during the course of a charter.

The operator provides the captain with additional instructions or advice where this is necessary, and applies the policies, the rules, and the procedures provided for by the company's management system. For him to be effective in communicating with the captain, he must be capable of placing himself in the place of the one who is receiving the instructions and is called upon to implement them (Kennedy, 2011). He should, then, have a good knowledge of the organization of the ship, and of the duties and roles for each job. In view of the fact that a large percentage of vessels nowadays are manned by crews of different nationalities, the operator must be able to handle the sensitive issue of cultural diversity (Theotokas and Progoulaki, 2007).

Another important department which supports the day-to-day operation of the vessels is the ships' **technical department**. Technical management is one of the most fundamental processes of a shipping enterprise since its effective functioning contributes to the improvement of the vessel's productivity and influences fundamentally the cost of the transportation services being provided. Furthermore, it includes a wide range of competencies, such as the scheduled maintenance and the inspections of the vessel, its repairs and dry-docking. Technical experts in co-operation with staff in ships carry out the activities of the technical department. They work closely with classification societies and surveyors and inspectors who ensure that the ships are properly maintained (Downard: 1990: 74).

The operational and technical management of a vessel are related to the process of safety, quality, and environmental responsibility management, which includes the development, operation, and administration of management systems which answer to the specifications of regulations such as the International Safety Management (ISM) Code and standards such as ISO 9001 and 14001. These standards set out the requirements for the development and implementation of a quality management system and an environmental management system, respectively.

At the same time, the existence of the necessary equipment (spare parts, engine supplies, lubricants, paints, etc.) and of the services required, as well as the provision of the necessary catering for the enterprise's crew, are required for the safe and uninterrupted operation of the vessel as a productive unit. The responsibility for this is that of the company's **supplies department**, which has to ensure an adequate supply of consumables and equipment on board the ship so that the voyage is not affected, and that risks do not arise either for the ship's crew or for the cargo because these are lacking.

Insurance cover against risks is another important process in the management of dry bulk vessels. The handling of the insurance covers of a shipping enterprise is undertaken by the specialist **insurance department**, which is responsible for ensuring the protection of the shipowner (an individual or an enterprise) from risks by insuring the vessel against total or partial loss, losses caused to third parties, or other risks, such as loss of profit or war risks. Also of importance are the monitoring and processing of any claims which may arise for the company.

3.2.4 Resources systems

Resources systems can be divided into support systems and control systems. Support systems include financial management and the accounts office, the management of information and communications, and the management of the workforce employed on the ships and in the offices of the enterprise, of which a separate account will be given in the rest of the article. The company's control systems do not necessarily involve specific processes, but activities which are diffused throughout all the other processes and have as their purpose the monitoring of the distribution and of the effective and efficient employment of the productive resources. For example, the assessment of the performance of the personnel in the offices is a control system which can be implemented both in the process of the human resources management and in each process separately by the person responsible for it. Control of the budget in the case of each ship and of that of the enterprise as a whole can be exercized by the department auditing the financial management and by their heads of operations in the areas of which they are in charge.

The above summary account is proposed as a framework for the analysis of the processes of a dry bulk shipping enterprise, which allows for extensions and adaptations, depending upon the particular requirements and the special characteristics of each shipping company. The company's development and competition strategy, the strategy for the employment of the vessels, the size of the fleet, the specialization of the ships and the level of technology, the quality of the workforce, and the company's culture are basic factors which determine the extent of the processes which the enterprise will develop. The above processes, as has already been pointed out, are necessary if the dry bulk shipping company is going to be able to provide the transportation services of its vessels. The company's strategy as regards its organization will determine how far these processes will be developed by the company itself or will be assigned to third-party enterprises within the framework of the outsourcing strategy[2].

3.3 The organization of dry bulk shipping companies

A systems approach[3] of the organizations provides the framework for an understanding of the interdependences which shipping companies manifest in their organization. A shipping enterprise can be analyzed as a system of interconnected and interdependent parts. Its administration is complex, because it includes the management of units of high capital value which are scattered in distant regions of the world, so that the day-to-day monitoring of their operation is difficult (Frankel, 1982: 103). For organizations that "perform the same funtions with the same division of labor and hierarchical arrangements in multiple locations" (Hall, 1996: 56) spatial dispersion is an element of their organizational complexity. Bulk shipping companies manage ships which, although identical in structure, differ from one another, and operate branches at different geographical positions, i.e. they are organisations with high spatial dispersion.

At the same time, the company's offices are organized in departments using the criterion of the management or support of the operation of the vessels. The performance of the ships is affected by physical factors, as well as by the acts and omissions of the crews on board of them and of those working in the enterprise's offices on land. This means that careful co-ordination and co-operation between the various departments and the ships are required for the achievement of the common objective. Furthermore, an estimation of the direct and indirect impact of specific decisions or actions taken either by a vessel or a department on the rest of the company's ships and departments is needed. Within this framework, communication between the different departments and the ships, which are the sub-systems of the system in the case of a shipping enterprise, is a precondition for effective functioning and the achievement of the aims both of each sub-system and of the enterprise as a whole.

The organization of shipping companies, like that of any other company, is characterized by standardization, that is, the degree to which expectations in connection with the means and the final result of its work are specified, written down, and enforced to the members of the organization; the concentration of power, that is, the degree to which decision-making remains at the highest levels of management or is decentralized to the other levels; and the complexity in the division of labour, that is, the degree to which there are different job titles or occupational groupings and different units or departments (Donnelly et al., 1995: 231).

Starting out from standardization, it should be noted that the introduction of regulations and codes which deal with safety and the quality of services led to an increase in the degree of standardization of jobs carried out by the human resources on land and on the vessels. This tendency appears to have also affected the degree of centralization and decentralization of decision-taking, as it has led to the ceding of decision-taking power to operational personnel of the enterprises, on the basis of the provisions of their management systems. The available infrastructure of communication between a company's ships and offices is also contributing in this direction.

With regard to complexity, this may be horizontal (number of departments in the enterprise), vertical (hierarchical levels), or geographical (dispersion of activities and personnel). Dry bulk shipping companies are organizations of relatively large horizontal complexity, which, of course, is a function of the size of the fleet which they manage, but also of the degree to which they carry out internally the whole of their management processes and do not outsource some of these to third parties. Further, dry bulk shipping companies are organizations of small vertical complexity, since their hierarchical levels are, usually, few. On the other hand, the ships display less horizontal complexity, but, as organizations with many hierarchical levels, they manifest great vertical complexity. Thus, bulk shipping companies' organization could be presented as a flat hierarchy; each ship as a vertical one. As regards geographical or spatial dispersion, shipping companies are systems containing complex organizations which carry out the same processes, have the same division of labour, and maintain the same hierarchical levels in branches which operate in many different locations (ships and offices). Spatial dispersion is a matter of size of the fleet managed by the company, as well as of the differentiation of the fleet. The higher the number of ships and the differentiation of the fleet are, the higher the spatial dispersion of the company is expected to be. For example, Oldendorff, which operates approximately 600 privately owned and chartered ships, is the world's leading dry bulk operator, with offices not only in Germany, where it is based, but in 16 different countries (Oldendorff, 2017a).

Of importance are factors related to the chartering strategy of the company and the extent to which they manage processes related to ship management internally or outsource them. For example, Torvald Klaveness owns 16 vessels but it commercially operates close to 135 vessels. The fact that technical management of ships is insourced, and that it provides commercial services to many vessels through the Klaveness Chartering and runs two dry bulk pools, led the company to operate chartering offices in Oslo, Singapore, and Shanghai, and offices in the Philippines, Romania, and South America for technical management services (Klaveness, 2017). Golden Ocean, which outsources technical management of ships, at the end of 2016 managed more than 70 capesize, panamax, kamsarmax, and supramax, and operated offices in Oslo and Singapore. The company contracted with independent ship management companies to manage and operate its vessels, while technical supervision services were provided by Frontline (Golden Ocean, 2017). It should be noted that Frontline itself implements a strategy of outsourcing management, crewing, and accounting services to independent ship management companies (Frontline, 2017).

The above-mentioned examples, however, should not lead to the conclusion that spatial dispersion is high for all dry bulk shipping companies. A great percentage of them operate fleets of small or medium size, which are managed from their head office, located in one of the main ship management centres such as Piraeus, Oslo, Singapore, or Hong Kong. For these companies, spatial dispersion is a dimension of organisational complexity related to the ships they operate.

3.4 The organizational structure and departmentalization of dry bulk shipping companies

Success for a shipping company is related with the existence of an organisational structure which facilitates organisational development, use of necessary know-how, change, simplicity, concentration on its aims and cost control (Lorange, 2005). The structuring of shipping companies is based on criteria such as interdependence and specialization of jobs and the pursuit of the best employment of resources. Furthermore, factors which are taken into consideration in the choice of structuring are the size of the enterprise, the spread of its activities, the complexity of the operational environment, the type of service which it provides, that is, the type of vessels which it manages, relations with the charterers, and the chartering strategies which it implements.

The strategy is one of the factors that define the organizational needs of the company and affect the choice of its structure. Different levels of strategy and the related alternative options affect the decision. In this context, strategies for ships' acquisition and finance, investment strategy, competitive strategy, chartering strategy, strategy for insourcing or outsourcing of processes, and strategy for ships' crewing define the vertical, horizontal, and spatial complexity of dry bulk shipping companies, i.e. their organizational structure.

An example can be given with regard to the investment strategy of the company, i.e. the choice between the long-run selling of shipping services or the beating of the market with sales and purchases of ships (Hope and Boe, 1981). The first choice mainly involves planning investments and purchasing ships in order to offer transport services over a long period, while the second sees ships as an asset with the aim of buying and selling ships on the markets. Companies active in second-hand market for ships employ personnel for the scanning of the market either to buy or to sell ships. The organisation of Oldendorff Carriers, for example, includes departments in Germany and Tokyo, responsible for the sale and purchase of ships (Oldendorff, 2017b). On the contrary, companies adopting the first choice invest in the development of their chartering operations.

The basic forms of structuring observable in dry bulk shipping are the following:

3.4.1 Functional structure

In functional structure, activities are grouped in departments on the basis of their operational specialization. This applies to companies with a small range of services which do not change over the course of time. It allows for central control, leads to a clear definition of competences, and at the same time facilitates concentration on operational issues, and therefore on the development of specialization among the personnel. At the same time, it has weaknesses which are connected precisely with the concentration of the personnel on their specialization, to the detriment, perhaps, of overall company objectives, with the emergence of problems of horizontal communication and difficulty in adapting to changes in the business environment.

In the case of a shipping company which applies a functional structure, there are departments which correspond to the processes which were analyzed in Section 3.2. A typical form of functional structuring according to the process involved is shown in Exhibit 3.2. The extent of functional structuring depends upon the size of the enterprise, and, consequently, upon the volume of jobs and the number of its personnel. In large-size companies which apply a functional structure, each process is organized into an independent department. Functional structure is the traditional form of organization in shipping companies also (Smith and Roggema, 1980). The majority of dry bulk shipping companies, especially those operating fleets of medium and small size, adopt the functional structure for their organization.

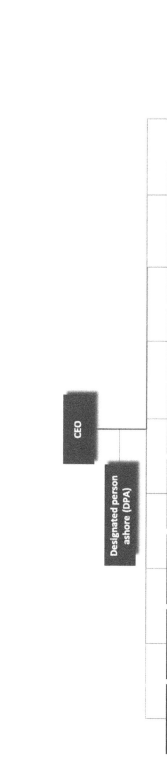

Exhibit 3.2 Functional structure.[4]

Source: Theotokas (2018: Figure 6.1).

3.4.2 Divisional structure

This is a structure by division of activity, which is often referred to as divisional structuring by product or service, or by strategic business units, groups activities, and processes on the basis of the organization's outflows (Daft, 2010: 105). In the case of the shipping industry, it is adopted by enterprises which manage diversified fleets with a large number of ships. The fleet is divided into groups, depending on the specialization of the vessels, and each group constitutes a division. Within each division, those processes which involve the management of the vessel and require specialization as regards its type, such as technical and operational management, are organized into a department, whereas support processes are organized into independent departments, which serve all areas of activity. Exhibit 3.3 shows an indicative form of divisional structure by product or service on the basis of the types of ships managed by the enterprise. The logic of this form of divisional structure is based on the fact that different divisions (types of ships) require different knowledge and skills.

Among the advantages of divisional structuring is the scope it provides for rapid changes in an unstable environment, flexibility in the organization of each division, the co-ordination of different processes within each division, and the development of personnel with overall supervision of the company's processes.

Among the disadvantages of divisional structures are the increased cost of implementation, as it eliminates economies of scale in the operational departments, the likelihood of a conflict between the divisions over claims on business resources, and the addition of a further level of management.

Its full implementation in the shipping industry is observable only in enterprises with very large fleets and many types of vessel, each fleet being made up of a large number of ships.

Exhibit 3.3 Divisional structure.
Source: Theotokas (2018: Figure 6.2).

3.4.3 Matrix structure

The matrix form of organization involves the grouping of activities on the basis of process and activity and combines vertical and horizontal lines of power simultaneously. On the vertical axes are the company's various processes, and on the horizontal, the different areas of activity or the various tasks which the enterprise carries out (Carrell et al., 1997).

The matrix form increases flexibility and allows for adaptation to any rapid changes in the conditions of the operating environment of the enterprises. It makes possible the optimal use of specialized personnel and equipment, motivation, flexibility, encouragement of co-operation, staff development, creativity, and the creation and diffusion of knowledge. Of course, it possesses disadvantages which have to do with the existence of a system of duplicated power and responsibility and probably time-consuming procedures in the taking of decisions and the resolution of disputes.

This is a kind of departmentalization suitable for dry bulk shipping companies, which operate in a dynamic and uncertain environment. A shipping enterprise requires an organizational structure which is simultaneously centralizing and decentralizing, since it needs special decisions on technical fields of high specialization, such as technical management or the scheduling of movements of a ship, but also a high degree of unification of all these decisions. For this reason, the role of a matrix organization is considered substantive in shipping, as it permits the co-ordination of specializations both at the level of process and at that of activity (Frankel, 1982). Furthermore, departmentalization of a matrix form orientates to a greater extent the whole organization towards the vessel and favours decentralization through the entrusting of more decisions to its personnel (Downard, 1990). The diversification of fleets they manage and the need for greater efficiency to increase competitiveness were factors that favoured the implementation of matrix structure (Smith and Roggema, 1980).

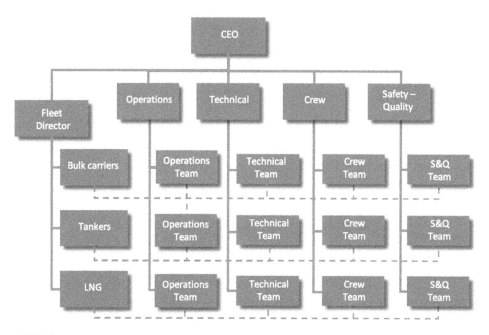

Exhibit 3.4 Matrix structure.
Source: Theotokas (2018: Figure 6.3).

3.4.4 Team structure

The structure of this form is based on interdepartmental teams. These teams include employees of differing specializations from different departments, a factor which leads to the development of new knowledge and its diffusion, while also contributing to the sound co-ordination of activities in the interior of each team. In effect, each team consists of employees with specializations which correspond to the processes of the satisfaction of demand, described in Section 3.2.

Team structuring constitutes a flexible structure as it keeps the hierarchy and the boundaries of the operational departments within limits. It is thought to increase the adaptability of organizations, improve the co-ordination between the functional specializations, and contribute to the proper employment of the human resources (Morgan, 1986: 82). Nevertheless, it is likely to cause an increase in complexity in the organization of the enterprise, particularly if that includes many small-size teams, resulting in difficulties arising with regard to control. For this reason, a factor crucial for the success of the teams is their unification (Mullern, 2000).

As by means of team structure an organization acquires a horizontal orientation, its flexibility is increased, while at the same time, decentralization in the decision-making and specialization of personnel who take on overall supervision of the task of management are facilitated. It is also important that the employees on land are orientated towards the result, that is, serving the ships so that they operate effectively. Each team is co-ordinated by the manager of the fleet, and itself undertakes the management of a group of the company's ships. Organization based on teams is thought to be appropriate for shipping enterprises (Korres and Thanopoulos, 2005: 109–110). Because it "reduces interfaces and waiting times, gives clear ownership and accountability of results", its adoption is considered as a best practice in ship management (Fraunhofer CML & GL 2013: 13).

Norden has adopted a similar approach (Norden, 2014). The technical department of the company (which actually brings together technical management of the fleet, crewing, safety and environment, inspections and purchase, and newbuildings), consists of four vessel groups (Norden, 2017d). Each vessel group is in charge of the technical operation of the vessels, which means that members of the group hold the responsibility of managing all issues for their vessels, either themselves or by asking for the assistance of support functions of the department which they need (Theotokas, 2018). An approach based on team structure adopts for its organisation the Thenamaris (Ships Management), who operates a diversified fleet of more than 90 ships (Thenamaris, 2017).

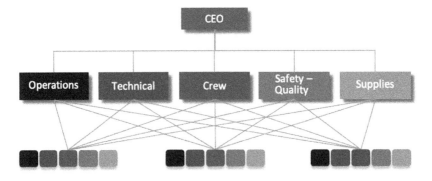

Exhibit 3.5 Team structure.
Source: Theotokas (2018: Figure 6.5).

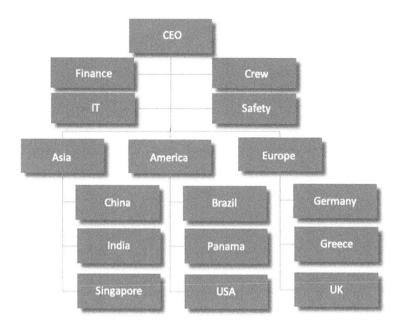

Exhibit 3.6 Geographical structure.
Source: Theotokas (2018: Figure 6.4).

3.4.5 Geographical structure

Geographical structuring is designed in light of the region in which the enterprise operates and is active, and is based on the logic of the concentration of all the activities associated with a region in one structure. The basic advantages of a geographical structure are better co-ordination of activities and scope for the decentralization of decisions. Nevertheless, its implementation precludes the possibility of making use of economies of scale, since it leads to the existence of many employees with the same duties in different geographical regions.

It is suggested for the organization of businesses which have activities at many geographical points, such as shipping enterprises, the central co-ordination of which is not always effective. Liner shipping companies mainly belong to this category, as they maintain extensive networks of agents in many ports all over the world. Enterprises with bulk shipping fleets of high specialization fall in the same category. By implementing this form of organization, they are able to have a better knowledge of the particular features of each market which they address, thus increasing their effectiveness. Oldendorff Carriers, for example, an operator specialized in transshipments, implements a structure similar to the geographical, as it can be seen in Table 3.1, where the different offices of the company and their responsibilities are presented. Commercial, operation and administration are the processes met in most of the offices' structures. Each structure, depending on the specific needs, size and resources, might adopt the functional, the matrix, the team structure, or a combination of them. Adopting a similar approach, Pacific Basin, who manages a fleet of over 200 handy-size and supramax bulk carriers, operates a network of 10 commercial offices and three technical/crewing offices around the world in order for its chartering and operations staff to be positioned close to customers and markets (Pacific Basin, 2017). Taking into account that large ship management companies have become international with established offices in the main maritime centres (Panayides, 2001), their organizational structure could be considered as geographical.

Table 3.1 Oldendorff Carriers Offices

Branch	Responsibilities							
	Commercial	Operations	Technical	Fleet Management	Research	Financial	Administration	Global Board
Germany	+	+		+	+	+	+	+
Singapore	+	+			+	+	+	
Dubai	+	+					+	
Abu Dhabi	+	+	+			+	+	
Mumbai	+	+			+	+	+	
Melbourne	+	+					+	
Vancouver	+	+					+	
Stamford	+	+					+	
London	+	+					+	
Tokyo	+	+					+	
Shanghai	+	+		+	+		+	
Trinidad	+							
Guyana	+	+	+			+	+	
Iskederun	+							
Hong Kong	+							
Santiago	+							
Copenhagen	+						+	

Source: Based on data from Oldendorff (2017b)

Exhibit 3.7 Network structure.
Source: Theotokas (2018: Figure 6.6).

3.4.6 Network structure

The network structure is implemented by companies which outsource many of their manage-ment processes to other enterprises in the same group or to external associates, and maintain a small-scale structure with a co-ordinating role. This form of organization provides the company with maximum flexibility and makes it possible for it to concentrate more effectively on the processes which it carries out itself or that it regards as crucial for its competitiveness. This, of course, is likely to lead to a reduction of control over the processes which it outsources to external associates. Network structure orientates the company towards cost control by means of a search for effective options in terms of cost and towards the avoidance of overlapping in its internal operation (Lorange, 2005). Among the advantages of this structure are a reduction of cost and increased flexibility and innovation, while the disadvantages include difficulties in co-ordination and control, together with probable competition on the part of external associates who may extend their activities. A crucial factor for the effectiveness of the network structure is the IT-based linkage between the partners, which permits their control and co-ordination by the central structure. Golden Ocean, as already mentioned, outsources extensively operating a limited structure, which is linked with independent ship managers to whom the technical man-agement of vessels is assigned (Golden Ocean, 2017).

3.4.7 Combination of forms

In the case of many shipping companies, there might be a combination of the above forms of organizational structure so as to respond to their individual characteristics, strategies, resources, and needs. Thus, they develop mixed forms of structuring, basic combinations of which are the following:

- the combination of structuring by functions and divisional structuring. This is implemented by enterprises which manage a diversified fleet. Depending on the strategic approach of the company, divisions may be based on type of vessels or on type of services provided. Rickmers Group, for example, operated two segments or divisions, one for Maritime Assets

(Rickmers, 2017a), which provided services related to financial and commercial management of vessels, and one for Maritime Services (Rickmers, 2017b), which provided technical and operational ship management for own and third-party vessels. In each division, services are provided by specialized companies. In a similar approach, Chinese Maritime Transport (CMT), a diversified shipping group, organizes in departments the finance, the general administration, the information technology and the personnel, and in divisions each one of the sectors to which is active, i.e. shipping, inland trucking, terminal & logistics and agency & travel, respectively (CMT, 2017);

- the combination of functional and team structuring. This is usually adopted by large enterprises. Within groups of core functions, such as technical, team structuring is followed. In the case of the rest of the line and staff departments, functional structuring is applied. For example, in case of Danaos, a company operating container vessels chartered by liner operators, the technical department of the company, whose aim is high vessel utilization, cost-effective efficiency, and the promotion of environmental awareness, consists of teams, with each team responsible for a certain number of vessels (Danaos, 2016);
- the combination of functional, divisional and geographical structuring. Large companies are likely to have offices in different maritime centres, each of which is capable of undertaking specific processes for one of the types of vessels which they manage. Large diversified groups, whose dry bulk activities form part of their activities, as for example Mitsui O.S.K. Lines (MOL, 2017), implement this approach.

3.5 Crewing issues

The workforce of ships, the crew, constitutes a special category of employees, for reasons which have to do with the nature of the work which they carry out. The working environment of a ship itself gives rise to conditions which differ significantly from the corresponding conditions on land. Furthermore, while in the case of the human resources of the offices, the labour market has geographical limits, in that of the crews, this does not apply, as the seamen's labour market is global.

Technological developments in the design, building, and equipping of ships have significantly reduced the number of members of a crew required, but, at the same time, the working conditions for seafarers have intensified. In the last ten years in particular, with the introduction of a series of regulations concerning the operation of a vessel, the workload has increased considerably for seamen. Attention should be drawn particularly to the negative experience produced among seafarers by the fact that the burden of bureaucracy which they have to manage is particularly large, complex, and time-consuming (Danish Maritime Authority, 2013). The regulations seek to focus on the human factor and to regulate matters concerned with training and safety, but, since in their drafting, factors relating to the seamen's workload are not taken into consideration to the necessary extent, they do not fully succeed in this objective.

At the same time, the search for low-cost seamen has led to the existence of multicultural crews, but attention has not always been given to the socialization of crew members, resulting in the creation of conditions of alienation. This, in conjunction with the introduction of regulations such as the International Ship and Port Facility Security Code (ISPS Code), which restricts seamen's shore leave in ports, gives rise to conditions which could be compared to those of "house arrest" on land (Horck, 2005).

Many enterprises seek to exploit the advantages provided by communications technology, both in the effective management itself of the vessel, and in the satisfaction and cohesion of the crew. With the passage of time and the creation of the necessary technological conditions, the provision for those employed on the ship of conditions of unimpeded and constant communication with the external environment will be the rule for well-organized shipping companies, given that one of the factors which contribute to the attraction and retention of crews is the possibility of communication with their families during the course of the voyage. As can be seen from recent research, a lack of proper communication with the family appears to be the most important reason for the abandonment of the seafarer's profession (Papachristou et al., 2015).

The management of the vessels' workforce is the responsibility of the crewing department. The task of the crewing department is the selection and staffing of ships with capable and qualified individuals, their training, and the planning of their career, as well as the resolution of any related issue.

The need for there to be a separate crewing department is due to the fact that, even in the case of small enterprises, the number of the crew and the special characteristics of the seafarers' profession call for the presence of personnel in the offices who are concerned with the management of their labour issues. If in the offices of a shipping company which manages ten ships with 25–30 shore staff, its crews can number in excess of 280 seamen, including those onboard, as well as those on shore leave. The need for a separate department for crew management applies to those shipping companies that do not implement the strategy of outsourcing the crew management processes to external associates.

The staffing of the crewing department is based on former seafarers, that is, on individuals who have experience of working on a ship and are in a position to understand the seafarers' attitudes and behaviours and to appreciate their needs.

Given that the crew of every ship is a team which lives and works at a great distance from the shipping company's headquarters, the choice as to its composition has to be made in a way which ensures its cohesion and efficiency, as well as its ability to perform well and safely, both in normal and in emergency conditions. To safeguard this last characteristic becomes even more difficult in the case of ships which employ crews of differing nationalities. Several studies which focus on the management of cultural diversity, as well as on the safety management of shipping companies, reveal the importance of national culture and of other factors that lead to differentiation among the crew members (Havold, 2007; Progoulaki and Theotokas, 2016).

The world seafarer's labour market is made up of individual markets, the existence of which makes possible a distinction between groups of seamen and the payment of differing remuneration to them (Leggate and McConville, 2002). For shipping companies to be able to exploit these differences, they must be in a position not only to identify the individual markets, but to attract and engage high-quality seamen from them. If those who take the decisions do not possess the knowledge and information necessary for this choice, and if, at the same time, the cost of their acquisition is great and in excess of the potential benefits, the outsourcing of the relevant activity to enterprises which possess the appropriate know-how is an attractive strategic option (Theotokas, 2018).

In light of the above, the management of crews may be carried out either by a special department within the enterprise or by a specialist subsidiary, or be outsourced in its entirety to third-party enterprises (ship management or crew agents). The choice is determined, *inter alia*, by the approach which is followed for the development of its ships' human resources. (Papadimitriou et al., 2005)

3.6 Concluding remarks

Dry bulk shipping companies operate in a dynamic and changing environment. In order for them to respond to the demands to which this gives rise, it is necessary to maintain degrees of flexibility which make it possible for them to engage in the necessary adjustments. In spite of the fact that as a whole they are active and operate competitively in the world markets, differentiating factors, such as size, strategies, the level of technology, or the culture, lead to different approaches to their organization and management.

It is precisely because of this characteristic that an analysis of the organizational and management phenomena of these enterprises should take into account the way these interact and define. In this direction, further research on the differentiating factors mentioned above and the way they affect the organization of dry bulk shipping companies, and create the need for specific adjustments to it, could contribute in the expansion of the research field. Furthermore, enrichment of existing literature with research focusing on approaches adopted by dry bulk shipping companies in various national contexts could offer better understanding of their organization.

Notes

1 Basic points in the analysis contained in this chapter are drawn from Theotokas I. (2018).
2 For the strategy of outsourcing activities in shipping see Panayides, (2001); Theotokas (2018).
3 For the systems theory, and the organisations as open systems, see Clegg and Dunkerley, (1999: 198–212).
4 This chart as well as those presented in Exhibits 3–7 are indicative of the way in which the structure they describe are developed. It should be noted that the charts don't describe nor include the complete range of the departments of a shipping enterprise.

References

Alizadeh, A.H. & Nomikos N.K. (2010) 'An overview of the dry bulk shipping industry' in Grammenos, Th. (ed.), *The Handbook of Maritime Economics*. 2nd ed. London: Lloyd's List, pp. 319–353.
Carrell, M.R., Jennings, D.F., & Heavrin, C. (1997) *Fundamentals of Organizational Behavior*. New Jersey: Prentice Hall.
Clegg, S. & Dunkerley, D. (1999) *Organization, Class and Control*. London: Routledge.
CMT (2017) 'CMT organization chart', *Chinese Maritime Transport Ltd* http://www.agcmt.com.tw/html/e-organization.html [accessed 27 December 2017].
Daft, R.L. (2010) *Management*. 9th ed. Mason: South-Western Cengage.
Daft, R.L. (2010) *Organization Theory and Design*. 10th ed. Mason: South-Western Cengage Learning.
Danaos (2016) *Corporate Social Responsibility Report 2016*. Danaos Shipping Co. Ltd.
Danish Maritime Authority (2013) *Survey on Administrative Burdens among International Seafarers. Final report*. Kongens Lyngby: COWI.
Donnelly, J.H., –Gibson, J.L., & Ivancevich, J.M. (1995) *Fundamentals of Management*, 9th ed. Chicago: Irwin.
Downard, J.M. (1990) *Managing Ships*. London: Fairplay Publications.
Eagle Bulk (2017) Annual Report 2016 *Eagle Bulk Shipping*.
Frankel, E. (1982) *Management and Operations of American Shipping*. Boston: Auburn House.
Fraunhofer C.M.L. & G.L. (2013) *Best Practice Ship Management Study 2013*. Germanicher Lloyd: Fraunhofer CML.
Frontiline (2017) Form 20-F. Frontline Ltd.
Golden Ocean (2017) Form 20-F. Golden Ocean.
Goulielmos, A.M. (1996) *Management of Shipping Companies*. Vol.II Athens: Stamoulis Publications.
Grammenos, C. Th. (2010) 'Revisiting credit risk, analysis and policy in bank shipping finance' in C. Th. Grammenos (ed.) *The Handbook of Maritime Economics and Business*, London: LLP Publications, pp. 777–810.
Hall, R.H. (1996) *Organizations – Structures, Processes, Outcomes*. 6th ed. New Jersey: Prentice Hall.
Havold, J.I. (2007) 'National cultures and safety orientation: A study of seafarers working for Norwegian shipping companies', *Work & Stress*. 21 (2) 173–195.
Hope, E. & Boe, O. (1981) 'Investment behaviour in Norwegian bulk shipping' in Hope, E. (ed.), *Studies in Shipping Economics in Honour of Professor Arnljot Stromme Svendsen*. Oslo: Bedriftsokonomens Forlag A/S.
Horck, J. (2005) 'Getting the best from multi-cultural manning' *BIMCO Bulletin*. 100 (4) 28–36.
Kavussanos, M.G. (1996) 'Comparisons of volatility in the dry-cargo ship sector: Spot versus time charters, and smaller versus larger vessels', *Journal of Transport Economics and Policy* 30 (1) 67–82.

Kavussanos, M.G. & Visvikis, I.D. (2006) 'Shipping freight derivatives: a survey of recent evidence', *Maritime Policy and Management* 33 (3) 233–255.

Kennedy, M.B. (2011) 'Crew – The operator's greatest challenge', *Alert – The International Human Element Bulletin* 25 January, p. 2.

Klaveness (2017) Activities *Klaveness* https://klaveness.com/activities/#overview [assessed 27 December 2017].

Korres, A.I. & Thanopoulos, I. (2005) *Ναυτιλιακή θεωρία και επιχειρηματικότητα στην εποχή της ποιότητας* [*Shipping Theory and Entrepreneurism in the Age of Quality*] Athens: Interbooks [in Greek].

Leggate, H. & McConville, J. (2002) 'The economics of the seafaring labour market in Grammenos, C.T. (ed.) *The Handbook of Maritime Economics and Business*. London: Lloyd's of London Press pp. 443–468.

Lorange, P. (2005) *Shipping Company Strategies*. Oxford: Elsevier.

Miller, A. (1998) *Strategic Management*. New York: McGraw-Hill.

MOL (2017) 'Organization' *Mitsui O.S.K. Lines.* http://www.mol.co.jp/en/corporate/organization/index.html [accessed 27 December 2017].

Morgan, G. (1986) *Images of Organization*. London: Sage Publications.

Mullern, T. (2000) 'Integrating the team-based structure in the business rocesses' in Pettigrew, A.M. & Fenton, E.M. (eds), *The Innovating Organization* London: Sage Publications pp. 236–255.

Nomikos, N.K. & Alizadeh, A.H. (2010) 'Managing Freight Rate Risk Using Freight Derivatives: An Overview of the Empirical Evidence', in Grammenos, Th. (ed.), *The Handbook of Maritime Economics*. 2nd ed. London: Lloyd's List pp. 745–775.

Norden News (2014) 'Technical department future proofed', *Norden News*, Summer pp. 4–6.

Norden (2017) 'Organisation overview' Norden http://www.ds-norden.com/profile/organisation/overview/ [accessed 14 July 2017].

Oldendorff (2017a) 'At a glance', *Oldendorff Carriers.* https://www.oldendorff.com/pages/company [accessed 21 December 2017].

Oldendorff (2017b) 'Finder. Offices', *Oldendorff Carriers.* https://www.oldendorff.com/finder [accessed 21 December 2017].

Pacific Basin (2017) 'Our global network', *Pacific Basin* http://www.pacificbasin.com/en/customers/global_network.php [accessed 28 December 2017].

Panayides, Ph.M. (2001) *Professional Ship Management – Marketing and Strategy.* Aldershot: Ashgate.

Papachristou, A., Stanchev D., & Theotokas, I. (2015) 'The role of communication to the retention of seafarers in the profession', *WMU Journal of Maritime Affairs.* 14 (1) 159–176.

Papadimitriou, G., Progoulaki, M., & Theotokas, I. (2005) 'Manning strategies in shipping – The role of outsourcing', Proceedings of International Association of Maritime Economists (IAME) Conference, *Contemporary Developments in Shipping: Efficiency, Productivity, Competitiveness*, Cyprus (22–25 June).

Progoulaki, M. & Theotokas, I. (2016) 'Managing culturally diverse maritime human resources as a shipping company's core competence', *Maritime Policy and Management* 43 (7) 860–873.

Rickmers (2017a) 'Maritime assets', *Rickmers Group* http://www.rickmers.com/index.php?id=1170 [accessed 28 December 2017].

Rickmers (2017b) 'Maritime services', *Rickmers Group* http://www.rickmers.com/index.php?id=1167&no_cache=1 [accessed 28 December 2017].

Smith, M.H. & Roggema, J. (1980) 'Emerging organizational values in shipping – Part 4: Decentralization – The redefinition of authority in shipping company organization', *Maritime Policy and Management*, 7 (4) 255–269

Star Bulk (2017a) 'Business strategy', *Star Bulk* http://www.starbulk.com/en/business-strategy [accessed 27 December 2017].

Star Bulk (2017b) 'Star Bulk Carriers Corp. announces closing of private placement of 6.310.272 common shares', *Star Bulk Carriers.*

Syriopoulos, Th. C. (2007) 'Financing Greek shipping: Modern instruments, methods and markets' in A. A. Pallis (ed.), *Maritime Transport – The Greek paradigm*, Oxford: Elsevier pp. 171–219.

Thenamaris (2017) 'On Shore', *Thenamaris.* http://www.thenamaris.com/careers/on-shore/ [accessed 8 December 2017].

Theotokas I. (2018) *Organization and Management of Shipping Companies.* Abingdon: Routledge.

Theotokas, I. & Progoulaki, M. (2007) 'Cultural diversity, manning strategies and management practices in Greek shipping', *Maritime Policy and Management* 34 (3) 383–40.

Organization and management of tanker shipping companies

D. V. Lyridis and C. Papaleonidas

4.1 Introduction

The significance of the shipping industry and the tanker market in particular is well known and described by many researchers and professionals. However, the market is not a standalone "organism", but rather a resultant of the multiple tanker companies operating in a competitive environment. This operation is based on organizational concepts and management tools that simultaneously have both market-general and company-specific elements. In the end, the significance of the tanker market is reflected upon the significance of the management of tanker companies that encompasses the organization of numerous departments, human and material resources, and activities.

The aim of this chapter is to elaborate on different aspects of management of tanker shipping companies, crucial to the implementation of corporate policy guidelines and strategy that affect long-term business viability.

In the first part, general information about the tanker industry is presented, including nomenclature and information on the tanker shipping market in the context of the oil and gas market as a whole. Building upon this information, the chapter focuses on widespread concepts of organizational structure, and provides a description of a standard organizational chart of tanker companies.

The second part of the chapter analyzes organizational structures of shipping companies, while the third part of the chapter deals with selected management issues of tanker companies and contemporary tools utilized in the management process.

Finally, the chapter ends with an outline of future technological trends, which may be implemented by the tanker shipping companies, with emphasis on blockchain technology and sea traffic management systems and enhance the management of said companies.

4.2 General information on tanker shipping

4.2.1 Nomenclature

Tanker shipping refers to the waterborne transportation of liquid bulk products in specialized vessels. The tanker market includes the transportation of crude oil, chemicals, liquefied petroleum gas (LPG), and liquefied natural gas (LNG).

Tanker vessels can be classified according to their cargo. Oil tankers (crude and product) constitute the largest segment of the tanker fleet, whereas gas carriers – specialized vessels used exclusively for the transportation of LPG and LNG – tend to follow the growing consumption needs for natural gas (UNCATD 2017).

Crude oil tanker vessels, as their name suggests, are utilized to transport crude oil or oil products such as diesel oil and residual fuel. The vessels connect the upstream and downstream parts of the oil supply chain, from production sites to oil terminals and refineries. Depending on the transportation route from the supply site to the demand site and its restrictions, crude oil tankers vary in size and transportation capacity.

Apart from crude oil tankers, smaller product tanker vessels transport petroleum-based products of the refinery process (gasoline, naphtha, kerosene, jet or fuel oil, gas oil, etc.) to the end segment of the downstream part of the supply chain for consumption. In order to achieve this, a clean-up process is necessary whenever a change of cargo type takes place. However, this is not easy and different cargoes are stored separately during all processes (parcel tanker) and circulated through a complex piping network and valve system on board.

Gas carriers carry natural gas and petroleum gas in liquid form in order to store greater volume of the gas. The liquefied gas is transferred with the use of pumps, through appropriate infrastructure, to specific tanks within the ship. The specific mechanism and its technical characteristics vary from cargo to cargo.

The LPG ships can carry propane, butane, ammonia, propylene, and ethylene. Common to all these gases is the low boiling point (–44 °C to 0 °C) and high vapour pressure.

The LNG carriers are used to transport natural gas from which major impurities like sulphur and carbon dioxide have been removed. The liquefaction of the natural gas is achieved at temperatures down to approximately –163 °C, either onshore at a liquefaction plant or offshore at an appropriately converted barge and on the spot at the production site with the utilization of an LNG floating production storage offloading unit (FPSO/FLNG).

Groups of tanker vessels are differentiated according to their size, (e.g. ULCC, VLCC, Suezmax, etc.). The ship's design and size and consequently her storage capacity range depend on a number of factors that fit the business and the specific goals of the ship-owner. Namely, the type of cargo, the loading and unloading port, and the routes along which it will be deployed. Nevertheless, there is significant differentiation in DWT tonnage for each ship type. A widely used classification is depicted in Tables 4.1 and 4.2.

Tanker shipping of liquid bulk cargo is preferred as an economical and convenient way for transportation (Lun et al. 2013). The relation between the ship's cargo capacity, hence her size and economics, is related as depicted by the unit cost function (Stopford 2009):

$$Unit\,Cost = \frac{LC + OPEX + CH}{PS}$$

Where, LC is the capital cost of the ship, OPEX is the operating cost over her life, CH is the cost of handling the cargo, and PS is the tonnage of the cargo. Apparently, cargo capacity (PS) is the critical factor for achieving economies of scale, since its increase does not come with a reciprocal increase of the costs in the numerator. For example, a VLCC can have the triple DWT and only twice the cost of a Panamax. Thus, VLCC and ULCC tankers are most feasible when deployed on long distance routes, whereas Suezmax and Aframax tankers are better on medium distance routes.

The transportation process of crude oil can be characterized as unidirectional, since ships return empty to the oil production site. The same applies for LNG carriers, as the terminal of discharge includes regasification facilities in order for the natural gas to be induced in the local network.

Table 4.1 Tanker Vessel Types

Vessel Type	Typical DWT	Cargo Type	Active Vessels (Excl. Laid up)
VLCC/ULCC	>200,000	Crude Oil	734
Suezmax	120,000–200,000	Crude Oil/Refined Products	557
LR-2	80,000–159,999	Refined Products	341
Aframax & Neo Panamax	80,000–119,999	Crude Oil	649
Panamax	60,000–79,999	Crude Oil	87
LR-1	45,000–79,999	Refined Products	361
MR	25,000–44,999	Refined Products	1,952
Handysize	10,000–59,999	Crude Oil	1,880
Small Product/Chemical/ General Purpose	<10,000	Refined Products/Other	5,390

Source: Clarksons * retrieved on 08/01/2018. Includes only active vessels

Table 4.2 Gas Carrier Vessel Types

Vessel Type	Typical Capacity (m^3)	Cargo Type	Active Vessels (excl. Laid Up)
Q-MAX	>220,000	LNG	15
Q-FLEX	209,000–219,000	LNG	31
UPPER CONVENTIONAL	145,000–208,999	LNG	276
LOWER CONVENTIONAL	90,000–144,999	LNG	113
MED MAX	36,000–89,999	LNG	9
SMALL SCALE	<36,000	LNG	37
VLGC	60,000–99,999	LPG	273
LGC	40,000–59,999	LPG	18
MIDSIZE GAS	20,000–39,000	LPG	178
HANDYSIZE GAS	10,000–19,999	LPG	86
SEMI REF/ETH GAS	5,000–9,999	LPG	267
SMALL SEMI-REF/ETH GAS	<4,999	LPG	620

Source: Clarksons * retrieved on 08/01/2018. Includes only active vessels

On the contrary, all other tankers (product, LPG) can be better utilized when transferring their cargo from terminal to terminal, because this option has the advantage of servicing multiple destinations.

A shipping company managing a fleet of tankers is active in four different yet linked markets (Lun et al. 2013): the newbuilding market where orders for new ships are placed, the freight market where shipping services for the transportation of a specific cargo are sought in exchange for a predetermined charter, the sale and purchase market where a company can sell one of its vessels and acquire a second-hand vessel, and the demolition market where ships, usually old, are scrapped and their parts are recycled.

4.2.2 Oil and gas market

The conditions of the tanker shipping market and the managerial decisions of the companies operating in the respective markets are intertwined with the oil and gas market. In this respect,

Table 4.3 Key Crude Tanker Trade Routes

Route Name	Locations
TD1	Middle East Gulf to US Gulf
TD2	Middle East Gulf to Singapore
TD3	Middle East Gulf to Japan
TD4	West Africa to US Gulf
TD7	North Sea to Continental Europe
TD8	Kuwait to Singapore
TD9	Caribbean to US Gulf
TD12	Amsterdam-Rotterdam-Antwerp to US Gulf
TD14	South East Asia to east coast Australia
TD15	West Africa to China
TD17	Baltic to UK-Continental Europe (UKC)
TD18	Baltic to UKC
TD19	Cross Mediterranean
TD20	West Africa to Continental Europe
TD21	Caribbean to US Gulf

Source: Tradewinds

Table 4.4 Key Product Tanker Trade Routes

Route Name	Locations
TC1	Ras Tanura, Saudi Arabia, to Yokohama, Japan
TC5	Ras Tanura to Yokohama
TC8	Jubail, Saudi Arabia, to Rotterdam
TC2	Rotterdam to New York
TC3	Caribbean to US Atlantic coast
TC4	Singapore to Japan
TC6	Skikda, Algeria, to Marseilles, France
TC7	Singapore to Sydney
TC10	Yeosu, South Korea, to Los Angeles
TC11	Yeosu to Singapore
TC12	Sikka, India, to Chiba, Japan
TC14	Houston to Amsterdam

Source: Tradewinds

it is essential to describe the concepts of supply, demand, and pricing for crude oil, as this is the most significant factor that determines the prices of refinery products and in some occasions the price of natural gas and LNG.

Crude oil and its products are used in many production processes and still cover a large percentage of the global energy consumption, whereas natural gas presents a steady increase (Figures 4.1 and 4.2).

The naturally unequal distribution of oil and gas reserves and production sites, along with the unequal energy needs per country (see Figures 4.3 and 4.4), are the driving force for the transportation of oil.

The supply and demand of hydrocarbons is a complex matter determined by many factors (Holditch & Chianelli 2008). Supply of crude oil is greatly affected by high oil price, which

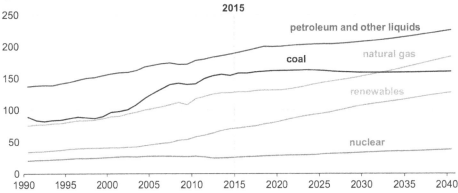

World energy consumption by energy source
quadrillion Btu

Figure 4.1 Global energy consumption by energy source.
Source: US Energy Information Administration, International Energy Outlook 2017.

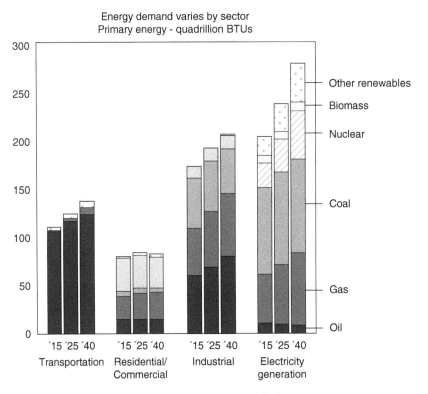

Figure 4.2 Global energy demand by sector and fuel.
Source: Exxon outlook for energy 2017.

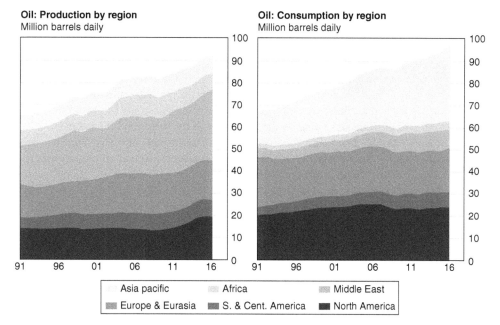

Figure 4.3 Global oil production and consumption by region.
Source: BP Outlook 2017.

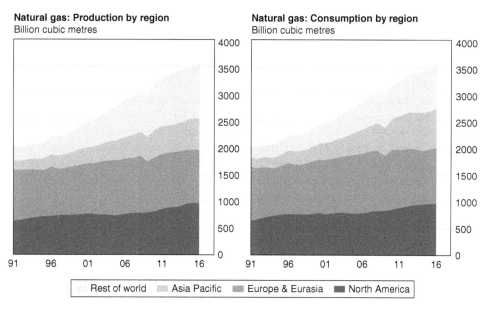

Figure 4.4 Global gas production and consumption by region.
Source: BP Outlook 2017.

leads to capital expenditure for oil exploration, development, and production of proven reserves. Specialized and experienced manpower scarcity is a subject raised in recent years prompted by the low oil price environment. A direct consequence of that is major personnel restructure of oil and gas companies (Helman, 2015), which in turn can possibly decelerate oil production. Another important obstacle for a possible rise in oil supply is limited access to oil resources (Holditch & Chianelli 2008), which in conjunction with the available capacity of refineries is an additional variable that affects the supply of oil products. Hydrocarbons can be feasibly transported via ship or pipeline depending on the geography of the region and the distance.

Global economic development is the major cause for an increase of the oil demand, especially in a low oil price environment. Policies and regulations for limitation of emissions and environmentally friendly operations could confine oil demand (Holditch & Chianelli 2008) but may favour other hydrocarbons such as LNG (IEA, Shell, BP, EXXON). Last but not least, research of new economically feasible technologies could limit the use of oil and its products, albeit not drastically.

4.2.3 Tanker shipping market

The tanker shipping market is often characterized as one operating under "perfect" competition (Zannetos 1964, Lyridis & Zacharioudakis 2012, Lun et al. 2013). This statement is based on several facts, the first of which is the plethora of ship-owners, relatively to other markets that provide identical shipping services. Complementary to this, the transparency regarding the freight rates proves to be a barrier for freight rate manipulation. The tanker shipping market is a relatively open market in terms of laws, regulations, and economic factors for placing or withdrawing capital in the form of a ship. Notwithstanding the aforementioned conditions, a relatively higher capital investment is required to acquire ships either new or second-hand.

The vessels at the market are contracted-chartered by brokers and shipbrokers to transfer cargo according to a specific freight arrangement. The contracts under which a ship is chartered can vary between the following: voyage charter, time charter, bareboat charter, consecutive voyages, and contract of affreightment (CoA) (Brodie 2006, Stopford 2009). Long-term contracts (e.g. time charters) engage the ship and her crew for a pre-arranged period, whereas short-term contracts (e.g. time charter trip) can last for just a single voyage (Lyridis & Zacharioudakis 2012). Especially in certain markets such as the LNG shipping market, long-term charters hold a dominant position compared to short-term charters trade in the spot market (see also Figure 4.5) (IGU 2017). However, this is subject to change in a similar way to the oil tanker industry, but an in-depth examination of this evolving market is beyond the limits of this chapter.

The supply of tanker shipping services is linked with the world tanker fleet and its productivity, the newbuilding order book, the scrapping of – usually old – vessels, and of course the freight rates (Stopford 2009). The demand of the global seaborne oil trade is affected by the state of the global economy and the oil trade (Lun et al. 2013), transport costs, significant political events (Stopford 2009), as well as possible refinery margins, oil stock building policies, etc. (UNCATD 2016).

The tanker shipping market presents fundamental differences from other shipping markets such as liner shipping (Stopford 2009). The first of those differences being its flexibility due to the absence of a regular fixed shipping schedule. Thus, tanker operators can adjust to the fluctuation of supply and demand in contrast with a liner company, which has no other choice but to service ports according to a specific schedule. Furthermore, the discrete nature of the liner cargo, which is transported in containers, makes its optimum management a rather complicated

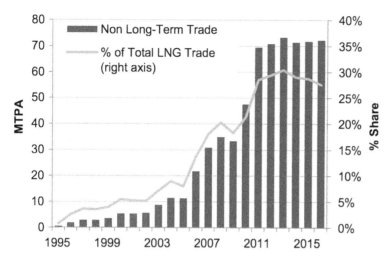

Figure 4.5 LNG short-term trade compared to total LNG trade.
Source: IGU Report 2017.

issue in terms of logistics. On the contrary, cargo management in tanker shipping maybe simpler logistically but has strict safety procedures, especially in LNG shipping.

Tanker vessels offering their services are operated either by shipping companies, which are subsidiaries of integrated oil groups (industrial shipping), or by individual ship-owners (tramp shipping) (Christiansen et al. 2007, Lyridis & Zacharioudakis 2012). In the first case, the ship operator usually owns the cargo and aims at the minimization of the shipping cost. Although industrial shipping represents the minority of the tanker shipping market, major oil companies can influence the tanker market because they are important charterers and they hold a signifi-cant market share in oil production. In the case of an individual ship-owner, the ship is operated according to a contract specifying the type and the quantity of cargo, the shipping time frame, and the payment, thus aiming to maximize the profit of the ship operation.

The findings of the study conducted by Glen and Martin (1998) remain topical, listing a variety of factors that have favoured the growth of tramp shipping against industrial shipping in the tanker market:

1 the evolution and growth of the spot oil tanker market;
2 managerial change of the logistics strategy of major oil companies;
3 stricter environmental protection regulations for oil tanker operations.

Indeed, in the 1970–80s, major oil companies shifted away from oil transportation as a core busi-ness following the 1970s oil crises, in order to limit their exposure (Lun et al. 2013). Thus, inde-pendent ship-owners adjust to fluctuation in oil transportation demand. Specialization of their services does not bound capital to other industries, thus offering them a larger economical capacity.

Furthermore, independent shipping companies are characterized by managerial and admin-istrative flexibility regarding decision such as building or buying new vessels, fleet deployment, etc. This flexibility proves ideal to exploit liquid market conditions, higher freight rates, or lower vessels' value. Moreover, they are relatively independent players in terms of shipping services for oil companies, as well as being less exposed to political pressures.

Table 4.5 World Industrial LNG Carrier Fleet

LNG Company	# of Vessels
ADNOC	8
BP	7
Brunei Gas Carriers	4
Chevron	7
CNOOC	1
ENGIE	4
Hyundai LNG Shipping	9
Japan Liquid Gas	1
Mitsubishi Corp	2
Mitsui & Co.	1
Mitsui O.S.K. Lines	26
Nakilat, JC	8
Nigeria LNG Ltd.	13
Petronas	28
Qatar Gas (Nakilat)	29
Shell	17
SNAM SpA	2
Sonangol	3
Sonatrach Petroleum	5
Tokyo LNG Tanker Co.	5
Total Industrial LNG Fleet	**180**
Total LNG Fleet	**505**
Industrial/Total Ratio	**35.64%**

Source: Clarksons * retrieved on 08/01/2018. Includes only active vessels

Based on the aforementioned facts, chartering a tanker vessel from an independent shipping company has been established as a more feasible solution for oil companies that they usually resort to instead of building their own fleet (Lyridis & Zacharioudakis 2012). This fact is also proved for the world fleet of LNG carriers, despite the fact that at least 25% is owned directly by large LNG producers as depicted in Table 4.5.

For a more detailed review of the liquid bulk shipping market the reader can refer to the work of Lyridis and Zacharioudakis (2012) and Lun et al. (2013). The scope of this chapter is to provide valuable insight into the structure and management methods applied by companies that provide the ship management services in the tanker shipping market.

4.3 Company organizational structures

Over the years, shipping companies evolved in their form and structure, with Stopford's (2009) presented examples of typical shipping company structures remaining timely to this day. The case of private companies owned and managed by their owners is one of the elements of the tanker shipping market conditions that prevent market manipulation and cartelization. In more recent years, diversified shipping groups were formed, as a result of growth and consolidation of fleet, which was supported by ship-owners' access to capital markets and other alternative sources of funding (e.g. investment fund placements, leasing). All these co-existing company forms are not in conflict with each other, as a shipping group may compose of both publicly listed companies and separate private companies.

Another common characteristic within the shipping business and tanker companies, in particular, is the separation of the ownership of the vessels and their operational management. Hence, tanker shipping companies can be categorized as (Lun et al. 2013):

- owners only;
- managers only (third-party ship management);
- owners and managers under the roof of the same parent organization, via subsidiaries or affiliated companies (wholly owned or joint venture).

The first occasion is straightforward and has distinct managerial procedures relating to ownership strategy. "When and in what ships should the company invest in", "should they be newly built or bought second-hand", "what ships should be scrapped" are subjects that concern a ship-owning company. Third-party ship management is a usual option for ship-owners who outsource the technical management to specialized companies. The main reason behind this decision is the technical expertise of the administrator company, which provides the ship-owner with a competitive solution in fleet administration. An additional advantage is that it allows ship-owners to focus on their ownership decisions as described above. Among the ship-owners who resort to third-party ship management are institutional ship-owners such as banks or investment funds, because of the nature of their involvement in shipping. However, the last case of parent companies combining ownership and in-house ship management will be further analyzed below, as it proves more complex in its managerial requirements.

Such a company will normally operate from its main office at the country usually connected with the ship-owner, even if it registers its headquarters or its vessels in a country with favourable economic environment (taxes, etc.). A company responsible with their technical management and companies providing services such as brokering, etc. are frequently independent companies with whom the parent holding company has fixed contracts.

Complementary to these, shipping companies prefer to use firms familiar with the local conditions in specific countries and maintain company representatives abroad, for example superintendents and inspectors at shipyards.

4.3.1 One ship – one company structure

The views of Thorburn (1960) and Zannetos (1964) placed the ship as the primary economic unit, whereas the shipping company, as a whole, played a secondary role. Recently, their opinion was contested by Lun et al. (2013) who state that instead of defining the ship-owning company as a company owning one ship, we should define it as that company that owns a set of ships; therefore, the company is the central economic unit.

Bearing in mind the aforementioned opinions, the tanker shipping market should be examined not statically, but instead in a dynamic fashion, analyzing properly the recent developments in company structures. In particular, the tanker shipping market conditions favour fragmentation due to the conducive and accessible circumstances for entering the market. Fewer obstacles translate to multiple players in the tanker market that cannot significantly consolidate, contrary to other industries, as the freight rates cannot be manipulated. Apart from that, consolidation is not a definitive option for companies considering the fact that meaningful economies of scale can be achieved more in terms of ship size than in fleet size (Lyridis & Zacharioudakis 2012).

The concept of vessels owned by single companies had been first observed in 1981–87 (Lun et al. 2013). Thirty years later, this case has been generalized in the market, as more and more tanker companies opt to found one separate company per each vessel. An obvious benefit of this option is the allotment of economic and financial elements to multiple entities, which mitigates the parent company's exposure to risk (including the risk for liabilities due to accidents) (Lyridis & Zacharioudakis 2012).

4.3.2 Pool structures

Shipping pools are a well-known concept between tanker companies, especially in Europe (Haifeng 2000). They are defined as:

> joint ventures between ship-owners to pool vessels of similar types, with central administration, which are marketed as a single entity, negotiating voyage/time charter parties and contracts of affreightment, where the revenues are pooled and distributed to owners.
>
> *(Murray 1994)*

Haralambides (1996) listed the shipping pool's key characteristics, which remain unchanged:

> Similar tonnage; central administration (pool management company); joint marketing; negotiation of freight rates; centralization of voyage costs; freight collection; weighing system; revenue distribution; fair share.

The main function of tanker companies participating with their fleet to a pool has remained unhinged, namely the transportation of cargo according to a charter, typically a CoA (Stopford 2009).

Thus, the formation of a shipping pool has a twofold goal: to secure a constant revenue flow (from CoAs, spot charters, etc.) for a company and to reduce its risk exposure (Haralambides 1996, Haifeng 2000). More tanker companies can participate in the pool, as it offers a greater possibility to sign CoA and minimize ballast voyage legs and idle time for their ships. Thus, exploiting the conditions of the spot charter market or even performing speculative moves in the sale and purchase market is of limited effect for a tanker pool.

The size of a liquid bulk pool grew on average over the years, from 15.2 vessels (1974) to 32.4 vessels (2000) (Haifeng 2000). This can be regarded as a natural development for the pools in order to sustain their goal and satisfy their customers' demand. Efficient operations and performance are critical to service the agreed contract up to an expected standard. Consolidation of management is complemented by dissemination of relevant data and information to all pool members (see also Figure 4.6).

As described above, the operational and commercial management of the combined tanker fleets are handled by a single separate company or by a member of the pool (Haralambides 1996). This company operates under the supervision of the vessel owners, usually through an executive committee.

The income of the pool is distributed to its members on the basis of a formula, which integrates multiple variables, instead of calculating each ship's income (Figure 4.7).

4.3.3 Organizational chart

The careful study of company structures, on a single company level, should examine the specific organizational chart. The organizational structure of a shipping company depends on both the nature of the trade in which it operates and on the scale of its activities. Whatever the size of the company, its structure should be designed to permit swift decision-making. A typical organizational structure is depicted on Figure 4.8.

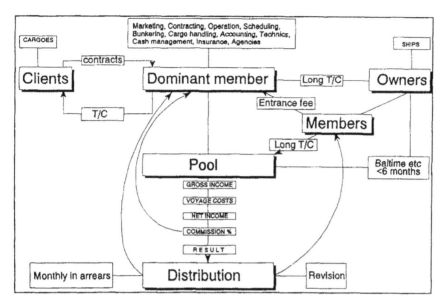

Figure 4.6 Shipping pool structure and operation.
Source: Haralmbides, 1996.

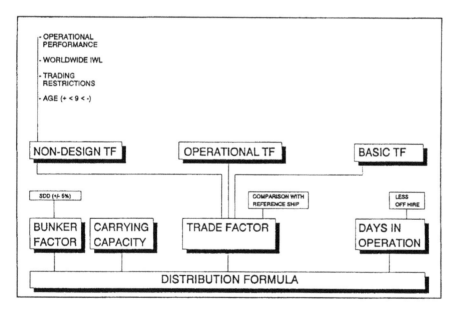

Figure 4.7 Weighting factors in the pool distribution formula.
Source: Haralmbides, 1996.

The board of directors (BoD), where the ship-owners are represented, is responsible for strategic decisions and corporate policy. A chief executive officer (CEO) is usually appointed by the BoD, tasked with the implementation of the corporate policy and strategy via executive decisions aided by a secretariat in charge of general administrative matters.

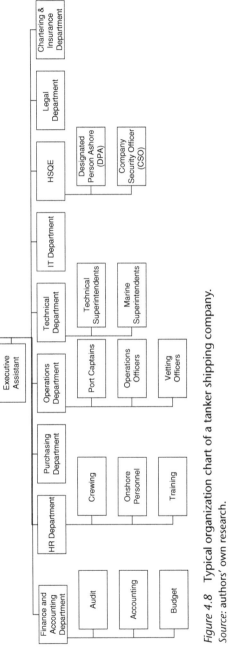

Figure 4.8 Typical organization chart of a tanker shipping company.
Source: authors' own research.

The operations department's duty is the management of the fleet and specifically the optimization of the ship performance as an economic unit. Fleet management includes ship operation, ship–terminal compatibility in order to enable more terminal calls, routing and crew schedules, and maintenance scheduling.

Another critical component of the organizational structure is the technical department. This department is in charge of ship dry dockings, overhauls, technical repairs, maintenance, spares inventory (utilizing the Planned Maintenance System – PMS), and research on optimizing aspects of the ship operation. Also, the department is usually responsible for new buildings, often handled by a separate team.

The health, safety, quality and environment (HSQE) department is primarily charged with the company's compliance with the national and international environmental legislation, laws and mandatory guidelines, rules and regulations recommended by IMO, ILO, flag administrations, classification societies, and maritime industry organizations.

The finance and accounting department covers budget planning and controlling issues, accounting, and finance of company's projects. It produces financial data necessary for decision-making in the form of regular reports for the company, the fleet, and each ship. Moreover, it implements audits and is also responsible for credit control issues.

The human resources (HR) department recruits and manages onshore and offshore personnel and plans their continuous training. The human capital is critical to the company operations. For that reason, the employment policy and the systematic training are critical duties.

The insurance and chartering department handles all the insurance formalities and arranges ship employment on a certain charter. Frequently, the insurance matters may be handled by the legal department.

The IT department's activities include all the secure operation and maintenance of information and technology infrastructure of the company, software, and hardware.

The legal department manages all legal affairs of the company's operations and provides the BoD and CEO with legal counsel in the subjects of company law and national and international taxes. It is definitely involved in contracts for new buildings, sales, and purchases of ships. A senior company lawyer cooperates directly with the CEO and is appointed to the BoD.

Apart from the general organizational structure, shipping companies normally build around key personnel and form flexible departments different from those mentioned above.

The aim of a tanker shipping company is to achieve efficiency and effectiveness through the best possible structure and integration between the aforementioned departments and people. Naturally, the organization chart clearly depicts a hierarchical structure that includes regulated tasks and work behaviour for each department and its employees. Centralized control by the ship-owner and/or other stakeholders is also clear along with hierarchically emphasized chain of commanding (Bielic 2009).

A decentralized form of management including the horizontal scope of business process management (BPM) may improve interaction between departments within a company, via information exchange and subsequent coordination (Bielic 2009). However, this form of management and its respective company organization can result in loose control and lost opportunities for a tanker company operating in an extremely competitive market with the volatility described above. This factor is taken into account by many companies, which opt for a "matrix organizational structure" (Bielic 2009) that consolidates multiple duties on fleet management to specific personnel, while encouraging the initiative of the personnel on-board the ship. Thus, elements of decentralization are incorporated to the role of the fleet manager who gains a holistic view of the company's interests through its own specific responsibilities.

4.4 Issues and tools of company management

The management of a tramp shipping company is no different than that of any other company, in the sense that it entails the organization of resources and coordination of activities in order to achieve defined objectives. In an environment such as the tanker shipping market, of intense competition and market volatility, the ability to plan and implement effective innovative company policies as well as the art of managing are especially important.

Management decisions are hierarchically separated in three levels: strategic, tactical, and operational (Christiansen et al. 2007). The ship-owner via the board of directors plans the course of the company by mapping out strategic long-term decisions. Strategic decisions of a tanker company range from fleet size and specific types of ships to long-term contracts with specific customers. It is on the basis of these decisions that the company will be governed year-to-year by the executive management. Day-to-day operational decisions focus on voyage scheduling problems, speed adjustment, and spot cargo chartering (Christiansen et al. 2007).

Financial aspects of corporate governance are of importance and tanker companies present no exception, since every management decision must take into account revenue, cost, and ultimately profits in order to reach specific goals set on all the aforementioned levels. For a company operating a fleet of tankers, its revenue is generated by freight rates for the transported cargo. On the other hand, it has a variety of fixed and variable expenses, which charge the ship-owner or the charterer depending on the terms set by the contract. Capital costs are fixed expenses relating to the acquisition of the tanker vessel. Running costs are fixed and variable expenses that include crew salaries, maintenance expenses, procurement, lubricants, administration expenses, and dry-docking costs. Voyage costs are variable expenses (fuel costs, tugging, and port and canal costs), depending on the voyage distance and the selected route and burden the charterer (Lyridis & Zacharioudakis 2012).

The utilization of software for management decisions in shipping companies has grown over the years. The technological barriers and reluctance shown by companies that were described over 25 years ago by Magirou et al. (1992) have changed. Today, most tanker shipping companies use integrated software for the majority of their operations and combine the experience of their executives with the capability of modern management support tools.

Further below, three key management issues will be presented: vetting, key performance indicators, and decision support systems. These are of importance for all tanker companies, as they constitute useful tools that support the decisions and functions of management on all levels.

4.4.1 Vetting

Vetting has been adopted as a tool to mitigate risks related initially with tramp shipping. Its development initiated when the portion of industrial tanker ownership was reduced and the market share of independent ship-owners rose respectively (Nigro et al. 2005). This development meant the tanker fleet available at the spot market included shipping services of varying quality, ranging from recognized, experienced shipping companies to substandard companies of new non-traditional shipping investors.

Vetting assessments are conducted by oil and gas companies-based information for specific vessels and the overall effectiveness of ship operator's management system. The information, in turn, is collected through inspectors using procedures and guidelines in line with two international systems, Ship Inspection Report Programme (SIRE) and Chemical Distribution Institute (CDI-Marine). Oil Companies International Marine Forum (OCIMF) and Chemical Distribution Institute (CDI) launched the internationally recognized SIRE and the CDI-M respectively to improve the safety and quality performance of oil, LPG, chemical product, and LNG shipping services.

Once the inspection is completed, a report based on standardized form is provided by the inspector to the ship operator for their response and together with the operator's response will be uploaded onto the SIRE or CDI database, available to company members of OCIMF and CDI. Then the company will make a specific screening decision based on the report, the input by the tanker company's vetting department, the Port State Control record, etc. and according to the particular charter's details (cargo, loading-unloading ports, length and route of the voyage, and time of year) (Snaith 2011).

4.4.2 Key performance indicators

The performance of a tanker company can be measured through sets of objectives established by its management on strategic, tactical, and operational levels, as they are held accountable by the customers, the ship-owner, and/or stakeholders if the company's stock is listed (Panayides 2003). In order to calculate up to what extent each of these objectives is achieved, specific parameters measuring each objective need to be defined: not ad hoc but in a concise and comprehensive manner. Thus, a full set of key performance indicators (KPIs) is considered to be a critical part of the broader business improvement system applied in a company (Kaplan and Norton, 2001).

The establishment of KPIs in the shipping industry and the tanker market is very important due to the extremely competitive nature of the market. Not only can they assist towards quantifying and monitoring the envisaged outcome of the adopted strategies of the company (Panayides, 2003), but they also enable the benchmarking of tanker shipping companies (Plomaritou and Konsta, 2013). An interesting issue that extends beyond the content of the present chapter is the one examined by Duru et al. (2013) concerning how the ship-owner's requirements for a third-party ship-manager can be monitored through generic KPIs.

At an organizational level, the top management of a tanker company utilizes KPIs as a measure that reflects the degree to which the company is achieving its goals according to its strategic direction and compared to its peers. KPIs comprise of selected information used to measure and assess performance (Konsta and Plomaritou 2012) and should include economic, commercial, technical, operational, as well as societal indices at a micro and at a macro level. Konsta and Plomaritou (2012), through literature review study, summarized general characteristics that KPIs development should follow:

1 link to strategic goals and critical success factors of the company;
2 include financial and non-financial measures;
3 use different measurements for different areas of the company;
4 evolve over time in order to reflect changes in strategy and operation;
5 be simple and easy to use;
6 give quick feedback to operators and managers;
7 aim at teaching rather than monitoring and controlling;
8 use benchmarking to set target characteristics of performance measurement systems found in world-class companies.

Notwithstanding the fact that the financial data on business performance are crucial, they can neither display the overall performance nor be used for accurate benchmarking (Panayides, 2003). When referring to tanker companies, specific aspects of performance must be incorporated in the KPIs used, including technical and operational efficiency for the fleet, safety and security issues, and environmental factors. For instance, tanker vessels carry hazardous or potentially harmful cargo, the transportation of which is subject to strict rules and regulations (Plomaritou and Konsta, 2013).

Another application of KPIs by a tanker company could serve the evaluation of its safety management system (SMS) and its compliance to International Safety Management (ISM) code requirements, the most known being the Tanker Management and Self-Assessment (TMSA) programme. The TMSA was first introduced in 2004 as a tool for ship managing companies to measure and improve their SMS. This can be achieved by providing tanker companies with certain KPIs to be benchmarked against. In that way, reports from different companies could be used to disseminate best practices to an industry-wide scale, thus the whole tanker market

Table 4.6 SPIs

SPI	KPI
Health and Safety	Flawless port state control performance
	Lost time injury frequency
	Health and safety deficiencies
	Lost time sickness frequency
HR Management Performance	Crew disciplinary frequency
	Crew planning
	HR deficiencies
	Cadets per ship
	Officer retention rate
	Officers experience rate
	Training days per officer
Environmental Performance	Releases of substances as def by MARPOLAnnex 1-6
	Ballast water management violations
	Contained spills
	Environmental deficiencies
Navigational Safety Performance	Navigational deficiencies
	Navigational incidents
Operational Performance	Budget performance
	Drydocking planning performance
	Cargo-related incidents
	Operational deficiencies
	Port state control detention
	Ship availability
	Vetting deficiencies
Security Performance	Port state control performance
	Security deficiencies
Technical Performance	Condition of class
	Failure of critical equipment and systems
Other	CO_2 efficiency [g/tonmile]
	Fire and explosions
	NOx efficiency [g/cargo unit] mile
	Port state control deficiency ratio
	SOx efficiency [g/cargo unit] mile

Source: BIMCO

will constantly attain high standards of safety. According to Snaith (2011), the second version of TMSA includes:

- 245 KPIs associated with best practice guidance;
- 101 reworded KPIs;
- 84 updated best practices;
- 52 stages in elements rearranged.

Another notable framework of performance measurement, including KPIs, has been set by InterManager in 2011 and subsequently Baltic and International Maritime Council (BIMCO) in 2015. BIMCO's Shipping KPI System includes 34 different KPIs enabling benchmarking of different companies by collecting and sharing anonymously aggregated data. The KPIs can be calculated using the measured values of 64 performance indicators (PIs) for each ship of the fleet. Tanker companies can use the Shipping KPI System to compare their business performance against peers and identify improvement margins.

The aforementioned attempts by international tanker-related shipping associations could be regarded as guidelines for tanker management companies to further develop their own KPIs, according to their goals, and different types and sizes of the vessels.

4.4.3 Decision support systems

Decision support systems (DSS) are tools first developed in 1970s (Power 2002) and still evolving up to date. The aim of a shipping-related DSS is to aid the ship-owner and the senior management in the decision-making process with the support of information technology. A plethora of DSS for any segment of the shipping industry, charter, and liner, are available, the majority of which focuses on various tactical or operational issues rather than strategic planning that relies mainly on the judgement of the ship-owner. Further below, this section will provide a comprehensive view on paradigms of practical uses of DSS in the context of tanker ship management.

In general terms, a tanker company can enhance different aspects of ship management with the implementation of an appropriate DSS. Maritime DSS were proposed focusing on specific problems such as ship design and operation Friis-Hansen 2000) or to provide support towards the general implementation of the International Ship and Port Security (ISPS) Code, and the development and maintenance of the associated security plans (Tzannatos 2003).

The aspect of the business performance of the tanker company can be assessed by various DSS that utilize different concepts and scientific methods such as the one proposed by Chou and Liang (2001), which combines fuzzy set theory, analytic hierarchy process (AHP), and concept of entropy, a fuzzy multiple criteria decision-making (MCDM) model for shipping company performance evaluation.

More recently, DSS are growing in complexity with regards to data input and expected results. A characteristic instance is the concept of Mansouri et al. (2015) that is based on multi-objective optimization to improve sustainability in shipping, focusing on environmental sustainability and trade-offs between economic and operational objectives. This direction is well aligned with the complexity of managing a modern tanker company in a challenging market environment that requires meeting both financial and operational objectives and aligning with new environmental regulations and policy. However, it is not commercially implemented by tanker shipping companies on a wide scale as it requires specialized knowledge, skills, and of course respective personnel training.

Several DSS prove to be useful for tanker companies operating at the spot market, as the better their understanding of the charter market, the higher the possibility for the company to be better placed in the future. A DSS providing knowledge of future conditions of the charter market allows the company to address many problems such as purchase/sale of vessels, chartering strategy, and risk management. Innovative methods, such as Artificial Neural Networks (ANN), have been used to create explanatory models for the freight market and then simulate a range of outcomes (Zacharioudakis 2007).

Other DSS can process data available in the tanker company, albeit with simplistic assumptions, and provide results that can support the managerial decisions. The input data include port information (cargo type, quantity, date and port of loading/offloading) and ship information (name, size, loadable types of cargo, date, position, operating cost, and revenues backlog initially available on the planning horizon). For instance, the DSS could either provide the tanker company with a schedule for all its vessels and their matching cargoes (Kim and Lee, 1997) or support strategic planning in tramp and industrial shipping, dealing with more complex problems such as fleet size and mix as well as short-term routing and scheduling problems (Fagerholt et al. 2010).

For long-term time charters during which tankers need to be allocated to dedicated terminals and operate on specific routes, DSS utilized by liner companies for fleet deployment should be put on trial. Multiple variations (Ting and Tzeng 2004, Fagerholt et al. 2009) of such DSS have been proposed with the common element being the optimum economic results.

Last but not least, from a sales and purchases, newbuilding market point of view, a DSS can be used by tanker companies in order to provide data on the best possible period to perform the respective action. A variety of tools, which provide useful information for sales and purchase decisions, are based on forecasting techniques (Karaindros 2005, Celik et al. 2009, Bulut et al. 2012, Guerra and Jenssen 2014).

4.5 Future trends

4.5.1 Blockchain application for tanker companies

Nowadays, management processes of tanker companies involve a lot of paperwork related to the ship and the cargo (sales contracts, lading bills, port documents, etc.). Lading bills are a characteristic example of the time-consuming procedure concerning shipping transactions where, starting from the load port shippers, they pass through several banks until reaching the receiver.

In order to make the processes more efficient, tanker companies may use blockchain, which is a technology based on an open-source software, enabling decentralized management of all transactions collectively by the network. For the management of the transactions, this contemporary technological novelty uses a chain of blocks (hence its name – blockchain), which is cryptographically secured and which is used as a public ledger that records all the bitcoin transactions (OPENSEA.PRO 2018). After the information is stored in the block, it cannot change or be deleted unless the majority of the network accepts the change or the deletion, and this makes user's interference in the blockchain impossible.

Tanker shipping companies may be inspired by the implementation of blockchain by the executive management of liner shipping companies. Maersk, leading a joint industrial project with IBM, found that a single shipment of refrigerated goods from East Africa to Europe could go through nearly 30 people and organizations, resulting in more than 200 different interactions and communications among them. Most of those communications have until recently remained paper-based due to concerns about authenticity and fraud. Furthermore, trade documentation processing and administration costs have been estimated to reach a level of one-fifth of the actual transportation costs (IBM, 2017). Projects run between IBM and Maersk aim at the implementation of blockchain in order to reduce the cost and complexity of trading, to make global trade more accessible to a bigger number of players, and to establish transparency among them.

The implementation and scale-up of blockchain application by tanker shipping companies could allow them to:

- reduce risk and improve the security by keeping sensitive information private and permissioned, which provides them with end-to-end visibility;
- promote transparency of transactions and the highly secure sharing of information among partners via managing and tracking paper trail by digitizing tanker operations from end-to-end;
- adopt micro-payments and skip intermediaries-imposed fees;
- establish new revenue models and financial and insurance services for their fleet. For example, the finance for an order of newbuilding tanker(s) could be better serviced; insurance may cover the lifetime of a vessel, rather than her current owner;
- create value exchanges amongst shipping companies, enhancing pool operations and shared fleet management via peer-to-peer platforms;
- optimize their operational and technical performance by examining real-time data recorded to a blockchain.

4.6 Summary

Tankers are operated either by subsidiaries of integrated oil groups (industrial shipping companies) or by individual ship-owners. However, industrial shipping is a minority in the tanker shipping market.

Independent tanker shipping companies are characterized by administrative and managerial flexibility regarding decision-making, being independent players in terms of shipping services for oil companies and less exposed to political pressures. An increasing number of tanker companies opt to found one separate company per vessel in order to allot economic and financial elements to multiple entities and to limit the exposure to risks.

Complementary to the one one-ship company business concept, shipping pools are a well-known concept in order to secure a constant revenue flow for a company and to reduce its risk exposure. More tanker companies can participate in the pool since it offers a greater possibility to sign CoA and minimize ship idle time.

Many tanker companies adopt a "matrix organizational structure" consolidating multiple duties on fleet management to specific personnel. Also, the utilization of software (tools) for management decisions in shipping companies has grown over the years and today most of these companies use the software for the majority of their operations.

Vetting, key performance indicators, and decision support systems are significant and useful management tools supporting tanker companies. KPIs are used by the tanker companies as a measure that reflects the degree to which the company is achieving its goals according to its strategic direction and compared to its peers and helps the company to identify improvement margins. Decision support systems contribute significantly in the decision-making process via the support of information technology. The majority of DSS focus on tactical or operational issues rather than strategic issues.

Concurrently with established management tools, tanker shipping companies will soon be faced with emerging and very promising technologies such as blockchain technology. This contemporary tool may prove to be more useful than expected, as specific gains for its application by liner shipping companies will shine through.

References

Bielic, T. (2009). Influence of shipping company organization on ship's team work effectiveness. Retrieved from https://bib.irb.hr/datoteka/405047.Bielic.pdf.

Brodie, P. (2006). *Commercial Shipping Handbook*. 2nd edittion, Informa Law, London: Routledge.

Bulut, E., Duru, O., Kececi, T. and Yoshida, S. (2012). Use of consistency index, expert prioritization and direct numerical inputs for generic fuzzy-AHP modeling: A process model for shipping asset management. *Expert Syst. Appl.* 39 (2): 1911–1923, doi:10.1016/j.eswa.2011.08.056.

Celik, M., Cebi, S., Kahraman, C. and Er, I. (2009). An integrated fuzzy QFD model proposal on routing of shipping investment decisions in crude oil tanker market. *Expert Systems with Applications*, 36 (3): 6227–35, doi:10.1016/j.eswa.2008.07.031.

Chou, T. and Liang, G. (2001). Application of a fuzzy multi-criteria decision-making model for shipping company performance evaluation. *Maritime Policy & Management*, 28 (4): 375–392, doi:10.1080/0308 8830110049951.

Christiansen, M. Fagerholt, K., Nygreen, B. and Ronen, D. (2007). Maritime Transportation. Editors C. Barnhart, G. Laporte. *Handbook in OR & MS* Volume 14, pp. 189–284, Amsterdam: Elsevier.

Duru, O., Bulut, E., Huang, S. and Yoshida, S. (2013). Shipping performance assessment and the role of key performance indicators (KPIs): 'Quality function deployment' for transforming shipowner's expectation. *SSRN Electronic Journal*. doi.org/10.2139/ssrn.2195984.

Fagerholt, K., Christiansen, M., Hvattum, L., Johnsen, T. and Vabo, T. (2010). *A Decision Support Methodology for Strategic Planning in Maritime Transportation*. Omega, 38 (6): 465–74, doi:10.1016/j.omega.2009.12.003.

Fagerholt, K., Trond, A., Johnsen, V. and Lindstad, H. (2009). Fleet deployment in liner shipping: A case study. *Maritime Policy & Management*, 36 (5): 397–409, doi:10.1080/03088830903187143.

Friis-Hansen, A. (2000). *Bayesian Networks as a Decision Support Tool in Marine Applications*. Master Thesis. Copenhagen: Technical University of Denmark.

Glen, D. and Martin, B. (1998). Conditional modelling of tanker market risk using route specific freight rates. *Maritime Policy and Management*, 25 (2): 117–128, doi:10.1080/03088839800000023.

Guerra, A. and Jenssen, M. (2014). *Multi Criteria Decision Analysis (MCDA) in the Norwegian Maritime Sector: Adding Environmental Criteria in Maritime Decision Support Systems*. Master Thesis. Trondheim: Norwegian University of Science and Technology.

Haifeng, W. (2000). Shipping pools in bulk shipping markets. Master Thesis. Malmö: World Maritime University.

Haralambides, H. (1996). The economics of bulk shipping pools. *Maritime Policy and Management*, 23 (3): 221–237.

Helman, C. (2015). As oil layoffs hit 200,000 a head-hunter looks at the bright side, *Forbes*, October 22, accessed April, 9, 2017.

Holditch, S. and Chianelli, R. (2008). Factors that will influence oil and gas supply and demand in the 21st century. *MRS Bulletin*, 33(4): 317–323.

IBM (2017). *Maersk and IBM Unveil First Industry-wide Cross-border Supply Chain Solution on Blockchain*. Retrieved from http://www-03.ibm.com/press/us/en/pressrelease/51712.wss

IGU. (2017). *World LNG Report*. International Gas Union.

Kaplan, R. S. and Norton, D. (2001). *The Strategy – Focused Organization*. Harvard: Harvard Business School Press.

Karaindros, A. (2005). Decision support tool for the tanker second-hand market using data mining techniques. Master Thesis. Massachusetts Institute of Technology. Retrieved from https://dspace.mit.edu/bitstream/handle/1721.1/33898/66528511-MIT.pdf.

Kim, S. And Lee, K. (1997). An optimization-based decision support system for ship scheduling. *Computers & Industrial Engineering* 33 (3): 689–92, doi:10.1016/S0360-8352(97)00223-4.

Konsta, K. and Plomaritou, E. (2012). Key performance indicators (KPIs) and shipping companies performance evaluation: The case of Greek tanker shipping companies. *International Journal of Business and Management*, 7 (10): 142–155.

Lun, Y., Hilmola, O., Goulielmos, A., Lai, K. And Cheng T. (2013). The tanker shipping market. *Oil transport management, Shipping and Transport Logistics*. Springer-Verlag: London.

Lyridis, D. and Zacharioudakis, P. (2012). Liquid bulk shipping. Editor Wayne K. Talley. *The Blackwell Companion to Maritime Economics*, First edition, pp. 205–229, Hoboken, NJ: Blackwell Publishing Ltd.

Magirou, E., Psaraftis, H. and Christodoulakis, N. (1992). Quantitative methods in shipping: A survey of current use and future trends. Report No. E115, Athens: Athens University of Economics and Business, Center for Economic Research.

Mansouri, S., Lee, H. and Aluko, O. (2015). Multi-objective decision support to enhance environmental sustainability in maritime shipping: A review and future directions. *Transportation Research Part E: Logistics and Transportation Review* 78: 3–18, doi:10.1016/j.tre.2015.01.012.

Murray, R. (1994, March). Shipping pools and EC competition law. Paper delivered at *EC Competition Law: A Guide for the Shipping Industry*, London.

Nigro, A., Brunori, L., Guassardo, G. and Panebianco, C. (2005, March). *Risk Based Approach to Oil Tankers and Bulk Carriers Vetting.* Paper presented at the Offshore Mediterranean Conference and Exhibition, Ravenna, Italy.

OPENSEA.PRO. (2018). *How Can the Shipping Industry take Advantage of the Blockchain Technology?* Retrieved from https://opensea.pro/blog/blockchain-for-shipping-industry.

Panayides, P. (2003). Competitive strategies and organizational performance in ship management. *Maritime Policy and Management*, 30 (2): 123–140.

Plomaritou, E. and Konsta, K. (2013). Key performance indicators (KPIs), shipping marketing and safety orientation: The case of greek tanker shipping companies. *Journal of Economics and Business*, 63, 3-4: 83–101.

Power, D. (2002). *Decision support systems: concepts and resources for managers.* Westport, Quorum Books.

Snaith, H. (2011, April*). Inspection vetting & screening.* INTERTANKO. Paris MoU PSC Familiarisation Course (Part 2).

Stopford, M. (2009). *Maritime economics.* Second edition, New York, Routledge.

Thorburn, T. (1960). *Supply and Demand of Water Transport.* Stockholm: Business Research Institute, Stockholm School of Economics.

Ting, S. and Tzeng, G. (2004). An Optimal Containership Slot Allocation for Liner Shipping Revenue Management. *Maritime Policy & Management* 31 (3): 199–211, doi:10.1080/0308883032000209553.

Tzannatos, E. (2003). *A Decision Support System for the Promotion of Security in Shipping. Disaster Prevention and Management: An International Journal*, 12 (3): 222–29, doi:10.1108/09653560310480703.

UNCATD. (2017). Review of maritime transport. Report by the UNCTAD secretariat.

Zacharioudakis, P. (2007). Development of decision support tools in shipping. PhD Thesis, National Technical University of Athens.

Zannetos, Z. (1964). *The theory of oil tankship rates: An economic analysis of tankship operations.* Massachusetts Institute of Technology, Cambridge.

Environmental management in shipping

Theory and practice of energy-efficient ship operation

Roar Adland, Kristoffer Thomassen, and Erland Østensen

5.1 Introduction

Energy efficiency is defined as doing more useful work with the same amount of energy consumption (IMO, 2009). It applies to both the design and the operation of ships and can mainly be improved in two ways: firstly, by enhancing technical efficiency through optimizing the hull shape and propulsion system. Secondly, by improving operational efficiency, mainly through voyage optimization, improved fleet management, and energy management.

While better fuel efficiency typically translates into a lower fuel bill, all else equal, there are other potential transmission mechanisms connecting economics and sustainable ship operation. Firstly, "greener designs" may obtain higher utilization in the market (e.g. reduced waiting time between contracts), thus improving the realized revenue. Secondly, in an increasingly environmentally conscious corporate world, buyers of ocean transportation may be willing to pay higher freight rates for the use of vessels that are operated with lower fuel consumption and emissions per cargo unit (or transportation work). Given the increasing focus on corporate sustainability (see Elkington, 1997, for a thorough discussion), the existence of a two-tier market based on energy efficiency is no longer far-fetched, even in the traditionally conservative shipping business. Importantly, there is an increasing risk of abrupt policy changes that will benefit standard bearers, e.g. introducing mandatory standards for vessel characteristics and operational management. Hence, being precautionary and having the ability and fleet to handle such potential regulatory changes may offer sustainable competitiveness.

In this chapter we present a comprehensive review of findings in the literature on energy-efficient ship operation in the shipping markets. We focus on two key areas: 1) the interaction between regulations, market conditions, and the sailing speed and emissions of ships, and 2) the relationship between energy efficiency and market prices. In both cases, it is critical to evaluate whether observed market behaviour is consistent with economic theory, both from a policy and a commercial point of view. If ships are not operated in a manner consistent with economic theory, then environmental policy developed on the basis that market agents behave rationally may not have the intended positive impact. Similarly, if the markets do not price energy efficiency correctly, then this will, on the one hand, slow down technological development and adoption of energy-efficient solutions and, on the other hand, offer low-risk commercial opportunities to those who know how to take advantage of such mispricing. We illustrate our discussion with an empirical case study on the tanker spot market. Specifically, we evaluate whether charterers are willing to pay a spot freight rate premium for energy-efficient tonnage in the voyage charter market for VLCCs trading on the Arabian Gulf–Asia routes. For the first time in the literature, our investigation is based on the merger of fixture data and real-life speed data derived from the automated identification system (AIS), enabling us to evaluate whether operational efficiency is rewarded. Finally, we discuss the managerial implications of the findings in our own analysis and the literature.

5.2 Compliance with emission regulations

Annex VI of the International Convention for the Prevention of Pollution from ships (MARPOL) sets limits on sulphur oxide (SOx) and nitrogen oxide (NOx) emissions from ship exhausts. In 2016 the International Maritime Organization (IMO) agreed on the latest version, stipulating that *global* limits on the sulphur content in marine fuels of 3.5% would be reduced to 0.50% in 2020. Until then, MARPOL defines four Emission Control Areas (ECAs) with particularly stringent limits on sulphur content in marine fuels: the Baltic Sea, the North Sea and English Channel, the North American coast, and the US Caribbean coast. The latter two areas also regulate NOx and particulate matter (PM) emissions. There are principally three technological solutions available to comply with these regional MARPOL regulations. The simplest approach is a modification of a vessel's fuel tank system to enable switching from heavy fuel oil (HFO) consumed outside ECAs to ultra-low-sulphur HFO or marine gas oil inside an ECA. Alternatives include natural gas-powered propulsion (LNG) and the installation of exhaust cleaning systems for SOx (scrubbers). Many studies have investigated the optimal compliance strategy (see, for instance, Lindstad et al., 2015; Yang et al., 2012; Balland et al, 2012, 2013; Brynolf et al., 2014; Jiang et al., 2014, Schinas and Stefanakos, 2012), typically by assessing criteria such as investment and operating costs, reliability, and maintenance requirements. It is recognized that the optimal solution is subject to uncertain future price differences of alternative fuels as well as technological and regulatory uncertainty. However, the effects of scrubber or LNG installation on the revenue potential through reduction in cargo-carrying capacity for space or stability reasons is generally not considered. Moreover, in a perfectly competitive freight market, mandating high-cost low-sulphur marine fuels, or any other increase in voyage costs, will merely increase freight rates accordingly (Adland and Strandenes, 2007). This implies that shipowners should favour compliance strategies that affect variable costs only (i.e. choosing fuel switching as opposed to additional investment in scrubbers or LNG retrofit). This important aspect is poorly understood in the literature on regulatory compliance.

Another branch of the literature considers the impact of MARPOL fuel regulations on the operating patterns of vessels, notably vessel speed and routing. Based on the common assumption that a vessel's fuel consumption (and therefore emissions) per time unit is proportional to the cube of speed, Ronen (1982) showed that the profit-maximizing speed in a one-period setting is a function of the square root of the ratio between the freight rate and fuel price. Accordingly, the higher price of low-sulphur fuels should lead to reduced sailing speeds within the ECAs, all else equal. Recent computational studies show, at least for the special case of liner shipping (Doudnikoff and Lacoste, 2014; Fagerholt et al., 2015), that a consequence of reduced sailing speeds within ECAs is that vessels must speed up outside to compensate for lost time, and that this will increase overall fuel consumption and CO_2 emissions. Fagerholt et al. (2015) also show that a likely effect of the regulations is that ship operators will choose to sail longer distances to avoid or reduce the sailing distances within the ECAs. These are temporary challenges that will be largely resolved when global regulations on the sulphur content of marine fuels come into force in 2020.

Recent surveys present a substantial literature on theoretically optimal sailing speeds (Psaraftis and Kontovas, 2013, 2014). Early works acknowledged the "cubic" relationship between fuel consumption and speed and focused on speed reduction as a cost-minimization measure (Manning, 1956; Avi-Itzhak, 1974; Artz Jr., 1975). The impact of fuel costs on freight rates was subsequently introduced implicitly through transport supply modelling, as in Norman and Wergeland (1979). However, explicit theories for optimal speed based on profit optimization, with freight rates and fuel cost as input variables, were not introduced until the early 1980s (Alderton, 1981; Ronen, 1982). While Alderton points to the impact of weather and ship-specific variables in governing potential speed and the influence of schedules on the preferred speed, such additional operational or technical variables are not modelled explicitly in the theoretical literature. Instead, recent works have elaborated on the environmental benefits of slow steaming, given the substantial reductions in fuel consumption and carbon emissions (see, for instance, Corbett et al., 2009; Lindstad et al. (2011), Wang and Meng, 2012; Maloni et al., 2013, Zis et al., 2014, Ferrari et al., 2015).

Improving availability of ship position and speed data from the automated identification system (AIS) for the tracking of vessels has allowed recent empirical studies to evaluate whether the classical speed-optimization theory can explain observed vessel speeds, both for entire voyages and when vessels are switching between different regulatory regimes (inside/outside ECA). Thus far, the results are not very favourable for either the classical speed-optimization theory or for the computational studies on ECA behaviour. Assmann et al. (2015) investigate average voyage speeds for VLCCs departing the Arabian Gulf and find that the elasticity of speed with regards to fuel price and freight rates is much lower than that implied by theory, and only statistically significant for the ballast voyage. Adland and Jia (2016a) expand the analysis of speed determinants to also include proxies for organizational constraints, operator quality, trading pattern, loading conditions, technical constraints, and ship-specific variables. Using average voyage speeds from the Capesize market, they also find that owners do not appear to adjust vessel speeds based on freight market conditions and fuel prices, as argued in classical maritime economic theory. Instead, vessel-specific variables such as age and design speed, as well as operational factors such as loading conditions, show some explanatory power. Adland and Jia (2016b) perform a similar analysis using weekly average speeds for VLCC tankers and reach the same conclusion. In the first study of empirical vessel behaviour in ECAs, Adland et al. (2017a) investigate changes in vessel speeds when vessels cross the ECA border. Their findings do not support the assertion that the introduction of stricter sulphur regulation inside the Emission Control Areas affects vessel speeds in any economically significant manner. Again, vessel speeds are not generally determined by fuel prices or freight rates but rather by voyage-specific variables such as whether a vessel is heading towards or away from heavily trafficked areas or ports of call, whether it is a tanker or cargo vessel, and seasonal weather factors. These empirical findings are important in the context of environmental policy design. Specifically, regulations or market-based measures (e.g. CO_2 levies and tradable quotas) that target the fuel price are not likely to affect ship operations in the desired way. Depending on the nature of commercial contracts and pricing power in the various shipping segments, the additional costs of low-sulphur fuels are borne by both consumers and vessel operators. This may lead to increased non-compliance from shipping companies. This would not only weaken the positive effect on emissions; it would also be a major competitive disadvantage for the companies that comply with the regulation (Adland et al., 2017a).

5.3 Do markets reward energy efficiency?

A key question is whether energy efficiency is properly recognized and rewarded in the pricing of charter contracts and ships in the markets. Improving technical efficiency through hull optimization and more sophisticated propulsion systems (e.g. hybrid systems, Lindstad et al., 2017) is costly. Accordingly, if more energy-efficient vessels are not rewarded through better utilization, higher freight rates (depending on contract type), and improved asset values compared to less environmentally friendly designs, the incentive to develop and operate such vessels will not be present. This will slow down the take-up rate for new technology and leave markets prone to regulation as the only way to force reductions in shipping emissions.

To the best of our knowledge, the empirical literature on price formation for individual contracts (fixtures) started with Bates (1969), who investigated freight rates in the global sugar trade. Economists have since been concerned mainly with whether there is evidence of price differentiation with regards to perceived quality-related variables. In the voyage charter market, Tamvakis (1995) tests whether there is a freight rate premium paid to tanker vessels of lower age, vessels with double-hull construction, or vessels trading to the United States, with mixed results. Tamvakis and Thanopoulou (2000) investigate the existence of a two-tier spot freight market for bulk carriers and find no significant age premium in the freight rate. Alizadeh and Talley (2011a, b) include the lead time between the contracting date and loading, as well as macroeconomic proxies representing the market freight rate level and its volatility. Alizadeh and Talley (2011a) confirm that single-hull tankers must offer a discount in the market over double-hull tankers though find no support of a separate vessel age discount. Using a more recent dataset, Adland et al. (2016) show in the case of Capesize bulk carriers and VLCC tankers that modern vessels generally attract a premium voyage charter rate over the market rate, while older vessels must accept a discount, and that this relationship is non-linear with respect to vessel age. Importantly, Adland et al. (2016) account for the heterogeneity of owners, charterers, and their relationships (matches) as fixed effects and find that this improves the explanatory power of their regression models substantially. One interpretation of this finding is that buyer and seller identity matters for the micro-markets where individual fixtures are negotiated, for instance, as a result of pricing power.

The existence of a two-tier market for timecharters was first investigated by Köhn and Thanopoulou (2011) using generalized additive models. They control for contract-specific effects such as place of delivery, lead time, charter duration, vessel size, and fuel consumption, and find evidence for the existence of a two-tier market for Panamax bulk carriers during the boom years of 2003–2007. Specifically, they find evidence of a non-linear age discount, with proportionately larger discounts for very old tonnage. Importantly for our discussion of energy efficiency, they also find a non-linear relationship between the daily fuel consumption for a vessel and the discount in TC rates, where only vessels in the highest quartile of the sample (in terms of daily fuel consumption) must accept a discount in TC rates.

However, when evaluating whether the markets reward energy efficiency, the question is not merely whether such price differentiation exists but to which extent the magnitude of any relative premium or discount reflects the value of the expected fuel savings. Specifically, in the timecharter market, where charterers pay for the fuel, charterers should be willing to pay a premium in the TC rate equivalent to the daily savings in fuel costs. Agnolucci et al. (2014) investigate the existence of a rate premium for fuel efficiency in the Panamax drybulk TC market during the period 2008–2012 and find that owners recoup approximately 40% of the fuel savings through higher rates. Adland et al. (2017b) extend the analysis both by ship size and by sample size (2001–2016) and show that energy efficiency is only rewarded during normal market conditions, and then only by 14–27% of the savings, while energy *inefficient* vessels are rewarded during boom periods. They suggest that it is in fact rational to value speed and capacity highly when the value of time is high (i.e. high TC rates, $/day) relative to the value of fuel savings. These mixed empirical results reflect the varied opinions in the policy-related literature. For instance, Kollamthodi et al. (2008), based on an interview with the Norwegian Shipowners' Association, claim that charterers are willing to pay higher rates for fuel-efficient ships if this entails a reduction in their fuel costs. However, Faber et al. (2011) conclude that charter rates do not reflect fuel efficiency, and that the owners who invest in fuel efficiency usually do not redeem their investments.

Existing studies investigating the presence of an energy-efficiency premium share one common shortcoming: they all use nominal design values to measure energy efficiency. That is, they evaluate technical efficiency rather than operational efficiency. Adland et al. (2017b) present the most comprehensive list of energy-efficiency variables and include daily fuel consumption, fuel consumption per tonnemile, the Existing Vessel Design Index (EVDI) of Rightship.com, and the difference in daily fuel cost from fleet average. However, the significance of these variables is evaluated at design speed. Prakash et al. (2016) evaluate preferences for energy efficiency using GHG Ratings (www.rightship.com), which can be considered a derivative of the EVDI and, thus, is also a nominal measure of efficiency. Adland et al. (2017b) acknowledge that this is a weakness in the literature and that the presence of an energy-efficiency premium should be evaluated at the true sailing speed, particularly during periods when the fleet is known to be slow steaming. For instance, Adland and Jia (2016b) show that average laden VLCC speeds between January 2013 and February 2015 are only 12.1 knots compared to an average design speed of about 15.8 knots, equivalent to a 23% speed reduction.

This observation has two important consequences for research on the existence of an energy-efficiency premium in observed fixture rates. Firstly, as the relationship between the speed and fuel consumption roughly follows the "cubic rule" (Ronen, 1982), slow-steaming vessels have substantially lower fuel costs than that implied by design values. Specifically, in our VLCC case, an average 23% speed reduction is equivalent to $1 - (12.1/15.8)^3 = 56\%$ reduction in fuel costs. Secondly, it is unlikely that speed reductions are evenly distributed across the fleet. Conceivably, vessels that are energy *inefficient* in nominal terms can compensate for poor design specifications by being operated more economically and still compete with vessels that have seemingly better energy-efficiency parameters. As pointed out by Adland et al. (2017b), establishing the statistical significance of energy-efficiency variables becomes much harder when absolute fuel consumption is lower, and the differences across the fleet are correspondingly smaller. It follows that the results in the literature concerning the importance of technical efficiency may not be robust if we evaluate the presence of an energy-efficiency premium at true sailing speeds (operational efficiency).

Finally, all the recent studies (Alizadeh and Talley, 2011a, b; Köhn and Thanopoulou, 2011; Agnolucci et al., 2014; Adland et al., 2016; Adland et al., 2017b) include a market index as one of the dependent variables. The logic is that in controlling for the "market effect", which should explain a large share of price movements in a perfectly competitive market, we are left only with the influence of heterogeneity in contractual terms and vessel specifications. Adland et al. (2017c) point to two potential flaws in this approach. Firstly, the market index itself captures part of the heterogeneity that we are trying to evaluate, as it is typically based on some standard vessel specification and route composition that can change at discrete points in time. Secondly, researchers are effectively trying to explain micro-data from transactions by a macro-variable (the market index), which is itself derived from the micro-data (circularity). Consequently, the effect of vessel characteristics in regressions explaining fixtures is likely to be biased since part of the vessel influence will be already accounted for in the market index. Adland et al. (2017c) propose to instead control for market conditions separately as a time fixed effect.

The above literature review has identified two important gaps in the literature. Firstly, there is a clear need to evaluate the presence of an energy-efficiency premium subject to real operating conditions rather than in nominal design terms. Secondly, the presence of an energy-efficiency premium, or indeed any micro-level heterogeneous effect, cannot be properly evaluated by including a market index, such as those supplied by Clarkson Research (2016) or the Baltic Exchange, as a control variable. In the next section, we present a study on the VLCC spot market that attempts to fill these gaps in the literature. The empirical study contributes to the literature in the following two ways. Firstly, our empirical data consists of fixture and vessel information merged with AIS-derived data on actual vessel speeds. This allows us to account for variations in true sailing speeds, and the corresponding estimated fuel consumption, across individual laden voyages with known pricing information. Secondly, we propose and estimate a new model of price formation in the voyage charter market for tankers that incorporates numerous sources of heterogeneity: vessel specifications, contractual terms, charterer and owner fixed effects, but with time fixed effects accounting for market conditions instead of an "exogeneous" market index.

5.4 A case study: the tanker spot market

The purpose of this section is to investigate whether more energy-efficient vessels attract a rate premium (or equivalently, whether less energy-efficient ships have to offer a discount) in the spot market for very large crude carriers (VLCCs). Specifically, our empirical analysis relates to laden trips between the Persian Gulf (PG) and Asia, the dominant trading route for such tonnage, between January 2013 and March 2016. Under a voyage charter, fuel costs and other voyage costs are borne in full by the shipowner. Since owners can pocket any fuel savings, energy efficiency is, in theory, already rewarded. Thus, if greater energy efficiency also leads to a premium in the freight rate, this would suggest that charterers are willing to pay to be environmentally friendly.

Our choice of variables largely follows the literature on microeconomic determinants of freight rates as referenced above, with some adaptations to account for the fact that we consider operational efficiency rather than technical efficiency in design terms. Considering the contract-specific variables, we account for the lead time (*Forward Days*) between the fixture date and the first layday (i.e. the start of the period within which the vessel is supposed to present for loading). The expected relationship between the Forward Days variable and fixture rates is positive, where vessels are fixed further ahead in strong markets (when there is a risk of transportation shortage) and nearer to the loading date when there is an oversupply of tonnage. It is also necessary to control for the wide geographical spread of discharge ports for the Arabian Gulf (AG) loadings in our sample, ranging from Singapore (Route TD2) to Japan (Route TD3). In this context, we create a simple dummy variable (*TD2_D*) for ports southwest of Hong Kong designed to pick up variations in fixture rate levels due to distance[1].

Moving on to our ship-specific variables, the deadweight capacity of each vessel (*DWT*) accounts for heterogeneity in vessel size. Following Tamvakis and Thanopoulou (2000), we expect a negative relationship between DWT and voyage charter rates within a size segment due to economies of scale. Similarly, older vessels (*Age*) are expected to receive a discount in the spot freight market, as found in Adland et al. (2016) and Alizadeh et al. (2011a, b). This relationship is often found to be non-linear in the literature, so we also include the squared age as a variable (*Age^2*). Following Adland et al. (2016) and Alizadeh et al. (2011a, b), we also consider the vessel's *load factor*, defined as the ratio between the reported cargo size and a vessel's DWT. As argued by Alizadeh and Talley (2011a), a negative sign for the coefficient of this variable is expected to compensate the owner for such "short loading".

Continuing with our energy-efficiency variables, we define three different measures to check the robustness of any findings of a voyage rate premium. Firstly, we calculate the estimated daily consumption at actual speed (*Est. cons.*) in Equation 5.1:

$$F_a = F_d \times \left(\frac{V_a}{V_d}\right)^{\beta} \tag{5.1}$$

where F_a is the estimated consumption at actual speed V_a, F_d is the vessel's nominal consumption at design speed V_d, and β is the fuel consumption exponent which is, for VLCCs, typically between 2,6, and 3,0 (Assmann et al. 2015). Unfortunately, the fuel exponent is effectively unobservable for individual vessels and so we resort to applying a constant $\beta = 2.738$ as obtained from industry sources. We note that, in practice, the actual fuel consumption in the seaway will also depend on, for instance, local weather and hull condition, though such information is not yet consistently available across the fleet. Secondly, we calculate the *Fuel Efficiency Index (FEI)*, defined in Equation 5.2 as:

$$FEI = \left(\frac{Consumption}{(DWT \times Speed \times 24)}\right) \times 10^6 \tag{5.2}$$

where *consumption* is the estimated consumption from Equation 5.1, *DWT* is the ship's deadweight capacity, and *speed* is the actual laden speed for the voyage. This is a measure of fuel consumption on a "grams per tonnemile" basis[2]. Thirdly, we estimate the fuel costs per tonne oil carried for each individual fixture. We first calculate the number of sailing days on the laden voyage:

$$Days\,laden = \frac{Distance\,laden}{(Actual\,speed \times 24)} \tag{5.3}$$

where the *distance laden* corresponds to the distance between the loading port and the discharge port, quoted in nautical miles. The next step is to calculate the total fuel cost incurred by each vessel:

$$Total\,fuel\,costs = (Days\,laden \times Estimated\,Consumption \times Fuel\,price) \tag{5.4}$$

where *days laden* comes from Equation 5.3, *estimated consumption* from Equation 5.1, and the *fuel price* corresponds to the prevailing HFO spot price at Fujairah[3] on the loading date. By using Equations 5.3 and 5.4, we can calculate the fuel cost per tonne carried for each fixture:

$$Fuel\,cost\,per\,tonne\,oil\,carried = \frac{Total\,fuel\,costs}{Quantity\,carried} \tag{5.5}$$

where *total fuel costs* are given by Equation 5.4 and the *quantity carried* is the reported cargo size in metric tonnes. We note that for all three energy efficiency variables, a higher reading means lower energy efficiency. Hence, we expect negative coefficients with regards to the freight rate.

Following the presentation in Adland et al. (2017c), let F_{covi} be the freight rate observed for fixture $i(t)$ signed on date t between charterer c and owner o for a vessel v. In the remainder, we simplify this notation to F_i across specifications. In the simplest specification, we consider the monthly time fixed effect only, by estimating the following linear model:

$$F_i = \sum_{t=1}^{T} \delta_t * \mathbb{I}_t + \varepsilon_i \tag{5.6}$$

where $\mathbb{I}_t$ is a dummy variable such that $\mathbb{I}_t = 1$ for time unit t and $\mathbb{I}_t = 0$ otherwise, and ε_i is a random perturbation such that $E(\varepsilon_i) = 0$ and $Var(\varepsilon_i) = \sigma^2$. Here, the various coefficients δ_t (with $t = 1, \ldots, T$) effectively correspond to the average freight rate for each time unit t.

Next, we want to account for the contract and ship-specific characteristics. Let $R_{i,j}$ be the set of j contract-specific variables and $S_{i,k}$ be the set of k ship-specific variables. We can then estimate the following fixed effect model:

$$F_i = \sum_{t=1}^{T} \delta_t * \mathbb{I}_t + \Sigma_j \theta_j R_{i,j} + \Sigma_j \omega_j S_{i,k} + \varepsilon_i \tag{5.7}$$

Finally, the results in Adland et al. (2016) suggest that it is necessary to control for the time-invariant unobserved heterogeneity of the market participants (charterers and owners). Thus, in our last specification we denote the two heterogeneity terms specific to the charterer c and owner o by γ_c and Ω_o respectively.

When the number of owners and charterers is not too high, as in our dataset, we can estimate the two-way fixed effects regression presented in Abowd et al. (1999):

$$F_i = \sum_{t=1}^{T} \delta_t * \mathbb{I}_t + \Sigma_j \theta_j R_{i,j} + \Sigma_j \omega_j S_{i,k} + \sum_c I_c \gamma_c + \sum_o I_o \Omega_o + \varepsilon_i \tag{5.8}$$

where I_c and I_o are dummy variables associated with the various charterers and owners, respectively. We note that our fixed effects specification allow for some correlation between either the charterer or owner fixed effects, and the set of contract and vessel characteristics. This may for instance relate to an oil major charterer who has preference for larger ships.

To control for heteroscedasticity, we use robust (Huber-White) standard errors. Furthermore, even though it is not optimized for panel data, we test for multicollinearity using the variance inflation factor (VIF) test. The variables are said to be prone to multicollinearity if the test statistic exceeds 10.

Our dataset is a result of merging several sources. Clarkson Research (2016) provided fixture data reported from the VLCC spot market for the Arabian Gulf to East Asia trades as well as technical vessel specifications for the 686 VLCCs in operation during the period under investigation. Clipper Data Ltd. provided verified laden voyage data with names of the loading terminal and discharge terminals, as well as loading and discharge dates. AIS-derived speed data for the voyage was obtained from ORBCOMM. The average speed for the voyage is approximated as the average of observations between the loading and discharge dates, filtering out observations below 7 knots to exclude periods where the vessel is drifting, at anchorage or alongside in port. After matching the fixture information with AIS-derived speed data, we are left with 1,007 laden voyages with loading date between 3 January 2013 and 24 February 2016. We note that the Clarkson vessel data is sometimes incomplete, particularly with regards to a ship's nominal fuel consumption. Where possible, we correct for this by identifying vessels with similar main engine, age, and DWT, for which fuel consumption is known.

Table 5.1 below summarizes the descriptive statistics for our chosen variables. The monthly mean freight rate of the observed fixtures is WS50, with a minimum of WS26.5 and a maximum of WS95. We note that 346 of 1,007 fixtures had South East Asia as their place of delivery, which accounts for about 34% of all transactions. The vessels are reported fixed on average about 16 days prior to the first layday, varying from zero days as the minimum to 34 days for the longest lead time. The average size VLCC on this trade is 307,000 DWT and the average size of the cargo carried is 270,000, leading to an average utilization ratio of about 88%. The average vessel age is ten years.

Figure 5.1 illustrates the distribution of actual sailing speeds compared to design speed. We notice that while the design speed of most ships falls between 15 and 17 knots, the observed speed for the fleet is noticeably lower, centred around 12 knots. Figure 5.2 illustrates how the reduced sailing speed affects the distribution of fuel consumption. Both figures clearly illustrate that evaluating the existence of an energy-efficiency premium based on nominal speeds and fuel consumption data (technical efficiency), as has been the approach in the literature until now, is not very representative of reality.

Finally, Table 5.2 lists the top-ten owners and charterers for the VLCC fixtures in our sample. The top-ten charterers represent approximately 73% of all fixtures, while the top-ten owners only account for 43% of the 1,007 transactions. As noted by Adland et al. (2016), the large share captured by the ten largest market participants, for both charterers and owners, may indicate that attributes such as bargaining power have an impact on the freight rates.

Table 5.3 shows the regression results for our model specifications in Equation 5.6 (1a) and Equation 5.7 (2a–c). We note that market conditions, interpreted here as the monthly dummies representing time fixed effects, dominate in terms of explanatory power. The addition of vessel- and contract-specific variables increases R^2 by only about 1%-point. Forward Days, DWT and the load factor are significant and their coefficients have the expected signs based on earlier results in the literature. Broadly speaking, our *TD2_D* dummy picks up the same route effects

Table 5.1 Descriptive Statistics

Variable	Obs.	Mean	Std.Dev	Min	Max
Contract rate (WS)	1,007	50.2	13.9	26.5	95
Market rate (TD3)	1,007	51.01	14.58	28.82	115.7
South East Asia	346				
Forward Days	1,007	15.7	3.79	0	34
DWT	1,007	306,635	10,709	265,539	323,182
Age	1,007	10.69	4.95	1	22
Age^2	1,007	138.74	109.74	1	484
LF	1,007	88.07	3.24	81.28	101.68
Estimated Cons.	1,007	46.54	11.19	13.93	89.05
FEI Actual	1,007	0.52	0.1	0.3	1.03
Fueltonne	1,007	1.46	0.62	0.22	3.57
Slow-steaming statistics:					
Observed speed	1,007	12.17	0.87	8.09	15.06
Design speed	1,007	15.82	0.93	12.25	21.50
Nom. Cons.	1,007	93.75	12.16	65.00	120.00
FEI Nominal	1,007	0.81	0.10	0.53	1.05

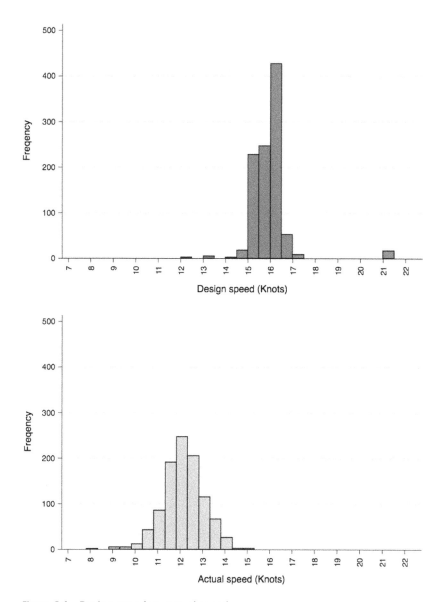

Figure 5.1 Design speed vs. actual speed.

as found in Alizadeh and Talley (2011a), with shorter routes to Asia generally having higher WS rates, though they consider a much finer geographical resolution than we do here. Importantly in our context, neither vessel age nor any of our fuel efficiency variables are found to be significant for these model specifications.

Finally, Table 5.4 shows the results for our model when we include owner and charterer fixed effects in addition to time fixed effects (1b) and vessel- and contract-specific variables (3a–c). This leads to a further increase in the R-squared by 2.86% compared to the case where only time fixed effects and contract and vessel characteristics are considered (from 0.8419 to 0.8705). This suggests that observed and unobserved characteristics of both charterers and

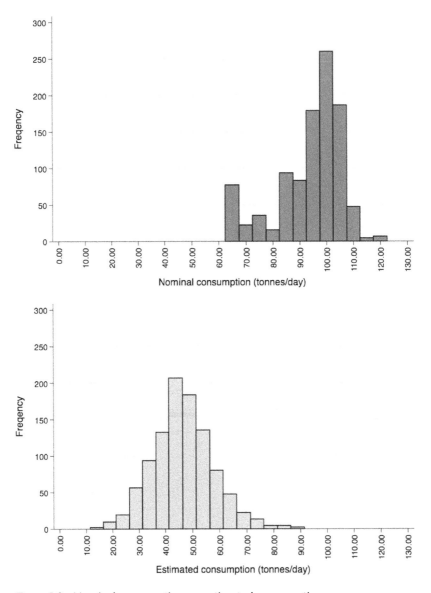

Figure 5.2 Nominal consumption vs. estimated consumption.

owners play an important role in the determination of the freight rates, as also shown by Adland et al. (2016).

Interestingly, after adding charterer and owner fixed effects, most of the independent variables that proved significant in Table 5.3 have become insignificant. The only exception is *Forward Days*, which still is significant at the 99% level and has an even larger coefficient. The reason some of our variables are losing their significance can be explained by charterers' and owners' preferences. For instance, it is reasonable to assume that a specific charterer – which is typically here also a refinery owner – has undertaken long-term crude oil purchasing agreements with oil producers in the AG. With the pattern of exporting and importing terminals largely fixed for

Table 5.2 Top Owners and Charterers

Charterer	Fixtures	Percentage	Cumul.	Owner	Fixtures	Percentage	Cumul.
UNIPEC	166	16.48	16.48	SK SHIPPING	79	7.85	7.85
PTT	100	9.93	26.42	MARAN TANKERS MNGT.	60	5.96	13.80
CHEVTEX	98	9.73	36.15	ALTOMARE S.A.	49	4.87	18.67
S.OIL	91	9.04	45.18	OCEAN TANKERS	48	4.77	23.44
SHELL	60	5.96	51.14	SHIP FINANCE INTER.	43	4.27	27.71
HYUNDAI	54	5.36	56.50	SHPG CORP. OF INDIA	34	3.38	31.08
DAY HARVEST	52	5.16	61.67	MITSUI & CO. LTD.	32	3.18	34.26
GLASFORD	45	4.47	66.14	EASTERN MED. MAR.	31	3.08	37.34
FORMOSA	36	3.57	69.71	AELOS MANAGEMENT	29	2.88	40.22
CPC	33	3.28	72.99	DYNACOM TANKERS MNGT.	28	2.78	43.00
OTHER	272	27.01	100.00	OTHER	574	57.00	100.00
TOTAL	1,007	100.00		TOTAL	1,007	100.00	

Source: Authors' calculations, data from Clarkson Research

Table 5.3 Regression Results (Time Fixed Effect Only)

VARIABLES	(1a)	(2a)	(2b)	(2c)
ForwardDays		0.2222***	0.2227***	0.2241***
		(0.000)	(0.000)	(0.000)
DWT/1000		−0.2022***	−0.2037***	−0.2055***
		(0.002)	(0.002)	(0.001)
Age		0.0736	0.0778	0.0852
		(0.676)	(0.659)	(0.629)
Age2		−0.0113	−0.0117	−0.0123
		(0.139)	(0.128)	(0.111)
LoadFactor*100		−0.5952***	−0.5987***	−0.5992***
		(0.004)	(0.004)	(0.004)
TD2_D		2.0727***	2.0854***	1.9397***
		(0.000)	(0.000)	(0.000)
EstCons		0.0072		
		(0.677)		
FEIAct			0.1541	
			(0.938)	
Fueltonne				−0.3106
				(0.545)
Constant	39.6429***	150.7193***	151.7597***	153.1759***
	(0.000)	(0.000)	(0.000)	(0.000)
Monthly dummy	YES	YES	YES	YES
Charter FE	NO	NO	NO	NO
Owner FE	NO	NO	NO	NO
R-squared	0.831	0.842	0.842	0.842
Observations	1,007	1,007	1,007	1,007

Robust p-values in parentheses, *** p<0.01, ** p<0.05, * p<0.1

each charterer, this will impose a correlation between charterer identity and the geographical routes of the vessels. Similarly, to the extent that physical constraints in the ports (e.g. maximum draft) play a role, there may be a correlation between the identity of the charterer, vessel size, and load factor. Hence, the correlation between the charterers' unobserved heterogeneity and the vessels' characteristics accounts for some of the other variables' significance, when controlling for charterers' and owners' fixed effects.

Importantly, after controlling for charterer and owner fixed effects, our energy efficiency variable *Fueltonne* becomes significant at the 95% level, with the *FEI Actual* variable nearly significant at the 90% level. All energy-efficiency coefficients have a negative sign, which implies a discount in the market for more inefficient ships. Consequently, we have some empirical evidence of a two-tier market based on energy efficiency when we evaluate operational efficiency and control for charterer and owner fixed effects.

5.4.1 Limitations

We acknowledge that our study has some weaknesses related to data quality and coverage. Firstly, public fixture coverage is known to be incomplete, and a large share of reported fixtures does not contain information on the agreed freight rate. We cannot be certain that the transactions

Table 5.4 Regression Results with Owner and Charterer Fixed Effects

VARIABLES	(1b)	(3a)	(3b)	(3c)
ForwardDays		0.305***	0.306***	0.311***
		(0.000)	(0.000)	(0.000)
DWT/1000		–0.054	–0.057	–0.060
		(0.555)	(0.532)	(0.507)
Age		0.280	0.274	0.277
		(0.299)	(0.312)	(0.299)
Age2		–0.015	–0.015	–0.015
		(0.196)	(0.197)	(0.180)
LoadFactor100		–0.173	–0.165	–0.191
		(0.547)	(0.565)	(0.505)
TD2_D		0.946	0.943	0.285
		(0.121)	(0.122)	(0.681)
EstCons		–0.026		
		(0.240)		
FEIAct			–4.456	
			(0.105)	
Fueltonne				–1.507**
				(0.026)
Constant	35.712***	65.260	66.718	70.962
	(0.000)	(0.205)	(0.194)	(0.165)
Monthly dummy	YES	YES	YES	YES
Charter FE	YES	YES	YES	YES
Owner FE	YES	YES	YES	YES
R-squared	0.8654	0.8701	0.8703	0.8705
Observations	1,007	1,007	1,007	1,007

Robust p-values in parentheses, *** p<0.01, ** p<0.05, * p<0.1

we include represent an unbiased sample of overall activity. Secondly, the process of mapping AIS-derived voyages to fixtures tend to further reduce the sample, for instance, because the terms of the reported fixture were ultimately changed (e.g. by changing load date or area). Thirdly, our process of filling in missing data for nominal fuel consumption may have introduced some measurement errors. Unfortunately, the alternative is a much-reduced sample. Fourthly, we would have liked to use the true speed–fuel consumption relationship for individual vessels, though such detailed technical information is not available in practice. Finally, the period under consideration is relatively short, but this is limited by the availability of satellite AIS data which did not start flowing into the public domain until 2012. Unfortunately, the above weaknesses are not possible to address, simply because better data is not available.

5.5 Conclusion and managerial implications

In this chapter we have reviewed the theory and practice of environmental management in ship operations. From this review, we can extract several research questions that are of crucial practical interest but also represent gaps in the literature:

1   How are the rewards for energy efficiency (i.e. fuel cost savings) shared between charterers and shipowners under different charterparty types, market conditions, and shipping segments?

2 Are charterers willing to pay a premium freight rate for more energy-efficient tonnage even if they do not share in the fuel savings (such as under a voyage charter)?

3 Do energy-efficient vessels instead increase their true earnings through increased utilization (i.e. lower unemployment between contracts, lower ballast ratio)?

The recent empirical literature has tried to tackle the first question, with Adland et al. (2017b) and Agnolucci et al. (2014) suggesting that only a fraction of fuel cost savings accrue to the owner through a premium in timecharter rates, and possibly only in poor market conditions. In this chapter we have pointed out that even these findings can be questioned on the basis that researchers use design values for speed and fuel consumption. Given that slow steaming has been prevalent in recent years (Adland and Jia, 2016a,b), evaluation of any energy-efficiency premium (discount) in freight rates must account for the true fuel consumption at actual sailing speeds to be meaningful. Unfortunately, empirical fuel consumption data is typically available to the researcher on a very small scale and, even then, it is hard to control for heterogeneity in operating conditions (see Meng et al, 2016). This also points to a possible key reason why energy efficiency is seemingly not "priced in" in timecharter rates to a greater extent: fuel consumption as a function of vessel speed in the real seaway is an extremely uncertain function, with actual consumption easily surpassing nominal "flat water" consumption by 50% due to fouling, currents, and weather conditions. Consequently, risk-averse charterers are reluctant to pay a fixed premium in the charter hire in exchange for highly uncertain fuel savings, particularly in oversupplied markets where "high-spec" vessels can be had for the cost of less energy-efficient vessels.

In our case study from the tanker freight market, we addressed the second question: whether charterers are willing to pay a premium freight rate for more energy-efficient tonnage under a voyage charter. Our empirical results suggest that the focus on sustainability in recent years may be starting to manifest itself in market pricing. We show that operational efficiency, evaluated at true sailing speeds, appears to be rewarded in the market for VLCC voyage charters, at least as long as we control for the unobservable heterogeneity of owner and charterer in a fixed effects model. This is the first empirical evidence of a two-tier market for tankers with respect to energy efficiency in the literature.

The managerial implications of this study are in fact all pointing in the same direction. An owner of an energy-efficient vessel should operate it in the voyage charter market wherever possible. The outcomes will be that all fuel savings will accrue for the benefit of the owner, and there may be an additional reward in the voyage freight rate (as per our VLCC study). Additionally, as owners remain in operational control of the vessel, they are free to take advantage of additional gains from speed optimization, subject to external constraints. In the timecharter market, at best, only a relatively small share of the savings from operating energy-efficient tonnage will pass through to owners by way of higher TC rates. Conversely, ship operators should charter in highly energy-efficient tonnage in the TC market and sublet the vessels in the voyage charter market, pocketing the difference. For all agents involved, it is crucial to reduce the uncertainty surrounding the monetary gains from energy-efficient operation, for instance by devoting resources to measure the true fuel consumption in the seaway, and disseminating such information to charterers. In the short term, it is only improved quality of information that can contribute to fairer pricing of energy efficiency and environmentally friendly operation in the markets.

The discussion and results in this chapter highlight several areas of importance for future research. Firstly, it is necessary to merge the emerging literature on vessel performance (e.g. fuel consumption) with that on the pricing of freight contracts and, particularly, the impact of energy efficiency. While improved availability of satellite AIS data has provided better information on the true sailing speed of vessels in recent years, the analysis of commercial data on the warranted speed and fuel consumption in charterparties or, alternatively, empirical fuel consumption data from noon reports, remain scarce. The hypothesis of an energy-efficiency premium in the freight market can only be evaluated properly once the true operating conditions – and the inherent uncertainty – are properly accounted for. Secondly, there is a need for research on whether energy-efficient vessels benefit indirectly through mechanisms other than freight contract pricing, for instance by having higher utilization (i.e. less ballasting, less idleness). While Prakash et al. (2016) scratches the surface here, this is currently a wide-open empirical research area. Thirdly, there is a need for research on the proper structure of commercial freight contracts in shipping. Largely unchanged for centuries, these contracts do not explicitly allow for the sharing of the benefits from fuel efficiency and energy-efficient operation in general. For instance, the existence of demurrage, often at rates higher than those for the freight itself, gives owners a perverse (from an environmental point of view) incentive to sail as fast as possible to the destination port only to wait at anchorage and, where possible, collect demurrage. The removal of such barriers to energy-efficient operation currently represents much lower-hanging fruit than the optimization of classical hull forms.

Notes

1 Since our VLCC vessels are larger than the Worldscale reference ship (75,000DWT), the spot freight rates for individual fixtures are not strictly comparable across routes and so some residual "route effect" will remain and is largely a function of sailing distance.
2 We have multiplied by $\$10^6$, to convert from tonnes to grams for ease of presentation.
3 Weekly fuel prices for Fujairah provided by Clarkson Research.

References

Abowd, J.M., Kramarz, F., Margolis, D. 1999. High wage workers and high wage firms. *Econometrica*, 67(2), 251–333.

Adland, R. and Jia, H. 2016a. Dynamic speed choice in bulk shipping. *Maritime Economics and Policy*, doi:10.1057/s41278-016-0002-3.

Adland, R. and Jia, H. 2016b. *Vessel Speed Analytics Using Satellite-based Ship Position Data.* IEEE proceedings of the IEEM, doi: 10.1109/IEEM.2016.7798088.

Adland, R. and Strandenes, S. P. 2007. A discrete-time stochastic partial equilibrium model of the spot freight market. *Journal of Transport Economics and Policy*, 41(2), 1– 30.

Adland, R., Cariou, P., Wolff F. C. 2016. The influence of charterers and owners on bulk shipping freight rates. *Transportation Research Part E*, 86, 69–82.

Adland, R., Fonnes, G., Jia, H., Lampe, O.D., Strandenes, S.P. 2017a. The impact of market conditions and regional environmental regulations on vessel speed. *Transportation Research Part D*, forthcoming.

Adland, R., Alger, H., Banyte, J., and Jia, H. 2017b. Does fuel efficiency pay? Empirical evidence from the drybulk timecharter market revisited. *Transportation Research Part A*, 95, 1–12.

Adland, R., Cariou, P., Wolff, F-C. 2017c. What makes a freight market index? An empirical analysis of vessel fixtures in the offshore market, Transportation Research Part E, 150–164. working paper,

Agnolucci, P., Smith, T., Rehmatullah, N. 2014. Energy efficiency and time charter rates: Energy efficiency savings recovered by ship owners in the Panamax market. *Transportation Research Part A*, 66, 173–184.

Alderton, P. 1981. The optimum speed of ships. *Journal of Navigation*, 34, 341–355.

Alizadeh, A.H., Talley, W.K. 2011a. Vessel and voyage determinants of tanker freight rates and contract times. *Transport Policy*, 18, 665–675.

Alizadeh, A.H. and Talley, W.K. 2011b. Microeconomic determinants of dry bulk shipping freight rates and contract times. *Transportation*, 38, 561–579.

Artz Jr., J. 1975. The economics of tanker slowdown: an observation. *Maritime Policy & Management*, 2(4), 244–249.

Assmann, L., Andersson, J., Eskeland, G. 2015. Missing in action? Speed optimization and slow steaming in maritime shipping. NHH Dept. of Business and Management Science Discussion Paper No. 2015/13.

Avi-Itzhak, J. 1974. Speed, fuel consumption and output of ships: some quantitative economical and national implications of the oil crisis. *Transportation Research*, 10(3), 137–221.

Balland, O., Erikstad, S., Fagerholt, K. 2012. Optimized selection of air emission controls for vessels. *Maritime Policy & Management*, 39(4), 387–400.

Balland, O., Erikstad, S., Fagerholt, K.,Wallace, S. 2013. Planning vessel air emission regulations compliance under uncertainty. *Journal of Marine Science and Technology*, 18(3), 349–357.

Bates, T. H. 1969. A linear regression analysis of ocean tramp rates. *Transportation Research*, 3, 377–395.

Brynolf, S., Magnusson, M., Fridell, E., and Andersson, K. 2014. Compliance possibilities for the future ECA regulations through the use of abatement technologies or change of fuels. *Transportation Research Part D: Transport and Environment*, 28, 6–18.

Clarkson Research, 2016. Shipping intelligence network. www.clarksons.net.

Corbett, J.J., Wang, H.F., and Winebrake, J.J. 2009. The effectiveness and costs of speed reduction on emissions from international shipping. *Transportation Research Part D – Transport and Environment*, 14(8), 593–598.

Doudnikoff, M. and Lacoste, R. 2014. Effect of a speed reduction of containerships in response to higher energy costs in Sulphur Emission Control Areas. *Transportation Research Part D: Transport and Environment*, 27, 19–29.

Elkington, J. 1997. Cannibals with forks. The triple bottom line of 21st century business. Gabriola Island, BC: New Society Publishers.

Faber, J., Behrends, B., Nelissen, D. 2011. *Analysis of GHG Marginal Abatement Cost Curves*. CE Delft, Delft.

Fagerholt, K., Gausel, N.T., Rakke, J.G., Psaraftis, H. 2015. Maritime routing and speed optimization with emission control areas. *Transportation Research Part C: Emerging Technologies*, 52, 57–73.

Ferrari, CL, F. Parola, A. Tei. 2015. Determinants of slow steaming and implications on service patterns. *Maritime Policy & Management*, 42, 636–652.

IMO. 2009. *Prevention of Air Pollution from Ships. Second IMO GHG Study 2009*. Paper MEPC 59/INF. 10. Annex. International Maritime Organization, London, UK.

Jiang, L., Kronbak, J. Christensen, L. 2014. The costs and benefits of sulphur reduction measures: Sulphur scrubbers versus marine gas oil. *Transportation Research Part D: Transport and Environment*, 28, 19–27.

Köhn, S. and Thanopolou, H. 2011. A GAM assessment of quality premia in the drybulk timecharter market. *Transportation Research Part E*, 47(5), 709–721.

Kollamthodi, S., Brannigan, C., Harfoot, M., Skinner, I.,Whall, C., Lavric, L., Noden, R., Lee, D., Buhaug, Ø., Martinussen, K., Skejic, R.,Valberg, I., Brembo, J., Eyring,V., Faber, J. 2008. *Greenhouse Gas Emissions from Shipping: Trends Projections and Abatement Potential*. AEA Energy & Environment, Didcot.

Lindstad, H., Asbjørnslett, B. E., Strømman, A. H. 2011. Reductions in greenhouse gas emissions and cost by shipping at lower speeds. *Energy Policy*, 39(6), 3456–3464.

Lindstad, H., I. Sandaas, and A. H. Stromman. 2015. Assessment of cost as a function of abatement options in maritime emission control areas. *Transportation Research Part D: Transport and Environment*, 38, 41–48.

Lindstad, H. E., Eskeland, G. S., Rialland, A. 2017. Batteries in offshore support vessels – Pollution, climate impact and economics. *Transportation Research Part D: Transport and Environment*, 50, 409–417.

Maloni, M., J.A. Paul, D.M. Gligor. 2013. Slow steaming impacts on ocean carriers and shippers. *Maritime Economics & Logistics*, 15(2), 151–171.

Manning, G. 1956. *The Theory and Technique of Ship Design; a Study of the Basic Principles and the processes Employed in the Design of Ships of all Classes*. The MIT Press, Cambridge.

Meng, Q., Du, Y., Wang, Y. 2016. Shipping log data based container ship fuel efficiency modeling. *Transportation Research Part B: Methodological*, 83, 207–229.

Norman, V. and Wergeland, T. 1979. *Oil Prices and World Shipping*. Oslo: Platou Report.

Prakash, V., Smith, T., Rehmatulla, N., Mitchell, Adland, R. 2016. *Revealed Preferences for Energy Efficiency in the Shipping Markets*. UCL, London, UK . Obtained 3 September 2016: http://shippingefficiency.org/sites/shippingefficiency.org

Psaraftis, H. and Kontovas, C. 2013. Speed models for energy-efficient maritime transportation: a taxonomy and survey. *Transportation Research Part C: Emerging Technologies*, 26, 331–351.

Psaraftis, H. and Kontovas, C. 2014. Ship speed optimization: Concepts, models and combined speed-routing scenarios. *Transportation Research Part C: Emerging Technologies*, 44, 52–69.

Ronen, D. 1982. The effect of oil price on the optimal speed of ships. *Journal of the Operational Research Society*, 33: 1035–1040.

Schinas, O., and Stefanakos, C. N. 2012. Cost assessment of environmental regulation and options for marine operators. *Transportation Research Part C: Emerging Technologies*, 25, 81–99.

Tamvakis, M.N. 1995. An investigation into the existence of a two-tier spot freight market for crude oil tankers. *Maritime Policy and Management*, 22 (1), 81–90.

Tamvakis, M.N., Thanopoulou, H.A. 2000. Does quality pay? The case of the dry bulk market. *Transportation Research Part E*, 36 (4), 297–307.

Wang, S. and Q. Meng. 2012. Sailing speed optimization for container ships in a liner shipping network. *Transportation Research Part E*, 48, 701–714.

Yang, Z., Zhang, D., Caglayan, O., Jankinson, I., Bonsall, S., Wang, J., Huang, M., Yan, X. 2012. Selection of techniques for reducing shipping NOx and SOx emissions. *Transportation Research Part D: Transport and Environment*, 17, 478–486.

Zis, T., North, R.J., Angeloudis, P., Ochieng, W.Y., Bell, M.G.H. 2014. Evaluation of cold ironing and speed reduction policies to reduce ship emissions near and at ports. *Maritime Economics & Logistics*, 16(4), 371–398.

Sustainability, maritime governance, and business performance in a self-regulated shipping industry

A study on the BIMCO Shipping KPI Standard

Evangelos F. Darousos, Maximo Q. Mejia Jr., and Ilias D. Visvikis

6.1 Introduction

Representing more than 80 per cent by volume in Q4 2017 (almost 10.6 billion tons) and trending upwards, maritime transport, with shipping at its core, plays a leading role for international trade (UNCTAD, 2017). The undisputed value of shipping for sustainable global economic and social prosperity is reflected upon its consideration by all the major global policy framework milestones. Indicatively, the importance of shipping as a crucial element of international trade and development is recognized by the Addis Ababa Action Agenda, which addresses the issue of financing sustainable, economical, social, and environmental projects (UN, 2015). Accordingly, the 14th Sustainable Development Goal (SDG) of the UN Agenda 2030 refers directly to the need for sustainable use of the oceans and the seas as conduits for trade and transportation, calling for international cooperation and coordination (United Nations General Assembly, 2015).

The existing maritime and ocean governance mechanisms, comprised by international, regional, and national policy-making, implementing and monitoring authorities and stakeholders alike, make constant efforts to ensure the sustainability of shipping operations in a seriously deteriorating oceanic environment. Undeniably, the shipping sector is structurally situated within a diverse and ever-evolving legal and policy framework, assessed and formulated through international and multilevel monitoring, control and surveillance (OECD, 2016). However, despite it being carefully orchestrated within an evolving framework of international standards and supported by international and domestic maritime legal instruments, it is not uncommon for unforeseen accidents to take place. These accidents that frequently result in disastrous consequences in the form of commercial deficiencies, safety and security issues, and environmental degradation, cast reasonable doubt on the effectiveness of the current maritime governance status quo.

Considering the vigorous system already built around shipping, this study does not address the existence of such failures in shipping by trying to identify gaps of a legal and policy nature. Instead, it considers the exercise of governance in the current hierarchical, pyramid-shaped institutional model of the shipping industry as the remote factor behind the majority of those failures in shipping. At the top of the current governance structure, the study places the "formal" authorities overarched by the International Maritime Organization (IMO), including international, regional, and national regulators and policymakers. Likewise, the top level of this structure includes all the organizations dealing with the implementation and monitoring of the relevant policies and measures. On the basis of the structure we identify the "informal" stakeholders: the shipping markets including the ship-owning and management companies, non-governmental organizations (NGOs), and of course the communities affected by the shipping industry, economically, environmentally (in terms of coastal areas), or otherwise. More specifically, it aspires to contribute to the ongoing public discourse about whether or not the various multilevel signs of failure in shipping are only due to their respective *causa proxima* or lack of good governance in the industry (indicatively, see Roe 2013; 2016).

This study aims to deal with two main issues. First is the identification of a reliable system to measure non-financial and non-accounting types of performance in the shipping industry. While other relevant initiatives exist, such as the EU Monitoring, Reporting, Verification (MRV) for measuring CO_2 emissions from shipping, past research indicates gaps regarding both the existence of non-financial and non-accounting performance in shipping, and ways of enabling internal and external communication of shipping environmental information (see Panayides et *al*, 2010; Andersson, 2016, amongst others). This study aims to fill those gaps by considering the full potential of the Shipping Key Performance Indicator (KPI) Standard of the Baltic and International Maritime Council (BIMCO). This market-driven instrument is not only addressed as a benchmarking tool for the shipping industry, but as a potential basis towards the creation of an instrument that will facilitate the measurement of the majority of shipping business performance types. Under this presupposition, the Shipping KPI Standard is also examined as to its accordance with some of the most important elements of good governance, which leads to the second main issue of this study.

Second is the consideration of a successful way to identify a different model of maritime governance, one that will allow for important dimensions of good governance to be expressed. Based on the assumption that the proliferation of deficiencies and accidents is not a mere issue of poor management, but the final stage of an ineffective model of governance, this study examines the potential of a decentralized model of maritime governance. The model is largely based on self-regulation and voluntary cooperation between formal and informal shipping stakeholders. While it is not the first time that the current model of governance in the maritime sector is challenged, this study fills a gap in the literature by examining a different approach in connection with specific elements of good governance, towards the enhancement of shipping performance.

The main questions explored in this maritime governance context include:

(i) Can the Shipping KPI Standard managed by BIMCO as a benchmarking system serve a greater purpose such as measuring shipping performance?

(ii) How can particular dimensions of good governance, or goals such as measurement of shipping business performance, be incorporated into a maritime governance regime in such a way as to promote sustainability in the shipping industry?

(iii) How can formal authorities ensure active stakeholder participation and greater competence towards achieving sustainability goals? Do more decentralized approaches based in collaboration and self-regulation represent a viable counterexample in the case of shipping?

The rest of this chapter is organized as follows. Section 6.2 investigates the Shipping KPI Standard. Section 6.3 presents various approaches to governance and maritime governance, highlighting the importance of good governance for sustainable development. Section 6.4 identifies the relation of the Shipping KPI Standard with some of the most common elements of good governance. Finally, Section 6.5 presents the conclusions of the chapter.

6.2 The Shipping KPI System by BIMCO

6.2.1 An overview

The Shipping KPI System began its development in 2003 led by InterManager, the international trade association for the ship management industry, in close collaboration with the Norwegian Research Council, consultants of Marintek, and maritime IT specialists from SOFTImpact. Starting 2011, the System was superintended by the independent KPI Association Ltd. In 2015 BIMCO, after acquiring the Shipping KPI System and along with the IT support of SOFTImpact, has been operating and developing it until the time of publication (BIMCO, 2015b).

The version of the System considered by this study (version 2.6) is based on a customized standard of 64 different KPIs to allow the most specific and accurate comparison of ships, across different types and sectors that are currently available, in order to allow to the companies using it to "... *drive sustainable improvements*" (BIMCO, 2018). The BIMCO KPI Standard is built up in a hierarchical orientation with seven (7) Shipping Performance Indices (SPIs), 34 KPIs, and 66 Performance Indicators (PIs). SPIs (high level indices) are calculated from KPIs, and then KPIs are calculated from PIs (lowest level); finally, on the highest level the KPIs are combined into SPIs in order to express performance. The types of performance measured by BIMCO by the version 2.6 of the Shipping KPI Standard included environmental, health, and safety management, HR management, navigational safety, and operational, security, and technical performance (BIMCO, 2015a). (See Table A6.1 in the Appendix.)

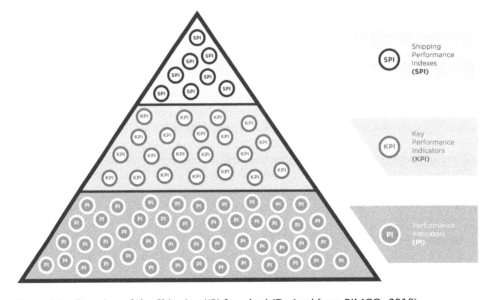

Figure 6.1   Overview of the Shipping KPI Standard (Derived from BIMCO, 2018).

The SPIs constitute the aggregated expression of the various types of performance. The data is presented as a weighted average of KPI ratings on a scale between 0 and 100 (BIMCO, 2018). PIs are captured and reported by ships, and generally KPIs and SPIs are also calculated on a ship basis. Due to the difficulty of expressing certain performance indicators on a single ship basis, though, the Shipping KPI System uses the strategic business units (SBUs or BUs). A BU is, simply put, "*an organizational sub-entity of a shipping company responsible for a subset of the ships*" (BIMCO, 2018). The size of a BU might vary from the national office of a shipping company up to one of its branches or regions. All the PIs which are fleet-wide defined are measured by the respective BU, which is the one to define the fleet and all ships within a BU share the same PI value.

In April 2018, BIMCO relaunched the Shipping KPI System in order to better conform with industry standards and improved the validity of the data, for example, by removing invalid IMO-numbers from the database. A major change is the upgrading of the port state control system performance indicator from a KPI to a new, eighth SPI, followed by certain changes regarding the PIs and the KPIs. For example, the importance of CO_2, SO_x and NO_x efficiency was already recognized in version 2.6 as highly relevant for the Environmental Performance SPI (SPI001). However, despite being recorded, they were not expressed on an SPI level due to being considered inconsistent as an expression of the ship manager's performance. Starting from version 3.0, they will be normally accounted for in the calculation of the SPI001. (See Table A6.2 in the Appendix)

6.3 Governance: a fundamental concept

Despite the wide use of the term, there remains no universally accepted definition of governance. There is a vast body of literature examining this issue, presenting definitions that exhibit similarities and differences with each other. However, whether its popularity is due to its ambiguity or not (Peters, 2012), it is a fact that the term has been widely used in a great range including organizations related to international policy-making and global governing bodies, as well as firms in the private sector.

The concept of governance has been fundamental in explaining the complex and constantly evolving nature of modern and late-modern forms of socio-political structures, particularly those which have emerged in the form of a networked-system between the state, market, civil society, and their interrelated institutions and market stakeholders. Campbell et al. (1991) define the term as the processes coordinating the activities of economic actors, while Fukuyama (2013) describes it as the ability of a government to produce and enforce regulations and provide services. Rhodes (1996) considers the concept of governance as being perceived in different ways depending on the context and suggests six different definitions and forms of governance, including an efficient public service, an independent public auditor, responsible to a representative legislature, and a pluralistic institutional structure.

It should be noted that what the term embodies is always subject to the point of view of the respective researchers, and their investigative scope and interests. Perhaps, trying to endorse static elements on such a highly volatile concept and to claim an absolute, fixed definition for it would even be anti-dialectic. For the purposes of this study, governance is treated as "... *the establishment and operation of social institutions (in the sense of rules of the game that serve to define social practices, assign roles, and guide interactions among the occupants of these roles) capable of resolving conflicts, facilitating cooperation, or, more generally, alleviating collective-action problems in a world of interdependent actors*" (Young, 1994).

6.3.1 Maritime and ocean governance: the key to sustainable shipping

Deductively, the absence of a universal definition specifically concerning the governance of maritime affairs is only to be expected. To begin with, there is a tendency to fuse maritime and ocean/marine governance under one umbrella definition, as has been for example previously done by the European Commission, when referring to the need for an integrated maritime policy, holistically covering all oceanic and maritime aspects (European Commission, 2007) or, by the World Ocean Council (2014), which addressed the whole of the maritime industry as one multi-sectoral business and industry suggesting a holistic treatment, in terms of global policy-making, of all the maritime activities. However, despite the frequent overlap in areas such law and policy, ocean governance is most recurrently attributed to the interaction between human activities and the marine environment (Chang, 2012) and marine processes, species, and ecosystems (Hildebrand and Bellefontaine, 2017). In contrast, the term maritime mostly refers to "… *issues such as ports and harbours, shipping, transportation and other sectoral oriented activities, including naval interests*" (Haward and Vince, 2008) and maritime governance is mostly involved in discussions regarding several areas in an context mostly related to shipping and shipping policy formation (Roe 2013; 2016; Mukherjee & Brownrigg, 2013) and relevant discussions, even with regards to port governance (Woo et al, 2011), shipping environmental governance (Lister et al., 2015), and maritime economics and policy (Duru, 2014). Hildebrand and Schröder-Hinrichs (2014) have also offered a cogent attempt to disentangle issues related to overlaps, specificities, and imprecisions in the use of the terms marine and maritime.

This study, though, treats maritime governance as "…*the sharing of policy-making competencies in a system of negotiation between nested governmental institutions at several levels (international, supranational, national, regional and local) on the one hand, and state actors, market parties and civil society organizations on the other hand in order to govern the activity of shipping and its consequences*" along with all the efforts, at regulatory level, to increase the sustainability of the shipping industry (Van Leeuwen, 2015).

Sustainability refers to the mindful use of natural resources considering their supply and continued viability. In other words, the maximization of the economic benefits from the high seas in a sustainable way, both environmentally and otherwise (Rothwell et al, 2006; Global Ocean Commission, 2014). The concept of sustainability and sustainable development are considered to lead the path towards progressive economic and societal transformation globally (World Commission on Environment and Development, 1987). Ambiguities notwithstanding, maritime and ocean governance both deal with the assurance of long-term sustainability, equity in resource allocation and the creation of the necessary conditions for the growth of the blue economy (Pauli, 2010; World Wildlife Fund 2015; Hildebrand and Bellefontaine, 2017; The World Bank, 2017). Even within the fragmented post-modern reality, the governance of maritime affairs still is more than the sum of its parts, meaning that policy-making, implementation and monitoring mechanisms led by, and derived from the formal power structure, do not stand not alone in ensuring the sustainability and sustainable development of the sector. Following a global structural shift towards neoliberalism, the role of states and other traditional centralized sources of power has been diminishing and a new, decentralized model of governance that includes multiple stakeholders – whether public, private, profit, or non-profit – has been emerging.

6.3.2 Links between shipping performance and sustainability

Good governance is an important element of achieving sustainability and this is the case for the maritime industry as well, where elements of good governance could be more easily nurtured if the current model of maritime governance allowed for a collaborative approach between the interdependent market stakeholders. Sustainability and sustainable development, however, are in turn in a lockstep with the performance of the shipping companies.

The best example derives from good corporate governance, which is considered to play a positive role in environmental performance (Walls et al., 2012). The environmental performance is the outcome of a firm's strategic activities that manage (or not) its impact on the natural environment (Walls et al., 2012). Not unexpectedly, the importance of the reduction of marine pollution of all kinds and the enhancement, conservation and sustainable use of oceans and their resources is also reflected in Goal 14 of the UN's 2030 Agenda for Sustainable Development, a plan of strategic importance for the global community which is expected to set the pace of governance strategies and initiatives towards achieving environmental sustainability.

The issue of environmental performance and the adoption of environmentally green initiatives has been addressed before, and there is sufficient evidence of shipping companies adopting 'green' measures to mitigate the environmental risk in shipping operations and reduce the negative impacts in handling shipping activities, and practices such as counting the carbon footprint of shipping routes and using alternative transportation equipment towards reducing environmental damage in shipping (Lun, 2013; Lun et al., 2015). A good example would be the Fair Winds Charter (FWC), an industry-led, voluntary, at-berth fuel-switching programme for ocean-going vessels calling at Hong Kong. Participating vessels of Maersk and 18 other shipping companies switch to low sulphur fuel (0.5% sulphur content or less) while at berth in Hong Kong (Civic Exchange, 2013; Helfre and Boot, 2013). Another example is the Maritime Singapore Green Initiative as a part of which Singapore-flagged ships surpassing the requirements of IMO's Energy Efficiency Design Index enjoy a 50% reduction of initial registration fees (IRF) and a 20% rebate on Annual Tonnage Tax (ATT) payable (Safety4Sea, 2011).

The comparison of shipping to other, more CO_2 emitting and polluting modes of transportation, continues to support its "green" image. However, the serious lag in transnational environmental governance in the shipping industry is increasingly responsible for the substantial environmental footprint of maritime activities (Lister et al., 2015). In a previous study, Panayides et al. (2010) suggest the importance of investigating and evaluating the non-financial and non-accounting performance dimensions of global shipping companies, both in-country and cross-border. Especially given its rapid growth rate, the need to successfully address the issue of the environmental performance of shipping companies seems to be pressing today more than ever.

6.4 Does the Shipping KPI System express good governance dimensions?

As in every situation requiring cross-sectional cooperation, the need for a common system of reference, a common "language", is required by institutional and market stakeholders. In this specific case, it is also synonymous with the need for a mutual tool of environmental performance measurement. The possible solution to those two challenges may interestingly be provided by a market-generated and oriented instrument managed by BIMCO, currently used for internal and external benchmarking of shipping companies.

This instrument, BIMCO's Shipping KPI System, is arguably the first KPI Standard developed specifically to serve the needs of the shipping industry. While the said System assesses performance at the micro-level of shipping companies, it shows potential for adaptation to the macro-level of the global shipping community and development as the common standard instrument for assessing performance of all stakeholders, whether commercial or regulatory.

There are specific guidelines concerning the KPIs included in the system. Specifically, the KPIs need to have the following characteristics (BIMCO, 2018):

1 observable and quantifiable;
2 valid indicator of performance;
3 robust against manipulation;
4 sensitive to change;
5 transparent and easy to understand;
6 compatible.

The inclusion of those guidelines by BIMCO is an important step towards the expression of specific good governance elements in shipping via performance measurement. As part of his work on ocean governance, Chang (2012) followed a mathematical approach to identify the most emphasized elements in relation to good governance, based on both international literature and practice. This study assessed the eight most crucial elements of good governance, together with commentaries on whether and how they correlate with indicators in the BIMCO Shipping KPI System.

6.4.1 Accountability

One way to classify accountability is according to the person, group, or institution to which the accountable entity answers (OECD, 2014). Currently, there is no legal instrument describing how, and to whom, shipping companies are accountable for the impact of their performance. It has been suggested, though, that the existence of market-based mechanisms (MBMs) holding global companies accountable for their performance towards their extensive stakeholder circle has been very effective in certain industries. In the specific case of the maritime industry, strengthening MBMs relevant to the accountability of the shipping companies is considered to be vital for the betterment of their performance. This is done initially by exposing shipping companies to the risk of losing their competitiveness in the market and, second, by allowing their clientele to pressure them towards performing responsibly (Rahim et al, 2016). In order to move in this direction, though, it is important to guarantee the disclosure of information about the performance of the companies both to the authorities and the public stakeholders. Besides, KPIs in general serve three purposes: (a) the monitoring of important findings, (b) the interpretation of their measures, and (c) the initiation of action when such is required (Barr, 2015). In the case of the BIMCO Shipping KPI System, the shipping company may be held accountable at each of those three distinct stages, during the monitoring and interpretation of disturbing findings, and the initiation of necessary actions to treat potential issues. The Shipping KPI System is therefore relevant to the expression of accountability of shipping companies, as well as to the communication and utilization of performance-related information. The inter-related issue of transparency, however, is examined separately below.

6.4.2 Effectiveness and efficiency

The System aims at the improvement of the internal performance of the shipping firms through the identification of potential deficiencies and, ultimately, at enhancing the quality of the service delivery. Since any given KPI System aims, by definition, at operational efficiency and effective performance data measurement and monitoring, the Shipping KPI System allows for effectiveness and efficiency to be expressed. However, there are two important points which should be considered. Every KPI Standard is as reliable as the collection of the performance data by each respective department.

In this respect, the shipping company should ensure that the environmental indicators are carefully collected in order to reflect the actual performance of the company at any given time. Furthermore, in order to be efficient, the KPI Standard needs to provide suitable indicators to reflect environmental performance properly. In other words, BIMCO should be ready to adapt to necessary changes and adopt new indicators if the situation demands it (e.g., if new technological advancements or scientific research require change or adaptation). The guidelines of BIMCO highlight the necessity for accurate and non-manipulated performance indicators on behalf of the shipping companies, in order to guarantee maximum effectiveness and efficiency. Therefore, the Shipping KPI System may serve as the necessary tool for effective and efficient performance, under the assumption that the management guarantee the legitimate gathering of information.

6.4.3 Rule of law

In the shipping industry, the United Nations Convention on the Law of the Sea (UNCLOS) allows states to decide "… *the best practicable means at their disposal and in accordance with their capabilities*" to prevent and mitigate marine pollution. In a collaborative, self-regulated model of governance the shipping firms, as stakeholders, would share a part of this duty and therefore be partly responsible for ensuring compatibility with the current rule of law. The Shipping KPI System is therefore related to the rule of law in the shipping industry, in that it provides the way of monitoring the compliance of the shipping company with the international legal framework. Furthermore, in a collaborative regime of governance or in the case where shipping firms were forced or encouraged to reveal their performance indicators *by using* the Shipping KPI System, shipping companies could become further engaged in maritime governance and subsequently in the rule of law.

6.4.4 Transparency and public access to environmental information

As mentioned in Section 6.2 of this study, the Shipping KPI System does not allow for transparency and/or public access to environmental information (SPI001). The reason is that the overall performance of a shipping firm is considered as sensitive market data, and BIMCO addresses this issue with the highest confidentiality, even for research purposes. However, an important part of environmental management is to facilitate internal and external communication on environmental issues. The level and quality of environmental reports vary, especially in the use of numbers as indicators of specific goals. The different cultures in companies and in different countries regarding information that should be released to the public are also factors. Regional initiatives that make sustainability reporting compulsory already exist. Foremost of these is the European Parliament's Directive 2014/95/EU on disclosure of non-financial and diversity information by certain large companies, which entered into force in December 2014. The directive requires companies to disclose, in their management report, information on policies, risks, and outcomes as regards environmental matters, social and employee aspects, respect for human rights, anticorruption and bribery issues, and diversity in their board of directors. This directive is expected to become national law in two years, with the first company reports being published in 2018 for the 2017–2018 financial year. The rules will apply to companies with more than 500 employees, and approximately 6,000 companies will be affected (Andersson, 2016). The Shipping KPI System allows for transparency as an element of good governance to be expressed *internally*, for business purposes and information of the shipping company's shareholders. However, in order to serve purposes relevant to the *external* environment of the company, transparency and public access to environmental information need to be expressed, in the form of disclosure of the SPIs to corresponding authorities and wide stakeholders.

6.4.5 Predictability

The Standard does not currently take predictability into consideration, as the indicators only reflect the number of separate incidents on a quarterly basis. However, there is a research gap regarding potential forecasting methods based on past measurements, which could potentially allow for predictions on the overall performance measurement of shipping firms.

6.4.6 Participation

The Shipping KPI System allows for participation in the case of a change in the current model of governance in the shipping sector. If the international government authorities adopt a cooperative stance, useful results concerning the amelioration of the overall performance in the maritime sector could be extracted by considering the self-monitoring capabilities of ship management firms.

6.4.7 Responsiveness

The Shipping KPI System is based on the presupposition that the performance measurements and the benchmarking process will lead not only to the efficient communication between the internal and external stakeholders of shipping firms, but also to effective changes at all managerial levels, in order to counteract the deficiencies. As a dimension of good governance, responsiveness would be expressed on the recurrence – or not – of the same or similar deficiencies, tracked through the System.

6.4.8 Suggestions

The inclusion of numerous and diverse shipping performance indicators in the Shipping KPI System and the consideration of SPIs relevant to sustainability, such as the Environmental Performance SPI001, seem to satisfy the potential internal needs of shipping companies. At its current version, the Shipping KPI Standard may sufficiently facilitate internal and external communication on operational, environmental, and other types of performance. In that way, it may be used as a tool of reporting for all stakeholders to communicate and extract crucial information. However, it should be noted that certain important elements of good governance may not currently be expressed (and thus, measured) by the Shipping KPI System. As any KPI Standard, it may always be subject to customization by its users; as such, the creation of new indicators to measure important governance elements is highly suggested, always in accordance to the BIMCO guidelines for the inclusion of KPIs.

6.5 Conclusion

Public discourse is dominated by the concept of sustainable development in this era of UN Agenda 2030. Shipping, the environmental footprint of which – despite its significance for major trade and its growth – has kept it unaccountable in comparison with other major means of transport, now needs to adopt a different pace in order to meet the sustainability goals deriving from its growing impact. Considering the need for sustainable "blue" growth, the maritime industry should perhaps follow the transformative curve of the modern economy, towards a more decentralized and less hierarchical model of governance, allowing for actual involvement and participation. The adoption of a more decentralized model, favouring the conditions for collaboration between public and private shipping stakeholders, could allow particular dimensions of good governance to be implemented within the maritime governance regime. These are dimensions of good governance that are currently unexpressed, but which are generally considered as interlinked to shipping business performance and sustainability. Collaboration and self-regulation should be considered as rational alternatives in the place of top-down regulatory measures and policies. By allowing shipping firms to actively participate as major stakeholders and therefore be further accountable for their performance and everyday operation, the shipping industry might take important steps towards a more sustainable direction.

The need for good governance of the shipping sector, either regarding the internal environment of shipping companies or the external, industry-wide, environment, is highlighted by the fact that despite the diverse and evolving legal and regulatory framework, disasters regarding various aspects of shipping still take place. The need for exchange of information regarding the performance levels of the global commercial fleet can be satisfied by the adoption of an appropriate tool of information exchange. The Shipping KPI Standard is an appropriate tool allowing for standardized exchange of shipping performance information. However, the development and adoption of other indicators, allowing for the expression of good governance elements such as participation in decision-making, control of corruption, or transparency are highly advised. Future empirical analysis of aggregated SPIs and KPIs by BIMCO databases should highlight specific issues concerning shipping performance in different types of shipping and geographical regions.

References

Andersson, K. (2016). Environmental management. In Andersson, K., Brynolf, S., Lindgren, J. F., Wilewska-Bien, M. (eds.), *Shipping and the Environment*. Berlin and Heidelberg: Springer-Verlag.

Barr, S. (2015). *What is a KPI Owner Accountable For?* Retrieved from: https://www.staceybarr.com/measure-up/what-is-a-kpi-owner-accountable-for/. Last accessed January 31 2019.

BIMCO. (2015a). *The Shipping KPI Standard V2.6*. Retrieved from Baltic and International Maritime Council website: https://www.shipping-kpi.org/public/downloads/documentation/Shipping_KPI_Quicksheet_V2.6.pdf#?kpiProfileId=1. Last accessed 28 April 2018.

BIMCO. (2015b). *BIMCO takes Ownership of Unique Shipping KPI System*. Retrieved 2 June 2017, from Shippin-KPI.org, available at: https://www.shipping-kpi.org/public/downloads/pressreleases/BIMCO_PRESS_RELEASE.pdf, last accessed: 12 October 2017.

BIMCO. (2018). *The Shipping KPI Standard V.3.0*. Retrieved from Baltic and International Maritime Council. Available at: https://www.shipping-kpi.org/book/pages/concepts#?kpiProfileId=1. Last accessed 28 April 2018.

Campbell, J., Hollingsworth, J., & Lindberg, L.N. (1991). *Governance of the American Economy*. Cambridge: Cambridge University Press.

Chang, Y.-C. (2012). *Ocean Governance A Way Forward*. Netherlands: Springer.

Civic Exchange. (2013). *The Fair Winds Charter 2013*. Available at: http://www.civic-exchange.org/materials/theme/files/FWC.html. Last accessed: April 28, 2018.

Duru, O. (2014). Irrationality in politics and governance of maritime affairs: The collapse of sovereign maritime governance. *International Journal of e-Navigation and Maritime Economy*, 1, 48–59.

European Commission. (2007). Communication from the Commission to the European Parliament, the Council, the European Economic and Social Committee and the Committee of the Regions. *An Integrated Maritime Policy for the European Union*, COM (2007) 575 final.

Fukuyama, F. (2013). What is governance? *Governance*, 26, 347–368.

Global Ocean Commission. (2014). *From Decline to Recovery: A Rescue Package for the Ocean*. Retrieved from http://www.some.ox.ac.uk/wpcontent/uploads/2016/03/GOC_report_2015.July_2.pdf. Last accessed 12 October 2017.

Haward, M. and Vince, J. (2008). *Oceans Governance in the Twenty-First Century: Managing the Blue Planet*. Cheltenham: Edward Elgar Publishing Limited.

Helfre, J.-F. and Boot, P. (2013). *Emission Reduction in the Shipping Industry: Regulations, Exposure and Solutions*. Available at: http://www.sustainalytics.com/sites/default/files/shippingemissions_july2013.pdf. Last accessed: 28 April 2018.

Hildebrand, L. and Bellefontaine, N. (2017). Ocean governance and sustainability in *Shipping Operations Management*, I.D. Visvikis and P.M. Panayides (eds.), New York: Springer International.

Hildebrand, L. and Schröder-Hinrichs, J.-U. (2014). Maritime and marine: Synonyms, solitudes or schizophrenia? *WMU Journal of Maritime Affairs*. 13, 173–176.

Lister, J., Taudal Poulsen, R., and Ponte, S. (2015). Orchestrating transnational environmental governance in maritime shipping. *Global Environmental Change,* 34, 185–195.

Lun, Y. H. (2013). Development of green shipping network to enhance environmental and economic performance. *Polish Maritime Research,* 20(Special Issue), 13–19.

Lun, Y.H., Lai, Kee-hung, Wong, Christina, and Cheng, T.C.E. (2015). Environmental governance mechanisms in shipping firms and their environmental performance. *Transportation Research Part E: Logistics and Transportation Review,* 78.

Mukherjee, P. and Brownrigg, M. (2013). *Farthing on International Shipping* (4th ed.). Heidelberg: Springer.

OECD. (2014). *Accountability and Democratic Governance: Orientations and Principles for Development, DAC Guidelines and Reference Series*. Paris: OECD Publishing.

OECD. (2016). *Better Policies for Sustainable Development 2016: A New Framework for Policy Coherence*. Paris: OECD Publishing.

Panayides P., Gong, S., and Lambertides, N. (2010). Measuring Business Performance in Shipping. In C.Th. Grammenos (ed.) *The Handbook of Maritime Economics and Business*, 2nd edition: 625–655.

Pauli, G. (2010), Sustainable transport: A case study of Rhine navigation. *Natural Resources Forum*, 34, 236–254.

Peters, G.B. (2012). Governance as political theory. In D. Levi-Faur (ed.), *The Oxford Handbook of Governance*, pp. 19–32. Oxford: Oxford University Press.

Rahim, M.M., Islam, T., and Kuruppu, S. (2016). Regulating global shipping corporations' accountability for reducing greenhouse gas emissions in the seas. *Marine Policy*, 69, 159 –170.

Rhodes, R.A.W. (1996). The new governance: Governing without government. *Political Studies*, 44(4), 652–667.

Roe, M. (2013). *Maritime Governance and Policy-Making*. London: Springer-Verlag.

Roe, M. (2016). *Maritime Governance. Speed, Flow, Form Process*. Switzerland: Springer International Publishing.

Rothwell, D. R., and Vanderzwaag, A. (2006). *Towards Principled Oceans Governance: Australian and Canadian Approaches and Challenges*. Abington: Routledge.

Safety4Sea. (July 01, 2011). Details of the green ship programme under the Maritime Singapore Green. Available at https://safety4sea.com/details-of-the-green-ship-programme-under-the-maritime-singapore-green-initiativ/. Last accessed: 30 June 2018.

UNCTAD. (2017). *Review of Maritime Transport 2017, UNCTAD/RMT/2017*. New York and Geneva: United Nations.

United Nations (2015). *Transforming Our World: The 2030 Agenda for Sustainable Development*. New York: UN Publishing.

United Nations General Assembly. (2015). *Addis Ababa Action Agenda of the Third International Conference on Financing for Development (Addis Ababa Action Agenda). A/ RES/69/313*. New York: United Nations.

Van Leeuwen, J. (2015). The regionalization of maritime governance: Towards a polycentric governance system for sustainable shipping in the European Union. *Ocean and Coastal Management*, 117, 23–31.

Walls, J.L., Berrone P., and Phan P.H. 2012. Corporate governance and environmental performance: Is there really a link? *Strategic Management Journal* 33(8), 885–913.

Woo, S., Pettit, S.J., Kwak, D. W., & Beresford, A. K. C. (2011). Seaport research: A structured literature review on methodological issues since the 1980s. *Transportation Research Part A*, 45, 667–685.

World Ocean Council. (2014). *International Ocean Governance: Policy Brief*. Honolulu.

World Wildlife Fund. (2015). All hands on deck – Setting course towards a sustainable blue economy. *WWF Baltic Ecoregion Programme*. Available at: http://d2ouvy59p0dg6k.cloudfront.net/downloads/15_6802_final_all_hands_on_deck_lr_1.

Young, O. R. (1994). *International Governance: Protecting the Environment in a Stateless Society*. Ithaca (N.Y.): Cornell University Press.

APPENDICES

Appendix I: Table A6.1

Table A6.1 BIMCO Shipping KPI Standard Version 2.6 Quick Sheet

SPI	KPI	PI
Health and Safety Performance	Flawless Port state control performance	Number of PSC inspections resulting in zero deficiencies
		Number of PSC inspections
	Lost Time Injury Frequency	Number of fatalities due to work injuries
		Number of lost workday cases
		Number of permanent total disabilities (PTD)
		Number of permanent partial disabilities (PPD)
		Total exposure hours
	Health and Safety deficiencies	Number of health and safety related deficiencies
		Number of recorded external inspections
	Lost Time Sickness Frequency	Number of cases where a crew member is sick for more than 24 hours
		Number of fatalities due to sickness
		Total exposure hours
	Passenger Injury Ratio	Number of passengers injured
		Passenger exposure hours
HR Management Performance	Crew disciplinary frequency	Number of absconded crew
		Number of charges of criminal offences
		Number of cases where drugs or alcohol is abused
		Number of dismissed crew
		Number of logged warnings
		Total exposure hours
	Crew planning	Number of seafarers not relieved on time
		Number of violation of rest hours
	HR deficiencies	Number of HR related deficiencies
		Number of recorded external inspections
	Cadets per ship	Number of cadets under training with the ship manager
		Number of ships operated under DOC holder
	Officer retention rate	Number of officer terminations from whatever cause
		Number of unavoidable officer terminations
		Number of beneficial officer terminations
		Average number of officers employed
	Officers experience rate	Number of officer experience points
		Number of officers onboard
	Training days per officer	Number of officer trainee man days
		Number of officer days onboard all ships under technical management (DOC)
Environmental Performance	Releases of substances as def by MARPOL Annex 1–6	Number of releases of solid substances to the environment
		Number of oil spills
	Ballast water management violations	Number of ballast water management violations
	Contained spills	Number of contained spills of liquid
	Environmental deficiencies	Number of environmental related deficiencies
		Number of recorded external inspections

(Continued)

Table A6.1 Continued

SPI	KPI	PI
Navigational Safety Performance	Navigational deficiencies	Number of navigational related deficiencies
		Number of recorded external inspections
	Navigational incidents	Number of collisions
		Number of allisions
		Number of groundings
Operational Performance	Budget performance	Last year's running cost budget
		Last year's actual running costs and accruals
		Last year's AAE (Additional Authorized Expenses)
	Drydocking planning performance**	Agreed drydocking duration
		Actual drydocking duration
		Agreed drydocking budget
		Actual drydocking costs
	Cargo related incidents	Number of cargo related incidents
	Operational deficiencies	Number of operational related deficiencies
		Number of recorded external inspections
	Passenger injury ratio	Number of passengers injured
		Passenger exposure hours
	Port state control detention	Number of PSC detentions
		Number of PSC inspections
	Ship availability	Actual unavailability
		Planned unavailability
	Vetting deficiencies	Number of observations during commercial inspections
		Number of commercial inspections
Security Performance	Port State Control performance	Number of PSC inspections resulting in zero deficiencies
		Number of PSC inspections
	Security deficiencies	Number of security related deficiencies
		Number of recorded external inspections
Technical Performance	Condition of class	Number of conditions of class
	Failure of critical equipment and systems	Number of failures of critical equipment and systems
These KPIs has no association to an SPI	CO_2 efficiency [g/tonmile]	Emitted mass of CO_2[ton]
		Transport work
	Fire and Explosions	Number of fire incidents
		Number of explosion incidents
	NOx efficiency [g/Cargo Unit] mile	Emitted mass of NOx[kg]
		Transport work
	Port state control deficiency ratio	Number of PSC deficiencies
		Number of PSC inspections
	SOx efficiency [g/Cargo Unit] mile	Emitted mass of SOx[kg]
		Transport work

Derived from BIMCO, 2015a

Table A6.2 BIMCO Shipping KPI Standard Version 3.0 Quick Sheet

SPI	KPI	PI
SPI001: **Environmental** **Performance**	KPI028: Releases of substances	Number of releases of substances to the environment Number of oil spills
	KPI001: Ballast water management violations	Number of ballast water management violations
	KPI007: Contained spills	Number of contained spills of liquid
	KPI011: Environmental deficiencies	Number of environmental related deficiencies Number of recorded external inspections
	KPI005: CO_2 efficiency	Emitted mass of CO_2 Transport work
	KPI021: NOx efficiency	Emitted mass of NOx Transport work
	KPI030: SOx efficiency	Emitted mass of SOx Transport work
SPI002: **Health and Safety** **Performance**	KPI013: Fire and Explosions	Number of fire incidents Number of explosion incidents
	KPI017: Lost Time Injury Frequency	Number of fatalities due to work injuries Number of lost workday cases Number of permanent total disabilities (PTD) Number of permanent partial disabilities Total exposure hours
	KPI015: Health and Safety deficiencies	Number of health and safety related deficiencies Number of recorded external inspections
	KPI018: Lost Time Sickness Frequency	Number of cases where a crew member is sick for more than 24 hours Number of fatalities due to sickness Total exposure hours
	KPI025: Passenger Injury Ratio	Number of passengers injured Passenger exposure hours
SPI003: **HR Management** **Performance**	KPI008: Crew disciplinary frequency	Number of absconded crew Number of charges of criminal offences Number of cases where drugs or alcohol is abused Number of dismissals Number of logged warnings Total exposure hours
	KPI009: Crew planning	Number of seafarers not relieved on time Number of violation of rest hours
	KPI016: HR deficiencies	Number of HR related deficiencies Number of recorded external inspections
	KPI003: Cadets per ship	Number of cadets under training with the DOC holder Number of ships operated under the DOC holder
	KPI022: Officer retention rate	Number of officer terminations from whatever cause Number of unavoidable officer terminations Number of beneficial officer terminations Number of officers employed

(Continued)

SPI	KPI	PI
	KPI023: Officers experience rate	Number of officer experience points Number of officers onboard
	KPI031: Training days per officer	Number of officer trainee man days Number of officer days onboard all ships with the DOC holder
SPI004: Navigational Safety Performance	KPI019: Navigational deficiencies	Number of navigational related deficiencies Number of recorded external inspections
	KPI020: Navigational incidents	Number of collisions Number of allisions Number of groundings
SPI005: Operational Performance	KPI002: Budget performance	Last year's running cost budget Last year's actual running costs and accruals Last year's AAE (Additional Authorized Expenses)
	KPI010: Drydocking planning performance	Agreed drydocking duration Actual drydocking duration Agreed drydocking budget Actual drydocking costs
	KPI004: Cargo related incidents	Number of cargo related incidents
	KPI024: Operational deficiencies	Number of operational related deficiencies Number of recorded external inspections
	KPI032: Ship availability	Actual unavailability Planned unavailability
	KPI033: Vetting deficiencies	Number of observations during commercial inspections Number of commercial inspections
SPI006: Security Performance	KPI029: Security deficiencies	Number of security related deficiencies Number of recorded external inspections
SPI007: Technical Performance	KPI006: Condition of class	Number of conditions of class
	KPI012: Failure of critical equipment and systems	Number of failures of critical equipment and systems
SPI009: Port State Control Performance	KPI027: Port state control detention	Number of PSC detentions Number of PSC inspections
	KPI026: Port state control deficiency ratio	Number of PSC deficiencies Number of PSC inspections
	KPI014: Port state control performance	Number of PSC inspections resulting in zero deficiencies Number of PSC inspections

Derived from BIMCO, 2018

7

An overview to contemporary maritime logistics and supply chain management decision areas

*Tobias Buer, Hans-Dietrich Haasis,
Aseem Kinra, and Herbert Kotzab*

7.1 Introduction

In today's world, companies are operating in a global environment with constantly changing competitive conditions. The era of highly individualized production of products and services has replaced mass production as well as mass customization. The use of modern technology in combination with rather cheap transport possibilities leads to the exploitation of time advantages over the whole globe (see e.g. Song and Lee 2009, Song and Panayides 2015). Consequently, maritime transport is seen as the most important transport mode and the backbone for the facilitation of global trade (see Cheng et al., 2015).

Contemporary supply chains can be characterized in accordance to Handfield and Nichols (1999, 2) as "all activities associated with the flow and transformation of goods from raw materials stage (extraction), through the end user, as well as the associated information flows", hence, on a global level. Consequently, logistics and supply chain management (SCM) are understood as the catalytic converters that are required to successfully link sources with sinks on a global level (Song and Panayides 2015). Global transport or freight chains are typically intermodal, combining sea and land ways (Gudehus and Kotzab 2012, 734). From this point of view, the objective of logistics and SCM is to move cargo at minimal operating costs, fuel consumption, and emissions; this requires the design, implementation, and operation of optimal shipping and maritime transport chains (see Gudehus and Kotzab 2016, Panayides and Song 2013, Andersen et al., 2017).

The logistics industry has thereby been facing significant challenges in terms of offering more integrated and sophisticated logistics and transportation services for more than one decade (Heaver 2005, Lee et al., 2011). The actors of the shipping industry also turned from being an efficient port-to-port operator to customer-oriented integrated supply chain service providers (see Hingorani et al., 2005).

Since the beginning of the new century, experts recommend that shipping companies should change their current strategies from sea-based transport to vertically integrated sea- and land-based logistics systems (e.g. Panayides 2006, 2015). This also requires more involvement in terminal management and intermodal services as well as value-adding logistics services which turns traditional shipping companies into integrated supply chain service providers (e.g. Heaver 2005,

Hingorani et al., 2005, Lee and Lee 2015, Sys et al., 2015). While the generic drivers for supply chain execution refer to decision making in the areas of facilities, transport, inventory, and information (following the notions of Chopra and Meindl 2015), a maritime perspective would widen the view on the inclusion of sea leg as well as port operations into this context (see Panayides and Song 2015).

In this paper we present and discuss some contemporary maritime logistics and SCM-related decision areas which are of particular interest for the shipping industry. They include terminal operations, hinterland logistics, and knowledge labs for maritime clusters as well as digital innovation and emerging technologies.

7.2 Contemporary maritime logistics and supply chain management decision areas

7.2.1 Decision area maritime container terminals

Following Rodrigue et al., (2017), a freight terminal is a facility where freight originates, terminates, or is handled in the transport process. All spatial flows of freight use terminals. Terminals such as airports, railway stations, or marine ports provide a substantial infrastructure which requires significant capital investments and influences their surrounding area. Therefore, terminals are essential links in transportation networks.

The function of a terminal is to consolidate and disperse freight flows. A terminal is either used as a point to switch between transport modes, e.g. street to air, or as point to interchange within the same modal system, e.g. rail to rail. Terminals are the only points where freight can enter or exit a transport network. Therefore, they are an interface which connects transport networks by providing handling equipment and a buffer area. If something goes wrong in a terminal, it quickly becomes a bottleneck in many supply chains. Therefore, efficient and robust terminal operations are very important.

Container terminals offer a plethora of planning problems. The planning of day to day operations highly depends on the structure and available equipment at a container terminal. With respect to daily operations, Vis and Koster (2003) identify five main processes at container terminals: ship arrival, unloading and loading of the ship, horizontal transport of containers within the yard, container stacking, and inter-terminal transportation. The main areas of a terminal are: seaside (with berth and quay), landside (with storage yard and gate), and transport area. Figure 7.1 shows a conceptual view of these areas.

Seaside operations include the arrival of a ship as well as its loading and unloading. Operational problems include the berth allocation and quay crane assignment and scheduling (Bierwirth and Meisel, 2010; Bierwirth and Meisel, 2015):

- **berth allocation problem (BAP)**: each container vessel that arrives at a terminal is assigned a quay space and a service time. Typically, the BAP assumes that the berth layout of the terminal and a set of vessels which has to be serviced within the planning period are given (Bierwirth and Meisel, 2010). Further data usually include vessel dimensions, arrival times, or estimated handling times. Vessels may not use the same quay space at the same time. Therefore, a feasible berth plan is an assignment of each vessel to a berth position and time such that no overlapping of the vessels with respect to space and time occurs. A frequently used measure to characterize the quality of a berth plan is the completion time of the vessels, i.e. the earliest time when all loading and unloading operations are completed. Further performance measures of berth plans which are used in the literature are discussed by Bierwirth and Meisel (2010);

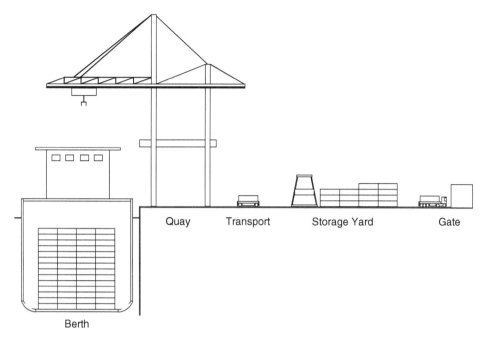

Berth

Figure 7.1 Five interdependent decision areas in container terminals (Carlo et al., 2014a).

- **quay crane scheduling**: based on a feasible berth plan, a quay crane assignment and scheduling problem is solved. The terminal operator decides for each vessel in the berth plan by how many quay cranes the vessel is serviced. Usually it is assumed that all quay cranes are able to service each vessel. However, as quay cranes are heavy and voluminous, they are not able to overtake each other. Two cranes that operate next to each other have to keep a safety distance. The workload, i.e. the loading and unloading operations, at each ship is divided into tasks. A task includes the loading or unloading of all containers stored in a) several bays, b) a single bay, c) a stack, or d) included in the same group (Bierwirth and Meisel, 2010). A group is usually defined on some container attributes such as the same destination. Among the tasks are precedence relations, e.g. unloading before loading. With respect to the cranes, additional constraints may apply. For example, a crane may be available during some time windows due to maintenance operations. The goal of quay crane scheduling problems is usually related to minimizing the ship handling time. Recent approaches take into account the strong interdependencies between a berth plan and a quay crane schedule. In order to improve the performance of terminals, solution methods which integrate the berth allocation and the quay crane scheduling problem are developed. Furthermore, new equipment such as twin cranes which allow double cycling require new models (Goodchild and Daganzo, 2007).

Landside operations in container terminals include, among others, storage decisions of containers in the yard as well as the gate-in and gate-out process:

- **container storage and handling in the yard**: Carlo et al., (2014b) provide a literature review on storage yard operations. Crucial for the yard operations is the used material handling equipment. The most prominent are straddle carriers and gantry cranes. A straddle carrier performs the horizontal transport of containers in the yard as well as vertical transport during loading and unloading within a block of containers. This makes them very flexible and there are also automated straddle carrier terminals (Steenken et al., 2004). Even more popular than straddle carriers are gantry crane-based terminals. There are two main variants of gantry cranes: rubber-tyred gantry cranes (RTGs) and rail-mounted gantry cranes (RMGs). Rail-mounted gantry cranes are less flexible because they require a track system. However, they are easier to semi-automate. A gantry crane usually spans eight to 12 rows and is able to stack up to ten containers on top of each other (Steenken et al., 2004). Recent versions of gantry cranes include dual passing RMGs which can be found in Container Terminal Altenwerder in the port of Hamburg, Germany Carlo et al., 2014b). In a dual passing RMG configuration, there are two cranes of different sizes. Since the cranes operate on different rails, the smaller one is able to pass under the larger one. This increases flexibility but has high requirements for safety and precision, therefore these configurations are only used with automated RMGs. An extension are Triple RMG systems, where one larger and two smaller yard cranes operate on two rails. Speer and Fischer (2017) compare the performance of different automated RMG systems including dual passing RMG and triple RMG systems. They provide sophisticated exact and heuristic algorithms to solve these problems which lay the groundwork to further automate terminal operations;

- **truck appointment system**: trucks play a dominant role for the gate-in or gate-out process at most container terminals. Shippers and consignees request trucking companies to pick up and delivery containers at a terminal. This process is often uncoordinated between the trucking companies and the terminal Phan and Kim, 2016). Therefore, trucks may arrive all at once at the terminal. This results in congestion and inappropriate waiting times of trucks; it also creates an uneven demand for terminal equipment which can result in an overload at the storage yard. Truck appointment systems offer a way to communicate the available capacity at the gates to trucking companies. A simple but common approach is to estimate the available gate handling capacity per time slot. If the capacity of a time slot is consumed, all further applications for this time slot are rejected (Phan and Kim, 2016). Truck appointment systems are operated by the terminal. Naturally, they focus more on the interests of the terminal operator and less on the interests of the trucking companies. In order to improve acceptance of truck appointment systems, Phan and Kim (2016) propose one such system that includes a negotiation process between the terminal and the trucking companies. With this decentral approach, the needs of the trucking companies can be better accounted for. Furthermore, a good decision for the whole system can be made without revealing too much private information. By using these negotiation-based truck appointment systems, the terminal avoids high congestions because peak arrivals are reduced. On the other hand, trucking companies have the opportunity to send their trucks to less-crowded time windows, incorporate this information in their vehicle routing, and save inefficient waiting times.

Transport operations are mainly concerned with the transport of containers from the quay to the yard or vice versa. However, inter-terminal transport between neighboring terminals and connections to the hinterland transport system are becoming more important:

- **horizontal transport of containers within the yard:** Carlo et al., (2014a) provide a review on transport operations within a terminal. In a terminal operated by RTGs or RMGs, the horizontal transport between quay, storage yard, and gate is performed by yard trucks. Horizontal transport can also be performed by means of automated guided vehicles (AGVs). AGVs usually operate on a fixed wire grid integrated in the ground. New technologies allow more precise and autonomous control of the vehicles by using GPS and laser-based systems. AGVs create new challenges within a terminal with respect to automated traffic management and deadlock prevention. Although automation offers the opportunity to smoothen the container handling processes on the ground and save labour cost, AGV systems come with considerable drawbacks: they require a lot of space, have high demands on safety, and are often controlled by a central instance. A rather small failure may lead to the shutdown of the whole AGV horizontal transport system due to safety reasons. Therefore, the decision in favor of AGVs is by no means an obvious one and needs careful consideration. In contrast to truck-based or AGV-based transportation in RMG and RGT terminals, a straddle carrier terminal requires no additional trucks to perform the horizontal transport. The decision of where to store containers in the yard affects the number of required vehicles, the routing of the vehicles, and the congestion in the yard. Therefore, Voß et al., (2016) study simultaneous container storage and transport decisions;

- **inter-terminal transportation:** seaports routinely contain a number of terminals. Often these terminals share some joint infrastructure such as access to rail, barge, or container ships (Tierney et al., 2014). When a switch in the mode of transport, e.g. from rail to ship, is necessary, transportation of containers between terminals is required. Furthermore, a container may arrive via vessel at one terminal and leave by another vessel from another terminal within the same port. Empty containers are also relocated among terminals. The organization of an efficient transfer of containers among terminals is referred to as the inter-terminal transportation problem (Tierney et al., 2014). Avoiding congestions plays an important role. Heilig and Voß (2017) provide an overview of the literature on inter-terminal transportation.

7.2.2 Decision area maritime facilities: hinterland logistics, and transport corridors

Efficient and well-developed transport corridors are important for setting up global supply chain networks that link major production sites with their procurement and sales markets. Their design and expansion are aimed at ensuring efficient accessibility of supply and demand, increasing the attractiveness and visibility of regions along transport corridors, increasing the reliability as well as cost-effectiveness and safety of transport, and ensuring sustainable, future-oriented networks of economic regions (see Li et al., 2016; Tran and Haasis 2015; Tran et al., 2017).

The successful implementation and execution of transport corridors will facilitate global trade and thus guarantee economic and social prosperity (Streit-Juotsa et al., 2018). Examples can be currently found in the one-belt-one-road initiative for setting up the new silk road by linking European–Asian railway corridors or the North–South as well as East–West transport corridors of the European Union with an aim to better link Scandinavia to the Iberian Peninsula, Paris via Budapest with Kiev with connections to the Adriatic ports, or the Port of Duisburg via Warsaw to Moscow with the connections East Sea–Black Sea (Ye and Haasis 2018).

By realizing these corridors, the hinterland will gain importance in terms of generating demand for intermodal transportation that needs to be efficiently realized under conditions of restricted infrastructure. Overall, there is a need for improved system integration of the traffic means road, water, and railway (Müller and Haasis 2018). The main deficiencies so far for inefficient intermodal transport lie in poor management of the interfaces when shifting transport modes (see Kotzab and Unseld 2010a, 2010b). The question on what the impact of future development in technology on efficiency of hinterland logistics will be can be posed. The impact would be more felt in logistics processes, information analysis, and cargo flow controls within the hinterland logistics rather than in the cargo handling hardware systems in the ports (Ho Thi Thu and Haasis 2017).

7.2.3 Decision area information: knowledge labs for maritime logistics clusters

The critical success factors for regional as well as global logistics and SCM are nowadays services, informatics, and innovation. These factors need to be combined and executed to allow an interconnected and flexible trade flow on a global level (Kulibu and Haasis 2015). As such, this ensures distributed production in dynamic environments on regional as well as global scale. Due to the upcoming of new customer requirements, new digital business models, new allocation of tasks, and value-added services, international supply chain networks turn from centrally organized networks to partly/fully autonomous decision making units (Haasis et al., 2015).

These developments are confronted with present and future challenges on climate change as well as on international security aspects. Knowledge management and knowledge labs for groups of decision makers can support the quality of the design and of the sustainable operation of these relations, and by this of the innovative design and management of usual services and of smart services (Kreeb and Haasis 2017).

Furthermore, facilities are not only considered for ensuring the physical processes and movement of goods; decision makers should also focus on facilities for improved information exchange as well as knowledge-driven transport infrastructure and regional knowledge management, urban logistics clusters, additive manufacturing, and cloud logistics as well as cyber-physical systems. Innovative maritime logistics clusters emphasize digital economy, society, and sustainability as well as intelligent freight and mobility. Within the EU, the framework program for research and development "Horizon 2020" promotes the topics of intelligent and integrated freight transportation (see Haasis et al., 2015).

7.2.4 Decision area digital innovation and emerging technologies

Digital innovations are the engines for a digital transformation of our life, focusing on the customer and their data as well as on networking and integration. Examples can be seen in line with smart ports, smart factories, smart logistics, and smart mobility. For the organization of data, new platform solutions can be implemented, as for example a digital logistics mall as one part of cloud logistics (see Haasis et al., 2015).

The management of the global supply chain relies heavily on a streamlined flow of information between the different actors of the supply chain. The information system becomes the glue of the supply chain, the most important contribution of which is to bring visibility to the entire supply chain (Hsuan et al., 2015). Lately thus there has been a lot of focus on digitization and information technology upgrading in the shipping industry. A part of this discussion also relates to technologies for better supply chain management, especially related to aspects of trust, risk, and control in the maritime value chain. Two such emerging technologies that have far-reaching capabilities for global supply chain management are the blockchain and the Remote Container Management. In this section we briefly describe the technologies and their supply chain management-enabling capabilities.

Information technology can automate processes such as documentation and internal operation routines. Blockchain is one such technology that holds vast potential for the maritime supply chain. It has been credited for its innovation and versatility. Loklindt et al. (2018) explore blockchains within the shipping context, and define these as self-governing decentralized and open information infrastructures that mediate the exchange of cryptographically verified information in permanent blocks of data. According to them, blockchain technology consists of three elements: (1) database, (2) peer-to-peer network, and (3) cryptography, see Figure 7.2.

Firstly, all blockchains use some kind of off-the-shelf database solution (Bitcoin uses BerkeleyDB, Ethereum uses LevelDB, etc.). Second, there can be numerous databases involved, and these are interconnected in a peer-to-peer network. The benefit of using a peer-to-peer network is that computing and storage costs can be distributed and shared amongst all users involved in the information exchange. Third, the entire network of the interconnected databases is aligned. This is done by running all data through a hash-algorithm, which is a cryptographic function that represents the content of a file in a unique ID. This fingerprint of the data is then inserted into the contents of the next file added to the database. This way all files (called blocks) in the database are chained together with hash-representations of the data in the previous file. The main innovation that this technology creates is the inability to go back and alter historic data entries, since it would cause a change to every hash-representation since then. One of the main selling features of blockchain is thus claimed to be immutability, which leads to a tamper-proof system with revolutionary applications within information systems (Mougayar, 2016).

Blockchain is essentially an information technology that enables supply chain management. Trust, coordination, and control are some of the most important components that bind together a supply chain. The lack of coordination and information sharing in the international transportation chain can often result in little transparency and a general lack of trust between the involved parties. Blockchain technology aims to establish trust at the intersection between parties that need to agree on ownership and rights, such as in a transaction (Brandon, 2016;

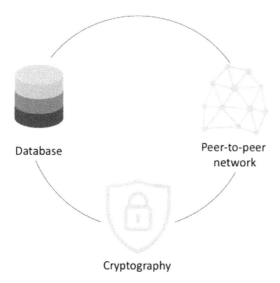

Database

Peer-to-peer
network

Cryptography

Figure 7.2 The three elements of blockchain technology (Loklindt et al., 2018).

Mougayar, 2016). Blockchain technology thus aims to reduce frictions between the transacting parties and locations in the global supply chain. Similarly, with its promising design features such as immutability, security, and territoriality, the technology can ensurebetter control and. ultimately, the reduction of inefficiencies attributed to paper-based information systems in the global supply chain (Loklindt et al., 2018).

Another emerging supply chain technology that has recently gained momentum is an IOT (Internet-of-things)-based solution, namely Remote Container Management (RCM). In short, RCM is an innovative technology within the transport of refrigerated goods, which allows the shipper to monitor the conditions inside a container from the moment the goods are locked inside, right up to delivery at their final destination (https://www.maerskline.com/en/ship ping/what-is-rcm). This technology has been pioneered by global shipping giant Maersk Line. The complex technology development project that has taken about five years to complete is now in full operation. It has GPS tracking capabilities and by June 2017 it had eliminated more than 100,000 manual pre-trip inspections (Rasmussen, 2017).

Remote Container Management (RCM) is a device installed on a refrigerated container (reefer), which collects data from the reefer controller and sends it to a central server. The device allows for continuous and remote monitoring of the status of reefer containers, thereby providing greater transparency throughout the supply chain. By providing real-time information (24/7) regarding reefer location, equipment status, reefer temperature, pressure, or plug-in status, the shipping company can rapidly react to alarm problems, manage hardware, and track reefer performance. This improves operational efficiency and ultimately data-driven supply chain efficiency for the supply chain partners through the sharing of: a) shipment overview of all containers with journey assessment parameters; b) temperature graphs; c) visuals on container positions; d) journey assessments; and e) consolidated list of notifications. As Vincent Clark, the present chief commercial fficer at Maersk Line mentions, "RCM has the capabilities that our customers have wanted from us for a very long time. It is going to insert an unprecedented level of visibility and reliability into their supply chains that will make their business better" (Clark, 2017). Figure 7.3 provides a visualization about how the technology works and its current functionalities.

Just like blockchain, RCM is also a supply chain management-enabling technology. According to Kinra and Kotzab (2008), an essential component of supply chain management

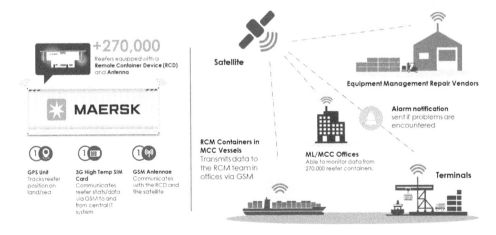

Figure 7.3   How RCM Works (https://www.mcc.com.sg/news/2017/09/04/mcc-welcomes-re mote-container-management).

is to manage logistics environmental complexity. Based upon Child (1972), logistics environmental complexity faced by a firm involved in international shipping and maritime logistics may be understood as the complexity created by the heterogeneity and range of the organization's activities in relation to the international movement and handling of cargo. RCM, like many other (geographic) information systems, may moderate the effects of logistics environmental complexity on the performance of firms involved in international logistics and shipping (Holmvik and Gilbro, 2016).

For container shipping companies, logistics environmental complexity may largely be driven by aspects such as goal diversity, process diversity, supplier diversity, customer diversity, labour diversity, movement diversity, and geographical diversity. For example, goal diversity for these types of companies arises because of the different market and product segments that the company services. Similarly, supplier diversity arises because of the diversity of suppliers such as container manufacturers, port and terminal operators, container repair companies, and logistics service providers that the company is involved with in its supply chain relationships. Investment in new, innovative information systems (such as RCM) then constitutes a specific group of information processing alternatives (Flynn & Flynn, 1999) that the shipping firm has in order to moderate the effects of the complexity it faces on its performance (Holmvik and Gilbro, 2016).

7.3 Conclusion and outlook

The goal of this section was to present and to discuss contemporary maritime logistics and SCM-related decision areas. The shipping industry has faced and will always face dynamic changes which affect the decisions, principles, and methods of maritime logistics (see Lee and Cullinane, 2016).

Our discussion showed that contemporary decision areas represent infrastructural issues around the core area of maritime logistics, especially in regards to facilities and their sea – as well as landside operations and information technology. In regard to the value creation processes by maritime logistics as suggested by Lee et al. (2015), primary as well as secondary activities are influenced by those.

The core of maritime logistics remains stable but innovative technical and managerial solutions allow larger capacities, faster operations, less use of energy, and improved performances as well as extended maritime supply chain services (see Gudehus and Kotzab, 2012). Lee and Lee (2016) characterized this development as a transition towards economies of flow and connection assisted by fusion technology. Consequently, decision makers in the shipping industry need to identify the macro-drivers for achieving efficient, effective, as well as competitive maritime logistics and supply chain networks and systems (in accordance with Gudehus and Kotzab, 2012).

References

Andersen, K., Andersson, H., Christiansen, M., Groenhaug, R. Sjamsutdinov, A. (2017). Designing a maritime supply chain for distribution of wood pellets: a case study from southern Norway. In: *Flexible Services and Manufacturing Journal*, Vol. 29, No. 3–4, 572–600.

Bierwirth, C., Meisel, F. (2010). A survey of berth allocation and quay crane scheduling problems in container terminals. In: *European Journal of Operational Research*, Vol. 202, No. 3, 615–627. DOI: 10.1016/j.ejor.2009.05.031.

Bierwirth, C., Meisel, F. (2015). A follow-up survey of berth allocation and quay crane scheduing problems in container terminals. In: *European Journal of Operational Research*, Vol. 244, Nr. 3, 675–689. DOI: 10.1016/j.ejor.2014.12.030.

Brandon, D. (2016). The blockchain: The future of business information systems? In: *International Journal of the Academic Business World*, Vol. 10, No. 2, 33–40.

Carlo, H.J., Vis, I.F., Roodbergen, K.J. (2014a). Storage yard operations in container terminals: Literature overview, trends, and research directions. In: *European Journal of Operational Research*, Vol. 235, No. 2, 412–430. DOI: 10.1016/j.ejor.2013.10.054.

Carlo, H.J., Vis, I.F., Roodbergen, K.J. (2014b). Transport operations in container terminals: Literature overview, trends, research directions and classification scheme. In: *European Journal of Operational Research* Vol. 236, No. 1, 1–13. DOI: https://doi.org/10.1016/j.ejor.2013.11.023.

Cheng, T.C.E., Fahrani, R., Lai, K.-H., Sarkis, J. (2015). Sustainability in maritime supply chains: Challenges and opportunities for theory and practice. In: *Transportation Research Part E*, Vol. 78, June, 1–2.

Child, J. (1972). Organizational structure, environment and performance: The role of strategic choice. In: *Sociology*, Vol. 6, No. 1, 1–22.

Chopra, S., Meindl, P. (2015). *Supply Chain Management: Strategy, Planning and Operation.* 6th edition, Pearson, Upper Saddle River NJ.

Clark, V. (2017). Press release 26/06/2017, accessed 29/05/2018 22:58 (https://www.maerskline.com/en/news/2017/06/26/maersk-line-launches-remote-container-management-for-customers).

Flynn, B.B., Flynn, E.J. (1999). Information-processing alternatives for coping with manufacturing environment complexity. In: *Decision Sciences*, Vol. 30, No. 4, 1021–1048.

Goodchild, A.V. and Daganzo, C. (2007). Crane double cycling in container ports: Planning methods and evaluation. In: *Transportation Research Part B: Methodological* Vol. 41, No. 8, 875–891.

Gudehus, T., Kotzab, H. (2012). *Comprehensive Logistics*, 2nd edition, Springer, Berlin.

Gudehus, T., Kotzab, H. (2016). Economic ship travel speed and consequences for operating strategies of container shipping companies. In: Kotzab, H., Pannek, J., Thoben, K.-D. (eds.): *Dynamics in Logistics. Proceedings of the 4th International Conference* LDIC, 2014 Bremen, Germany, 407–415.

Haasis, H.-D., Landwehr, T., Kille, G., Obsadny, M. (2015). Cloud-based eBusiness standardization in the maritime supply chain. In: Dethloff, J.; Haasis, H.-D.; Kopfer, H.; Kotzab, H.; Schönberger, J. (eds.): *Logistics Management. Products, Actors, Technologies*, Springer, Cham, Heidelberg, New York, Dordrecht, London, pp. 265–276.

Handfield, R., Nichols E. (1999). *Introduction to Supply Chain Management.* Prentice-Hall, Upper Saddle River, NJ.

Heaver, T. (2005). Supply chain and logistics management: Implications for liner shipping. In: Grammenos, C. (ed.): *The Handbook of Maritime Economics and Business*, MPG Books Ltd, Bodmin, Cornwall, pp. 375–396.

Heilig, L., Voß, S. (2017). Inter-terminal transportation: an annotated bibliography and research agenda. In: *Flexible Services and Manufacturing Journal*, Vol. 29, No. 1, 35–63. DOI: 10.1007/s10696-016-9237-7.

Hingorani, N., Moore, D., Tornquist, K. (2005). *Setting a new course in the container shipping industry*, IBM Global Services, Somers New York.

Ho Thi Thu, H., Haasis, H.-D. (2017). Improving value chain through efficient port logistics. In: *Management Studies*, Vol. 5, No. 4, 321–335.

Holmvik, C., Gilbro, M. (2016). *Logistical Environmental Complexity and The Role of Information*, Master thesis, CBS.

Hsuan, J., Skjøtt-Larsen, T., Kinra, A., Kotzab, H. (2015). *Managing the Global Supply Chain*, 4th ed., CBS Press, Copenhagen.

Kilubi, I., Haasis, H.-D. (2015). Supply chain risk management enablers – A framework development through systematic review of literature from 2000 to 2015. In: *International Journal of Business Science and Applied Management*, Vol. 10, No. 1, 35–54.

Kinra, A., Kotzab, H. (2008). Understanding and measuring macro institutional complexity of logistics systems environment. In: *Journal of Business Logistics*, Vol. 29, No. 1, 327–346.

Kreeb, M., Haasis, H.-D. (2017). Sustainable cooperate information portals: Digital knowledge communities for SME, in: Osburg, T., Lohrmann, C. (eds.): *Sustainability in a Digital World. New Opportunities Through New Technologies*, Cham, Springer, 145–158.

Lee, P., Cullinane, K. (2016). Introduction. In: Lee, P., Cullinance, K. (eds.): *Dynamic shipping and port development in the globalized economy*, Vol. 1: *Applying theory to practice in maritime logistics*, Palgrave Macmillan, Hampshire, New York, pp. 1–11.

Lee, P., Lee, T.-C. (2016). New concepts in the economies of flow, connection and fusion technology in maritime logistics. In: Lee, P., Cullinance, K. (eds.): *Dynamic shipping and port development in the globalized economy*, Vol. 1: *Applying theory to practice in maritime logistics*, Palgrave Macmillan, Hampshire, New York, pp. 198–218.

Lee, E.-S., Nam, H.-S., Song, D.-W. (2015). Defining maritime logistics and its value. In: Song, D.-W., Panayides, P. (eds.): *Maritime Logistics. A Guide to Contemporary Shipping and Port Management*, 2nd edition, Kogan Page, London, pp. 53–66.

Lee, L.-H., Chew, E., Zhen, L., Gan, C., Shao, J. (2011). Recent development of maritime logistics. In: Chew, E., Loo, H., Tang, L. (eds.): *Advances in maritime logistics and supply chain systems*, World Scientific, New Jersey, London, Singapore, Beijing, Shanghai, Hong Kong, Taipei, Chennai, pp. 49–68.

Li, F., Schwarz, L., Haasis, H.-D. (2016). A framework and risk analysis for supply chain emission trading. In: *Logistics Research*, Vol. 9, No. 10, 2–10.

Loklindt, C., Moeller, M-P, Kinra, A. (2018). How blockchain could be implemented for exchanging documentation in the shipping industry. In: Michael Freitag; Herbert Kotzab; Jürgen Pannek (eds.): *Dynamics in Logistics*. Proceedings of the 6th International Conference LDIC 2018, Bremen, Germany. Springer, Cham, pp. 194–198.

Mougayar, W. (2016). *The Business Blockchain: Promise, Practice, and Application of the Next Internet Technology*, Wiley, New Jersey.

Müller, R., Haasis, H.-D. (2018). Security in maritime logistics – learning by gaming. In: Freitag, M., Kotzab, H., Pannek, J. (eds.): *Dynamics in Logistics*, Springer, Proceedings of the 6th International Conference LDIC 2018, Bremen, Germany. Springer, Cham, pp. 189–193.

Panayides, P. (2006). Maritime logistics and global supply chains: Towards a research agenda. In: *Maritime Economics & Logistics*, Vol. 8, No. 1, 3–18.

Panayides, P., Song, D.-W. (2013). Maritime logistics as an emerging discipline. In: *Maritime Policy & Management*, Vol. 40, No. 3, 295–308.

Panayides, P., Song, D.-W. (2015). Looking ahead. In: Song, D.-W., Panayides, P. (eds): *Maritime Logistics. A Guide to Contemporary Shipping and Port Management*, 2nd edition, Kogan Page, London, pp. 427–434.

Phan, M.-H., Kim, K.H. (2016). Collaborative truck scheduling and appointments for trucking companies and container terminals. In: *Transportation Research Part B: Methodological* 86, 37–50.

Rasmussen, C.H. (2017). Podcast, 16/06/2017, accessed 29/05/2018 22:58 https://shippingpodcast.com/catja-hjorth-rasmussen-head-equipment-excellence-maersk-line/.

Rodrigue, J.-P., Comtois, C., Slack, B. (2017). *The Geography of Transport Systems*. Routledge, New York.

Song, D.-W., Lee, P. (2009). Maritime logistics in the global supply chain. In: *International Journal of Logistics: Research and Application*, Vol. 12, No. 2, 83–84.

Song, D.-W., Panayides, P. (2015). Introduction to maritime logistics. In: Song, D.-W., Panayides, P. (eds): *Maritime Logistics. A Guide to Contemporary Shipping and Port Management*, 2nd edition, Kogan Page, London, pp. 3–10.

Speer, U., K. Fischer (2017). Scheduling of different automated yard crane systems at container terminals. In: *Transportation Science*, Vol. 51, No. 1, 305–324. DOI: 10.1287/trsc.2016.0687.

Steenken, D., Voß, S., Stahlbock, R. (2004). Container terminal operation and operations research – a classification and literature review. In: *OR Spectrum*, Vol. 26, No. 1, 3–49. DOI: 10.1007/s00291-003-0157-z.

Streit-Juotsa, L., Haasis, H.-D., Schumann-Bölsche, D. (2018). Dependency of pharmaceutical logistics in Sub-Sahara Africa from seaport performance. In: Freitag, M.; Kotzab, H.; Pannek, J. (eds.): *Dynamics in Logistics*, Springer, Cham, 2018, pp. 178–183.

Sys, C., Vanelslander, T., Carlan, V. (2015). *Innovative concepts in the maritime supply chain*, Antwerp. Retrieved from www.google.com/url?sa=t&rct=j&q=&esrc=ssource=web&cd=2&ved=2ahUKEwjmo8bE7sngAhUJz6YKHTOlBHcQFjABegQICRAB&url=https%3A%2F%2Frepository.uantwerpen.be%2Fdocman%2Firua%2Fb0dde7%2F132165.pdf&usg=AOvVaw0EUBaK05tOOZZN2eNtrChr.

Tierney, K., Voß, S., Stahlbock, R. (2014). A mathematical model of inter-terminal transportation. In: *European Journal of Operational Research*, Vol. 235, No. 2, 448–460.

Tran, N. K.; Haasis, H.-D. (2015). An empirical study of fleet expansion and growth of ship size in container liner shipping. In: *International Journal of Production Economics*, Vol. 159, 241–253.

Tran, N. K.; Haasis, H.-D. (2015). Literature survey of network optimization in container liner shipping. In: *Flexible Services and Manufacturing Journal*, Vol. 27, 139–179.

Tran, N. K.; Haasis, H.-D.; Buer, T. (2017). Container shipping route design incorporating the costs of shipping, inland/feeder transport, inventory and CO_2 emission. In: *Maritime Economics & Logistics*, Vol. 19, No. 4, 667–694.

Vis, I. F. A., de Koster, R. (2003). Transshipment of containers at a container terminal: An overview. In: *European Journal of Operational Research*, Vol. 147, No. 1, 1–16. DOI: 10.1016/s0377-2217(02)00293-x.

Voß, A., Guckenbiehl, G., Schütt, H., Buer, T. (2016). An online storage strategy with dynamic bay reservations for container terminals. In: 2016 IEEE Symposium Series on Computational Intelligence (SSCI), 1–8. DOI: 10.1109/SSCI.2016.7850059.

Ye, J., Haasis, H.-D. 2018. Impacts of the BRI on international logistics network. In: Freitag, M., Kotzab, H., Pannek, J. (eds.): *Dynamics in Logistics*, Springer, Cham, pp. 250–254.

8

Using the bunker adjustment factor as a strategic decision instrument

Christa Sys, Hilde Meersman, Yasmine Rashed,
Eddy Van de Voorde, and Thierry Vanelslander

8.1 Introduction

The bunkering adjustment factor (BAF) is an additional charge levied and payable by the shippers in order to compensate for fluctuations in the bunker price of the ship's fuel. The BAF has been used in the liner shipping industry in case of full container loads since the 1950s. After the oil shock in the 1970s, this surcharge gained importance (Cariou and Wolff, 2006; Meersman et al., 2015a). In other shipping segments and less than container load (LCL), the BAF is either a lump sum or a percentage based on weight or measurement (W/M). This surcharge is calculated separately for each trade lane based on a typical vessel operating on that lane. The strategic decision is different per trade lane. A floating BAF allows transferring the risk of bunker price volatility to the shipper or sharing savings when crude oil and bunker prices respectively go up or down. Meersman et al. (2015a) provide a detailed theoretical framework of this relationship.

In the present chapter, the central research question is whether the BAF can be used as a strategic decision instrument. To answer this question, first, a co-integration test is used to find out whether there is a stable long-run relationship between the bunker price (BP) and the BAF. This relation can then be estimated by means of an error-correction model. Subsequently, these results allow studying how a change in the BP will affect the BAF. The analysis is applied to a panel of top-14 liner carriers to see whether there are significant differences, which could be indicative for differences in BAF strategies in the container liner shipping industry (CLSI).

The research contributes to the academic literature which previously focused on reviewing the BAF (Slack and Gouvernal, 2011), calculating the bunker cost (Boutsikas, 2004; Notteboom and Vernimmen, 2009; Stopford, 2009; van Hassel et al., 2014), examining the relationship with the freight rate (Cariou and Wolff, 2006; De Oliveira, 2014; Meersman et al., 2015a; Notteboom and Cariou, 2013; Slack and Gouvernal, 2011; Wang et al., 2011), transferring risk to the shipper (Menachof and Dicer, 2001) using alternative fuels (and facilities) (Aronietis et al., 2016), and emission standards regulation (Sys et al., 2016).

The research is relevant for all actors involved, given the new EU pricing rules on price transparency (i.e. base rate and surcharges) (European Commission, 2016). From a scientific viewpoint, the present research aims to understand the full cost recovery of the bunkering cost at carrier level. This insight also contributes to management decision making. Transparency regarding long-run elasticities of the BAF with respect to a change in the BP at carrier level and insight of why these elasticities diverge contribute to professional practice.

This research is especially relevant to liner operators and shippers, particularly in the context of contract renewals. It not only puts forward an overall picture of the relationship between BP and BAF, but also gives an insight into the long-run elasticity of the BAF with respect to a change in the BP at carrier level. Given bunker price uncertainty and volatility, in particular, setting the BAF raises a challenge for the managers of liner operators.

The further structure of the paper is as follows: Section 8.2 describes the rationale of the present research. The used data and research methods are presented in Section 8.3. Section 8.4 presents the empirical results. Conclusions are drawn in Section 8.5.

8.2 Setting the scene

As of 2009, liner operators started publishing price levels through relevant announcements, known as General Rate Increases (GRI), as well as surcharges on a given trade lane publicized on their companies' websites (Chen, 2017; Munin and Schramm, 2017). Since 2015, most liner operators got rid of BAF calculators on their websites (as customers benefitted most from low oil price) and moved to all-in freight rates, where all surcharges are included in the overall price (Meersman et al., 2015a). The European Commission was concerned whether these practices on routes to and from Europe harmed competition and customers. On the other hand, according to Meersman et al. (2015b), given the low freight rates, the container liner shipping industry (CLSI) has no need for regulation in the short run. It is sufficient to monitor the market and the significant decision variables, viz. freight rates and surcharges. In order to respond to the commission's concerns, fourteen liner carriers started to commit to transparent pricing including base rate and surcharges (i.e. bunker charges, terminal handling charges, peak season charges, security fee, container weight fee, emission control fee) (European Commission, 2016).[1] According to Evans (2005), currency and bunkering adjustment factors (CAF) and terminal handling surcharges (THC) mount to about 30% of the total freight rate. Kontainer (2016) states that the additional charges (CAF, BAF, THC, documentation charges, and customs clearance) account for 43% of the freight rate.

At strategic level, setting the BAF raises a challenge for the managers of liner operators. They need to take into account the bunker purchasing policy (the annual bunker volume, the bunker port selection), the bunker cost of vessel lay-up, the empty repositioning of containers[2] due to the imbalance in shipping flows, and/or an overflow of equipment at (inland) depots, as well as to manage bunker price uncertainty and volatility. Based on cost accounting alone, the total bunker cost of an entire round trip can easily be calculated. Following Blauwens et al. (2016), the challenge then arises how to allocate the extra costs (due to the imbalance, empty repositioning of containers, and idling of ships) to both legs of which one is dominant (i.e. transporting more loaded, hence paying, then empty containers). In practice, two models are applied by the carriers. In the first model, the BAF surcharge of a loaded container comprises a contribution needed to compensate for the annual bunker cost. A virtual example illustrates: based on cost accounting, the BAF surcharge is for instance $150 for both the front and back haul. Taking into account the imbalance between loaded and empty containers, however, the loaded container pays $250 ($150 BAF + $100 contribution). This research cannot specify further how this contribution is determined. In the second model, all trips must yield earnings that are sufficient to cover the annual bunker cost. This results in a BAF surcharge above the bunker cost for the trade lane. According to Blauwens et al. (2016), the latter depends on the commercial possibilities or on the market's willingness to pay. Setting the BAF surcharge over the portfolio trade lanes proves a difficult challenge.

At operational level, the biggest challenge is enforcing this surcharge, because freight rate nego-tiations often result in a lower BAF and key account clients are rewarded with a BAF-free "all-in" contract (Drewry, 2015; Meersman et al., 2015a). Hence, in terms of management decision mak-ing, knowledge of the long-run relationship between BP and BAF is useful to cover and control the costs (e.g. to trigger the BAF formula) without infringing the freight rate. With regard to bun-ker price volatility, the International Energy Agency (2016) and the World Bank (2016) estimate that the crude oil price (COP) is expected to increase, mainly due to further supply disruptions. Crude oil prices (average spot) are projected to increase to $65.6 (*$57.1*) per barrel in 2020 and $82.6 (*$66.3*) per barrel in 2025 (nominal US dollars – in italics: constant US dollars) (World Bank, 2016)[3]. In parallel to Meersman et al. (2015), the lead–lag relationship between crude oil price (BRENT) and bunker price (IFO 380 Rotterdam) over the period January 2000–December 2016 shows that a change in the COP will affect instantaneously (with no lead or lag) the BP (Meersman et al., 2015a). Hence, the BP is also assumed to increase. To compensate for fluctua-tions in the BP, liner operators fix a BAF, based on the prevailing bunker oil price. Meersman et al. (2015a) found that the BP leads the BAF by two months. In the case of a changed BP, this cor-responds to the practice of informing the shipper in month+1 and invoicing in month+2.

Figure 8.1 gives a first indication for the fact that the BAF can be used as a strategic deci-sion tool. The figure shows, for October 2009 –December 2016, the evolution of the Shanghai Containerized Freight Index (SCFI), the spot rates (not-contractual rates) from China (e.g. Shanghai) to the rest of the world (October 2009 = 1,000), and the average BAF level (MBAF) charged by the top-14 carriers on the Far East to Northern Europe ($/TEU) trade lane. The SCFI is inclusive of the MBAF. The shaded area reflects the MBAF.

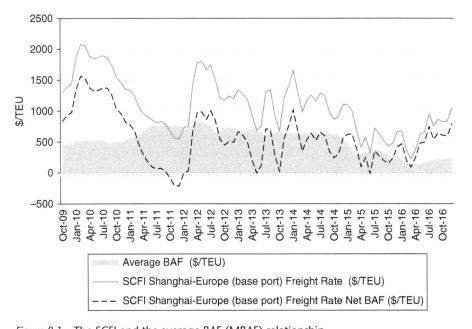

Figure 8.1 The SCFI and the average BAF (MBAF) relationship.

Source: own compilation based on Clarkson Research (2016) and Alphaliner Monthly Monitor (various editions). [i] The impact of the new EU price rules and the (further) consolidation will become clear in spring 2017 when new contracts will be negotiated.

A first observation is the high volatility of the SCFI over the period concerned. Given the low operating margins, liner operators firstly focused on minimizing costs (among others, reduction of fuel cost, e.g. slow steaming) (Ferrari et al., 2015; Notteboom and Cariou, 2013), and refuelling decisions (e.g. selection of bunkering ports) (Aydin et al., 2017; Ghosh et al., 2015). With respect to revenue optimizing, during the past five years, the focus shifted to the additional charges, viz. BAF and demurrage and detention. Secondly, during the mid-2013–December 2016 period, the MBAF curve shows a decline after a period between mid-2011 and mid-2013 of fluctuating between $600/TEU and $800/TEU, while the SCFI was very volatile. According to Meersman et al. (2015a), the volatility of the freight rate is determined by other factors (supply/demand) or surcharges than the cost of the bunker price. Furthermore, Figure 8.1 shows that the adjusted SCFI became negative from October 2011 to January 2012. This suggests that the BAF surcharge not only serves as a hedging tool against bunker price volatility (Sun and Ding, 2017), but that it sometimes also creates a source of profit (Meersman et al., 2015a). In both 2013 and 2015, the adjusted SCFI came close to zero, suggesting a learning process. The question is whether monitoring freight rates and surcharges might be used by individual liner companies as a strategic decision tool.

Regarding the MBAF curve, there is a clear difference before/after the abolishment of conferences, where common surcharges were determined[4]. This is clearly noticeable when the monthly percentage changes of the MBAF are compared to the monthly percentage changes of the COP and BP (Figure 8.2). Before 2009, the monthly percentage changes of the average MBAF were much stronger than those of the COP and BP. As of 2009, the changes in the three-time series are following a more similar path. Several academic and other studies (Cariou and Wolff, 2006; De Oliveira, 2014; Notteboom and Cariou, 2013; Slack and Gouvernal, 2011; Wang et al., 2011), all dating from before the 2008 downturn, concur that BAF does not reflect the actual bunker costs incurred by liner operators.

The evolution of the BAF before and after the abolishment of the conferences is even more interesting if the analysis of the BAF is conducted by liner carrier (Figure 8.3). The rationale for

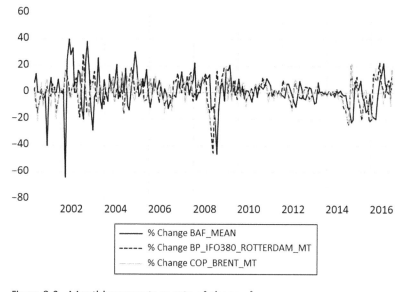

Figure 8.2 Monthly percentage rate of change.[5]
Source: own compilation based on EIA (2016) and Alphaliner Monthly Monitor (various editions).

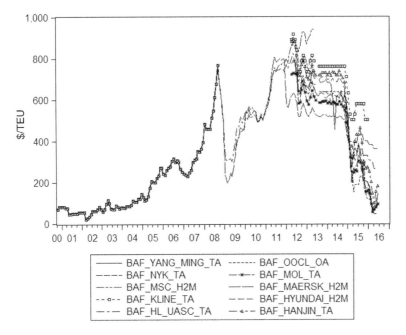

Figure 8.3 Evolution of fuel charges on the Far East to Northern Europe trade route ($/TEU).
Source: own compilation based on Alphaliner Monthly Newsletter (various editions).

the selected liner carriers and trade lane is data availability. For a number of liner carriers, there is no information available during some periods. The individual statistics for the different carriers, grouped by alliances, are shown in Annex 8.1 (Alphaliner, various editions).

Although the BAFs are highly correlated (>0.80), within the sample, a different pattern can be observed. Another observation is that there is a clear consensus in rising bunker fuel prices, but not when they stagnate or fall. A possible explanation can be found in the different hedging strategy and/or cost policy (i.e. cost division within an alliance). For the studied period, there is a difference between independent carriers (Maersk Line and CMA CGM) and carriers involved in alliances. Maersk Line is clearly the leader (e.g. changing strategy in January 2012 and January 2015), while the other carriers follow. This will be explained in-depth in the following subsections.

8.3 Description of the data and research method used

Section 8.3 describes the data used and presents the research methods.

8.3.1 Data used

For the purpose of analysis and testing, monthly data is collected about the BRENT COP, the price of IFO380 in Rotterdam (BP) (Clarkson Research, 2016), and the MBAF for the 2000–2016 period. The data for the COP is available through EIA open data (US Energy Information Administration, 2016); while the data for the other time series was collected from Alphaliner Monthly (various editions). The test shows that the first differences of the logarithms of the COP, the BP, and the MBAF are stationary.

8.3.2 Research methods used

Central to the analysis is the relationship between the BAF and the BP, or in logarithms (ln)

$$\ln\left(BAF_t\right)=\beta_0+\beta_1\ln\left(BP_t\right)+\varepsilon_t \tag{8.1}$$

where β_1 is the elasticity of the BAF with respect to a change in the BP. It indicates by what percentage the BAF will change if the BP changes by 1%. To get reliable traditional OLS estimates for β_0 and β_1, it is necessary that the error term ε_t is distributed around a zero mean with a constant variance. This will only be the case if both lnBAF and lnBP are stationary variables. If not, the simple relationship in Eq. 8.1 is not a correct representation of the process, which relates the BAF to the BP. Therefore, it is crucial to first test whether the variables are stationary.

Using the Augmented Dickey-Fuller unit root test (ADF) (Engle and Granger, 1991), none of the variables in natural logarithms is stationary, but the first differences are[6]. This means that the relation between the BAF and the BP can be represented by

$$\Delta\ln\left(BAF_t\right)=\alpha_0+\alpha_1\Delta\ln\left(BP_t\right)+\epsilon_t \tag{8.2}$$

The problem with this specification is that there is no long-run equilibrium relation holding the BAF and the BP together. However, if it can be shown that such a long-run equilibrium relation exists, the relation between the BAF and the BP must be represented by an error-correction model (ECM) (Engle and Granger, 1987)

$$\Delta\ln\left(BAF_t\right)=\alpha_0+\alpha_1\Delta\ln\left(BP_t\right)+\delta\left(\ln\left(BAF_{t-1}\right)-\beta_0-\beta_1\ln\left(BP_{t-1}\right)\right)+\epsilon_t \tag{8.3}$$

where $\ln\left(BAF_{t-1}\right)-\beta_0-\beta_1\ln\left(BP_{t-1}\right)$ represents the long-run equilibrium relationship, also known as the co-integrating relation; β_1 is the long-run elasticity of the BAF to a change in BP; the coefficients α_0, α_1, and δ determine the short-run fluctuations of the BAF and the BP around the long-run equilibrium, where more specifically δ indicates how strongly the BAF reacts to correct for a deviation from the long-run equilibrium in the previous period; ϵ_t is white noise. To test whether there exists a long-run relationship between the BAF and the BP, one has to test whether the variables are co-integrated or whether $\left(\ln\left(BAF_t\right)-\beta_0-\beta_1\ln\left(BP_t\right)\right)$ is stationary[7].

8.4 Empirical analysis

The above-mentioned framework is used first to test whether for the trade lane from the Far East to Europe, the relationship between the BAF and the BP has changed after the conferences have been banned, and second to see whether this relationship differs over the different liner companies.

8.4.1 Relationship between MBAF and BP

In the empirical analysis, the focus is first on the relationship between the MBAF and the BP in order to test whether this relationship has changed after the conferences were banned in October 2008. Therefore, a dummy variable DC_t was created which has the value 0 until October 2008 (Eq. 8.5) and the value 1 from November 2008 on (Eq. 8.6). It was also taken into account that the BAF adjusts to the BP with a lag of two months (Meersman et al., 2015a).

Testing for co-integration shows that ln(MBAF) and ln(BP) are co-integrated. The error-correction model, including the dummy variable DC, is

$$\Delta \ln\left(MBAF_t\right) = \alpha_1\left(1 + \gamma_1 DC_{t-2}\right)\Delta \ln\left(BP_{t-2}\right)$$
$$+ \delta\left(\ln\left(MBAF_{t-1}\right) - \beta_0\left(1 + \lambda_0 DC_{t-3}\right)\right) \qquad (8.4)$$
$$- \beta_1\left(1 + \lambda_1 DC_{t-3}\right)\ln\left(BP_{t-3}\right)\right) + \epsilon_t$$

which becomes for observations until October 2008 (DC = 0)

$$\Delta \ln\left(MBAF_t\right) = \alpha_1\Delta \ln\left(BP_{t-2}\right) + \delta\left(\ln\left(MBAF_{t-1}\right) - \beta_0 - \beta_1 \ln\left(BP_{t-3}\right)\right) + \epsilon_t \qquad (8.5)$$

and for observations from November 2008 (DC = 1)

$$\Delta \ln\left(MBAF_t\right) = (\alpha_1 + \gamma_1)\Delta \ln\left(BP_{t-2}\right) + \delta\left(\ln\left(MBAF_{t-1}\right) - \left(\beta_0 + \lambda_0\right)\right.$$
$$\left. - \left(\beta_1 + \lambda_1\right)\ln\left(BP_{t-3}\right)\right) + \epsilon_t \qquad (8.6)$$

The ECM is estimated using the two-step Engle-Granger method where the co-integrating relation is estimated with dynamic ordinary least squares (DOLS). The results of the estimation are reported in Table 8.1.

As λ_0, λ_1, and γ_1 are all significantly different from zero, there is a significant change in the long-run relation between the MBAF and the BP, as well as in the dynamic adjustment after the abolishment of the conferences. Until October 2008, the long-run equilibrium relation indicates that a 1% change of the BP would lead to a 1.73% change of the MBAF at (t-3), i.e. the change in the BP affects the MBAF after three months; from November 2008 on, this would only be 1.107%. This suggests that since the end of the conferences, the MBAF follows much more closely the evolution of the bunker prices.

As Figure 8.3 shows, the evolution of the BAFs per liner is not exactly the same. Therefore, for each liner, the relation between the BAF and the BP is modelled individually for the

Table 8.1 Estimates of the Relation between the MBAF and the BP

$\Delta \ln(MBAF_t) = \alpha_1(1 + \gamma_1 DC_{t-2})\Delta \ln(BP_{t-2})$

$+ \delta\left(\ln(MBAF_{t-1}) - \beta_0(1 + \lambda_0 DC_{t-3}) - \beta_1(1 + \lambda_1 DC_{t-3})\ln(BP_{t-3})\right) + \epsilon_t$

Coefficient	Estimate	Std. Error	t-Statistic		
α_1	1.025	0.076	13.54	Adjusted R-squared	0.51
γ_1	−0.061	0.023	−2.69	S.E. of regression	0.10
δ	−0.088	0.022	−3.95	Sum squared resid	1.85
λ_0	3.716*	0.476*	7.8*	Log likelihood	186.00
λ_1	−0.623*	0.083*	−7.5*	Durbin-Watson stat	2.06
β_0	−4.259*	0.301*	−14.17*	Mean dependent var	0.01
β_1	1.73*	0.057*	30.36*	S.D. dependent var	0.14
Sample (adjusted): 2000M04 2016M12				Included observations: 201 after adjustments	

* coefficients, standard errors and t-statistics based on DOLS estimation of the co-integrating relation

post-conferences period. For each of the liners, lnBAF and lnBP are co-integrated, with the exception of K-LINE, because they have brought the BAF to zero as from January 2016. When for K-LINE, the year 2016 is excluded from the analysis, the BAF and the BP are also co-integrated. The long-run equilibrium relation together with the dynamic adjustment was estimated using a vector error-correction model (Annex 8.2).

The estimated co-integrating relations give a long-run elasticity per individual carrier varying from 0.463 (K-Line) to 1.688 (OOCL). Figure 8.4 gives an overview of the long-run elasticities according to their ranking; while Figure 8.5 groups the results per alliance.

In the case of Maersk Line, the elasticity of the BAF regarding the BP is positive and significant, meaning that 1% change in the BP results in an increase of 0.564% in the BAF. In comparison with the other liner operators in the panel, a lower elasticity might be part of their broader bunkering

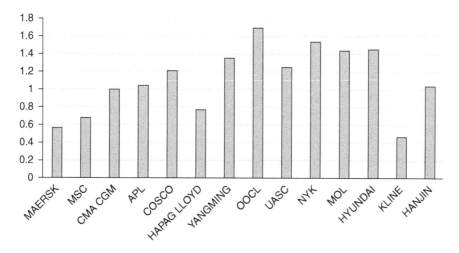

Figure 8.4   Relation between BAF and BP (in elasticities).
Source: own compilation using Eviews 9 and based on Alphaliner Monthly Newsletter (various editions).

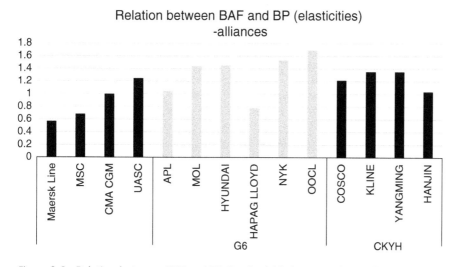

Figure 8.5   Relation between BAF and BP (in elasticities) grouped per alliance.
Source: own compilation using Eviews 9 and based on Alphaliner Monthly Newsletter (various editions).

fuel management (optimal bunker port selection, amount, ship speed, hedging), resulting in a competitive advantage. CMA CGM, APL, and Hanjin before its bankruptcy follow closely the evolution of the BP. Except for Hapag Lloyd, the long-run elasticities for carriers involved in alliances are above unity. An explanation might be found in the bunker price (often bunkering in Asian ports), the number of trade lanes (the more trade routes, the better empty containers repositioning from recovering bunker fuel cost perspective), the logistics of empty equipment (more merchant haulage), or the imbalance of shipping flows. In the case of NYK, taking into account the imbalance of cargo flows results in a different BAF eastbound versus westbound. The results of MSC might be affected as the BAF rolled into freight-all-kind (FAK) from June 2013. The findings for K-LINE might be biased by the fact that for this carrier, 2016 is not included in the analysis. Figure 8.5 clearly shows differences in and between alliances.

8.4.2 BAF strategy at carrier level

The aim of this subsection is to see whether the liner carriers' strategy potentially helps explaining why these elasticities diverge. For this purpose, and in function of data availability, Figure 8.6 gives a visual impression of the carrier-level BAF (shaded area), the bunker price (Rotterdam), and the MBAF.

An interesting observation concerns Mediterranean Shipping Company (MSC), which stopped from June 2013 imposing bunker surcharges on top of freight charges on the Asia-to-Europe trade route (Figure 8.6). Following the EU rules, as of December 2016, MSC publishes advisable freight-all-kind (FAK) rates, including Origin THC (OTHC), International Ship and Port Security (ISPS), Bunkering Utilization Contribution (BUC), Piracy Risk Surcharge (PRS), Suez Canal Surcharge (SCS), Carrier Security Fee (CSF), and Peak Season Surcharge, if any.

Next, in the case of Maersk Line, three periods can be distinguished among: introducing a BAF surcharge calculation tool with predefined parameters (i.e. the oil price) (October 2008–January 2012), revising the BAF formula (monthly updated) in January 2012 (for changing fleet characteristics), and opting for a quarterly BAF surcharge based on actual changes in their fuel costs (January 2015) (Grønvald Raun, 2015). As of April 2015, the BAF surcharge published by Maersk Line turns out to be the highest in the industry (Alphaliner, 2008–2017).

The fuel surcharge imposed by CMA CGM initially followed the surcharge imposed by MSC. From July 2012 onwards, CMA CGM applies a revised BAF calculator tool. Up until January 2015, the BAF surcharge of CMA CGM remains in line with the surcharge published by Maersk Line (Alphaliner, various editions; Meersman et al., 2015a); afterwards, it continues to lag the bunker price by two months.

Within alliances, the BAF surcharges of Hapag Lloyd exceed during the entire period the level of the BP. Until March 2015, it appears that the BAF surcharges of OOCL and NYK, formerly members of the Grand Alliance, and from 2011 onwards of the G6, do not deviate substantially from the surcharge levels imposed by Hapag Lloyd. Except for the fuel surcharge applied by Yang Ming, the BAF surcharges of COSCO, Hanjin, and K-LINE were higher than the average BAF. This observation is also applicable to HMM, with the exception of 2016; while the BAF surcharge of the other alliance members of the former New World Alliance, viz. APL and MOL, is closely related by a two months' delay to the BP.

In sum, in terms of pricing strategy for the BAF, there is a difference between the top-three carriers and the lower-ranked carriers involved in an alliance. Moreover, the pricing strategy on liner operators' behaviour changed in the 2015–2016 period. An explanation might be found in the freight rates at loss-making level. Given that no disaggregate data with respect to operating margin at trade level is available, it is yet not possible to examine the relationship between the operating margin and freight rates at trade level.

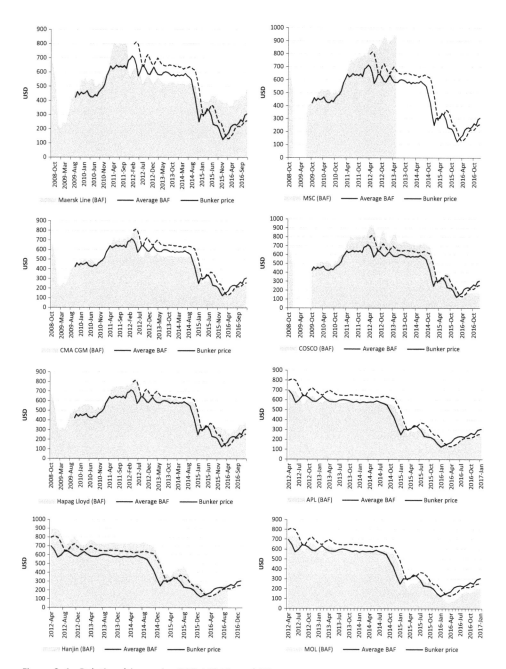

Figure 8.6 Relationship carrier BAF, MBAF, and BP.

Source: own compilation based on Alphaliner Monthly Newsletter (various editions).

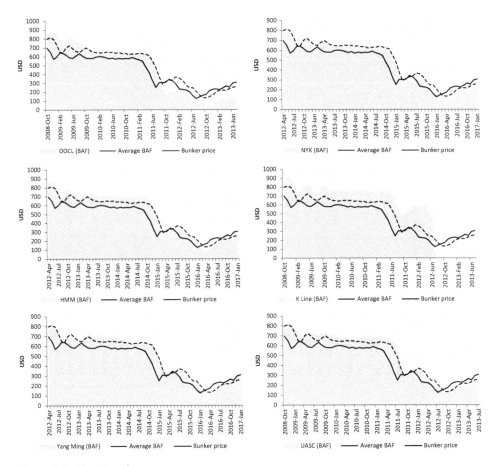

Figure 8.6 Continued.

8.5 Conclusions

In this chapter, the central research question is whether the bunkering adjustment factor (BAF) can be used as a strategic decision tool. To answer this question, a co-integration test is used to test whether there is a stable long-run relationship between the bunker price (BP) and the BAF. A database of the top-14 liner carriers is used for the estimations to see whether there are significant differences, which could be indicative for differences in BAF strategies in the container liner shipping industry.

Some conclusions can be formulated. First, the analysis of the evolution of the freight rate shows that the BAF was used as a strategic decision tool: either to compensate for fluctuations in the BP up to the maximum or lower (responsive to price elasticity), or to increase the market share. Further, if hedging guaranteed positive results, two options were possible: either maximizing profit or using the BAF as a tool to increase competitiveness. Secondly, from the empirical analysis, a significant change in the long-run relation between the average BAF and the BP, as well as in the dynamic adjustment after the abolishment of the conferences to/from Europe, is found. Until October 2008, the long-run equilibrium relation indicates that a 1% change of the BP would lead to a 1.73% change of the MBAF at (t-3); from November 2008 on, this would only be 1.12%. After the abolishment of the conferences, the average BAF follows more closely the evolution of the BP.

Thirdly, a different strategy between the top-three liner carriers and the lower-ranked carriers involved in alliances can be observed. This is also reflected in the long-run elasticities. The long-run elasticities for the lower-ranked carriers are above unity.

In the light of management decision making, this study is especially relevant. It gives insight in the long-run relationship between BP and BAF (allow optimizing the bunker formula) and their bunker price elasticity compared to other carriers. This research at carrier level is also relevant to shippers, particularly in the context of contract renewals. It puts forward an overall picture of the parameters (bunker port selection, imbalance of shipping flows, empty repositioning, penalty/bonus) taking into account by the carrier in setting the BAF surcharge and a comparison of the long-run bunker price elasticity of different carriers. For low-volume shippers often active in the sport market, they are paying the increased surcharge.

However, the BAF is only one of the KPIs to monitor from both carrier and shipper perspective. Further research might take overcapacity, cash flow, and the currency adjustment factor (compensating for losses or gains resulting from variations in exchange rates) at trade level into account. Given that most payments are done in USD currency and the forecast USD to EUR exchange rate is expected to increase by 10 to 15% over the 2017–2019 period, low freight rates may be offset by more interesting payments. In addition, further research is needed, taking into account more trade routes, imbalance in shipping flows, and empty repositioning (including fuel cost of land transport).

Acknowledgment

The authors wish to thank managers of CMA CGM, COSCO, Maersk Line, and NYK for the interesting conversations validating the research results.

Notes

1 As of December 2016, CMA CGM quotes its prices as per EU rules and publishes the basic freight rate and the surcharges separately on its website (http://www.cma-cgm.com/static/News/Attachments/ CMACGM_Commitments_20161205.pdf); while MSC reports EU price announcements for different trade lanes (https://www.msc.com/mrt/notices).
2 The more trade routes, the better empty containers repositioning from recovering bunker fuel cost perspective.
3 The International Monetary Fund (IMF) ($57,65/bbl) and the Organization for Economic Co-operation and Development (OECD) ($45,00/bbl) are slightly more pessimistic in their forecasts (IMF, 2016; OECD, 2016).
4 On 25 September 2006, the council agreed to repeal Regulation 4056/86. By consequence, it puts an end to the coordination of prices, charges, and surcharges as well as coordinated capacity management in European Union trades as of October 2008. Since that date, liner operators have had to fix their own freight rates and any surcharge (European Commission, 2007, 1997; Sys, 2010).
5 The change in March 2002 corresponds with cutting oil production by OPEC and non-OPEC countries.
6 All results of stationarity and co-integration tests are available from the authors.
7 There exist several co-integration tests of which the Engle-Granger test and the Johansen test are the most used (Engle and Granger, 1987; Johansen, 1988; Verbeek, 2008).

References

Alphaliner, 2008–2017. *Alphaliner Monthly Newsletter.*
Alphaliner, 2008–2017. *Alphaliner Weekly Newsletter.*

Aronietis, R., Sys, C., van Hassel, E., Vanelslander, T., 2016. Forecasting port-level demand for LNG as a ship fuel: the case of the port of Antwerp. J. Shipp. Trade 1. doi:10.1186/s41072-016-0007-1

Aydin, N., Lee, H., Mansouri, S.A., 2017. Speed optimization and bunkering in liner shipping in the presence of uncertain service times and time windows at ports. *European Journal of Operational Research*. 259(1), pp.143–154.

Blauwens, G., De Baere, P., Van De Voorde, E., 2016. *Transport Economics*. De Boeck, Berchem.

Boutsikas, A., 2004. The bunkering industry and its effect on shipping tanker operations (thesis). Massachusetts Institute of Technology.

Cariou, P., Wolff, F.-C., 2006. An analysis of bunker adjustment factors and freight rates in the Europe/Far East market (2000–2004). *Marit. Econ. Logist.* 8, 187–201. doi:10.1057/palgrave.mel.9100156

Chen, G., 2017. Pre-announcements of price increase intentions in liner shipping spot markets. *Transp. Res. Part Policy Pract.* 95, 109–125. doi:10.1016/j.tra.2016.11.004

Clarkson Research, 2016. Shipping intelligence network [WWW Document].

De Oliveira, G.F., 2014. Determinants of European freight rates: The role of market power and trade imbalance. *Transp. Res. Part E Logist. Transp. Rev.* 62, 23–33.

Drewry, 2015. Fuel speed ahead? *Container Insight Weekly*. Retrieved from www.drewry.co.uk/container-insight-weekly

Engle, R.F., Granger, C.W.J., 1987. Co-Integration and error correction: Representation, estimation, and testing. *Econometrica*. 55, 251–276.

Engle, R.F., Granger, C.W.J., 1991. Introduction, in: Engle, R.F., Granger, C.W.J. (Eds.) *Long-Run Economic Relationships: Readings in Cointegration*. Oxford University Press, pp. 1–16.

European Commission, 1997. Commission notice on the definition of relevant market for the purposes of Community competition law.

European Commission, 2007. Guidelines on the application of Article 81 of the EC Treaty to maritime transport services – draft.

European Commission, 2016. Antitrust: Commission accepts commitments by container liner shipping companies on price transparency.

Evans, L., 2005. Competition developments affecting the maritime sector. *Eur. Marit. Law Organ.* Lond.

Ferrari, C., Parola, F., Tei, A., 2015. Determinants of slow steaming and implications on service patterns. *Marit. Policy Manag.* 42, 636–652. doi:10.1080/03088839.2015.1078011

Ghosh, S., Lee, L.H., Ng, S.H., 2015. Bunkering decisions for a shipping liner in an uncertain environment with service contract. *Eur. J. Oper. Res.* 244, 792–802.

Grønvald Raun, K., 2015. Maersk Line changing course on fuel surcharge. Lloyds List.

IMF, 2016. IMF Commodity Price Forecasts till January 2021.

International Energy Agency, 2016. Oil market report.

Johansen, S., 1988. Statistical analysis of cointegrating vectors. *J. Econ. Dyn. Control* 12, 231–254.

Kontainer, 2016. Anatomy of container shipping rates [Figure], in 6 freight rates every shipper must know. *Port Technology International*. Retrieved from https://www.porttechnology.org/news/6_freight_rates_every_shipper_must_know

Meersman, H., Rashed, Y., Sys, C., Van de Voorde, E., Vanelslander, T., 2015a. Consequences of applying a bunker adjustment factor, in: Altosole, M., Francescutto, A. (Eds.) 18th International Conference on Ships and Shipping Research 2015. Lecco, Italy, pp. 704–716.

Meersman, H., Sys, C., Van de Voorde, E., Vanelslander, T., 2015b. L'histoire se répète? Current competition issues in container liner shipping. OECD Work. Party No 2 Compet. Regul. 11.

Menachof, D.A., Dicer, G.N., 2001. Risk management methods for the liner shipping industry: the case of the Bunker Adjustment Factor. *Marit. Policy Manag.* 28, 141–155. doi:http://dx.doi.org/10.1080/0308 88301750147654

Munin, Z.H., Schramm, H.J., 2017. Forecasting container shipping freight rates for the Far East–Northern Europe trade lane. *Marit Econ Logist.* 19, 106–125. doi:http://dx.doi.org/10.1057/s41278-016-0051-7

Notteboom, T., Cariou, P., 2013. Slow steaming in container liner shipping: is there any impact on fuel surcharge practices? *Int. J. Logist. Manag.* 24(1), 73–86.

Notteboom, T., Vernimmen, B., 2009. The effect of high fuel costs on liner service configuration in container shipping. *J. Transp. Geogr.* 17, 325–337.

OECD, 2016. Economic outlook no 99, June 2016.

Slack, B., Gouvernal, E., 2011. Container freight rates and the role of surcharges. *J. Transp. Geogr.* 19, 1482–1489. doi:10.1016/j.jtrangeo.2011.09.003

Stopford, M., 2009. *Maritime Economics*. Routledge, Oxon.

Sun, X., Ding, S., 2017. Bunker hedging with expected loss control by buffered probability of exceedance and conditional value-at-risk. Presented at the IAME 2017 Conference, Kyoto, Japan.

Sys, C., 2010. Inside the box: assessing the competitive conditions, the concentration and the market structure of the container liner shipping industry (dissertation). Ghent University.

Sys, C., Vanelslander, T., Adriaenssens, M., Van Rillaer, I., 2016. International emission regulation in sea transport: Economic feasibility and impact. *Transp. Res. Part Transp. Environ.* 45, 139–151. doi:10.1016/j.trd.2015.06.009

U.S. Energy Information Administration, 2016. Europe BRENT spot price FOB [WWW Document]. URL http://www.eia.gov/dnav/pet/hist/LeafHandler.ashx?n=PET&s=RBRTE&f=M (accessed 20 January 2017).

van Hassel, E., Meersman, H., Van de Voorde, E., Vanelslander, T., 2014. Impact of scale increase of container ships on the generalized chain cost. Presented at the International Association of Maritime Economists, Norfolk.

Verbeek, M., 2008. *A Guide to Modern Econometrics*. John Wiley & Sons, Chichester.

Wang, D.-H., Chen, C.-C., Lai, C.-S., 2011. The rationale behind and effects of bunker adjustment factors. *J. Transp. Geogr.* 19, 467–474. doi:10.1016/j.jtrangeo.2009.11.002

World Bank, 2016. Commodity Markets Outlook.

Annex 8.1 BAF ($/TEU) on the Route from the Far East to Northern Europe by Liner Operator

Shipping Line	Mean	Max.	Min.	Std. Dev	Skew.	Kurtosis	J-B	Prob.	Period	Obs.
2M										
MAERSK	501.96	805.00	195.00	129.11	0.25	3.62	2.69	0.26	10M2008-12M2106	99
MSC[a]	674.10	940.00	335.00	179.40	-0.03	1.55	4.32	0.11	10M2008-04M2013	53
Ocean Alliance[b]										
CMA CGM	458.16	800.00	121.00	175.54	-0.18	2.14	8.09	0.20	10M2008-12M2106	99
APL	444.66	693.00	124.00	174.54	-0.43	1.67	5.87	0.05	04M2012-12M2016	56
									04M2012-12M2016	
COSCO	573.97	931.00	94.00	232.05	-0.59	2.14	8.09	0.02	(except 01M2009-09M2009)	90
OOCL	467.11	864.00	47.00	286.58	-0.24	1.39	6.54	0.03	04M2012-12M2016	56
UASC[c]	511.61	828.00	119.00	242.35	-0.42	1.45	7.26	0.03	04M2012-12M2016	56
THE Alliance										
HANJIN[d]	567.83	895.00	100.00	232.63	-0.56	1.82	5.83	0.47	04M2012-09M2016	56
Hapag Lloyd	530.75	821.00	263.00	158.28	-0.20	1.83	6.23	0.04	10M2008-12M2106	99
HMM	513.08	879.00	74.00	256.74	-0.36	1.49	6.51	0.03	04M2012-12M2016	56
K-Line	565.66	917.00	0.00	310.95	-1.08	2.56	11.62	0.00	04M2012-12M2016	55
MOL	430.21	729.00	55.00	217.76	-0.37	1.53	6.31	0.04	04M2012-12M2016	56
NYK	457.05	788.00	58.00	235.71	-0.37	1.49	6.62	0.03	04M2012-12M2016	56
YANG MING	485.73	792.00	63.00	227.44	-0.42	1.66	5.87	0.05	04M2012-12M2016	56

Source: own compilation based on Alphaliner Monthly Monitor (various editions)
Notes: (a) MSC rolled BAF into the base freight rate from June 2013 for all FE-Europe cargo, (b) Evergreen (July 2009), the recently merged CSCL (August 2009), applies an Emergency Bunker Surcharge (EBS), i.e. the changing bunker price is included in the base freight rate, as well as K-Line; (c) UASC continues in the Ocean Alliance until end of March 2017; (d) insolvency of Hanjin just beyond scope of research.

Annex 8.2 Vector Error-correction Model

#vec in eviews IRF_carrier	liner	const.	trend	lnBP	const	trend	dynamic adjustment					adj.R²	#obs
							coint coef	d(lnBAF(-1))	d(lnBAF(-2))	d(lnBP(-1))	d(lnBP(-2))		
1	APL	0.29		1.042			-0.545	-0.063	0.046	-0.61	0.477	0.9666	44
3	COSCO	1.11		1.21			-0.615	0.057	0.073	-0.932	0.463	0.878	78
5	CMA CGM	0.126	-0.0015	0.994	0.023	-0.00088	-0.718	0.103		-0.701		0.781	91
6	HANJIN			1.033			-0.920	0.255	0.225	-0.877	-0.481	0.646	44
8	Hapag Lloyd	1.56		0.771			-0.432	0.156		-0.192		0.529	91
11	HYUNDAI	-2.77	0.003	1.451	-0.074		-0.863	0.053		-1.306		0.877	46
14	KLINE	3.68		0.463			-0.535	0.342		-0.143		0.654	39
17	MAERSK	2.75		0.564			-0.231	0.373		0.041*		0.341	91
20	MOL	2.78		1.438			-0.711	0.010*		-1.27		0.703	46
21	MSC	1.87	0.0107	0.679	0.011		-0.629	0.055*		-0.559		0.777	46
23	NYK	-3.41	0.0036	1.53	-0.074		-0.751	0.101		-1.297		0.884	46
25	OOCL	-3.79	-0.005	1.688	-0.122		-0.674	0.087	0.088	-1.201	-1.154	0.814	44
28	YANGMING	-2.12		1.35			-0.630	0.010*		-0.769		0.545	46
30	UASC	1.39		1.245			-0.331	0.16	-0.04	0.41	-0.166	0.317	50

Slow steaming in the maritime industry

Pierre Cariou, Claudio Ferrari, Francesco Parola, and Alessio Tei

9.1 Introduction

Shipping has always been a cyclical industry (Stopford, 2010) characterized by high volatility in freight rates (e.g. Kavussanos, 1996) and potential excess of capacity (e.g. Cariou, 2008). These characteristics vary considerably depending on the specific sector (e.g. container, dry bulk, tanker markets) but they are a strategic issue for all the shipping operators. Thus, shipping companies have always tried to mitigate cyclical effects – impacting on both competition and business uncertainty – through a series of collaborative actions (e.g. Haralambides, 1996; Heaver et al., 2000).

Even if cycles are considered a structural component of the shipping industry, an exceptional scenario occurred in the second half of the '00s when high fuel cost dynamics coincided with a long period of low demand for all the main shipping sectors, generating a persisting deterioration of the business.

Thus, starting from 2008, the reduction of the commercial speed (i.e. slow steaming) represented a shipping operators' strategy that assured savings of bunker costs in a period of high fuel price and a reduction in demand. Savings were guaranteed by the direct relationship between fuel consumption and ship speed (e.g. Bialystocki and Konovessis, 2016). The effects of slow steaming practice on the shipping services' organization were dramatic: increasing duration of the ship turnaround, modification of the fleet deployment and effect of cascading, and rationalization of the ports of calls, among others. Side effects of slow steaming were also related to a reduction of the environmental impact of the shipping – proportional to the reduction in fuel consumption – and the new required characteristics for the ordered vessels (e.g. lower design speed). While slow steaming was initially meant to be a short-term strategy to allow shipping companies to deal with unprecedented market conditions, after almost a decade average shipping speed hasn't returned to previous levels. The long-lasting strategy of slow steaming is mostly related to the volatility of the market that still affects shipping operators' revenues, even though forecast of the fuel price drastically changed in the last year, foreseeing a low bunker cost level for the coming years.

While reasons for applying slow steaming have always been clear to scholars, real effects on the market and on the environment have often been questioned. For this reason, several scholars and international agencies (e.g. the International Maritime Organization) investigated the effects of speed reduction. These investigations – that began even before the term "slow steaming" became common – focused on understanding the wider effects of modification in average sailing speed on the industry. Initial studies (e.g. Kågeson, 1999; Cariou and Wolff, 2006) highlighted the economic incentives in reducing emissions through fuel savings. Those studies were not directly linked to the slow steaming practice but to the general idea of finding a relation between speed reductions and shipping emissions. Only further technical studies (e.g. Buhaug et al., 2009; Corbett et al., 2009; Faber et al. 2012) underlined the conditions under which the overall environmental impact of shipping is reduced by decreasing speed. In general terms, engine typology and load factor together with the level of speed reduction affect the overall pollution generated by the navigation and then the net effect of slow steaming on the environment. Moreover, Tai and Lin (2013) claimed that increasing benefits of slow steaming on the environment can be obtained only with mixed routing strategies aiming at optimizing ship utilization. For this reason, Song et al. (2015) used a multi-objective model in order to find an optimal scenario able to achieve different shipping company goals when adopting slow steaming. Thus, slow steaming can be considered an environmentally friendly strategy but only under certain conditions (e.g. Wang and Meng, 2012).

While the relation between shipping environmental impact and speed is one of the first reasons why speed reduction has been examined by many scholars, during the second part of the '00s, the financial and economic effects of speed reduction were mainly investigated by researchers. In fact, as noted by Notteboom and Venminnen (2009), fuel consumption represents the main component of the shipping voyage and operating costs, varying from more than 60% up to 75% depending on the ship size and trip characteristics (e.g. Ronen, 2011; Ferrari et al., 2015). In a period of high fuel cost, slow steaming became then a major strategic tool to contain operational costs. Cariou (2011) suggested a threshold of fuel costs around 350–400 dollars per tonne as the limit that makes the fuel savings sustainable in relation to other market conditions. Despite this, the persistency of slow steaming in 2017 (with bunker cost around 200 dollars per tonne) demonstrates the possible convenience of shipping companies in adopting slow steaming as a long-term strategy. Finnsgård et al. (2016) highlighted that current slow steaming advantages are more related to other competitive factors (e.g. fleet deployment, reduction of overcapacity) than to just fuel savings. These differentiated advantages have been translated in the possibility for forwarders to guarantee a premium to shipping operators for increasing current service speed. Thus, while the strategy of cutting operating costs was the traditional driver for implementing slow steaming, now the main reasons behind the adoption of this strategy have changed.

The current operational condition introduces different challenges in terms of ship technology (i.e. engine efficiency, as discussed in Corbett et al., 2009) but also competitive and managerial implications. Among these latter ones, Zacharioudakis et al. (2011) underlined the effects in shipping routing while Ferrari et al. (2015) discussed the implications related to port competition and selection criteria. In fact, in order to maintain a given level of service, shipping companies rescheduled traditional services, calling at a reduced number of ports. The rescheduling affected the port selection strategy (e.g. Yap and Notteboom, 2011) and pushed companies to rationalize their network. Therefore, slow steaming had a different impact on several shipping-related markets.

In the context of this background, this chapter aims to discuss the main effects of slow steaming on the shipping business, by referring to industry reports and the extant literature, classifying those effects into three main categories:

- economic implications;
- environmental implications and;
- service-related implications.

After a background section, the following parts of the chapter will then focus on the three main aspects introduced above with the aim to understand the different effects of slow steaming on the shipping industry.

9.2 Background

As mentioned, slow steaming was generalized around 2008 to respond to the extreme conditions the shipping markets were facing. Figure 9.1 collates the main shipping market trends of the last 20 years. Average fuel and freight rates (the latter represented by the ClarkSea Index) are always correlated and represent the cyclical movement of the shipping industry. The economic boom of the early '00s (mainly led by China) pushed the market to unprecedented levels, achieving its peak between 2007 and 2008. Despite the depressing effects of the 2008 financial crisis on the shipping market lasting only for a short period of time (at least for many shipping sectors), afterwards the pace of growth decreased compared to the previous years. The crisis (and the slowdown in the market rate of growth) generated an excess of capacity that was worsened by the orders made during the previous market peak. Figure 9.1 shows, as an example, the increased discrepancy between the container exports growth and the container fleet capacity growth (starting from 2007). In the same period of time – and quite unusually – freight rates (the ClarkSea Index as proxy) and bunker price diverged pushing into a situation of high fuel prices, overcapacity, low rate of growth, and low freight rates.

This situation – which lasted for almost a decade – pushed shipping companies, especially in the liner sector, to find new ways to be competitive. Together with alliances, consortia, and new routing strategies, one of the most adopted techniques was to slow steam.

In general terms, slow steaming represents a reduction of the average ship commercial speed aiming at: a) reducing the fuel consumption and b) reducing the level of overcapacity (Sanguri, 2012). The first goal is a direct effect of the declining speed. Lee and Song (2017) underline how

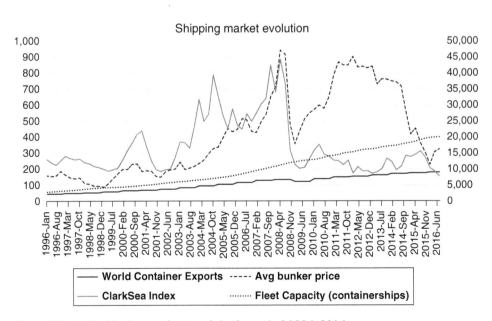

Figure 9.1 Main shipping market trends in the period 1996–2016.
Source: Own elaboration from Clarkson SIN data, 2016.

slow steaming decreased the sailing speed from an average of 23–26 knots on the main routes to a speed of about 21 knots (normal slow steaming) with minimum values of about 15 knots (super slow steaming). Thus, this practice generated an average speed reduction of nearly 30% with peaks of 40%. As discussed by Buhaug et al. (2009) and Faber et al. (2012), the relation between fuel consumption and speed is proportional only if a certain variation range is maintained, otherwise the effects are no longer linear. Thus, many shipping companies, in a period of high fuel prices, decided to reduce their own operating costs by decreasing sailing speed. According to Ronen (2011), reducing the commercial speed by 20% brings savings up to 50% on the daily fuel consumption.

On the other hand, reduction of speed pushed shipping companies to reschedule many services due to the increasing travel time. In order to maintain frequencies in ports, shipping companies had to increase the number of ships per route and this generated a limitation in the overall deployed capacity (positively affecting the market).

As mentioned in several papers (e.g. Notteboom and Cariou, 2013; Ferrari et al., 2015), this strategy generated a series of further positive consequences, such as a reduction of the negative environmental impact of shipping activity and the possibility to sell different services depending on the scheduled transit time (e.g. Daily Maersk service). Nevertheless, not all these positive effects were achieved, and some negative issues influenced the industry as well. Among the latter, the re-routing of many ships affected the degree of competition in the port market, while sailing times and the increased delays in many services affected the overall quality of services (Drewry Maritime Research, 2013). Figure 9.2 portrays the main reasons and effects of the slow steaming practice, as described above.

A further interesting issue is that slow steaming impacted differently the several shipping markets. While all the main shipping sectors adopted slow steaming (e.g. very large crude carrier (VLCC) reduced their speed by over 30% after 2010 [e.g. Psaraftis and Kontovas, 2013]), as stated by Ronen (1982) oil price affects ship speed differently depending on the market organization (e.g. tramp vs liner). In fact, in the tramp sector (and then in the majority of the bulk markets), ballast voyages can be easily developed promoting slow steaming, but once a deal

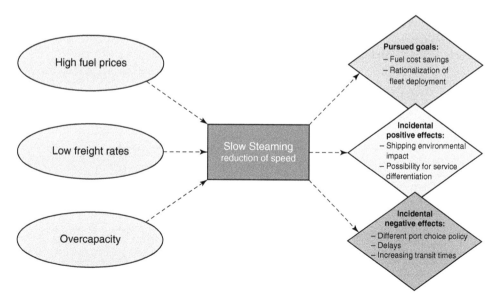

Figure 9.2 Slow steaming rationale.

with a cargo owner is achieved, reduced speed can be a less effective tool for the increase of daily earnings (since there is a need for a flexible and rapid capability to answer to the market needs). Long-term deals (e.g. time charter) or scheduled maritime services (i.e. liner shipping) can more easily extend the benefits of slow steaming as a means to both reduce cost and manage overcapacity, given the rigid structure of their service (and then the different way to meet supply and demand). For this reason, the majority of studies have been performed on liner shipping (and this will be the main point of view of the chapter). Despite this issue, many of the considerations that follow can also be applied to the bulk sector.

9.3 Economic implications of slow steaming for shipping lines

The practice of deliberately slowing down the speed of a vessel is a common operating choice of players in the current shipping market as a way to cut costs by lowering fuel consumption (Cariou and Wolff, 2006; Maloni et al., 2013). As indicated above, slow steaming was adopted between 2007 and 2008, when shipping lines started to experience tonnage overcapacity, declining freight rates, and increasing bunker prices (Lindstad et al., 2011). Later on, ship-owners encountered higher bunker costs not only because of volatile bunker prices, but also due to the legal obligation of using more expensive low-sulphur fuel oil (LSFO); for instance, when operating in sulphur emission control areas (SECAs). Over the last few years, bunker prices collapsed but the practice of slow steaming is still adopted by major shipping lines.

The above practice demonstrates that the economic implications of slow steaming reach much beyond fuel costs reduction and cost leadership, and include other strategic goals, such as the differentiation of shipping services and the preservation of the supply–demand balance as illustrated in Figure 9.3.

9.3.1 Cost leadership

As widely recognized, shipping lines are forced to pursue cost leadership strategies to restore their financial margins and withstand competitive pressures. Although slow steaming is not the only approach for reducing fuel consumption and cutting costs, it seems to be the least time and money consuming. On the basis of a study by the Boston Consulting Group (2012), this is what probably makes the strategy so widely adopted worldwide among shipping carriers.

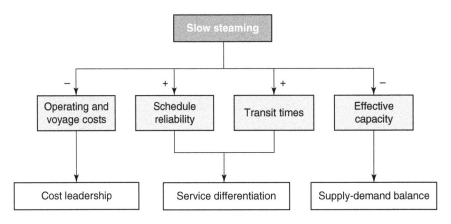

Figure 9.3 Economic implications of slow steaming strategies.

Notably, slow steaming brings substantial economic benefits. Taking into account direct costs (fuel consumption, crew, capital costs), indirect costs (additional inventory costs, adjustment of logistical chains), and external costs (impacts of emissions on human health and ecosystems, climate impacts), the pros of slow steaming outweigh its costs.

Sailing ships at slower speeds significantly reduces fuel consumption. Lowering engine speed by 10% cuts engine power by 27%, and reduces the overall energy required for the voyage by 19% (Cariou, 2011; Kloch, 2013). Ocean carriers have broadly resorted to the slow steaming strategy manifested by an operating speed of 20 knots. As mentioned above, some players have even implemented super-slow steaming with speeds of 15 knots. Slow steaming enables operators to utilize less fuel, and fuel constitutes a large share of operating costs: when oil prices were at their peak, fuel accounted for as much as 50% of the total cost of sailing a vessel (Notteboom and Vermminen, 2009).

In addition, besides the well-known reduction of fuel costs, slow steaming provides environmental benefits that translate into immediate economic implications (Psaraftis and Kontovas, 2010). In fact, in some port regions, ocean carriers can enjoy savings in other running costs components, thanks to the discount in port dues and local taxes. For instance, the two busiest ports in the USA (Long Beach and Los Angeles) have launched a series of voluntary incentive-based programs. Indeed, the two ports offer a 15% discount on dockage fees to vessels that voluntary comply with the "Vessel Speed Reduction Programme" and decrease their speed to 12 knots while entering or leaving the ports (Port of Long Beach, 2009). In addition, in many ports worldwide, port authorities have introduced environmentally differentiated port dues (Kågeson, 1999).

In economic terms, however, it is worth questioning the extent to which some of these savings are "distributed" to shippers. Longer transit times raise shippers' costs, through the increase in inventory costs. After considering factors such as depreciation and insurance, the added inventory costs that accrue to shippers when cargo is sailing on the oceans are roughly USD 170 million (Kloch, 2013). In addition, longer sailing times can also impact shippers' cash flow, as the time span from production to sale is extended. It is widely understood that this can become more problematic for time-sensitive commodities.

9.3.2 Service differentiation

These arguments lead to a second important area of economic impacts for slow steaming, i.e. service differentiation. Indeed, shipping line customers may obtain some advantages from slow steaming because of the improvement in terms of transit time reliability (Finnsgård et al., 2015). Slow steaming vessels are more likely to arrive at a port on schedule. When a ship sails at full speed, it has no "buffer time" if it is delayed by weather conditions, congestion issues, or tidal constraints at ports. Conversely, in case of slow steaming the ship can increase speed to make up for the lost time.

For manufacturers, retailers, importers, and exporters, supply chain reliability is more important than transit time or freight rates. Delivering on time as promised is the basis for business success and ensures the loyalty of customers (Kloch, 2013). Superior reliability enables shippers to decrease the inventory they hold in the country of destination, thus counteracting the rising inventory levels needed for slow steaming. Indeed, shippers can hold less buffer stock as they can be sure new stock will arrive on schedule.

Another important effect of slow steaming in terms of service differentiation is the introduction of diverse service patterns (port rotation) and transit times. Contrary to traditional long-haul services that were carried out by running at a standard commercial speed (24–26 knots), slow steaming offers a spectrum of speed solutions that depends on fuel prices and market conditions. Based on a market survey sampling of over 200 liner and tramp companies, 75% apply slow steaming to various extents (Seatrade Maritime News, 2014). In such a way, ocean carriers can modulate the commercial speed and offer differentiated transit times to shippers, thus serving cargo of different value and time sensitiveness. In this regard, it is worth to note that time sensitiveness can also vary for seasonality issues during the year, e.g. launch of new products or peak periods for consumption (e.g. Christmas, Chinese New Year).

9.4 Impact of slow steaming on the environment

The practice of slow steaming also brings the advantages of being the most cost-effective measure to reduce CO_2 emissions. It has been one of the main arguments used by shipping lines to justify that they were slowing down vessels and investing in large containerships for which the amount of emissions per container is lower. This was particularly used at a time when the successive IMO studies (Buhaug et al. 2009; 2014) were pointing out the contribution of international shipping to greenhouse gas emissions and therefore to global warming. In this context, the Third International Maritime Organization (IMO) on GHG emissions from ships (2014) brought some positive news to the shipping community. This report shows that CO_2 emissions from international shipping have globally decreased by 11% since 2007, from 885 million tons to 796 million in tons in 2012. Shipping-related CO_2 emissions that were representing 2.8% of worldwide CO_2 emissions in 2007 went down to 2.2% in 2012. Slow steaming of containerships is the main contributor to this reduction. However, some factors tend to limit these effects and the long-term sustainability of slow steaming (Cariou 2011).

Firstly, some technical elements may still represent limits to the expected reduction in emissions associated with speed reduction. Indeed, and apart from the modern vessels such as the Maersk Triple E which are built to operate under low speed mode, the generalization of slow steaming means that most containerships' engines are running outside their designed operating mode. This range, estimated at less than 55% of the maximum continuous rate according to Sanguri (2012), leads to some potential increase in the specific fuel oil consumption and the need for engines retrofitting.

Secondly, the impact of slow steaming on the amount of CO_2 emitted per TEU or tons transported, and not based on the vessel, can be questioned. The reduction in transit time may mean that less cargo is transported, and more vessels are needed to transport these cargoes. It therefore means that, similarly to economies of scale, the effectiveness of slow steaming to the reduction in emissions can only be judged when considering the impact on trade, and the impact of changes in service characteristics on the level of demand.

Thirdly, the total amount of CO_2 emitted by a containership is not solely related to the main engine. For instance, for some trade, containerships are transporting a significant amount of reefer containers for which, due to the increase in transit time, a large proportion of emissions come from the auxiliary engine. When transit time increases, this effect may cancel out the potential gains brought by the reduction in emissions from the main engine. These elements were investigated by Cheaitou and Cariou (2012) for a container liner service deployed from Northern Europe to the East Coast of South America, where a significant portion of transport is for fresh products in reefer containers. The existence of a trade-off between total savings in fuel consumption (main and auxiliary engines) and the decrease in transported quantities when demand is elastic to the transit time can alter the positive impact brought by slow steaming.

To conclude, the positive effect from slow steaming on the reduction in CO_2 emissions is significant and, so far, mostly explained by gains shipping lines get from its implementation in terms of fuel savings and, more generally, of reduction in slot costs. Even in a time when bunker prices are low, as expressed earlier, this strategy does not change as long as freight rates remain at low levels. In the long run, the internalization of CO_2 emissions, either through taxation or the introduction of cap-and-trade market, could represent incentives to maintain and even to increase even further the economic positive benefits from slow steaming, and therefore its contribution to curb emissions from container shipping.

9.5 Impact of slow steaming on the current structure of shipping services

A possible starting point of slow steaming practice is 2006 when both the Grand Alliance and CMA CGM decided to add a ninth ship to one of their respective Asia–Europe routes to cope with the high bunker price. As stated by Vernimmen et al. (2007), the resulting bunker cost savings encountered by the other eight vessels more than compensated for the cost of hiring and operating the additional (ninth) vessel.

This practice was also helpful in avoiding piracy along some routes and, when the economic crisis came about, a different reason justified the adoption of slow steaming: the reduction of navigation speed helped liner companies in facing the drop of demand. It represented a third leverage – together with the tonnage lay-up and ship scrapping – to reduce the tonnage supply.

The earnings due to the reduced vessels' speed were so relevant that this practice was soon adopted in all maritime transport sectors, including liner and tramp services.

Nowadays, a decade after the adoption of slow steaming practice, the economic conditions are totally different: several countries have completely recovered from the economic crisis, oil price is low, but the liner shipping industry is still facing an oversupply of tonnage. Therefore, it is worthwhile to discuss if this practice is still profitable and what implications it has on the structure of maritime services, mainly on the liner shipping industry due to its complexity.

First of all, it is important to note that while in 2006 slow steaming and super-slow steaming represented a practical attempt to reduce the shipping costs, namely adopted on the backhaul trip, nowadays they have been "embedded" in the design process of ships. In fact, as reported in Psaraftis and Kontovas (2014) Maersk's new Triple E ships (with a nominal capacity of around 18,000 TEU) have a design speed of 17.8 knots, well below the 22–25 knots considered as the normal range of speed of the former generation of vessels.

As indicated above, since the ships have a lower (than in the recent past) cruising speed, the number of vessels employed on a single route must be higher (than in the past). This is confirmed by data collected by Drewry (2016, 2013, 2010, and 2008) in its "slow steaming monitor": taking into account the number of vessels employed by liner carriers in a sample of shipping routes, it is quite evident that there is an increasing number of vessels employed in each service. At the same time the introduction in the fleet of ever bigger vessels, often "shared" among the carriers through slot charter agreements or vessels sharing agreements, has progressively reduced the number of liner services needed in order to accommodate transport demand. Figures 9.4, 9.5, and 9.6 show this "scissors effect" for the Far East–Europe trade lane and for the route linking Eastern Asia to the East Coast of North America through the Panama Canal.

In the context of the low price of fuel seen in recent times, it has been suggested that shipping lines might return to running faster services. The competitive advantage of slowing down ships when fuel costs significantly decrease is less compelling, but the opinion of some senior

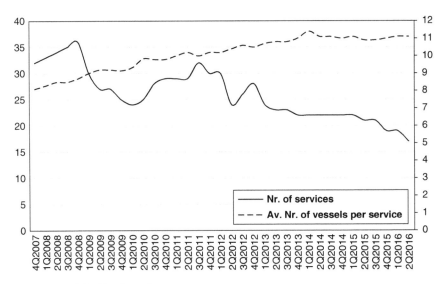

Figure 9.4 Asia–Northern Europe.
Source: Compiled from Drewry data, several years.

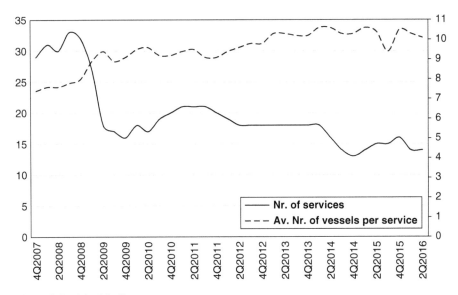

Figure 9.5 Asia–Mediterranean.
Source: Compiled from Drewry data, several years.

CEOs in the industry is that no operators are about to suddenly reverse their policy on slow steaming. The willingness to preserve the bargaining power towards shippers and the need of avoiding price wars among shipping lines are expected to prevail, at least under the current market conditions. Looking at the more recent data, none of the services serving the main routes has increased the number of ships deployed. This would confirm that slow steaming is still being adopted by carriers but no longer developing. Namely, in the main routes, the main

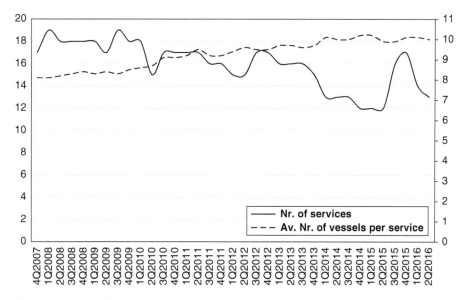

Figure 9.6 Asia–ECNA via Panama.
Source: Compiled from Drewry data, several years.

efforts of carriers will focus on restructuring the scheduling of services in consequence to the recent mergers and changes happening in the industry (such as the bankruptcy of Hanjin at the end of August 2016) instead of adding new ships to their loops.

Another interesting fact monitored by Drewry (2016) is the number of vessels deployed by carriers on the main routes and their service use on different services. The comparison between the current number of ships deployed and the number of services offered allows us to better understand the differences in the use of the ships in comparison with the 2007 value (i.e. the hypothetical number of vessels that would be currently deployed in the case of the same number of ships and the same number of loops as had been deployed in late 2007). These three figures are shown in Figure 9.7 for the main shipping routes. To sum up, in the second quarter of 2016, 763 ships are deployed in the eight monitored routes, while there were 894 in late 2007 (−14.7%); there would actually be 1,118 assuming the same service level as in 2007. In the same period of time (2007–2016), UNCTAD (2015) estimates that, globally, the containerized cargo loaded has grown from 1,193 million tons in 2007 to 1,631 million tons (+36.7%).

Slow steaming coupled with the deployment of ever bigger vessels has had a relevant impact also on ports, determining a reduction in the number of calls. Taking into consideration the shipping services on the route Far East–Mediterranean as monitored by Drewry, while in July 2007 there were 46 services and 584 port calls, at the beginning of 2016 the services were reduced to 23 and the port calls dropped to 396. The number of ports interested by these services remained the same (89 vs 88) but the average number of calls per port dropped from 6.6 to 4.4. This is the result of the evolution of the system of alliances among the carriers; each carrier is actually behaving as before the economic crisis, calling at each port around 1.5–2.5 times (considering solely the services on the Far East–Mediterranean route); the range was 1.7–2.6 times in 2007. The progressive diffusion of alliances has determined that the same range of calls per port is currently recorded for a fewer number of allied carriers. This means that the seaport container terminals have to move a greater volume of containers in a few hours and that most

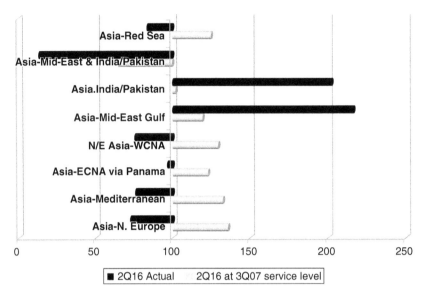

Figure 9.7   Actual ships (2Q2016) deployed on main shipping routes compared with 3Q2007 (equal to 100) and ships deployed at 3Q2007 service level.
Source: Compiled from Drewry data, several years.

of the time the berths are unattended; at the same time, the opportunity cost that a ship could bear in case the berth is not free is higher due to the "cascading" effect. Any delays in the port operations in a slow steaming regime may be tackled by an increase of the speed of the ship or by skipping a port call; both solutions have negative results in terms of higher costs or lower affordability of the service.

It is possible that, in the future, if the industry faces proliferation of M&As, the number of ports called at by the main shipping services will also be reduced as a result of the further drive to achieve economies of scale by the shipping lines.

9.6 Conclusion

Slow steaming is a common practice in the shipping industry and was introduced in the early 2000s in order to face some unexpected market conditions (i.e. fuel prices, overcapacity, high bunker price, and low freight rates). Despite its origin as a solution for uncommon events, slow steaming has become a shipping practice applied by several shipping companies, mainly in liner shipping, and is now established as current business practice even in a time of low bunker price and higher freight rates. The reasons behind this long-lasting phase are mainly related to the further advantages that slow steaming can guarantee, in terms of fleet organization and possibility for further service differentiation.

Slow steaming generated different intended and unintended effects over the years. Firstly, the main economic effects were related to a cost-cutting strategy of the bunker costs; nevertheless, its main long-lasting effects were related to the fleet management costs (e.g. reduction of the overcapacity) and a more rational use of the fleet. These last considerations partially explain why slow steaming has been primarily linked to liner shipping rather than to the tramp sector, where ship management is done considering different strategic variables. The positive effects of slow steaming are entirely gained by the newest ships, i.e. the ships specifically designed to regularly perform at low commercial speed, and this affects the maintenance costs. Similarly, while slow steaming has been commonly considered as an environmental strategy – drawing a direct connection between fuel consumption and emission reduction – actual emission savings are disputable. This last consideration is mainly related to the studies connected to the actual ratio between carried capacity and CO_2 emissions and not on the general ship performance. This discrepancy is mainly linked to the increased number of ships used to assure a certain service. In fact, the main general effect of slow steaming is on the routing plan of the shipping companies: during slow steaming implementation, the structure of several services was changed in order to deal with different market conditions.

While slow steaming was firstly considered as a temporary practice, it is now considered a long-term strategy that is indirectly increasing port competition – due to the need for reducing port calls – and the possibility for further increasing the level of differentiation of shipping services. The low demand growth in many shipping sectors – at least in comparison with the previous capacity growth – is pushing shipping operators to preserve slow steaming and reduce the number of "fast" services. Moreover, given the fact that qualitative service attributes (such as punctuality and reliability) have acquired increased importance (more than speed or frequency) in many logistics chains, slow steaming appears as a useful tool to reduce unforeseen delays (e.g. giving the chance to speed up the vessel in case of need).

Interestingly, in a time when shipping seems to confirm slow steaming, some infrastructural projects (e.g. the Belt and Road Initiative) try to create an alternative to traditional shipping trade lines, guaranteeing faster connections. These new potential solutions could generate a new kind of intermodal transport competition in which cargo that needs reliable and cheaper – but slower – services still focuses on shipping while richer cargo could be served by these new transport corridors.

Eventually, the slow steaming practice is creating longer supply chains and impacting on the perceived quality of shipping services, often determining extra costs for the shippers (despite the possibility of reducing potential delays). These disadvantages will probably make up the next challenges for the survival of the slow steaming practice in the shipping industry of the future.

References

Bialystocki N., Konovessis D. (2016). On the estimation of ship's fuel consumption and speed curve: A statistical approach. *Journal of Ocean Engineering and Science*, 1, 157–166.

Boston Consulting Group (2012). *Charting a new course – restoring profitability to container shipping*. The Boston Consulting Group, Boston, MA.

Buhaug Ø., Corbett J.J., Endresen Ø., Eyring V., Faber J., Hanayama S., Lee D.S., Lee D., Lindstad H., Markowska A.Z., Mjelde A., Nelissen D., Nilsen J., Pålsson C., Winebrake J.J., Wu W., Yoshida K. (2009). Second IMO GHG Study 2009, International Maritime Organization (IMO) London.

Buhaug Ø., Corbett J.J., Endresen Ø., Eyring V., Faber J., Hanayama S., Lee D.S., Lee D., Lindstad H., Markowska A.Z., Mjelde A., Nelissen D., Nilsen J., Pålsson C., Winebrake J.J., Wu W., Yoshida K. (2014). Third IMO GHG Study 2014, International Maritime Organization (IMO), London.

Cariou P. (2008). Liner shipping strategies: an overview. *International Journal of Ocean Systems Management*, 1, 2–13.

Cariou P. (2011). Is slow steaming a sustainable means of reducing CO_2 emissions from container shipping? *Transportation Research Part D*, 16, 260–264.

Cariou P., Cheaitou A. (2012). Liner shipping service optimization with reefers container capacity: an application to Northern Europe/South America trade. *Maritime Policy and Management*, 39, 589–602.

Cariou P. and Wolff F.-C. (2006). An analysis of bunker adjustment factors and freight rates in the Europe/ Far East market (2000–2004). *Maritime Economics & Logistics*, 8, 187 –201.

Corbett J.J., Wang H., Winebrake J.J. (2009). The effectiveness and costs of speed reductions on emissions from international shipping,. *Transportation Research Part D*, 14, 593–598.

Drewry Maritime Research (2013). Container Forecast. Quarterly Drewry Report. London: Drewry.

Drewry Shipping Consultants (2008). Container forecaster – Quarter 4, London, UK.

Drewry Shipping Consultants (2010). Container forecaster – Quarter 4, London, UK.

Drewry Shipping Consultants (2013). Container forecaster – Quarter 3, London, UK.

Drewry Shipping Consultants (2016). Container forecaster – Quarter 2, London, UK.

Faber J., Nelissen D., Hon G., Wang H., Tsimplis M. (2012). An assessment of options, costs and benefits, regulated slow steaming in maritime transport. CE Delft report.

Ferrari C., Parola F., Tei A. (2015). Determinants of slow steaming and implications on service patterns. *Maritime Policy & Management*, 42, 636–652.

Finnsgård C., Kalantari, J., Roso, V., Woxenius, J. (2015). Slow steaming from the shippers' perspective. In 2015 METRANS International Urban Freight Conference (I-NUF), October 21–23 2015. Long Beach, California.

Finnsgård C., Kalantari J., Roso V., Woxenius J., Raza Z. (2016). Shipper strategies for coping with slow-steaming in deep sea container shipping. Proceedings of WCTR conference, Shanghai.

Haralambides H. (1996). The economics of bulk shipping pools. *Maritime Policy & Management*, 23, 221–237.

Heaver T., Meersmann H., Moglia F., Van de Voorde E. (2000). Do mergers and alliances influence European shipping and port competition? *Maritime Policy & Management*, 27, 363–373.

Kågeson P. (1999). *Economic instruments for reducing emissions from sea transport*. European Federation for Transport and Environment.

Kavussanos M. (1996). Comparisons of volatility in the dry-cargo ship sector: spot versus time charters, and smaller versus larger vessels. *Journal of Transport Economics and Policy*, 30, 67–82.

Kloch L. (2013). Is slow steaming good for the supply chain? *Inbound Logistics*, April, 72.

Lee C.Y., Song D.P. (2017). Ocean container transport in global supply chains: overview and research opportunities. *Transportation Research Part B*, 95, 442–474.

Lindstad, H., Asbjørnslett, B.E., Strømman, A. H. (2011). Reductions in greenhouse gas emissions and cost by shipping at lower speeds. *Energy Policy*, 39, 3456–3464.

Maloni, M., Paul, J.A., Gligor, D.M. (2013). Slow steaming impacts on ocean carriers and shippers. *Maritime Economics & Logistics*, 15(2), 151–171.

Notteboom T., Cariou P. (2013). Slow steaming in container liner shipping: is there any impact on fuel surcharge practices? *The International Journal of Logistics Management*, 24, 73–86.

Notteboom T., Vernimmen B. (2009). The effect of high fuel costs on liner service configuration in container shipping. *Journal of Transport Geography*, 17, 325–337.

Port of Long Beach (2009). Building the port of the future. Annual Report, Long Beach.

Psaraftis H.N., Kontovas C.A. (2010). Balancing the economic and environmental performance of maritime transportation. *Transportation Research Part D: Transport and Environment*, 15(8), 458–462.

Psaraftis H.N., Kontovas C.A. (2013). Speed models for energy-efficient maritime transportation: A taxonomy and survey. *Transportation Research Part C*, 26, 331–351.

Psaraftis HN., Kontovas, C.A. (2014). Ship speed optimization: concepts, models and combined speed-routing scenarios. *Transportation Research Part C*, 52–69.

Ronen D. (1982). The effect of oil price on the optimal speed of ships. *Journal of the Operational Research Society*, 33, 1035–1040.

Ronen, D. (2011). The effect of oil price on containership speed and fleet size. *Journal of Operation Research Society*, 62, 211–216.

Sanguri M. (2012). The guide to slow steaming on ships. *Marine Insight*. London: Lloyd's List. https://www. marineinsight.com/wp-content/uploads/2013/01/The-guide-to-slow-steaming-on-ships.pdf

Seatrade Maritime News (2014). http://www.seatrade-maritime.com/news/americas/the-economics-of-slow-steaming.html.

Song D.P., Li D., Drake P. (2015). Multi-objective optimization for planning liner shipping service with uncertain port times, *Transportation Research Part E*, 84, 1–22.

Stopford M. (2010). Shipping market cycles. In Grammenos C., *The Handbook of Maritime Economics and Business*, 235–258.

Tai H.H., Lin D.Y. (2013). Comparing the unit emissions of daily frequency and slow steaming strategies on trunk route deployment in international container shipping. *Transportation Research Part D*, 21, 26–31.

UNCTAD (2015). *Review of Maritime Transport 2015*, Geneva.

Vernimmen B., Dullaert W., Engelen S. (2007). Schedule unreliability in liner shipping: origins and consequences for the hinterland supply chain. *Maritime Economics and Logistics*, 9, 193–213.

Wang S., Meng Q. (2012). Sailing speed optimization for container ships in a liner shipping network. *Transportation Research Part E*, 48, 701–714.

Yap W., Notteboom T. (2011). Dynamics of liner shipping service scheduling and their impact on container port competition. *Maritime Policy & Management*, 38, 471–485.

Zacharioudakis P., Iordanis S., Lyridis D., Psaraftis H. (2011). Liner shipping cycle cost modelling, fleet deployment optimization and what-if analysis. *Maritime Economics & Logistics*, 13, 278–297.

Determinants of ship management fees

Antonis A. Michis

10.1 Introduction

The ship management industry has evolved considerably in recent years in response to changes in maritime regulations and the increasing considerations of ship owners regarding the efficient operation of their vessels. The traditional model of vertically integrating the ship management and ship owning operations under the same group structure is gradually being replaced by the third-party and hybrid models of ship management. Unlike the hybrid model, which combines in-house operations with selected outsourcing, the third-party management model outsources all vessel operations to third-party companies.

Outsourcing enables ship owners to assign the technical, crewing, and commercial (financial, logistics, procurement, and marketing) operations of their vessels to specialized third-party ship management companies. These companies tend to be associated with superior technical and operational skills in the following areas: implementation of modern technologies in ship operations, cost efficiency in crewing, precision in technical and commercial operations, superior knowledge and expertise in managing the ship capital, and specialization in crew training (see Branch and Robarts, 2014; Panayides and Cullinane, 2002; Mitroussi, 2004a, 2004b). In addition, they are well trained in securing the effective adaptation of the ship capital to changes in maritime regulations and certifications, such as the implementation of the International Ship Management Code (ISM).

Sea transport operations tend to be influenced by several economic, regulatory, and commercial factors such as volume changes in the international trade of goods, volatility in freight rates, unexpected rises in the cost of fuels, amendments in safety and environmental regulations, and cyclical changes in the supply and demand for ships. The uncertainty associated with these factors underlines the importance of the ship management industry for the safe and efficient operation of vessels with the ultimate purpose of controlling costs, increasing competitiveness, and ensuring the viability of the sea transport industry. This key role assumed by ship management companies calls for an in-depth investigation of the determinants of ship management fees.

Apart from the operational costs associated with the technical, crew, and commercial management of vessels, the fees charged in the industry are also expected to vary with market forces. These market forces are, essentially, the formation of market power and the pricing tactics used by the companies operating in the industry. All these determinants are analyzed in the rest of the chapter and, in addition, several econometric methods are discussed which can be used for the empirical analysis of movements in ship management fees. First, a general panel data hedonic regression model is proposed to identify the factors that influence the level of fees charged by ship management companies. These factors include the technical characteristics of ships under consideration, the characteristics of ship management contracts, information on the associated ship owning companies, as well as some general market conditions such as the level of concentration in the industry.

Second, an empirical case study is presented using a log-linear hedonic regression model for crew management fees. The model was estimated using a cross-sectional dataset compiled from actual ship management contracts. In addition, several other econometric topics are discussed, such as the use of discreet choice models for the identification of switching costs and the use of market power models for evaluating the level of competition in the ship management industry.

The rest of the chapter is organized into 6 sections. Section 10.2 outlines the main categories of expenses incurred by ship management companies and Section 10.3 examines the efficiency gains associated with ship management operations. Section 10.4 concentrates on the market forces that influence the level of fees charged in the industry, such as the acquisition of market power by dominant firms, the influence of ship owners' switching costs, and geographic price discrimination. Section 10.5 discusses several econometric methods that can be employed to analyze the determinants of ship management fees, and Section 10.6 provides actual market results from the estimation of a model for crew management fees. Section 10.7 concludes with some recommended topics for future research.

10.2 Classification of ship management expenses

Ship management companies tend to be associated with three broad categories of expenses that vary depending on the type of ship management service provided: (a) crew (labour) expenses, (b) expenses related with technical ship management operations, and (c) financial and other administrative expenses. Accordingly, the ship management fee is defined as the total annual amount paid by a ship owner to an independent ship management company for the provision of crew and technical or commercial management services, which are the primary outsourced activities in vessel management (Cariou and Wolff, 2011). The fees are usually subject to annual reviews when ship management contracts are renewed and are frequently paid in instalments. Contracts with shorter duration (e.g. 6 months) are also possible. In addition to the aforementioned expenses and a profit margin, the fees are also influenced by several market forces that are examined in Section 10.4.

Given the international scope of ship management operations, the first two categories of expenses usually involve large amounts of cross-border transactions, which are recorded in the balance of payments (Haralambides, 1989) of the ship management company's country of registration. In particular, these expenses are recorded under the transport services sector of the current account as outflows (International Monetary Fund, 2009) and can exert considerable influence on the net current account balance of a country that is associated with a large shipping sector.

Labour expenses concern primarily crew earnings and other expenses related to the technical staff assigned on vessels such as training expenses, provident fund contributions, health insurance premiums, and medical expenses. Most commonly, ship management companies employ seafarers from various countries, therefore salary payments to crew staff employed on board are considered as imports of services and recorded as debits in the balance of payments. Together with the rising cost of fuels, crew wages constitute one of the main factors contributing to the rising cost of vessel operations in recent years.

Expenses related to technical ship management operations refer to all expenses incurred during the technical supervision, maintenance, and mechanical operation of the vessel. Typical expenses in this category include dry-docking, spare parts, lubricants, superintendents' expenses, repairs, and maintenance costs. Also included are expenses related to the licensing and compliance procedures required by international shipping regulations (e.g. the ISM code), operation and maintenance of electronic communication and documentation systems, flag registration expenses, and port expenses.

Financial and other administrative expenses include all expenses deemed as necessary for the operation of fully-fledged offices at various locations. These include business-related expenses such as auditing, legal, insurance and banking fees, as well as taxes, rents, IT expenses, and various other frequently recurring costs. Financial and administrative expenses consist mainly of transactions incurred in countries where ship management companies establish fully-fledged offices. They are considered as less important for balance of payments purposes, particularly in cases where a ship management company establishes its management and control in its country of registration.

10.3 Efficiency in ship management operations

Third-party ship management companies can provide significant economies of scale in ship operations and help ship owners reduce the operational cost of their vessels (Cariou and Wolff, 2011). This is most commonly achieved by concentrating on volume contracts with suppliers such as ship chandlers, fuel receiving (bunkering) stations, shipyards, and spare-parts suppliers. Additional economies of scale can be achieved through synchronization of the technical and commercial operations of vessels in full management contracts, which outsource all types of ship management services to the same provider. For example, Branch and Robarts (2014) emphasize that strategic decisions such as the choice of ports and shipyards for ship surveys, bunkering, and technical repairs should be integrated efficiently in the vessel's sailing programme to minimize costly disruptions.

Another example of the benefits associated with the synchronization of technical and commercial operations in full management contracts concerns the implementation of IT-based purchasing systems that provide ship owners with real-time updating of their accounting and logistics operations. This is important for activities such as ordering, invoicing, delivery notification, and purchases of fuels and materials, since it can minimize costly delays in payment procedures and facilitate working capital management.

In crew management operations, efficiency can be achieved in crew scheduling and planning with the aid of modern software environments that provide optimization capabilities (Yuan, 2016). The main objective in these applications is to solve complex problems in crew scheduling under the constraint of cost minimization such as: the optimal number of professionals needed by area of expertise, the optimal crew composition on board, and the efficient allocation of hundreds of seafarers to dozens of ships. The range of applications also include the optimal allocation of the crew working, training, and resting hours in accordance with the guidelines of the Maritime Labour Convention 2006 (DNV GL – Maritime, 2015).

In technical management, the most important activities concern maintenance and repair scheduling. Some of these activities can be performed on board, however; the most important maintenance and repair operations are performed when the vessel is anchored at a harbour and frequently involve the use of a dockyard. Efficiency and optimization are important considerations in repair and maintenance scheduling and are nowadays performed with the aid of specialized software systems. The main objective in these applications is to optimally plan all necessary operations given the available resources. Mourtzis (2005) and Deris et al. (1999) provide examples of software applications for harbour-based repair and maintenance scheduling respectively. When scheduling for maintenance operations performed on board, the optimization problem is further complicated by two additional parameters: the number of seafarers employed on board and limitations concerning the available working hours. The primary objective in this case is to minimize both early and delayed maintenance (Yuan, 2016). Early maintenance increases crew workload and the total cost of spare parts, while delayed maintenance increases operational risk.

It is also worth noting the two kinds of contracts that are prevalent in ship management operations and their efficiency implications: lump-sum and cost-sum contracts. In cost-sum contracts, the ship management company has the right to claim all the expenses incurred during the completion of the operations specified in the ship management contract. In contrast, lump-sum contracts specify a fixed budget for the provision of the ship management service. The tasks and terms of service are thoroughly specified in the contracts and no additional costs can be imposed on the ship owner.

Lump-sum contracts are designed to promote efficiency and are frequently preferred by ship owners in technical management operations that may require the use of expensive materials, special equipment, and spare parts. In a recent study, Michis (2017) provided an average estimate of the difference between the levels of fees paid by ship owners who use lump-sum instead of cost-sum contracts. The estimate was based on econometric methods that control for other factors that may differentiate the level of fees specified in a contract such as the type, size, and age of a vessel. On average, lump-sum contracts were found to be associated with a 22.7% reduction in ship management fees when compared with cost-sum contracts, which suggests superior efficiency.

Lump-sum contracts are also used in other shipping services. For example, lump-sum charters represent fixed amounts paid for the use of a vessel (based on its carrying capacity), irrespective of the cargo or the quantity to be transported. Similarly, lump-sum freights represent fixed amounts paid to a ship owner for the availability of a specific amount of space and maximum weight on a vessel, irrespective of the composition of the cargo to be carried (Branch and Robarts, 2014).

10.4 Economic determinants of ship management fees

In addition to the main cost determinants outlined in Section 10.2, ship management fees are also influenced by several market forces such as the evolution of market structure and the pricing tactics used by the companies operating in the industry. In this section, three related topics are examined in detail using results from the industrial organization literature: the acquisition of market power by dominant firms, geographic price discrimination, and switching costs. In the analysis that follows, the above-mentioned topics will be examined in the context of imperfectly competitive market structures (such as oligopolies and monopolies) that can provide valuable insights regarding the level of fees charged in the ship management industry. Sanchez and Wilmsmeier (2011) emphasize that the application of industrial organization methods in transport markets can provide many useful insights regarding the influence of competition, expansion, and concentration in these markets.

Branch and Robarts (2014) provided a list of the five most important ship management companies in the world, which suggests an oligopolistic market structure (similar rankings were provided by Cariou and Wolff, 2011). The existence of concentration and market power in shipping markets is also supported by many academic studies. Sjostrom (1989) and Pirrong (1992) examined the determinants of cartels in shipping, while Clyde and Reitzes (1998), Marin and Sicotte (2003) and Hummels et al. (2009) found evidence of market power in liner shipping markets. Similarly,

Deltas et al. (2008) found evidence of cartel behaviour in passenger shipping and Morton (1997) and Podolny and Morton (1999) investigated the pricing behaviour of shipping cartels in Britain.

Market power refers to the ability of a business entity to set the price charged for a product or service above marginal cost (Cabral, 2000). The measurement of market power is of great importance in order to identify market phenomena such as monopolistic and oligopolistic pricing and the formation of cartels. Companies operating in industries with low levels of competition are generally expected to possess varying degrees of market power. In the next subsection, three indices are presented for investigating the existence of market power in the ship management industry in the context of the Structure-Conduct-Performance (S-C-P) and Relative Efficiency Hypothesis (REH) models in the industrial organization literature: the Lerner index, the m-company concentration ratio, and the Herfindahl–Hirschman index.

In addition, two methods from the New Empirical Industrial Organization (NEIO) literature are discussed that can be used for measuring market power in the ship management industry. NEIO methods have also been recommended by Sanchez and Wilmsmeier (2011) with the purpose of examining imperfect competition issues in liner shipping networks. Such issues can exist even in shipping markets with a large number of participants, as in the case of alliances that frequently involve pricing agreements. The NEIO methods are based on structural models that can be estimated with econometric methods using actual market data, to infer the level of competition in the ship management industry.

10.4.1 Market power

A standard method used for measuring market power is the Lerner index, which is based on the difference between price (p) and marginal cost (mc):

$$Lerner\ Index = \frac{p - mc}{p}$$

Large values of this index tend to be associated with the formation of market power and lack of competition. In empirical studies, the measurement of market power is frequently complicated by the limited availability of detailed cost and pricing data. Another complication that is particularly relevant for the shipping industry refers to the orientation of the boundaries of the market for a shipping-related service. Specifically, the geographical boundaries of the market in question and the set of products or services that can be considered as close substitutes and therefore constitute a separate market.

Early studies of industries with market power in the industrial organization literature employed indices of industry concentration such as the m-company concentration ratio (C_m) or the Herfindahl–Hirschman index (HHI) to identify changes in market structure and therefore the level of competition in a market. Both indices are constructed using the market shares (s_i) of the companies. For the m-company concentration ratio, market shares are first ranked in decreasing order of size, which is then followed by addition of the shares of the first m-companies: $C_m = \sum_{i=1}^{m} s_i$. Values of the m-company concentration ratio (e.g. C_3 or C_4) close to 1 suggest a highly concentrated market where market power is likely to exist.

The Herfindahl–Hirschman index is more comprehensive since information on all (N) companies in the market is required for its computation, through the addition of their squared market shares (s_i^2) as follows: $HHI = \sum_{i=1}^{N} s_i^2$. This index can also be expressed in percentage terms. Values close to 0 suggest a perfectly competitive market, while values above 1800 are indicative of a highly concentrated market. Sanchez and Wilmsmeier (2011) note that rising market concentration can be related with changes in market entrance and efficiency, which both influence the level of competition in the shipping industry. They also note that market concentration is likely to be associated with more severe effects in small shipping markets. Although informative, the C_m and HHI indices cannot be directly linked with market power estimates since several important factors are ignored from their computation, such as product differentiation and capacity constraints (Belleflamme and Peitz 2010).

In studies of industries with market power, these concentration indices can be interpreted in the context of the Structure-Conduct-Performance (S-C-P) and Relative Efficiency Hypothesis (REH) models in the industrial organization literature. The principal hypothesis underlying the S-C-P model (Cabral, 2000) is that rising market concentration (changes in structure) enables dominant firms with market power to set higher prices (conduct), thereby achieving higher profits (performance). Unlike competitive markets, inefficient companies are not forced out of the market and the model assumes in addition that these markets are characterized by barriers to entry. Sanchez and Wilmsmeier (2011) used the S-C-P model in the context of liner shipping networks and emphasize that, historically, the shipping industry has exhibited trends towards higher concentration in an effort to take advantage of the benefits associated with positive network effects and economies of density.

The REH model (Demsetz, 1973), considers markets where companies differ in terms of efficiency due to factors such as technological progress or management expertise. More efficient companies have the ability to set lower prices (due to lower cost of production) and therefore increase their market shares. Market concentration increases in this case too but, unlike in the S-C-P model, the direction of the price–concentration relationship is negative (Heffernan, 2005).

In the NEIO literature, the empirical measurement of market power is based on profit maximization principles and sophisticated econometric models. Market power is estimated endogenously, in the context of econometric models that are usually specified as systems of simultaneous equations which include detailed cost and demand factors. Two methods that have been used extensively in the NEIO literature and can be used for market power studies in the ship management industry are the conjectural variations and Panzar-Rose methods.

In conjectural variations models, the strategic interactions among firms are considered by evaluating partial derivatives of the following form: $\partial q_B / \partial q_A$ or $\partial p_B / \partial p_A$ (see Church and Ware, 2000). These partial derivatives quantify how competitive company B reacts to quantity (q_A) or price (p_A) change decisions by company A. The principal aim is to quantify the expectations (conjectures) a company has regarding the reactions of its rivals to price or quantity changes.

In markets with large numbers of companies ($i = 1,...,N$) it is possible to write the first order profit maximization condition for a company in terms of the Lerner index (see Belleflamme and Peitz, 2010), recognizing that in equilibrium $q_i = q / N$ and the conjectural variation parameter $\lambda = \partial q_{-i} / \partial q_i$ can be expressed with respect to the output of all competitors ($-i$) of company i. Monopolistic markets are associated with values of the conjectural variation parameter equal to one ($\lambda = 1$) and competitive markets with values equal to minus one ($\lambda = -1$). The Lerner index then equals the ratio of the market power index ($\theta = (1 + \lambda) / N$) to the price elasticity of demand (η). Consequently, estimation of the conjectural variation parameter enables the calculation of the Lerner index, which is very useful for evaluating imperfectly competitive market structures that lie between the extremes of monopoly and perfect competition.

$$Lerner\ Index = \frac{p - mc(q)}{p} = -\theta \cdot \frac{\partial p(q)}{\partial q} \cdot \frac{q}{p} = \frac{\theta}{\eta}$$

The Panzar-Rose (1987) method for measuring market power examines how changes in input prices affect the equilibrium revenues (R) of companies. In empirical studies, revenues are defined as functions of the prices of input factors ($w_1, ..., w_m$) such as crew wages and the prices of fuels, a vector of exogenous cost determinants (X) such as port and licensing expenses, and a vector of demand factors (Y). Inference regarding the level of competition in a market is achieved by estimating and summing the elasticities of revenues with respect to changes in each one of the input prices:

$$H = \sum_{i=1}^{m} \frac{\partial R(w_1, ..., w_m, X, Y)}{\partial w_i} \cdot \frac{\partial w_i}{\partial R}$$

Monopolies are expected to generate values of the index lower than zero ($H < 0$) since increases in input prices (marginal cost) will tend to reduce the revenues of the monopolist. Following a similar line of reasoning, perfectly competitive markets are expected to generate values equal to one ($H = 1$) since increases in input prices will tend to generate proportionate increases in revenues.

Sanchez and Wilmsmeier (2011) discuss the application of NEIO methods and the Herfindahl–Hirschman index in shipping in order to examine different hypotheses regarding the level of competition in shipping markets. The authors also provide several interesting observations concerning the South American container shipping market which suggest the possession of market power by dominant firms, such as the existence of mergers and acquisitions, conference agreements, and alliances.

10.4.2 Geographic price discrimination

The location where a product or service is purchased is frequently used as a price segmentation fence by companies (Schindler, 2012), which gives rise to geographic price discrimination. Such price differences between otherwise identical products are usually observed across countries or regions. Geographic price discrimination exists when the observed differences in prices cannot be attributed to cost differences but derive from differences in margins (Belleflamme and Peitz, 2010).

Geographic price discrimination has been documented for many products and industries such as, for example, textbooks (Cabolis et al., 2007) and cars (Goldberg and Verboven, 2001, 2004; Brenkers and Verboven, 2006). The empirical studies conducted for these markets support the assertion that the observed price differences across countries are primarily the result of differences in margins. A key difficulty encountered in empirical studies of geographic price discrimination concerns the lack of detailed data on production costs that are necessary in order to effectively decompose price differences into their profit margin, cost, and exchange rate components.

Ship management companies usually provide their services to many different ship owners across nations, which provides opportunities for the exercise of geographic price discrimination. The industry is also characterized by long-term customer relationships in the form of repeated short-term contracts, which enable companies to improve their knowledge of key client characteristics such as profitability, price sensitivity, local market conditions, and willingness to pay for specific types of ship management services. Knowledge of such client characteristics provides the opportunity for the exercise of geographic price discrimination, using characteristics such as the ship owner's country of origin as a price segmentation fence.

The industrial organization literature provides illuminating theoretical insights regarding the market structures that can be associated with the exercise of geographic price discrimination. To motivate the discussion, I first briefly present some key results for the monopoly case which are essential for understanding geographic price discrimination in the context of oligopolistic shipping markets. For a monopolist selling a product in N separate geographical areas, the optimal pricing strategy is to charge higher prices in areas with a lower elasticity of demand. This is a straightforward extension of the classic profit maximization condition for a monopolist: for any geographical area i, in equilibrium, the price mark-up is inversely related to the price elasticity of demand (η_i)

$$\frac{p_i - mc(q_i)}{p_i} = \frac{1}{\eta_i}.$$

Consequently, the monopolist will tend to charge higher prices in geographical areas with less price sensitive consumers that exhibit a higher willingness to pay for the monopolist's product. This result is valid provided that resale arbitrage (buying the product from a low-price market and selling it in a high-price market) is not possible or forbidden.

Shy (1995) considers the case when the provision of a product by a supplier is tied with the provision of a local service to the consumer (e.g. after sale maintenance). Under specific conditions, tying enables the monopolist to geographically segment the market and therefore to price discriminate with the purpose of increasing profits. In the case of two countries with homogeneous consumers, this strategy is profitable as long as the value of the local service to the consumers of each country is higher that their differences in product valuation.

When local markets are more closely related to oligopolistic structures, price discrimination might not be the most profitable pricing strategy. Belleflamme and Peitz (2010) consider an oligopoly model with two retailers, three independent markets (two monopolies and one market where the two retailers compete), and identical consumers with linear-quadratic utilities. The authors analyzed the pricing policies of the retailers in the context of a two-stage game as follows: in stage one retailers choose between local and uniform pricing (charging the same price in all markets) and in stage two they compete according to the pricing policies chosen in stage one.

The key insight derived from the solution of this model resembles the prisoners' dilemma. When companies hold monopoly positions in small local markets but face competition in large markets, price discrimination is not the most profitable strategy. Both retailers would be better off if they cooperated in setting a uniform price. However, they frequently consider their pricing policies in isolation and therefore choose to price discriminate in local markets.

Abandoning the monopoly price in the small local market initially reduces profits. However, increasing the price in the large contested market prompts a similar price reaction by the competitor, which raises profits for both retailers. When local markets are sufficiently small, the increase in profits achieved in the large common market is higher than the decrease in profits incurred from abandoning monopoly pricing in the small markets. Consequently, adopting a uniform pricing policy provides a credible way for increasing prices and reducing price competition (Belleflamme and Peitz, 2010).

To investigate the use of geographic price discrimination in ship management services, Michis (2017) examined a large number of ship management contracts collected by the Cyprus Shipping Chamber. The analysis was based on a two-stage procedure. First, a hedonic regression model was estimated to decompose the fees charged by the ship management companies into their main components. As will be explained in Section 10.5, these include the technical characteristics of ships, the characteristics of ship management contracts, as well as information on the associated ship owning companies (whose ships were managed by the ship managements companies) and markets under consideration.

This decomposition enabled the estimation of individual components for the ship owners' countries of origin that represent the "partial prices" (excluding all other characteristics in the hedonic model) charged by the ship management companies in each country. In a second stage, these country components were incorporated in a new econometric model to examine how the country specific "partial prices" vary with the GDP of the ship owner's country of origin (a proxy for income). The results suggest the exercise of geographic price discrimination since the ship management companies included in the sample were found to charge higher fees to ship owners based in high-GDP countries.

10.4.3 Switching costs

Switching costs arise when consumers are forced to incur learning, pecuniary, or psychological costs when changing a product or service provider. Such costs exist in a variety of forms in the economy. For example, Belleflamme and Peitz (2010) mention: contractual costs (e.g. discount coupons), compatibility costs (e.g. for complementary products), learning costs (e.g. operating a new software), uncertainty costs (e.g. adopting an unknown brand), psychological costs (e.g. quality and trust associated with a specific service provider), and transaction costs (e.g. loss of customer specific information).

Switching costs are frequently encountered in markets for "follow-on" products where contracts are individually negotiated, companies can distinguish between old and new customers, and short-term contracts are repeatedly renewed over long periods of time (Klemperer, 2008). These characteristics are also encountered in the ship management industry. Previous empirical studies in this field have investigated a variety of industries such as electricity supply (Waterson, 2003), television services (Shcherbakov, 2016), phone services (Shi et al., 2006), credit cards (Calem and Mester, 1995) and automobile insurance (Israel, 2005).

Klemperer (1995) first noted that in shipping, switching costs commonly exist in the form of "loyalty contracts". Shipping companies provide customers with discount coupons who in return commit to pay a "damage fee" in case they decide to terminate the contract and switch to another service provider. Loyalty contracts are also common in the ship management industry and constitute a form of endogenous switching cost created strategically by companies. The cumulative present value of these discount coupons is equal to the damage fee.

Chao and Chen (2015) provide examples of exogenous switching costs in shipping (not created by companies or as a result of consumer decisions). Nowadays, many ocean carriers invest in software systems that enable the transmission of data on the status and progress of shipments. These applications are highly valued by consumers of transportation services and tend to lower the probability of a customer switching to another carrier. Similar costs exist in the ship management industry through the installation of: (a) electronic performance monitoring systems that are important for cost efficiency evaluations and (b) software environments that generate the information that is deemed necessary for the creation of all the documents required by the ISM code and the vessel certification procedures. Frequently, custom-made systems are also developed (see Dickie, 2014), which further increases the difficulty of a competitive customer switch.

Another example of the formation of switching costs in the ship management industry concerns the integration of maintenance, procurement (purchasing) and quality-safety software systems (DNV GL – Maritime, 2015). When these software applications are assigned to the same vendor, important benefits can be achieved such as reductions in interfaces, faster processing of information, synchronization in software updates, and the compilation of more detailed databases. The installation of such integrated software systems tends to reduce the possibility of a competitive switch by a ship owning company. Furthermore, the assignment of dedicated teams consisting of senior technical officers and superintendents that work on the same fleet for many years promotes commitment, in-depth knowledge and expertise concerning the status and maintenance of specific groups of vessels (DNV GL – Maritime, 2015). These competencies are valued by ship owners and further reduce the possibility of a competitive switch.

In all these cases, repeat purchase from the same supplier is associated with a premium that consumers are expected to lose if they decide to switch to another product or service provider. When this premium is sufficiently high, consumers are locked-in and become more valuable to suppliers. For this reason, companies compete more aggressively *ex ante* for customer acquisition with the purpose of benefiting from customer inertia *ex post*. In effect, companies acquire market power and charge higher prices *ex post*. As a result, switching costs can lower consumer welfare and increase corporate profits.

These differences in *ex ante* and *ex post* pricing behaviour suggest a "bargain-then rip-off" (or "lo-hi") pricing pattern and it is not clear whether markets become more or less competitive due to the existence of switching costs. Several models have been proposed in the literature that are illuminating in this respect. A key insight of this research is that the effects of exogenous switching costs vary with market conditions and consumer preferences. In a monopoly context, switching costs do not exert any influence on average prices (Belleflamme and Peitz, 2010). In a two-period model, consumers receive a discount on the average price *ex ante* in order to lock-in, which the monopolist collects back *ex-post* by charging a higher price. However, of more interest for the ship management industry are models of imperfectly competitive markets.

Villas-Boas (2015) describes an insightful imperfect competition model that incorporates exogenous switching costs and consists of two periods and two companies.

The impact of switching costs on prices and competition was found to depend on the stability of consumers' preferences (degree of "lock-in") and the forward-looking characteristics of companies and consumers. In most cases a "bargain-then-rip-off" pricing pattern was involved where first period prices tended to be lower than second period prices. Therefore, the existence of switching costs in a market does not always imply the formation of market power. A slightly different version of this model is discussed by Klemperer (1987), while Villas-Boas (2006) confirmed the previous findings using an infinite horizon model with overlapping generations of consumers that live for two periods.

Discount coupons constitute a form of endogenous switching cost since they are strategically created by companies in order to facilitate consumer lock-in and they are frequently used in the shipping industry (Klemperer 1995). To understand the impact of endogenous switching costs on prices, Belleflamme and Peitz (2010) used the aforementioned two-period model (with some additional assumptions). The key insight provided by their analysis is that price competition declines when coupons exist and companies increase their profits. Even though second period prices are lower for loyal customers, both first and second period prices are higher when compared with the case when coupons do not exist.

More recent research in this field has examined the link between the existing market structure in a market and the competitive effects of switching costs. Fabra and Garcia (2015) distinguished between the long-term and short-term effects of switching costs. In the long-term, switching costs were found to always increase competition. In the short-term, switching costs relax competition in markets that are relatively concentrated but intensify competition in markets that are not concentrated. Similar findings were also reported by Cabral (2016). Switching costs reduce competition in markets that are *ex ante* less competitive but increase competition in markets that are *ex ante* more competitive. The empirical identification and measurement of switching costs is discussed in Section 10.5, including the results of an empirical study for the ship management industry that was based on information from actual ship management contracts.

10.5 Econometric modelling of ship management fees

Econometric models of the determinants of ship management fees can be developed using the hedonic regression methodology that is extensively used in applied microeconomics. Hedonic price models are based on the assumption that the utility derived from the consumption of a product or services is related with the technical and quality characteristics of the product (Lancaster, 1966). Building on this framework, Rosen (1974) proposed a profit and utility maximization model for the determination of hedonic price functions, where equilibrium prices were found to be functions of the implicit prices of the technical characteristics of the products.

Hedonic price functions are also influenced by the level of competition and the distribution of buyers and sellers in the market (Nesheim, 2008) and can be extended to include a price mark-up, over and above marginal cost, as in market power models (Pakes, 2003). In empirical economics, hedonic price functions are developed as regression models to decompose the observed prices of products or services into their technical and quality components and to attach consumer valuations to them. They are also used by national statistical agencies and organizations for the construction of price indices that can account for changes in the quality of products over time (Sopranzetti, 2015).

A panel data hedonic regression model for ship management fees ($FEES_{it}$), varying over contracts i and periods t, can be developed using the following broad categories of explanatory variables: (a) the technical characteristics of ships, (b) the characteristics of ship management contracts, and (c) information on the associated ship owning companies and markets under consideration. In an empirical study, Cariou and Wolff (2011) investigated the factors influencing a ship owner's decision to outsource vessel management. According to their findings, this decision is mainly influenced by the characteristics of the vessels as well as the characteristics of the ship owning company.

The first category of technical characteristics can include variables such as the age of the vessel specified in contract i in period t (AGE_{it}); the number of crew staff employed on board ($CREW\_SIZE_{it}$); the deadweight tonnage (DWT_{it}) and twenty-foot equivalent units (TEU_{it}) capacity of the vessel specified in contract i in period t ; as well as the country of flag registration ($FLAG_{mit}$) and type (l) of each vessel ($VESSEL_{lit}$) (container, tanker etc.).

The second category includes variables such as the type of ship management service ($SERVICE_{it}$) that is provided to the ship owner according to contract i in period t and the time interval (e.g. number of months) for which the services will be provided ($DURATION_{it}$). The third category of variables includes a market concentration measure such as the Herfindahl–Hirschman index ($HERFINDAHL_t$) that varies over time periods and is frequently used in pricing models (see for example Michis, 2016); indicator variables for each ship management company j ($FIRM_j$) included in the sample of contracts; a time trend regressor ($TIME_t$); and indicator variables for the countries associated with the beneficial owners of the vessels ($COUNTRY_k$). A linear regression model consisting of the aforementioned variables will have the following form:

$$FEES_{it} = a + \sum_{j=1}^{J} \delta_j . FIRM_{jit} + \sum_{k=1}^{K} \gamma_k . COUNTRY_{kit} + \beta_1 . AGE_{it}$$

$$+ \beta_2 . CREW\_SIZE_{it} + \beta_3 . DWT_{it} + \beta_4 . TEU_{it} + \beta_5 . DURATION_{it}$$

$$+ \beta_6 . TIME_t + \beta_7 HERFINDAHL_t + \sum_{m=1}^{M} \zeta_m . FLAG_{mit} + \sum_{l=1}^{L} \theta_l . VESSEL_{lit}$$

$$+ \sum_{r=1}^{R} \phi_r . SERVICE_{rit} + ERROR_{it}.$$

Hedonic regression models are most commonly formulated in log-linear or semi-log-linear format and estimated using ordinary least squares (OLS). The coefficients estimates provide valuable information concerning the influence (size and direction of the effect) of each variable on the level of ship management fees. The estimation results can also be used to construct a ship management price index with the purpose of tracking the period-by-period movements in the average level of ship management fees. Section 10.6 includes results from the estimation of a representative model for crew management fees.

The identification and measurement of switching costs is predominantly conducted using discreet choice models that are extensively used in the industrial organization literature (see for example Lee et al., 2006). Nearly all of the studies in this area proceed by comparing the choice probabilities of old versus new customers. Switching costs are said to exist when old customers choose previously bought products with higher probability than new customers. In addition, discreet choice models enable the estimation of partial prices for product attributes, which is useful for evaluating the product characteristics that are directly related to switching costs.

For example, Dubé et al. (2009) proposed a discreet choice model to investigate the impact of switching costs on choice probabilities and prices. It is based on the following utility index:

$$u_{it} = \delta_i + \beta\, p_{it} + \gamma\, I\big[s_t \neq i\big] + \varepsilon_{it}.$$

The utility derived by a consumer when choosing product i in period t is a function of the price of the product (p_{it}), a brand intercept (δ_i), and an indicator variable for changes in brand loyalty in period t $\big(I[.]\big)$. Consumers who were loyal to product i in period $t-1$ ($s_{t-1} = i$) will experience a reduction in their utility equal to γ if they decide to switch to product k ($s_t = k \neq i$) in period t $\big(I[s_t \neq i]\big)$. The utility index includes, in addition, a random utility element ε_{it}. In studies of consumer demand, it is also common to include in the modelling framework variables that represent product and consumer characteristics. The consumer's choice probability can be represented with the following logit model where loyalty to product i in period $t-1$ should be expected to increase the probability of choosing the same product again in period t

$$P_i\big(s_t, p_t\big) = \frac{\exp\big(\delta_i + \beta\, p_{it} + \gamma\, I[s_t \neq i]\big)}{\sum_{k=0}^{N} \exp\big(\delta_i + \beta\, p_{it} + \gamma\, I[s_t \neq i]\big)}.$$

Michis (2017) proposed a cross-sectional, semiparametric model for comparing the prices charged to old versus new customers in the ship management industry that was calibrated on actual data from ship management contracts. In addition to the hedonic characteristics presented above, the econometric model in this study included a variable reflecting the number of years a professional cooperation existed between the ship management and ship owning companies described in each contract. This variable was used to distinguish between old and new customers in the sample and was included in the model in non-parametric form to estimate the "fees charged – years of cooperation" relationship. The estimation procedure generated a positive, monotonic relationship that is consistent with the "lo-hi" pricing tactic described in Subsection 10.3, which suggests that the fees charged by the ship management companies tend to be higher for older ("locked-in") customers.

Other methods that have been proposed in the literature for a variety of industries proceed by estimating the cross-price consumption elasticities between subsequent periods (e.g. whether an increase in consumption in the previous period tends to be associated with an increase in consumption in the current period) or by directly estimating the impact on prices of product changes related with switching costs (Belleflamme and Peitz 2010).

10.6 Case study: determinants of crew management fees

In this section, an econometric model for crew management fees is estimated using data derived from actual crew management contracts. Crew expenses constitute a high-cost area in shipping, which is also associated with high training expenses in order to keep up to date with the technological improvements in naval technology, operations, and equipment (Alderton, 2004). The dataset was kindly provided by the Cyprus Shipping Chamber and consists of information from contracts that were active on 31 December 2011. Cyprus is one of the largest ship management centres in the European Union (Michis and Nason, 2017) and currently has the tenth largest ship registry in the world. Based on the information and variables included in the dataset, a hedonic regression model was developed to identify the determinants of crew management fees.

The dataset consists of 2212 cross sectional observations. Each observation refers to a separate crew management contract for the provision of services to a specific vessel. Several ship management companies are represented in the sample that includes information on all the vessels under their management on 31 December 2011. Since the dataset consists of only cross-sectional observations, the model presented in this section does not include variables that vary in time such as the Herfindahl–Hirschman index. Nevertheless, all the variables included in the model are compatible with the definitions provided in Section 10.5. Table 10.1 includes summary statistics of all the continuous variables included in the model.

The model includes in addition indicator variables for each ship management company represented in the sample, the countries associated with the ships' beneficial owners, the types

Table 10.1 Summary Statistics

Variable	Mean	Std Dev	Min	Max
FEES (€)	121,674.983	2,635.157	65,000	1,733,115.690
AGE	10.087	0.167	0.200	52.000
CREW_SIZE	12.146	0.222	0.000	200.000
DWT	24,188.013	686.194	0.000	684,563.000
TEU	1,192.306	56.755	0.000	71,634.000
DURATION	7.287	0.053	0.400	12.000

of vessels serviced, and their flag registrations specified in the contracts. It is worth noting that the average duration of crew management contracts is 7.287 months and the average number of seafarers ($CREW\_SIZE_i$) employed on board is 12.146. The zero minimum value of this variable refers to contracts that include crew services other than assigning crew staff on board (e.g. training). The average age of the vessels included in the sample is 10.087 years. Greenwood and Hanson (2015) emphasize that in the market for ships age and size are among the main factors that determine the value of ship capital.

$$\log(FEES_i) = a + \sum_{j=1}^{J} \delta_{ji}.FIRM_j + \sum_{k=1}^{K} \gamma_{ki}.COUNTRY_k + \beta_1.\log(AGE_i)$$

$$+ \beta_2.\log(CREW\_SIZE_i) + \beta_3.\log(DWT_i) + \beta_4.\log(TEU_i)$$

$$+ \beta_5.\log(DURATION_i) + \sum_{m=1}^{M} \zeta_m.FLAG_{mi}$$

$$+ \sum_{l=1}^{L} \theta_i.VESSEL_{li} + ERROR_i$$

The model was estimated using OLS and the coefficient estimates for the continuous variables are included in Table 10.2. The coefficients for the indicator variables (countries, flags, and types of ship management services) are not reported due to space limitations. The model has a good fit to the data as indicated by the high R-squared value and the F-test for the joint significance of all the coefficients. All the coefficients have the expected sign and are statistically significant at the 5% level.

The coefficient for the age variable suggests that newer vessels tend to be associated with higher crew management fees. This is mainly due to the increasing complexity and sophistication of navigations systems and equipment installed in modern vessels, which require crew staff with superior technical skills and training for their operation. On average, a 1% decrease in the age of a vessel increases crew management fees by 0.024%.

The coefficients for deadweight tonnage capacity (DWT) and twenty-foot equivalent units (TEU) are positive, which suggests that large vessels tend to be charged higher crew management fees. Similarly, the coefficient for the number of crew staff employed on board is positive.

Table 10.2 OLS Estimation Results

Coefficient	Estimates	Robust std errors	t test
Intercept	9.677	0.117	82.846
log (AGE)	−0.024	0.001	−58.702
log (CREW_SIZE)	0.555	0.002	240.985
log (DWT)	0.078	0.001	230.550
log (TEU)	0.043	0.001	617.816
log (DURATION)	0.979	0.016	62.536

R squared: 0.864
F-statistic: 161.2
Sample size: 2212 obs.

On average, a 1% increase in the number of seafarers employed on board increases crew management fees by 0.555%. The coefficient for the duration variable is also positive and suggests that a 1% increase in the period (months) of service provision increases fees by 0.979%.

10.7 Conclusions and topics for future research

Third-party ship management constitutes a dynamic and growing component of world transport that provides a key link between the efficient transportation of goods and passengers and the compliance of vessel operations with maritime and safety regulations. The growing importance of this industry calls for an in-depth investigation of the fees charged by the companies participating in the industry, which will help clarify several issues concerning the cost of modern maritime transport. It will also provide valuable insights in the process of regulating the industry and designing tax incentives and policies that will facilitate international trade. In this context, there are several research areas worth investigating regarding the pricing policies used in the industry.

The development of market power models for the ship management industry in the form of systems of equations that will include demand, price, and marginal cost specifications is a fruitful area for future research. The main difficulty encountered in these studies refers to the acquisition of detailed price and cost data at the company level and the correct orientation of the boundaries of the market. The shipping sector provides services globally and for this reason competition in the industry is by definition international. Monitoring and assessment of the level of competition in the various shipping markets will be feasible only with the development of detailed international databases.

Ship management companies most commonly provide their services to ship owners located in many different countries, which facilitates the exercise of geographic price discrimination. However, the ability to price discriminate using the country location as a price discrimination fence is frequently reduced when competition exists from local ship management companies. Geographic price discrimination is further complicated when local governments provide subsidies or other forms of government support (e.g. tax exemptions) to local producers (Schindler, 2012). A recent study by Kalouptsidi (2016) suggests that the impact of government subsidies in shipping is important. It would be interesting to perform similar investigations in the ship management industry with the purpose of understanding the impact of government subsidies on the exercise of price discrimination.

Future research can also investigate the different types of switching costs inherent in ship management operations and their varying implications for prices and profitability. Villas-Boas (2015) suggests three broad classifications for switching costs, which can differ considerably in terms of their market effects: (i) termination, (ii) search and evaluation, and (iii) adoption. Investigating each one of these sources and their manifestations in shipping will enhance our understanding of shipping markets and shed light on several related issues, such as the impact of uncertainty (e.g. regarding the size of termination costs), customer heterogeneity (e.g. differences in search and evaluation costs), and company size (e.g. new entrants, small in size, entail a higher cost of adoption for consumers) on prices.

To address these topics effectively, it would be necessary to explore new panel datasets with large samples of cross-sectional and time series observations, in conjunction with novel applications of econometric methods. Further, several exogenous factors are known to influence the dissemination of switching costs in a market such as changes in interest rates, the phase of the business cycle, and exchange rate movements (Klemperer, 2008). Since the shipping industry is strongly influenced by these factors (see Stopford, 2008 and Kalouptsidi, 2014), it would be interesting to investigate how they influence the adoption of switching cost strategies by ship management companies.

References

Alderton, P.M. (2004) *Reeds Sea Transport: Operation and Economics*, 5th edition, London: Adlard Coles Nautical.

Belleflamme, P. and Peitz, M. (2010) *Industrial Organization: Markets and Strategies*, NY: Cambridge University Press.

Branch, A.E. and Robarts, M. (2014) *Branch's Elements of Shipping*, 9th ed., Abingdon: Routledge.

Brenkers, R. and Verboven, F. (2006) "Liberalizing a distribution system: the European car market" *Journal of the European Economic Association*, 4, 216–251.

Cabolis, C., Clerides, S., Ioannou, I., and Senft, L. (2007) "A textbook example of international price discrimination" *Economics Letters*, 95, 91–95.

Cabral, L. (2016) "Dynamic pricing in customer markets with switching costs" *Review of Economic Dynamics*, 20, 43–62.

Cabral, L.M.B. (2000) *Introduction to Industrial Organization*, Cambridge, Massachusetts: MIT press.

Calem, P. and Mester, L. (1995) "Consumer behavior and the stickiness of credit-card interest rates" *American Economic Review*, 85, 1327–1336.

Cariou, P. and Wolff, F-C (2011) "Ship-owners' decisions to outsource vessel management" *Transport Reviews*, 31, 709–724.

Chao, S-L. and Chen, B-C. (2015) "Effects of switching costs on customer loyalty in the liner shipping industry" *Maritime Economics & Logistics*, 17, 341–358.

Church, J. and Ware, R. (2000) *Industrial Organisation: A Strategic Approach*, Boston: McGraw-Hill.

Clyde, P.S. and Reitzes, J.D. (1998) "Market power and collusion in the ocean shipping industry: is a bigger cartel a better cartel?" *Economic Inquiry*, 36, 292–304.

Deltas, G., Sicotte, R., and Tomczak, P. (2008) "Passenger shipping cartels and their effect on trans-atlantic migration" *Review of Economics and Statistics*, 90, 119–133.

Demsetz, H. (1973) "Industry structure, market rivalry and public policy" *Journal of Law and Economics*, 16, 1 –10.

Deris, S., Omatu, S., Ohta, H., Kutar, L.C.S., and Samat, P.A. (1999) "Ship maintenance scheduling by genetic algorithm and constraint-based reasoning" *European Journal of Operational Research*, 112(3):489–502.

Dickie, J.W. (2014) *Reeds 21st Century Ship Management*, London: Bloomsbury Publishing.

DNV GL – Maritime (2015) "Best practice ship management" DNV GL – Maritime, Global communications 02/2015, Print: ID 820479.

Dubé, J-P., Hitsch, J., and Rossi, P. (2009) "Do switching costs make markets less competitive?" *Journal of Marketing Research*, 46, 435 –445.

Fabra, N. and Garcia, A. (2015) "Market structure and the competitive effects of switching costs" *Economic Letters*, 126, 150–155.

Goldberg, P.K. and Verboven, F. (2001) "The Evolution of price dispersion in the European car market" *Review of Economic Studies*, 68, 811–848.

Goldberg, P.K. and Verboven, F. (2004) "Cross-country price dispersion in the Euro era: a case study of the European car market" *Economic Policy*, 40, 484–521.

Greenwood, R. and Hanson, S.G. (2015) "Waves in ship prices and investment" *Quarterly Journal of Economics*, 130, 55–109.

Haralambides, H.E. (1989) "Shipping transactions in the balance of payments statistics: a tabular approach" *Marine Policy Reports*, 1, 119–134.

Heffernan, S. (2005) *Modern Banking*, Chichester, UK: John Wiley and Sons Ltd.

Hummels, D., Lugovskyy, V., and Skiba, A. (2009) "The trade reducing effects of market power in international shipping" *Journal of Development Economics*, 89, 84–97.

International Monetary Fund (2009) *Balance of Payments and International Investment Position Manual*, International Monetary Fund publication services: Washington D.C.

Israel, M.A. (2005) "Tenure dependence in consumer–company relationships: An empirical analysis of consumer departures from automobile insurance companies" *RAND Journal of Economics*, 36, 165–192.

Kalouptsidi, M. (2014) "Time to build and fluctuations in bulk shipping" *American Economic Review*, 104, 564–608.

Kalouptsidi, M. (2016) "Detection and impact of industrial subsidies: The case of world shipbuilding" NBER Working Paper 20119.

Klemperer, P.D. (1987) "The competitiveness of markets with switching costs" *Rand Journal of Economics*, 18, 138–150.

Klemperer, P.D. (1995) "Competition when consumers have switching costs: an overview with applications to industrial organization, macroeconomics and international trade" *Review of Economic Studies*, 62, 515–539.

Klemperer, P.D. (2008) "Switching costs" in Durlauf, S.N., Blume, L.E. (eds.) *The New Palgrave: A Dictionary of Economics*, second ed., Basingstoke: Palgrave-Macmillan.

Lancaster, K. (1966) "A new approach to consumer theory" *Journal of Political Economy*, 74, 132–157.

Lee, J., Kim, Y., Lee J-D., and Park, Y. (2006) "Estimating the extent of potential competition in the Korean mobile telecommunications market: switching costs and number portability" *International Journal of Industrial Organization*, 24, 107–124.

Marin, P.L. and Sicotte, R. (2003) "Exclusive contracts and market power: evidence from ocean shipping" *Journal of Industrial Economics*, 51, 193–213.

Michis, A.A. (2016) "Market concentration and nonlinear pricing in European banking" *Journal of Economics and Business* 85, 1–12.

Michis, A.A. (2017) "Switching costs and geographic price discrimination in the ship management industry" Working Paper, Central Bank of Cyprus.

Michis, A.A. and Nason G.P. (2017) "Case study: Shipping trend estimation and prediction via multiscale variance stabilisation" *Journal of Applied Statistics*, 44, 2672–2684.

Mitroussi, K. (2004a) "The ship owners' stance on third party ship management: an empirical study" *Maritime Policy and Management*, 31, 31–45.

Mitroussi, K. (2004b) "The role of organisational characteristics of ship owning firms in the use of third party ship management" *Marine Policy*, 28, 325–333.

Morton, S.F. (1997) "Entry and predation: British shipping cartels, 1879–1929" *Journal of Economics and Management Strategy*, 6, 679–724.

Mourtzis, D. (2005) "An integrated system for managing ship repair operations" *International Journal of Computer Integrated Manufacturing*, 18, 721–733.

Nesheim, L. (2008) "Hedonic price functions", in S. N. Durlauf and L.E. Blume (eds.), *The New Palgrave Dictionary of Economics*, 2nd Edition, New York: Palgrave Macmillan.

Pakes A. (2003) "A reconsideration of hedonic price indexes with an application to PC's" *American Economic Review*, 93, 1578–1596.

Panayides, P.M. and Cullinane, K.P.B (2002) "The vertical disintegration of ship management: choice criteria for third party selection and evaluation" *Maritime Policy and Management*, 29, 45–64.

Panzar, J.C. and Rosse, J.N. (1987) "Testing for monopoly equilibrium" *Journal of Industrial Economics*, 35, 443–456.

Pirrong, S.C. (1992) "An application of core theory to the analysis of ocean shipping markets" *Journal of Law and Economics*, 35, 89–131.

Podolny, J. and Morton, S.F. (1999) "Social status, entry and predation: the case of British shipping cartels, 1879–1929" *Journal of Industrial Economics*, 47, 41–67.

Rosen, S. (1974) "Hedonic prices and implicit markets: product differentiation in pure competition" *Journal of Political Economy*, 82, 34–55.

Sanchez, R.J. and Wilmsmeier, G. (2011) "Liner shipping networks and market concentration" in K. Cullinane (eds.) *International Handbook of Maritime Economics*, Cheltenham, UK: Edward Elgar Publishing.

Schindler, R.M. (2012) *Pricing Strategies: A Marketing Approach*, Thousand Oaks, CA: Sage Publications.

Shcherbakov, O. (2016) "Measuring consumer switching costs in the television industry" *Rand Journal of Economics*, 47, 366–393.

Shi, M., Chiang, J., and Rhee, B. (2006) "Price competition with reduced consumer switching costs: The case of 'wireless number portability' in the cellular phone industry" *Management Science*, 52, 27–38.

Shy, O. (1995) *Industrial Organisation: Theory and Applications*, Cambridge, MA: MIT press.

Sjostrom, W. (1989) "Collusion in ocean shipping: a test of monopoly and empty core models" *Journal of Political Economy*, 97, 1160–79.

Sopranzetti, B.J. (2015) "Hedonic regression models" in C.-F. Lee and J. Lee (eds.), *Handbook of Financial Econometrics and Statistics*, NY: Springer.

Stopford, M. (2008) *Maritime Economics*, 3rd ed., Abingdon: Routledge.

Villas-Boas, J.M. (2015) "A short survey on switching costs and dynamic competition" *International Journal of Research in Marketing*, 32, 219–222.

Villas-Boas, J.M. (2006) "Dynamic competition with experience goods" *Journal of Economics and Management Strategy*, 15, 37–66.

Waterson, M. (2003) "The role of consumers in competition and competition policy" *International Journal of Industrial Organization*, 21, 129–150.

Yuan, Z. (2016) "A brief literature review on ship management in maritime transportation" Technical Report, TR\IRIDIA\2016-1, Université Libre de Bruxelles.

11

Corporate governance in the shipping industry

Konstantinos D. Melas

11.1 Introduction

Maritime business is as old as the need of humans to transport goods. However, shipping companies in the modern era of maritime transport are looking up to a corporatist approach in their spectrum of business. This is evident from the gradual changes in internal structures and management (Notteboom 2004), the strategies adopted, such as strategic alliances (Panayides and Widmer, 2011), mergers, and acquisitions (Alexandrou et al. 2014) as well as the new approaches to raising finance (Merikas et al. 2009) that have inevitably lead to greater attention on corporate governance in the shipping industry.

The governance of shipping enterprises faces various issues that may lead to problematic situations in the smooth operation of the entities. The most predominant factor that affects the industry is the high volatility of the companies' earnings, which derive from a highly cyclical freight rate market. These extreme deviations of earnings affect various aspects of the enterprise both financially and operationally. For example, the number of vessels in the market (Bakkehaug et al. 2014), the number of demolitions (Kagkarakis et al. 2016), or even the speed of the vessels (Lindstad et al. 2013). Additionally, =in a number of companies the concertation of the majority of shares between family members is evident. This gives raise to agency problems (Jensen and Meckling 1976) that need to be tackled. Thus, corporate governance mechanisms are a measure to enhance a holistically undisruptive business environment.

In the current chapter, light is shed on the corporate governance of maritime enterprises, given that their safeguarding systems aim both to enhance businesses with defenses against corporate frictions and to create teams which will invigorate the enterprises both operationally and financially in the context of international financial markets. Initially, a literature review of the relevant bibliography reveals the unique characteristics of the shipping industry as far as corporate practices and their outcomes are concerned. Moreover, the chapter discusses how corporate governance affects enterprises at large and why both academics and professionals have been active in the field trying both to grasp the conundrum of corporate boards and to create ameliorating policies. Finally, exploratory research is conducted to reveal the demographic profile of the corporate boards. The revealed trends of the last 15 years will provide the reader of the following chapter with an insight of the practices that maritime enterprises have been using in order to provide better mechanisms of governance that can safeguard the entities as a whole.

11.2 Corporate governance in the maritime sector

Corporate governance has been defined on various occasions both on an academic and on a policy basis (US Congress 2002). Nevertheless, the definition of Goergen and Renneboog (2008, p. 4) gives a thorough treatment of the topic: "*Corporate governance system is the combination of mechanisms which ensure that the management (the agent) runs the firm for the benefit of one or several stakeholders (principals). Such stakeholders may cover shareholders, creditors, suppliers, clients, employees, and other parties with whom the firm conducts its business*".

It goes without saying that apart from having a strict corporate perspective, each enterprise also serves as an active cell of the community. Thus, companies cannot act solely with the perspective of profit maximization, since their operations can create externalities that influence their environment. Since shipping is one of the few sectors whose businesses have global economic scope, these dimensions are various. From the rise of the internet technology, to the free trade agreements and to inter-modalism (Roe 2007), the shipping industry is currently affected by a spectrum of diversified factors. But the main problem is how a shipping enterprise can be managed officially under such a volatile and multifaceted environment.

After 2000, maritime enterprises have started to float in the global stock markets mainly as a means for raising equity finance due to monetary reasons (Kavussanos and Visvikis, 2016). The freight rate prices have risen to very high values and thus the acquisition of both new and second-hand vessels became capital intensive, as it can be observed in Figure 11.1. The booming environment and the infusion of money in the industry give rise to agencies' problems that are harmful for the whole spectrum of the stakeholders. Thus, corporate governance mechanisms have been established in order to avoid potential threats.

The literature on corporate governance of the maritime listed companies is still limited given the fruitful setting that the industry is providing. Both the inherent volatile environment of the industry and the nature of the sector's core assets create a multifaceted managerial environment that corporate governance should protect. Most of the studies have been focusing on the board of directors and how its demographic characteristics are correlated with the entities' performance measures. The only attempt so far to review the bibliography on corporate

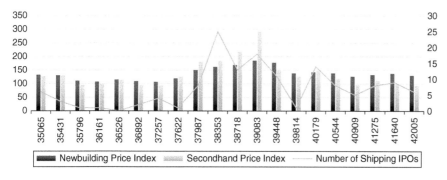

Figure 11.1   Newbuilt and secondhand price indices and number of shipping IPOs per year.

governance has been conducted by Giannakopoulou et al. (2016). Research by Andreou et al. (2014), Syriopoulos and Tsatsaronis (2012), Randøy et al. (2003), and Koufopoulos et al. (2010) represent the bulk of academic publications that focus on corporate governance in shipping (Figure 11.2).

Nevertheless, this research is still inconclusive on whether CEOs should have a predominant role in the enterprise by also serving as chairmen of the board of directors, and on the question of whether or not larger boards of directors are better in increasing the performance of a company. The most recent and thorough research on the matter has been conducted by Andreou et al. (2014), and focuses on a broader sample compared to previous ones. More precisely, this study uses data from the US stock markets for the period between 1999 and 2010, and the sample consists of 46 firms and 273 firm-year observations. Andreou et al. (2014) have found that the number of the board members matters. More precisely, their evidence shows that the larger the number of the board members of a shipping company, the lower the sub-optimal investments will be. In addition, in their research, they shed light on the duality of the CEO/chairperson. They show that the latter duality can in fact have a positive outcome on the financial performance of the shipping companies, while the percentage of ownership of the board also has a positive relation with financial performance. This means that maritime enterprises, more often than not, are managed by their founding members (or their extended family) and tend to perform better when compared to their counterparts. On the contrary, Syriopoulos and Tsatsaronis (2011) have found evidence that contradict the previous research. Nevertheless, it should be mentioned that their sample consists of 11 Nasdaq listed Greek maritime companies for the period from 2004 to 2008. While Andreou et al. (2014) show evidence that the higher the numerical composition of board members of the shipping company, the lower the sub-optimal investments will be, Syriopoulos and Tsatsaronis (2011) found that small boards can better serve the economic targets of a shipping company. Interestingly though, both researchers found that CEO duality is a favourable board characteristic, since it increases the company's performance. Randøy et al. (2003) has shown evidence that founding

Corporate Governance of Shipping Firms				
BoD Measure	**Investment**	**Performance**	**Profitability**	**Earnings Management**
Founding Family CEOs		+ (Randøy et al. 2003)		
Board Independence		~ (Syriopoulos & Tsatsaronis 2011)	+ (Randøy et al. 2003)	
Level of ownership by the board (plus officers & directors)		+ (Andreou et al. 2014) ~ (Syriopoulos & Tsatsaronis 2011)	~ (Randøy et al. 2003)	+ (Andreou et al. 2014)
Corporate Governance Committee		+ (Andreou et al. 2014)		
CEO Duality		+ (Andreou et al. 2014) – (Syriopoulos & Tsatsaronis 2012)		
Busy Directors		– (Andreou et al. 2014)		
Number of Directors	– (Andreou et al. 2014)			
Founding Family CEO		+ (Syriopoulos & Tsatsaronis 2011)		
+ :Positive Correlation, –: Negative Correlation, ~ : No Correlation				

Figure 11.2 Representation of the findings of the literature concerning different BoD measures and different financial performance indicators.

CEOs and a greater board independence can increase the profitability of a maritime company. However, contrary to Andreou et al. (2014), who find that insider ownership improves performance, Randøy et al. (2003) didn't find any significant relation. It is critical though to mention that the work of Randøy et al. (2003) focused on the Scandinavian market by examining 50 listed maritime enterprises with headquarters either in Norway or Sweden for the years from 1996 to 1998. The latter is a significant differentiation given the different legislation that was in place in the Nordic countries at the time. A more comprehensive analysis has been carried out by Koufopoulos et al. (2010). In their research, data was acquired through questionnaires that were answered by maritime executives who served in Greek listed companies. The research was conducted between 2006 and 2007 and 179 managing directors of maritime companies were asked to participate. The final response rate was 20.3%. Despite the targeted research group that Koufopoulos et al. (2010) used, their results are highly valuable for the bibliography in the maritime context given the gap that exists in survey results. In their research, the prominent role of the family members of the founder was revealed. Furthermore, the CEO/chairman duality is prominent in more than half of the examined companies. Also, for the majority of companies, the outside directors are a relatively small fraction of the board of directors. Furthermore, a critical point that has been raised for the first time in the maritime context is the frequency with which the board of directors convenes. Results show that most boards of directors (30,8% of the sample) have weekly meetings. As for the remaining boards of directors, the trend is towards meetings held every three months (23.1%) or every month (11.5%). For this reason, assumptions can be made on the close relation that directors have with the company's performance, its plans, and the market in general. Furthermore, it should be mentioned that a very large number of meetings will eventually prohibit outside directors to join the team given the considerable effort that should be made in this engagement, while the actual economic benefit that one could have for serving on a shipping corporate governance board has not yet been researched.

Last but not least, the novel work of Lambertides and Louca (2008) focuses on the ownership structure of the maritime enterprises and on how it affects their performance. Ownership concertation is an additional factor affecting enterprises. High-shares concertation with accompanying voting rights means that the majority of shareholders can act harmfully towards the rest of the shareholders according to the previously discussed agency problems. Lambertides and Louca (2008) focused on the European listed enterprises for the period covering 2002, 2003, and 2004, and they had a sample of 312 firm-year observations. However, what one can observe in their research is that the operating performance of the maritime entities is positively associated with foreign shareholders and with investment firms. That is to say, block holders that decide to invest in shipping companies chose entities that have stable operating function rather than companies that perform on a more gain maximization level.

Finally, recent research has tried to shed light into different aspects of the corporate governance conundrum and not solely focus on financial indicators. Lee and Han (2016), in their research on the containership enterprises for 2015, show evidence that while corporate governance does not directly affect the financial performance of entities, it does however affect their business scope. Additionally, Lee and Han (2016) provide survey results on the way the corporate governance of shipping companies can tackle problems that have arisen due to globalization.

11.3 Theoretical aspects of corporate governance

While corporate governance is a concept that applies to all enterprises, more often than not it is the board of directors of the publicly listed firms that comes under scrutiny. This is because, in their majority, privately held companies are managed by their shareholders. This is not to say of course that the latter combined role is of little importance, but given the significance that board of directors' decisions may have on the value of the shareholders' investments in monetary terms, it is reasonable that the socio-economic environment (policy-makers, professionals, and academics) be mainly concerned about the listed companies where the separation of ownership and management is more predominant.

The spectrum of the shareholders, the top management team, and the stakeholders of the companies create a dynamic environment where different individuals collaborate to create value for an enterprise in a multinational environment. Corporate governance can be examined both on the level of the relation between the management and shareholders and stakeholders and on a microlevel regarding examination of the management per se. The literature provides two different schools of thought regarding the relation between the management of the companies and the investors of the company. On the one hand, the stewardship theory considers the managers as stewards that act in the best interest of both the shareholders the value of the entity (Davis et al. 1997). On the other hand, agency theory suggests that the agents (i.e. managers) will primarily act in an individualistic manner, as they will try to benefit themselves, and thus the relation that exists between them and their principals (i.e. shareholders) is endogenously frictional (Jensen and Meckling 1976). Two different types of problems can arise as far as agency theory is concerned. "Problem I" is the state when agents try to make themselves better off by acting for their own benefit rather than for the benefit of their managers (i.e. shareholders). Subsequently, "Problem II" exists when shareholders who hold big blocks of shares try to expropriate benefits from minor shareholders (Villalonga and Amit 2006). Despite the significant research that has been conducted over the years, it is still not clear why some agents tend to have self-seeking behaviors while others do not. Nevertheless, the novel work of Wiseman and Gomez-Mejia (1998) on the behavioural aspects of the managerial process does give some insights on thisambiguity.

When it comes to the mechanisms through which the principals try to control the agents of the firm to avoid any malicious acts on their part, both internal and external functions should be in place. As it can be seen in Figure 11.3, actions can be taken both internally by the principals of the company, so they can be protected, but also externally. External mechanisms that are in place are policies that can be either attributed to government or to institution initiatives. On the contrary, the internal mechanisms are in place mostly due to the shareholders of the company.

A system that is universally accepted as a positive enhancement to the companies' control on the principal–agent frictional relationship is the board of directors that serves as a supervisory body in the operation of a given company. The board of directors, most of the times, consists of internal and external directors who oversee the operations of the company, periodically, to maximize the company's value. It goes without saying that the board of directors' function is not to account for all the daily operations of the company but, on the contrary, to make decisions for any critical issues. A critical issue that is thoroughly examined in the bibliography is the composition of the board of directors per se and its optimal structure that can lead the corporation to achieve a positive and sustainable performance. It is sound to believe that different corporations need different management approaches not only on their daily operations but furthermore on their overall strategy. Financial performance (Core et al., 1999), investment decisions (Billett et al. 2011), and earnings quality (Larcker et al., 2007) are all crucial factors that strongly affect the value of the company (whether positive or negative), and which are discussed and decided in the board of directors' meetings. Various aspects of the board's composition have been researched and the results give us an outline of the most suitable composition. More precisely, boards of directors that have a more pluralistic composition either demographically or on terms of human or social capital appear to drive their companies towards a more sustainable business environment (Johnson et al. 2013).

Figure 11.3 Graphic representation of the internal and external mechanisms that exist for the control and the safeguarding of companies' operations and performance.
Source: Giannakopoulou et al. (2016).

More precisely, recent research has been thorough on the effects demographic characteristic have on the businesses' entrepreneurial outcomes. Initially, the demographical diversification of the board (Erhardt et al. 2003) shows what can have a significant effect on the company's performance. More precisely, the boards of directors that combine people who come from different geographic positions can actually tackle problems of the enterprise from different contextual prisms and thus enhance the corporate value. Likewise, differentiations in cognitive skills of the BoDs members also enhance the dynamics of the team.

The size of the board is considered an important factor (Cheng, 2008) since there is a clear cost and benefit relation in the number of people who sit on the board. While more individuals mean more expertise, decisions take longer to be made. Thus, the literature suggests that high-growth enterprises are better off when they keep small boards of directors in order for decisions to be taken in a timely manner (Coles et al. 2008). On the contrary, enterprises that are not part of sectors which are experiencing high-growth opportunities are better off when they are composed of bigger boards of directors. It is crucial to mention here the distinctive position of the maritime industry in this subject. High levels of volatility are an endogenic part of the industry.

Additionally, the percentage of outside directors (Booth and Deli 1996) is researched thoroughly in the literature of corporate governance. Outside directors are considered to possess relevant experience and expertise, and serving on the board gives them a broader perspective on corporate issues. However, a critical concern that may arise is the degree of independence that these members have. A recent stream of the literature suggests that despite the fact that, from a legislative perspective, directors are considered independent, they tend to be overly sympathetic with the company's management (Cohen et al. 2012). It should also be mentioned that under certain national contexts, it can be the case that not all the criteria are met when independency is considered and thus listed companies may perform their obligations on the fringe of the law (Santella et al. 2006).

Coming to another part of major importance, the board of directors has a chairman that acts as the one responsible for the meetings. Various academics have reported on the outcomes when one single person is not only the chairman of the board but also the CEO of the company. The results are mainly inconclusive, since a stream of research states that the combination of the two roles has negative effects on the company's performance (Charitou and Louca 2013), while other scholars state the opposite (Rechner and Dalton 1991). Nevertheless, it is still not clear whether this inconclusiveness depends of endogeneity issues or issues related to agency problems vs. stewardship (Krause et al. 2014).

Last but not least, attention has been given lately to the mixture of genders in the BoDs. This is important not only in the context of equality, but also in relation to the optimum performance of the companies that invite more women on the boards. Research has provided evidence that women, under the corporate governance context, show less overconfidence characteristics, and thus their approach towards investments (M&As) is less aggressive/expansive (Terjesen et al. 2009).

11.4 Research results on the corporate governance of the maritime sector

As already discussed, the tendency in the last 15 years has been for shipping companies to be floated on the international markets. In this section, demographic data of the boards of directors of shipping companies listed in the global stock markets are presented starting from January 2000 until December 2015. In order to collect this data, all ship-owning enterprises that are listed (or had been listed floating) on the financial markets have been accounted for. In the current sample, the companies that have as a sole operation the transportation of goods by sea have been accounted for. That is to say, listed companies that are diversified in a bouquet of different sectors have not been included in the current sample. As a next step, Boardex Global has been used in order to retrieve all the available information that exists for the board of directors of the shipping companies. 106 ship-owning companies are included in the final database that has been used. The collected data are demographic characteristics of the board members.

As it can be seen in Figure 11.4, most of the companies in our sample have their headquarters in Greece. It should be mentioned that this is in high correlation with the fact that Greece is one of the countries with the highest tonnage owned as a percentage of the world fleet. This is one of the reasons why a significant number of research projects on the corporate governance of maritime enterprises focuses on Greek shipping companies (Syriopoulos and Tsatsaronis 2011; Harlaftis and Theotokas 2004). The second country of incorporation is Bermuda, and the third one is the United States of America. Bermudan and American companies are more likely to be listed in the US markets according to our findings. However, the Greek stock exchange market is not an option when new IPOs are considered.

In Figure 11.3, it can be observed that the US markets are the prime market where maritime enterprises are heading to float. Thus, it must be concluded that the distrust of the Greek ship-owners towards the financial institutions of their country is not only a recent event that precipitated after the 2008 financial crisis but has a long-lasting history. On the contrary, jurisdictions such as Norway and Hong Kong both host a considerable number of ship-owning companies and also provide them with financial markets that can be trusted (Figure 11.5).

Coming to the second critical aspect of the board's composition, the relevant information shows that there is a tendency, since 2010, for the members of the boards to be older compared

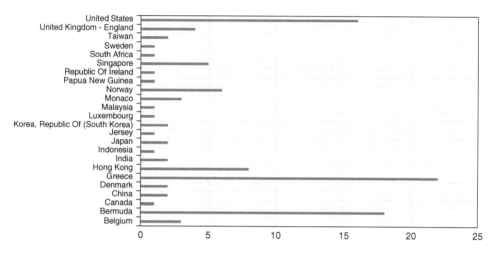

Figure 11.4 Number of companies per country.

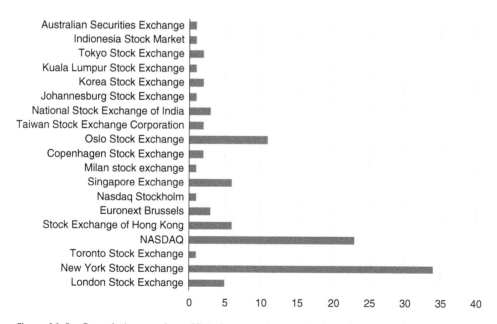

Figure 11.5 Cumulative number of listed companies per stock exchange market.

to their counterparts, especially before the crisis. More precisely, while in the pre-crisis period the average age was 56 years in 2015, the average age is now approximately 59 years. This shows the tendency of the industry to enhance the expertise and knowledge of board members, given the high volatility that freight rate markets are experiencing since the crisis, and not to provide the opportunities to younger people (Figure 11.6).

Moreover, there is a tendency towards a growing number of board members. While for a long period of time the average number of directors serving on the board was approximately seven, in the years after the crisis, on average, the board of directors has consisted of eight members. This fact leads us to two different conclusions. On the one hand, the companies' directors are more willing to serve on bigger boards in order to have more expertise. However, this is closely related to a slower pace as far as negotiations and conclusions on the business matters discussed are concerned. On the other hand, it can be the case that shareholders are pushing for more board members so as to alleviate any potential agency costs. There are various occasions where shipping companies are de-listed as fast as they have been listed, leaving their shareholders with big losses given the destruction of the company's value (Figure 11.7).

As far as the independence of the board is concerned, until 2004, companies' directors were reluctant to include independent members on the board. However, the increase in independent members has been stable ever since, and in the last years the independent members that serve on the board have accounted approximately for 60% of the board. However, the actual independence of the directors in the shipping companies has not been researched yet, thus promising a fruitful area given the social interlinks that people can have in an industry where special interest groups are predominant (Figure 11.8).

Another topic of major importance in the corporate governance literature is the separation of the roles of the chief executive officer and the chairman of the board. As it can be observed from Figure 11.9, in the initial phase of the period examined, it was the main practice of the companies not to combine the two roles. However, as the companies that decided to go public have increased, it can be observed that a considerable amount of them choose not to separate the

Figure 11.6 Average age of the board.

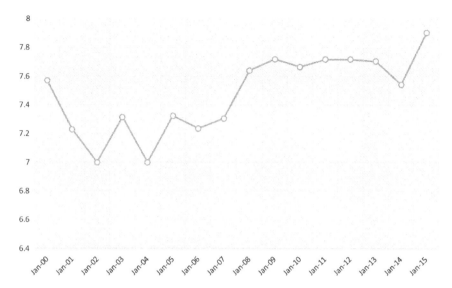

Figure 11.7 Average number of directors.

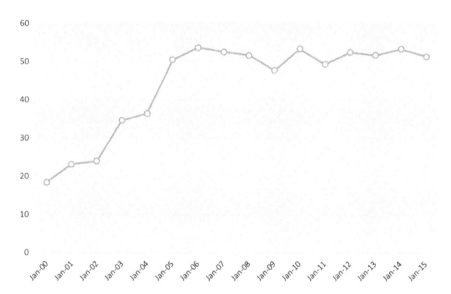

Figure 11.8 Average percentage of independent directors sitting in the board.

two roles. More precisely, in the last decade, the number has been about 40%. The latter increase in the CEO/chairman duality is evident due to the decision of highly closely held companies to list in the stock markets, especially after 2002. The research of Syriopoulos and Tsatsaronis (2011) shows that shipping family companies at that time were reluctant to relinquish all their power over the firms. Nevertheless, it was the case that, despite the latter, this duality was having a positive effect on the performance of the companies.

Konstantinos D. Melas

A major advance, however, in the composition of the boards is the steady increase in female members. Female board members consistently seem to add positive value to the boards that they are serving irrespective of the sector or the geographic area researched (Campbell and Minguez-Vera 2008; Rose and Rose 2007). Likewise, female board members have increased their representation in the shipping companies' boards. While in 2000 the females serving on the boards were around 4%, in 2015 the number is approximately 11% (Figure 11.10).

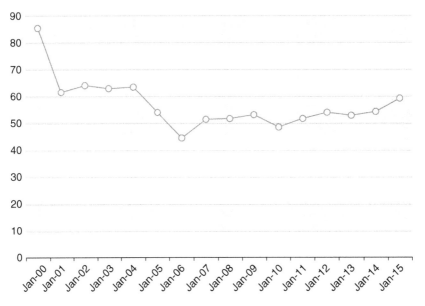

Figure 11.9 Percentage of companies that distinguish the roles of CEO & Chairman of the BoD.

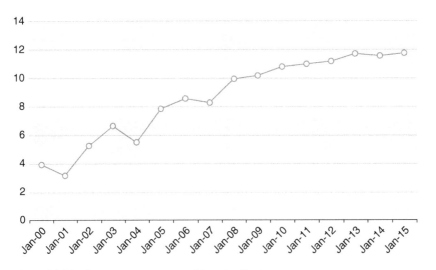

Figure 11.10 Average percentage of female directors.

11.5 Literature contribution

The corporate governance mechanisms for the good practice of the firms' management is of paramount importance given the recent economic scandals that have erupted in the financial world. As far as the maritime enterprises are concerned, the externalities of the industry (sea hazards, water pollution, trades disruptions) imposes demands on the management of the firms to keep high performance standards. Moreover, given the rising number of companies that are willing to float in the markets as well as the recent Hanjin Shipping bankruptcy filing in September 2016 (Guardian, 2016), the governance of maritime entities is and will further be under the public eye. The current chapter has developed a general framework of the corporate governance conundrum and how it can be applied to the shipping context. Moreover, apart from the theoretical aspect, evidence is shown of the current world practices regarding the matter. It should be mentioned that the data collected cover all the international stock markets and have a time span of 15 years, making the current research thorough.

11.6 Future agenda

From an academic perspective, the research has focused on the financial performance measures and their relationship with the corporate governance indicators, and more precisely with the board of directors' demographics and the ownership structure of the companies. When the internal measures of corporate governance are considered, it is fair to say that there has not been any research on the internal policies that companies themselves have in practice so as to protect their status quo. Furthermore, as far as external measures are concerned, apart from the paper of Alexandrou et al. (2014) that gives insight on the positive market reactions of mergers and acquisitions in the industry, academic research has not focused extensively on the legislative and regulative systems (on international or regional basis) and how they interact in the corporate governance concept. Given the numerous IPOs that have taken place, data on shipping companies are easier to be found either in databases or in published reports. Consequently, future research should focus on alternative decisions that intrinsically bear the opinion of the BoD, such as investment decisions, diversification, fleet mix, etc. Additionally, the close ties that exist between shipping professionals (Harlaftis and Theotokas 2007) should not be overlooked, as they can lead to agency problems due to the personal relationships that exist (Westphal 1999). However, a serious setback often encountered in maritime research is the lack of data, since most maritime enterprises are not listed in the stock markets. Consequently, maritime research is deluged with the implications of corporate governance for shareholders rather than the broader audience of stakeholders.

11.7 Conclusion

The shipping sector has changed dramatically through the past years. Due to changes in the trade context, the management of maritime companies could not have remained the same. Corporate boards are now in place and have the obligation to protect and add value not only to the investment of the shareholders but also to that of the stakeholders of the company, given the severe externalities that the industry can have (Lan et al. 2014). Thus, shipping companies that have joined the stock markets or are thinking of joining them should consider how their boards will be constructed to create a dynamic team that can cope with a highly volatile economic environment. As it has already been discussed, the first wave of the shipping companies that have been listed maintained a pool of numerous investors, which subsequently led to a market-led approach to the creation of the board of directors. As the markets started to become more willing to invest in the sector, the second wave of IPOs that took place was of previously tightly held (family-owned) companies that decided to raise funds in the markets. While one would believe that the family companies would be reluctant to evolve and modernize their operations to business professional standards, this was not the case. The statistical tables show a high increase in the independent directors who were hired to add value to board. Furthermore, the total number of directors and the number of non-executive directors has been increasing especially after the 2008 financial crisis. Summing up, this chapter provides both the theoretical framework and the statistical data concerning the evolution of corporate governance in the shipping sector. Future opportunities, thus, are arising on further research regarding the role of the governance mechanisms and their effectiveness on the entrepreneurial management.

Bibliography

Alexandrou, G., Gounopoulos, D. & Thomas, H.M., 2014. Mergers and acquisitions in shipping. *Transportation Research Part E: Logistics and Transportation Review*, 61, 212–234. Available at: http://lin kinghub.elsevier.com/retrieve/pii/S1366554513001919 [Accessed 17 June 2014].

Andreou, P.C., Louca, C., & Panayides, P.M., 2014. Corporate governance, financial management decisions and firm performance: Evidence from the maritime industry. *Transportation Research Part E: Logistics and Transportation Review*, 63, 59–78.

Bakkehaug, R. et al., 2014. A stochastic programming formulation for strategic fleet renewal in shipping. *Transportation Research Part E: Logistics and Transportation Review*, 72, 60–76. Available at: http://dx.doi. org/10.1016/j.tre.2014.09.010.

Billett, M.T., Garfinkel, J. A., Jiang, Y., 2011. The influence of governance on investment: Evidence from a hazard model. *Journal of Financial Economics*, 102(3), 643–670. Available at: http://dx.doi.org/10.1016/ j.jfineco.2011.07.004.

Booth, J.R. & Deli, D.N., 1996. Factors affecting the number of outside directorships held by CEOs. *Journal of Financial Economics*, 40(1), 81–104.

Campbell, K. & Minguez-Vera, A., 2008. Gender diversity in the boardroom and firm financial performance. *Journal of Business Ethics*, 83(3), 435–451.

Charitou, A. & Louca, C., 2013. *Corporate Governance, Agency Problems, and Firm Performance: Empirical Evidence from an Emerging European Market*, Available at: https://papers.ssrn.com/sol3/papers.cfm?abstract_id= 2221612.

Cheng, S., 2008. Board size and the variability of corporate performance. *Journal of Financial Economics*, 87(1), 157–176.

Cohen, L., Frazzini, A., & Malloy, C.J., 2012. Hiring cheerleaders: board appointments of "independent" directors. *Management Science*, 58(6), 1039–1058.

Coles, J.L., Daniel, N.D., & Naveen, L., 2008. Boards: Does one size fit all? *Journal of Financial Economics*, 87(2), 329–356.

Core, J.E., Holthausen, R.W., & Larcker, D.F., 1999. Corporate governance, chief executive officer compensation, and firm performance. *Journal of Financial Economics*, 51, 371–406.

Davis, J.H., Schoorman, F.D., & Donaldson, L., 1997. Toward a stewardship theory of management. *Academy of Management Review*, 22(1), 20–47.

Erhardt, N.L., Werbel, J.D., & Shrader, C.B., 2003. Board of director diversity and firm financial performance. *Corporate Governance*, 11(2), 102–111.

Giannakopoulou, E.N., Thalassinos, E.I., & Stamatopoulos, T.V., 2016. Corporate governance in shipping: an overview. *Maritime Policy & Management*, 43(1), 19–38. Available at: http://dx.doi.org/10.1080/0308 8839.2015.1009185.

Goergen, M. & Renneboog, L., 2008. Corporate governance and shareholder value. In D. Lowe, ed. *Commercial Management of Projects: Defining the Discipline*, Oxford: Blackwell Publishing Ltd., p. 464.

Guardian, 2016. Hanjin Shipping bankruptcy causes turmoil in global sea freight. *Guardian*. Available at: https://www.theguardian.com/business/2016/sep/02/hanjin-shipping-bankruptcy-causes-turmoil-in-global-sea-freight.

Harlaftis, G. & Theotokas, G., 2007. *Greek shipowners and shipping companies – Organization, management and strategy*, Athens: Alexandria Publications.

Harlaftis, G. & Theotokas, J., 2004. European family firms in international business: British and Greek tramp-shipping firms. *Business History*, 46(2), 219–255. Available at: http://www.tandfonline.com/doi/abs/10.1080/0007679042000215115 [Accessed 12 June 2014].

Jensen, M.C. & Meckling, W.H., 1976. Theory of the firm: managerial behavior, agency costs and ownership structure. *Journal of Financial Economics*, 3(4), 305–360.

Johnson, S.G., Schnatterly, K. & Hill, A.D., 2013. Board composition beyond independence social capital, human capital, and demographics. *Journal of Management*, 39(1), 232–262. Available at: http://jom.sagepub.com/content/39/1/232%5Cnhttp://jom.sagepub.com/content/39/1/232.abstract%5Cnhttp://jom.sagepub.com/content/39/1/232.full.pdf%5Cnhttp://0-jom.sagepub.com.alpha2.latrobe.edu.au/content/39/1/232%5Cnhttp://0-jom.sagepub.com.alpha2.latrobe.e.

Kagkarakis, N.D., Merikas, A.G., & Merika, A., 2016. Modelling and forecasting the demolition market in shipping. *Maritime Policy and Management*, 43(8), 1021–1035. Available at: http://dx.doi.org/10.1080/03088839.2016.1185181.

Kavussanos, M.G. & Visvikis, I.D., 2016. *The International Handbook of Shipping Finance, Theory and Practice* 1st ed., Palgrave Macmillan.

Koufopoulos, D.N. et al., 2010. Corporate governance and board practices by Greek shipping management companies. *Corporate Governance*, 10(3), 261–278.

Krause, R., Semadeni, M., & Cannella, A.A., 2014. CEO duality: A review and research agenda. *Journal of Management*, 40(1), 256–286. Available at: http://jom.sagepub.com/cgi/doi/10.1177/0149206313503013.

Lambertides, N. & Louca, C., 2008. Ownership structure and operating performance: evidence from the European maritime industry. *Maritime Policy & Management*, 35(4), 395–409. Available at: http://dx.doi.org/10.1080/03088830802198308.

Lan, D. et al., 2014. Marine oil spill risk mapping for accidental pollution and its application in a coastal city. *Marine Pollution Bulletin*, 96(1–2), 220–225. Available at: http://dx.doi.org/10.1016/j.marpolbul.2015.05.023.

Larcker, D.F., Richardson, S. A., & Tuna, I., 2007. Corporate governance, accounting outcomes, and organizational performance. *Accounting Review*, 82(4), 963–1008.

Lee, T.T.H. & Han, J.K., 2016. Global carriers' governance and business scope. *Asian Journal of Shipping and Logistics*, 32(3), 173–178. Available at: http://dx.doi.org/10.1016/j.ajsl.2016.09.006.

Lindstad, H., Asbjornslett, B.E., & Jullumstro, E., 2013. Assessment of profit, cost and emissions by varying speed as a function of sea conditions and freight market. *Transportation Research Part D: Transport and Environment*, 19, 5–12. Available at: http://dx.doi.org/10.1016/j.trd.2012.11.001.

Merikas, A., Gounopoulos, D., & Nounis, C., 2009. Global shipping IPOs performance. *Maritime Policy & Management*, 36(6), 481–505.

Notteboom, T.E., 2004. Container shipping and Ports: An overview. *Review of Network Economics*, 3(2), 86–106.

Panayides, P.M. & Wiedmer, R., 2001. Strategic alliances in container liner shipping. *Research in Transportation Economies*, 32(1), 25–38.

Randøy, T., Down, J., & Jenssen, J., 2003. Corporate governance and board effectiveness in maritime firms. *Maritime Economics & Logistics*, (5), 40–54.

Rechner, P.L. & Dalton, D.R., 1991. CEO duality and organizational performance: A longitudinal analysis. *Strategic Management Journal*, 12(2), 155–160.

Roe, M., 2007. Shipping, policy and multi-level governance. *Maritime Economics & Logistics*, 9(1), 84–103. Available at: http://link.springer.com/10.1057/palgrave.mel.9100173.

Rose, C. & Rose, C., 2007. Does female board representation influence firm performance? The Danish evidence. *Corporate Governance*, 15(2), 404–413.

Santella, P., Paone, G., & Drago, C., 2006. How independent are independent directors? The case of Italy, pp.1–37. Available at: http://papers.ssrn.com/sol3/Papers.cfm?abstract_id=839204.

Syriopoulos, T. & Tsatsaronis, M., 2011. The corporate governance model of the shipping firms: financial performance implications. *Maritime Policy & Management*, 38(6), 585–604.

Syriopoulos, T. & Tsatsaronis, M., 2012. Corporate governance mechanisms and financial performance: Ceo duality in shipping firms. *Eurasian Business Review*, 2(1), 1–30.

Terjesen, S., Sealy, R., & Singh, V., 2009. Women directors on corporate boards: A review and research agenda. *Corporate Governance: An International Review*, 17(3), 320–337.

US Congress, 2002. *The Sarbanes–Oxley Act of 2002*, U.S. Government Printing Office. Available at: http://www.gpo.gov/fdsys/pkg/PLAW-107publ204/content-detail.html%5Cnhttp://www.gpo.gov/fdsys/granule/STATUTE-116/STATUTE-116-Pg745/content-detail.html.

Villalonga, B. & Amit, R., 2006. How do family ownership, control and management affect firm value? *Journal of Financial Economics*, 80(2), 385–417.

Westphal, J.D., 1999. Collaboration in the boardroom: Behavioral and performance consequences of Ceo-board social ties. *Academy of Management Journal*, 42(1), 7–24.

Wiseman, R.M. & Gomez-Mejia, L.R., 1998. A behavioral agency model of managerial risk taking. *Academy of Management Review*, 23(1), 133–153.

12

The ownership structure of US listed shipping companies

Dimitris A. Tsouknidis

12.1 Introduction

Transportation by sea is the leading mode of transportation worldwide, carrying over 90% of the global trade in volume terms (United Nations Conference on Trade and Development [UNCTAD], 2018). The large bulk of sea transportation globally is facilitated by the US listed shipping companies[1,2]. Traditionally, public shipping companies exhibit a large concentration of ownership as specific individuals, families or holding companies hold large percentages of the total shares out held. Thus, it is very common for the owner to be also the CEO of the company.[3] However, institutional investors also hold a substantial percentage of ownership for the US listed shipping companies following the general trend of higher institutional ownership percentages for US listed firms (Schmidt and Fahlenbrach, 2017). Several large institutional investors build portfolios including listed shipping firms, as the great majority of the latter have adopted modern corporate structures which enable them to access the capital markets as a source of finance with favourable terms (Kavussanos and Tsouknidis, 2014; 2016). Despite the unique ownership structure of shipping companies and the importance of transportation by sea to the global economy and the international trade, little is known regarding the ownership structure of US listed shipping companies.

A unique feature of the commercial ocean-going shipping industry is its capital-intensive nature, as investment to a single newbuilding vessel can often require over $100 million, depending on ship type and size (Stopford, 2009). Even second-hand vessels command values of several million dollars, rendering the shipping industry one of the most capital demanding. Naturally, such amounts of capital are difficult to be raised by shipowners and shipping entrepreneurs. On this basis, shipping companies have turned to a range of potential sources of finance in order to raise the required capital for pursuing shipping projects. Historically, shipping bank loans have been the most popular source of capital for the shipping industry (Kavussanos and Tsouknidis, 2016). However, as shipping companies evolve from family businesses to modern corporations, other forms of finance have emerged as strong alternatives for raising the necessary capital for shipping projects. These include shipping bonds (Kavussanos and Tsouknidis, 2014) and initial public offerings (IPOs) (Syriopoulos, 2007)[4]

The proliferation of capital markets as a source of funds for ship finance has also brought about a number of challenges in the business of shipping, not least the implications that may arise due to the separation of ownership and management. Such issues have been examined and explained by agency theory (Jensen and Meckling, 1976) which also highlighted the conflicts of interest that may arise between controlling and non-controlling shareholders (Bebchuk and Weisbach, 2010). Both capital markets and ship-lending financial institutions have strong incentives to examine the ways in which shipping companies mitigate issues related to agency theory. The latter suggests that shareholders may alleviate agency problems by instilling corporate governance mechanisms (Jensen and Meckling, 1976).

Existing theories and empirical evidence suggest a direct link between the control-ownership structure and the firm's ability to raise external debt finance (Anderson et al., 2003; Crane et al., 2016; McConnell and Servaes, 1995). Specifically, agency theory is manifested when large shareholders pursue their own interests, such as, for example, when transferring assets and profits out of firms – sometimes in the form of dividends – or when they commit capital to non-profitable investments that provide private benefits. These practices are associated with high financial distress costs and likelihood of bankruptcy. Anderson et al. (2003) provide empirical evidence suggesting that concentrated ownership is associated with higher cost of capital for US listed companies. Since creditors assess these risks when granting a credit facility, a higher likelihood of negative outcomes results into higher financial costs. This increases the agency problem faced by the creditors and results into higher cost of debt financing. Among others, Lin et al. (2011) provide empirical evidence suggesting that concentrated ownership is associated with higher cost of capital for US listed companies.

It is evident from the theory on general management and corporate governance issues that ownership structure and subsequently the concentration of ownership form central issues for all companies worldwide. These issues become even more important in the shipping industry as it exhibits unique characteristics [5]such as its capital-intensive nature, its inherent uncertainty, and the excess volatility observed in freight rates and ship prices. These characteristics exacerbate agency problems and increase the likelihood for the management to engage into, for example, harmful earnings management practices. Given the importance of the shipping industry for the global trade the, ownership structure of shipping companies is an issue of paramount importance for several shipping market players. For these reasons, this study provides a comprehensive analysis of the ownership structure of US listed shipping companies and calculates for the first time in the shipping management literature the Herfindahl index to provide an accurate and consistent measurement of the concentration of ownership across shipping companies.

The contributions of this study to the literature are discussed below. This is the first study analyzing in such detail the ownership structure of US listed shipping companies. This is enabled through access to publicly available data regarding consolidated ownership percentages collected through the mandatory disclosure Forms of 13F, 13A/DG, and 20F under SEC's regulation for US listed shipping companies. These data have not been presented or discussed before in the literature. Moreover, this study reveals that US listed shipping companies exhibit high concentration of ownership, as the largest shareholder holds an average ownership percentage equal to 23.70%. In addition, the main investor types being the largest shareholders of US listed shipping companies are shown to be: insider investors, holding companies, corporations, private equity, and other individual investors. This study also utilizes for the first time in the shipping literature the Herfindahl index to measure concentration of ownership in US listed shipping companies and reveals the dominant effect of the largest shareholder percentage of ownership on this index. This is achieved by comparing the Herfindahl index for the ten largest shareholders with the same index but excluding the largest shareholder.

The rest of this chapter is organized as follows: Section 12.2 reviews the related literature and builds the theoretical background regarding the importance of the ownership structure for shipping firms; Section 12.3 describes briefly the data and outlines the methodology adopted in this chapter; Section 12.4 presents in detail the empirical results; Section 12.5 discusses the main findings and compares these with the prior literature on the issue, and Section 12.6 concludes the chapter.

12.2 Literature review and theoretical background

The literature devoted to the ownership structure of shipping companies is relatively thin. Prior studies have revealed that shipping companies follow a family business model, and consequently, business decisions and control of the company are concentrated on one individual and/or a few members of the founding family (Harlaftis and Theotokas, 2004). This can be attributed to the fact that shipowners seek immediate control over business decisions through bypassing the complex and time-consuming procedures of modern corporations, such as, for example, adopting a strict corporate governance model.

One step further, a number of studies focus on the interaction between ownership structure and firm performance in the shipping industry. There are two primary mechanisms through which concentrated ownership may affect the management and financial performance of a shipping company. First, concentrated ownership might provide better control to a few individuals or a holding company, but at the same time increases the cost of capital the company faces. This is because a creditor may be more reluctant against the management abilities of a single individual, e.g. due to overconfidence. Second, dispersed ownership as opposed to concentrated ownership might lead to better financial performance as the business decisions are better discussed and planned among a group of individuals and/or companies (board of directors), who in turn face alternative pressures from multiple owners.

12.2.1 The interaction of the ownership structure and firm performance in the shipping industry

As discussed earlier in this chapter, only a few studies have been devoted to the interaction of the ownership structure and firm performance in the shipping industry. Specifically, Andreou et al. (2014) examine the relationship between corporate governance performance and firm performance, utilizing data from COMPUSTAT and Boardex for a US listed sample varying from 26 to 32 shipping firms according to data availability, over the period 1999–2010. The authors report significant positive associations between corporate governance mechanisms – one out of the three dimensions of environmental, social, and corporate governance performance – and firm performance. Evidence presented supports that the shipping industry differs from the general corporate framework regarding the effect of corporate governance on firm performance and financial management decisions[6].

In another study, Lambertides and Louca (2008) examined the relationship of ownership structure and operating performance, utilizing 92 listed shipping firms in European stock exchanges, over the period 2002–2004. The authors provide evidence of a significant positive impact of the percentage of shares held by foreign shareholders on operating performance. They attribute this to foreign shareholders' greater efficiency on facilitating corporate governance and monitor management. In a related study, Syriopoulos and Tsatsaronis (2011) examine the impact of CEO duality – where the same person is the manager and the chairman of the board of directors – on firm performance, by utilizing a sample of 11 Greek shipping firms listed on NYSE and NASDAQ stock exchanges, over the period 2004–2008. They reveal weak evidence of a negative association between the two.

Finally, Tsionas et al. (2012) examine the cross-sectional relationship, for the year 2009 only, between concentrated ownership and firm performance for a sample of 107 globally listed firms. The authors find a positive relationship between concentration of ownership and firm performance in the shipping industry, which they attribute to the increased control of management over a shipping company having a few large shareholders. As no prior study has examined systematically the historical evolution of the ownership structure of US listed shipping companies to date, this study fills this gap in the literature by exploring and discussing in detail the ownership structure of the world's largest shipping companies which are primarily listed in the US stock exchanges of NYSE and NASDAQ.

12.3 Data and methodology

The data examined in this study comprise quarterly ownership data for the US listed shipping companies over the period 2002 Q1 to 2016 Q3, consisting of a total of 59 quarters. The sources of information which have been cross-matched to identify the list of cargo-carrying ocean shipping companies include: Datastream, Bloomberg, Lloyd's List, Marine Money, and Clarkson's Research. In total, 43 shipping companies listed in NYSE and NASDAQ stock exchanges are identified. Shipping firms are those with business activities in deep-sea foreign transportation of freight, classified into several categories such as dry bulk, tankers, container, general cargo, offshore, and vehicle carrier. In order for a shipping company to be included in the sample examined, the majority (over 50%) of its income should be earned from shipping transportation activities. Table 12.1 reports the list of shipping companies examined in this study along with their stock trading tickers, the stock exchange they are listed in, the shipping sector they operate in, and their market capitalization as of 2016 Q3. These companies exhibit an aggregate market value of $23.58 billion as of 2016 Q3, which renders them largely representative of the global shipping industry. After filtering the data for missing values, the final sample contains 1,909 firm-quarter observations.

Consolidated ownership data including percentages of shares out held and the detailed characteristics for the 50 largest shareholders of each US listed shipping company are obtained through Thomson Reuters Eikon. However, all data examined are originally disclosed in multiple mandatory forms as per Stock Exchange Committee's (SEC's) regulations. Specifically, the dominant original source of data is the mandatory Form 13F[7], which applies to all listed firms in NYSE/NASDAQ stock exchanges. Form 13F is filled in on a quarterly basis by "institutional investment managers" and contains all equity assets under management of at least $100 million in value. In this way, Form 13F provides position-level disclosure of all institutional investment managers with more than $100 million in assets under management with relevant long US holdings.

Apart from Form 13F, Schedule 13D is another SEC filing that must be submitted to the US Securities and Exchange Commission within ten days, by anyone who acquires beneficial ownership of more than 5% of any class of publicly traded securities in a public company. A filer must promptly update the Schedule 13D filing to reflect any material change in the facts disclosed, including, among other things, the acquisition or disposition of 1% or more of the class of securities that are the subject of the filing. In turn, Schedule 13G is an alternative SEC filing for the 13D which must be filed by anyone who acquires ownership in a public company of more than 5% of the outstanding stock. The 13G filing is considered a more passive version of the 13D since it includes fewer reporting requirements[8]. Finally, Form 20F is another SEC filing submitted to the US Securities and Exchange Commission used by certain foreign private issuers to provide information.

Table 12.1 List of US Listed Shipping Companies

Number	Name	Ticker	Stock exchange	Sector	Market capitalization (as of 2016 Q3)
1	AEGEAN MARINE PETROLM NETWK	ANW	New York Stock Exchange	Tanker	500.3685
2	Alexander & Baldwin Inc	ALEX	New York Stock Exchange	Dry bulk	1883.339
3	XOB SHIPS INC	TEU	New York Stock Exchange	Container	0.67186
4	COSTAMARE INC	CMRE	New York Stock Exchange	Container	689.1414
5	DANAOS CORP	DAC	New York Stock Exchange	Container	294.2151
6	DHT HOLDINGS INC	DHT	New York Stock Exchange	Tanker	391.2038
7	DIANA CONTAINERSHIPS INC	DCIX	NASDAQ	Container	30.79859
8	DIANA SHIPPING INC	DSX	New York Stock Exchange	Dry bulk	221.9036
9	DryShips Inc	DRYS	NASDAQ	Multi-sector	7.100009
10	EAGLE BULK SHIPPING INC	EGLE	NASDAQ	Dry bulk	340.3323
11	EUROSEAS LTD	ESEA	NASDAQ	Multi-sector	16.47348
12	FREESEAS INC	FREE	NASDAQ	Dry bulk	0.0069647
13	GASLOG LTD	GLOG	New York Stock Exchange	Gas	1172.05
14	GENCO SHIPPING & TRADING	GNK	New York Stock Exchange	Dry bulk	33.68338
15	GENCORP INC	GY	New York Stock Exchange	Multi-sector	1223.568
16	GLOBAL SHIP LEASE INC	GSL	New York Stock Exchange	Container	91.25524
17	GLOBUS MARITIME LTD	GLBS	NASDAQ	Dry bulk	7.495911
18	GOLAR LNG LTD	GLNG	NASDAQ	Gas	1973.72
19	Golden Ocean Group Ltd	GLF	New York Stock Exchange	Dry bulk	45.08494
20	GULFMARK OFFSHORE INC	GOG	New York Stock Exchange	Tanker	429.0782
21	HORNBECK OFFSHORE SVCS INC	HOS	New York Stock Exchange	Multi-sector	199.8521
22	INTL SHIPHOLDING CORP	ISH	New York Stock Exchange	Multi-sector	0.5175384
23	KIRBY CORP	KEX	New York Stock Exchange	Barge	3347.689
24	MATSON INC	MATX	New York Stock Exchange	Container	1708.478
25	MC SHIPPING	MCX	New York Stock Exchange	Gas	85.953598
26	NAVIOS MARITIME ACQUISITION	NNA	New York Stock Exchange	Tanker	203.557
27	NAVIOS MARITIME HOLDINGS INC	NM	New York Stock Exchange	Dry bulk	132.517
28	NEWLEAD HOLDINGS LTD	NEWL	NASDAQ	Multi-sector	0.0017866
29	NORDIC AMERICAN TANKERS LTD	NAT	New York Stock Exchange	Tanker	901.63
30	PARAGON SHIPPING INC	PRGN	NASDAQ	Dry bulk	0.1980659
31	QUINTANA MARITIME LTD	QMAR	NASDAQ	Dry bulk	1324.3629
32	SAFE BULKERS INC	SB	New York Stock Exchange	Dry bulk	117.7038

(Continued)

Table 12.1 Continued

Number	Name	Ticker	Stock exchange	Sector	Market capitalization (as of 2016 Q3)
33	SEACOR HOLDINGS INC	CKH	New York Stock Exchange	Multi-sector	1030.413
34	SEANERGY MARITIME HLDGS CORP	SHIP	NASDAQ	Dry bulk	63.94573
35	SEASPAN CORP	SSW	New York Stock Exchange	Container	1408.277
36	SHIP FINANCE INTL LTD	SFL	New York Stock Exchange	Multi-sector	1377.322
37	Star Bulk Carriers Corp	SBLK	NASDAQ	Dry bulk	254.5617
38	STEALTHGAS INC	GASS	NASDAQ	Gas	140.5963
39	STELMAR SHIPPING LTD	SJH	New York Stock Exchange	Tanker	825.6543
40	TEEKAY CORP	TK	New York Stock Exchange	Tanker	560.517
41	TIDEWATER INC	TDW	New York Stock Exchange	Tanker	132.7313
42	TOP SHIPS INC	TOPS	NASDAQ	Tanker	16.18214
43	TSAKOS ENERGY NAVIGATION LTD	TNP	New York Stock Exchange	Tanker	405.6251

12.3.1 Measurement of concentrated ownership

The Herfindahl-Hirschman index (HHI) is used as a measure of concentration of ownership by several studies in the literature (Demsetz and Lehn, 1985; Hou et al., 2016). The Herfindahl index is calculated as the sum of the squared ownership shares of the ten largest shareholders for each shipping company examined in this study. The higher the value of the Herfindahl index, the more concentrated the ownership of the company. Specifically, the Herfindahl index is calculated to measure the ownership concentration (H) of stock i for quarter q. The calculation involves the percentage share (w) of each owner j that is present in each shipping stock:

$$H_{i,q} = \sum_{j=1}^{J} w_{i,q,j}^2 \qquad (12.1)$$

In addition, the $Hex1_{i,q}$ variable is computed as the sum of the percentage of shares owned by the ten largest shareholders but excluding the largest one (Demsetz and Villalonga, 2001; Omran, 2009). This measure is used as an alternative ownership concentration measure to highlight the importance of the largest shareholder when measuring the concentration of ownership in the shipping industry. The cross-sectional average values of $H_{i,q}$ and $Hex1_{i,q}$ are also computed as *hhi* and *hhi_ex*1, respectively.

12.4 Results

The results of this study reveal several important features of the ownership structure of US listed shipping companies. In particular, Table 12.2 presents the descriptive statistics for the percentage of shares out held (PSOH) for each one the ten largest shareholders; while the last column of Table 12.2 presents the descriptive statistics for the summation of the percentage of shares out held for the 50 largest shareholders (SPSOH 1–50). As observed, the average percentage of ownership for the largest shareholder is equal to 23.70%, followed by 8.62% for the second, and

Table 12.2 Descriptive Statistics for the Percentage of Shares Out Held (PSOH) by Ranking of Owner and the Summation of the Percentage of Shares Out Held (SPSOH 1-50) for the 50 Largest Owners

Statistic	PSOH1	PSOH2	PSOH3	PSOH4	PSOH5	PSOH6	PSOH7	PSOH8	PSOH9	PSOH10	SPSOH 1-50
Mean	23.70	8.62	5.66	4.08	3.21	2.63	2.24	1.92	1.65	1.45	62.96
Median	14.85	7.55	5.49	3.96	3.00	2.47	2.02	1.75	1.49	1.28	70.65
Standard deviation	19.55	5.36	3.00	2.17	1.90	1.65	1.48	1.31	1.12	0.97	27.45
Minimum	1.3	0.82	0.35	0.24	0.16	0.15	0.11	0.08	0.05	0.07	10.7
Maximum	80.09	25.73	13.95	9.21	7.76	6.57	5.68	5.08	4.29	3.57	96.38
Skewness	1.11	1.35	0.597	0.31	0.41	0.47	0.51	0.56	0.51	0.45	−0.66
Kurtosis	3.41	4.92	3.32	2.46	2.41	2.41	2.39	2.45	2.32	2.15	2.21
JB p-value	[0.000]	[0.000]	[0.000]	[0.000]	[0.000]	[0.000]	[0.000]	[0.000]	[0.000]	[0.000]	[0.000]

Notes: This table shows the descriptive statistics for the percentage of ownership for the first ten largest owners. Mean, median minimum, and maximum are the arithmetic average, the 50th percentile, the minimum, and the maximum monthly observations of the sample data, respectively. Skewness and kurtosis are the estimated centralized third and fourth moments of the data. JB is the Jarque and Bera (1980) test for normality; the statistic is $\chi^2(2)$ distributed. Sample period 2002–2016.

5.66% for the third largest shareholder. Smaller shareholders exhibit average percentages lower than 5%. Median values are close to the aforementioned mean values – 14.85%, 7.55%, and 5.49% for the first, second, and third shareholder, respectively – indicating the limited existence of outliers. The standard deviations of the average ownership percentages follow a similar pattern as they are equal to 19.55%, 5.36%, and 3.00% for the first, second, and third largest shareholders, respectively. The ownership percentage for the largest shareholder ranges from 1.3% to 80.09%; these values correspond to the companies exhibiting the highest dispersion and highest concentration of ownership, respectively. The range of ownership percentage for the smaller shareholders is significantly smaller, as it takes values between 0.82%–25.73% and 0.35%–13.95% for the second and third largest shareholders, respectively. The aggregate ownership percentage for the 50 largest shareholders exhibits a mean value equal to 62.96% and a standard deviation of 27.45%. This result shows that the aggregate ownership percentage of the 50 largest shareholders exhibits large dispersion across the shipping companies examined in this study. The p-values for the Jarque and Bera (1980) test reject the null hypothesis of normality for the ownership percentages at the 5% significance level and across all rankings of shareholders. In most cases, this can be attributed to excess skewness of the data and not so much to excess kurtosis.

Table 12.3 reports the frequencies for the different sources of ownership data for the first ten largest shareholders (Owner1–Owner10). There are in total 13 different filing types from where the ownership percentages originate. Overall, the large majority of ownership data across the ten largest shareholders comes from Forms 13F, 20F, 13G, and 13D; while very few of these data come from the rest of the sources listed in Table 12.3. As observed, the vast majority of the data examined in this study across the ten largest shareholders come from Form 13F, which is filled in on a quarterly basis by "institutional investment managers" and contains all equity assets under management of at least $100 million in value. Specifically, Form 13F is the source for 37.91%, 62.13%, and 74.60% of the total ownership data for the first, second, and third largest shareholders, respectively. The same values for Form 20F are 23.26%, 12.94%, and 7.13%, respectively; while for Form 13D 17.63%, 6.58%, and 3.79%, respectively.

It is important to note that Form 13F exhibits an increasing frequency as a source of ownership data as the ranking of shareholder decreases in terms of the magnitude of percentage ownership, i.e. from Owner1 to Owner10. This can be attributed to the fact that Form 13F discloses ownership percentages of institutional investors. This result reveals that institutional investors are unlikely to be the largest shareholders of shipping companies. This can be attributed to the rather concentrated and family-oriented ownership of shipping companies. However, as observed in Table 12.3, institutional ownership is quite common for the lower-ranked shareholders in terms of ownership percentages. The exact opposite pattern holds for Forms 13D/G, which list all the persons owning more than 5% of a specific equity entity. In particular, these forms exhibit a high percentage as a source for ownership data for the first shareholder – Form 13D: 17.63% and Form 13G: 14.01% – rather than for the rest of the shareholders. This result reveals that in several cases specific individuals or subsidies entities control a large percentage of the ownership of shipping companies. The same pattern applies for Form 20F which lists the ownership percentages of foreign private investors.

In turn, Table 12.4 shows the average percentage of ownership per type of investor for the ten largest shareholders (Owner1–Owner10). The last column of Table 12.4 presents the average percentage of ownership per type of investor and across the first ten largest shareholders to enable aggregate comparisons across the different types of investors in shipping companies. As observed, the average percentage of ownership for the largest shareholder (Owner1) is equal to 46.47% for the investor type *other insider investor*, i.e. the individual investor who holds the vast majority of shares of the company. The same statistic is equal to 39.91% for *holding company*,

Table 12.3 Frequencies of Sources of Ownership Data – Filing Types

Frequencies	Owner1	Owner2	Owner3	Owner4	Owner5	Owner6	Owner7	Owner8	Owner9	Owner10
10K	0.52%	0.39%	0.39%	0.50%	0.51%	0.45%	0.73%	0.45%	0.57%	0.74%
13D	17.63%	6.58%	3.79%	3.35%	1.12%	0.73%	1.02%	0.57%	0.34%	0.57%
13F	37.91%	62.13%	74.60%	82.01%	84.29%	84.20%	82.19%	85.73%	87.26%	86.19%
13G	14.01%	11.54%	8.52%	3.58%	2.75%	1.97%	1.98%	1.25%	0.80%	0.45%
20F	23.26%	12.94%	7.13%	5.81%	5.44%	5.45%	5.43%	4.30%	4.21%	5.06%
Aggregate MFs	0.69%	2.57%	2.51%	2.68%	3.20%	3.15%	3.67%	3.45%	3.13%	2.96%
Insider Update	2.01%	1.56%	1.06%	0.67%	1.07%	1.85%	2.32%	1.81%	1.59%	1.36%
Prospectus	0.06%	0.06%	0.00%	0.06%	0.11%	0.06%	0.00%	0.06%	0.00%	0.00%
Proxy	2.41%	1.73%	1.45%	1.17%	0.73%	1.41%	1.75%	1.87%	1.59%	2.16%
Registration Statement	0.00%	0.28%	0.11%	0.00%	0.00%	0.06%	0.17%	0.06%	0.11%	0.06%
Regulatory News Service	0.40%	0.17%	0.17%	0.11%	0.17%	0.17%	0.28%	0.28%	0.06%	0.17%
Shareholder Report	0.17%	0.00%	0.00%	0.00%	0.00%	0.00%	0.00%	0.00%	0.00%	0.00%
Trade Report	0.92%	0.06%	0.28%	0.50%	0.56%	0.34%	0.34	0.17%	0.34%	0.28%
Sum	100.00%	100.00%	100.00%	100.00%	100.00%	100.00%	100.00%	100.00%	100.00%	100.00%

Notes: This table shows the frequencies for each source used to collect data on the consolidated ownership percentages.

Table 12.4 Average Percentage of Ownership per Type of Investor and Ranking of Ownership Percentage

Mean percentage of ownership	Owner 1	Owner 2	Owner 3	Owner 4	Owner 5	Owner 6	Owner 7	Owner 8	Owner 9	Owner 10	Average Owner 1 to 10 (ignoring zeros)
Bank and Trust	7.98%	8.4%	4.91%	4.86%	1.21%	3.65%	0.98%	1.47%	1.66%	2.06%	3.72%
Corporation	36.58%	11.41%	7.69%	5.68%	4.73%	4.21%	3.77%	4.17%	3.32%	2.42%	8.40%
Hedge Fund	11.42%	7.72%	5.77%	4.07%	2.95%	2.42%	1.84%	1.65%	1.96%	1.99%	4.18%
Holding Company	39.91%	8.71%	6.87%	1.79%	0.00%	1.79%	0.00%	0.00%	0.00%	0.00%	11.81%
Individual Investor	21.91%	13.71%	7.26%	3.65%	3.10%	2.39%	2.23%	2.11%	1.73%	1.85%	5.99%
Insurance Company	0.00%	3.42%	3.39%	1.8%	3.44%	1.51%	0.82%	0.00%	0.08%	0.84%	1.91%
Investment Advisor	7.82%	7.07%	5.28%	4.20%	3.35%	2.83%	2.44%	2.07%	2.03%	1.97%	3.91%
Investment Advisor/ Hedge Fund	11.71%	6.98%	5.23%	3.90%	3.19%	2.79%	2.37%	2.02%	2.04%	2.09%	4.23%
Other Insider Investor	46.47%	0.00%	0.00%	0.00%	0.00%	0.00%	0.00%	0.00%	0.00%	0.00%	46.47%
Pension Fund	2.58%	3.67%	2.05%	2.24%	1.81%	0.82%	1.14%	1.01%	1.38%	1.23%	1.79%
Private Equity	23.03%	18.24%	4.65%	4.45%	3.19%	1.61%	2.81%	1.82%	2.53%	0.00%	6.93%
Research Firm	13.84	3.59%	3.25%	2.05%	1.93%	1.41%	1.33%	1.21%	0.66%	1.24%	3.05%
Sovereign Wealth Fund	0.00%	0.00%	0.00%	0.82%	0.71%	1.11%	0.99%	0.68%	0.77%	1.07%	0.88%
Venture Capital	0.00%	0.00%	10.04%	0.00%	0.00%	0.00%	4.51%	0.00%	4.17%	4.11%	5.71%

Notes: This table shows the average percentage of ownership per ranking of ownership percentage (Owner 1, Owner 2, etc.) and per type of investor (bank and trust, corporation, etc.). The last column shows the average ownership across all ten largest owners for each type of investor.

i.e. usually a subsidiary of the founding person (or family) of the shipping company; while it is 36.58% for *corporation*, i.e. another public or private entity. These three types of investors are the largest shareholders for the vast majority of the US listed shipping companies. Furthermore, the average percentages of ownership are equal to 23.03% and 21.91% for *private equity* investors and *individual investors*, respectively. The aforementioned average percentages of ownership per type of investor are several times lower for the second largest shareholder (Owner2). This result highlights the existence of largely concentrated ownership in US listed shipping firms. The ranking among different types of investors in terms of the average percentages of ownership is preserved in the last column of Table 12.4, which shows the average percentages of ownership per type of investor across all ten largest shareholders; that is, the ranking is still: other insider investor, holding company, corporation, private equity and individual investor.

Regarding the historical evolution of the ownership percentages for listed shipping firms, Figure 12.1 depicts the cross-sectional average for the total percentage ownership of the 50 largest shareholders together (AvgOwn_mean). In addition, Figure 12.1 depicts the median value (AvgOwn_median) along with the 25th percentile (AvgOwn_p25) and the 75th percentile (AvgOwn_p75) values. As observed, the mean and median values are close with one another and fluctuate within the 60–80% range over the sample period examined. The median aggregate percentage ownership for the 50 largest shareholders increases notably from less or close to 60% to almost 80% during the period 2002–2007. This period coincides with a notable increase in freight rates and ship prices for the shipping industry. By contrast, the median value remains close to 60% during the period 2007–2012 to increase again almost to 80% over the period 2012–2016. The interquartile range – the difference between p75 and p25 – is around 80% at the start of the sample period (2002–2005) examined, but narrows down to around 25% during

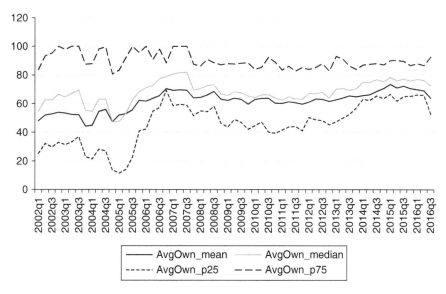

Figure 12.1 The historical evolution of the average percentage of ownership for the combined holding of the 50 largest owners of US listed shipping firms.

Notes: This figure depicts the historical evolution of the average percentage of ownership for the combined holdings of the 50 largest shareholders of US listed shipping companies. AvgOwn_mean, AvgOwn_median, AvgOwn_p25, and AvgOwn_p75 correspond to the mean, median, 25th percentile, and 75th percentile values for the average percentage of ownership of the 50 largest shareholders, respectively.

Dimitris A. Tsouknidis

the end of the sample period (2014–2016). Overall, Figure 12.1 documents the existence of a large concentration of ownership for the US listed shipping companies when the aggregate ownership of the 50 largest shareholders is examined.

The information provided in Figure 12.1 provides some indication for the concentration of ownership in listed shipping firms but it is not indicative regarding the degree of concentrated ownership in the first few shareholders in terms of ownership held. In order to provide some further insight in this direction, Figure 12.2 depicts the average Herfindahl concentration index over time for the ten largest shareholders (*hhi*) and the same index when the largest shareholder is excluded (*hhi_ex1*). As observed, throughout the whole period examined, the difference between the two Herfindahl indices is large. This result documents the dominant effect of the largest shareholder on the concentration of ownership for US listed shipping companies. In addition, *hhi* increases substantially over the period 2002–2007 and remains at these levels with some significant fluctuations during the period 2008–2016. In contrast, hhi_ex1 exhibits lower values and fluctuations over the whole time period examined. This result reveals that, for US listed shipping companies, fluctuations in measures of concentrated ownership are primarily driven by the changes of ownership for the largest shareholder rather than the rest of the shareholders.

Overall, these results indicate that the average ownership structure of the largest shareholder is high and equal to 23.70%. Further analysis of the data examined in this study also reveals the large concentration of ownership to one individual – insider investor – or a corporate entity – holding company or other corporation – in the shipping industry. Private equity investors and individual investors also maintain relatively large percentages of ownership in US shipping listed companies. In addition, this study provides novel statistics regarding the ownership percentages of the 50 largest shareholders of US listed shipping companies and their evolution over time; revealing that the average ownership percentage has been increased notably during the period 2002–2007 and remains relatively stable thereafter. Finally, this study quantifies for the first time in the literature the degree of concentration of shipping companies by calculating the Herfindahl index for the ten largest shareholders and the same index excluding the largest shareholder.

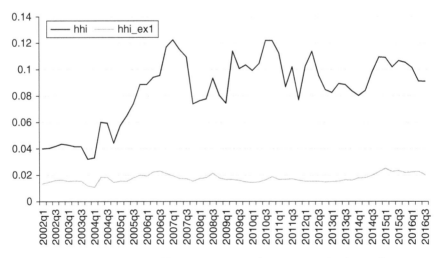

Figure 12.2 Average Herfindahl concentration index over time for the ten largest owners of US listed shipping firms (*hhi*) and excluding the largest owner (*hhi_ex1*).

Notes: This figure reports the cross-sectional average Herfindahl index (*hhi*) and the same index excluding the largest shareholder (*hhi_ex1*) as measures of concentrated ownership for the US listed shipping companies. The calculation of the indices is described in Eq. (12.1).

12.5 Discussion

The results of this study document the existence of a large concentration of ownership to one or a few shareholders based on a sample of US listed shipping firms over the period 2002–2016. The large concentration of ownership for US listed shipping companies is to some extent expected as it facilitates the necessary flexibility and speed in their business decision-making process. Moreover, such flexibility and speed might be a critical factor when negotiating short-lived shipping investment opportunities. The documented large concentration of ownership may also be attributed to the fact that shipping business forms an extremely competitive industry which traditionally attracts investors with large risk appetites. However, the large concentration of ownership for US listed shipping firms is in sharp contrast with the case of the rest of the equities sectors, which exhibit historically much more dispersed ownership structures. Such dispersed ownership structures are also due to large investments by institutional investors in the equities markets, which have held large percentages of ownership of US listed firms across different equities sectors (Schmidt and Fahlenbrach, 2017).

Regarding the implications of the ownership structure of US listed shipping companies for potential investors, it seems that investments in public shipping companies which manage to maintain their traditional person-based (or family-based) decision-making process are favoured by potential investors over the rest. This implies that the maintenance of a person-based business decision-making process may be a critical factor when operating within a global and very competitive industry such as shipping. This is because investment opportunities might arise for very small periods of time and in regions way beyond the headquarters of the company. Supporting this rationale with empirical evidence, Tsionas et al. (2012) reveal a positive relationship between concentrated ownership – mainly concentrated on the founding person or family of a shipping firm – and firm performance for listed shipping companies. Furthermore, the results of this paper point to the fact that shipping companies need to be very careful regarding substantial changes of their ownership structure – especially if these happen after going public. This is because it might be the case that a large percentage of institutional ownership weakens their family-type concentrated ownership structure and results in harming their future firm performance.

A research question of significant importance which stems from the above discussion and findings is whether the reported large percentages of institutional ownership lead eventually to higher firm performance for US listed shipping companies. High percentages of institutional ownership are also expected to substantially affect business decision-making and operations of companies. This is due to the fact that institutional investors have become increasingly willing to use their ownership rights to exert pressure on managers to act in the best interest of the shareholders. In this way, institutional investors may act as a mechanism for monitoring the quality of management decisions (Cornett et al., 2007). The rationale behind this mechanism is that due to high costs of monitoring only large shareholders, such as institutional investors, can achieve sufficient benefits to have an incentive to monitor managers (Grossman and Hart, 1980; Shleifer and Vishny, 1986). Furthermore, institutional shareholders have the resources and ability required to monitor and influence managers (Smith, 1996; Del Guercio and Hawkins, 1999).

On the other hand, if the relationship between institutional ownership and firm performance is negative, it would underpin the value of maintaining a flexible decision-making when operating within the shipping industry. Moreover, it may be argued that institutional investors exert to the management of a shipping company extra monitoring cost which might delay its decision-making process and in this way harm its future financial performance. In addition, if institutional investors exhibit an opportunistic short-term profit view for their shareholdings on a specific shipping company, it might be the case that they encourage – or do not argue against – risky projects, which may eventually harm the future performance of the company. In addition, a negative relationship between institutional ownership and firm performance would imply that the benefits of shipping IPOs might be reduced in the long-term due to the dilution of the ownership structure of the shipping company, especially if its shares are held to a large extent by institutional investors after becoming listed. For this reason, alternative sources of finance for shipping projects, such as the traditionally popular shipping bank loans and shipping bond issues, might be more prominent for financing longer-term shipping projects as these sources of finance do not alter the ownership structure of the shipping firm. Another way through which institutional ownership might affect the firm performance of a shipping firm may be the fact that changes in the ownership structure are typically associated with costs of adjustment during the initial phase of implementation. Adopting new decision-making processes and monitoring mechanisms takes time and might face short-run denial from the management team and employees.

Overall, the results of this study are novel and distinct from the extant literature on the issue. The importance of the global shipping industry for the global supply chain of transportation and its unique characteristics underpin the necessity of exploring the ownership structure – including institutional ownership – effect on firm performance for shipping companies. One step further, such analysis can be generalized for industries with similar characteristics, i.e. capital intensive, excess volatility in revenues, concentrated ownership structure, such as airlines and transportation firms.

12.6 Conclusion

This study discusses in detail the ownership structure for the US listed shipping companies. The contributions of this study to the literature are the following: first, it explores the ownership structure of US listed shipping companies in detail for the first time in the literature. This is enabled through access to publically available data regarding consolidated ownership percentages collected primarily through Forms 13F, 13A/DG, and 20F under SEC's regulation for US listed shipping companies. Second, this study reveals that US listed shipping companies exhibit high concentration of ownership, as the largest shareholder holds an average ownership percentage equal to 23.70%. In addition, the main investor types being the largest shareholders of US listed shipping companies are shown to be – ranked by descending percentage of ownership – insider investors, holding companies, corporations, private equity, and other individual investors. Third, this study utilizes for the first time in the shipping literature the Herfindahl index to measure concentration of ownership in US listed shipping companies and reveals the very large effect of the biggest shareholder percentage of ownership on Herfindahl's index values. Finally, the Herfindahl indices computed are shown to exhibit notable increases – indicating higher concentration of ownership – during the period 2002–2007 but remain relatively more stable during the period 2008–2016.

Notes

1 The shipping sector overall contributes around $380bil a year to the global economy (Catalyst Global Shipping Market Report, 2016) and during the period 2006 to 2016 more than $130bil per annum is invested in ocean going cargo vessels according to data from Clarksons Platou.
2 The largest in terms of capitalization global listed shipping companies are the ones listed in NYSE and NASDAQ stock exchanges (Drobetz et al., 2013).

3 In addition, shipping firms usually operate under the one-ship-one-company offshore legal framework and involve high levels of anonymity of ownership through the use of flags of convenience.

4 While shipping bank loans preserve anonymity for the parties involved, IPO's lack this feature; which is often preferred in an industry not keen on revealing owners, vessel trading strategies, use of freight derivatives and other business strategies capable of providing a competitive advantage for a specific shipping company. This explains partly the small number of studies devoted on the ownership structure of shipping companies. For an overview of sources of capital in shipping see Albertijn et al. (2011).

5 The high operational and business risks in the shipping industry are explained in detail in (Kavussanos and Visvikis, 2006); for example the segmentation effect between different segments and sub-segments of the vessels increases risk (volatility) spillovers among these (for details on this see, Tsouknidis, 2016)

6 For example, in the shipping industry board size, insiders' ownership, busy directors and CEO duality are all associated with firm operating performance, while not all of these variables are found significant in the general corporate finance framework. This is mainly attributed to the unique characteristics of the shipping industry such as its concentrated ownership, capital intensive nature and excess volatility in freight rates and vessel prices.

7 Form 13F covers institutional investment managers, which include Registered Investment Advisers (RIAs), banks, insurance companies, hedge funds, trust companies, pension funds, mutual funds, among natural persons or entities with investment discretion over its own account or another's.

8 Activist practices are not permitted by 13G filers unless they refile a 13D. The security holder of more than 5% but less than 10% must file within 45 days after the end of the calendar year in which the Exchange Act registration becomes effective. If the security holder holds more than 10%, then the holder must file within 10 business days once the threshold is met.

References

Albertijn, S., Bessler, W., Drobetz, W., 2011. Financing shipping companies and shipping operations: a risk-management perspective. *Journal of Applied Corporate Finance* 23, 70–82. doi:10.1111/j.1745-6622.2011.00353.x

Anderson, R.C., Mansi, S.A., Reeb, D.M., 2003. Founding family ownership and the agency cost of debt. *Journal of Financial Economics* 68, 263–285. doi:10.1016/S0304-405X(03)00067-9

Andreou, P.C., Louca, C., Panayides, P.M., 2014. Corporate governance, financial management decisions and firm performance: Evidence from the maritime industry. *Transportation Research Part E: Logistics and Transportation Review* 63, 59–78.

Bebchuk, L.A., Weisbach, M.S., 2010. The state of corporate governance research. *Rev. Financ. Stud.* 23, 939–961. doi:10.1093/rfs/hhp121

Catalyst, 2016. Global shipping market report. https://www.uk.alantra.com/research-documents/2016/catalyst-corporate-finance-global-shipping-report---spring-2016.pdf.

Cornett, M.M., Marcus, A.J., Saunders, A., Tehranian, H., 2007. The impact of institutional ownership on corporate operating performance. *Journal of Banking & Finance* 31, 1771–1794.

Crane, A.D., Michenaud, S., Weston, J.P., 2016. The effect of institutional ownership on payout policy: evidence from index thresholds. *Rev Financ Stud* 29, 1377–1408. doi:10.1093/rfs/hhw012

Demsetz, H., Lehn, K., 1985. The structure of corporate ownership: causes and consequences. *Journal of Political Economy* 93, 1155–1177.

Demsetz, H., Villalonga, B., 2001. Ownership structure and corporate performance. *Journal of Corporate Finance* 7, 209–233. doi:10.1016/S0929-1199(01)00020-7

Grossman, S.J., Hart, O.D., 1980. Takeover bids, the free-rider problem, and the theory of the corporation. *The Bell Journal of Economics* 11, 42–64.

Harlaftis, G., Theotokas, J., 2004. European family firms in international business: British and Greek tramp-shipping firms. *Business History* 46, 219–255. doi:10.1080/0007679042000215115

Hou, W., Lee, E., Stathopoulos, K., Tong, Z., 2016. Executive compensation and the split share structure reform in China. *The European Journal of Finance* 22, 506–528. doi:10.1080/1351847X.2013.802250

Jarque, C.M., Bera, A.K., 1980. Efficient tests for normality, homoscedasticity and serial independence of regression residuals. *Economics Letters* 6, 255–259.

Jensen, M.C., Meckling, W.H., 1976. Theory of the firm: Managerial behavior, agency costs and ownership structure. *Journal of Financial Economics* 3, 305–360. doi:10.1016/0304-405X(76)90026-X

Kavussanos, M.G., Tsouknidis, D.A., 2014. The determinants of credit spreads changes in global shipping bonds. *Transportation Research Part E: Logistics and Transportation Review* 70, 55–75. doi:10.1016/j. tre.2014.06.001

Kavussanos, M.G., Tsouknidis, D.A., 2016. Default risk drivers in shipping bank loans. *Transportation Research Part E: Logistics and Transportation Review* 94, 71–94. doi:10.1016/j.tre.2016.07.008

Kavussanos, M.G., Visvikis, I.D., 2006. *Derivatives and Risk Management in Shipping.* Witherbys, London.

Lin, C., Ma, Y., Malatesta, P., Xuan, Y., 2011. Ownership structure and the cost of corporate borrowing. *Journal of Financial Economics* 100, 1–23. doi:10.1016/j.jfineco.2010.10.012

McConnell, J.J., Servaes, H., 1995. Equity ownership and the two faces of debt. *Journal of Financial Economics* 39, 131–157. doi:10.1016/0304-405X(95)00824-X

Omran, M., 2009. Post-privatization corporate governance and firm performance: the role of private ownership concentration, identity and board composition. *Journal of Comparative Economics* 37, 658–673. doi:10.1016/j.jce.2009.02.002

Schmidt, C., Fahlenbrach, R., 2017. Do exogenous changes in passive institutional ownership affect corporate governance and firm value? *Journal of Financial Economics* 124, 285–306.

Shleifer, A., Vishny, R.W., 1986. Large shareholders and corporate control. *Journal of Political Economy* 94, 461–488.

Smith, M.P., 1996. Shareholder activism by institutional investors: evidence from CalPERS. *The Journal of Finance* 51, 227–252.

Stopford, M., 2009. *Maritime Economics,* 3rd ed. Routledge, London and New York.

Syriopoulos, T., 2007. Chapter 6 Financing Greek shipping: modern instruments, methods and markets. *Research in Transportation Economics, Maritime Transport: The Greek Paradigm* 21, 171–219. doi:10.1016/S0739-8859(07)21006-6

Syriopoulos, T., Tsatsaronis, M., 2011. The corporate governance model of the shipping firms financial performance implications. *Maritime Policy & Management* 38, 585–604. doi:10.1080/03088839.2011.615867

Tsionas, M.G., Merikas, A.G., Merika, A.A., 2012. Concentrated ownership and corporate performance revisited: the case of shipping. *Transportation Research Part E: Logistics and Transportation Review* 48, 843–852. doi:10.1016/j.tre.2012.01.004

Tsouknidis, D.A., 2016. Dynamic volatility spillovers across shipping freight markets. *Transportation Research Part E: Logistics and Transportation Review* 91, 90–111. doi:10.1016/j.tre.2016.04.001

UNCTAD, 2018. *Review of Maritime Transport, United Nations,* https://unctad.org/en/PublicationsLibrary/rmt2018_en.pdf.

13

A critical review of the ship investment literature

Panayiotis C. Andreou and Isabella Karasamani

13.1 Introduction

Central questions during scientific inquiry in shipping finance have been the ability of firms to identify in time potentially viable investment opportunities in ships, to raise capital, and also to manage the investments and achieve specific financial objectives. For instance, Kalouptsidi (2014) explores the nature of fluctuations in world bulk shipping by quantifying the impact of time to build and demand uncertainty on investment and prices; Bendall & Stent (2003) rely on real option analysis to model strategic flexibility planning pertaining to investment decisions under swings in shipping demand driven by periods of uncertainty and declining profitability; and Merikas et al. (2009) analyze the price performance of global shipping initial public offerings (IPOs).

Studies of this nature dealing with the timing, viability, raising of funds, and management of investments have been undertaken at various stages over the years giving rise to the need for a review and critique of the expanding and diversified knowledge base of the topic as it continues to develop, and to address new and emerging topics that would benefit from a holistic conceptualization and synthesis of the literature to date. As these questions have been investigated for many years, this research domain has matured and the size of its literature has grown, hence a literature review is a necessary step in structuring and developing further the theory in this research field.

The objective of this paper is to identify and review studies of the main pillars of ship investment research and integrate theoretical thinking. An integrative review is composed of critical analysis and examination of the given topic culminating in precipitation of the need for new research. A literature review is essential for providing a sense of focus and a direction for new research. Although no review is completely inclusive, the critical review approach we follow allows us to synthesize and integrate the vast and diverse literature on ship investment. In this respect, this paper contributes to the extant literature by proceeding with classification of the studies regarding the timing during which the investment is made, the appraisal of the investment, and the management of the investment to identify gaps, issues, and opportunities for further research, as well as to offer new understandings and, possibly, significant reconceptualization of the theme under investigation.

13.2 Method

To ensure the achievement of a systematic review of the "ship investment" literature, the method applied two stages as suggested by Alves et al. (2016) viz. (1) planning the review which indicates how the systematic approach was planned and (2) conducting the review and analyzing the implications, which sets out the description of how the review was carried out and the systematization of the selected literature.

In conducting a critical review, it is important to identify, assess, and systematically review all relevant studies using a transparent process that will safeguard replicability (Petticrew and Roberts, 2008, Tranfield et al., 2003). The process is described and entails the paper selection/exclusion criteria and the synthesis and interpretation-based assessment that would ensure a systematic review (Macpherson and Holt, 2007, Thorpe et al., 2005, Tranfield et al., 2003).

Our review relies on information derived from 43 journal articles, books, and book chapters extracted in a four-step procedure. First, we focused on searches from leading maritime journals (the titles are provided in Appendix A.1). We accessed our targeted journals directly from the publishers' website and carefully read abstracts from all published issues since 1984 to identify the most relevant ones. Second, given the multidisciplinary nature of ship investment research, especially with financial economics, we searched via Scopus and Google Scholar for additional economics and finance related journals, including in our information set studies published in the journals listed in Appendix A.2. Third, we reviewed shipping and/or shipping finance related books to include the relevant chapters from the books listed in Appendix A.3. Finally, after reading very carefully each article or book chapter, we kept only those that are related to the scope of our investigation, in particular, the timing and viability of investment, sources of finance, and management of the investment. In addition, we kept book chapters from books that were deemed to have undergone a peer-review process of the same quality as that of an academic journal.

In the fourth and final phase of our study, we completed content analysis and systematized the 43 articles. Based on these results, we extracted summarized information on the subject to analyze in terms of the type of study, type of analysis, conclusions, scope, and similarities among the studies.

Key elements of our literature search in terms of studies published in journals are summarized in Tables 13.1 and 13.2, and reveal the following. First, in the entire set of 43 articles, the vast majority refers to empirical studies. Second, most of the studies are published in shipping related journals and books since only 12% is published in other journals. In addition, a chronological segmentation of the studies reveals an increased interest in the topics under review over time. Third, regarding the topics, 18% of the articles relate to the timing and appraisal of investments, 18% relate to the sources of finance and 7% to the viability and appraisal of ship investments. In summary, our literature search reveals that there is an increasing number of quantitative, empirical studies in this domain involving statistical modelling and analysis of variables and there is an overall balance of studies across the different ship investment topics with a notable small number of studies in the part of the viability and appraisal of ship investment.

13.3 Ship investment review

In the following sections, we critically review the ship investment literature separately for the three topics of interest, namely, when and how to invest, how to manage the investment, and how to raise the funds for the investment. In each case, the aim is to provide the structure of the extant studies, their nature, and the provision of implications and recommendations for future research.

Table 13.1 Literature Search Results

Journal	Empirical	Event study	Case study	Survey/in-depth interview	Simulations	Theoretical	Total
Maritime Policy and Management	8 (61)	1 (8)	0 (0)	0 (0)	0 (0)	4 (31)	13 (30)
Transportation Research Part E	9 (100)	0 (0)	0 (0)	0 (0)	0 (0)	0 (0)	9 (21)
The Handbook of Maritime Economics and Business	0 (0)	0 (0)	0 (0)	0 (0)	0 (0)	3 (100)	3 (7)
Unpublished/Working Papers	0 (0)	0 (0)	0 (0)	0 (0)	2 (100)	0 (0)	2 (5)
International Journal of Maritime Economics	1 (50)	1 (50)	0 (0)	0 (0)	0 (0)	0 (0)	2 (5)
Maritime Economics and Logistics	1 (100)	0 (0)	0 (0)	0 (0)	0 (0)	0 (0)	1 (2)
Research in Transportation Economics	1 (100)	0 (0)	0 (0)	0 (0)	0 (0)	0 (0)	1 (2)
The Asian Journal of Shipping and Logistics	1 (100)	0 (0)	0 (0)	0 (0)	0 (0)	0 (0)	1 (2)
Journal of Transport Economics and Policy	0 (0)	0 (0)	0 (0)	0 (0)	1 (100)	0 (0)	1 (2)
Marine Money Offshore	1 (100)	0 (0)	0 (0)	0 (0)	0 (0)	0 (0)	1 (2)
South East European Journal of Economics and Business	0 (0)	0 (0)	0 (0)	1 (100)	0 (0)	0 (0)	1 (2)
Transportation Journal	1 (100)	0 (0)	0 (0)	0 (0)	0 (0)	0 (0)	1 (2)
Witherbys Publishing & Seamanship International	0 (0)	0 (0)	0 (0)	0 (0)	0 (0)	1 (100)	1 (2)
International Journal of Financial Services Management	0 (0)	1 (100)	0 (0)	0 (0)	0 (0)	0 (0)	1 (2)
Journal of Applied Business Research	1 (100)	0 (0)	0 (0)	0 (0)	0 (0)	0 (0)	1 (2)
Journal of Applied Corporate Finance	0 (0)	0 (0)	0 (0)	0 (0)	0 (0)	1 (100)	1 (2)
Munich Personal RePEc Archive	0 (0)	0 (0)	0 (0)	0 (0)	0 (0)	1 (100)	1 (2)
Industrial Management and Data Systems	0 (0)	0 (0)	1 (100)	0 (0)	0 (0)	0 (0)	1 (2)
The American Economic Review	1 (100)	0 (0)	0 (0)	0 (0)	0 (0)	0 (0)	1 (2)

This table tabulates the literature search findings resulted from published journal articles. The numbers report articles used in case. Numbers inside the parentheses report relevant percentage (%) in each case.

Table 13.2 Literature Search Results

Years and topics	Empirical	Event study	Case study	In-depth interview	Simulations	Theoretical	Total
Publication years							
1980 – 1989	0 (0)	0 (0)	0 (0)	0 (0)	2 (67)	1 (33)	3 (7)
1990 – 1995	1 (100)	0 (0)	0 (0)	0 (0)	0 (0)	0 (0)	1 (2)
1996 – 2000	4 (80)	0 (0)	0 (0)	0 (0)	0 (0)	1 (20)	5 (12)
2001 – 2005	4 (50)	1 (13)	0 (0)	0 (0)	1 (13)	2 (25)	8 (19)
2006 – 2010	5 (38)	2 (15)	2 (15)	1 (8)	0 (0)	3 (23)	13 (30)
2011 – 2015	11 (85)	0 (0)	0 (0)	0 (0)	0 (0)	2 (15)	13 (30)
Data							
Global	14 (78)	1 (6)	0 (0)	0 (0)	2 (11)	1 (6)	18 (42)
US	8 (89)	1 (11)	0 (0)	0 (0)	0 (0)	0 (0)	9 (21)
Europe	2 (50)	1 (25)	0 (0)	1(25)	0 (0)	0 (0)	4 (9)
Asia	1 (50)	0 (0)	0 (0)	0 (0)	1 (50)	0 (0)	2 (5)
Scandinavia	0 (0)	0 (0)	1 (100)	0 (0)	0 (0)	0 (0)	1 (2)
Topics of ship investments							
Timing, type, and appraisal	11 (61)	3 (17)	1 (6)	0 (0)	0 (0)	3 (17)	18 (42)
Viability and appraisal of ship investments	1 (14)	0 (0)	1 (14)	0 (0)	3 (43)	2 (29)	7 (16)
Raising funds for ship purchase	13(72)	0 (0)	0 (0)	1(6)	0 (0)	4 (22)	18 (42)

This table tabulates the literature search findings resulted from published journal articles in terms of publication year, data, and topic. The numbers report articles used in case. Numbers inside the parentheses report relevant percentage (%) in each case.

13.3.1 When and how to invest: market efficiency and ship investments

13.3.1.1 Market efficiency

Second-hand ship trading preserves market competitiveness through the ease in entering or exiting freight markets. Demand and supply in new-building vessels as well as prices are highly dependent on cyclical fluctuations. Such fluctuations have on several occasions led to collapses, causing serious financial difficulties and even defaults to shipping firms and shipyards (Tsolakis et al., 2003).

This strand in the literature identified the necessity of investigating whether the markets for second-hand and new-building vessels are efficient and whether assets are priced rationally, since a rejection of the efficient market hypothesis (EMH) may be a sign of arbitrage opportunities. Publications relevant to this component centre on the methodologies employed to test the efficiency of the market for ships. In early work, Strandenes (1984), who utilized a present value framework to explore prices in the dry bulk and tanker sectors, revealed that prices are more affected by changes in the long-term equilibrium profits than by changes in operating profits. Under the assumption that current market rates and equilibrium rates reflect ship prices, she concludes that such a finding supports the semi-rational expectations assumption in the formation of ship prices. In an earlier study, Beenstock (1985), under the assumption of rational expectations and efficient markets, employs a dynamic general equilibrium model for the determination of ship prices, suggesting that prices are explained by current and expected freight rates and economic activity. Hale and Vanags (1992) report the existence of cointegration between the three-time series of second-hand prices, questioning market efficiency for three sizes of dry bulk second-hand vessels. Extending the Hale and Vanags (1992) method, Glen (1997) tested the informational efficiency for three tanker ship sizes as well as dry bulk ships. Applying the powerful tool of Johansen's maximum likelihood method, the author posed doubts on the existence of efficient markets in the tanker and dry cargo markets. Glen (1997) further argued that even the existence of cointegration does not necessarily mean market inefficiency, if the factors that create the common trends are stochastic in nature. Kavussanos and Alizadeh (2002) extended the vector autoregressive models proposed by Campbell and Shiller (1988) and determined the presence of time-varying risk premia that rejected the efficient market hypothesis in the markets for new-building and second-hand dry bulk vessels, also supporting the existence of rational bubbles in the formation of ship prices.

A later study by Tsolakis et al. (2003) applied an autoregressive model for all ship types and found that second-hand ship prices are largely influenced by new-building prices and time-charter rates in most cases both in the short and long run. The cost of capital appeared to solely affect bulk carriers, while order-book exhibited a negative relationship with the price of second-hand vessels only in the long run and only in large and Panamax tankers. Consistent with the notion that new-building prices are cost driven, shipbuilding costs were found to have the highest impact on new-building prices for all ship types, while time-charter rates appeared to influence only a few ship segments. Actual exchange rates do not influence shipbuilding prices directly, but indirectly through cost variations, due to exchange rate fluctuations. Results relating to the order-book showed that shipyards' extension policy targets high-value ships such as tankers rather than bulk carriers. The results obtained by Tsolakis et al. (2003) suggested also that new-building prices for certain ship types may be partially influenced by asset pricing and speculation.

A daunting issue relates to trading costs and the effects of the illiquid shipping market (e.g., delays in the execution of a buy or sell decision and the deviation from the desired buy or sell price) which are rarely considered in the investigation of price efficiency and would definitely impact returns. Another issue is whether there is a common stochastic trend in the data (e.g., caused by trade growth and costs to asset price behaviour) which could imply that the series are still not forecastable in the long run, even if cointegration exists.

The literature addresses the issue of ship price composition, on testing the efficiency of shipping markets, and on investigating the behaviour of ship prices and volatility. However, there has been a lack of comprehensive evidence as to the profitability of sale and purchase decisions of ships based on fundamental analysis. An exception to this is the recent study by Kalouptsidi (2014), who explores the nature of fluctuations in world bulk shipping by quantifying the impact of time to build and demand uncertainty on investment and prices. The author examines the impact of both construction lags and their lengthening in periods of high investment activity by constructing a dynamic model of ship entry and exit, and finds that moving from time-varying to constant to no time to build reduces prices, while significantly increasing both the level and volatility of investment. Future research should also focus on more theoretical and rigorous developments to result into seminal work which obviously could provide a strong basis for furthering this scientific field in terms of better understanding the timing of ship investments; in this respect, studies would have clear implications for policy makers and decision makers alike.

13.3.1.2 Ship investments

Compared to the other areas of shipping investments, mergers and acquisitions (M&As) is one of the most commonly represented topics in the pool of the examined papers. Further, although the prevailing literature in shipping finance concentrated on investment choices of financial assets, shipbuilding cycles, and the speculative behaviour characterizing second-hand ship investments due to the long delivery time of new ships, studies turned their attention to the efficiency of new-building and second-hand markets. Second-hand ship trading has a tremendous economic impact on the shipping industry as it facilitates the direct buying and selling of ships and preserves market competitiveness through the ease in entering or exiting freight markets. Similarly, demand and supply in new-building vessels as well as prices are highly dependent on cyclical fluctuations. Such fluctuations have on several occasions led to collapses, causing serious financial difficulties and even defaults to shipping firms and shipyards (Andreou et al., 2014; Tsolakis et al., 2003).

13.3.1.2.1 MERGERS AND ACQUISITIONS (M&AS)

The efforts of shipping firms to adapt to the dynamic environment influenced the development of strategies directed to market value enhancement rather than simply profit maximizing. In this context, the last decades have seen an increasing number of M&As).

The prevailing theoretical framework of these studies is centred predominantly on the motives and the underlying environmental conditions inducing M&As (Midoro and Pitto, 2000, Panayides and Gong, 2002b, Brooks and Ritchie, 2006, Yeo, 2013) addressed by the prospect of the combined economic value generated by the merged firm.

Brooks and Ritchie (2006) developed a typology to explain the motives driving M&As particularly in the transport sector, and to verify whether they are satisfactorily addressed by the scope of the typology. The suggested typology revealed two crucial motives characterizing target-driven acquisitions in the transportation sector: (1) financial, e.g., due to debt obligations and (2) redefining of the core business whereby an acquirer would assume activities outside the firm's strategic direction. The second classification in terms of economic value refers to the value-neutral theories which signify the managers' exaggerated self-confidence or hubris in deciding upon an acquisition of a target (Roll, 1986). Identifying the variations among countries not only in respect to the frequency of takeover attempts, but also to the possibility of a the merger being friendly or hostile, the presence of cross-border mergers, the premiums offered, and the method of payment i.e., cash or stocks, the literature on shipping M&As appeared to equally examine the US market (e.g., Andreou et al., 2012) as well as the global market to avoid potential country-specific biases arising from the effects of regulatory and legal constraints (Alexandrou et al., 2014).

Studies on mergers and acquisitions in the shipping industry, while often quite rich and comprehensive, have tended to be largely qualitative in nature, being observed in the form of event and case studies of a single merger case and in the form of survey and interview data (Panayides and Gong, 2002b, Syriopoulos and Theotokas, 2007, Solesvik and Westhead, 2010); nonetheless, in certain instances, maintaining a quantitative approach for case studies of multiple mergers (Samitas and Kenourgios, 2007, Alexandrou, et al., 2014). More recent studies emerged in the form of panel data analysis seeking relationships in models linking various hypothesized causal variables to various valuation, proximity, and financial measures being analyzed through univariate and multivariate regressions as well as multiple logit and Cox regressions (Andreou, et al., 2012, Merikas, et al., 2011, Das, 2011, Yeo, 2013, Alexandrou et al., 2014).

In general, the inference from this strand of literature suggests that M&As in shipping add to the value of the firms that decide to pursue them (Andreou et al., 2012). Studies indicated that, in general, stock prices rise rapidly on the announcement of the proposed consolidation, a fact that is long anticipated by the industry, and in addition the share price of the target companies increases more than the share price of the bidder companies' due to the announcement of the major strategic move (Panayides and Gong, 2002a). Additionally, Samitas and Kenourgios (2007), results revealed that M&As have a direct positive impact on shipping firms' stock prices and increase financial value; these firms also become larger in terms of the deadweight tonnage terms due to the overall fleet expansion. Brooks and Ritchie (2006) reviewed all mergers and acquisitions globally and presented a consolidation tendency in the shipping sector while arguing that the industry does not notably differ from other sectors of the transport industry. Brooks and Ritchie (2006) suggest considering targets' motivations in addition to the usual focus on acquirer motives, to confer further attention on the geographic dimension and minority acquisitions. The geographic component of mergers was addressed in a later study by Yeo (2013), who stressed the importance of geographical closeness as a noteworthy reason for consolidations due to the low costs of acquiring information regarding targets. Yeo (2013) also inferred that larger targets appear to be more attractive for inter-continental consolidations because of economies of scale, confirming to a certain extent that the prime motivation of M&As is to accomplish synergy effects.

Future research is required to provide further evidence regarding the changing motivations behind merger activities which are highly influenced by the prevailing environmental factors and appear frequently as a natural response to various elements in the industry structure or to distinct phases of the business cycle. In addition, apart from a few exceptions, studies generally use case analysis and small samples, which suggests the need for new studies with long-term data. In this respect, longitudinal rather than cross-sectional studies will provide additional insights relating to time-specific issues, and the scale, nature, processes, costs, and benefits associated with alternative inter-firm investment strategies. Further, future research should also investigate the determinants of long-run returns/operating performance of mergers and acquisitions as well as the possible differential valuation effects in the supply chain (i.e., upstream or downstream in the transportation chain). Strategic motives, not only from the side of the acquirer but also from the target, should also be looked at. Finally, current literature M&As totally lack evidence relating to the motives behind the wealth effects and economic synergies that emerge from fleet diversification and the timing of acquisitions.

13.3.2 Viability and appraisal of ship investments

Conventional literature on modelling ship prices primarily based its analysis on general and partial equilibrium models and employed structural relations between certain variables including order-book, new-building deliveries, scrapping rates, freight rates, and bunker prices (for example Strandenes, 1984, Beenstock and Vergottis, 1989). Other literature (Bendall and Stent, 2003, Bendall, 2010, Axarloglou et al., 2013), recognizing the characteristics of the shipping industry, argued for real options analysis for establishing ship prices under uncertainty and other market fluctuations. Studies dedicated to real options analysis referred to Black and Scholes (1973), Merton (1973), and the binomial approach of Cox, Ross, and Rubinstein (1979) for pricing financial options. In this respect, a real option is the right, but not the obligation, to take a future action which will alter the value of an investment. Following these grounds, the analysis is based on proposed scenarios with hypothetical examples distinguishing between static and flexible investment strategies and simulation analysis (e.g., Bendall and Stent 2003, 2004, 2007).

A prerequisite for real options analysis is operational flexibility in managing ships, entailing flexibility in entering or exiting the market, employing vessels in the spot or the time-charter market, moving between lay-up and trading statuses, expanding operations, and switching inputs or outputs (Bendall and Stent, 2003, 2004, 2007). As a result, this strand of literature firmly supported that shipping is dependent upon many changing variables which stipulate ongoing strategic planning assessments to adjust to differing economic cycles.

The empirical part of most of the studies dealing with real options analysis utilized case studies with proposed investments (Bendall and Stent, 2003, 2004, 2007). These scenarios were based on actual trade data and constituted appropriate settings to understand investment dilemmas encountered by ship-owners showing the efficacy of real options analysis as an appropriate valuation method. To value the proposed strategies, simulation models are built to represent underlying assets and provide estimates of present values which were eventually used as market prices. The studies also provide estimates of respective volatilities and correlations which are used to model the evolution of prices in a second step, when options are valued.

Bendall and Stent (2003) argued that, as with other sectors, shipping firms operate in a volatile market environment; hence, choices directed to trade rationalization can significantly impact the firm's long-term competitive posture. This would suggest that at times of depressed market conditions, shipping firms should be flexible to exit the market and re-enter at favourable conditions. Because of the high uncertainty in the shipping market and the costs associated with such a strategy, exiting the market until conditions improve would pose a threat of losing market share from competitors. As a result, such a strategy cannot simply be evaluated in terms of exiting and entering the market and, more importantly, traditional capital budgeting techniques fail to assimilate the arrival of new information into their investment assessments (Bendall and Stent, 2003, 2004, 2007). Consequently, the passive or static nature of traditional discounted cash flows (DCF) and net present value (NPV) analysis is regarded as of limited application in the valuation of projects which require management flexibility to adapt to future contingencies.

Bendall and Stent (2003, 2004, 2007) argued that real options analysis can serve as a more appropriate technique because it values explicitly operational flexibility, treating it like a financial option with the use of non-arbitrage. It is then added to the present value of the original strategy to give the present value of the flexible strategy. Hence, management does not assess investments as mutually exclusive options, but rather, as a switching option exercise. This framework enables management to decide between market entrance and exit, operating in spot and period time-charter, and switching between lay-up and trading; thus, it facilitates the exchange of one risky income stream related to a strategy for that of another.

However, the limited extant literature also suffers from methodological limitations. For instance, sample sizes are rather limited to a very small number of ships or even to only one ship. In addition, geographic coverage is non-existent, and the analysis refers only to the countries where the hypothetical service would be based, which may be very restrictive. Future research should also accommodate the decision of managers to postpone the commitment of their resources for later on, and thus pursue some extra flexibility, which allows managers to reverse their commitment of resources before the expiration time of the projects. Future research may also consider severe demand shocks such as unprecedented economic crises.

Finally, the implications of the real options framework should ultimately validate the managerial decision-making process. In this vein, only the study by Axarloglou et al. (2013) employed a real options approach to theoretically determine the way managers and ship-owners operate their vessels by chartering them for different ranges of time spans. This decision-making directly influences the variations in the volume of voyage and the prospective fixtures of time-charters; thus, it highly impacts the spread between voyage and time-charter rates. Axarloglou et al. (2013) derived the spread between voyage and time-charter rates, illustrating that when a time-charter contract is compared to a stream of voyage contracts of the same time period, several separate real options appear that cover a common time horizon with the time-charter contract. Empirical evidence suggested that managers or ship-owners decide upon expending their firm's resources for a short period (long period) during boom market conditions in order to maintain a flexible (commitment) approach and take advantage of impending opportunities whilst charterers behave in the opposite manner. Future research should follow a similar paradigm to provide well justified empirical inferences which would give support to the real option models.

13.3.3 Raising funds for ship purchase

The financing perspective remains a momentous pillar for shipping firms which are required to tie internal and external financing decisions to the intensive capital requirements related to the underlying real assets and the cyclical and volatile nature of the industry. Hence, the financing pillar defines its own sub-universe in shipping finance with three primary areas that are critically examined in this section: capital structure, bond financing, and initial public offerings.

13.3.3.1 Capital structure

The preference of bank finance and capital markets as dominant options for financing shipping firms can be explained by the central financial theoretical perspective of the pecking order theory; yet, the idiosyncratic conditions of the industry should not be undermined (Grammenos and Papapostolou, 2012). Shipping companies have come through two stages that could possibly explain capital structure choices; in the 1990s, the pecking order theory seems to justify shipping firms' financing preferences, while for 2000 and onwards the market timing theory seems to better explain these preferences (Grammenos and Papapostolou, 2012). The market timing theory seemed to gain some merit especially for the period of 2003–2010 when the capital markets experienced a wave of initial public and secondary offerings by shipping firms as well as increasing tendencies in high-yield bonds issuances. This is indicative of the fact that preference in financing is dependent upon the firm's perception of the costs of debt and equity in conjunction with the industry's specific characteristics.

Merikas, et al. (2011) suggested that a shipping firm's capital structure should be determined in conjunction with its commercial strategy. Thus, the decision of whether firms will operate their vessels in the period charter market or in the spot charter market should be dependent on the corporate risk profile (market risk plus financial risk) adopted by the firm. Time-charter commercial strategies which assume lower market risks are, therefore, more likely to appear in highly levered capital structures, while firms exposing spot market profiles will tend to adopt a debt-free capital structure with low financial risk. The highly cyclical macroeconomic environment and its impact on freight rate volatility and cash flow uncertainty inevitably make market risk a factor constantly demanding monitoring. In addition, the continuous and intense capital requirements of the industry endorse a shift towards debt markets. An additional way to determine the shipping firm's capital structure is by assessing how the cyclicality on the asset side of the balance sheet affects the liability side. The high volatility of asset values of shipping companies compared to non-shipping counterparts (Dobretz et al., 2013), along with the high operational leverage and financial leverage characterizing the industry (Kavussanos and Visvikis, 2006), point to the vulnerability of these firms to vessel price risks. Because of high costs of financial distress, shipping firms incur large costs diverging from the target leverage ratios. Nonetheless, the optimality of the past excessive leverage ratios should be an issue of reconsideration since the limited asset redeployment ability in recession times along with the high regulatory requirements imposed to shipping banks will increase the need for equity financing, and, as a result, decrease expected returns to equity in the industry (Albertijn et al., 2011, Dobretz et al., 2013, Kavussanos and Visvikis, 2006).

The global capital markets have become a valid option for shipping firms; decisions made to correspond to the industry's heavy reliance on capital, either with debt or equity, are critical in market value creation. Studies pertinent to the capital structure of shipping firms are limited in number; yet, they appear to provide an adequate starting point in terms of magnitude and depth of investigation, hence cultivating a solid ground for future research in the area. These studies identified the aforesaid factors and primarily attempted to tie capital structure issues to the intensive capital requirements related to the underlying real assets, which are directly related to increased financial risks and therefore possible adverse results. To determine the factors affecting the capital structure of shipping firms, studies concentrated both on smaller samples focusing solely on US listed firms for a narrow time period, providing results through correlational inferences (Merikas et al., 2011), as well as on global firms analyzing rather large panels of data and enhancing the analysis through different dynamic panel estimators (Drobetz et al., 2013).

The central theoretical perspectives used to examine the capital structure of shipping firms predominantly discussed four prominent theories: the trade-off theory (Myers, 1977, Jensen and Meckling, 1976, Jensen, 1986), the shipping corporate risk trade-off hypothesis (Merikas et al., 2011), the pecking order theory (Myers 1984, 2001, Myers and Majiluf 1984), and the market timing theory (Baker and Wurgler, 2002). Regarding the decision to raise funds externally, through either equity or debt, discussions pertinent to the trade-off theory may need to be altered to suit the industry's peculiarities. For instance, the effective tax rate becomes negligible in many countries which have either offered certain tax incentives to relax the tax liability of shipping firms or established a tonnage tax regime, where the payable tax is based on the tonnage of the vessel and not on accounting figures realized from vessel exploitation. Often shipping firms select to position their operations in those countries offering tax-efficient regimes. Future studies should take into account these elements and revisit the capital structure in the shipping industry. Regarding the pecking order theory, in the financial economics literature, this has experienced a time of supremacy around the 1990s, but its supposed drivers are still at odds, especially during economic downturns (Huang and Ritter, 2009); more recently the market timing theory seems to better explain capital structure choices. The effect of the exceedingly cyclical macroeconomic environment of shipping firms on freight rates and cash flow uncertainty as well as the observed problem of over-leverage make the overall corporate risk of the firm a burning issue in shipping corporate risk management, as they increase the probability of financial distress and impair financial flexibility. Therefore, future studies should revisit the capital structure choices since recent periods provide a fresh domain for investigation and perform a horse-race of the four prominent theories.

Future studies should also provide more in-depth multivariate analysis, making efforts to establish causal relationships and moving forward from the extant attempts to empirically investigate hypotheses through a correlational approach which establishes only statistical associations, and, at the same time, they should employ global datasets which would result in large sample sizes covering longer time periods. Finally, as suggested by Merikas et al. (2011), future research should also take into account that a shipping firm's capital structure should be determined in conjunction with its commercial strategy.

13.3.3.2 Bonds financing

Studies exploring the bond dimension of shipping financing mainly discussed the corporate and investment perspective of bonds. The corporate perspective entailed a comparison of bond financing with traditional bank finance and equity. This perspective deems bond financing as an advantageous financing instrument due to the positive cash flow effect resulting from the non-amortization of interest, the long periods of coupon repayment, and the possibility of converting the bond into equity which potentially does not require any repayment at all (Grammenos et al., 2008, Grammenos and Arkoulis, 2003, Grammenos, et al., 2007). The investment perspective of bonds referred to the investor whose perception on shipping bonds partly stems from the assessments done by rating agencies providing an indication of the default risk in bonds. For that reason, most of the studies utilized credit ratings as one key factor in their analysis, since credit ratings are intended to reveal the likelihood that a firm will repay its debt on time (Grammenos and Arkoulis, 2003, Grammenos et al., 2007, Grammenos et al., 2008).

The major factors that may have pushed many shipping firms to issue equity have also influenced these firms to shift or combine traditional banking finance with private placements and public issues of debt over the last 20 years. The reports that began to emerge after the early dismissal of bond issues in the 2000s anticipated that the shipping industry would need considerable capital requirements resulting from increasing trade flows and ageing fleets. The early dismissals were attributed to the high coupon requirements amplified by the speculative ratings of shipping bonds ascribed by the rating agencies. According to Leggate (2000), these issues conveyed that bond finance largely depends on the perception of the shipping industry by the investment community. The shipping industry appears weak in promoting investor confidence; nonetheless, investors seem to have a more optimistic stance than credit agencies. A good indication of this phenomenon can be found in defaulted bonds, which have experienced increased prices and falling yields since default. Fridson and Garman (1998) argue further that this difference in the perception of leverage and market conditions between credit agencies and the market when assessing and pricing high yield bonds gives rise to agency conflicts between the agencies and their customers comprised by shipping firms.

Despite the reduction in the numbers of shipping high yield bond issues after 1999 due to the high number of defaults of shipping companies, the market has seen an increase of new issues mainly because of the strong shipping market. Primary and secondary dynamics of yield premia are of key importance both for the investment community, since information on changes in yield premia can be used for investment and asset allocation purposes, and for shipping firms who need bond financing to keep up with intensified capital requirements. Credit rating is the major determinant of the yield premia on primary pricing (Grammenos and Arkoulis,

2003, Fridson and Garman, 1998, Garman, 2000) and financial leverage as well as shipping market conditions are found to explain a significant part of the price variability (Fridson and Garman, 1998). The drivers of the spreads of global cargo carrying high yield bonds – the only sample being investigated separately up to now – are found to be liquidity of the bond issue, market-wide volatility, cyclical bond factors, freight earnings, and the credit rating of the issue (Kavussanos and Tsouknidis, 2014). Such a focus on a specific shipping sub-sector is important because of the distinct cycles underlying different shipping sectors, which can affect the ability of a bond issuer to meet loan obligations.

Seasoned high yield bond premia appear to be related to macroeconomic factors, i.e., the ten-year Treasuries as well as the Merrill Lynch single-B index (Grammenos et al., 2007). Furthermore, the lower the credit rating and the earnings in the shipping market, the larger – and wider throughout the passage of time until maturity – seasoned high yield premiums seem to be. The credit rating's significance is marked as dominant; yet, the shipping market — proxied by earnings — also captures an important share in determining the spread. This denotes that investors not only asses the shipping market, but they also consider the credit ratings while deciding upon investments in shipping high yield bonds (Grammenos et al., 2007).

After the 1999 recession in the shipping market, many shipping companies who operated their fleet mainly in the spot market were found incapable of meeting their debt obligations in the US high yield bond market (Grammenos et al., 2008). Grammenos et al. (2008) highlighted certain financial variables that can, in fact, provide a signal on issues that have a high likelihood to default. Specifically, higher gearing levels are found to be associated with increased probabilities of default when these levels reach 65% or more, and if the amount to be raised surpasses total assets by 80%. On the contrary, working capital over total assets ratio, and retained earnings over total assets ratio as well as the industry-specific variable capturing of shipping market conditions at the time of issuance, seems to negatively predict the probability of default.

In conclusion, the use of panel methodology is highlighted in investigating the determinants of credit spread changes in the bond financing frame. Also, geographical coverage is rather broad and standard compared to the other strands of literature, focusing on global, EU, and US bond issues. These studies draw on the benefits and limitations of panel data and conclude that the shipping industry entails a heterogeneous group of companies exhibiting variables which are difficult to measure and quantify monthly. Thus, it is highly supported that any future attempt to capture this heterogeneity should be done by the utilization of a fixed effects model (Grammenos et al., 2008). As suggested by Kavussanos and Tsouknidis (2014), the technical handling of panel data estimations is a critical aspect driving research findings in shipping bond spreads. Extensive use of wider samples to global bonds and longer time periods capturing complete shipping business cycles are also factors that received limited attention in the literature but are considered as key in providing insights with respect to shipping bond financing (Kavussanos and Tsouknidis, 2014). Moreover, future research is called to conduct a careful selection of the sample of the shipping bonds to make sure that the variable of freight earnings adequately reflects the returns of the bond issuer. Such a selection is deemed crucial as investors tend to evaluate the ability of a firm to repay its loans by assessing the freight market segment the firm operates, its cyclicality, and its income generation (Kavussanos and Tsouknidis, 2014).

13.3.3.3 IPOs

Regardless of their critical role in investment funding, equity markets have traditionally demonstrated limited contribution in shipping finance. This is attributed to the perseverance of these firms on a family-owned structure, the disinclination of ship-owners to disseminate firm control, and the lack of transparency of important firm information. Moreover, as highlighted by Kavussanos and Marcoulis (2000), the perception of the investment community regarding the riskiness of shipping stocks compared to other stocks, largely due to the highly volatile environment of the industry in which these firms operate, further added to the stock market abstinence of shipping firms. Recently, however, the over-leverage issue along with the bank difficulties in providing adequate capital on a timely manner and in meeting the ever-increasing legal requirements and tightening credit facilities; the elevated vessel prices; the demands for larger vessel sizes; the structural adjustments of shipping firms; the appetite for greater visibility and prestige to attract institutional and private investors; and the preference for international capital markets expressed by younger generations of ship-owners, constitute some of the reasons that shifted the interest of several shipping firms from the traditional wherewithal of financing to equity financing and global markets (Sambracos and Maniati, 2013, Grammenos and Papapostolou, 2012, Syriopoulos, 2010).

Motives that have been identified to urge shipping firms to IPO issues include vessel acquisition, asset play, and debt repayment. Debt repayment appeared to induce firms that were larger than those induced by vessel acquisition purposes (Grammenos and Marcoulis, 1996). Factors taken into consideration for IPO stock performance vary from gross proceeds of the IPO issue, to firm size and age, equity stake offered, and fleet age, with gearing level being the most important amongst all. IPO performance is mainly assessed with short-term and long-term abnormal returns. These include the percentage change in the first day closing price relative to the offer price for short-term abnormal returns, whilst for long-term returns benchmarks employed are the cumulative average returns (CARs), the buy-and-hold abnormal returns (BHARs), and the Fama and French (1996) three-factor (FF3F) model. It generally seems that there is a declining over-performance as moving towards six months after listing. Moreover, consistent with information signalling theories, under-pricing is found to positively relate to the age of the firm, implying a type of private valuation undertaken by ship-owners into the age of the firm before going public (Merikas et al., 2009). Other features that elucidate first trading day returns relate to the reputation of the stock market and the IPO market conditions prevailing at the time of the issue, while the reputation of the underwriter appears to negatively affect under-pricing. US stock exchanges, however, seem to suffer from a less severe under-pricing on initial trading day (Merikas et al., 2010), which indicates extraordinary maturity levels in the shipping sector; whilst this difference in the results compared to global IPOs for one-, two-, three-year holding period returns poses doubts on whether investing in US shipping IPOs is a guaranteed investment by those maintaining a long-term investment philosophy.

With regards to the probability of US shipping IPOs being under-priced, the main focus should essentially be on the existence of asymmetric information. Under-pricing often arises from informational asymmetry between market players; specifically, the issuing firm, the underwriter, the initial investors, and the secondary market investors. In this respect, Cullinane and Gong (2002) focused on the hypothesis of the divergence of opinion originally proposed by Miller (1977), which has received limited attention. The hypothesis of the divergence of opinion assumes that mispricing results from the heterogeneity in investors estimates of the intrinsic value and the expected returns of unseasoned equity issues. Naturally, the divergence of opinion would be more pronounced during the stock's first issuance. Cullinane and Gong (2002) argued that in the context of transportation IPOs, it would seem that Miller's (1977) hypothesis of the divergence of opinion is particularly relevant, a conclusion that sits well with the notion that in the shipping IPOs, it is rational to anticipate higher initial day returns since there exists higher *ex ante* uncertainty as to their intrinsic values. In similar vein, Grammenos and Papapostolou (2012) evinced that there is no information asymmetry between participants in shipping IPOs and that readily available public information prior to the IPO is partially adjusted into the final offer price. Underwriters of shipping IPOs seem to compensate private or institutional investors for disclosing their information about the issuing company in the registration period, and this compensation is reflected in the form of partial adjustment in the final offer price.

Regarding IPOs, the number of publications concentrating on this thematic area has been limited in number; nevertheless, the rate is increasing. It seems that the increasing presence of shipping firms in the capital markets and more particularly in the US markets has attracted considerable interest in recent research. To understand the shipping IPO market in depth, additional research should concentrate on the share allocation to private and institutional investors. These investors are looking for alternative investments; thus, a comprehensive analysis of stock volatility for appropriate portfolio management and efficient asset allocation, as well as firm valuation, is a crucial aspect in shipping financing. Merikas et al. (2009) suggest a search into three categories of allocation mechanisms: fixed-price offerings, auctions, and book building. Further studies may also concentrate on the accuracy of earning forecasts. Given that investors rely on the forecasts provided in the prospectuses of IPO firms to subscribe to the new issue or to invest on the first day of trading, the accuracy of such a forecast is vital (Chen et al., 2001). Research should be produced with the employment of error metrics to examine the forecast accuracy of the shipping sector.

The puzzling evidence with respect to the buy-and-hold returns that US listed shipping IPOs experience should be examined in conjunction with the unique characteristics of the shipping industry including sophistication, innovation, and complexity (Merikas et al., 2010). Many critical factors should be taken into consideration, including the derived nature of the demand for shipping services (which is sensitive to economic growth), the idiosyncratic characteristics of the shipping industry, and the cyclicality of freight rates and vessel prices.

Moreover, although most of the IPOs are introduced in the form of cross-listings, this particularity has not been given the adequate attention in the literature of shipping IPOs. It appears that under favourable prevailing economy, equity market, and industry conditions at the time of the IPO decision, cross-listed IPOs enjoy an unexpected range of benefits, including corporate image enhancement, wider reach of existing and potential stockholders, as well as greater bargaining power over their creditors (Mourdoukoutas and Stefanidis, 2007). As the market matures, researchers should examine IPOs of such a regime with reference to the appropriate venues to list shares, to the timing of the listing, and to indirect effects of the IPO other than the direct outcome of immediate capital growth.

The empirical approaches examined in the prevailing literature on shipping IPOs vary from in-depth interviews and surveys (questionnaires) establishing associations between the variables examined (Mourdoukoutas and Stefanidis, 2009), to standard finance methodologies for assessing the existence and scale of mispricing by computing average initial day raw returns by place of listing as well as by nature of service and by group (freight v. passenger) (Cullinane and Gong, 2002), cross-sectional regressions in short and post-listing returns (Merikas et al., 2009; Merikas et al., 2010), and logit techniques which assign score to each firm by weighting the independent variables to determine the probability of shipping IPOs being under-priced (Grammenos and Papapostolou, 2012). In addition, the geographic orientation of these publications appears to be broadly skewed. Only two papers reviewed are based on samples of US listed shipping firms. The rest of the papers vary in geographic focus, concentrating on samples of shipping IPOs in global stock exchanges, on transportation companies that went public in the Chinese mainland and Hong Kong, and on Greek firms choosing to be listed in US stock exchanges. The coverage of topic areas relative to the articles summarized in this section is relatively narrow. Under-pricing is the most commonly represented topic, complemented by factors that may explain first trading day returns.

Unlike other areas of shipping finance research, recent studies in shipping IPOs attempt not only to use long periods of examination and the geographical spectrum but also to incorporate aftermarket returns for shipping IPOs. These studies take into account short- and long-term performance and they unveil a chronological progress, enriching already researched subject matters while shedding light on new aspects of the performance of shipping IPOs. Further, these studies (Merikas et al., 2009, Merikas et al. 2010, Grammenos and Papapostolou, 2012) displayed unanimous interest in exploiting specific market or firm characteristics such as the underwriter's reputation, the size of the IPO, the reputation of the stock exchange in which the shipping IPO occurred, and the period of listing (defined as hot or cold in terms of cyclical patterns in the IPO market). More research is required on the allocation of shares to institutional and individual investors that could inform the general literature on the allocation mechanisms between fixed-price offerings, auctions, and book building. In addition, the literature needs to also consider seasoned equity offerings (SEOs), which constitute another means of equity financing following a firm's IPO.

13.4 Conclusion

We identified 43 studies on the timing, viability, raising of funds, and management of shipping investments, evidence that academic research recognizes the prominence of this topic in the broader area of shipping finance. This research stream gains from theoretical as well as applied perspectives, which complement and antagonize based on the particular topic and methodology. A key goal for future research should be to examine fields of overlap and omission among the pertinent studies, with special emphasis on their applicability on the highly cyclical and notoriously volatile shipping environment. Moreover, although the trend towards empirical quantitative analysis is obvious in the studies examined, an extensive focus on methodological issues with regards to these studies is required so that research in the field facilitates both the utility and comparability of future work. Lastly, the focus of earlier work needs to be more diverse emphasizing a more integrative picture of what has been done in the past and covering geographic spheres in a more proportionate trend. As it is emphasized in the study, what we offer is not an exhaustive list of the factors that influence shipping investments. By integrating prior work and critically identifying promising research gaps, we hope to stimulate further research on the topic.

APPENDIX A

A.1

Transportation Research Part B, Transportation Research Part E, Transport Reviews, Maritime Policy and Management, Economics of Transportation, Transportation, Maritime Economics and Logistics (formerly International Journal of Maritime Economics), International Journal of Shipping and Transport Logistics, Research in Transportation Economics, Transportation Journal, Asian Journal of Shipping and Logistics, Marine Money Offshore, Munich Personal RePEc Archive.

A.2

Journal of Finance, Review of Financial Studies, Journal of Financial Economics, Journal of Accounting and Economics, Review of Finance, European Economic Review, Journal of World Business, The Quarterly Review of Economics and Finance, International Journal of Business in

Society, Industrial Management and Data Systems, The American Economic Review, Journal of Alternative Investments, Journal of Applied Corporate Finance, International Journal of Financial Services Management, Applied Economics, South East European Journal of Economics and Business, Journal of Applied Business Research, Eurasian Business Review.

A.3

Maritime Economics, Shipping Finance, The Handbook of Maritime Economics and Business, The International Handbook of Maritime Economics, The Blackwell Companion to Maritime Economics, Derivatives and Risk Management in Shipping.

References

Albertijn, S., Bessler, W., and Drobetz, W. (2011) Financing shipping companies and shipping operations: A risk-management perspective. *Journal of Applied Corporate Finance* 23(4): 70–82.

Alexandrou, G., Gounopoulos, D., and Thomas, H.M. (2014) Mergers and acquisitions in shipping. *Transportation Research Part E: Logistics and Transportation Review* 61: 212–234.

Alves, H., Fernandes, C., and Raposo, M. (2016) Social media marketing: A literature review and implications. *Psychology & Marketing* 33(12): 1029–1038.

Andreou, P.C., Louca, C., and Panayides, P.M. (2012) Valuation effects of mergers and acquisitions in freight transportation. *Transportation Research Part E: Logistics and Transportation Review* 48(6):1221–1234.

Andreou, P.C., Louca, C., and Panayides, P.M. (2014) Corporate governance, financial management decisions and firm performance: Evidence from the maritime industry. *Transportation Research Part E: Logistics and Transportation Review* 63: 59–78.

Axarloglou, K., Visvikis, I., and Zarkos, S. (2013) The time dimension and value of flexibility in resource allocation: The case of the maritime industry. *Transportation Research Part E: Logistics and Transportation Review* 52:35–48.

Baker, M. and Wurgler, J. (2002) Market timing and capital structure. *The Journal of Finance* 57(1): 1–32.

Beenstock, M. (1985) A theory of ship prices. *Maritime Policy and Management* 12(3): 215–225.

Beenstock, M. and Vergottis, A. (1989) An econometric model of the world tanker market. *Journal of Transport Economics and Policy.* 23(3): 263–280.

Bendall, H. (2010) Valuing maritime investments with real options: The right course to chart. In: C.T. Grammenos (ed.) *The Handbook of Maritime Economics and Business* 2nd ed. London: Lloyd's List, pp. 683–708.

Bendall, H.B. and Stent, A.F. (2003) Investment strategies in market uncertainty. *Maritime Policy & Management* 30(4): 293–303.

Bendall, H.B. and Stent, A.F. (2004) Ship investment under uncertainty: a real option approach. In: University of Otago Department of Finance Seminar Series.

Bendall, H.B. and Stent, A.F. (2007) Maritime investment strategies with a portfolio of real options. *Maritime Policy & Management* 34(5): 441–452.

Black, F. and Scholes, M. (1973) The pricing of options and corporate liabilities. *The Journal of Political Economy*, 81(3): 637–654.

Brooks, M.R. and Ritchie, P. (2006) Mergers and acquisitions in the maritime transport industry 1996–2000. *Transportation Journal* 45(2): 7–22.

Campbell, J.Y. and Shiller, R.J. (1988) Stock prices, earnings and expected dividends. *The Journal of Finance* 43(3): 661–676.

Chen, G., Firth, M., and Krishnan, G.V. (2001) Earnings forecast errors in IPO prospectuses and their associations with initial stock returns. *Journal of Multinational Financial Management* 11(2): 225–240.

Cox, J.C., Ross, S.A., and Rubinstein, M. (1979) Option pricing: A simplified approach. *Journal of Financial Economics* 7(3): 229–263.

Cullinane, K. and Gong, X. (2002) The mispricing of transportation initial public offerings in the Chinese mainland and Hong Kong. *Maritime Policy & Management* 29(2): 107–118.

Das, S.S. (2011) To partner or to acquire? A longitudinal study of alliances in the shipping industry. *Maritime Policy & Management* 38(2): 111–128.

Drobetz, W., Gounopoulos, D., Merikas, A., and Schröder, H. (2013) Capital structure decisions of globally-listed shipping companies. *Transportation Research Part E: Logistics and Transportation Review* 52: 49–76.

Fama, E.F. and French, K.R. (1996) Multifactor explanations of asset pricing anomalies. *The Journal of Finance* 51(1): 55–84.

Fridson, M.S. and Garman, C.M. (1998) Determinants of spreads on new high-yield bonds. *Financial Analysts Journal* 54(2): 28–39.

Garman, C. M. (2000) Pricing European high-yield new issues. *The Journal of Fixed Income* 9(4): 35–42.

Glen, D.R. (1997) The market for second-hand ships: Further results on efficiency using cointegration analysis. *Maritime Policy and Management* 24(3): 245–260.

Gounopoulos, D., Merikas, A.G., and Nounis, C.P. (2009) Global shipping IPOs performance. *Maritime Policy and Management* 36(6): 481–505.

Grammenos, C.T., Alizadeh, A.H., and Papapostolou, N.C. (2007) Factors affecting the dynamics of yield premia on shipping seasoned high yield bonds. *Transportation Research Part E: Logistics and Transportation Review* 43(5): 549–564.

Grammenos, C.T. and Arkoulis, A.G. (2003) Determinants of spreads on new high yield bonds of shipping companies. *Transportation Research Part E: Logistics and Transportation Review* 39(6): 459–471.

Grammenos, C.T., Nomikos, N.K., and Papapostolou, N.C. (2008) Estimating the probability of default for shipping high yield bond issues. *Transportation Research Part E: Logistics and Transportation Review* 44(6): 1123–1138.

Grammenos, C.T. and Marcoulis, S. (1996) *Shipping Initial Public Offerings: A Cross Country Analysis. Empirical Issues in Raising Equity Capital.* Oxford: Elsevier, pp. 379–400.

Grammenos, C.T. and Papapostolou, N.C. (2012) US shipping initial public offerings: Do prospectus and market information matter? *Transportation Research Part E: Logistics and Transportation Review* 48(1): 276–295.

Hale, C. and Vanags, A. (1992) The market for second-hand ships: some results on efficiency using cointegration. *Maritime Policy & Management* 19(1): 31–39.

Huang, R. and Ritter, J.R. (2009) Testing theories of capital structure and estimating the speed of adjustment. *Journal of Financial and Quantitative Analysis* 44(02): 237–271.

Jensen, M.C. (1986) Agency cost of free cash flow corporate finance, and takeovers. Corporate Finance and Takeovers. *American Economic Review* 76(2): 323–329.

Jensen, M.C. and Meckling, W.H. (1976) Theory of the firm: Managerial behavior agency costs and ownership structure. *Journal of Financial Economics* 3(4): 305–360.

Kalouptsidi, M. (2014) Time to build and fluctuations in bulk shipping. *The American Economic Review* 104(2): 564–608.

Kavussanos, M.G. and Alizadeh, A.H. (2002) Efficient pricing of ships in the dry bulk sector of the shipping industry. *Maritime Policy & Management* 29(3): 303–330.

Kavussanos, M.G. and Marcoulis, S.N. (2000) The stock market perception of industry risk through the utilisation of a general multifactor model. *International Journal of Transport Economics/Rivista internazionale di economia dei trasporti*, 77–98.

Kavussanos, M.G. and Tsouknidis, D.A. (2014) The determinants of credit spreads changes in global shipping bonds. *Transportation Research Part E: Logistics and Transportation Review* 70: 55–75.

Kavussanos, M.G. and Visvikis, I.D. (2006) *Derivatives and Risk Management in Shipping.* London: Witherby Seamanship International.

Leggate, H.K. (2000) A European perspective on bond finance for the maritime industry. *Maritime Policy & Management* 27(4): 353–362.

Macpherson, A. and Holt, R. (2007) Knowledge, learning and small firm growth: A systematic review of the evidence. *Research Policy* 36: 172–192.

Merikas, A., Gounopoulos, D. and Karli, C. (2010) Market performance of US-listed Shipping IPOs. *Maritime Economics & Logistics* 12(1): 36–64.

Merikas, A., Sigalas, C., and Drobetz, W. (2011) The shipping corporate risk trade-off hypothesis. *Marine Money* 27(6): 40–43.

Merton, R.C. (1973) Theory of rational option pricing. *The Bell Journal of Economics and Management Science* 4(1): 141–183.

Midoro, R. and Pitto, A. (2000). A critical evaluation of strategic alliances in liner shipping. *Maritime Policy & Management* 27(1): 31–40.

Miller, E.M. (1977) Risk uncertainty, and divergence of opinion. *The Journal of Finance* 32(4): 1151–1168.

Mourdoukoutas, P. and Stefanidis, A. (2009) To list or not to list: expectations versus reality for Greek shipping IPOs. *South East European Journal of Economics and Business* 4(1): 125–134.

Myers, S.C. (1977) Determinants of corporate borrowing. *Journal of Financial Economics* 5(2): 147–175.

Myers, S.C. (1984) The capital structure puzzle. *The Journal of Finance* 39(3): 574–592.

Myers, S.C. (2001) Capital structure. *The Journal of Economic Perspectives* 15(2): 81–102.

Myers, S.C. and Majluf, N.S. (1984) Corporate financing and investment decisions when firms have information that investors do not have. *Journal of Financial Economics* 13(2): 187–221.

Panayides, P.M. and Gong, X. (2002a) The stock market reaction to merger and acquisition announcements in liner shipping. *International Journal of Maritime Economics* 4(1): 55–80.

Panayides, P.M. and Gong, X. (2002b) Consolidation, mergers and acquisitions in the shipping industry. *The Handbook of Maritime Economics and Business*, pp. 598–620, London: LLP.

Petticrew, M. and Roberts, H. (2008) *Systematic Reviews in the Social Sciences: A Practical Guide*. Malden MA: Blackwell Publishing Ltd.

Roll, R. (1986) The hubris hypothesis of corporate takeovers. *Journal of Business* 59(2): 197–216.

Sambracos, E. and Maniati, M. (2013) *Shipping Market Financing: Special Features & the Impact of Basel III*. Available at SSRN 2337919.

Samitas, A.G. and Kenourgios, D.F. (2007) Impact of mergers and acquisitions on stock returns of tramp shipping firms. *International Journal of Financial Services Management*, 2(4): 327–343.

Solesvik, M.Z. and Westhead, P. (2010) Partner selection for strategic alliances: case study insights from the maritime industry. *Industrial Management & Data Systems* 110(6): 841–860.

Strandenes, S.P. (1984) Price determination in the time charter and second hand markets. Center for Applied Research, Norwegian School of Economics and Business Administration, working paper MU, 6.

Syriopoulos, T. (2010) *Shipping Finance and International Capital Markets. The Handbook of Maritime Economics and Business*. London: Lloyd's List, pp. 811–849.

Syriopoulos, T. and Theotokas, I. (2007). Value creation through corporate destruction? Corporate governance in shipping takeovers. *Maritime Policy & Management* 34(3): 225–242.

Thorpe, R., Holt, R., MacPherson, A., and Pittaway, L. (2005) Using knowledge within small and medium sized firms: A systematic review of the evidence. *International Journal of Management Reviews* 7: 257–281.

Tranfield, D., Denyer, and Smart, P. (2003) Towards a methodology for developing evidence informed management knowledge by means of systematic review. *British Journal of Management* 14: 207–222.

Tsolakis, S.D., Cridland, C., and Haralambides, H.E. (2003) Econometric modelling of second-hand ship prices. *Maritime Economics & Logistics* 5(4): 347–377.

Yeo, H.J. (2013) Geography of mergers and acquisitions in the container shipping industry. *The Asian Journal of Shipping and Logistics* 29(3): 291–314.

14

Development of ship finance centre

The case of Singapore

Jasmine Siu Lee Lam and Sun Xi

14.1 Introduction

The shipping industry is characterized by high market volatility and a capital-intensive nature. With the increasing size of the world commercial fleet, the demand for capital in the shipping industry has been growing over the years (Cai, 2011). This places emphasis on the importance of a well-developed ship finance sector. As an integral part of a maritime cluster, ship finance acts as a key contributor to the development of an international maritime centre (IMC). A number of maritime cities such as Hong Kong, London, Oslo, Shanghai, and Singapore strive to attain or maintain the status of a world-class international maritime centre by actively engaging in the ship finance market (Zhang and Lam, 2013). With reference to these maritime cities, an IMC means an international hub for maritime business and activities. A ship finance centre specializes in ship finance business and activities. An attractive ship finance centre has many ship owners choosing the maritime city to finance their ships and companies. Various innovative and dynamic sources of financing are made available to meet the increasing demand for capital. Besides the traditional way of bank loans, there are many other models suited to the financing of ships, structured by means of finance houses, brokers, leasing companies, shipping funds, and shipbuilding credit schemes. These models allow ship owners and operators to have an easier access to capital, both in terms of the flexibility of financing structures and of the size of capital.

Due in part to its strategic location, Singapore is both a global shipping hub and an Asian banking centre. As the gateway to South East Asia, Singapore has been the world's largest transhipment hub and bunkering port for many years (Lam, 2016). In 2016, the maritime industry contributed 7% of Singapore's Gross Domestic Product (GDP) and the total cargo throughput hit 593.3 million tonnes. In terms of container cargoes, the throughput was 30.9 million TEUs (MPA, 2017). However, as Singapore aims to build itself into a leading IMC, its maritime service sector such as ship finance needs to be broadened and enhanced.

While various studies have been done on analyzing the development of finance centres in general as well as maritime clusters, very little research has been conducted on understanding the development of a ship finance centre. In order to contribute to the narrowing of this literature gap, the first objective of this chapter is to analyze the critical success factors of a ship finance centre. The second objective is to conduct a case study of Singapore and to examine the landscape of Singapore's ship finance sector. In order to address these two objectives, this chapter is organized as follows: the next section reviews the critical success factors for the development of a ship finance centre in general. After that, the case study of Singapore's ship finance sector will be presented, followed by practical implications and recommendations.

14.2 Critical success factors of a ship finance centre

We conducted a review of literature, market reports, country reports, and creditable internet sources to derive the critical success factors of a ship finance centre. Such factors can be categorized by three aspects, namely government, maritime cluster, and financial development as summarized in Table 14.1.

14.2.1 Government aspect

The stability of the political environment is the premise of economic and social development. Henisz (2002) defined political stability as the degree to which the governing policies of a country are stable. By this definition, companies in politically stable regions are not likely to be affected by the unexpected change of policies or regulations, as the multiple veto points in government or political coalitions make it difficult to change existing policies without much political debate or warning (Kim and Li, 2012). This provides a favourable environment for business development where investors are confident to inject their money, thus bringing in both private investment and Foreign Direct Investment (FDI) which contribute to economic growth (Panayides et al., 2015). One favourable example is London: the long-lasting stable political environment of the United Kingdom enables London to secure its place as the world's premier maritime centre. Since the 18th century, political stability has been drawing more capital and investment to London, boosting the economy and making it a leading financial centre. With the increasing demand for shipping activities/services and the availability of capital, London is now one of the most established ship finance centres.

Another factor for the successful development of a ship finance centre is the incentive policies from the government, which encourage the holistic development of the industry as well as shaping its structure (Bondonio and Greenbaum, 2007). This is essential for developing maritime cities such as Hong Kong, Singapore, and Shanghai, which are in their transitional period to grow from physical shipping centres toward having more maritime services (Zhang and Lam, 2013). For instance, the Maritime and Port Authority of Singapore (MPA) has launched the Maritime Finance Incentive (MFI) Scheme since 2006, seeking to encourage international ship owners and operators to establish their commercial shipping operations in Singapore through tax concession and exemption (MPA, 2016). The MFI Scheme also provides more alternatives in ship financing, thus attracting more capital that is crucial for the development of a ship finance market. More details will be discussed in Section 14.3.

14.2.2 Maritime cluster aspect

Economists define the concept of a cluster as groups of companies and institutions co-located in a specific geographic region and linked by interdependencies in providing a related group of products and/or services (Ketels, 2003). The existence of clusters enables firms and institutions to achieve a higher level of efficiency and innovation compared to a situation where they work in isolation (Chang, 2011). According to Benito et al. (2003), a cluster is established when

Table 14.1 Critical Success Factors of a Ship Finance Centre

Aspect	Factor	Examples from the maritime industry	Reference
Government	1. Stable government (political stability)	The long-lasting stable political environment enables London to secure its place as the world's premier maritime centre. It encourages both private investment and FDI, thus bringing economic growth, more shipping activities, and an increasing request for maritime services such as ship finance in the UK.	Kim and Li (2012) Jackowicz, Oskar, and Łukasz (2013)
	2. Incentive policies	In Singapore's case, the Maritime Finance Incentive Scheme seeks to encourage international ship owners and operators to establish their commercial shipping operations in Singapore through tax concession and exemption. The MFI Scheme also provides more alternatives in ship financing, thus attracting more capital, which is crucial for the development of a ship finance market.	MPA (2016) Bondonio and Greenbaum (2007)
Maritime cluster	1. More advanced structure of maritime cluster that enables its holistic development	Through regulations and incentive schemes, the governments of developing maritime nations/regions such as Hong Kong and Singapore are directing the evolution of the maritime cluster towards a more comprehensive status, so they can function as a maritime services centres instead of performing only physical shipping.	Zhang and Lam (2013) Othman, Bruce, and Hamid (2011) Chang (2011)
	2. Availability of a wide range of maritime services	With a large merchant marine fleet and a well-developed shipping market, Norway is established as an international maritime centre and actively involved in a wide range of maritime sectors.	Viederyte (2013) Benito et al. (2003) Lam and Cullinane (2003)
	3. Number of shipping-related MNC regional headquarters	Multinational corporations' regional headquarters and high-order financial activities are usually located side by side. They share similar requirements for location choice, i.e. accessibility and accuracy of information to reduce asymmetric information. With a favourable business and regulatory environment, Singapore has attracted over 4,200 foreign companies (MNCs) that now have their regional activities in the city, and some 26,000 international companies that maintain offices there.	Sim, et al. (2003) Zhao, Zhang, and Wang (2004) MPA (2016)

(Continued)

Table 14.1 Continued

Aspect	Factor	Examples from the maritime industry	Reference
Financial	1. Investor risk appetite	Investor risk appetite will influence the size and type of the shipping capital market.	Goetz (2007)
	2. Dynamic and innovative sources of ship financing	The increasing size of ships brings an increasing demand for capital, making the traditional way of financing less favorable. The availability of new sources for financing that can provide larger capital is crucial in attracting more financial activities. Shipping funds such as German KG and Norwegian KS provide an alternative in raising capital in shipping markets.	Jarvis (2011) Cai (2011) Drobetz and Merikas (2013)
	3. Performance of financial institutions	With local financial institutions focusing more on the ship finance sector and an increasing number of international banks with expertise on ship finance setting up their offices in Singapore, it will be easier and more flexible for ship owners/operators to finance their ships in terms of the size of the capital and less regulation constraint.	Marine Money Group (2015) Molyneux, Nguyen and Xie (2013)

Source: Compiled by authors.

all parts of a value-creating system are available, thus the development of maritime cluster in a city is based on the availability of a wide range of maritime services. In the analysis of the maritime sector in Norway, it is concluded that with a large merchant marine fleet as well as a well-developed shipping market consisting of various maritime-oriented services, Norway has developed a strong and dynamic maritime cluster which is actively involved in a wide range of maritime sectors (Viederyte, 2013).

Another essential factor is the evolution towards a more advanced structure of maritime cluster that enables its holistic development. This is done by enhancing the main function from purely cargo handling and distribution to high-value-added maritime related-services. Currently, cities such as Hong Kong and Singapore are identified as type 3 maritime clusters where the main function includes allocation of the integrated resources. Through regulations and incentive schemes, the governments of these developing maritime nations/regions are directing the development of the maritime cluster to a more comprehensive status, which functions as a maritime services centre with a variety of maritime services provided (Zhang and Lam, 2013).

The number of shipping-related multinational corporation (MNC) regional headquarters is another success factor of a maritime cluster. MNC regional headquarters and high-order financial activities are usually located alongside (Zhao et al., 2004). They both share similar requirements for location choice, i.e. accessibility and accuracy of information to reduce asymmetric information. For example, with a favourable business and regulatory environment, Singapore has attracted over 7,000 foreign MNCs which now have their regional activities there and some 26,000 international companies which maintain offices in the city (MPA, 2016).

14.2.3 Financial aspect

As a capital-intensive industry, shipping requires huge amounts of capital investment with a long return period; it also bears a high risk due to the volatility of the shipping market (Cai, 2011). All these factors determine the fact that it is not likely, or it might even be impossible, for shipping firms to involve in investment activities on themselves. This stresses the importance of ship finance. Furthermore, the recent trend towards an increasing size of ships makes the demand for capital even stronger, rendering the traditional way of financing less favourable (Drobetz and Merikas, 2013). The availability of new sources for ship finance that can provide larger capital is crucial in attracting more financial activities in a region/nation; this may include equity financing, bond issue, shipyard credit, and leasing. Some of the established shipping funds, such as German KG and Norwegian KS, provide an alternative for raising capital in shipping markets.

The performance of financial institutions also has a great impact on the enhancement of the ship finance sector (Molyneux et al., 2013). With local financial institutions focusing more on the ship finance sector and an increasing number of international banks with expertise on ship finance setting up their offices (Marine Money Group, 2015), it will be easier and more flexible for ship owners/operators to finance their ships in terms of the size of the capital and lower regulation constraint.

As another critical success factor, investor risk appetite will influence the size and type of shipping capital market. According to Gai and Vause (2006), risk appetite is defined as the willingness of investors to bear risk, and depends on both the degree to which investors dislike such uncertainty and the level of that uncertainty. During peak years or recovery periods of the shipping market cycle, the uncertainty level of shipping declines, and investors are more confident about the future and thus have higher risk appetite (Jarvis, 2011). The shipping capital market expands with more investors entering the market. It is the reverse during a trough period and times when markets collapse. A ship finance centre should attract and retain investors having a risk appetite on the shipping capital market.

14.3 Case study of Singapore as a ship finance centre

MPA has an aim to build Singapore as a leading IMC. As such, maritime services including ship finance are being broadened and enhanced. Singapore has achieved highly commendable ship finance performance in a relatively short time span. It is ranked number two in ship financial services (Zhang and Lam, 2016) and number four in maritime finance and law (Menon Economics and DNV GL, 2017) in the world. Therefore, Singapore is an interesting case for analyzing the development of a ship finance centre. Located at the southern tip of the Malay Peninsula, Singapore has a very small total area as a city-state. With limited natural resources and agricultural capacities, its economic growth heavily depends on the development of value-added services and on the level of capital and investment (Jarvis, 2011). Ever since its independence in 1965, Singapore has been experiencing constant economic growth under a stable political environment. Over the years, the government of Singapore has been building its reputation as a global business and finance centre by initiating incentive policies, producing a favourable tax system, and creating a competitive business environment. US-based research institute Business Environment Risk Intelligence (BERI) ranked Singapore as the most favourable investment destination in terms of investment potential (BERI report 2011-II, 2011 August), which is assessed by the easy access of the market, political risk, and overall business environment.

Singapore has been building itself towards an international maritime centre. A series of development initiatives including tax incentives and monetary policies are released by the MPA, aiming at convincing more ship owners and operators as well as maritime service providers to establish their business in Singapore (MPA, 2016).

MPA introduced the Maritime Sector Incentive (MSI) Scheme in June 2011. It consolidates and updates the tax incentives previously offered, categorizing them into three major sectors: shipping operations, maritime leasing arrangements, and shipping support services. Among the three categories, the maritime leasing award (MSI-ML Award) is the most essential one for promoting the development of the ship finance sector in Singapore. It is largely based on the previous Maritime Finance Incentive (MFI) Scheme, targeting ship-leasing companies, shipping business trusts, and shipping funds which provide financing services for vessels as well as the ones used for the offshore oil and gas sector (MPA, 2016).

The main body of the scheme is tax concession and exemption for eligible parties. By showing a strong track record, a demonstrable business plan, and a commitment to expand shipping and container financing operations in Singapore, these parties may apply for the MSI-ML Award. Once approved, a tax concession of 10% up to ten years or an exemption up to five years may apply on the qualified income of the entity. For Approved Ship Investment Managers (ASIM), there will be a concessionary tax rate of 10% on qualifying management-related income for a period of ten years, while for leasing companies, funds, business trusts, or partnerships, tax exemption for up to five years on their qualifying leasing income from both finance and operating leases will be applicable. The scheme has encouraged international ship owners and operators to establish their commercial shipping operations in Singapore as well as promoting alternatives in ship financing such as shipping fund and shipping trust.

Compared with other traditional maritime countries such as the UK and Norway, Singapore stepped up efforts in developing ship finance activities only about ten years ago, yet it has attained very good performance in terms of its ranking in industry survey and performance analysis (Menon Economics and DNV GL, 2017; Zhang and Lam, 2016). To provide a holistic view, Table 14.2 compiles the key characteristics of London, Oslo, and Singapore ship finance centres. All three centres provide various incentives from their respective governments to attract ship finance business. The major approach is tax reduction or exemption. London is recognized as a very established ship finance centre. However, in recent years, ship financing has a trend of turning to capital markets, including initial public offerings and bond markets. The UK lost out as it has limited maritime capital markets activity (PwC, 2016b). On the other hand, Oslo and Singapore have gained more market share in maritime capital markets. Also, UK and European banks have significantly reduced exposure to the maritime sector in recent years (PwC, 2016). This funding gap is largely being filled by Asian banks who have been gaining a share of the total loan book, particularly since 2011.

These incentive schemes as discussed above also have a great impact on shaping the structure of the maritime cluster, directing Singapore's maritime cluster to a more advanced type that functions as a maritime services centre instead of mainly physical shipping. Zhang and Lam (2013) classified the world's major maritime clusters into four categories based on the assessment of maritime services offered. Fisher Associates (2004) has also identified the type of maritime services as the principal feature for different stages of maritime clusters. As one of the world's top container ports, currently Singapore's port main function is still cargo handling and distribution. To be a leading IMC, Singapore's maritime cluster has to offer comprehensive and wide-ranging types of services. As such, maritime services including ship finance are being broadened and enhanced. A key development is that the Singapore Exchange (SGX) acquired the Baltic Exchange Limited in 2016, which enables SGX to diversify into the commodities and shipping finance markets (Vasagar, 2016).

Table 14.2 Comparison of London, Oslo and Singapore Ship finance Centers

	London	Oslo	Singapore
Ranking in overall ship finance	Number one in ship financial service (Zhang and Lam, 2016) and number one in maritime finance and law (Menon Economics and DNV GL, 2017).	Number seven in ship financial service (Zhang and Lam, 2016) and number two in maritime finance and law (Menon Economics and DNV GL, 2017).	Number two in ship financial service (Zhang and Lam, 2016) and number four in maritime finance and law (Menon Economics and DNV GL, 2017).
Ranking in banks offering ship finance	Number six regarding existing shipping portfolio of top 40 shipping banks in dollars (Menon Economics and DNV GL, 2017).	Number two regarding existing shipping portfolio of top 40 shipping banks in dollars (Menon Economics & DNV GL, 2017).	Number ten regarding existing shipping portfolio of top 40 shipping banks in dollars (Menon Economics & DNV GL, 2017).
Key features and development	1. London's strength in ship finance has historically been in debt finance, with very little activity in capital markets occurring in the maritime sector (PwC, 2016). 2. UK and European banks have significantly reduced exposure to the maritime sector in recent years (PwC, 2016).	1. Oslo is home to the world's two leading shipping banks and has a strong position in a maritime focused stock exchange. 2. Oslo is strong in capital markets for shipping (PwC, 2016).	1. Singapore has three local banks providing shipping bank services – DBS, UOB, & OCBC. DBS, as the first and the largest local shipping bank player, ranks 29 in the world in terms of bank lending to shipping based on a survey conducted by Petrofin Bank Research (2017). 2. In 2016, Singapore Exchange (SGX) acquired the Baltic Exchange Limited, which enables SGX to diversify into the commodities and shipping finance markets (Vasagar, 2016).
Key incentives from government	1. Tax credits are available for small, medium, and large enterprises. Large companies can attract 130% tax deductions and SMEs 225% tax deductions for qualifying R&D expenditure (HM Government, 2013). 2. The UK has 48 Enterprise Zones offering businesses simplified planning processes and discounts on business rates (HM Government, 2017). 3. The UK operated successive reductions in corporation tax down to 20% in 2015. Also, it reduced the top rate of income tax from 50% to 45% (HM Government, 2013).	1. Norwegian tonnage tax regime (for qualified companies or assets only): instead of normal tax on general income, a company under this special tax arrangement pays a tonnage tax based on the net tonnage of relevant vessels (Norwegian Maritime Authority, 2012). 2. Grant scheme for the employment of seafarers to any organization operating ships registered in the Norwegian Ordinary Ship Register (NOR) or Norwegian and meeting certain requirements (Ministry of Trade Industry and Fisheries of Norway, 2016).	Maritime Sector Incentive (MSI) Scheme (MPA, 2016): 1. Concessionary tax rate of 10% on qualifying management-related income for Approved Ship Investment Managers (ASIM) for a period of ten years. 2. Tax exemption on qualifying income (from both finance and operating leases) derived by Approved Ship Investment Vehicles. 3. Withholding tax exemption on interest and related payments made in respect of loans obtained to finance the purchase or construction of ships, containers and intermodal equipment.

Source: Compiled by authors.

Furthermore, recognized as one of the most important business and financial centres in South Asia, Singapore keeps its competitiveness through attracting regional headquarters of MNCs (Sim et al., 2003). Zhao et al. (2004) have identified the number of MNC headquarters as an indicator of the city's international business status. By 2015, over 7,000 MNCs have set up their business in Singapore and they have brought in $1,235.4 billion of foreign direct investment (Singapore Department of Statistics, 2016).

The success of business development comes together with increasing financial activities. Numerous finance companies are operating in Singapore where most of the major banks set their regional headquarters. This is especially beneficial for the maritime industry as currently lending is still the main form of ship financing in Singapore (Chang, 2011). The presence of these major banks allows ship owners and operators to acquire capital in a more efficient way, especially in terms of the capital size.

Although ship finance has not been their traditional area of business for the three local banks – Development Bank of Singapore (DBS), United Overseas Bank (UOB), and Oversea-Chinese Banking Corporation (OCBC) – they have been actively building up the ship finance sector for the past few years. There is a trend of growing presence of local banks in Singapore's ship finance sector. For example, DBS played a major role as the lead arranger in Singapore's first shipping trust deal, Pacific Shipping Trust, in May 2006.

Another important factor for the development of Singapore's ship finance is the performance of the Asian market. The booming of the Asian economies and globalization has brought about 40% of the world's commercial tonnage to Asian countries (Marine Money Offshore, 2015), resulting in a strong demand for various shipping services especially the demand for capital. The shift of the weight of shipping activities towards Asia has had great benefits for Singapore as it brings more shipping activities and encourages the holistic development of the Singapore maritime cluster (Benito et al., 2003).

14.4 Practical implications and recommendations

Looking at the globe, currently most of the fast-growing maritime centres such as Hong Kong, Shanghai, and Singapore are located in East Asia. As the rise of Asia's economy brings great opportunities for these maritime cities, the competition among them has also become more intensive.

Unlike other well-developed maritime cites in Europe such as Norway and London, Asian cities are still in the way of building the structure of their maritime clusters. Originally, most of them functioned mainly as container ports with their key business being cargo handling. However, with the emergence of other Chinese and Malaysian ports such as Ningbo and Tanjung Pelepas, which share similar geographical advantages but have lower costs, these cities must upgrade their maritime clusters in order to maintain their competitiveness (Yap et al., 2011). In this case, government intervention is especially important in shaping the maritime cluster in terms of its composition and direction. A more service-oriented cluster is needed while the development of ship finance is one of the most essential parts of it. As discussed above, the critical success factors of a ship finance centre consist of three main categories: government, maritime cluster, and financial performance. As such, various initiatives can be taken to encourage the buildup of a ship finance centre by fulfilling these three main aspects. Experience from other maritime cities such as London can also be learned from and adopted.

In Singapore's case, the costs of conducting business such as labour and rental expenses continue to increase. For future development, instead of competing by cost, Singapore should continue to strengthen high-value-added services, such as ship finance. The implication is that for Singapore to maintain its competitiveness as the global maritime hub, there must be a strong presence of financial and legal service providers (Verhetsel and Sel, 2009). To upgrade Singapore's maritime cluster to a shipping service-oriented type, more initiatives such as incentive policies should be taken by the authorities to promote more dynamic sources of ship financing. By providing the market with more financing options and higher return investment opportunities, there will be an increase in investor appetite and thus a boost in the demand in the ship finance market. One successful example is the establishment of shipping funds in Singapore.

Unlike Singapore, whose development as a maritime centre is achieved largely through active government policies, Hong Kong has been adopting a more laissez-faire policy to promote entrepreneurial inflow (Huat, 2004). The less-intervention policy of the government allows a flexible business environment, promoting growth in different maritime sectors (Kriz, 2007). However, there are certain aspects where the intervention of government can bring in huge benefits. Hong Kong also offers tax incentives, e.g. companies are subject to profits tax of no more than 16.5%, while salaries tax on individuals does not exceed 15%, and it does not levy global tax (HKMPB, 2016). Furthermore, the government is a suitable party to provide a roadmap for maritime cluster development. One example is that the interrelationship among different maritime sectors should be taken into consideration such that the promotion of one sector should not suppress the development of other sectors (Zhang and Lam, 2013). For instance, the promotion of the ship finance sector allows easier access to capital which is beneficial for the shipbuilding sector. While these two sectors are positively correlated, there may be other cases where the expansion of one sector will restrict other sectors. In this case, the impact of one sector on the others should be fully assessed by the government authority in order to achieve holistic development.

The launch of Shanghai Free Trade Zone in September 2013 has intensified the competition among these Asian maritime centres. With tax incentive policies that allow enterprises to enjoy tax exemption and reduction for certain periods based on the enterprises' operating nature, Shanghai is aiming at attracting more international business and foreign investment. There are also policies made specifically for promoting the maritime industry, for instance Chinese-invested banks within the zone are permitted to engage in offshore business and for financial leasing companies, and no minimum registered capital restriction is imposed on the set up of single machine/single ship subsidiaries. These leasing companies are also allowed to be engaged concurrently in the commercial factoring business relating to their principal business (China (Shanghai) Pilot Free Trade Zone, 2016). Additionally, opening up to foreign investors may also have a positive impact on the trading volume of the Shanghai stock exchange, bring prosperity to China's bond market, and intensify the competition for capital in East Asia.

14.5 Concluding remarks

This chapter studies one of the most important aspects of the maritime industry: the development of ship finance centres. Given the very limited literature on the topic, the study presents an original contribution to identify the critical success factors for an international ship finance centre and classifies them into three main categories: government stability and intervention, presence of a well-developed maritime cluster, and performance of financial institutions. The contributions of these factors are studied and assessed by real examples of ship finance centres from various regions such as London, Oslo, Hong Kong, and Singapore.

The chapter is also among the first in the literature to conduct a case study of Singapore's ship finance sector. The performances of the factors listed in the three categories are studied accordingly under Singapore's environment. As an international shipping hub, Singapore has a strong presence in the physical shipping sector as a major container port and bunker centre. It is also an established finance centre in South Asia with most of the world's major banks setting up their regional headquarters in the city-state.

Practical recommendations are given in Section 14.4 of the chapter based on the previous discussion. For maritime centres that are still in a developing stage, various initiatives can be adopted by different centres based on their business and political environment. In the case of Singapore, the launch of government incentive policies is perceived to be an efficient way, since Singapore's success has been furthered by the government creating and maintaining Singapore's advantages in the ship finance market by providing competitive tax structures and a sound and stable financial system. While, for Hong Kong, adaptive government intervention may be beneficial to ensure the holistic development of the maritime cluster, on the other side, Shanghai may seize the opportunity of the opening of the Free Trade Zone, taking full advantage of the increasing business opportunity and enhancing its ship finance market (Lai, 2006).

As a whole, this chapter advances ship finance studies in a new area, especially for the developing maritime centres. The research findings presented can be applied in the enhancement of the ship finance sector. Areas for future research should seek to assess the interrelationship among ship financing and other maritime services. In other words, it is recommended that researchers investigate how the enhancement of the ship finance sector affects the performance of other sectors in the maritime cluster. Thus, a comprehensive model can be developed for the establishment of a strong maritime cluster.

References

Benito, G.R.G., Berger, E., Forest, M., and Shum, J. (2003), A cluster analysis of the maritime sector in Norway, *International Journal of Transport Management* 1(4): 203–215.

Bondonio, D. and Greenbaum, R. T. (2007), Do local tax incentives affect economic growth? What mean impacts miss in the analysis of enterprise zone policies, *Regional Science and Urban Economics* 37(1): 121–136.

Cai, Y.C. (2011), Ship industry funds—innovation of shipping finance, *Shipbuilding of China* 2011(4).

Chang, Y. (2011), Maritime clusters: What can be learnt from the south west of England, *Ocean & Coastal Management* 54(6): 488–494.

China (Shanghai) Pilot Free Trade Zone (2016), website: www.shftz.gov.cn, last accessed in 16 March 2016.

Drobetz, W. and Merikas, A. G. (2013), Maritime financial management, *Transportation Research Part E: Logistics and Transportation Review* 52(special issue): 1–2.

Fisher Associates (2004), *The future of London's Maritime Services Cluster: A Call for Action*, Corporation of London, London.

Gai, P. and Vause, N. (2006), Measuring investors' risk appetite, *International Journal of Central Banking* 2(1): 167–188.

Goetz, V.P. (2007), International banking centres: A network perspective, *BIS Quarterly Review* working paper. Available at SSRN: http://ssrn.com/abstract=1075205

Henisz, W.J. (2002), The institutional environment for infrastructure investment, *Industrial and Corporate Change* 11(2): 355–389.

HKMPB. (2017), The Hong Kong maritime and port board. Retrieved October 29, 2017 from https://www.hkmpb.gov.hk/en/index.html

HM Government. (2013), Open for maritime business. Retrieved 27 October 2017 from https://www.gov.uk/government/publications/open-for-maritime-business-what-the-uk-has-to-offer-to-the-global-shipping-community

HM Government. (2017), Enterprise zone finder. Retrieved 29 October 2017 from http://enterprisezones.communities.gov.uk/enterprise-zone-finder/

Huat, T.C. (2004), Competing international financial centers: A comparative study between Hong Kong and Singapore. Saw Centre for Financial Studies and ISEAS Conference.

Jackowicz, K., Oskar, K., and Łukasz, K. (2013), The influence of political factors on commercial banks in central European countries, *Journal of Financial Stability* 9(4): 759–777.

Jarvis, D.S.L. (2011), Race for the money: international financial centres in Asia, *Journal of International Relations & Development* 14(1): 60–95.

Ketels, C.H.M. (2003), The development of the cluster concept: present experiences and further developments. Dr. Christian Ketels, Harvard Business School, paper prepared for NRW Conference on Clusters, Duisburg, Germany.

Kim, P.H. and Li, M.X. (2012), Injecting demand through spillovers: Foreign direct investment, domestic socio-political conditions, and host-country, *Journal of Business Venturing* 29(2): 210–231.

Kriz, P. N. (2007), *Comment on Hong Kong and Shanghai: Yesterday, Today and Tomorrow, Financial Sector Development in the Pacific Rim, East Asia Seminar on Economics, Volume 18*. University of Chicago Press, Chicago.

Lai, K. (2006), *Developing Shanghai as an International Financial Centre: Progress and Prospects*, Discussion Paper 4, China Policy Institute, University of Nottingham.

Lam, J.S.L. (2016), Strategy of a transshipment hub: The case of Port of Singapore, in Lee, P.T.W. and Cullinane, K. (eds.) *Dynamic Shipping and Port Development in the Globalized Economy* Vol. 1. Palgrave Macmillan, Basingstoke.

Lam, J.S.L. and Cullinane, K. (2003), Shanghai as an international maritime centre: Implications for the East Asian regional economy. Proceedings of the Eastern Asia Society for Transportation Studies, Eastern Asia Society for Transportation Studies, Fukuoka, Japan, 29 Oct–1 Nov 2003.

Marine Money Offshore (2015), website: www.marinemoneyoffshore.com/node/3971, last accessed 29 January 2015.

Maritime and Port Authority of Singapore (2016), website: www.mpa.gov.sg, last accessed 24 August 2016.

Maritime and Port Authority of Singapore (2017), Singapore's 2016 maritime performance. Last accessed 27 October 2017, from http://www.mpa.gov.sg/web/portal/home/media-centre/news-releases/detail/05460688-fe49-42e7-9740-4ce88b157b46

Menon Economics and DNV GL. (2017), The leading maritime capitals of the world 2017. Retrieved from https://www.menon.no/wp-content/uploads/2017-28-LMC-report.pdf

Ministry of Trade Industry and Fisheries of Norway (2016), Regulations on grants for the employment of employees at sea. Retrieved 3 November 2017 from https://www.sjofartsdir.no/contentassets/5783 46d8a3244c5ba06ebae8d3e48215/26-february-2016-no.-214-grants-for-the-employment-of-em ployees-at-sea.pdf?t=1509260698042

Molyneux, P., Nguyen, L. H., and Xie, R. (2013), Foreign bank entry in South East Asia, *International Review of Financial Analysis* 30: 26–35.

MPA. (2017), Leading International Maritime Centre (IMC), www.mpa.gov.sg/sites/maritime_singapore/what_is_maritime_singapore/leading_imc.page, last accessed 24 August 2016.

Norwegian Maritime Authority (2012), Norwegian tonnage tax regime – Norwegian Maritime Authority. Retrieved 29 October 2017, from https://www.sjofartsdir.no/en/shipping/registration-of-commercial -vessels-in-nisnor/new-registration-nis/norwegian-tonnage-tax-regime/

Othman, M.R., Bruce, G.J., and Hamid, S.A. (2011), The strength of Malaysian maritime cluster: The development of maritime policy, *Ocean & Coastal Management* 54(8): 557–568.

Panayides, P.M., Parola, F., and Lam, J.S.L. (2015), The effect of institutional factors on public-private partnership success in ports, *Transportation Research Part A*, 71: 110–127.

Petrofin Bank Research. (2017), Key Developments and growth in global ship-finance. Retrieved 28 October 2017 from http://www.petrofin.gr/Upload/Petrofin_Global_Bank_Research_and_Petrof in_Index_of_Global_Ship_Finance-end2016.pdf

PwC. (2016), The UK's global maritime professional services: contribution and trends. Retrieved 30 October 2017 from https://www.maritimeuk.org/media-centre/publications/uks-global-maritime-professional-services-contribution-and-trends_/

Sim, L., Ong, S., Agarwal, A., Parsa, A., and Keivani, R. (2003), Singapore's competitiveness as a global city: development strategy, institutions and business environment, *Cities* 20(2): 115–127.

Singapore Department of Statistics (2016), Foreign equity investment in Singapore website: www.singstat. gov.sg, last accessed 15 October 2016.

Vasagar, J. (22 August 2016), Singapore bourse and Baltic Exchange agree terms. Retrieved 29 October 2017, from https://www.ft.com/content/fb5598be-6870-11e6-a0b1-d87a9fea034f?mhq5j=e5

Verhetsel, A. and Sel, S. (2009), World maritime cities: From which cities do container shipping companies make decisions? *Transport Policy* 16(5): 240–250.

Viederyte, R. (2013), Maritime cluster organizations: Enhancing role of maritime industry development, *Procedia – Social and Behavioral Sciences* 81: 624–611.

Yap, W.Y., Lam, J.S.L. and Cullinane, K. (2011), A theoretical framework for the evaluation of competition between container terminal operators, *Singapore Economic Review* 56(4): 535–559.

Zhang, W. and Lam, J.S.L. (2013), Maritime cluster evolution based on symbiosis theory and Lotka-Volterra model, *Maritime Policy & Management* 40(2): 161–176.

Zhang, W. and Lam, J.S.L. (2016), Comparison on competitive advantages of major world maritime clusters, Proceedings of the International Association of Maritime Economists Annual Conference, Hamburg, 24–26 August 2016.

Zhao, X.B.S., Zhang, L., and Wang, D.T. (2004), Determining factors of the development of a national financial center: the case of China, *Geoforum* 35(5): 577–592.

15

Appraisal of shipping investment projects using real options

Christoforos Andreou, Neophytos Lambertides,
and Photis M. Panayides

15.1 Introduction

This chapter intends to describe the use of real options in shipping providing simple practical examples. Shipping companies operate in a highly volatile market where their investment decisions are of vital importance. Companies make their investments having the following as their main objectives: to maximize their profits, to remain competitive, and of course to increase their market value. This implies that they should assess their investment opportunities as efficiently as possible in order to avoid making two serious investment errors: to invest in a project that they should not consider or to not invest in a project that they should have considered. The capital budgeting methods that are commonly used by the majority of firms generally (Kester et al., 1999; Ryan and Ryan, 2002) and shipping companies to assess their investments are based on *traditional discount cash flows (DCF)* methods. The most widespread DCF methods used by most CFOs regardless of the type of company are the *net present value (NPV)* and the *internal rate of return (IRR)* (Graham and Harvey, 2001).

Over the past half-century, DCF methods have been criticized by decision scientists and many scholars (Hayes and Abernathy, 1980; Hayes and Garvin, 1982; Myers, 1984; Hooder and Riggs, 1985; Trigeorgis and Mason, 1987) where one of the main problems of DCF methods is that they do not have the ability to properly capture the management's flexibility that is associated with a specific investment (Dixit and Pindyck, 1994; Trigeorgis, 1995, 1996). For instance, NPV makes an implicit assumption that an investment under assessment is rigid (without managerial flexibility) ignoring the options that managers have to alter an initial investment which implies that cash flows and cost of capital will be constant until the maturity of the investment. In reality, this assumption rarely remains valid because most of the investments, especially in shipping, offer the flexibility to the management to revise initial decisions of investment in response to future market developments. However, in the absence of managerial flexibility, NPV is a remarkable valuation method to assess rigid or static investments. According to standard finance books (Copeland et al., 2004; Brealey et. al., 2009; Smart et al., 2010), NPV is better than other traditional valuation measures (IRR, accounting rate of return, payback period, etc.) to assess investments without managerial flexibility.

Several scholars (Hertz, 1964; Magee, 1964; Salazar and Sen, 1968) try to overcome the problems of DCF methods by developing new valuation approaches such as *simulation techniques* and *decision-tree analysis (DTA)*. Hertz (1964) introduced a new evaluation method of capital investments using the simulation approach: this method is well known as risk analysis in capital budgeting. In a few words, this method takes a random sampling and finds the probability distribution of important variables for an investment. However, simulation is not suitable for investments with managerial flexibility due to the inability to handle the asymmetries arising due to managerial flexibility (Trigeorgis, 1996). Magee (1964) suggested the decision-tree analysis (DTA), which maps all the potential alternatives that have the management based on a specific investment. Even if it is a good approach for capital budgeting, DTA is subject to a serious problem about the determination of the appropriate discount rate (Trigeorgis and Mason, 1987; Trigeorgis, 1996).

Real options analysis (ROA) is the capital budgeting method that can overcome all the aforementioned problems. Real options, as in financial options, give the right but not the obligation, in a firm, to make or alter an investment.[1] The term *real options* was used for the first time by Myers in 1977. Myers (1977), in his seminal study in this field, indicated that a firm's investment is like a financial option where investment cost is the exercise price of an option and the present value of cash flows that derived from an investment is the underlying asset. The main advantage of ROA over the DCF methods is that it can properly capture the managerial flexibility related to an investment. However, this does not mean DCF methods (i.e. NPV) should be ignored or abolished because DCF provides necessary input to ROA. For example, if there is no similar asset with the under-assessed project, then, in order to estimate the present value of the underlying asset that would be used in ROA, we use the NPV approach to estimate the present value of the project by discounting the anticipated cash flows which will be used as the present value of the underlying asset in ROA. A detailed explanation of the practical use of ROA will be given in the next sections.

A question that arises at this point is why investment analysts in the shipping industry should use ROA to assess their investment since real options seem at first sight more complicated than the simpler DCF methods. The answer is simple: because the shipping industry is characterized by a combination of volatile markets and a high uncertainty which lead managers to adjust their strategies/investments based on market information flow. Hence, ROA is a very efficient capital budgeting technique in such an environment. For instance, real options enable the managers of a shipping company to make rational investment decisions (the right decision at the right time) such as whether to buy or sell ships increasing their investment value on upside potential opportunities or mitigate losses on unfavourable market conditions.

15.2 Types of real options in shipping

In shipping, there are a number of valuable real options that investors regularly use without realizing the benefits that may arise from the proper assessment of these options. These options are separated into two main categories similar to financial options: call options and put options. Call options are used mainly when the shipping market moves favourably, while put options are used when the market moves unfavourably. At this point, it is good to see the analogy of financial options and real options. According to Trigeorgis (1996), call options of stocks are similar to real options on a project. Specifically, the necessary inputs of call options on stocks are 1) the current value of stock, 2) the exercise price, 3) the time to expiration, 4) the stock value uncertainty and the risk-free interest rate which are corresponding/analogous to the following inputs of real options on a project: 1) the present value of expected cash flows, 2) the investment cost, 3) the time until opportunities "expire", 4) the project value uncertainty, and 5) the risk-free interest rate which remains the same (Trigeorgis, 1996). Real options are also distinguished into European and American options as financial options. European real options are exercised on a scheduled day, while American options can be exercised any time before opportunities disappear. Most real options in shipping are American-type options because of the unexpected and dynamic profile of the shipping market.

The most common real options in shipping are the option to expand, growth option, time-to-build option, option to defer, option to abandon, option to contract, option to lay-up, option to switch, option to default. Following is a brief description of each.

15.2.1 Option to expand

If a specific shipping market (e.g. tanker market) has an upward trend, then many shipping companies decide to increase the scale of their operation in several ways: purchasing new or second-hand ships, entering into a new market (from dry to wet), etc. Consider a company that has the option to purchase new or second-hand vessels by investing an amount which equals I_E, in order to have an additional benefit from favourable market developments. This company will decide to invest (exercise expand option) only if the additional increase (e%) of the firm value is higher than the investment cost (I_E, exercised price).[2] Bendall and Stent (2005, 2007) show that a shipping company that has the flexibility to expand or contract will be in better economic position than when operating in any rigid strategy as assumed by DCF methods.

15.2.2 Time-to-build option, option to defer, and option to abandon

During a shortage of ships, there is an increase in the demand for new ships. A shipping company, before deciding whether or not to invest in a new ship, should take into consideration all the embedded options of this investment. The purchase of a new vessel is completed after a shipping company pays (usually) five instalments; this procedure gives some additional flexibility to the company.[3] At the time of the first payment, a company has an American call option which can be called either *time-to-build option* or *option to defer*.[4]

This option will be exercised if the investment opportunity's value is higher than the corresponding outlay. From the second payment onwards, the company will face two mutually exclusive options: the first one is the option to continue the building procedure (time-to-build option) or to defer (option to defer) the payment for a given period, given that the contract of the building of a new ship has a clause that allows the shipowner to delay their installments, and the second option is the *option to abandon* for the salvage value. The second one is an American put option with a maturity equal to the maturity of the time-to-build option or the option to defer. The maturity of the option to defer depends mainly on the shipbuilding contract; usually, a shipping company has a maximum period of one year to the settlement of the payment (one-year delay). Particularly, this option has been widely used by dry bulk shipping companies during the first quarter of 2016 because of the unprecedented crisis in the dry bulk market, when shipping companies, by delaying their payments, gave time to the market to recover. The abandon option can be exercised if the price of the ship's salvage value (exercise price) under construction is higher than the value of the current project (the present value of future free cash flows of this new ship), then the company should abandon the investment for its salvage value by selling to a shipowner who is willing to undertake this investment by paying the salvage value.

The salvage value is not usually predetermined as it happens to most financial options, hence the valuation of such options should be done based on rational assumptions and reassessing from time to time.

15.2.3 Option to contract

The option to contract is useful when the shipping markets (i.e. dry bulk market) fluctuate on lower levels than expected. In this case, a shipping company has several options in order to reduce its operating costs. For instance, if the ship's operating costs (exercise price) are higher than the revenue for more than a certain period (e.g. two weeks), then a company can take out (lay-up) the ship until the market recovers, saving in this way the operating costs. Dixit and Pindyck (1994) and Tvedt (1999) try to value the option to lay-up assuming that freight revenues follow a geometric Brownian process, while Mossin (1968), in his seminal study, assumes that freight revenues follow a stochastic process based on stationary random walk. Another option to contract in shipping is that to sell the ship in the second-hand market if it is possible. This option (option to sell the ship in the second-hand market) is an American-type option that can be exercised if the present value of the future revenues based on the current market conditions is lower than the selling price in the second-hand market. Also, some other options to contract may be related with the ship's operation by a way that reduces the outlays. Such an option to contract can be that to decrease the ship's speed, saving a significant amount of fuel costs and reducing the short-term ship supply a bit. This type of option is an American put option which is exercised if the potential cost savings (I_s) (exercise cost) are higher than the reducing project's value (rV, r is the percentage reduction change of the project's value), giving $\max(I_s - rV, 0)$ (Trigeorgis, 1993b, 1996).

15.2.4 Option to switch

Switching options give the right to the decision maker to switch from one mode of operation to another that is more profitable after accounting for the switching cost, if it exists. This type of option is valuable because of technological improvements and the alternative services that a shipping company can provide. Sodal et al. (2008) use a real options model to value the switching option that arises from combined carriers (COMBO). Specifically, a combined carrier has the option to carry either wet or dry bulk, which makes combination carriers more expensive than tankers or dry bulk carriers of comparable size. For that reason, they try to assess this flexibility using a closed-form solution based on real options theory. Also, a similar model developed by Sodal et al. (2009) tries to value the flexibility that a shipping company has to switch from dry bulk market to tanker market, using the assumption that a shipping company owns only one ship that operates in exactly one of the two markets. Another strategic tradeoff that a shipping company has is the flexibility to switch their ships from time charter to spot market and vice versa, or to switch between several alternative routes based on the most profitable choice. A shipping company that "holds" any option to switch should take into consideration which of its options is more profitable in each period, taking into account the switching costs because they are important factors in the valuation of such options (Kulatilaka and Trigeorgis, 1994). More specifically, Kulatilaka and Trigeorgis (1994) show that if there is no cost to switch from one operating mode to another, then the value of the flexible project (e.g. combined carrier) can be seen as the value of the rigid project (e.g. tanker or dry bulk carrier) plus the values of the option to switch in the future; this means that option value additivity holds. However, in the presence of asymmetric switching costs between alternatives, operating strategies create interactions that lead option value additivity to break down.

15.2.5 Growth options

In a dynamic and unpredictable industry such as shipping, growth options play a key role. Growth options are related to a firm's strategic planning and future investment opportunities, strengthening the company's presence and competitive positioning. This type of option includes many other real options such as the option to expand, the option to acquire, the option to alliance, and generally any investment (call) option that tends to increase the firm's or project's value. Growth options are more intense in the shipbuilding market because shipbuilding companies invest huge amounts in research and development (R&D) in order to enhance or retain their market positioning. Firms that usually invest in R&D have a series of growth options (or staged investment), high investment uncertainty and possibly a negative NPV. However, in the case that the follow-up options (e.g., applying the new innovative technology on the ships, gaining new ship orders) are taken into account using ROA, this investment opportunity can turn into a valuable investment. A growth option example in the shipping industry can be the option of a dry bulk shipping company to enter into the tanker by making a strategic acquisition. During unfavorable tanker market conditions, this investment may seem worthless, but taking into account all the embedded future growth opportunities that are associated with this investment decision, maybe really worth. Such opportunities can mean that the acquirer, after a year of the acquisition, may have the option to replace some of the existing tankers with new larger vessels with new technologies in order to enter into a new agreement with a big oil company which needs a transportation partner who owns technologically developed ships. In this example, the first option is a compound option (strategic acquisition) which has a follow-up switching option (option to replace existing ships with new ones). Another example of growth options is when a liner shipping company can invest in a container terminal (e.g. COSCO Group) and use it for its own benefit, gaining a substantial advantage over the other liner companies that use this container terminal. A liner shipping company can invest in bigger vessels and add more routes, which can boost the company's operation providing a substantial strategic value that can also push out of the market many of its competitors.

15.3 Application of real options analysis in shipping

This section shows how real options can be used in various shipping investments. The examples that follow use a binomial option pricing model rather than closed-form solutions in order to make it easier for the readers to understand how ROA works. This implies that the various shipping assets follow a multiplicative binomial process (Cox et al., 1979) similarly to Tvent (1999), Bendall and Stent (2005, 2007), Alizadeh and Nomikos (2009).[5] In each example, ROA results are compared with those of NPV in order to clarify why ROA is a superior capital budgeting approach.

Based on ROA, the real project value (Expanded NPV) is equal to the standard NPV of cash flows plus the option premium that arises from the managerial flexibility of active management (Trigeorgis (1996, p. 124)) that is given by,

$$\text{Expanded NPV} = \text{NPV of expected cash Flows} + \text{Option Premium} \qquad (15.1)$$

The first example is a simple generic example that intends to show the differences between ROA and DCF (NPV) in the absence and presence of management flexibility.

15.3.1 Generic example of ROA

The following example includes a simple generic example based on ROA that intends to explain briefly the idea of risk-neutral valuation and the difference between ROA and DCF methods.

Assume that a company is considering investing in a new project that costs \$22 million. The present value of the future cash flows (project value or underlying asset) is \$20 million and in one year this project is expected to be either \$34 million if the market moves favourably or \$12 million if the market moves unfavourably. This means that the project value follows the multiplicative binomial process with upward factor equal to 1.7 and downward factor equal to 0.6.[6] There is an equal probability for the market to move up (P_u) or down (P_d), which is equal to 0.5 or 50%. The cost of capital in this project, based on given information, can be estimated as follows:[7]

$$r_c = \frac{0.5 \times V_1^+ + 0.5 \times V_1^-}{V_0} - 1 = \frac{0.5 \times 32 + 0.5 \times 12}{20} - 1 = 0.1 \text{ or } 10\% \tag{15.2}$$

We expect the two methods to conclude in the same decision, whether to accept or to reject the project, since this project does not provide any flexibility.

15.3.2 DCF methods (NPV)

The project's value is equal to \$20 million. This could be also found using the equation:[8]

$$V_0 = \frac{P_{DCF} \times V_1^+ + (1 - P_{DCF}) \times V_1^-}{1 + k} = \frac{0.5 \times 32 + 0.5 \times 12}{1.10} = 20 \tag{15.3}$$

The NPV is given by the following equation:

$$\text{NPV} = V_0 - I_0 = 20 - 22 = -2 \text{ million} \tag{15.4}$$

The NPV of this project is −2 million, which means that it should be rejected by the firm.

15.3.3 ROA

The ROA using binomial trees also assumes that the project value follows the multiplicative binomial process with the difference that the probabilities of the underlying asset to move up or down are estimated using risk-neutral probabilities that allow the expected values of the project to be discounted at the risk-free rate $(r_f = 4\%)$ (Cox et al., 1979).[9] The risk-neutral probabilities are estimated in the same manner as in financial options (for more information see Trigeorgis, 1996, Chapter 5). The following equations show how to estimate the risk-neutral probabilities for the one-step binomial tree (Figure 15.1).

$$\text{Probability of up movement} = P_{ROA} = \frac{(1 + r_f) \times V_0 - V_1^-}{V_1^+ - V_1^-} = \frac{(1.04) \times 20 - 12}{32 - 12} 0.44 \tag{15.5a}$$

$$1 - P_{ROA} = 0.56 \tag{15.5b}$$

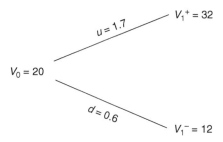

Figure 15.1   One-step binomial lattice using risk-neutral valuation method (ROA).

The expanded NPV is equal to the value of the option to invest today or not. The value of this option is given by Equation (15.6) and it equals to zero, which implies that the firm should not invest in this project today.

$$E_0 = \max\left(V_0 - I_0, 0\right) = \max\left(20 - 22, 0\right) = 0 \tag{15.6}$$

In the absence of managerial or operating flexibility, the two methods (DCF and ROA) provide the same decision (rejection of the investment) because this project does not include any operation or managerial flexibility. In reality, most investments give several types of flexibility (expand, defer, contract, and so forth) where DCF is unable to take into account these options and may lead investors to wrong decisions.

Let's see what happens in the presence of managerial flexibility. In the previous example, supposedly, a firm has the option to wait to invest for a year. Hence, a firm, by waiting a year to decide when to invest or not, will benefit from the availability of new information, which will make its investment decision easier than a year before, since the uncertainty will have been reduced to a large extent.

The underlying asset price evolution lattice is the same as before, but now we have to value the option to defer (OD) where the project value should be adjusted for it (Figure 15.2).

The investment cost in one year forward is estimated using the risk-free interest rate, similarly to what happens with the exercise price of financial options: $I_1 = 22 \times (1.04) = 22.88$

The expanded NPV (NPV plus the option to defer) of the investment can be estimated using the option pricing technique for one step:

$$E_0 = \frac{P E^+ + (1-P)E^-}{(1+r_f)} = \frac{0.44 * 9.12 + 0.56 * 0}{1.04} = 3.86 \text{ million} \tag{15.7}$$

The value of the option to defer is equal to the actual project value including the flexibility to defer (expanded NPV) minus the NPV value from DCF.

Option Premium = Expanded NPV $-$ (DCF) NPV

Option Premium $= 3.86 - (-2) = 5.86$ million

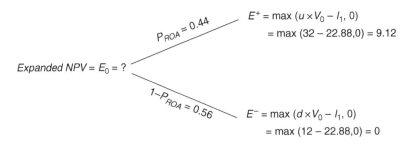

$$E^+ = \max(u \times V_0 - I_1, 0)$$
$$= \max(32 - 22.88, 0) = 9.12$$

Expanded NPV = E_0 = ?

$P_{ROA} = 0.44$

$1 - P_{ROA} = 0.56$

$$E^- = \max(d \times V_0 - I_1, 0)$$
$$= \max(12 - 22.88, 0) = 0$$

Figure 15.2 Option to defer (one step).

DTA can also capture the value of waiting to invest but may lead to different/misleading results because of the use of different probabilities and a discount factor which, as it has already been mentioned, is the main drawback of DTA (see Trigeorgis, 1996, p.160):

$$\text{Project Value} = \frac{P_{DCF}E^+ + (1 - P_{DCF})E^-}{1 + k} = \frac{0.5 * 9.12 + 0.5 * 0}{1.10} = 4.15$$

There is a difference between DTA and ROA, about 0.3 (= 4.15 − 3.86) where DTA seems to lead to an overestimation of the project.

Example 1: option to defer in shipping

This example shows how the option to defer can be applied in shipping, using market data. Assume that in April 2014, a shipping company that operates in oil transportation considered investing in two five-year-old (modern) Aframax Tankers in order to benefit from future market developments in freight rates. The cost of this investment today (May 2014) is assumed to be $75 million.[10] The shipping company, after the purchase, will operate those using five-years' time charters.[11] Based on this information, the present value (in April 2014) of future free cash flows (FCF) for both vessels is assumed to be $73 million.[12] Hence, the NPV of this investment is −2.5 million,

NPV = 73 − 75 = −2.5 millions

For that reason, the shipping company based on traditional DCF should reject this investment. However, this investment gives the option to defer the investment for a year, which provides additional flexibility to the firm and, of course, increases the investment value because the option to defer gives some time for the market to be improved. This option cannot be properly captured by DCF, but ROA can do it.

The first step to the valuing of real options is to create the lattice for the evolution of the underlying asset (the present value of future cash flow of the investment) using binomial trees. Binomial trees are estimated in a similar way to financial options valuation, using up and down multipliers based on the multiplicative binomial process. For the estimation of up (u) and down (d) multipliers, the standard deviation of the underlying assets and the duration of each step in binomial tree, Δ_t are required. The standard deviation of the underlying asset is assumed to be equal to the standard deviation of logarithmic returns of five years' time charters freight rates. To estimate the standard deviation, we use the monthly data from Clarkson Shipping Intelligence Network (CSIN), taking all the available historical

(70 monthly observations) logarithmic returns of five years' time charters freight rates (CSIN code 69839).[13] The steps for the option to defer are assumed to be four and the maturity one year, hence $\Delta_t = 0.25$ (= number of steps/maturity of the option). The following formulas calculate the multiplicative factors (u and d):

$$u = e^{\sigma\sqrt{\Delta_t}} \Rightarrow u = e^{0.091\sqrt{0.25}} = 1.05 \tag{15.8}$$

$$d = e^{-\sigma\sqrt{\Delta_t}} \ldots \Rightarrow d = e^{-0.091\sqrt{0.25}} = 0.96 \quad \text{or} \quad d = \frac{1}{u} = \frac{1}{1.835} = 0.96 \tag{15.9}$$

The risk-neutral probabilities for upward and downward movements of discrete prices are given as follows:[14]

$$P_u = \frac{e^{r_f(\Delta_t)} - d}{u - d} = \frac{e^{4\%(0.25)} - 0.954}{1.046 - 0.954} = 0.60 \tag{15.10a}$$

$$P_d = 1 - P_u = 0.40 \tag{15.10b}$$

After the estimation of all the necessary intermediate inputs, we can proceed to the real option valuation (Figure 15.3). Figures 15.4 and 15.5 present the project's value evaluation lattice and the option to defer valuation lattice respectively. The project's values in Figure 15.4 are estimated from left to right. Specifically, if the project's value moves only right, then it is (increased) multiplied by u, but if it moves right and down, it is (decreased) multiplied by d. For example, the value of the project in the second step, if we assume that it will move

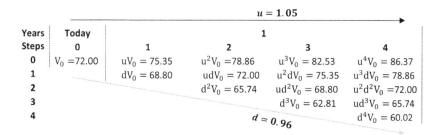

Figure 15.3   Project's value evolution lattice.

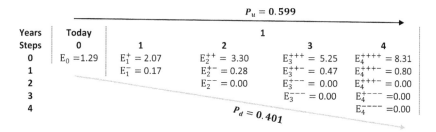

Figure 15.4   Option to defer valuation lattice.

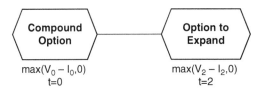

max($V_0 - I_0, 0$) max($V_2 - I_2, 0$)
t=0   t=2

Figure 15.5 Option map.

upwards for two consecutive years, will be $V_2^{++} = u^2 \times V_0 = 1.05^2 \times 72 = \$78.86$ million. All the values in the following figures are presented in millions.

To estimate the option to defer value, we have to start our assessment procedure from the final step (fourth step). The option prices (payoffs) in the fourth (final) step in the option valuation lattice are estimated using the maximum function, comparing the value of the project at step four minus the investment cost and zero. For instance, the value of the node E_4^{+++-} is equal to the corresponding project's value $\left(u^3 dV_0 = 78.86\right)$ minus the investment cost $\left(75 \times e^{0.04(0.25 \times 4)}\right)$ at step four or zero, max $\left(78.86 - 78.06, 0\right) = \$0.8$ million . The option prices from the third step and earlier are calculated using the backward induction method for American options that includes a maximum function comparing the options prices $\left((P_u E_{t+1}^+ + P_d E_{t+1}^+)e^{-rf \Delta t}\right)$ and the payoffs of early exercise/investment $\left(V_t - I_0 e^{rf(t)}\right)$. For instance, the option value at node E_3^{+++} derives from the following equation:

$$E_3^{+++} = \max\left(\left(P_u \times E_4^{++++} + P_{dx} E_4^{+++-}\right)e^{-rf \times \Delta t}, u^3 \times V_0 - I_0 \times e^{rf \times (3 \times \Delta t)}\right)$$

$$E_3^{+++} = \max\left(\left(0.599 \times 8.311 + 0.401 \times 0.799\right)e^{-4\% \times (0.25)},\right.$$

$$\left.1.045^3 \times 72 - 75e^{4\% \times (3 \times 0.25)}\right)$$

The expanded NPV for this investment is $1.293 million, which means that the investment should not be rejected as suggested by traditional (passive) NPV, but it should be kept alive for a year. The positive value of expanded NPV arises from the option to defer where its value is $3.793 million (1.293–(–2.5)), which is equal to about to 5% of the project's gross value. It is worth noting that there is no early exercise of the option to invest since the project's value does not erode by any dividend-type payout rates such as competitive erosion.

Example 2: Compound/sequential option and expand option

A dry bulk shipping company, due to the recent unprecedented crisis in dry bulk shipping (January 2016), considers diversifying in a new shipping market by investing in two modern (five years old) Suezmax oil tankers (160K DWT). The cost of this investment is assumed to be $100 million $\left(I_0\right)$. Additionally, two years after this investment, the firm has the opportunity to be the main oil transportation company of a specific oil company that operates in specific oilfields, but the shipping company should buy two additional VLCC tankers (260K DWT) that will cost $180 million $\left(I_2\right)$.[15] The first option is a compound option whose value derived from the follow-on option, which is similar to the expand option that gives the opportunity to the firm to expand its operations by investing an additional amount ($180 million).[16] Both options are assumed to be European-type options. The present value of future FCF from Suezmax vessels is assumed to be $87 million, and for VLCC it is $155 million. Hence, the present value of the first investment (V_0) is $87 million and its annual volatility is equal to 18%, which is estimated as the average of standard deviation for one, three, and five years' time charters (CSIN code 48989, 49108, and 69838 respectively) for the previous 36 months (from March 2013 to March 2016) since the firm plan to operate its new ships through time charter contracts. If the company decides to expand its operations in oil transportation by incurring the follow-on cost, it will benefit by an additional part $((e\% = 85\%)$ of the investment in Suezmax ships; this benefit implies that the present value of FCF from VLCC tankers is $160.95 million $\left(= 1.85 \times 87 = (1 + e\%) \times V_0\right)$. The risk-free interest rate is 5%. The total NPV for the whole project, and for each investment opportunity, is as follows:

NPV of the first investment:

$$NPV_0 = V_0 - PV(I_0) => NPV = 87 - 100 = -\$13 \text{ million}$$

NPV of the second investment:[17]

$$NPV_2 = (1 + e\%) \times V_0 - PV(I_0) => NPV = 160.95 - 180 \times e^{-5\% \times 2} = -1.92 \text{ million}$$

Total NPV of the project:

$$\text{Total}(\text{Passive})NPV = NPV_0 + NPV_2 = -13 - 1.92 = -\$14.92 \text{ million}$$

The NPVs from the first and the follow-on investments are −$13 and −$1.92 million respectively. Consequently, the shipping company should reject the whole investment opportunity since the total (traditional) NPV is −14.92 million. These investment options include a certain level of flexibility, the option to expand in two years for which DCF methods are unable to assess them properly. Hence, we can deal with this investment using ROA.

Figure 15.6 shows the option map of the company's investment opportunity to get into a new shipping market, which is a simple growth compound option. Firstly, the option to expand should be assessed because the value of the compound option derives from a combination of the follow-on option.

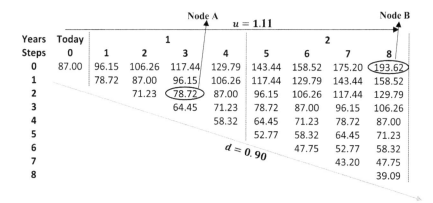

Figure 15.6 Underlying asset.

Table 15.1 presents the necessary input parameters for the evaluation of these real options. All the intermediate parameters are estimated in a similar way as the previous example. The value of the asset increases and decreases in each step of binomial lattice (see Figure 15.6) by up ($u = 1.11$) and down ($d = 0.90$) multifactors respectively. Also, the risk-neutral probability for upward and downward movement is 55% and 45% respectively. More specifically, the nodes A and B from Figure 15.7 are calculated as follows:

$$\text{Node A} = V_0 \times d^2 \times u^1 = 87 \times 0.90^2 \times 1.11^1 = \$78.72 \text{ million}$$

where $d = 0.9048 \cong 0.90$ and $u = 1.1052 \approx 1.11$

$$\text{Node B} = V_0 \times u^{12} = 87 \times 1.11^{12} = \$256.19 \text{ million}$$

Figures 15.7 and 15.8 illustrate the payoffs for expand and compound options respectively.[18] The payoffs of the option to expand at maturity and on earlier steps are measured as follows:

$$\text{Node A} = \max\left((1+e\%) \times V_0 - I_3, 0\right) = \max\left(1.85 \times 193.62 - 180, 0\right) = \$178.20 \text{ million}$$

Table 15.1 ROA Parameters

Panel A: Input Parameters		Panel B: Intermediate Parameters	
V_0	$87 million	Δ_t	0.25
I_1	$105 million	$e^{-rf \times (\Delta_t)}$	1.01
I_3	$180 million	$u\left(= e^{\sigma\sqrt{\Delta_t}}\right)$	1.09
Σ	20%	$d\left(= e^{-\sigma\sqrt{\Delta_t}}\right)$	0.90
r_f	0.05	$P_u\left(= \dfrac{e^{r(\Delta_t)} - d}{u - d}\right)$	54%
T	2	$P_d = (1 - P_u)$	46%
Steps	8	$e\%$	85%

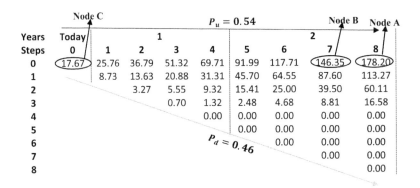

Years	Today		1					2	
Steps	0	1	2	3	4	5	6	7	8
0	17.67	25.76	36.79	51.32	69.71	91.99	117.71	146.35	178.20
1		8.73	13.63	20.88	31.31	45.70	64.55	87.60	113.27
2			3.27	5.55	9.32	15.41	25.00	39.50	60.11
3				0.70	1.32	2.48	4.68	8.81	16.58
4					0.00	0.00	0.00	0.00	0.00
5						0.00	0.00	0.00	0.00
6							0.00	0.00	0.00
7								0.00	0.00
8									0.00

Node C $P_u = 0.54$ Node B Node A $P_d = 0.46$

Figure 15.7 Option to expand.

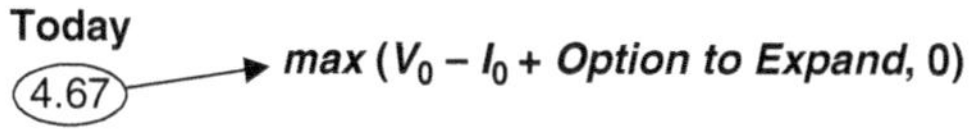

Today
(4.67) ⟶ *max (V$_0$ − I$_0$ + Option to Expand, 0)*

Figure 15.8 Compound option (expanded NPV).

$$\text{Node B} = \left(0.54 \times 178.20 + 0.46 \times 113.27\right)e^{-5\% \times 0.25} = \$146.35 \text{ million}$$

$$\text{Node C} = \left(0.54 \times 25.76 + 0.46 \times 8.73\right)e^{-5\% \times 0.25} = \$17.67 \text{ million}$$

The value of the option to expand is equal to $17.67 million, where this option can also be valued using the Black and Scholes (1973) formula since it can be exercised only upon maturity ($t = $ 2nd year). The value of the option to expand from the Black and Scholes formula is $17.26 million, which is close to the value that is derived from binomial option pricing model.[19] However, the formula of Black and Scholes assumes infinite steps (continues time) where if it is possible to use such closed-form solution, it is preferable to do it because it is more accurate.

The value of the first option (compound option) is equal to:

$$\text{Expanded NPV} = \max\left(V_0 - I_0 + \text{Option to Expand}, 0\right)$$

$$= 87 - 100 + 17.26 = \$4.26 \text{ million}$$

Therefore, the project's expanded NPV that incorporates the value of the option to expand is equal to $4.26 million, which implies that the project should be accepted by the firm and not be rejected as suggested by traditional NPV (DCF methods). Hence, the value of the compound option (including the option to expand) can also be given by:

$$\text{Option to Expand} = \text{Expanded NPV} - \left(\text{traditional}\right)\text{NPV}$$

$$= 4.26 - \left(-13\right) = \$17.26 \text{ million}$$

which is equal to almost 20% (17.26/87) of the initial investment on the Suezmax vessels.

15.4 Conclusion

The aim of this chapter is threefold. Firstly, it intends to explain the real options analysis in a simple way. More specifically, ROA is a valuation method that can properly capture the managerial flexibility and handle the uncertainty that is associated with an investment. Secondly, this chapter tries to explain the superior position of ROA relative to alternative capital budgeting techniques. Also, it gives a brief description of the main real options in shipping industry which are the option to expand, the option to defer, the option to abandon, the option to contract, the option to switch, and growth options. Additionally, we show how ROA can be applied to evaluate shipping investments using two different examples. The first one refers to the option to defer which is really valuable during trough or recovery stages of the shipping cycle. The second example shows how to assess an investment that unlocks an expansion investment. The first investment of this example is similar to a compound option where its value depends on the follow-on investment/option. Moreover, each example is also evaluated using the net present value in order for the results of both valuation methods to be compared.

In the shipping industry, which is characterized by unpredictable market movements and high uncertainty, ROA could be an essential tool for capital budgeting decisions. Furthermore, it can increase the efficiency of the shipping economy by helping shipping companies to react rationally at the right time when the shipping market moves favourably or unfavourably. The future of a shipping company will be determined by rational investment options; therefore, a better evaluation method (ROA) leads to a promising future.

Notes

1 Knowledge of financial options is considered essential for the understanding of real options. For a review of financial options see Black and Scholes (1973), Merton (1973), Smith (1976),Cox, Ross and Rubinstein andHull (2012).
2 An expansion option will be exercised if its payoff (max(eV-I_E, 0)) is higher than zero, where eV is the additional value that arises by investing I_E.
3 It is worth to note that a new ship needs about two to three years before being 'delivered from the first payment.
4 For more information about time-to-build option and option to defer, see McDonald and Siegel (1986), Majd and Pindyck (1987), Paddock et al. (1988), Trigeorgis (1993a), Trigeorgis (1996), Milne and Elizabeth (2000).
5 Bjerksund and Ekern (1995), Sodal et al. (2008, 2009) use ROA in shipping by assuming that the shipping assets (i.e. freight rates) follow a mean-reverting process.
6 The formulas for the estimation of up and down multiplicative factors along with risk-neutral probabilities for multiple-steps binomial trees are presented in Equations (15.8, 15.9, 15.10a and 15.10b) respectively.
7 Commonly, the cost of capital is estimated by traditional the Weighted Average Cost of Capital (WACC) formula of Modigliani and Miller (1958, 1963). Two important components of the WACC formula are the cost of debt and the cost of equity. The first one is easy to identify but the second one needs a significant effort, and practitioners usually use the Capital Asset Pricing Model (CAPM) or some arbitrage pricing models such as the three and five factor model of Fama and French (1993, 2015). The number of operating years of this ship is assumed to be 20, hence it has an additional 15 years before being removed from the market. In the end of its useful life, the ship is sold for scrapping, where this scrap value is adjusted on the last predicted FCF.
8 In the case that we have the forecasts of FCF and we wish to estimate the present value of this project, we should use the following equation:

$$V_0 = \sum_{t=1}^{N} \frac{FCF_t}{(1+r_c)^t}$$

where N refers to the final future FCF, t is the time, and r_c is the project's cost of capital.
9 Real options analysis in several studies is referred as contingent claim analysis (CCA).
10 In reality the new or second-hand ship prices are stochastic, where they usually follow a mean-reverting process. In order to avoid the complexity with two stochastic or discrete variables, we assume that the ship prices are constant and are adjusted in time using the risk-free rate. Time charter freight rates are assumed to be a stochastic variable. That is the main factor that affects the present value of project's FCFs, representing the current price of the underlying asset.
11 The expected life of these ships is assumed to be 20 years, hence the shipping company will exploit them for 15 years and then it will sell them for their scrap value, which should be adjusted in the analysis. The firm will have the opportunity to use three five years' time charters. In reality, a shipping company has more than one option to operate their ships, which can be priced using ROA (or else CCA), see for example Bjerksund and Ekern (1995).
12 FCF is equal to the future operating revenues minus the total expenses (operating costs, maintenance costs, and so on). It is not in the objectives of the present chapter to show how to forecast the shipping markets and consequently the cash flows of shipping investments, hence, the numbers that are used

in various examples are hypothetical. The present value of FCF (of project) is derived by discounting predicted FCF by cost of capital.

13 After the estimation, monthly standard deviation should be transformed to annual frequency (i.e. $\sigma_{monthly} * \sqrt{12} = \sigma_{yearly}$).

14 The risk-free rate is assumed to be 4%.

15 The oil company set as a requirement to a potential transportation partner to be operated in the oil transportation industry for at least two years in order to have the experience and the expertise to keep a high level of customer satisfaction. Hence this option will be available only if the first option takes place today.

16 Compound option or sequential option is an option whose underlying asset derived from the follow-on option price. This type of option was valued using a closed-form solution by Geske (1979), who replaced the standard normal distribution (Black and Scholes (1973)) with a bi-variate normal distribution.

17 The investment cost for the expand strategy is $180 million, which should be discounted by risk-free rate for two years to be compared with the present value of the project $180\ e^{-0.05 \times 2} = 162.87$.

18 Both options are European type options, hence at intermediate steps do not have the opportunity for early exercise.

19 $\text{Option to expand} = \left(\left(1 + e\% \right) \times V_0 \right) \times N\left(d_1 \right) - I_3 \times N\left(d_2 \right) \times e^{r_f \times T}$ (15.11)

$$d_1 = \frac{ln\left(\dfrac{\left(\left(1 + e\% \right) \times V_0 \right)}{I_3} \right) + \left(r_{f-} \dfrac{\sigma^2}{2} \right) \times T}{\sigma\sqrt{T}}$$ (15.11a) and $d_2 = d_1 - \sigma \times \sqrt{T}$ (15.11b)

References

Alizadeh, A.H., & Nomikos N. (2009). *Shipping derivatives and risk management*. Basingstoke Stoke: Palgrave Macmillan.

Bendall, H.B., & Stent, A.F. (2005). Ship investment under uncertainty: Valuing a real option on the maximum of several strategies. *Maritime Economics & Logistics*, 7(1), 19–35.

Bendall, H.B., & Stent, A.F. (2007). Maritime investment strategies with a portfolio of real options. *Maritime Policy & Management*, 34(5), 441.

Bjerksund, P., & Ekern, S. (1995). Contingent claims evaluation of mean-reverting cash flows in shipping. In *Real options in capital investment: Models, strategies, and applications* (pp. 207–219). London: Preager.

Black, F., & Scholes, M. (1973). The pricing of options and corporate liabilities. *Journal of Political Economy*, 81(3), 637.

Brealey, R.A., Myers, S.C., & Allen, F. (2009). *Principles of corporate finance*. New York: Tata McGraw-Hill Education.

Copeland, T.E., Weston, J.F., & Shastri, K. (2004). *Financial theory and corporate policy*. New York: Pearson.

Cox, J.C., Ross, S.A., & Rubinstein, M. (1979). Option pricing: A simplified approach. *Journal of Financial Economics*, 7(3), 229–263.

Dixit, A.K., & Pindyck, R.S. (1994). *Investment under uncertainty*. Princeton University Press.

Fama, E.F., & French, K.R. (1993). Common risk factors in the returns on stocks and bonds. *Journal of Financial Economics*, 33(1), 3–56.

Geske, R. (1979). The valuation of compound options. *Journal of Financial Economics*, 7(1), 63–81.

Graham, J.R., & Harvey, C.R. (2001). The theory and practice of corporate finance: Evidence from the field. *Journal of Financial Economics*, 60(2–3), 187–243.

Hayes, R.H., & Abernathy, W.J. (1980). Managing our way to economic decline. *Harvard Business Review* 58(4 OP), 67–77.

Hayes, R.H., & Garvin, D.A. (1982). Managing as if tomorrow mattered. *Harvard Business Review*, 60(3), 70.

Hertz, D.B. (1964). Risk analysis in capital investment. *Harvard Business Review*, 42(1), 95–106.

Hodder, J.E., & Riggs, H.E. (1985). Pitfalls in evaluating risky projects. *Harvard Business Review: HBR*, 63(1), 128–135.

Hull, J. (2012). *Options, futures, and other derivatives* 8th edition. New York: Pearson.

Kester, G.W., Chang, R.P., Echanis, E.S., Haikal, S., Isa, M.M., Skully, M.T., Tsui, K.-C., & Wang, C.-J. (1999). Capital budgeting practices in the Asia-Pacific region: Australia, Hong Kong, Indonesia, Malaysia, Philippines, and Singapore. *Financial Practice & Education*, *9*(1), 25.

Kulatilaka, N., & Trigeorgis, L. (1994). The general flexibility to switch: Real options revisited. *International Journal of Finance*, *6*(2), 179–198.

Magee, J.F. (1964). Decision trees for decision making. *Harvard Business Review*, *42*(4), 126–138. Retrieved from http://prx.library.gatech.edu/login

Majd, S., & Pindyck, R.S. (1987). Time to build, option value, and investment decisions. *Journal of Financial Economics*, *18*(1), 7.

McDonald, R. L., & Siegel, D. (1986). The value of waiting to invest. *The Quarterly Journal of Economics*, *101*(4), 707–727.

Merton, R.C. (1973). Theory of rational o pricing. *The Bell Journal of Economics and Management Science*, *4*(1), 141–183.

Milne, A., & Elizabeth A.W. (2000). "Time to build, option value and investment decisions": a comment. *Journal of Financial Economics*, *56*(2), 325.

Modigliani, F., & Miller, M.H. (1958). The cost of capital, corporation finance and the theory of investment. *The American Economic Review*, *XLVII*(3), 261–297.

Modigliani, F., & Miller, M.H. (1963). Corporate income taxes and the cost of capital: A correction. *American Economic Review*, *53*(3), 433–443.

Mossin, J. (1968). An optimal policy for lay-up decisions. *The Swedish Journal of Economics*, *70*(3), 170.

Myers, S.C. (1977). Determinants of corporate borrowing. *Journal of Financial Economics*, *5*, 147–175.

Myers, S.C. (1984). Finance theory and financial strategy. *Interfaces*, *14*(1), 126–137.

Paddock, J.L., Siegel, D.R., & Smith, J.L. (1988). Option valuation of claims on real assets: The case of offshore petroleum leases. *The Quarterly Journal of Economics*, *103*(3), 479.

Ryan, P.A., & Ryan, G.P. (2002). Capital budgeting practices of the fortune 1000: How have things changed? *Journal of Business & Management*, *8*(4), 355.

Salazar, R.C., & Sen, S.K. (1968). A simulation model of capital budgeting under uncertainty. *Management Science*, *15*(4), B161–B179.

Sigbjorn Sodal, S., Koekebakker, & Aadland, R. (2008). Market switching in shipping – A real option model applied to the valuation of combination carriers. *Review of Financial Economics*, *17*(3), 183–203.

Smart, S.B., Megginson, W.L., & Graham, J. (2010). *Financial Management*. Nashville: South-Western.

Smith, C.W. (1976). Option pricing: A review. *Journal of Financial Economics*, *3*(1), 3–51.

Sodal, S., Koekebakker, S., & Adland, R. (2009). Value based trading of real assets in shipping under stochastic freight rates. *Applied Economics*, *41*(22), 2793–2807.

Trigeorgis, L. (1993a). The nature of option interactions and the valuation of investments with multiple real options. *Journal of Financial and Quantitative Analysis*, *28*(1), 1–20.

Trigeorgis, L. (1993b). Real options and interactions with financial flexibility. *Financial Management*, *22*(3) 202–224.

Trigeorgis, L. (1995). *Real options in capital investment: models, strategies, and applications*. London: Praeger.

Trigeorgis, L. (1996). *Real options: managerial flexibility and strategy in resource allocation*. Cambridge, MA: MIT Press.

Trigeorgis, L., & Mason, P.S. (1987). Valuing managerial flexibility. *Midland Corporate Finance Journal*, *5*(1), 14–21.

Tvedt, J. (1999). The ship lay-up option and equilibrium freight rates. In M.J. Brennan & L. Trigeorgis (eds.), *Project flexibility, agency, and competition: new developments in the theory and application of real options* (pp. 340–349). Oxford: Oxford University Press.

16

Credit risk analysis, measurement, and management in the shipping industry

Manolis G. Kavussanos and Dimitris A. Tsouknidis

16.1 Introduction

Shipping business involves a large number of bilateral private transactions which entail (promised) future payments. This exposes shipping market participants to significant levels of credit risk, which is inherent in all bilateral agreements. Credit risk can be broadly defined as the risk each party in a deal faces that the other party will not have the ability or the willingness to honour the contract and fulfil the agreed terms of the contract.[1]

Credit risk is particularly important in the shipping business environment as it is directly linked with two notable features of the industry: first, shipping business is capital intensive, as investment on even a single vessel can often require funds of several million, depending on type and size. Second, operating within the shipping industry involves significant operational and commercial risks (see Kavussanos, 2002; Kavussanos and Visvikis, 2006). For example, shipping firms and charterers are exposed to extreme fluctuations in their cash flows which stem from pronounced volatility in freight rates and ship prices in all segments of the industry (see Kavussanos, 1996, 1997, 2002, 2003, 2010; Tsouknidis, 2016). This volatility increases the probability of default for shipping market participants. For instance, on 31 August 2016, the shipping company Hanjin filed for bankruptcy protection at the Seoul Central District Court and requested the court to freeze its assets. This was because Hanjin had long-term time-charter agreements to hire in vessels with a number of shipowners around the world. As freight rates remained at very low levels in the aftermath of the global financial crisis (2007–2009) with only moderate short-lived increases thereafter, Hanjin was not able to receive revenues based on the new freight rates – which would have enabled it to service its earlier obligations. Massive losses led the company to bankruptcy. According to Wikipedia, at the time of its default, Hanjin shipping operated 60 liner and tramper services around the globe, transporting over 100 million tons of cargo annually using a fleet of 200 containerships, bulk, and LNG carriers.[2] Hanjin Shipping's dissolution was the largest and most significant bankruptcy in the container transport industry and caused worldwide disruption in shipping as cargo ships were "trapped" at ports and canals waiting for cash payments. This default event created a massive ripple effect as several other businesses that rely on physical products found themselves without the expected revenue from inventory that became stuck at sea; moreover, a number of shipping companies that chartered out their vessels to Hanjin faced financial difficulties or bankruptcy, which also affected their own creditors and suppliers.

Given the importance of credit risk for the shipping industry, this chapter presents the main types, measures, and sources of credit risk in the sector. Furthermore, it provides a comprehensive discussion of the tools available to manage it effectively. The next section presents the potential sources of credit risk in the industry, while Section 16.3 defines its main types and measures. Section 16.4 discusses the tools available for managing this type of risk effectively, while Section 16.5 concludes the chapter.

16.2 Sources of credit risk in the shipping industry

Shipping business agreements comprise primarily bilateral private transactions which entail significant levels of credit risk. This can be viewed from different points of view, including those of shipowners, investors, suppliers, or other parties involved in the industry. Examples of parties and contracts involved include charterparty contracts between shipowners and charterers; newbuilding agreements between shipping investors and shipyards; bunker agreements between shipowners/charterers and bunker suppliers; supplies and spare parts or lubricants between shipowners/operators operating vessels and the corresponding suppliers of these commodities; shipping bank loans between banks and shipowners; shipping bonds between shipping companies borrowing money and investors in these bonds; positions in Over the Counter (OTC) Forward Freight Agreements (FFAs); acquisition contracts for second-hand vessels among shipping investors; individual and institutional investors who are interested in investing in a shipping bond or equity and financiers (bankers) who wish to assess a credit facility to finance shipping projects; shipping and insurance companies involved in insurance contracts, such as insurance for the vessel hull, machinery, pollution, etc. In this latter case, both the shipping company and the insurers face credit risk, while problems of asymmetric information between the insurer and the insured can complicate issues further.

The shipping market participants who are involved in all the aforementioned bilateral agreements face the risk of an economic loss in case the other party does not fulfil the contractual obligations. Thus, shipowners, charterers, shipyards, bunker suppliers, spare parts and lubricants suppliers, and banks among others have to carefully assess the creditworthiness of their counterparties in all these bilateral agreements and be aware of the tools available to mitigate them in order to avoid losses in case of default.

16.3 Types and measures of credit risk

16.3.1 Types of credit risk

Generally speaking, credit risk comes in different forms. Namely "default risk", "technical default risk", "credit-spread risk", and "downgrade risk":

- *default risk* is the most important type of credit risk, defined as the risk of a party failing to meet the agreed payments of a deal as scheduled. For example, a shipowner not fulfilling the repayment schedule of a shipping bank loan or a charterer not meeting the promised payments as agreed on a charter contract;
- *technical default risk* is defined as the risk that one of the two parties in an agreement stops satisfying one or more clauses of the agreement. Such an example could be, for example: a shipowner who has obtained finance for the acquisition of a newbuilding vessel through

a bank loan stops satisfying a contractual restriction posed by the creditor. This restriction may be for instance that the shipowner needs to maintain the asset cover ratio (ACR), i.e. the ratio of the vessel's value over the loan's value, above a specific level, say 125%, throughout the period of repayment of the loan. In case the ACR falls below this level, say due to a severe drop in second-hand vessel prices, the obligor (the shipowner) faces a technical default and the creditor (bank) may require additional collateral – typically in the form of cash – in order to raise the asset cover ratio above the agreed level of 125%;

- **credit spread risk** is the risk that the bondholder faces from adverse movements in the bond's spread. For example, say a shipping company raises capital through a bond issue, promising the bondholders (investors) a series of coupon payments and repayment of the initial capital (the principal) at the maturity date of the bond. Once issued, bonds trade in markets, with their price fluctuating according to the prevailing demand and supply conditions. Investors can calculate their return on investment through the yield-to-maturity (YTM) of the bond.[3] The credit spread of this bond is defined as the difference between its YTM and the YTM of a risk-free asset of the same maturity, say the US Treasury bond. The size of the credit spread indicates the bond market's assessment of the creditworthiness of the bond issuer; that is, the possibility that the issuing company does not honour the aforementioned promised payments of the bond issue;

- **downgrade risk** represents the risk that the credit rating assigned by a credit rating agency (CRA) to a specific company decreases. Such an event indicates an increase in the probability of default for this company. An immediate consequence of a downgrade event is the increase in the cost of borrowing for the company, i.e. larger margins would be required on bond issues or loans and the value of these debt instruments would be lower.

16.3.2 Measures of credit risk

The following measures are used to quantify the exposure/loss of the counterparty in case of default:

- *probability of default (PD)* is the probability of a party in a deal failing to meet the agreed terms on time;
- *distance to default (DD)* measures the number of standard deviations the asset value of the company needs to drop in order to trigger a default event;
- *exposure at default (EAD)* is the economic value, measured in monetary terms (say in dollars), of the defaulted deal for the counterparty;
- *loss given default (LGD)* is the actual economic loss as a percentage of the whole amount invested for the counterparty in case of a default.

The above measures are interrelated. For instance, the DD and PD measures have an inverse relationship, as the lower the distance to default (DD) the higher the probability of default (PD) and vice versa. Furthermore, EAD and LGD are not equal because recovery rates are typically included in a deal. Thus, the initial and typically larger exposure-at-default (EAD) of a party in a deal is limited to a typically lower actual loss given default (LGD). This is due to the existence of a recovery rate which partly offsets the initial exposure at default (EAD).

It is important to note that credit risk measures can be estimated at the company-level, assessing the creditworthiness of a specific company, or at the debt instrument/deal-level, assessing the credit riskiness of specific debt instruments or deals, such as bond issues, bank loan agreements, or charter contracts. Small deviations may be observed in the probability of default (PD) of a shipping company and that of its associated debt instruments. This is because a bond issue or a bank loan may be asset-backed up with collateral of high value – resulting into a higher recovery rate – and in this way provide better protection to the creditor in case of a default event.

From the point of view of the creditor, the decision of granting a bank loan or investing in a bond issue is enhanced given an accurate credit risk evaluation. Thus, several methodologies have been developed over time to compute different credit risk measures. These measures provide an assessment of the creditworthiness of a specific company and are important for potential creditors, investors, and suppliers of a company who require a credit risk assessment to help them decide whether and under what terms to grant a bank loan, invest in a bond issue or stock equity, etc. The most popular ones are: i) those used by credit rating agencies to assign credit ratings to companies issuing bonds; ii) credit scoring models, which build on Altman's 1968 z-score using financial accounting data comprising five different financial ratios; and iii) market-based models, which build on the seminal work of Merton (1974) and use a combination of market data, such as equity prices, and financial accounting data, such as current liabilities, long-term debt, and total assets. Credit risk measures aim to estimate probabilities of default (PD).

With the exception of the Merton (1974) market-based model, the aforementioned credit risk measures can be used to assess the credit risk of a specific entity, a specific debt instrument (bond), or a credit facility (bank loan). However, it is important to note that it is not legal for an obligor to select to honour one payment obligation against another, a notion known as a cross-default trigger. The existing legal framework, consisting of bankruptcy codes and contract law, prevents selective default. Essentially, an obligor must honour all his obligations and his creditworthiness refers exactly to this definition.

16.3.2.1 Credit ratings and credit rating agencies (CRAs)

Credit rating agencies (CRAs) produce credit ratings in order to assess the creditworthiness of a debt issue (bond) and its issuer in a simple and intuitive way. Credit ratings are popular measures of the creditworthiness of bond issuer(s) and are used by a number of participants in the global financial system, such as banks, private and institutional investors, and regulatory authorities, amongst others. CRAs use a variety of tailor-made methodologies in order to assess the creditworthiness of a bond issue(r) and assign a single credit rating. The credit rating assigned reflects information from a large number of company, industry, and macroeconomic factors.

Table 16.1 presents credit rating grading scales for three dominant CRAs, namely Moody's, Standard and Poor's (S&P), and Fitch. As observed, credit ratings are broadly classified into investment and non-investment grades;[4] corporate or government bonds rated in the range Aaa/AAA (Moody's/S&P's) to Baa/BBB (Moody's/S&P's) are considered as "*investment grade*", whereas those rated Ba/BB (Moody's/S&P's) or below are considered "*non-investment high-yield*" or junk bonds. Fitch and S&P share the same notation for their rating classes. CRAs have introduced one additional level of classification for their credit ratings by adding notches to each rating. In this way, each credit rating assigned can carry a plus or minus for S&P or numbers 1, 2, and 3 for Moody's in order to provide further refined credit ratings. For example, a company can be rated by S&P or Fitch as BB–, indicating lower creditworthiness (outlook) compared to BB+ or BB.

16.3.2.2 Credit ratings in the shipping industry

Credit ratings assigned to shipping debt instruments and issuers need to reflect the unique characteristics of the shipping industry and the high level of risks shipping market participants are exposed to. CRAs, such as Moody's (2005), have developed customized shipping-specific rating methodologies in order to assess accurately the creditworthiness of shipping debt

Table 16.1 Bond Credit Ratings Scales for the Three Dominant Credit Rating Agencies

	Moody's	Standard & Poor's	Fitch	Description
Investment Grade	Aaa1	AAA+	AAA+	Prime
	Aaa2	AAA	AAA	
	Aaa3	AAA-	AAA-	
	Aa1	AA+	AA+	High grade
	Aa2	AA	AA	
	Aa3	AA-	AA-	
	A1	A+	A+	Upper medium grade
	A2	A	A	
	A3	A-	A-	
	Baa1	BBB+	BBB+	Lower medium grade
	Baa2	BBB	BBB	
	Baa3	BBB-	BBB-	
Non-Investment Grade	Ba1	BB+	BB+	Non-investment grade
	Ba2	BB	BB	speculative
	Ba3	BB-	BB-	
	B1	B+	B+	Highly speculative
	B2	B	B	
	B3	B-	B-	
	Caa1	CCC+	CCC	Substantial risks
	Caa2	CCC		Extremely speculative
	Caa3	CCC-		Close to default with little
	Ca	CC		prospect for recovery
Default		D	DDD	In default
			DD	
			D	

instruments and entities. Specifically, for the shipping industry, Moody's (2005) recognizes that industry-specific factors are especially important when assessing the creditworthiness of shipping companies, as owning and operating ocean-cargo vessels exposes participants to substantial ownership and operational risks. According to Moody's, the following characteristics of the shipping industry are recognized as important for assigning a credit rating: high cyclicality of freight rates and asset values, commodity product fragmentation of the industry, competition and cooperation, capital intensity, different vessel funding structures, cost management, fleet management, and high volatility of financials. Table 16.2 presents the rating factors, their weightings, and the proxies used by Moody's (2005) in order to assign a credit rating to a shipping company; similar rating factors are employed by Fitch (2010).

16.3.2.3 Credit spreads of shipping bonds

Since the mid-90s, issuing public debt has become relatively popular as a source of funds for the ocean-going shipping industry. This has been facilitated by the corporate structure modern shipping companies have adopted, as they move from traditional family-centred entities to modern corporate structures. Furthermore, these companies have realized the tax advantages associated with bond issues when compared to other sources of capital, such as Initial public offerings (IPOs). The tax benefits arise as, accounting wise, interest rate payments are treated as

Table 16.2 Moody's Credit Rating Factors for Shipping Companies

Rating Factor	Weight (importance)	Rating Factor Definition
Company Size and Diversification	25%	Size: absolute revenues and number of vessels. Diversification: segment and geographical diversification and customer structure.
Revenue Characteristics	10%	Volatility of revenues and contract structure.
Operating Efficiency and Flexibility	15%	Fleet age and profitability.
Cash Flow Variability	10%	Free cash flow generation throughout the business cycle, change in the average fleet age, balanced investment strategy.
Financial Strategy and Capital Structure	15%	Average length of debt maturities, the ratio of cash and cash equivalents to total assets, the notional value of committed funding sources, value of unencumbered vessels.
Credit Metrics	25%	Adjusted retained cash flow/net adjusted debt, gross adjusted debt/EBITDA, total coverage ratio, free cash flow/gross adjusted debt.

Notes: Revenue volatility is defined as the average change in revenue growth rate over the last five years. Gross adjusted debt over EBITDA is equal to (gross debt + modified PV lease valuation + underfunded pension liabilities + "basket adjusted" hybrids + accounts receivable securitization outstanding + guarantees of debt obligations + off-balance sheet debt-like obligations + other debt like items) / (pre-tax income +/- exceptional charges/revenues – interest expense (including interest component of rent expense) + depreciation + amortization of goodwill).
Source: Moody's, Standard & Poors, and Fitch.

costs, and in this way, they reduce the tax bill. Another reason for the popularity of bond issues as a source of finance for the shipping industry is that they provide an attractive alternative to traditional bank finance, especially during periods of tight liquidity in the banking sector, such as the one which followed the onset of the global financial crisis in 2007.

Table 16.3 presents key characteristics for all shipping bonds issued over the period 2003–2016, see also Kavussanos and Tsouknidis (2014). As observed, a substantial number of bond issues offerings took place after 2003, during the booming years of freight markets. This fell to zero in 2009 and 2010, and picked up again, in the absence of bank finance, reaching a high in 2012 and 2013, and declined thereafter to only four issues in 2016. Typically, the average credit rating of these bond issues fell in the high-yield segment. The high coupon rate of these bonds as well as their spread reflect this rating; the latter has declined during the period 2004–2007 primarily due to increasing freight rates and ship prices, thereby reducing the risk level perceived by the market. This spread increased substantially during the period 2008–2010 as a result of the global financial crisis of 2007 and the ensuing shipping crisis of 2008–2009. A related pattern is also observed for the average maturity of the active bond issues: in 2004 it stood at approximately eight years; however, by the crisis years it declined to 4.83 years, went up again by 2014, and down again to 4.75 years in 2016.

The yield-to-maturity (YTM) of a bond issue is another important figure to consider. It reflects the return required by investors, under the current market conditions, to invest their funds on the bond issue. This return is a function of the risks investors bear when placing funds on the specific instrument. Similarly, bond spreads, that is risk premiums, YTM of bonds above YTM of risk-free instrument, indicate the market's assessment of the risks involved in a bond issue, including the creditworthiness of the bond issuer. Deteriorating creditworthiness of the

Table 16.3 Shipping Bond Characteristics by Year of Issuance

Year	Number of Active Bond Issues	Number of New Bond Issues	Average Spread of Active Bonds (bps)	St. Deviation of Spreads of Active Bonds (bps)	Total Market Value ($ Millions) of Active Bonds	Average Market Value ($ Millions) of Active Bonds	Average Coupon (%) of Active Bonds	Average Maturity of Active Issues (Years)	Median Moody's Rating
2003	13	–	795.88	605.26	2,116	109	9.45	6.16	B1
2004	38	25	393.92	251.88	8,987	187	8.23	8.09	Ba3
2005	42	4	351.65	294.66	9,952	241	7.75	7.84	Ba3
2006	46	4	425.93	691.09	10,604	235	7.86	6.85	Ba3
2007	50	4	466.48	808.20	11,037	238	7.89	6.24	Ba3
2008	47	2	631.44	649.31	10,125	250	7.95	6.13	Ba3
2009	44	0	882.13	900.54	9,598	233	7.97	5.42	Ba2
2010	41	0	753.74	927.05	9,471	236	8.02	4.83	Ba2
2011	43	4	551.76	506.35	9,045	260	7.21	5.88	B1
2012	60	19	783.75	632.51	9,307	251	8.24	5.19	B1
2013	70	18	632.01	747.44	16,227	338	7.53	5.62	B2
2014	65	13	617.88	980.24	23,318	387	7.95	5.84	B2
2015	64	5	585.21	250.61	23,325	380	6.94	5.54	B3
2016	60	4	725.12	369.76	19,678	315	9.65	4.75	B2

Notes: This table presents the characteristics over time of the shipping bonds examined in Kavussanos and Tsouknidis (2014), updated up to year 2016. Bond spreads are winsorized at the 1st and 99th percentiles. The number of active bonds refers to the number of shipping bonds which were available in the bond market during a specific year; each year some new bond issues are offered and some bond issues are maturing and exit the market. The number of new bonds refers to the number of issues which are first issued each year. Average spread of active bonds refers to the arithmetic average of the spread of the active bonds during each year, while the next column refers to their corresponding standard deviations. Total market value refers to the sum of the market values of all active shipping bonds at the end of each year. The average market value refers to the average amount outstanding for all the active bonds during the specific year. The same principle holds for the average coupon and the average maturity of the bond issues which were active during the specific year. Last, the median rating refers to the median average Moody's rating, as defined in Table 16.1, for all the active bonds on a yearly basis.

Source: Kavussanos and Tsouknidis (2014) and author's calculations based on data from Thomson Reuters Datastream over the period 2011–2016.

issuer indicates more uncertainty regarding the fulfilment of the bond's promised payments, higher PD, lower credit rating, and larger bond spread. It is important to note that bond spreads reflect a set of risks, the most important of which are the following: default risk, defined as the PD of a bond issue; liquidity risk, representing the risk that a bondholder cannot sell a bond at will within a short period of time or without a substantial discount in its price; and market risk, which refers to the risk of there being a significant discount in the market price of a bond as a consequence of a depressed market.

Several financial institutions publish bond indices. They reflect the level of YTMs in the global corporate bond markets. Figure 16.1 presents the weighted average YTM of five bond indices for the US market as published by Bank of America Merrill Lynch. As observed, broadly speaking, the US high-yield transportation sector excluding air/rail exhibits the largest weighted average YTM in comparison to all other indices. The index of transportation excluding air/rail (H0SH) can be considered the closest to the shipping bond market. Other indices depicted

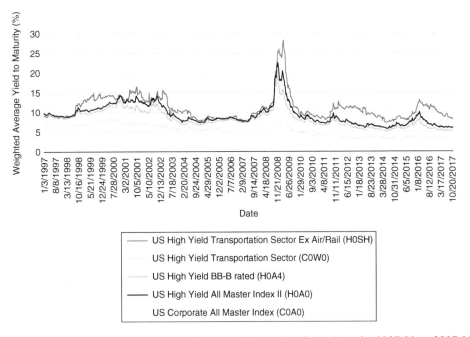

Figure 16.1 Bank of America Merrill Lynch US Bond Indices: Sample 1997:01 – 2017:11.
Notes: The above indices represent the effective yields of the BofA Merrill Lynch indices. Specifically, the US Corporate All Master Index (C0A0) tracks the performance of the US dollar denominated investment grade rated corporate debt publically issued in the US domestic market. To qualify for inclusion in the index, securities must have an investment grade rating (based on an average of Moody's, S&P, and Fitch) and an investment grade rated country of risk (based on an average of Moody's, S&P, and Fitch foreign currency long-term sovereign debt ratings). Each security must have greater than one year of remaining maturity, a fixed coupon schedule, and a minimum amount outstanding of $250 million. The same criteria apply for the US High Yield All Master Index II (H0A0) but this time a non-investment grade rating is required for the bond issues included in the index. US High Yield BB-B rated (H0A4) Index includes bond issues carrying a credit rating within the BB-B range of credit ratings. US High Yield Transportation Sector (C0W0) includes bond issues from issuers operating in the transportation industry and US High Yield Transportation Sector (H0SH) includes the same issues excluding the ones issued by air/rail issuers.
Source: Bloomberg.

in Figure 16.1 include the US High Yield Master II Index, which incorporates all high-yield bond issues for the US market and the US High Yield BB-B rated Index, which incorporates all high-yield bonds rated within the BB-B range. As expected, all these bond indices exhibit large increases during autumn–winter 2008, when the global financial crisis hit the global capital markets and Lehman Brothers collapsed.

16.3.2.4 Financial accounting measures of credit risk

Since Altman's (1968) influential paper, several studies have adopted multivariate discriminant analysis (MDA) or linear discriminant analysis (LDA) techniques in order to develop z-scores to assess the default risk of companies and/or bank loan agreements. However, the MDA approach exhibits restrictive assumptions, such as that discriminating variables are distributed as jointly multivariate normal and that the covariance matrices for failed and non-failed companies are equal (on this, see for e.g. Karels and Prakash, 1987). Typically, these assumptions are violated, thus limiting the appropriateness of the method, as it would lead to biased inferences. In contrast, a logistic regression model is free from such restrictive assumptions. In fact, as documented in the literature, logit and probit models overcome the problems of MDA and form superior methods of developing a credit scoring model for different markets, and for this reason, they are widely used in the literature (see for instance Campbell et al., 2008).

Altman's (1968) z-score utilizes five financial ratios to estimate the z-score of each company, namely: working capital (WC), retained earnings (RE), earnings before interest and taxes (EBIT), sales (S), total assets (TA), market value of equity (ME), and total liabilities (TL). The following weightings for the calculation of the z-score were estimated by Altman, utilizing a US market sample. Thus, the z-score for a company is given as:

$$z = 1.2 * (WC / TA) + 1.4 * (RE / TA)$$
$$+ 3.3 * (EBIT / TA) + 0.6 * (ME / TL) + 0.999 * (S / TA)$$

(16.1)

The ratio (WC/TA) captures the short-term liquidity of a firm, the RE/TA and EBIT/TA measure the historical and the current profitability respectively, the ME/TL is a measure of leverage, and finally the S/TA indicates the market competitiveness of a company. The model is constructed so that the higher the z-score, the less the default risk of a company. A z-score above 3 is an indication that default is very unlikely to happen, a z-score below 1.8 indicates that default is very likely, while values between 1.8 and 3 are a "grey" area. Kavussanos and Tsouknidis (2011; 2016) developed a credit scoring model for the assessment of default risk in shipping bank loan agreements.

16.3.2.5 Structural models of credit risk

The basic premise of structural models is that default risk can be assessed from market prices of securities whose values are affected by default, such as corporate bonds, equities, and credit derivatives. Securities prices should, in theory, provide more up-to-date and accurate measures of default risk since capital markets have access to a larger information set and investors have stronger incentives, such as arbitrage profits, to incorporate the available information into market prices. The first class of structural models is based on the work of Merton (1974), where default occurs when the value of the firm's assets is lower than its liabilities.

Market-based or structural models are widely used for the evaluation of the default risk of an issuer. The seminal work of Merton (1974) established the first class of these models by applying the valuation framework developed by Black and Scholes (BS) (1973). Structural models build on the efficient market hypothesis, which assumes that market prices encapsulate all the available information for a listed company including its probability of default. Therefore, credit risk can be assessed through market prices of equities.

Merton's framework identifies conditions under which we expect borrowers to default and then calculates the probability that these conditions will eventually occur. The key assumption of structural models is that default occurs when the value of the company's assets falls below a critical level. In the case of a limited liability company, default is expected to occur if the asset value is less than company's liabilities. Specifically, the following equation is true for all limited liability companies:

$$\text{Asset Value} = \text{Value of Equity} + \text{Value of Liabilities} \tag{16.2}$$

If the asset value is smaller than the value of the liabilities – the so-called default threshold – then the value of equity becomes negative for the equation to hold. When equity holders of a limited liability company own a negative value, they have the option to walk away and give up on the equity they hold. In this way, they leave the ownership of the company to its creditors such as banks or investors who financed the company. The option to walk away can be priced using the BS option pricing formula.

Merton (1974) considered the following simple set-up as depicted in Figure 16.2. The company's liabilities are assumed to consist of just one zero-coupon bond with notional value L maturing in T. There are no payments until T, and equity holders will wait until T before they decide whether to default or not. In this way, the probability of default is represented by the probability that, at time T, the value of the assets is below the value of the liabilities. Thus, holders are given an incentive to exercise the option of leaving the company to default – walking away – and avoid any losses associated with the negative value of equity they own.

The company's liability can be obtained through its balance sheet. However, we need to specify the company's asset value at maturity T. For this reason, we assume that the value of

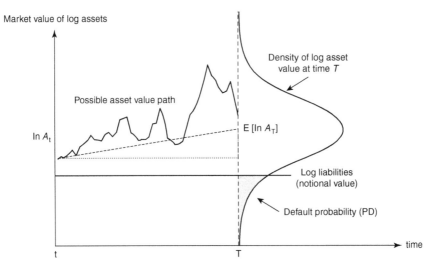

Figure 16.2 Default probability in the Merton (1974) model.
Source: Merton (1974).

financial assets follows a log-normal distribution, i.e. the logarithm of the asset value is normally distributed. The annual variance of the log asset values is σ^2, whereas the expected annual change in log asset values is $(\mu-\sigma)^2/2$, where μ is the drift parameter. Thus, the log asset value in T follows a normal distribution, where t denotes today. That is,

$$\ln A_T \sim N\left(\ln A_T + \left(\frac{\mu - \sigma^2}{2}\right)(T-t), \sigma^2(T-t)\right) \tag{16.3}$$

where, T-t is the remaining time until the option contract reaches maturity (T). The probability of a normally distributed variable x to fall below a threshold z – representing the default point in this case – is given by:

$$\Phi\left[\frac{z - E[x]}{\sigma(x)}\right] \tag{16.4}$$

where, Φ denotes the cumulative standard normal distribution. In this way, we can obtain an estimate of the default probability:

$$\Pr(Default) = \Phi\left[\frac{\ln\left(\frac{L}{A_t}\right) - \left(\frac{\mu - \sigma^2}{2}\right)(T-t)}{\sigma\sqrt{T-t}}\right] \tag{16.5}$$

In order to obtain the distance to default (DD) we drop the cumulative standard normal distribution operator Φ:

$$DD = \frac{\ln A_T + \left(\frac{\mu - \sigma^2}{2}\right)(T-t) - \ln L}{\sigma\sqrt{T-t}} \tag{16.6}$$

where, DD measures the number of standard deviations the expected asset value A_T is away from the default threshold. Following Merton's (1974) seminal paper on using the option pricing formula to derive a measure of probability of default, a number of structural models was introduced by Black and Cox (1976), Geske (1979), and Vasicek (1984). These subsequent models relax some unrealistic assumptions of Merton's original model thereby bringing it closer to reality. For example, Black and Cox (1976) introduce the possibility of more complex capital structures including subordinated debt; Geske (1979) includes interest-paying debt, while Vasicek (1984) distinguishes between short- and long-term liabilities. The last model was used in the derivation of the Kealhofer, McQuown, and Vasicek (KMV) model – introduced by the KMV company established in 1989 – which instead of predicting the probability of default on a target data measures default probability as a function of the distance relative to a moving floor that represents liabilities. This approach leads to expected default frequencies (EDFs) produced by KMV for companies worldwide. The established KMV Corporation was subsequently acquired by Moody's to form Moody's KMV.

16.4 Credit risk management

Credit risk management forms a challenging task for participants in shipping markets. This is due to two main factors: first, managing credit risk effectively requires the use of accurate credit risk measures, as discussed earlier in this chapter, and second, for credit risk management there is a need to develop the appropriate methods and tools to minimize the potential losses of a party in a deal if the other party defaults or its creditworthiness deteriorates significantly.

A wide set of methods and tools are available and have been used in practice to manage credit risk effectively. The most typical one is the use of collateral as protection for lending money, a method used since the invention of credit. Another popular method for minimizing the default risk of credit portfolios is diversification; that is, including different types of obligors in a lender's credit portfolio. These can be for example companies operating in different sectors or sub-sectors of the shipping industry. Apart from the traditional tools available for credit risk management mentioned above, the introduction of credit derivatives has changed considerably the way market participants handle credit risk. Credit derivatives enable participants in financial markets to trade credit as an asset, such as that involved in stocks or in bond issues. The following few sections discuss and illustrate through relevant examples how traditional and modern tools can be used to manage effectively exposures to credit risk.

16.4.1 The use of collateral for credit risk management

Collateral in a credit agreement is the oldest and most widely used tool to minimize credit risk emanating from either the non-ability or the non-willingness of an obligor to repay debt. The popularity of this method as a tool for minimizing credit risk is due to its simplicity and efficiency. Collateral is typically provided in the form of a valuable asset from the obligor to the creditor. The right of the creditor is exercised only in case the obligor defaults, in order to recover part or the whole value of the debt due. Thus, the use of collateral of high value increases the recovery rate of the creditor in case a default event happens. In addition, the use of collateral reduces or eliminates the creditor's cost to pursue the necessary legal procedure of the liquidation of the obligor's assets in case of a default event. In practice, the types of valuable assets used as collateral may vary widely depending on the notional value of the debt due and the type of credit agreement. For example, the collateral used in shipping bank loans is typically the financed vessel itself. In several cases, lenders may require additional collateral in the form of real estate, cash, or financial assets (bonds or stocks) or even personal guarantees from the obligor and/or a third party.

The value of collateral in a credit agreement is periodically marked-to-market to reflect changes in its value. This is a standard procedure followed by creditors in order to ensure that the current (market) value of the collateral is enough over time to cover the pre-specified percentage of the original value of the loan granted to the obligor. This practice is typically followed also in shipping bank loan agreements as ship prices may fluctuate substantially within small periods of time. Therefore, the value of the vessel used as collateral is periodically marked-to-market to reflect changes in the value of the vessel. In case the collateral's (vessel's) value is less than the agreed percentage of the notional value of debt, then the creditor reserves the right to ask for additional collateral to be committed in the agreement. In case the obligor fails to comply, a technical default may be triggered, i.e. a breach of the agreed terms of the credit facility may be declared.

To illustrate through an example, consider a shipowner who has financed the acquisition of a newbuilding vessel through a bank loan and faces a contractual restriction by the creditor to maintain the asset coverage ratio (ACR), i.e. the ratio of vessel's value over loan's value, above a specific level, say 125%, throughout the repayment period of the loan. In case the ACR falls below 125% due to, for example, a drop of the second-hand vessel prices, the obligor faces a technical default and the creditor may require additional collateral – typically in the form of cash – on top of the ship's current market price to raise the asset coverage ratio above the agreed level of 125%.

The collateral used in bond issues depends on their seniority, see Kavussanos and Tsouknidis (2014). The seniority can vary from senior secured bonds, which are covered with collateral of high value, to junior subordinated bonds, which have limited or zero collateral. As expected, senior secured bonds (junior subordinated bonds) carry much lower (higher) yield premiums in order to reflect the significantly lower (higher) credit risk they expose the bondholders to.

16.4.2 Credit enhancements

Credit enhancements are instruments which can be applied on top of the traditional collateral assets used in a credit facility to increase its credit quality; that is, to lower the credit risk the lender is exposed to. The primary use of credit enhancements is to improve the chances of the loan applications to be accepted by credit providers, which would otherwise be unacceptable due to their high risk. Typical credit enhancements may take the form of intangibles such as credit derivatives[5] or tangible assets such as real estate property. Other credit enhancements used in practice include the use of collateral of higher value, say in the form of additional cash, and/or personal guarantees which may use as collateral privately owned real estate assets of the ship-owner; requests for insurance or third-party assurances, say in the form of corporate guarantees by a subsidiary company; granting specific rights, say freight earnings earned to repay directly the bank loan agreement; and letters of credit.[6] Another commonly used credit enhancement is the so-called master agreement. This is defined as the legal documentation signed by the parties involved in a credit transaction, which facilitates cross-default triggers, and is used in a variety of transactions, including positions in derivatives and foreign exchange products.[7] The most popular type is the 1992 ISDA master agreement.[8] The master agreement is typically used to minimize credit risk in OTC financial transactions by specifying: default events, termination events, netting legislation, or early termination payments.

16.4.3 Diversification as a tool for credit risk management

Diversification benefits are well known for equity portfolios, where a well-diversified portfolio exhibits the minimum total portfolio risk by diversifying away its idiosyncratic component. This can be achieved by including in the portfolio assets with low correlation coefficients. Apart from equity portfolios, the same diversification benefits can be achieved in credit portfolios. Specifically, a well-diversified credit portfolio can diversify away the idiosyncratic component of credit risk and in this way minimize its total credit risk. This is achieved by adding different types of loans in a credit portfolio, that is loans of obligors operating in different industries and/or different segments of the same industry. The non-correlated default probabilities of these credit facilities diversify away the part of their credit risk which is due to idiosyncratic characteristics. In order to illustrate the benefits of credit portfolio diversification through an example, consider a ship-lending bank which currently holds a credit portfolio with obligors operating exclusively in one segment of the shipping market, say the tanker segment. Naturally, this financial institution is heavily exposed to the freight rate and ship-price fluctuations of the tanker market, as the repayment of its entire shipping credit portfolio depends on the cash-flow generating ability of obligors operating in tanker markets.[9] Therefore, large fluctuations in tanker market freight rate and ship prices would result into several defaults of the loans in the portfolio, given the higher correlation in their default probabilities. The ship-lending bank of this example can diversify away the idiosyncratic component of the credit risk of its portfolio by including credit facilities to obligors operating in different segments of the shipping industry, such as dry-bulk, wet-bulk, containerships, ferries, coastal shipping, offshore, and cruise shipping. This would lead to lower correlations between the default probabilities of the loans granted, and in this way decrease the overall credit risk exposure of the bank.

16.4.4 Downgrade triggers and credit risk management

Downgrade triggers are investment clauses which are included in a contract and give the option/ obligation to a market participant to cancel, liquidate, or change the terms of the contract if the credit rating of the other party downgrades below a pre-specified rating threshold. A typical downgrade trigger could be for a company to lose two credit rating notches within a year, or for a bond issue to be downgraded from the investment grade class to the non-investment grade class. In fact, this downgrading from investment to non-investment classes of a financial instrument is a frequently used downgrade trigger applied by institutional investors, such as pension funds.

To take an example from the shipping industry, a ship-lending bank may impose a downgrade trigger on a shipping company in the following case scenario: if the shipping company is downgraded from a BBB+ rating to one equal or below BB during the repayment of the loan, then the bank has the option to cancel or amend the agreement by requiring additional collateral in the form of cash; charging a higher margin for the remaining part of the debt due; and/or imposing additional terms to the original agreement, such as the renegotiation of the repayment schedule of the loan. In this way, the bank can mitigate its credit risk exposure to the specific company in case its creditworthiness decreases considerably during the repayment period of the loan, thereby casting doubt over the remaining payments of the loan due.

16.4.5 Netting of contracts

Another method to mitigate counterparty credit risk is through "*netting of contracts*". This is usually applied when two parties are involved in several OTC bilateral derivatives transactions between them. Consider the case where two parties include a netting of contracts clause for the agreed bilateral contracts between them and one-party defaults on one of the contracts. In this case, all contracts outstanding will be immediately considered in default and can be closed at their current market values. Thus, the netting of contracts clause prohibits one of the two parties in a deal to apply the so-called "*selective default*", i.e. to default only on specific – non-favourable for them – contracts. In this way, the netting of contracts clause protects the party of the deal that has not defaulted but is involved in several contracts with the defaulting party by limiting its losses and closing all the contracts outstanding at their current market values. The netting of contracts clause is usually applied in OTC derivatives contracts as it helps the parties involved avoid excess losses due to cross-defaults.

The following example illustrates how the netting of contracts clause works in practice. Consider a shipping company involved in four OTC FFA contracts with a specific charterer. The current values of these contracts for the shipping company are: +$4m, +$5m, −$4m, and −$3m, and these are due in one, six, twelve, and twenty-four months, respectively. The other party of the deal (e.g. a charterer) faces financial distress due to its deteriorating profitability, as freight rates have risen rapidly, and fails to pay the first contract of +$4m to the shipping company. In this scenario, the shipping company has the right to use the netting of contracts clause and require the closing of all four outstanding contracts at their current market values. This would result in a loss of $2m (= + $4m + $5m − $4m − 3$m) instead of $4m for the shipping company. In contrast, if the netting of contracts clause was not included in the OTC derivatives agreements between the two parties, the shipping company would incur a loss of $16m as the counterparty would default on the first two contracts ($4m and $5m) and claim the last two contracts (−$4m and −$3m).

16.4.6 Credit value-at-risk (VaR)

Financial institutions need to continuously monitor and rebalance their credit portfolios consisting of credit risky instruments, such as bonds, bank loans, financial derivatives, and other financial instruments. Monitoring and reporting their exposures is also a regulatory requirement under Basel I (1988), Basel II (2004), and Basel III (2010) agreements.[10] Correlations between default probabilities among different credit risky instruments may change over time and in this way increase/decrease the total credit risk of the credit portfolio. For this reason, bankers often require answers to questions such as *"How probable is it for the bank to lose more than $100m over a horizon of one day?"*. Such questions can be answered through a specific class of models which utilize the concept of value-at-risk and apply it to credit risky portfolios to form the so-called "Credit VaR" (CVaR) model. This model was originally developed in 1997 when a consortium of financial institutions, consisting of JP Morgan, Bank of America, KMV Corporation, UBS, and others, launched the CVaR model – also known as CreditMetrics. The CVaR model takes into account the possible extreme fluctuations of the asset values for the instruments included in a credit risky portfolio. In this way, it is able to provide answers regarding the worst-case scenario prediction for the maximum possible losses of credit risky instruments during a certain period of time.

16.4.7 Credit derivatives

Credit derivatives are a class of financial instruments traded since the late 90s and grew significantly in terms of trading volume after 2004. Despite their short history, credit derivatives are considered an innovative enhancement in the global financial system as they enable participants in the financial markets to trade credit risk like an asset. As depicted in Figure 16.3, credit derivatives experienced a steady reduction of total notional values outstanding, mainly due to the effect of the global financial crisis, to $15 trillion at the end of December 2015 and to $12 trillion at the end of June 2016. The latter value represents less than a quarter of its end-of-2007 historical peak of $58 trillion, according to the International Swaps and Derivatives Association (ISDA).

The payoffs of credit derivatives depend on default events or deteriorating creditworthiness of bond issues, bond issuers, or countries. The majority of credit derivatives contracts is cleared through clearing houses, such as LCH Clearnet and Intercontinental Exchange Inc. (ICE), and form bilateral agreements between a buyer and a seller (underwriter). The seller sells insurance (protection) against the credit risk of the reference entity to the buyer. In this way, credit derivatives can pass credit risk from one party (e.g. an investor) to another as the default risk of a specific deal can be transferred to a third entity other than the two entities of the original (reference) transaction. Thus, credit derivatives allow credit risk to be *"extracted"* from loans and bonds and be traded as a separate (derivative) asset in its own market.

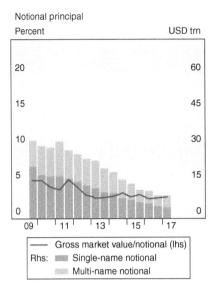

Figure 16.3 Total notional amount of outstanding CDS contracts.

Notes: Single-name CDS contracts provide default risk protection against only one reference entity, whereas multi-name CDS contracts provide default risk protection against a set of reference entities/assets/issuers.

Source: BIS OTC derivatives statistics at end-December 2017. Further information on the BIS derivatives statistics is available at www.bis.org/statistics/derstats.htm.

The transfer of default risk among different entities takes place without the need for the underlying assets to be exchanged. This feature of credit derivatives enables financial markets' participants to take positions in specific assets of their interest, such as bond issues, and at the same time pass away the default risk associated with the bond issue through entering a credit derivative contract. Several participants in financial markets and especially institutional investors hold positions in credit derivatives; they include commercial banks, mutual funds, hedge funds, etc. For instance, fund managers may use credit derivatives to hedge against adverse movements in credit spreads of the bond issues they hold.

16.4.7.1 Credit default swaps (CDS)

Credit default swaps (CDS) are the most heavily traded credit derivative products. The buyer of a CDS contract has the right to sell a bond issue at its face value to the seller of the CDS contract if the reference entity (the bond issuer) defaults. By entering a CDS contract the buyer agrees to make periodic payments to the seller of the contract until the maturity of the CDS or until a credit event of the reference entity occurs. On the opposite side, the seller of the CDS contract receives the periodic payments by the buyer of the contract throughout the life of the CDS contract with the obligation to buy the bond at its face value if the bond issuer defaults.[11] In other words, CDS contracts provide insurance against default risk of bond issues and can be used to hedge positions of market participants in bonds. The CDS spreads (premia) indicate the value required to enter a CDS agreement or equivalently to enter an agreement that protects against a default risk event for the reference asset. Even if CDS contracts provide insurance against the credit risk involved in a bond issue (the reference asset), they still expose CDS holders to the credit risk of the entity issuing (selling) the CDS.

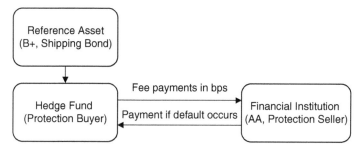

Figure 16.4 Structure of a typical credit default swap (CDS).

Figure 16.4 illustrates how a CDS derivative contract may be used between two financial markets' participants to trade credit risk. In this example, a hedge fund has made an investment in a bond of $20 million face value and 8% coupon, issued by a specific shipping company. The current credit rating of the shipping bonds purchased is B+ by Standard & Poor's (S&P), but the senior management of the hedge fund is concerned regarding the future creditworthiness of the issuer and their ability to pay back the promised payments; that is, the coupon payments during the life of the bond and the principal value at maturity. For this reason, the hedge fund enters into a credit default swap agreement with a third party (underwriter), say a financial institution which is currently rated AA and willing to pay back the face value of the bond issue in case the bond issuer defaults. The CDS agreement specifies that the CDS buyer will pay the CDS seller a standard annual fee until maturity of say 50 basis points (bps) (i.e. 0.5%) on the face value of the bond, which amounts to $100,000 (= $20m x 0.005). As mentioned earlier, credit risk is not really eliminated as the CDS protection seller may default also. If the bond issuer (the shipping company) defaults on the promised payments of the bond issue, then the financial institution (the underwriter) will pay to the hedge fund the notional value of $20million, irrespective of the current market value of the bond, which may have been reduced over time. The CDS premia (fee) are higher when the deviation observed in credit ratings between the reference entity and the underwriter of the CDS agreement is larger. By entering this CDS agreement, the hedge fund has upgraded its credit risk exposure from a low-rated (B+) shipping company (the reference entity) to a highly-rated (AA) financial institution (the underwriter) for the price of the CDS premium (fee).. By entering this CDS agreement, the hedge fund has upgraded its credit risk exposure from a low-rated shipping company (the reference entity) to a highly rated financial institution (the underwriter) for the price of the CDS premium (fee).

Several CDS indices have been developed in order to track CDS spreads in financial markets. Most notably, in 2004 two credit derivatives indices were introduced, namely, the five-year and ten-year Credit Default Index for North America investment grade issues (Ticker: CDX NA IG). These two indices track credit spreads for 125 large investment grade North American companies. The European equivalent indices are the five-year and ten-year iTraxx Europe, which track credit spreads for 125 investment grade large European companies. The construction of the aforementioned indices enables market participants to buy or sell a portfolio of credit default swaps by buying or selling the index, respectively. The so-called basket CDS swap is an important extension of the single-name CDS contract as it provides protection to its buyer against default event(s) of a basket of reference entities. The generic basket CDS contract may come in different specifications, such as: the add-up basket of CDS which pays off when any of the reference entities defaults; the first-to-default basket CDS which pays off when the first entity defaults; the second-to-default which pays off when the second entity defaults; and so on.

16.4.7.2 Total return swap (TRS)

Another class of credit derivatives is the so-called total return swaps (TRS). These are bilateral contracts under which the two parties of the deal agree to swap periodic payments during a pre-specified period of time. As their name suggests, one of the two parties in the deal receives the total return of a reference asset, which can be, for example, a bond issue. The term total return incorporates both capital gains or losses and interest payments of the reference asset. The other party of the deal agrees to receive a fixed (or floating) payment (fee) which is independent of the fluctuations to the price or the creditworthiness of the reference asset. The most widely used reference assets for total return swaps contracts are stocks, bonds, financial indices, or baskets of these.

To understand the mechanics of a TRS contract, consider the following example as depicted in Figure 16.5. Specifically, a hedge fund has currently an investment of $10m in a shipping bond issue with maturity five years. The hedge fund seeks to reduce its exposure to the credit risk and the market risk associated with this specific bond issue. This is especially important for the hedge fund as the bond issuer (the shipping company) has recently been downgraded to the non-investment class BB+ and the price of this bond issue in the market has fluctuated widely during the last months. In order for the fund to be protected against the credit risk and the market risk of this particular bond issue, it enters a total return swap deal with a financial institution, which is currently rated AA+ and willing to participate in this agreement.

The TRS contract specifies that for the next five years to maturity the fund will pay to the financial institution the total return of the shipping bonds during their lifetime and, in exchange, the fund will receive from the financial institution an annual fee equal to LIBOR plus 30bps on the face value of the bonds ($10m). The hedge fund is willing to participate in this agreement since it transfers its credit risk exposure from a BB+ rated shipping company to an investment grade AA+ rated financial institution. At the same time the hedge fund agrees to pay the financial institution the total return on the US$10m shipping bonds (avoiding the market risk associated with the specific bond issue), and in return receive one-year LIBOR plus 30 basis points on US$10m every year. Under this TRS agreement, price changes of the bond – including the possibility of default of the bond issuer – will be incurred by the financial institution and not by the hedge fund. This is the main difference between CDS and TRS contracts; that is, that CDS offer protection against credit events solely, whereas TRS protect against the loss of bonds' value in general.

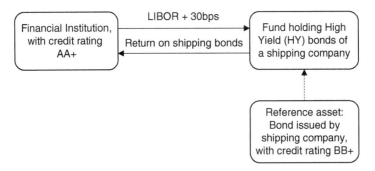

Figure 16.5 Structure of a total return swap (TRS).

16.4.7.3 Credit spread options (CSO)

As discussed earlier in this chapter, bond spreads reflect several risks faced by the bondholder. Kavussanos and Tsouknidis (2014) report that shipping bond spreads are larger on average when compared to spreads of corporate bonds. During the lifetime of a bond it may be the case that the prospects of the shipping company deteriorate, leading to even lower credit rating and increased bond spreads. Thus, it might be important for shipping bondholders to hedge their position against this credit spread risk; that is, against potential increases of the credit spread during the lifetime of the bond.

This can be achieved through credit spread options. They are a type of credit derivative contract that enables the transfer of credit spread risk from one participant to another. Specifically, the buyer of a credit spread option agrees to receive cash flows from the seller, which depend on the changes of the credit spread of the reference asset (the bond issue). Credit spread options are offered both as call and put options to serve the different buyers' and sellers' expectations regarding the evolution of credit spreads in the future. The payoffs of these call and put option contracts are defined respectively as: $\max[S\text{-}K, 0]$ and $\max[K\text{-}S, 0]$; where $S = y_c - y_{rf}$, S stands for the credit spread, defined as the difference of the yield to maturity of the shipping bond (y_c) and the risk-free interest rate (y_{rf}), and K is the exercise price (the spread) of the bond.

The following example illustrates the way a credit spread option works in practice. Assume an investor places $10m in a shipping bond with maturity in five years, issued two years ago by shipping company A. The company is currently rated BB– and the bond has a yield to maturity 7%. The current risk-free US Treasury bond with maturity five years has yield to maturity 3%. Therefore, the credit spread of the bond is 4% (= 7%–3%). The bondholder is concerned about the creditworthiness of company A over the next year and seeks protection against the possibility of the credit spread of the bond widening. A widening bond spread reflects the market's assessment that the company is not performing well and therefore the probability of defaulting on the bond's promised payments is increasing. The bondholder can protect himself against a widening bond spread by buying a credit spread call option from another party (underwriter), say with strike price 5% and expiry period one year. The credit spread option premium is paid upfront. In this way, the investor is protected against the situation where for any reason during the following year the prospects of the shipping company (the bond issuer) deteriorate, thereby leading to lower bond prices, increased yield to maturity and ultimately a spread over 5%. Thus, if the bond spread becomes greater than the strike spread of the option, say 6%, the option is exercised and the 1% difference between the "spot" price (6%) and the strike price of the call option (5%) is received. This difference will be paid on the bond's face value of $10m, thus resulting into a payment of $100,000 (= 1% x $10m). By buying the credit spread call option the bondholder has reduced his potential losses from the widening of the bond's spread.

16.5 Summary and conclusions

This chapter presented and discussed the critical subject of credit risk measurement and management in the shipping industry. Spectacular defaults in the past have resulted in multimillion-dollar losses in the industry. As presented earlier in the chapter, different types of credit risks emerge within a wide set of bilateral agreements in the shipping sector. These include charterparty contracts between shipowners and charterers; newbuilding agreements between shipping investors and shipyards; bunker agreements between shipowners/charterers and bunker suppliers; shipping bank loans between banks and shipowners; and positions in over-the-counter forward freight agreements. The risky and volatile nature of the industry highlights the importance of identifying these sources of credit risk, measuring them, and eventually using the appropriate tools to effectively manage them. They include the use of collateral; the diversification of the sources of credit risk through appropriate mixtures of assets in a credit risk portfolio; the use of downgrade triggers; netting of contracts; credit enhancements, and the use of credit derivatives, such as the CDS, TRS, and CSO. This chapter also presented working examples for the most popular credit risk management techniques used by shipping market participants.

Notes

1 Credit risk also includes the delay or postponement of the agreed payments beyond their due date in a transaction, even if these are honoured eventually.
2 The Wikipedia article for the Hanjin shipping default can be found here: https://en.wikipedia.org/wiki/Hanjin_Shipping (accessed on 16th of October 2017).
3 Yield-to-maturity (YTM) is the annualized return that an investor will have by buying the bond at today's market value and keeping it until its maturity.
4 Bonds rated in the non-investment grade are also known as junk bonds, speculative bonds, or high-yield (HY) bonds.
5 As explained in the next section of this chapter, credit derivatives are financial instruments whose pay-offs are linked with default events of bonds, companies, or countries.
6 A letter of credit is a letter issued by a financial institution guaranteeing that a buyer's payment to a seller will be received on time and for the correct amount. If the buyer is unable to make the payment on a specified date, the financial institution is required to cover the amount of the purchase.
7 Cross-default is a provision in a bond or loan agreement that sets a borrower in default if the borrower defaults on another obligation. For instance, a cross-default clause in a shipping bank loan agreement may impose that the borrower automatically defaults on the agreement if he fails to meet the coupon and principal payments due to its bondholders. The cross-default trigger exists to protect the interest of lenders, who desire to have equal rights to a borrower's assets in case of default on one of the loan contracts.
8 This can be found at www.isda.org.
9 Kavussanos and Tsouknidis (2014) have shown that shipping bond spreads and the associated default risks depend on the state of the shipping market as captured by the Clarksea freight earnings index.
10 In general, Basel III is focused on strengthening bank capital requirements by enhancing bank liquidity and limiting bank leverage (for details see Basel III, 2010). Financial institutions are required to comply with the proposed changes from 1 April 2013 until 31 March 2019.
11 The total face value of the bonds that can be sold is called the CDS's notional principal value.

References

Altman, E.I., 1968. Financial ratios, discriminant analysis and the prediction of corporate bankruptcy. *J. Finance* 23, 589–609. doi:10.1111/j.1540-6261.1968.tb00843.x

Basel I, C. on B.S., 1988. International convergence of capital measurement and capital standards. BIS report.

Basel II, C. on B.S., 2004. International convergence of capital measurement and capital standards: A revised framework. BIS report.

Basel III, 2010. Group of governors and heads of supervision announces higher global minimum capital standards. BIS report.

Black, F., Cox, J.C., 1976. Valuing corporate securities: Some effects of bond indenture provisions. *J. Finance* 31, 351–367.

Black, F., Scholes, M., 1973. The pricing of options and corporate liabilities. *Journal of Political Economy* 81(3), 637–654.

Campbell, J., Hilscher, J., and Szilagyi, J., 2008. In search of distress risk. *The Journal of Finance* 58(6), 2899–2939.

Fitch, 2010. *Report on the Global Shipping Companies*. Fitch Ratings Inc., New York.

Geske, R., 1979. The valuation of compound options. *J. Financ. Econ.* 7, 63–81. doi:10.1016/0304-405x(79)90022-9

Karels, G.V., Prakash, A.J., 1987. Multivariate normality and forecasting of business bankruptcy. *J. Bus. Finance Account.* 14, 573–593. doi:10.1111/j.1468-5957.1987.tb00113.x

Kavussanos, M.G., 1996. Price risk modelling of different size vessels in the tanker industry using Autoregressive Conditional Heteroskedasticity (ARCH) models. *Logist. Transp. Rev.* 32, 161–176.

Kavussanos, M.G., 1997. The dynamics of time-varying volatilities in different size second-hand ship prices of the dry-cargo sector. *Appl. Econ.* 29, 433–443.

Kavussanos, M.G., 2002. Business risk measurement and management in the cargo carrying sector of the shipping industry, in: *The Handbook of Maritime Economics*. Lloyd's List Publication, London.

Kavussanos, M.G., 2003. Time varying risks among segments of the tanker freight markets. *Marit. Econ. Logist.* 5, 227–250.

Kavussanos, M., 2010. Business risk measurement and management in the cargo carrying sector of the shipping industry – an update, in: *The Handbook of Maritime Economics and Business*. Lloyd's List Publications, London.

Kavussanos, M.G., Tsouknidis, D.A., 2011. Default risk drivers in shipping bank loans, in: Proceedings of the 15th International Association of Maritime Economists Conference.

Kavussanos, M.G., Tsouknidis, D.A., 2014. The determinants of credit spreads changes in global shipping bonds. *Transp. Res. Part E Logist. Transp. Rev.* 70, 55–75. doi:10.1016/j.tre.2014.06.001

Kavussanos, M.G., Tsouknidis, D.A., 2016. Default risk drivers in shipping bank loans. *Transp. Res. Part E Logist. Transp. Rev.* 94, 71–94. doi:10.1016/j.tre.2016.07.008

Kavussanos, M.G., Visvikis, I.D., 2006. *Derivatives and Risk Management in Shipping*. Witherbys, London.

Merton, R.C., 1974. On the pricing of corporate debt: The risk structure of interest rates. *J. Finance* 29, 449–470.

Moody's Investor Service, 2005. *Report on the Global Shipping Industry*. Moody's Corporation, New York.

Tsouknidis, D.A., 2016. Dynamic volatility spillovers across shipping freight markets. *Transp. Res. Part E Logist. Transp. Rev.* 91, 90–111. doi:10.1016/j.tre.2016.04.001

Vasicek, O.A., 1984. *Credit Valuation*. San Francisco: KMV Corp.

17

The dynamic Baltic Dry Index

An approach to improve the freight market index

Satya Sahoo and Stavros Karamperidis

17.1 Introduction to indices

Indices are developed to assist practitioners and academics in *inter alia* forecasting and managing risks that occur in the diverse, high-value environment of the maritime transport sector. According to Hermans et al. (2010), the interest in indices creation and use has increased in recent years, "An index number is a statistical measure that shows the percentage change in a variable from a fixed point in the past" (Collis and Hussey, 2009 p.279). Rodrigue et al. (2009 p.29) point out that: "Indices are more complex methods to represent the structural properties of a graph since they involve the comparison of one measure over another". An additional "interesting" quote for indices is that given by Jacques (2006 p.184): "Index numbers enable us to identify trends and relationships in the data". In short, indices that are complex statistical measurements could help the improvement of the maritime transport sector, as according to Harrington (1991 p.82), who has applied the following logic to the industrial sector: "If you cannot measure it, you cannot control it. If you cannot control it, you cannot manage it. If you cannot manage it, you cannot improve it". Indices have a broad application to the maritime transport sector, from freight rates to environmental performance (Karamperidis et al., 2013). For example, Maersk has applied the management logic mentioned by Harrington and has established some key performance indicators (KPIs) as scorecards. These scorecards measure the energy (environmental) performance of some of the company's vessels. The measurements recorded since 2009 have helped Maersk to save USD 90 million. It is essential to realise that the scorecards are only a valuable tool if they help facilitate decision making amongst stakeholders (Hellenic Shipping News Worldwide, 2012). One example of those measurements has led to the saving of 160,000 tons of fuel, due only to higher propulsion efficiency (Hellenic Shipping News Worldwide, 2012).

A variety of indices are used in the maritime transport sector in an attempt to predict market changes and behaviours; for example, Notis (2010) showed that freight indices often change before changes in sales and production. Therefore, indices have developed to assist practitioners and academics in *inter alia* forecasting and managing risks that occur in the diverse, high-value environment of the maritime transport sector.

17.1.1 Indices risk management tool

Some indices (which are mostly of a time series nature) are used within the maritime transport sector as forecasting models, in an attempt to anticipate future trends. These indices use various explanatory variables to forecast risk (FreightMetrics, 2003). Some of the freight indices are used in the shipping sector as measuring tools; for example, one of the most important forms of risk is been identified as the freight market risk. This refers to the possibility of financial losses arising from the unfavourable changes in the market (FreightMetrics, 2003).

As it is observed from the freight rates fluctuation, they could be extremely volatile. This was particularly so for the dry bulk sector, where a steep rise of the freight rates upwards was observed until the second quarter of 2008, caused by the inelastic short-term supply in the market with ships. That inelastic short-term supply caused by the limited number of shipyards around the globe and the time required to respond to market needs was, on average, 3.5 years (Clarksons, 2013). Therefore, the ship-building industry could not match the demand with the supply, which had a reverse effect when the economic crisis began and the demand for products had then fallen due to the oversupply of the market with available vessels. Thus, the shipping rates started to collapse in the last quarter of 2008. An example was the Baltic Dry Index, which from 20 May 2008 (11,793 points, which was the highest peak of the index since its creation) fell by 94% until 5 December 2008 (663 points – the lowest level since 1986) (The Baltic Exchange, 2010).

According to Karamperidis et al. (2013), the index which is most widely used in the maritime transport sector is the BDI. Thus, the improvement of the aforementioned index, which is used as a benchmark index in the maritime transport sector, will have a great impact on the maritime transport sector as it could help improve other maritime indices.

The Baltic indices derive their name from The Baltic Exchange, which is based in London and covers the dry (Baltic Dry Index, BDI) and the wet (Baltic International Tanker Routes, BITR) ship markets. Both indices are managed by The Baltic Exchange. The BDI covers dry bulk shipping rates while similarly the BITR the wet bulk shipping rates. The BDI is a number that is updated and issued five days per week. The index provides an assessment of the freight of moving the major raw materials by sea. Changes in the BDI can give insights into how the global trends of supply and demand are changing. Simply, the BDI reflects the costs of hiring (chartering) a vessel for transporting major bulk – raw materials (Bloomberg, 2010; Clarksons, 2010).

17.1.2 The Baltic Dry Index (BDI)

As mentioned above, the BDI is the most mentioned index in the maritime transport sector, and the improvement of the dominant index used in the maritime transport sector could achieve the improvement of other indices. To have an in-depth understanding of the BDI, we briefly demonstrate not only its history but also how the index has evolved over the last years. Later we will provide a comparison of the index with existing stock exchange indices which are using novel methods to be in line with the market and constantly up to date.

The Baltic Exchange is the largest global marketplace where shipbrokers, charterers, and shipowners gather to fix real-time freight market information for ocean transportation of industrial cargos. The Baltic Exchange produces more than 40 daily route assessments such as a sale and purchase index, forward prices, fixture lists, and market reports. It has a total membership of nearly 600 companies and 3000+ individuals (January 2012), and approximately 400 Baltic member companies are based in the UK. The Baltic also has a growing membership base in the US, Europe, and the Far East (The Baltic Exchange, 2018). The Baltic Exchange is headquartered in London with a regional office in Singapore. On 26 September 2016, The Baltic

Exchange was bought by the SGX Singapore Exchange (Saul, 2016). The Baltic Exchange emerged in 1744 from the "Virginia and Baltic Coffee House" where people met to arrange the transportation of goods.

The Baltic Exchange had introduced the first ocean freight index as the Baltic Freight Index (BFI) on 4 January 1985. BFI was a statistical index covering freight rates on different trade routes: grain, coal, iron ore, and trip charter. The details of the index composition are presented in Table 17.1.

BFI was calculated on a daily basis as the weighted average of actual rates of, initially, 13 voyage routes. If there were no charters, a panel of brokers independently submitted their estimates of what the charter rate would have been, and these were averaged. BFI provides accurate information about the level of freight rates across a variety of shipping routes, worldwide. BFI was also developed as a settlement mechanism for the newly established Baltic International Freight Futures Exchange (BIFFEX) futures contract. BIFFEX was opened to enable shippers, owners, and charterers to hedge against sudden changes in the freight rates. BFI information was extremely valuable for shipping market agents. BFI was an invaluable tool in their decision-making process particularly, for an industry such as shipping (The Baltic Exchange, 2018).

Subsequently, it was realised that the BFI was not reflecting the dry bulk freight market efficiently and needed segmentation of the industry rather than presenting a single dry freight index of 13 different routes, that is, it was essential to construct the index for the dry bulk sub-sectors based on the size of the vessels. This gave rise to the development of the Baltic Capesize Index (BCI), the Baltic Panamax Index (BPI), and the Baltic Handy Index (BHI)[1] for capturing the freight market movements of Capesize, Panamax, and Handysize bulk carriers respectively. A composite index comprising of BCI, BPI, and BHI was introduced on 1 November 1999 and is known as the Baltic Dry Index (BDI), which started gaining popularity. The details of the development and evolution of the BDI are presented in Section 3.1.

The BDI deals with raw materials (e.g. fuels, foodstuffs and fertilisers, construction materials, and other raw goods) moved by sea instead of finished goods. Thus, it is a measure of the price of shipping major raw materials such as metals, grains, and fossil fuels by sea. Dry cargo accounts for around two-thirds of seaborne trade volumes. BDI is created by the London Baltic Exchange based on daily assessments from a panel of shipbrokers, while it is considered to have a link with

Table 17.1 The Baltic Exchange Freight Index (BFI) Composition – 1985

Routes	Vessel size (DWT)	Cargo	Route description	Weights
1	55,000	Light cargo	US Gulf to ARA	20%
2	52,000	HSS	US Gulf to South Japan	20%
3	52,000	HSS	US Pacific Coast to South Japan	15%
4	21,000	HSS	US Gulf to Venezuela	5%
5	20,000	Barley	Antwerp (Belgium) to Red Sea	5%
6	120,000	Coal	Hampton Roads (US) to South Japan	5%
7	65,000	Coal	Hampton Roads (US) to ARA	5%
8	110,000	Coal	Queensland (Australia) to Rotterdam	5%
9	55,000	Coal	Vancouver (Canada) to Rotterdam (Netherlands)	5%
10	90,000	Iron ore	Monrovia (Liberia) to Rotterdam (Netherlands)	5%
11	20,000	Sugar	Recife (Brazil) to US East Coast	5%
12	20,000	Potash	Hamburg (Germany) to West Coast India	2.5%
13	14,000	Phosphate	Aqaba (Jordan) to West Coast India	2.5%

Source: The Baltic Exchange, 2018.

the global economy as it captures the transportation of vital goods for the world economy (Lin and Sim, 2013). The latter has seen a huge growth in the volume of seaborne cargo over the past 30 years, and this is reflected in the figures captured by the BDI (The Baltic Exchange, 2018).

17.1.3 Criticism

For a period of years, the BDI was referred to as being an economic indicator; however, as observed during the last years, it does not seem to be reacting that way. Thus, the board had changed the equation used for calculating the index several times in the last few years. Chambers (2010, p.11) mentions: "we should stop using the BDI as an economic barometer because it is not reacting like that". Therefore, the equation used for calculating the index should change based on new reliable data and methods.

Karamperidis et al. (2013) state that the maritime transport sector uses indices from other sectors, e.g. finance, economics, and stock markets. Stock market indices have developed efficiently over a period of time to capture the market fluctuations. Thus we use them as a "benchmark" to demonstrate how to improve maritime indices based on methods that they use.

17.2 Types of market indices

The market index first started from the stock market where the movement of certain stock prices is captured through a composite index. The first stock market index was developed in 1896 and is known as the Dow Jones Industrial Average index (Lakonishok and Smidt, 1988). Stocks, being a matured market, have gone through various evolutionary phases in order to develop different market indices whose efficiency has increased over time. Compared to the stock market, the freight market indices are relatively new. The Baltic Exchange developed the first ocean freight rate index, known as the Baltic Freight Index (BFI), which started only in 1985. As the ocean freight index is still evolving, for better understanding and construction of the freight market index to capture the market freight market movements efficiently, it is important to understand the history and evolution of the stock market index. Sections 2.1. and 2.2. explain the two main types of stock market index: price-weighted index and market-weighted index.

17.2.1 Price-weighted index

The price-weighted index, which is generally used in the stock markets, is calculated by adding the prices of each stock and dividing the total number of stocks which is used to determine the index value. Dow Jones Industrial Average (DJIA) is one of the well-known market indices calculated using the price-weighted index methodology (Milne, 1966). Since the development of DJIA in 1896, it was fairly successful in capturing the market movements of the major US-traded[2] stocks until practitioners realised the downside of the price-weighted index. A fluctuation for a stock traded at a higher price and with a lower market size/cap could have a greater impact on the compose index compared to a similar fluctuation on a stock traded at a lower price and with a larger market size/cap.

We could elaborate with the following example: Table 17.2 presents the stock composition of DJIA for 10 June 2018. JP Morgan Chase and Goldman Sachs share prices are traded at USD 106.62 and USD 226.85 on 10 June 2018 while they have a market cap of USD 352.12 billion and USD 83.36 billion respectively. In practice, a 10% drop in JP Morgan Chase share price will have a greater impact on the banking industry as compared to a 10% drop in Goldman Sachs share price as the former has a larger market capitalization. While in a similar situation, DJIA will

Satya Sahoo and Stavros Karamperidis

Table 17.2 Stock Composition of Dow Jones Industrial Average

No. of stock	Company name	Price	Change	% Change	Volume traded	Market cap
1	PFE Pfizer	37.43	0.27	0.0073	19,216,190	218.65B
2	CSCO Cisco	42.86	0.19	0.0045	20,224,631	201.75B
3	KO Coca-Cola	44.97	0.57	0.0128	10,606,148	192.39B
4	VZ Verizon	51.34	0.6	0.0118	9,614,559	215.23B
5	INTC Intel	52.16	0.3	0.0058	17,362,901	240.77B
6	MRK Merck	62.3	0.28	0.0045	10,750,468	168.09B
7	WBA Walgreen	63.2	−0.53	−0.0083	9,250,528	63.69B
8	DWDP DowDuPont Inc	67.81	1.06	0.0159	8,053,856	155.44B
9	NKE Nike	77.57	0.29	0.0038	6,281,841	123.73B
10	PG Procter & Gamble	79.82	1.96	0.0252	12,773,488	204.45B
11	XOM Exxon Mobil	83.66	0.76	0.0092	8,806,167	351.77B
12	WMT Wal-Mart	87.21	1.28	0.0149	6,048,406	253.09B
13	AXP American Express	99.91	0	0	4,675,451	84.76B
14	MSFT Microsoft	102.12	0.27	0.0027	19,293,140	779.29B
15	DIS Disney	106.03	0.01	0.0001	4,213,638	156.19B
16	JPM JPMorgan Chase	106.62	−0.66	−0.0062	14,575,873	352.12B
17	TRV Travelers Companies Inc	125.87	0.47	0.0037	1,367,042	33.42B
18	UTX United Technologies	127.06	0.38	0.003	3,198,926	100.63B
19	JNJ Johnson & Johnson	127.38	1.33	0.0106	5,075,638	340.84B
20	CVX Chevron	127.59	1.6	0.0127	5,092,075	240.24B
21	V Visa	136.69	1.17	0.0086	6,561,867	302.93B
22	CAT Caterpillar	141.25	0.28	0.002	3,761,653	81.13B
23	IBM IBM	144.71	0.32	0.0022	3,776,991	131.08B
24	MCD McDonald's	160.62	0.68	0.0043	2,187,530	125.71B
25	AAPL Apple	190.35	−0.23	−0.0012	15,939,149	922.78B
26	HD Home Depot	197.61	1.53	0.0078	2,842,359	226.09B
27	MMM 3M	201.48	0.95	0.0047	1,688,695	117.79B
28	GS Goldman Sachs	226.85	−1.14	−0.005	2,524,839	83.36B
29	UNH UnitedHealth	255.54	1.87	0.0074	2,012,223	242.75B
30	BA Boeing	347.16	5.24	0.0153	3,278,253	197.94B

Source: Dow Jones Industrial Average®.

be affected more by the fluctuation of Goldman Sachs as compared to JP Morgan Chase since the share price of Goldman Sachs is traded at a higher price compared to JP Morgan Chase.

Hence, the movement of the Dow Jones Industrial Average index could provide biased information about the market movements as an increase in the DJIA index does not necessarily correspond to the fluctuations of the entire stock market. This led to the development of the market-weighted index, also known as the capitalization-weighted index (Powell et al., 1989).

17.2.2 Market-weighted index

Following the downside of the Dow Jones Industrial Average index (due to its method of calculation of the composite index), a market-weighted index of 500 stock prices was developed in 1957, which is called the Standard & Poor's (S&P) 500 index (Wilson and Jones, 2002). The S&P 500 index proved successful compared to the DJIA index in capturing the stock market movements, which is attributed to two main reasons: (a) the S&P 500 considers a larger number of stocks for constructing the composite index compared to the DJIA index (that is, the S&P 500 index consists of 500 stock prices whereas the DJIA index only comprises of 30 stocks) and (b) the S&P 500 varies the weights of the stocks contributing to the index depending on the size of the company, whilst the DJIA index gives equal weight to all stock prices (Frankfurter, 1976). For example, in the S&P 500 index, Apple Inc. has the highest weight as its market cap is USD 922.78 billion, and Travelers Companies Inc. has the lowest weight as it has the lowest market cap of USD 33.42 billion within DJIA index stocks (see Table 17.2 for the market cap).

As the market capitalization parameter used for calculating the index reflects the market movements efficiently, the market-weighted index model is widely used to calculate various composite indices. Following the success of the S&P 500 index, some other market-weighted stock indices were also developed, such as the NASDAQ composite index, the Wilshire 5000 Total Market Index, the Hang Seng Index, and the MSCI EAFE Index, amongst others.

Inferences from the stock market-weighted index can be applied to the dry freight market index. Similar to the usage of market capitalization as a weighting factor used for individual shares, the deadweight tonnage (DWT) of the vessel types can be used as the weighting for every ship segment. For instance, if the total DWT of Capesize bulk carriers increases relative to the Handysize bulk carriers, the contribution of the Capesize freight rates in the construction of the dry bulk freight market index should increase as compared to the Handysize. Hence, the fluctuations of Capesize freight rates should have a greater impact on the freight market index as compared to the Handysize freight rates. Though using this analogy, less weight shall be allocated for the vessels which have lower total tonnage (or are niche); this will calibrate the dry bulk freight market index to reflect the overall dry market fluctuations, which are interesting to the majority of the market players.

17.3 The shipping freight index: development and construction

17.3.1 History and evolution of the Baltic Dry Index (BDI)

The Baltic Dry Index (BDI) was first introduced in 1999 and is a composite index of the Baltic Capesize Index (BCI), the Baltic Panamax Index (BPI), and the Baltic Handy Index (BHI). The BDI was calculated as the equal-weighted average of BCI, BPI, and BHI as presented in the following equation:

$$BDI = \left(0.33 * BCI + 0.33 * BPI + 0.33 * BHI\right) * k \qquad (17.1)$$

where, k represents the multiplication factor which is used to scale the index so that it matches the previous index value. The multiplication factor is always used while re-structuring the index to provide a smooth transition between the past and newly constructed index. The value of k on November 1999 was 0.998007990.

Later, in 2001, the Baltic Handy Index (BDI) was replaced with the Baltic Handymax Index (BHMI) for the calculation of the BDI. A new dry bulk subsector index, known as the Baltic Supramax Index (BSI), was introduced on 1 June 2005 and the BHMI ceased to exist. On 2 January 2007, the Baltic Handysize Index (BHSI) was introduced and started gaining popularity as a freight index for smaller dry bulk (Handysize) vessels.

Due to the increase in demand of the BHSI, there was a need to capture the Handysize freight rate fluctuations into the Baltic Dry Index (BDI) as the Handysize market is also a vital component of the dry bulk freight market. On 1 July 2009, the BDI was then calculated with equal weighting of the timecharter average of BCI, BPI, BSI, and BHSI as shown in the following equation:

$$BDI = \left(0.25 * BCI_{TCavg} + 0.25 * BPI_{TCavg}\right.$$
$$\left. +0.25 * BSI_{TCavg} + 0.25 * BHSI_{TCavg}\right) * k \qquad (17.2)$$

Where, BCI_{TCavg}, BPI_{TCavg}, BSI_{TCavg}, and $BHSI_{TCavg}$ denote the timecharter average of BCI, BPI, BSI, and BHSI respectively, and k represents a multiplication factor. k in this case was 0.113473601.

Following the major change in the calculation of BDI in 1999, recently the BDI has undergone another change in calculation. Since March 2018, the BHSI does not contribute to the estimation of the BDI. Presently, the BDI is calculated only with BCI, BPI, and BSI timecharter average where the corresponding timecharter average is weighted as 40%, 30%, and 30% respectively (Hellenic Shipping News, 2018), as shown in the following equation.

$$BDI = \left(0.4 * BCI_{TCavg} + 0.3 * BPI_{TCavg} + 0.3 * BSI_{TCavg}\right) * k \qquad (17.3)$$

where, the multiplying factor (k) is 0.1.

As the market changes dynamically, it is important to adjust the weight of the index compositions which will reflect the freight market efficiently. Simultaneously, it is also important to demonstrate the rationale of the construction of an index and the changes for the calculation of the index to gain the confidence of market practitioners, failing which the application of the new index shall be limited. This study attempts to provide a structural framework for the calculation of the Baltic Dry Index, thereby extending the application to other freight market indices.

17.3.2 Dynamic market-weighted index: application to The Baltic Exchange Dry Index

Due to the development of technology and motivation to achieve an economy of scale (Cullinane and Khanna, 1999, Jansson and Shneerson, 1982), ships are increasing in size over time. This leads to the increase in the total deadweight of the larger vessels compared to the smaller vessels. As shown in Figure 17.1, the total deadweight percentage of Capesize bulk carriers has increased over time whereas the total deadweight percentage of Handysize bulk carriers decreased gradually.

As observed in Figure 17.1, in 1998, Capesize and Handysize bulk carriers comprised of 30% of the total DWT, whereas in 2018, the percentage of Capesize bulk carriers increased to 40%while Handysize bulk carriers decreased to about 10%. Similarly, it is observed that the total deadweight tonnage of Panamax and Supramax bulk carriers has also increased. This gradual shift of the vessels tonnage towards the larger vessels is observed not only due to the technological advancement which makes the shipyards capable of building large vessels, but also due to the growth in port infrastructure to accommodate those vessels (Cullinane and Khanna, 2000) which in return helps to meet the economy of scale for the shipowners. Hence it is important to develop a model for estimating the freight market index for dynamically evolving shipping industry as the stationary or static freight market index[3] might cause biasness in the freight market. This study proposes a dynamic model to estimate the composite index for dry bulk freight market; henceforth this shall be referred to as the Dynamic Baltic Dry Index (DBDI). The DBDI comprises of the weighted average of the BCI, BPI, BSI, and BHSI representing the

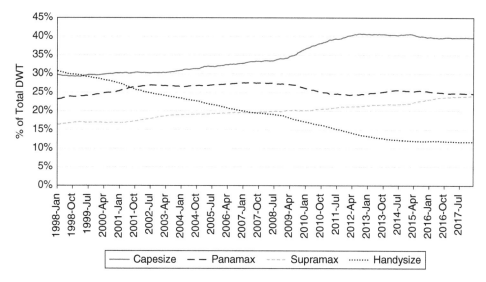

Figure 17.1 Dry bulk carrier fleet development (in percentage of deadweight tonne – DWT).
Source: Clarksons SIN (2018).

Capesize, Panamax, Supramax, and Handysize freight markets respectively, where the weights are calculated as the percentage of DWT of the corresponding subsectors similar to that of market-weighted index for the stock markets which uses the stock market capitalization as the weighting factor. The equation for DBDI is presented as follows:

$$
\begin{aligned}
DBDI &= \left[\frac{BCI \times Cape_{dwt} + BPI \times Pana_{dwt} + BSI \times Supra_{dwt} + BHSI \times Handy_{dwt}}{Total_{dwt}} \right] \times k \\
&= \left[BCI \times \frac{Cape_{dwt}}{Total_{dwt}} + BPI \times \frac{Pana_{dwt}}{Total_{dwt}} + BSI \times \frac{Supra_{dwt}}{Total_{dwt}} + BHSI \times \frac{Handy_{dwt}}{Total_{dwt}} \right] \times k \\
&= \left[BCI \times Cape_{dwt\%} + BPI \times Pana_{dwt\%} + BSI \times Supra_{dwt\%} + BHSI \times Handy_{dwt\%} \right] \times k
\end{aligned}
\tag{17.4}
$$

where, $Cape_{dwt}$, $Pana_{dwt}$, $Supra_{dwt}$, and $Handy_{dwt}$ are the total deadweight tonnage of Capesize, Panamax, Supramax, and Handymax bulk carriers respectively. $Total_{dwt}$ represents the sum of all dry bulk deadweight tonnage, while $Cape_{dwt\%}$, $Pana_{dwt\%}$, $Supra_{dwt\%}$, and $Handy_{dwt\%}$ denotes the percentage of Capesize, Panamax, Supramax, and Handysize deadweight tonnage with respect to the total dry bulk tonnage. k represents the multiplication factor for scaling the freight index.

17.3.3 Acceptable limits of the weights

This section presents the acceptable limit of the weights which are used for estimating the Dynamic Baltic Dry Index. Dynamic confidence interval technique is used to estimate this process. The observations for the first ten years (January 1998–December 2008) are used to calculate the 99% confidence interval for January 2009. This ten-year window (60 monthly observations) is then rolled over for the next period to calculate the confidence interval for February 2008 and so on until the end. The total sample size constitutes 242 monthly observations (January 1998–February 2018). The confidence interval for Capesize, Panamax, Supramax, and Handysize weights (based on their percentage of deadweight tonnage) is presented in Figure 17.2.

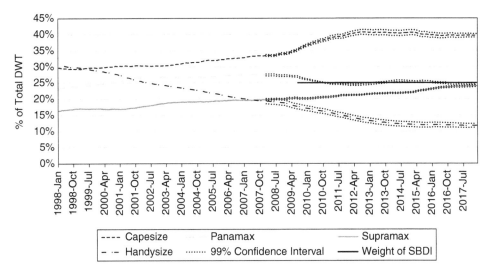

Figure 17.2 Acceptable limits for the weights of DBDI – 99% confidence interval.

Furthermore, the estimated confidence interval is compared to the equal weight of 25%for BDI, BPI, BSI, and BHSI which is used to calculate the Static Baltic Dry Index between July 1999 and February 2018. As observed in Figure 17.2, only Panamax weights are close to the 25% weight, while Supramax weights lie marginally below the 25% level, and Capesize and Handysize weights are distinctly above and below the 25% level, which is the multiplication factor used to estimate the Baltic Dry Index. Hence, allocating equal weight of 20%on Capesize, Panamax, Supramax, and Handysize freight rates for estimating the composite dry bulk index may provide a biased result.

17.3.4 Dynamic Baltic Dry Index vs Static Baltic Dry Index

As the difference between the weights for estimating the Dynamic Baltic Dry Index and Static Baltic Dry Index is significant (presented in the previous section), this section provides a comparative analysis between the benchmark Baltic Dry Index (denoted as Static Baltic Dry Index) and the newly constructed Dynamic Baltic Dry Index. The DBDI is estimated considering the weighted average of the total DWT for Capesize, Panamax, Supramax, and Handysize bulk carriers as presented in Equation 17.3. A graphical comparison between Dynamic Baltic Dry Index and Static Baltic Dry Index is presented in Figure 17.3.

It is observed from the figure above that there is a discrepancy between the Dynamic Baltic Dry Index and the Static Baltic Dry Index. An empirical test is conducted to quantify the difference between the DBDI and the SBDI as follows:

$$\Delta_{DBDI,SBDI} = \frac{\left(DBDI - SBDI\right)}{SBDI} \tag{17.5}$$

where, $\Delta_{DBDI,SBDI}$ denotes the percentage change in the index value of DBDI w.r.t. SBDI.

Between May 2006[4] and February 2018 (147 monthly observations), it is observed that $\Delta_{DBDI,SBDI}$ is positive and statistically significant at 99% confidence interval. The result is presented in Table 17.3.

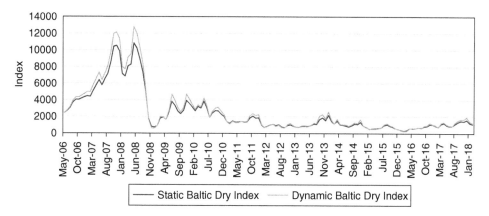

Figure 17.3 Dynamic Baltic Dry Index vs Static Baltic Dry Index.

Table 17.3 Percentage Change of DBDI w.r.t. SBDI

Coefficients	Standard Error	t Stat	P-value
0.066	0.008	8.841	0.000

From the table, it is deduced that the Dynamic Baltic Dry Index is on average 6.6% higher than the Static Baltic Dry Index. This difference is produced because the Static Baltic Dry Index between May 2006 and June 2009 is the equal-weighted average of Capesize, Panamax, and Supramax freight rates and equal-weighted average of Capesize, Panamax, Supramax, and Handysize freight rates between July 2009 and February 2018, whereas the Dynamic Baltic Dry Index considers the weighted average of Capesize, Panamax, Supramax, and Handysize indices with a varying weighted factor depending on the deadweight tonnage of each subsector.

17.4 Discussion and conclusion

This section highlights the importance of using the dynamic weighted-average index as compared to the static equal-weighted index. *Firstly*, the dynamically adjusted weights for calculating the composite index accurately reflect the return and volatility of the market, hence this index is more efficient than the static equal-weighted index (Fama, 1998). As the performance of the index for capturing the market movement and fluctuations increases, the Dynamic Baltic Dry Index will gain more popularity amongst the market practitioners as a benchmark for the dry bulk freight market as compared to the Static Dry Bulk Index. Additionally, this will also provide transparency in index calculation, which will not only avoid mispricing of the underlying index (Elliott et al., 2010) but also increase confidence amongst the market practitioners for using the Baltic Dry Index.

Secondly, the idea of the dynamic market index for freight rates is not just limited to the dry bulk freight rates index but can be extended to other freight market indices such as tanker (both dirty and clean) and container freight indices. Presently, the Baltic Dirty Tanker Index (BDTI) and the Baltic Clean Tanker Index (BCTI) are calculated as the equal-weighted average of 14 routes and six routes respectively[5]. While some of the routes have more trade volume as compared to others, for example TD3C (Middle East Gulf to China) and TC2_37 (Rotterdam to New York), which are the major routes amongst the crude oil and oil products trade (Alizadeh et al., 2015), they have the same weight as that of some unpopular routes in construction of BDTI and BCTI respectively. Along this line, the Shanghai Container Freight Index (SCFI) was developed by the Shanghai Shipping Exchange, and is one of the most widely used benchmarks for container freight rates. Though it provides different weights on liner trade routes (starting from Shanghai) in construction of composite index [6], the weights for the various routes do not change over time. These static weights not only cause confusion amongst the liner companies but, could also provide biased information disrupting the freight market. Furthermore, this discussion should be extended to the construction of various freight indices for the sub-sectors in shipping such as Capesize, Panamax, Supramax, and Handysize indices. For example, the Baltic Panamax Index (BPI) is calculated as the equal-weighted average of four different Panamax routes[7]. As the dry bulk freight market has seasonality (Kavussanos and Alizadeh-M, 2001), the importance of the routes changes over time and hence considering a constant and uniform weight for calculating the composite index, however easy it may be, at times can be misleading. Hence, the idea of the dynamic weighted-average index can have a wider application to various freight markets improving the efficiency of the existing static (constant) weighted-average freight indices.

The freight market index serves as the underlying index for developing and hedging various freight derivative products, such as freight forward assessments (FFAs) and freight options (Alizadeh and Nomikos, 2009, Kavussanos and Visvikis, 2006). The freight derivatives have low hedging effectiveness for minimising the freight rate fluctuations (Kavussanos and Visvikis, 2010, Alizadeh et al., 2015, Alexandridis et al., 2018). This could be attributed to the fact that the underlying index on which those financial products are developed fails to capture the physical market efficiently, similarly to the case of BIFFEX contracts (Kavussanos and Nomikos, 2000a, Kavussanos and Nomikos, 2000b). Hence *finally*, this chapter serves as a benchmark to re-construct physical freight rate indices with time-varying market weights which can help improve the hedging performances of the freight derivative contracts, thereby increasing the usage of freight derivative products and improving the stability of the highly risky shipping market.

By achieving that, shipowners and charterers (as the main users of the proposed index), along with other market practitioners including freight brokers, freight forwarders, and shipping investors amongst others, will be able to achieve better performance and profitability, as it will reduce the risk exposure and increase the yield from the freight derivatives. The application of the dynamic weighted-average index methodology in the maritime transport sector will bring contemporary management practices to a sector which is traditional in its operations.

Notes

1 Later BHI was converted into Baltic Handymax Index (BHMI) on January 2001.
2 DJIA comprises of 30 major stocks traded in the New York Stock Exchange and NASDAQ.
3 Stationary or static index refers to the composite index where the weights of the components are not changing over time.
4 The empirical test is conducted from May 2006 as the BHSI was published by The Baltic Exchange only from May 2006.
5 Details of the tanker routes: (i) the BDTI comprises of TD1 (280,000mt, Middle East Gulf to US Gulf), TD2 (270,000mt, Middle East Gulf to Singapore), TD3C (270,000mt, Middle East Gulf to China), TD6 (135,000mt, Black Sea/Mediterranean), TD7 (80,000mt, North Sea to Continent), TD8 (80,000mt, crude and/or DPP heat 135F, Kuwait to Singapore), TD9 (70,000mt, Caribbean to US Gulf), TD12 (55,000mt, fuel oil, Amsterdam-Rotterdam-Antwerp range to US Gulf), TD14 (80,000mt, no heat crude, SE Asia to EC Australia), TD15 (260,000mt, no heat crude, West Africa to China), TD17 (100,000mt crude, Baltic to UK/Cont), TD18 (30,000mt fuel oil, Baltic to UK/Cont), TD19

(80,000mt, cross-Mediterranean), TD20 (130,000mt, West Africa to Rotterdam); (ii) the BCTI comprises of TC1 (75,000mt CPP/UNL naphtha, Middle East Gulf to Japan), TC2_37 (37,000mt CPP/UNL, Rotterdam to New York), TC5 (55,000mt CPP/UNL naphtha, Ras Tanura to Yokohama), TC6 (30,000mt CPP/UNL, Euromed Skikda to Lavera), TC9 (30,000mt CPP/UNL/ULSD, Baltic to UK/Cont), TC16 (60,000mt CPP, Amsterdam to offshore Lome).

6   The Shanghai Container Freight Composite Index constitutes of 13 major liner routes from Shanghai to other ports globally.

7   The BPI constitutes of P1A_03 (transatlantic round voyage), P2A _03 (Skaw–Gibraltar range to Far East, redelivery Taiwan–Japan range), P3A_03 (Japan–South Korea range to Pacific round voyage, redelivery Japan–South Korea range), and P4_03 (Japan–South Korea range, redelivery Skaw–'Passero range).

References

Alexandridis, G., Sahoo, S., Song, D.-W., & Visvikis, I. 2018. Shipping risk management practice revisited: A new portfolio approach. *Transportation Research Part A: Policy and Practice*, 110, 274–290.

Alizadeh, A.H., Huang, C.-Y., & van Dellen, S. 2015. A regime switching approach for hedging tanker shipping freight rates. *Energy Economics*, 49, 44–59.

Alizadeh, A. & Nomikos, N. 2009. *Shipping Derivatives and Risk Management*. New York: Springer.

The Baltic Exchange 2010. *Indices*, http://www.balticexchange.com/default.asp?action=article&ID=45, accessed 12 November 2010.

The Baltic Exchange 2018. *History*, https://www.balticexchange.com/about-us/history/, accessed 18 August 2018.

Bloomberg 2010. *The Baltic Dry Index*, http://www.bloomberg.com/apps/quote?ticker=BDIY:IND, accessed 28 June 2010.

Chambers, S. 2010. Beware the doomsayers. *Seatrade* 4, (110).

Clarksons 2010. *The Baltic Dry Index*, http://www.clarksons.com/, accessed 10 April 2010.

Clarksons 2013. *Shipping Intelligence Weekly: 18 January 2013*. London: Clarkson Research Services Ltd.

Clarksons SIN 2018. *Timeseries; Graphs*, https://sin.clarksons.net/Timeseries, accessed 10 August 2018.

Collis, J. & Hussey, R. 2009. *Business Research: A Practical Guide for Undergraduate and Postgraduate Students*. 3rd ed. Basingstoke: Palgrave-Macmillan.

Cullinane, K. & Khanna, M. 1999. Economies of scale in large container ships. *Journal of Transport Economics and Policy*, 33(2), 185–207.

Cullinane, K. & Khanna, M. 2000. Economies of scale in large containerships: Optimal size and geographical implications. *Journal of Transport Geography*, 8, 181–195.

Elliott, W.B., Krische, S.D., & Peecher, M.E. 2010. Expected mispricing: The joint influence of accounting transparency and investor base. *Journal of Accounting Research*, 48, 343–381.

Fama, E.F. 1998. Market efficiency, long-term returns, and behavioral finance. *Journal of Financial Economics*, 49, 283–306.

Frankfurter, G.M. 1976. The effect of "market indexes" on the ex-post performance of the Sharpe Portfolio Selection Model. *The Journal of Finance*, 31, 949–955.

FreightMetrics 2003. *Risk Management in Shipping*, http://www.freightmetrics.com/downloads/Risk ManagementInShipping.pdf, accessed 26 March 2011.

Harrington, H. 1991. *Business Process Improvement: The Breakthrough Strategy for Total Quality, Productivity, and Competitiveness*. New York: McGraw-Hill.

Hellenic Shipping News Worldwide 2012. *Maersk: Vessel KPIs Save USD 90 Million on Energy*, http://www .hellenicshippingnews.com/News.aspx?ElementId=7e4f6d46-c420-41cd-b47b-78dd9aafc9d2&utm_source=newsletter&utm_medium=email&utm_campaign=daily, accessed 17 July 2012.

Hellenic Shipping News Worldwide 2018. *Baltic Exchange Applies Changes to BDI, Scraps Handysize Index*, http://www.hellenicshippingnews.com/baltic-exchange-applies-changes-to-bdi-scraps-handysize-index/, accessed 26 February 2018.

Hermans, E., Ruan, D., Brijs, T., Wets, G., & Vanhoof, K. 2010. Road safety risk evaluation by means of ordered weighted averaging operators and expert knowledge. *Knowledge-Based Systems* 23(1), 48–52.

Jacques, I. 2006. *Mathematics for Economics and Business*. 5th ed. Harlow: Pearson Education Ltd.

Jansson, J.O. & Shneerson, D. 1982. The optimal ship size. *Journal of Transport Economics and Policy*, 217–238.

Karamperidis, S., Jackson, E., & Mangan, J. 2013. The use of indices in the maritime transport sector. *Maritime Policy & Management*, 40(4), 339–350.

Kavussanos, M.G. & Alizadeh-M, A.H. 2001. Seasonality patterns in dry bulk shipping spot and time charter freight rates. *Transportation Research Part E: Logistics and Transportation Review*, 37, 443–467.

Kavussanos, M.G. & Nomikos, N.K. 2000a. Constant vs. time-varying hedge ratios and hedging efficiency in the Biffex Market. *Transportation Research Part E: Logistics and Transportation Review*, 36, 229–248.

Kavussanos, M.G. & Nomikos, N.K. 2000b. Futures hedging when the structure of the underlying asset changes: The case of the Biffex Contract. *Journal of Futures Markets: Futures, Options, and Other Derivative Products*, 20, 775–801.

Kavussanos, M.G. & Visvikis, I.D. 2006. *Derivatives and Risk Management in Shipping* 1st ed. London: Witherbys Publishing.

Kavussanos, M.G. & Visvikis, I.D. 2010. The hedging performance of the Capesize forward freight market. *International Handbook of Maritime Business*. Cheltenham: Edward Elgar Publishing.

Lakonishok, J. & Smidt, S. 1988. Are seasonal anomalies real? A ninety-year perspective. *The Review of Financial Studies*, 1, 403–425.

Lin, F. & Sim, N.C.S. 2013. Trade, income and the Baltic Dry Index. *European Economic Review*, 59, 1–18.

Milne, R.D. 1966. The Dow-Jones Industrial Average re-examined. *Financial Analysts Journal*, 22, 83–88.

Notis, K. 2010. *Overview of the Transportation Services Index*, http://www.bts.gov/video/tsi_overview/, accessed 2 July 2010.

Powell, J.L., Stock, J.H. & Stoker, T.M. 1989. Semiparametric estimation of index coefficients. *Econometrica: Journal of the Econometric Society*, 57(6),, 1403–1430.

Rodrigue, J.-P., Comtois, C., & Slack, B. 2009. *The Geography of Transport Systems*. 2nd ed. London: Routledge.

Saul, J. 2016. *Baltic Exchange Shareholders Approve Takeover by Singapore Exchange*, https://www.reuters.com/article/us-baltic-exchange-m-a-sgx/baltic-exchange-shareholders-approve-takeover-by-singapore-exchange-idUSKCN11W1TK, accessed 27 September 2016.

Wilson, J.W. & Jones, C.P. 2002. An analysis of the S&P 500 Index and Cowles's extensions: Price indexes and stock returns, 1870–1999. *The Journal of Business*, 75, 505–533.

18

Inter-organizational relationships of European port management entities

Athanasios A. Pallis and Paraskevi Kladaki

18.1 Introduction

Port management entities, or *port authorities,* are increasingly involved in collaborations with other ports, commercial entities, and institutions. As port authorities (PAs) "go international" via several strategies, they expand collaborations well beyond the notion of proximity. While they continue to be involved in various forms of collaboration with ports and other entities located in nearby regions, they also seek to establish and benefit by relationships with geographically non-proximate ports or stakeholders.

This chapter provides a conceptual and empirical understanding of the emerging patterns of the latter inter-organizational relationships, that is to say, those partnerships evolving on cross-border and, in many cases, cross-continental level.

Following a discussion about the drivers towards more extensive port collaboration (Section 18.2), the empirical part of the study (Section 18.3) explores the relevant practices developed by major European port authorities. This analysis develops a fitting typology of the behaviours observed with reference to the geography, objectives, and structures of the evolved collaborations. Beyond a synopsis of the latest (strategic) trends in the port industry, this typology also provides an essential background to link practices with *why* and *how* these strategies are emerging.

The chapter provides this linkage in a way that responds to calls to move port research towards management-focused firm-led concepts (see: Pallis et al., 2010; 2011; Woo et al., 2012; Notteboom et al, 2013): it employs non-port-related literature on the formation of inter-organizational relationships so as to better explore the structures of the *whys* and *hows* of the recorded collaborative activities. These explorations allow developing the framework for understanding whether port management bodies follow similar paths when initiating such relationships.

18.2 Inter-organizational relationships as core PA strategies

The restructuring of the port industry over the last 30 years has not let unaffected the role of modern port authorities. A changing economic environment produced by the globalization of production and distribution, changing forms of cargo transportation, technological break-throughs, and many more issues, have among others resulted in a revisiting of the role of PAs.

This revisiting refers to two strands. The first one is the positioning of PAs within the new institutional setting of port governance. The second one relates to the functions and activities of the management entities in modern ports, so as to better advance the competitiveness of the port(s) they manage and, to a lesser extent, operate.

The increasing presence of private terminal operators results in a rebalance of powers and a presence of different governance formats. These formats range from privatized to landlord and state-owned governed and operated ports, and are frequently associated with the separation of the management of the port from operations (services provision). The movement of governments to establish more commercialized port operations devolved the responsibility for port development to a port authority and has contributed to the realignment of the roles of those bodies previously managing ports.

The continuously adjusted activities and strategic choices of PAs have not been unnoticed by scholarly research focusing on port governance (cf. Goss, 1990; Cullinane and Song, 2001; Brooks and Pallis, 2012; contributions in: Brooks and Cullinane 2007; and Brooks and Pallis, 2013). These studies acknowledge that the centrality of PAs remains, while their mission and role change, not least as the new governance setting touches the core of the commonly called "landlord" model. In the biggest European port, for example, the Rotterdam PA has been corporatized, assuming responsibilities for commercial and financial affairs, investments in new development projects, mid-term business planning and implementation, and autonomous setting of long-term objectives. The purpose is to formalize substantial changes to the landlord function to enable adjustments, such as capital investment mobilization or the accommodation of increased traffic via the coordination of supply chain actors. Land scarcity, the oligopoly in terminal operations, and negative externalities of port development led to a more active coordinating role by the previously "passive" landlord PAs (Verhoeven, 2010). Similar examples are found in other European ports where corporatized PAs assume similar responsibilities to those held by Rotterdam.

In the contemporary setting, PAs are hybrid organizations that need to act "smart" (Chlomoudis and Pallis, 2004; Dooms et al, 2013) and develop beyond the management of the activities within the port zone: these are today the port management entities that act as "community" and "port cluster" managers (de Langen, 2004, 2007), engaged with stakeholders (Dooms and Verbeke, 2007; Notteboom et al, 2015). Meanwhile, in an increasing number of cases, they started extending their activities at regional or even at global level (van der Lugt and de Langen, 2007). This transition – which is driven by (i) port users looking for a business-oriented port authority, (ii) governments that reduce government spending on ports, implying that port authorities should become more financially self-sustaining, and (iii) NGOs that demand transparency and inclusion in decisions that affect stakeholders – leads to the inception of port authorities as *port development companies* (de Langen and van der Lugt, 2017).

Verhoeven (2010) provides a typology with three hypothetical options for a modern port authority. The first strategic option is to be a "conservator", concentrating on being a good housekeeper. The second one is to be a "facilitator", operating as a mediator and matchmaker between economic and societal interests within the port and beyond the port perimeter, and trying to engage in strategic regional partnerships. The third potential is to be an "entrepreneur", combining the main features of the facilitator with a more outspoken commercial attitude as investor, service provider, and consultant on local, regional, and global level.

To fulfil such different roles, PAs can choose different strategies. First, port authorities may be leaders in bringing together the various supply chain actors to provide integrated transportation services beneficial to all; and second, they may engage in *cooperation strategies* to develop business together.

While it is the second strategy that is of paramount interest in this paper, it would be beneficial to also briefly consider the first approach. *Coordination strategies* refer to an integrated transportation service beneficial to all the actors but especially to the port. Van der Horst and De Langen (2008) have developed the concept of coordination in hinterland accessibility using the lens of institutional economics to empirically examine coordination of supply chain actors and the role that ports may play. The degree of coordination among the supply chain actors focused on servicing a port and its hinterland impacts significantly on the port's ability not only to contribute to an efficient regional port infrastructure but also to ensure that inland hinterland areas are well serviced by the transportation and logistics companies using the port. From the public policy perspective, there are social welfare benefits arising from coordination. Bottlenecks impacting on local citizens will likely be mitigated or at least addressed, and the interests of citizens as a whole are better served by a more efficient trading network delivering national wealth.

18.2.1 Port collaboration

It is the second strategy, particularly those collaboration cases that do not result from geographical proximity or overlapping hinterlands produced by functional and spatial regionalization (Notteboom and Rodrigue, 2005), that is largely unexplored, and, thus, forms the theme of the empirical part of the chapter.

Collaboration between ports, in particular PAs, is not an entirely new practice. Going back in time, in the 1990s, UNCTAD (1996) and Juhel (2000) explored port cooperation aiming to adapt to more flexible traffic distribution patterns. Van Klink (1997) detailed the cooperation between Rotterdam and Baltic ports to strengthen the competitive position of the "home port". Avery (2000) proposed strategic alliances between adjacent container ports as a countervailing option against the growing market power in shipping lines.

A decade ago, in 2007, the PAs of the two major European ports (Rotterdam and Antwerp) supported an academic conference on "ports in proximity" to discuss the evolving complex relationships between ports located in proximate geographical areas, with the ways that such ports collaborate touched by various contributions (see Notteboom et al, 2009). Similar initiatives developed in Atlantic Canada, where PAs also supported research on the best forms of collaboration and coordination (see: Brooks et al, 2010). Song (2003) had earlier coined the term "port co-opetition" to describe the collaborating relations developed between competing terminal operators in neighbouring ports in China and Hong-Kong, in order to prevent wasting scarce resources on inter-port competition (also: Notteboom and Winkelmans, 2001).

Recently, a volume containing retrospective works on port reform and governance development in different countries during the past decade provided evidence that PAs have long expressed and established forms of cooperation within defined geographical limits (see: Brooks et al., 2017). Such examples have been observed, among others, between Spanish and Portuguese ports (Caldeirinha et al., 2017), the non-formalized tendency towards better cooperation among Belgian ports (Van De Voorde and Verhoeven, 2017), and the joint marketing agreements in order to tackle regional challenges between US ports (Knatz, 2017).

Since the early 2010s, however, the relationships between non-proximate PAs started attracting scholarly interest, a reflection of the pace that such activities are recorded at practical level. Dooms et al. (2013) conceptualize beyond borders collaboration as the "outward" component of PAs "internationalization" strategies that aim to establish a commercial representation abroad, transfer know-how, and invest abroad; whereas the "inwards" component develops at the "home port". PAs might have several motives and pursue diverse goals ranging from "selling the port" worldwide to controlling international transport networks or gaining competitive advantage. There are at least two cases that port cooperation might expand beyond adjacent ports. The first is cooperation between the two ends of a logistics corridor in order to optimize goods' traffic between the two regions. The second is "sister agreements" for exchange of information on port activities, management, organization, and technology via conferences, delegation visits, or informal contacts. Likewise, Song (2003) conceptualizes motives, stages, goals, and practices bringing concepts of international business, calling for further research on PA strategies.

Beyond the need to examine collaboration between non-proximate entities, these studies call for linking PA strategies with concepts concerning strategic management and having a more specific application to firms. Explicitly responding to the limited research applying strategic management perspectives to PAs, van der Lugt et al. (2015) surveyed the strategic scope of 94 PAs worldwide and concluded that these authorities often provide services that are not generally associated with the landlord role. PAs with more autonomy and a more business-like structure were found to have a wider strategic scope and more business-like goals. The scholars conclude that this might imply a shift in focus from goals at the macro level to goals at the firm level, as well as the moving of PAs towards a more entrepreneurial role which, apart from business development, involves "internationalization" strategies to expand in the future.

On these grounds, it was realized that it is worth to gain deeper insights into *what* a PA strategy looks like, *how* it is defined, and *why* a PA defines an internationalization strategy (van der Lugt, et al., 2013). The remainder of the chapter works towards these directions utilizing firm-level concepts aiming to approach inter-organizational relationships.

18.3 How to best understand inter-organizational relationships?

Answering *why* firms establish inter-organizational relationships and *how* they work on partner selection has been a core theme of scholarly research exploring the forms of such relationships. Scheme 18.1 provides a summary of the *whys* and *hows* of inter-organizational relations as explored by the related results.

The attainment of competitive advantage is a significant motive for the establishment of all such relationships (Soda and Furlotti, 2014). In this vein, Dyer and Singh (1998) argue that in

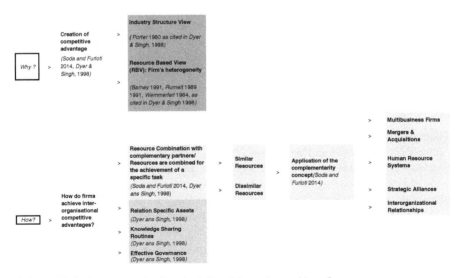

Scheme 18.1   Inter-organizational relationships: why and how?
Source: Elaborated by the authors, based on several sources.

order to explore this notion of competitive advantage when investigating the collaborative strategies of firms, one has to first explore the various relations between firms.

The potential patterns of relationships developed between firms differ. Snow (2015) distinguishes three potentials, namely *competition*, *cooperation*, and *collaboration*, which reflect a chain of evolving relationships between firms. The form of collaboration is the latest and most sophisticated trend, and is the result of the highly globalized economy where the essential rapid diffusion of information produces a revisiting of the traditional hierarchical organizational forms. In collaborative inter-organizational relationships, the trust between interacting partners is high, with firms having intrinsic motivations to work together, oriented towards specific and mutually determined objectives through an intense, open, and shared exchange of information and communications.

Achieving competitive advantages via inter-organization relationships is a notion formed around two pillars: the industry perspective (cf. Porter, 1990) and the resource-based view (Dyer and Singh, 1998) respectively. In the former case, the firm seeks to gain all benefits from its participation in an industry. In the latter case, a firm seeks to attain advantages from resources and capabilities (know-how, resources hard to imitate, etc.). Here, the reference is not only to advantages from resources that one firm possesses but also to the coupling of resources between firms. This coupling provides benefits such as "firm heterogeneity", which means the combination of different idiosyncrasies and capabilities which develop strong competitive advantages for the participant firms.

Referring to *how* firms and organizations form such coupling relationships in order to achieve a competitive advantage, four distinguished practices have been identified (Soda and Furlotti, 2014; Dyer and Singh, 1998): (a) the combination of resources between partners for the achievement of a specific task; (b) specific asset-related investments; (c) knowledge-sharing routines; and (d) more effective governance mechanisms. The combination of similar or dissimilar resources is related to the "inter-organizational resource complementarity", whereas under this practice, different relationships might be formed: multi–business firms; mergers and acquisitions; human resource systems, strategic, alliances and inter-organizational relationships (Soda and Furlotti, 2014).

Nooteboom (1999) put forward a comprehensive concept of inter-firm alliances interpreting the term "alliance" in a broad sense covering a wide spectrum of forms of cooperation between firms (from full integration to fully independent firms engaged in pure market contracting). Here the aims of strategic cooperation are threefold: to better use assets in terms of efficiency, scale and scope; to improve competencies; and to gain positional advantage that may potentially pre-empt the competition.

18.4 Inter-organizational relationships beyond proximity

Following content analysis of several port reports and desktop research, we constructed a dataset including all the identified inter-organizational relationships formed by European port management entities with other non-proximate ports, or other commercial entities and institutions. The constructed dataset refers to the identified cases that these attempts have developed further than a simple expression of interest, i.e. they have been implemented, formalized by signatory parties, disclosed in a report, or detailed further.

The constructed dataset includes a total of 17 collaboration initiatives by a given group of ports (Table 18.1). These observations reveal that ports located in the Northern European range dominate the scene as regards inter-organizational relationships formed beyond proximate entities. Across Europe, only port management bodies that belong to this range have so far included

Table 18.1 Inter-organizational Relationship Patterns Recorded (European Port Management Bodies)

Port	Country	Location	Port	Country	Location	Project	Form of Inter-organizational Relationship	Objectives seeking to be achieved	
A	A	A	B	B	B	(if any specific)		encoded in 2-digit categories*	1-digit
Port of Antwerp	BE	Europe	Port of Montreal	CA	East/Central Canada	–	MoU	CAT6.2 CAT10.1	6, 10
Port of Antwerp	BE	Europe	Port of Nagoya	JP	East Asia	–	MoU	CAT6.3 CAT10.1	6, 10
Port of Antwerp	BE	Europe	Panama Canal Authority	PA	Central America	–	Collaboration	CAT8.1 CAT6.5 CAT4.1	4, 6, 8
Port of Antwerp	BE	Europe	State of Sao Paulo and Sao Paulo Ports	BR	South America	–	Collaboration	CAT10.1 CAT1.4 CAT6.5	1, 6, 10
Port of Antwerp	BE	Europe	San Pedro	CI	West Africa	–	Collaboration	CAT5.2	5
Port of Antwerp	BE	Europe	Rosmorport	RU	Northern Eurasia	–	Collaboration	CAT5.2 CAT3.2 CAT5.3 CAT1.4	1, 3, 5
Port of Antwerp	BE	Europe	Essar Ports Limited	IN	Asia	–	Alliance	CAT10.1 CAT3.2	3, 10
Port of Antwerp	BE	Europe	Jawaharlal Nehru Port Trust (JNPT)	IN	Asia	JNPT APEC Port Training Centre	MoU	CAT6.5	6
Port of Amsterdam	NL	Europe	Aruba Ports Authority	AW	Carribean	–	MoU	CAT11	11
Port of Rotterdam	NL	Europe	Sohar Port and Free Zone	OM	Middle East	Sohar Port and Free Zone	Joint Venture / Investments	CAT10.1	10
Port of Rotterdam	NL	Europe	TPK Logistica	BR	South America	Porto Central	Joint Venture / Investments	CAT10.1 CAT5.1	5, 10
Port of Rotterdam	NL	Europe	Indian Ports Association	IN	Asia	–	Consultancy (Part A is the consultant)	CAT7.2 CAT7.1	7
Port of Rotterdam	NL	Europe	SKIL Infrastructure Limited	IN	Asia	Port West	Joint Venture / Investments	CAT5.2 CAT5.1	5
Port of Rotterdam	NL	Europe	Pelindo I	ID	South East Asia	Kuala Tanjung	Collaboration Agreement	CAT5.2	5
Port of Rotterdam	NL	Europe	Singapore	SG	South East Asia	–	MoU	CAT1.4 CAT6.3 CAT5.2	1, 5, 6
Port of Hamburg	DE	Europe	Port of Los Angeles	US	West Coast	–	Collaboration Agreement	CAT6.4 CAT6.3	6
Bremen-ports	DE	Europe	Iceland	IS	Northern Europe	Finna Fjord	Collaboration Agreement	CAT5.1	5

Legend:

CAT1	CAT2	CAT3	CAT4	CAT5	CAT6
Sustainability (Environmental)	Regional Growth	Logistics & Hinterland	Nautical/Technical Services	Infrastructure – Development	Share and Exchange of Know-How, raining
CAT7	CAT8	CAT9	CAT10	CAT11	
Port Management	Port Management: Commercial	Crisis Management	Port Growth	To be clarified	

*For main categories and subcategories, see also Table 18.2

Source: Elaborated by the authors, based on several sources.

such collaboration practices into their business. These are the ports of Antwerp, Amsterdam, Bremenports, Hamburg, and Rotterdam.

The PAs of Antwerp and Rotterdam are the two most active ones in the establishment of the relationships under examination. This group of port management bodies is referred to as the *Part A* participant aiming to define the reference point for our analysis (European ports), since this process can be as well identified vice versa. All *Part B* participants refer to port management bodies and (where this is applicable) other commercial entities that have established a certain form of collaboration relationship with a *Part A* participant.

Apart from the cases included in the dataset, there is also a case of the *partner ports* initiative developed by the port of Hamburg. The reason for excluding this initiative is the fact that it lacks any specific and formal pattern, whereas the information available lacked any hint that the announced *sister ports* initiatives for *knowledge sharing* are linked with concrete activities and results.

Still, these cases refer to cross-border *partnership relationships* of Hamburg with ports in many places in Asia (Busan Port Authority, Kaohsiung Harbour Bureau, Shanghai International Port, Shenxhen Municipal Port Authority, Yokohama Port Public Corporation), Africa (Tanzania Ports Authority), and the Americas (Administracion Nacional de Puertos, Port of Halifax), but also proximate ports (Port of Gothenburg, Port of Bronka).

Beyond these observations, certain cases were revealed that refer to US ports cross-border collaborations with non-European ports – these are beyond the scope to develop a typology founded on the exploration of the European forms paradigm.

Based on the official announcements and reports, Table 18.1 provides a number of the key characteristics regarding the forms of inter-organizational relationships established in each case, details concerning the parties involved (other ports or undertakings), as well as miscellaneous information that is essential for our subsequent typology analysis.

18.4.1 Configuration of objectives patterns

The column *Form of Inter-organizational Relationship* in Table 18.1 details all the objectives that PAs seek to achieve in each collaboration initiative empirically observed. Based on what has been quoted or stated by official sources, the objectives that the involved parties aim to achieve by establishing each of the identified inter-organizational relationships are categorized and encoded into ten plus one (11) main categories, which in turn are broken down further into two-digit subcategories (Table 18.2). To establish this categorization, we also took advantage of the objectives detailed in such collaborations that do not involve European ports.

Grounded on these, it is worth depicting the "objective patterns" that each collaboration agreement is aiming to form. Table 18.3 presents the frequency of appearance of these objectives (encoded in categories). The range of the objectives is wide and quite diverse. Each relationship reveals a unique blend of goals with the diversity of intentions ranging from purely environmental ones to more technical objectives. In several cases, specific collaboration activities aim to achieve more than one objective.

A certain trend is observed as regards the configuration patterns detailed: the goals selected most frequently are those falling under a triad of categories, these being *infrastructure/development/Greenfield projects development* (CAT5), *port growth* (CAT10), and *share and exchange of know-how/training* (CAT6) respectively. At the same time, another key observation is the diversity of these objectives (nine out of 11 potential categories of objectives have been selected and pursued). This observation is further detailed in Graph 18.1.

Table 18.2 Categorization of Collaboration Objective

Category	Objective	Category	Objective
CAT1 Sustainability (Environmental)		**CAT6 Share & Exchange of Know-how, Training**	
CAT1.1	Economic Fuel Development	CAT6.1	Exchange Expertise
CAT1.2	Environmental Policies	CAT6.2	Exchange Know-how
CAT1.3	Renewable Energy	CAT6.3	Share Best Practices
CAT1.4	Sustainability (Environmental)	CAT6.4	Share Strategies
		CAT6.5	Training Programmes
CAT2 Regional Growth		**CAT7 Port Management**	
CAT2.1	Job Growth	CAT7.1	Monitoring & Reporting Processes
CAT2.2	Boost Regional Economies	CAT7.2	Port Business Plan
CAT3 Logistics & Hinterland		**CAT8 Port Management: Commercial**	
CAT3.1	Expertise in Logistics	CAT8.1	Marketing
CAT 3.2	Hinterland and Logistics		
CAT4 Nautical/Technical Services		**CAT9 Crisis Management**	
CAT4.1	Very Large Vessels' Handling	CAT9.1	Disaster Prevention
CAT5 Infrastructure – Development		**CAT10 Port Growth**	
CAT5.1	Greenfield Projects	CAT10.1	Promote Trade
CAT5.2	Port Development		
CAT5.3	Port Infrastructure	**CAT11 To Be Clarified**	

* *The part that initiated the collaboration has not yet clarified any specific purpose/ objective.*
Source: Elaborated by the authors.

Table 18.3 Configuration of Objectives' Patterns

Port	Number of times each objective is officially stated in each port's collaboration agreement (objectives encoded in categories)					
	Amsterdam	Antwerp	Hamburg	Rotterdam	Bremenports	Total
Sustainability (Environmental)	2					2
Regional Growth						0
Logistics & Hinterland	2					2
Nautical/Technical Services	1					1
Infrastructure – Development	2			4	1	6
Share and Exchange of Know-how, Training	4	1				5
Port Management	1			1		2
Port Management: Commercial	1					1
Crisis Management						0
Port Growth		4		2		6
To be clarified	1					1
Total	1	17	1	7	1	27

Source: Elaborated by the authors.

The diversity of objectives for each participant port is notable, denoting a different strategy of engagement by the various PAs. The port of Antwerp is the port management entity with the wider range of objectives pursued with its inter-organization relationships; 17 different goals have been recorded lying within eight different categories of objectives. To achieve these diverse

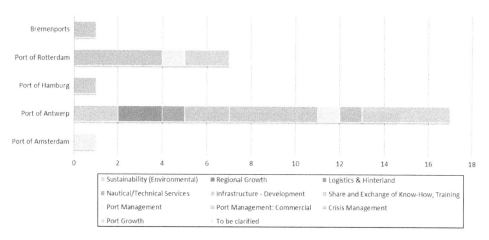

Graph 18.1 Configuration of objectives pursued per port.
Source: Elaborated by the authors.

objectives, it also stands as the PA with the more extensive portfolio of collaboration initiatives; its presence is recorded in right different agreements. The Port of Rotterdam Authority is also involved in a number of collaborative relationships (seven in total).

However, the objectives of the Rotterdam PA are more focused compared to those of Antwerp, i.e. they lie mostly in two categories: *infrastructure/Greenfield projects development* (CAT5) and *share and exchange of know-how* (CAT 6). The PAs of Amsterdam, Hamburg, and Bremenports are each involved in one single-objective cross-border collaboration agreement. However, the objective that each of them is seeking via this involvement is of different category compared to the one that the other two PAs seek in the respective collaborations that they have formed.

18.4.2 Configuration of collaboration patterns

Another element worth exploring is the type of relationship formed in each coupling of resources. Six types of inter-organizational relationship formats have been observed in the cases detailed in Table 18.1. These are:(a) *collaborations*; (b) *collaboration agreements*; (c) *joint ventures / investments*; (d) *alliances*; (e) *memorandum of understanding* (MoU); and (f) *consultancy* (where the European PA involved acts as the *consultant*). As regards the two first formats, the difference between them is that collaboration relationships have just been officially announced and are not followed by any other formal documentation, or such was not clearly stated or revealed publicly, whereas a *collaboration agreement* is one that implies an official agreement signed by both parts involved.

Graph 18.2 illustrates the structure of these relationships as developed by each PA. A certain preference in MOUs and collaboration agreements signing reveals a trend in validating officially most of the collaboration relationships established by port management entities.

As it might have been expected, the most active PAs insofar as the involvement in inter-organizational relationships is concerned, namely the PAs of Antwerp and Rotterdam, have also established more sophisticated forms of collaboration. The port of Rotterdam forms joint ventures but also acts as a consultant to other ports, while the port of Antwerp is involved in the forming of alliances. This observation can be attributed to the expanded business structures that have been established and activated lately by both ports. The relationships

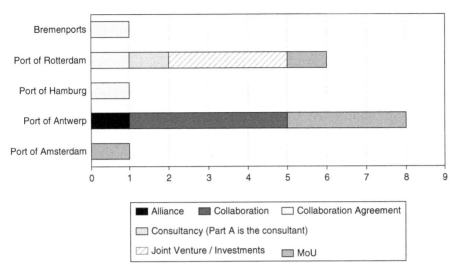

Graph 18.2 Structure of collaboration relationships.
Source: Elaborated by the authors.

established between the port of Antwerp and the ports of San Pedro and Rosmoport (see Table 18.1) are initiated by a business structure of the Port of Antwerp Authority called *Port of Antwerp International*, which is an investment subsidiary of Port of Antwerp Authority (Port of Antwerp International, 2016).

The corporatized Port of Rotterdam Authority also developed a similar business structure. The principal aim of the established *Port of Rotterdam International* (PORint) department is to promote trade with Rotterdam, by, among other things, developing a global port network (Port of Rotterdam International, 2016). PORint is the business structure that has initiated the collaboration relationships observed. In a similar pattern, the port of Amsterdam has also been involved in a collaboration relationship with the Aruba Ports Authority (see Table 18.1) through its international consultancy firm *Port of Amsterdam International* (Port of Amsterdam International 2016).

18.4.3 The geography of collaboration patterns

As regards the geography of the established relationships, Figure 18.1 presents the locational couplings of the identified collaborations in an effort to explore if there is any specific pattern followed. As the map illustrates, the geographic patterns is rather scattered across continents, with no possible specific strategic pattern in place. Nevertheless, we can observe a certain preference in conducting collaboration relationships with ports belonging to Asia (India) and South America (Brazil). These preferences are similar in the cases of the ports of Antwerp and Rotterdam.

18.4.4 Firm-based concepts in port practice

Reflecting the firm-based literature on collaboration between firms, one identifies a clear linkage with Snow's (2015) work. Especially the Antwerp and Rotterdam cases validate the relevant framework, both in terms of forms of collaboration and in terms of objectives. The patterns

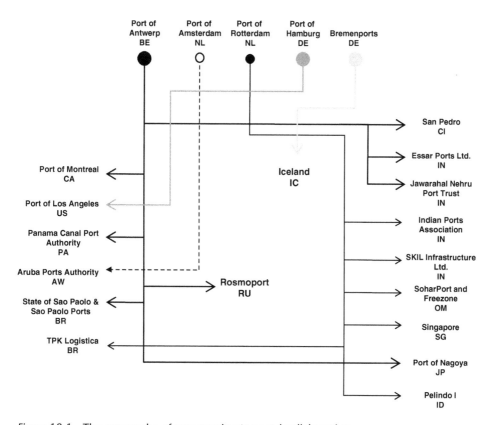

Figure 18.1 The geography of non-proximate ports' collaboration.

observed are intense, there is a high-level exchange of information, but, most importantly, the parties involved work together for the achievement of mutual objectives, by forming very specific and formally announced forms of relationships (MoUs, joint ventures, alliances, collaboration agreements), by working on specific objectives (see Table 18.1).

Moreover, the examined cases validate to a considerable extent the conceptual patterns referring to the *whys* and *hows* inter-organizational relationships develop (see Scheme 18.1). While not always clearly stated as an intention in our dataset's observations, the attainment of a competitive advantage is present at the introduction of international business departments (see the cases of Antwerp, Rotterdam, and Amsterdam). The way the port management bodies of our database respond to the *why they get involved in inter-organizational formations* question is more coherent with the suggested resource-based view (RBV) theory, in turn based on the heterogeneity of firms, rather than with the *industry structure concept*. The managing bodies of Antwerp, Rotterdam, and Bremenports have established relationships with other non-port related entities within an approach matching the RBV concept.

In parallel, the blending and combination of resources, know-how, and information exchange are all evident when exploring the objectives of all different cases, in other words, how the involved firms head to achieve inter-organizational competitive advantage. As depicted in Scheme 18.2, human resources systems and strategic alliances are present, yet more generalized forms of inter-organizational relationships are in most cases the preferred way forward.

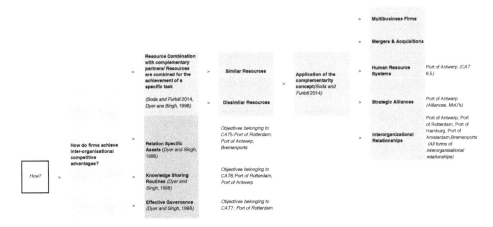

Scheme 18.2 Inter-organizational relationships: how?
Source: Elaborated by the authors.

18.5 The dynamic nature of inter-organizational relationships

Inter-organizational relationships between ports are of a highly dynamic nature, pushed further by new developments in the industry. Announcements are constantly recorded from port management bodies across the globe, which demonstrates a persistent flow of such initiatives.

The observed actions concern collaboration practices and/or such intentions in general, mostly within the framework developed in the previous sections. For that reason, some very recently announced cases (coming not only from the European continent), highlight this trend that characterizes the international port industry. Even though not all the following selected cases fall under the particular scope of the study, it is worth shedding light on this factual information that demonstrates the acceleration of collaboration between ports.

One such case is the intention of the port of Rotterdam to participate as a bidder at the auction for the sale of the Australian Fremantle port, a port privatization attempt back in early 2016. The privatization procedure of the port was delayed principally due to lack of wide political consensus, hence information on the interested parties cannot yet be validated in a formal way, and so this intention has yet to be formalized. Moreover, this case has little to do with the collaborative patterns explored in the present work. Yet it is an indicative paradigm of a process that seems to go beyond the delineated boundaries of the inter-organizational strategies of port management bodies. It entails, at least, a twist for the nature and the operational scope of the port's management body, since, for instance, such intention goes even beyond the port authority's international department (PoRint) stated responsibilities.

On the other hand, the port of Antwerp seems to continue its activity around the pursuance of mutual objectives along with other entities and/or port authorities, with a collaboration agreement sealed by a MoU signed with Shahid Rajaie Port Authority (port of Bandar Abbas) in Iran. The mutual objectives concern, among others, the exchange of information on statistics and port development projects, as well as collaboration in the field of training. Furthermore, the collaboration of the port of Antwerp with the port of San Pedro in Côte d'Ivoire (see Table 18.1) has been renewed in late 2016 for another five years.

Apart from the European cross-border initiatives, an indicative case from the other side of the globe is a formal announcement for an agreement on the formation of an alliance between six Malaysian and 11 Chinese ports. The alliance's objective is, apart from the joint promotion of the port-related industries (logistics, shipping, etc.) in both countries, the intention of the development of a new (third) deep-sea port at Port-Klang. This case is quite interesting, since this time the international strategy patterns engage in collaboration through the formation of same "nationality" groups of ports, each group belonging to a different country.

At the same time, it is worth noting that the continuation of the restructuring of liner shipping, foremost the identification of shipping alliances formation, seems to act as incentive for collaboration between both proximate and non-proximate port authorities.

To give an example, even though this is not a European case, Savannah and Norfolk port authorities have applied to the Federal Maritime Commission to get such permission with the stated angle being not to discuss commercial issues such as prices but to present to the newly formed liner shipping alliances a united front on a number of key issues. This is a case of two ports that are on the same coastline but 500 miles apart whose respective port authorities have applied to regulatory authorities for permission to work more closely together. As they are a long way from each other (and so do not compete head-to-head for their captive local cargo markets, only the longer-distance discretionary intermodal markets), these ports are seeking to work together on a range of topics such as coordinating vessel calls and berthing arrangements, marketing, and procurement, to make more efficient use of their facilities. All these are in addition to next-door neighbour ports forming alliances (e.g. ports of Seattle and Tacoma) or neighbour terminals forming cooperation agreements (e.g. the two terminals in Miami), or even terminal operating portfolios agreeing to work more closely together (e.g. CMA Terminals Holding and COSCO Shipping Ports).

18.6 Conclusions

Port management has been subject to redefinition in many fundamental respects. A key change refers to the structures and strategies of PAs. Disassociated from port operations, they do not remain passive landlord entities but assume a more active role in port development. Development of inter-organizational relations is part of the latter. Initially developed between ports in proximate geographical regions and overlapping hinterlands, this strategy expanded to collaborations with non-proximate port authorities or other entities.

The study identified a number of such practices developed by different European PAs; yet this is not a generalized practice, but a strategy limited to a group including the three major European ports and a couple of additional North European ports. It was also identified that the strategies of the PAs that are involved in such initiatives vary to a considerable extent, while in some collaborations develop with other entities than PAs.

Searching for a fitting typology of port collaboration beyond proximity, it was found that these initiatives are not single-purpose ones but might fit in one, or more, of 11 different categories. The initiatives are not single-scope but might have more than one objectives, whereas some PAs (in particular the PA of Antwerp) were found to be more active and dynamic than the others. With regard to the structures of these initiatives, again there is a lack of a single pattern, though the signing and implementation of formal agreements and memorandums of understanding are the most popular formats. Notably, the development of such relationships and the intention to further develop the international strategies alter the structures of PAs themselves, as PAs start establishing purpose-based entities to develop such initiatives.

Nonetheless, the form of inter-organization relationships established provides one perspective of developing strategies. With most of them being recently formed, researching how these agreements progress over time will be useful; it will allow understanding whether these agreements are followed by concrete results or fade away after public relations announcements, how many of them have achieved their initial objectives, and if and how these objectives might have been broadened in scope or progressively adjusted.

Searching for a fit of these collaborations with taxonomies and concepts aiming to understand *why* and *how* inter-organizational relationships between firms develop, it was observed that the configurations of relationship-formation patterns are extensively matching these particular frameworks. These observations confirm the validity of calls to move port research towards management-focused firm-led concepts.

The observations and the analysis conclude in two major leaders (ports of Antwerp and Rotterdam) that have significantly broadened their agendas with international-related strategies. It is also evident that these leading ports have already developed advanced strategies at a rather fast pace, whereas their most recent actions indicate a tendency to integrate such practices into their core strategic philosophies, along with an intention to progress with more advanced strategic actions.

It remains to be seen, though, if these ports are in reality leaders or followers, if there is a time-lag in the dataset's participants and if, in the future, other ports will follow. Monitoring development will also allow answering whether the *going international* strategies for the two leaders (Antwerp and Rotterdam), which currently focus on partnerships with ports in emerging countries, will be a modern drive for growth in overseas locations. Are, for instance, these strategies more than an exchange of know-how, or is this just a "selling" of technical skills? Is the driver a profit-making exercise or is it part of a development undertaken by market leaders who will eventually promote by these means a global business-thinking model with possible followers?

Notably, a parallel "going international" process has also marked the port industry: the one of international container terminal operators that emerged since the 1990s. While the analysis of ITOs behaviour in relation to changes in domestic and foreign markets remains beyond the scope of the present study (for such analyses: Olivier et al, 2007; Parola et al., 2013), it is worth for future research to examine the ways that the two types of internationalization intersect and the ways that the strategies and the balance of power between the various actors involved are affected (for a first attempt on the way that ITOs internationalization does so: Bichou and Bell, 2007).

In a nutshell, the findings suggest that strategic port management is redefined in at least two respects: first, by redefining the targets and activities of PAs, and second by redefining, in at least some cases, the intra-organizational structures of the managing bodies of ports. They also provide a base to further explore the rationale for these moves and the precise implications that they (will) have for strategic port management.

The above reveals a potential for strategic port management, not easily identified, however definitely anticipated. Port management is seen to have been opened up to a brand-new way of assessing targets. Although the recorded moves by PAs in some of the cases seem somewhat impulsive and not clearly introduced within a specific strategic frame, there are a lot of lessons and incentives there for CEOs: first, the port world is not that static at all and is on the threshold of changes. These changes affect the core management and will, in the future, bring new norms and business philosophies. Second, port managers need to be more vigilant and proactive and, why not, re-educated beyond the traditional port management setting, or to include in their workforce specially trained consultants. Targeting as an element of strategy seems to move beyond the attraction of cargoes and the inclusion of the port as a concrete node of the supply chain. Internationalization will be the principal issue that the port managers of the near future will be faced with, along with all possible departments of a port authority, especially legal departments (new forms of contracts, new forms of negotiations, and introduction of safety valves). The creation of specific departments such as those introduced by the port of Antwerp and the port of Rotterdam may be another issue that port managers may have to examine further.

Acknowledgements

The study has benefited by the Jean Monnet Action European Port Policy (5648484-EPP-1-20151), co-financed by the European Commission – Education and Culture DG.

References

Avery, P. (2000). *Strategies for Container Ports, A Cargo Systems Report*, London: IIR Ltd.

Bichou, K. and Bell, M.G.H. (2007). Internationalisation and consolidation of the container port industry: Assessment of channel structure and relationships. *Maritime Economics and Logistics*, 9(1), 35–51.

Brooks M.R., Cullinane K.P.B., and Pallis, A.A. (2017). Revisiting port governance and port reform: A multi-country examination. *Research in Transportation Business and Management*, 22, 1–10.

Brooks, M.R., Mccalla, R., Pallis, A.A., and van der Lugt, L. (2010). Strategic cooperation in peripheral ports: The case of Atlantic Canada's ports. *Canadian Journal of Transportation*, 4(1), 29–42.

Brooks M.R. and Pallis A.A. (2012). Port governance. In: Talley W.K. (ed.) *Maritime Economics – A Blackwell Companion*, London: Blackwell, 232–267.

Brooks M.R. and Pallis A.A. (2013). Advances in port performance and strategy. *Research in Transportation Business and Management*, 8, 1–6.

Caldeirinha, V., Felício, J.A., and da Cunha, S.F. (2017). Government policies and Portuguese port governance in the period from 2005 to 2015. *Research in Transportation Business & Management*, 22, 11–20.

Chlomoudis, C.I. and Pallis A.A. (2004). Port governance and the smart port authority: Key issues for the reinforcement of quality services in European ports. 10th *World Conference on Transport Research* (proceedings: CD-Rom format), Istanbul, Turkey, June.

Cullinane, K. and Brooks, M.R. (2007). Devolution, port performance and port governance. *Research in Transport Economics*, Volume 17, Bingley: JAI Press.

Cullinane, K. and Song, D.W. (2001). The administrative and ownership structure of Asian container ports. *Journal of Maritime Economics and Logistics*, 3, 175–197.

De Langen, P.W. (2004). *The Performance of Seaport Clusters*. PhD dissertation, ERIM, Erasmus Research Institute of Management.

De Langen, P.W. (2007). Stakeholders, conflicting interests and governance in port clusters. In: Brooks, M.R. and Cullinane, K. (eds), *Devolution, Port Governance and Port Performance*, Amsterdam: Elsevier, 457–477.

De Langen, P. and van der Lugt, L. (2017). Institutional reforms of port authorities in the Netherlands; the establishment of port development companies. *Research in Transportation Business & Management*, 22, 108–113.

Dooms, M., and Verbeke, M.A. (2007). Stakeholder management in ports: a conceptual framework integrating insights from research in strategy, corporate social responsibility and port management. *IAME 2007 Conference*, Athens, Greece.

Dooms, M., van der Lugt, L., Parola, F., Song, D.-W., and Satta, G. (2013). A conceptual framework for internationalization strategies of port authorities. *IAME 2013 Conference*, Marseille, France.

Dooms, M., Verbeke, A., and Haezendonck, E. (2013). Stakeholder management and path dependence in large-scale transport infrastructure development: the port of Antwerp case (1960–2010). *Journal of Transport Geography*, 1, 1–12.

Dyer, J.H. and Singh, H. (1998). The relational view: Cooperative strategy and sources of interorganizational competitive advantage. *Academy of Management Review*, 23(4), 660–679.

Goss, R. (1990). Economies policies and seaports: 2. The diversity of port policies. *Maritime Policy and Management*, 17, 221–234.

Gulati, R. and Singh, H. (1998). The architecture of cooperation: Managing coordination costs and appropriation concerns in strategic alliances. *Administrative Science Quarterly*, 43(4), 781–814.

Juhel, M. (2000). Globalization and partnerships in ports: trends for the 21st century. *Ports and Harbours*, 45, 9–14.

Knatz, G. (2017). How competition is driving change in port governance, strategic decision-making, and government policy in the United States, *Research in Transportation Business & Management*, 22, 67–77.

Nooteboom B. (1999). *Inter-Firm Alliances: Analysis and Design*. London: Routledge.

Notteboom, T., De Langen, P., and Jacobs, W. (2013). Institutional plasticity and path dependence in seaports: interactions between institutions, port governance reform and port authority routines. *Journal of Transport Geography*, 27, 26–35.

Notteboom T., Ducruet, C., and De Langen P.W. (2009). *Ports in Proximity: Competition and Coordination among Adjacent Seaports.* Aldershot: Ashgate.

Notteboom, T., Parola, F., Satta, G., and Penco, L. (2015). Disclosure as a tool in stakeholder relations management: a longitudinal study on the Port of Rotterdam. *International Journal of Logistics Research and Applications*, 18(3), 228–250.

Notteboom, T.E. and Rodrigue, J-P. (2005). Port regionalization: Towards a new phase in port development. *Maritime Policy and Management*, 32(3), 297–313.

Notteboom, T.E. and Winkelmans, W. (2001). Structural changes in logistics: how will port authorities face the challenge? *Maritime Policy and Management*, 28(1), 71–89.

Olivier, D., Parola, F., Slack, B., and Wang, J.J. (2007). The time scale of internationalisation: The case of the container port industry. *Maritime Economics and Logistics*, 9(1), 1–34.

Pallis A.A., Vitsounis T.K., and de Langen P.W., (2010). Research in port economics, policy and management: a review. *Transport Reviews*, 30(1), 115–161.

Pallis A.A., Vitsounis T.K., De Langen P.W., and Notteboom T.E. (2011). Port economics, policy and management: Content classification and survey. *Transport Reviews*, 31(4), 445–471.

Parola, F., Satta, G., and Caschili, S. (2013). Unveiling co-operative networks and "hidden families" in the container port industry. *Maritime Policy and Management*, 1, 1–21.

Porter, M., (1990), The competitive advantage of nations. *Harvard Business Review*, March–April, 73–91.

Port of Amsterdam International (2016). Our expertise, available at: http://www.portofamsterdaminternati onal.com/poai/Our-expertise (last visit: 14 March 2016).

Port of Antwerp International (2016). Investments as part of the foreland policy, available at: http://www .portofantwerp.com/nl/node/3842 (last visit: 14 March 2016).

Port of Rotterdam International (2016). Port of Rotterdam International, available at: https ://www.porto frotterdam.com/en/business-opportunities/global-port-network/port-of-rotterdam-international (last visit: 14 March 2016).

Snow, C.C. (2015). Organizing in the age of competition, cooperation, and collaboration. *Journal of Leadership & Organizational Studies*, 22(4), 433–442.

Soda, G. and Furlotti, M. (2014). Bringing tasks back in an organizational theory of resource complementarity and partner selection. *Journal of Management*, 43(2), 348–375.

Song, D.-W. (2003). Port co-opetition in concept and practice. *Maritime Policy and Management*, 30(1), 29–44.

UNCTAD (United Nations Conference on Trade and Development) (1996). *Potentialities for Regional Port Co-operation*, UNCTAD/SDD/PORT/5, Geneva: UN.

Van de Voorde, E. and Verhoeven, P. (2017). Port governance and policy changes in Belgium 2006–2016: A comprehensive assessment of process and impact. *Research in Transportation Business & Management*, 22, 123–134.

Van der Horst, M.R. and De Langen, P.W. (2008). Coordination in hinterland transport chains: a major challenge for the seaport community. *Maritime Economics & Logistics*, 10(1–2), 108–129.

Van der Lugt, L.M. and De Langen, P.W. (2007). Port authority strategy: Beyond the landlord – A conceptual approach. *IAME2007 Conference*, Athens, Greece.

Van der Lugt, L.M., De Langen, P.W., and Hagdorn, E. (2015). Beyond the landlord: worldwide empirical analysis of port authority strategies. *International Journal of Shipping and Transport Logistics*, 7(5), 570–596.

Van der Lugt, L.M., Dooms, M., and Parola, F., (2013). Strategy making by hybrid organizations: The case of the port authority. *Research in Transportation Business & Management*, 8, 103–113.

Van Klink, H.A. (1997). Creating port networks. *International Journal of Transport Economics*, 24(3), 393–408.

Verhoeven, P. (2010). A review of port authority functions: Towards a Renaissance? *Maritime Policy and Management*, 37(3), 247–270.

Woo, S-H., Pettit, S.J., Beresford, A., and Kwak, D-W. (2012). Seaport research: A decadal analysis of trends and themes since the 1980s. *Transport Reviews*, 32(3), 351–377.

19

Investments and financial instruments in port management

Giovanni Satta, Francesco Parola, and Enrico Musso

19.1 Background: investment and financial decisions in the container port industry

Over the last two decades, terminal and stevedoring industries have been experiencing a profound reorganization process produced by the port reform worldwide, the progressive opening of formerly monopolistic (local) markets, and a fast internationalization of the business. The new competitive environment determined a growing commitment of private investors in the (co-)funding and management of container port facilities, and reshaped major assumptions underlying investment and financial decisions in the industry. For exploiting open window opportunities originated by the reorganization of the sector, several private firms have undertaken a sequence of investments in foreign markets, along with aggressive internationalization paths. Leading international terminal operators (ITOs) were capable to build and run broad portfolios of infrastructures in multiple locations (Olivier, 2005; Notteboom and Rodrigue, 2012; Parola et al., 2013; Satta and Persico, 2015; Parola et al., 2015). In this context, strategic dimensions related to port investment decisions became even more complex due to the capital-intensive nature of the industry and the long pay-back period of port investments. Relatedly, the huge financial resources required for the development of greenfield mega-projects and the feeding of ITOs' overseas expansion (e.g. privatizations, merger & acquisitions, etc.) established new links between finance and the port terminal industry (Rodrigue et al., 2011).

Therefore, over the last two decades, in fact, the relation between the port industry and the financial sector has become much more intense, triggering scholars to coin the notion of financialization[1] of the port and terminal industry (Rodrigue et al., 2011; Notteboom and Rodrigue, 2012). Similar trends characterized the relationship between the shipping business and the financial sector since the '90s (Grammenos et al., 2007).

Although the intensity and the pervading nature of this trend emerged even more clearly in conjunction with the blast of the economic and financial crisis (2008), this phenomenon appears scarcely investigated and debated in port literature (Pallis and Syriopoulos, 2007; Rodrigue et al., 2011). As a result, significant literature gaps still persist.

In this perspective, the container port industry constitutes an insightful field for empirical investigations on the drivers of change affecting investment and financial decisions within the port context. The reason is twofold. First, some innate characteristics of this sector, such as its capital-intensive nature and the long pay-back period of investments in terminals and facilities, traditionally determine high financial needs for private firms (van De Voorde, 2005; Pallis and Syriopoulos, 2007; Soppé et al., 2009; Parola et al., 2014). Second, the sector has recently suffered commercial and institutional transformations, which imposed higher financial requirements for investing in the business, e.g. the increase of international maritime trade volume and the ongoing growth of ships' and terminals' size, the diffusion of new public management practices in port domain, the internationalization of leading container port operators, etc. (Hoyle and Charlier 1995; Notteboom 2002; Parola et al., 2013; Parola et al., 2014).

This chapter identifies the main drivers which shape investment and financial decisions in the industry, triggering towards a deeper financialization of the sector. In particular, the following issues are identified as the most salient trends:

- increasing magnitude of port investments, due to the development of greenfield mega-projects, the ITOs' overseas expansion, and the acceleration in M&A activity (Section 19.2);
- adoption of new sources of capital and the new role of international financial markets, e.g. initial public offerings (IPOs) and bond issuing (Section 19.3);
- changes in risk perception, which affects appetite for risk, asset pricing methodologies, and weighted average cost of capital (WACC) (Section 19.4);
- new policies in risk management and a wider diffusion of financial derivatives (Section 19.5);
- entry of financial investors in the industry, e.g. pension funds and insurance companies, sovereign wealth funds, investment banks and private equity funds, investment holding companies, multilateral financial institutions (Section 19.6).

19.2 Port investments and need for additional funds

The first financial driver affecting the container port industry refers to the growing magnitude of port investments which imposes the need to gather greater financial resources. Mega-projects, in particular, are becoming a common phenomenon in the development of container port infrastructure, with several implications in terms of investment decisions, technical and financial scale, duration, complexity, risks, and the number of parties involved (Flyvbjerg et al., 2003; Van Marrewijk, 2007; Parola et al., 2013; Satta and Persico, 2015). Port infrastructure projects indeed are characterized by tremendous barriers to entry as they impose huge up-front, non-divisible investments (typically, over 100 million USD). Due to their intrinsic illiquid nature in the short term and their managerial, organizational, and financial complexity port mega-projects determine high-transaction costs for starting and closing financial deals. As a result, the types and range of actors holding the financial size and the technical skills required for investing in this asset class still remain rather limited (Siemiatycki, 2015). A number of mega-projects have recently taken place in developing countries where the mismatch between limited supply and growing demand for port infrastructures (coupled with a significant availability of low-cost greenfield spaces) stimulated the attraction of private investments in major container facilities (Parola et al., 2013). In this perspective, public-private-partnership (PPP) and other forms of project finance emerged as viable solutions for ensuring private involvement and commitment (Guasch, 2004; Parola et al., 2015), as well as for overcoming public budgetary constraints and lack of expertise in operations (Flinders, 2005; Hammami et al., 2006). Table 19.1 shows the most significant greenfield mega-projects in container terminals realized within the 2000–2014 timeframe in developing countries, as reported by the Private Participation in Infrastructures (PPI) database of the World Bank. The 26 sample projects took place in 14 developing countries,

Table 19.1 Greenfield Mega-projects (above 300 million USD) in Container Terminals in Developing Countries (2000–2014)

Project name	Country	Private investments (in million USD)	Financial closure year	Contractual arrangement	Project status	Contract period	Private commitment (%)	Technology	Sponsors
Onne port expansion, phase 4B	Nigeria	2,900.00	2013	BOO	Construction	25	100	Multi-purpose terminal	Macquarie Infrastructure and real assets and other investors
Lekki Deep Seaport	Nigeria	1,500.00	2013	BOT	Construction	45	62	Multi-purpose terminal	Tolaram Group (62% / Singapore)
Pakistan Deep Water Container	Pakistan	1,200.00	2010	BOT	Construction	25	100	Container terminal	Hutchison Port Holdings (100% / Hong Kong, China)
Qingdao New Qianwan CT Joint Venture	China	1,000.00	2007	BOT	Construction	50	59	Container terminal	Dubai Holding (24% / United Arab Emirates), AP Moller – Maersk Group (16% / Denmark), Pan Asia International Shipping Ltd (20% / China)
APM Terminals Lazaro Cardenas	Mexico	900.00	2013	BOT	Construction	32	100	Container terminal	AP Moller – Maersk Group (95% / Denmark), ICA SA de CV (5% / Mexico)
Shenzhen Dachan Bay Container Terminals	China	858.00	2005	BOT	Construction	50	65	Container terminal	Modern Terminals Ltd (65% / Hong Kong, China)
Yantian International CT Phase III	China	845.00	2002	BOT	Construction	50	65	Container terminal	Hutchison Whampoa Ltd (65% / Hong Kong, China)
Brasil Terminal Portuario	Brazil	845.00	2011	BLT	Operational	NA	100	Container terminal, liquid bulk terminal	AP Moller – Maersk Group (50% / Denmark), Terminal Investments Ltd (50% / Netherlands)

(*Continued*)

Table 19.1 Continued

Project name	Country	Private investments (in million USD)	Financial closure year	Contractual arrangement	Project status	Contract period	Private commitment (%)	Technology	Sponsors
Tianjin Port North Gangchi CT Phase III	China	825.72	2007	BOT	Operational	50	49	Container terminal	PSA Corp (49% / Singapore)
Embraport	Brazil	800.00	2011	BOO	Operational	NA	67	Multi-purpose terminal	Odebrecht SA (26% / Brazil), Dubai Holding (26% / United Arab Emirates), Coimex (16% / Brazil)
Super Port Acu LLX Acu	Brazil	700.00	2012	BOO	Construction	25	100	Multi-purpose terminal	EBX Capital Partners (21% / Brazil), EIG Global Energy Partners (53% / United States), Small local investors (27% / ..)
Damietta Port	Egypt, Arab Rep.	640.00	2008	BOT	Construction	40	100	Container terminal	Kuwait and Gulf Link Holding Company (KGL Holding) (30% / Kuwait), China Shipping Group Company (20% / China), Terminal Link Company (20% / Egypt, Arab Rep.)
Dhamra Port Project Phase I	India	600.00	2007	BOT	Operational	34	100	Multi-purpose terminal	Adani Group (100% / India)
Colombo South Container Terminal	Sri Lanka	500.00	2011	BOT	Construction	35	55	Container terminal	China Harbour Engineering Company Ltd (55% / China), Aitken Spence & Company Ltd (30% / Sri Lanka)
Lome Container Terminal	Togo	495.00	2011	BOT	Operational	35	100	Container terminal	Mediterranean Shipping Company (MSC) (100% / Switzerland)
Container Terminal Cotonou Port	Benin	489.00	2009	BOT	Operational		100	Container terminal	Bollore Group (88% / France)
Shanghai Waigaoqiao Phase V Project	China	482.00	2005	BOT	Operational	50	50	Container terminal	Hutchison Whampoa Ltd (50% / Hong Kong, China)
Puducherry Port	India	467.00	2006	BOT	Construction	30	100	Multi-purpose terminal	Subhash Projects & Marketing Ltd (.. / India)
Callao South Dock Container Terminal	Peru	439.00	2008	BOT	Operational	30	100	Container terminal	DP World (70% / United Arab Emirates), Uniport SA (30% / Peru)

Project	Country	Investment	Year	Contract type	Status		%	Terminal type	Operator
Asya Port Container Terminal	Turkey	415.00	2013	BOO	Construction	NA	100	Container terminal	Mediterranean Shipping Company (MSC) (50% / Switzerland), Others (50% / ..)
Puerto Bahia	Colombia	400.00	2013	Merchant	Construction	NA	100	Multi-purpose terminal	Pacific Rubiales Corporation (100% / Canada)
Doraleh Container Terminal	Djibouti	396.00	2007	BOT	Operational	NA	100	Container terminal	DP World (100% / United Arab Emirates)
Gangavaram Port Limited	India	385.50	2005	BOT	Operational	30	89	Multi-purpose terminal	DP World (.. / United Arab Emirates), DVS Raju (.. / India)
Xiamen Songyu Container Terminal	China	364.25	2004	BOT	Construction	50	50	Container terminal	AP Moller – Maersk Group (50% / Denmark)
Tuxpan Container Terminal	Mexico	350.00	2014	BOT	Construction	20	100	Container terminal	Stevedoring Services of America (SSA) Inc. (.. / United States)
Manzanillo TEC II (Phase I)	Mexico	321.20	2012	BOT	Operational	34	100	Container terminal	International Container Terminal Services Inc. (ICTSI) (100% / Philippines)

Notes: BOT = Build-operate-transfer; BOO = Build-own-operate; BLT = build, lease, and transfer.
Source: Authors' own elaboration from PPI database World Bank (2015).

determining total private investments above 19.11 billion USD. The mean size of port terminal projects was above 0.735 billion USD, ranging from 2.90 (Onne port expansion, phase 4B in Nigeria) to 0.32 (Manzanillo TEC II, Phase I, in Mexico). Unexpectedly, the temporal distribution of the investments across the sampled period shows that the financial crisis did not affect significantly the amount of financial resources committed by the private sector to mega-container port projects in emerging countries (7.30 billion USD in the 2002–2008 period versus 11.81 billion USD in the following one). As for the geographical distribution of these investments, China (5,497 million USD), Nigeria (4,400), Brazil (3,985), and India (2,242) emerge as leading countries in terms of private financial commitment. The build-operate-transfer (BOT) scheme represents the most popular contractual arrangement (76.92%) followed by build-own-operate (BOO, 15.38%).

In addition, some multinational enterprises, leveraging on port reform opportunities, have expanded their container terminal business overseas, becoming international terminal operators (ITOs) (Peters, 2001; Bichou and Bell, 2007; Satta and Persico, 2015) and have positioned themselves as leading players capable of managing large portfolios of facilities in diverse nations (Olivier 2005; Satta et al., 2014). The new market structure and competitive environment increased the level of competition among terminal operators (Notteboom 2007), and induced leading ITOs to pursue aggressive corporate strategies based on growth and internationalization, aiming to stretch their market share, exploit the scale and network effects, and ensure higher financial returns (van De Voorde 2005; Olivier 2005; Satta et al., 2014).

These accelerated overseas expansion strategies are often grounded on external aggressive market entry strategies, namely, conventional acquisition (i.e. the takeover of a single facility/firm located in a single site), merger, and multiple acquisition (i.e. the simultaneous takeover of an entire terminal portfolio in a single transaction) (Parola et al., 2015). Overall, merger & acquisition (M&A) activity in the container port industry rapidly blew up since the beginning of the new century (Olivier et al., 2007; Notteboom and Rodrigue, 2012).

In the 2000–2014 timeframe, 49 major financial transactions (value above 100 million USD) have been closed with an overall amount of financial resources committed over 43.7 billion USD (calculated on the 40 financial deals with figures disclosed). Table 19.2 and Table 19.3 report major information on these M&A operations. On average, each deal included around six new facilities located in three countries, with a financial commitment slightly above 1.1 billion USD per transaction. A number of contractual arrangements have been used in order to take the control over additional terminals and facilities, including the simultaneous acquisition of different assets (AS), the takeover of an entire corporation/company (CO), the private negotiation of shares, or the acquisition of a determined stake from the market (SH).

During the sample period, the major financial transactions took place in 2006: among others, the acquisition of P&O Ports by Dubai Ports World (6.8 billion USD), that of a 23.33% stake in Associated British Ports (ABP) by Goldman Sachs (4.6), and that of a 20% HPH stake by PSA International in 2006 (4.4). One year later (2007), the wave of M&A activities continued, financial operators such as Goldman Sachs, RREEF (Deutsche Bank), and Ontario Teachers' Pension Plan (OTPP) being the major actors involved.

The financial crisis significantly decreased M&A deal flow in the industry, reducing company valuations (see Section 19.4). In the 2000–2007 period, each deal required on average financial resources of 1.69 billion USD, against values slightly above 0.52 billion USD in the 2008–2014 timeframe.

More recently, some valuable financial deals were closed; in 2011, Citi Infrastructure Investments acquired the control (75% stake) of the Australian DPW terminal network for

Table 19.2 Major M&A Operations in the Container Port Industry (2000–2007)

Year	Buyer Name	Buyer Headquarters	Target company Name	Target company Headquarters	Transaction data N. of terminals	N. of countries	Transaction type*	Transaction value (million USD)
2001	Hutchison Port Holdings (HPH)	Hong Kong	ECT Rotterdam	Netherlands	2	1	CO	589
2001	Hutchison Port Holdings (HPH)	Hong Kong	Int. Container Terminal Services Inc. (ICTSI)	Philippines	8	6	AS	563
2002	PSA Corporation (PSA)	Singapore	Hesse Noord Natie	Belgium	5	1	CO	717
2002	Hutchison Port Holdings (HPH)	Hong Kong	Hyundai Merchant Marine (Hyundai)	South Korea	4	1	AS	215
2002	Nippon Yusen Kaisha (NYK)	Japan	Ceres	USA	5	3	CO	250
2003	CMA-CGM	France	EGIS Ports	France	3	1	SH (80%)	Undisclosed
2003	P&O Ports	UK	EGIS Ports	France	4	1	SH (20%)	Undisclosed
2004	Dubai Ports World (DPW)	UAE	CSX World Terminals (CSX)	USA	7	6	CO	1,150
2005	PSA Corporation (PSA)	Singapore	Hong kong International Terminals (HIT)	Hong Kong	5	1	SH (20%)	925
2005	China Merchant Holdings (CHM)	Hong Kong	Shanghai Int. Port Group (SIPG)	China	9	1	SH (30%)	Undisclosed
2005	PSA Corporation (PSA)	Singapore	NWS Holding	Hong Kong	2	1	AS	386
2006	Babcock & Brown Infrastructures (B&B)	Australia	PD Ports	UK	4	2	CO	1,368
2006	RREEF (Deutsche Bank)	Germany	Maher Terminals	USA	2	2	CO	2,100
2006	Dubai Ports World (DPW)	UAE	P&O Ports	UK	33	15	CO	6,800
2006	Goldman Sachs	USA	Associated British Ports (ABP)	UK	7	1	SH (23.33%)	4,600
2006	Macquarie	Australia	Hanjin Terminals (Hanjin)	South Korea	6	3	SH (40%)	870
2006	APM Terminals (Maersk)	Denmark	P&O Nedlloyd (PONL)	UK–Netherlands	2	2	CO	Undisclosed

(Continued)

Table 19.2 (Continued)

Year	Buyer		Target company		Transaction data			Transaction type*	Transaction value (million USD)
	Name	Headquarters	Name	Headquarters	N. of terminals	N. of countries			
2006	PSA Corporation (PSA)	Singapore	Hutchison Port Holdings (HPH)	Hong Kong	38	18		SH (20%)	4,400
2007	RREEF (Deutsche Bank)	Germany	Peel Ports	UK	4	2		SH (49%)	1,430
2007	Goldman Sachs	USA	Stevedoring Services Association (SSA)	USA	12	4		SH (49%)	2,800
2007	Ontario Teachers Pension Fund (OTTP)	Canada	Orient Overseas Container Line (OOCL)	Hong Kong	4	2		AS	2,350
2007	Ports America (Highstar Capital)	USA	Dubai Ports World (DPW)	UAE	6	1		AS	1,100
2007	Ports America (Highstar Capital)	USA	Amports Terminal Baltimore	USA	6	1		AS	430
2007	Ports America (Highstar Capital)	USA	Marine Terminals Corporation (MTC)	USA	8	1		CO	800

* Transaction type: AS = asset acquisition; CO = company/firm acquisition; SH = acquisition of a share in a company.
Source: Authors' own elaboration from Drewry Shipping Consultants (2001–2015) and Corporate Annual Reports.

Table 19.3 Major M&A Operations in the Container Port Industry (2008–2014)

Year	Buyer		Target company		Transaction data			
	Name	Headquarters	Name	Headquarters	N. of terminals	N. of countries	Transaction	Transaction value
2009	Brookfield	Canada	Babcock & Brown Infrastructures (B&B)	Australia	4	1	AS	625
2009	Euroports	Luxembourg	Babcock & Brown Infrastructures (B&B)	Australia	4	2	AS	Undisclosed
2009	Nippon Yusen Kaisha (NYK)	Japan	Hutchison Port Holdings (HPH)	Hong Kong	2	1	SH (4.5%)	(equity swap)
2010	JP Morgan	USA	Dragados	Spain	5	1	AS	720
2011	Cosco Pacific	China	Yantian International Container terminal	China	1	1	SH (9.7%)	520
2011	China Merchant Holdings (CHM)	Hong Kong	Tin Can Container Terminal (from ZIM)	Nigeria	1	1	SH (47.5%)	154
2011	Yildirim Group	Turkey	Malta Freeport Container Terminal (from Terminal Link, CMA-CGM)	France	1	1	SH (50%)	285
2011	Mitsui	Japan	Portek International (from ICTSI and via trading on the market)	Singapore	5	5	SH (100%)	179
2011	CITI Infrastructure Investments	USA	Dubai Ports World (DPW) Australia	United Arab Emirates	5	1	SH (75%)	1,500
2012	APM Terminals (Maersk)	Denmark	Poti Seaport (from Ras Al Khaimah Investment Authority)	UAE	1	1	SH (80%)	100
2012	APM Terminals (Maersk)	Denmark	Ningbo Port	China	1	1	SH (25%)	674
2012	Xiamen Port Group	China	Xiamen Songyu Container Terminal (from APM Terminal, Maersk)	China	1	1	SH (50%)	Undisclosed
2012	Hutchison Port Holdings (HPH) Trust	Singapore	Asia Container Terminals Holdings (from PSA and DPW)	Hong Kong	1	1	AS	407
2012	Terminal Investment Limited (TIL – MSC Group)	Switzerland	CSM Italia – Gate (Medcenter Container Terminal)	Italy	1	1	SH (50%)	Undisclosed
2012	Forth Ports	UK	Tilbury Container Services (from DP World and ABP)	UK	1	1	AS	150
2013	APM Terminals (Maersk)	Denmark	Global Ports Investments (GPI)	Russia	7	3	SH (37.5%)	863

(Continued)

Table 19.3 Continued

| Year | Buyer | | Target company | | Transaction data | | | |
	Name	Headquarters	Name	Headquarters	N. of terminals	N. of countries	Transaction	Transaction value
2013	China Merchant Holdings (CHM)	Hong Kong	Terminal Link (from CMA-CGM)	France	15	8	SH (49%)	520
2013	Global Ports Investments (GPI)	Russia	Vostochny Container Terminal (from DPW)	Russia	1	1	SH (25%)	230
2013	Goodman	Hong Kong	Container Terminal 3 in Hong Kong, ex CSXWT (from DPW)	Hong Kong	1	1	AS	463
2013	Global Ports Investments (GPI)	Russia	Terminal Investment Limited (TIL - MSC Group)	Switzerland	25	17	SH (35%)	1,929
2014	Int. Container Terminal Services Inc. (ICT)	Philippines	Yantai Company Ltd (from DPW)	China	1	1	SH (51%)	Undisclosed
2014	Consortium (IBK Security Company and Korea Investment Partners Company)	South Korea	Aògericas Container Terminal	Spain	1	1	SH (70%)	168
2014	Cosco Pacific (40%) and China Shipping Terminal Development	China	Asia Container Terminals Holdings (from HPH Trust)	Hong Kong	1	1	SH (60%)	215
2014	Brookfield	Canada	TraPac (from Mitsui O.S.K. Lines, MOL)	USA	2	1	SH (49%)	200
2014	Fernando Chico Pardo	Mexico	SSA Marine (from Goldman Sachs)	USA	22	5	SH (49%)	Undisclosed

Transaction type: AS = asset acquisition; CO = company/firm acquisition; SH = acquisition of a share in a company.
Source: Authors' own elaboration from Drewry Shipping Consultants (2001–2015) and Corporate Annual Reports.

1.5 billion USD, while in 2013 Global Ports Investments (GPI) acquired a 35% stake in Terminal Investment Limited (TIL) from MSC Group, with an investment of 1.9 billion USD.

M&A transactions and multiple-entry strategies allowed ITOs to reduce the time required for entry in new markets and to overtake several economic, institutional, and legal barriers (De Langen and Pallis, 2007; Satta and Persico, 2015). The increase in M&A activity before the financial crisis, indeed, required large amounts of financial resources backed by financial institutions (Rodrigue et al., 2011). This trend originated a growing need for financial consultancy and advisory, as well as exposing ITOs to high sunk costs in case of divestitures (Pallis et al., 2010) (Table 19.4).

19.3 New sources of capital: international financial markets

The second driver of change affecting investment and financial decisions in the container port industry is the progressive introduction of a broad spectrum of new funding options. Self-sustained (internal) financing, bank loans (e.g. mortgage-backed loans, corporate loans, loan syndications), and in many countries also governmental support, have been historically among the most important sources of finance in the container port domain (Stopford, 2009; Grammenos, 2013). The increasing magnitude of investments, indeed, made these sources of capital insufficient and determined a growing resort to capital markets and special purpose vehicles (SPVs) as methods of raising funds (Pallis and Syriopoulos, 2007). (Initial) public offering and bond issuing recently emerged as viable financial solutions to finance ITOs growth strategies and new port investments.

19.3.1 Initial public offerings (IPOs) in the container port industry

By offering shares sold on international stock exchanges (subsequently traded on secondary markets), a number of terminal operators and corporatized ports were able to gather additional financial resources to support their investment plans. In some cases, the public listing of port authorities/port companies has come as the final step (part privatization) of a corporatization path, through which public sector undertakings have been transformed into companies under private corporate law and commercially driven autonomous port authorities (Pallis and Syriopoulos, 2007). Despite a growing interest of port actors in equity capital markets as a source of finance, port-related IPOs received limited attention in academic circles (Satta et al., 2017), especially when compared with studies focused on the shipping business (Merikas et al., 2009).

The major advantages related to this source of funding compared to traditional instruments are the higher strategic flexibility in investment choices and the longer "maturity"; moreover, by collecting financial resources from international stock exchanges, port-related companies are expected to improve their debt/equity ratio. Conversely, primary cons regard the costs related to institutional communication with financial markets (e.g., the development of an ad hoc "investor relations" department), the higher exposure to financial markets' volatility, and the need for minimum standards of transparency.

Since the beginning of the new century, the (container) port industry experienced a renewed interest toward listing, through initial public offering (IPO). In particular, in the 2000–2014 timeframe, 90 companies were listed in major stock exchanges. They include port companies and port authorities (28) which leveraged on IPO to accelerate the privatization process, terminal operators and stevedores (28), some vertically integrated carriers (7), as well as enterprises involved in ancillary services and port-related activities (27). Figure 19.1 reports the temporal

Table 19.4 Gross Proceeds from IPOs in the Container Port Industry (2000–2014)

Business type	Year	2000	2001	2002	2003	2004	2005	2006	2007	2008	2009	2010	2011	2012	2013	2014	Total
Port company/ authority	No. of IPO	–	1	–	1	–	3	5	3	–	1	6	–	1	2	5	28
	Gross proceeds (million USD)	–	16.98	–	63.86	–	196.54	1,824.21	378.76	–	0.80	2,374.32	–	2.27	1,191.73	390.47	6,439.93
Terminal Operator/ stevedore	No. of IPO	–	–	–	–	–	2	2	6	3	1	5	3	–	4	2	28
	Gross proceeds (million USD)	–	–	–	–	–	282.17	426.46	7,088.79	18.37	48.71	990.55	4,596.13	–	554.73	4.86	14,010.77
Carrier (integrated)	No. of IPO	–	–	–	–	2	3	–	2	–	–	–	–	–	–	–	7
	Gross proceeds (million USD)	–	–	–	–	1,178.75	2,604.86	–	3,496.05	–	–	–	–	–	–	–	7,279.66
Ancillary services and port-related activities	No. of IPO	–	–	–	–	–	4	5	3	2	2	4	3	1	3	–	27
	Gross proceeds (million USD)	–	–	–	–	–	713.54	247.67	205.11	122.52	87.64	360.91	225.47	42.68	602.56	–	2,608.10
Total	No. of IPO	–	1	–	1	2	12	12	14	5	4	15	6	2	9	7	90
	Gross proceeds (million USD)	–	16.98	–	63.86	1,178.75	3,797.11	2,498.34	11,168.71	140.89	137.15	3,725.78	4,821.60	44.95	2,349.02	395.33	30,338.46

Source: Authors' own elaboration from S&P Capital I-Q Database and corporate annual reports.

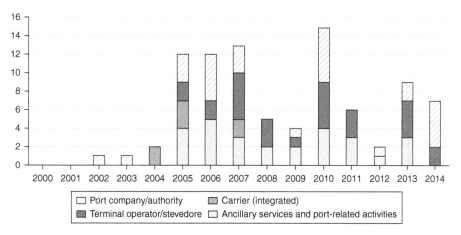

Figure 19.1 Temporal distribution of IPOs in the container port industry (2000–2014).
Source: Authors' own elaboration from S&P Capital I-Q Database and corporate annual reports.

distribution of sample IPOs within the sector. Data unveils how port-related companies understood public listing on international stock exchanges only recently: in particular, two main IPO waves are clearly identifiable between 2005 and 2007, as well as in the 2010–2011 period.

Overall, these 90 IPOs enable firms to raise more than 30 billion USD of equity resources from the private sector. The analysis of the gross proceeds' temporal distribution shows that 2007 was the "golden year" for the collection of additional financial resources in the industry (more than 11 billion USD per year). During the financial bubble, private and institutional investors, eager for higher-yielding assets, discovered the attractiveness of exchange-traded infrastructure companies and started to consider port-related companies as alternative assets for enhancing performance and diversification benefits (Inderst, 2010; Della Croce and Gatti, 2014; Siemiatycki, 2015).

As concerns the issuer's country of origin, the Far East and developing countries emerge as dominant areas for the recent listing activity, fueled by national economies' growth rates and the accelerated dynamics of international maritime trade (Kern, 2007). Issuers typically come from China (18 cases), Vietnam (10), Brazil (5), Hong Kong (4) and Malaysia (4), whereas advanced economies appear quite marginal. When considering the transaction value of sampled IPOs (gross proceeds), China still ranks first (9.91 billion USD), before United Arab Emirates (4.69), Singapore (3.97), Brazil (2.18), Hong Kong (1.62), and Germany (1.52). The Stock Exchange of Hong Kong, Nasdaq, Singapore Exchange, Shanghai Stock Exchange, and Bolsa de Valores de San Paulo are the most significant capital markets in terms of gross proceeds.

Table 19.5 reports main data on port companies and port authorities' IPOs. Port companies tended to choose global offerings when going public (16 global offerings vs. 12 domestic offerings), by devoting a portion of the offered shares to foreign investors. This decision enabled them to gather a significant amount of financial resources from international equity markets (3.82 billion USD, equivalent to 59.35% of the total gross proceeds from global offerings, respect to 2.61 billion USD from domestic offerings). The global offering approach seems to be the most popular option within the sector, as it allows to gather higher amounts of money, as well as to maximize issue proceeds (Chan et al., 2007).

Regarding the rationale for going public, empirical evidence suggests that port authorities and port companies' IPOs have been undertaken predominantly to channel fresh funds to the

Table 19.5 The IPOs of Port Companies and Port Authorities: Public Offerings Features (2000–2014)

Year	Issuer	Home country	Gross Proceeds ($USD million)	IPO Exchange	Global/Domestic Offering*	Securities Offered by Company/ Shareholders**
2001	Thessaloniki Port Authority S.A.	Greece	16.98	The Athens Stock Exchange	D	S
2003	Piraeus Port Authority SA	Greece	63.86	The Athens Stock Exchange	D	S
2005	Xiamen International Port Co., Ltd.	China	152.74	The Stock Exchange of Hong Kong Ltd	G	C&S
2005	Nanjing Port Co., Ltd.	China	34.52	Shenzhen Stock Exchange	D	C
2005	CIG Yangtze Ports PLC	Hong Kong	9.28	The Stock Exchange of Hong Kong Ltd	G	C
2006	Shanghai International Port (Group) Co., Ltd.***	China	800.00	Shanghai Stock Exchange/Hong Kong Stock Exchange	D	C&S
2006	MMX Mineração e Metalicos S.A.	Brazil	468.52	Bolsa de Valores de Sao Paulo	G	C
2006	Dalian Port (PDA) Company Limited	China	278.94	The Stock Exchange of Hong Kong Ltd	G	C
2006	Tianjin Port Development Holdings Limited	Hong Kong	140.12	The Stock Exchange of Hong Kong Ltd	G	C
2006	Rizhao Port Co., Ltd.	China	136.63	Shanghai Stock Exchange	D	C
2007	Triunfo Participações e Investimentos S.A.	Brazil	275.54	Bolsa de Valores de Sao Paulo	G	C&S
2007	Jiangsu Lianyungang Port Co., Ltd.	China	96.76	Shanghai Stock Exchange	D	C
2007	Grand Harbour Marina p.l.c.	Malta	6.46	Malta Stock Exchange	D	C
2009	Thi Xai Port Co.	Vietnam	0.80	Ho Chi Minh Stock Exchange	D	C
2010	Xingbo Port Company Limited	China	1,099.88	Shanghai Stock Exchange	D	C
2010	OHL Mexico SAB De CV	Mexico	791.99	Bolsa Mexicana de Valores	G	C&S
2010	TangShan Port Group CO., LTD.	China	242.10	Shanghai Stock Exchange	D	C
2010	Skil Ports & Logistics Limited	Channel Islands	121.05	London Stock Exchange	G	C
2010	Gujarat Pipavav Port Limited	India	118.08	Mumbai Stock Exchange	D	C&S
2010	My Thoi Port JSC	Vietnam	1.22	Ho Chi Minh Stock Exchange	D	C

Year	Company	Country	Value	Exchange	Global/Domestic	Securities offered by
2012	Tan Thuan Industrial Promotion Co., Ltd.	Vietnam	2.27	Ho Chi Minh Stock Exchange	G	C
2013	Westports Holdings Berhad	Malaysia	629.89	Bursa Malaysia	G	S
2013	Qinhuangdao Port Co., Ltd.	China	561.84	The Stock Exchange of Hong Kong Ltd	G	C&S
2014	Qingdao Port International Co., Ltd.	China	376.54	The Stock Exchange of Hong Kong Ltd	G	C&S
2014	Port of Hai Phong Joint Stock Company	Vietnam	11.26	Hanoi Stock Exchange	G	C&S
2014	Nghe Tinh Port Holding LLC	Vietnam	2.21	Hanoi Stock Exchange	G	S
2014	Quang Ninh Port Limited Liability Company	Vietnam	0.45	Hanoi Stock Exchange	G	C
2014	Can Tho Port Co., Ltd.	Vietnam	0.14	Ho Chi Minh Stock Exchange	G	C

* Global/Domestic offering: G = Global offering; D = Domestic offering.
** Securities offered by: C = the company; S = the shareholders; C&S = the company and the shareholders.
*** Technically the operation took place as a share swap, not as an intial public offering.
Source: Authors' own elaboration on S&P Capital I-Q Database and corporate annual reports.

firms and to finance business strategies and new investment projects, whereas IPOs constituted neither an exit strategy for pre-IPO shareholders nor a tool for revolutionizing the company's governance. In only 4 cases out of 27 (14%), securities offered in the IPO originated exclusively from pre-IPO owners, while in 16 cases (57%) the securities offered came entirely from a new emission, and in 8 cases (29%) securities were offered jointly by both the company and prior shareholders.

Table 19.6 shows IPOs performed by container terminal operators and vertically integrated global carriers. By going public, these companies were able to gather 21.29 billion USD in 15 years. The most valuable financial transactions were IPOs related to DP World Limited's IPO (4.21 billion USD), China Shipping Container Lines (2.02), HHLA (1.47), and Sinotrans Shipping Ltd (1.47) in 2007 as well as Hutchison Port Holdings Trust (3.83) and Global Ports Investments PLC in 2011 (0.53). Domestic and global offerings related to this category of firms seem to be balanced (18 vs. 17). Nevertheless, those companies that reached international financial markets were able to raise a wider amount of fresh funds. Overall, in global offerings, more than 16.73 billion USD were gathered (78.62% of total gross proceeds), against only 4.55 billion USD raised through domestic offerings (21.38%).

Almost 20% of IPOs performed by container terminal operators and integrated global carriers allowed pre-IPO shareholders to mitigate their financial exposure towards the listed company. The most appreciable case is the DP World Limited' IPO: in this case a 23% share was sold by the pre-IPO shareholder, i.e. the United Arab Emirates' sovereign wealth fund named "Investment Corporation of Dubai", in order to help repaying 3.5 billion USD of Islamic bonds and provide cash to the Dubai government. Conversely, the majority of the other sample IPOs aimed to finance the aggressive corporate growth strategies of the listed company (Parola et al., 2015; Satta and Persico, 2015). Global Ports Investments PLC (GPI), for example, was floated on the London Stock Exchange in 2011 and invested the financial resources gathered from the IPO both to start new greenfield projects (Drewry Shipping Consultants, 2001–2015) and to build up their container terminal network in the following years (e.g. the acquisition of both a 25% share in the Vostochny Container Terminal from DP World Limited and a 35% share in Terminal Investment Limited (TIL) from MSC Group in 2013).

19.3.2 Bond issuing

Several motivations have recently triggered port-related companies to issue bonds. In particular, this type of security has a number of advantages compared to other forms of debts or bank loans: i) bonds are typically characterized by tenors longer than other forms of medium- and long-term finance (often 10, but potentially also 15 years); ii) frequently the principal is not repaid until the security matures, favouring the distribution of positive/negative cash flows, especially during bearish market peaks (Stopford, 2009; Kavussanos and Tsouknidis, 2014; Kavussanos and Tsouknidis, 2016). Potential disadvantages include the timing for collecting financial resources, the potentially high cost of money, and the need to ensure secondary market's liquidity.

Within the 2000–2014 timeframe, 247 bond securities were issued by listed companies involved in container port activities, i.e. terminal operators and stevedores, port companies and port authorities, as well as vertically integrated container carriers (Table 19.7). Issued bond securities (136 still "active" and 111 by now "inactive") predominantly include corporate debentures (88.69%) and corporate convertibles (8.38%), but also other financial instruments (2.93%), such as foreign currency debentures, foreign governments/agencies' emissions, and Islamic bonds, i.e. "sukuk" securities.

Table 19.6 The IPOs of Container Terminal Operators and Integrated Carriers: Public Offerings Features (2000–2014)

Year	Issuer	Home Country	Type of Company	Gross Proceeds (million USD) million)	IPO Exchange	Global/Domestic Offering*	Securities Offered by Company/ Shareholders**
2004	China Shipping Container Lines Co. Ltd	China	Carrier (integrated)	963.75	The Stock Exchange of Hong Kong Ltd	G	C
2004	Royal P&O Nedlloyd NV	United Kingdom – The Netherlands	Carrier (integrated)	215.00	Dutch Stock Exchange	G	C&S
2005	China COSCO Holdings Company Limited	China	Carrier (integrated)	1,227.24	The Stock Exchange of Hong Kong Ltd	G	C&S
2005	China COSCO Holdings Company Limited	China	Carrier (integrated)	1,220.00	The Stock Exchange of Hong Kong Ltd	G	C
2005	Hyundai Glovis Co. Ltd.	South Korea	Carrier (integrated)	157.62	Korea Stock Exchange	D	C
2005	Sigdo Koppers S.A.	Chile	Terminal operator/ stevedore	157.17	Santiago Stock Exchange	G	C
2005	Horizon Lines, Inc.	United States	Terminal operator/ stevedore	125.00	Pink Sheets LLC	D	C
2006	Santos-Brasil Participações S.A.	Brazil	Terminal operator/ stevedore	391.23	Bolsa de Valores de Sao Paulo	G	C&S
2006	Azuma Shipping Co. Ltd.	Japan	Terminal operator/ stevedore	35.23	The Tokyo Stock Exchange	D	C&S
2007	DP World Limited	United Arab Emirates	Terminal operator/ stevedore	4,218.89	Nasdaq	G	S
2007	China Shipping Container Lines Co. Ltd	China	Carrier (integrated)	2,023.98	Shanghai Stock Exchange	D	C
2007	Sinotrans Shipping Ltd	Hong Kong	Carrier (integrated)	1,472.07	The Stock Exchange of Hong Kong Ltd	G	C
2007	Hamburger Hafen und Logistik AG	Germany	Terminal operator/ stevedore	1,471.26	Deutsche Boerse AG	D	C&S

(Continued)

Table 19.6 Continued

Year	Issuer	Home Country	Type of Company	Gross Proceeds (million USD)	IPO Exchange	Global/Domestic Offering*	Securities Offered by Company/ Shareholders**
2007	Adani Ports and Special Economic Zone Limited	India	Terminal operator/ stevedore	451.84	Mumbai Stock Exchange	G	C
2007	Log-In Logística Intermodal S.A.	Brazil	Terminal operator/ stevedore	389.03	Bolsa de Valores de Sao Paulo	G	C&S
2007	Wilson Sons Limited	Bermuda	Terminal operator/ stevedore	310.01	Bolsa de Valores de Sao Paulo	G	C&S
2007	Gulf Navigation Holding PJSC	United Arab Emirates	Terminal operator/ stevedore	247.76	Dubai Financial Market	D	C
2008	Sino-Global Shipping America Ltd	United States	Terminal operator/ stevedore	9.52	Nasdaq	D	C
2008	Naigai Trans Line Limited	Japan	Terminal operator/ stevedore	7.63	The Tokyo Stock Exchange	D	C&S
2008	Southern Waterborne Transport Corporation	Vietnam	Terminal operator/ stevedore	1.22	Hanoi Stock Exchange	D	C
2009	Bidvest Namibia Limited	Namibia	Terminal operator/ stevedore	48.71	Namibian Stock Exchange	D	C&S
2010	EcoRodovias Infraestrutura e Logística S.A.	Brazil	Terminal operator/ stevedore	661.95	Bolsa de Valores de Sao Paulo	G	C&S
2010	PT Krakatau Steel (Persero) Tbk	Indonesia	Terminal operator/ stevedore	301.15	Jakarta Stock Exchange	D	C
2010	Cogent Holdings Limited	Singapore	Terminal operator/ stevedore	14.36	Singapore Exchange	D	C&S
2010	Ocean Containers Ltd	Bangladesh	Terminal operator/ stevedore	12.47	Dhaka Stock Exchange Ltd	D	S
2010	Cargo Handlers Limited	Jamaica	Terminal operator/ stevedore	0.62	The Jamaica Stock Exchange	D	C

(Continued)

Year	Company	Country	Business	Value	Stock Exchange	Global/domestic	Securities
2011	Hutchison Port Holdings Trust	Singapore	Terminal operator/stevedore	3,833.50	Singapore Exchange	G	C
2011	Global Ports Investments PLC	Cyprus	Terminal operator/stevedore	534.09	London Stock Exchange	G	C&S
2011	PT ABM Investama Tbk	Indonesia	Terminal operator/stevedore	228.54	Jakarta Stock Exchange	G	C&S
2013	China Conch Venture Holdings Limited	China	Terminal operator/stevedore	463.51	The Stock Exchange of Hong Kong Ltd.	G	C
2013	Namyong Terminal Public Company Limited	Thailand	Terminal operator/stevedore	76.86	The Stock Exchange of Thailand	D	C
2013	Harbor Star Shipping Services, Inc.	Philippines	Terminal operator/stevedore	7.91	Philippines Stock Exchange	D	C
2013	Dafeng Port Heshun Technology Co. Ltd	Hong Kong	Terminal operator/stevedore	6.45	The Stock Exchange of Hong Kong Ltd	D	C
2014	Saif Powertec Limited	Bangladesh	Terminal operator/stevedore	4.64	Dhaka Stock Exchange Ltd	D	S
2014	Nha Trang Port Holding Limited Liability Company	Vietnam	Terminal operator/stevedore	0.22	Hanoi Stock Exchange	G	S

*Global/domestic offering: G = global offering; D = domestic offering.

**Securities offered by: C = the company; S = the shareholders; C&S = the company and the shareholders.

***Technically the operation took place as a share swap, not as an intial public offering.

Source: Authors' elaboration on S&P Capital I-Q Database and corporate annual reports.

Table 19.7 Bonds Issued by Listed Companies Operating in Container Port Activities (2000–2014)

Type of company	No. of emissions		Total offering amount	
	No.	%	Amount	%
Listed companies involved in	*247*	*100.00%*	*62,523.19*	*100.00%*
container port activities				
Corporate convertibles	18	7.29%	5,240.10	8.38%
Corporate debentures	210	85.02%	55,449.03	88.69%
Other financial instruments	19	7.69%	1,834.06	2.93%
Port company/authority	*60*	*100.00%*	*12,047.46*	*100.00%*
Corporate convertibles	1	1.67%	108.60	0.90%
Corporate debentures	51	85.00%	11,073.90	91.92%
Other financial instruments	8	13.33%	864.96	7.18%
Terminal operator/stevedore	*44*	*100.00%*	*13,422.91*	*100.00%*
Corporate convertibles	3	6.82%	1,254.20	9.34%
Corporate debentures	35	79.55%	11,803.00	87.93%
Other financial instruments	6	13.64%	365.71	2.72%
Carrier (integrated)	*143*	*100.00%*	*37,052.82*	*100%*
Corporate convertibles	14	9.79%	3,877.30	10.46%
Corporate debentures	124	86.71%	32,572.13	87.91%
Other financial instruments	5	3.50%	603.39	1.63%

Source: Authors' own elaboration from S&P Capital I-Q Database and corporate annual reports.

Table 19.8 Bond Issues' Offering Date

	No. of emissions			Offering amount		
	2000–2007	2008–2014	Total	2000–2007	2008–2014	Total
Carrier (integrated)	46	97	143	8,137.10	28,915.72	37,052.82
Port company/authority	3	57	60	277.80	11,769.66	12,047.46
Terminal operator/ stevedore	10	34	44	5,548.90	7,874.01	13,422.91
Total	*59*	*188*	*247*	*13,963.80*	*48,559.39*	*62,523.19*

Source: Authors' elaboration on S&P Capital I-Q Database and corporate annual reports.

By accessing the debt capital market, these companies were able to raise a significant amount of fresh funds within the timeframe (62.52 billion USD). In this perspective, carriers are found to be the most active players in the (primary) bond security markets, both in terms of number of emissions (143) and total offering amount (37.05 billion USB). The outcome originates from the longer shipping companies' track-record experience in bond markets (Grammenos and Arkoulis, 2003; Grammenos et al., 2008). Nevertheless, bond issuing emerges as a practical and attractive fundraising strategy also for port companies (12.07 billion USD) and terminal operators (13.42 billion USD). For port-related companies, this trend is even more evident when comparing the temporal distribution of bond issues (Table 19.8): almost 98% of the total offering amount, in fact, relates to the 2008–2014 timeframe and the geographical spread (Table 19.9).

Table 19.9 Geographical Spread of Port-related Companies Issuing Bonds: Breakdown per Type of Firm

Headquarter	Listed companies involved in container port activities		Port company/authority		Terminal operator/stevedore		Carrier (integrated)	
	No. of emissions	Total offering amount	No. of emissions	Total offering amount	No. of emissions	Total offering amount	No. of emissions	Total offering amount
Australia	2	463.40	2	463.40	–	–	–	–
Bermuda	3	144.70	–	–	3	144.70	–	–
Brazil	5	364.70	–	–	5	364.70	–	–
Canada	1	1.01	–	–	1	1.01	–	–
China	60	15,512.04	40	7,455.00	3	255.80	17	7,801.24
Cyprus	1	150.00	–	–	1	150.00	–	–
Denmark	16	7,554.10	–	–	–	–	16	7,554.10
France	11	4,681.00	–	–	–	–	11	4,681.00
Germany	12	2,838.39	–	–	–	–	12	2,838.39
Hong Kong	11	5,490.10	3	890.10	8	4,600.00	–	–
Indonesia	2	1,000.00	2	1,000.00	–	–	–	–
Japan	68	10,190.49	–	–	3	222.50	65	9,967.99
Malaysia	13	518.46	3	226.26	10	292.20	–	–
New Zealand	2	98.00	2	98.00	–	–	–	–
Norway	1	134.50	–	–	1	134.50	–	–
Peru	4	450.00	4	450.00	–	–	–	–
Philippines	3	757.50	–	–	3	757.50	–	–
Singapore	9	2,781.20	4	1,464.70	–	–	5	1,316.50
United Arab Emirates	4	6,000.00	–	–	4	6,000.00	–	–
United Kingdom	2	500.00	–	–	2	500.00	–	–
United States	17	2,893.60	–	–	–	–	17	2,893.60
Total	247	62,523.19	60	12,047.46	44	13,422.91	143	37,052.82

Note: Total offering amounts are expressed in million USD.
Source: Authors' own elaboration from S&P Capital I-Q Database and corporate annual reports.

After the 2008 crisis, the restricted liquidity experienced in the secondary market has made bond trading significantly more difficult, like what happened to shipping companies after the Asian crisis (Grammenos and Arkoulis, 2003).

19.4 Risk perception, asset pricing methodologies, and weighted average cost of capital

The unprecedented rise of the container port industry, combined with the substantial returns generated by the sector in the early 2000s, attracted a number of new investors catching sound opportunities in capital allocation. The apparent relentless growth and the availability of additional funding sources hid the intrinsically risky nature of the container port business (Notteboom and Rodrigue, 2012). This capital-intensive industry, in fact, is characterized by long pay-back periods, and investments in terminal assets and port related companies evaluation was 20 times higher, as reported by the financial multiple Enterprise Value on Earnings Before Interest, Taxes, Depreciation, and Amortization (EV/EBITDA) or by the ratio Transaction Value on Operating Value.

However, as the sector was increasingly profitable, several investors, unaware of potential risks, were induced to increase their financial exposure in the business, even without a solid background in the business. This trend led to a severe misperception of market treats (Rodrigue et al., 2011).

As fresh funds became easily available and cheaper for port firms, the financial evaluation of terminal assets neglected progressively to assess and weigh business-related risks.

Table 19.10 focuses on fluctuations in terminal assets' prices in selected acquisitions during the 2000–2014 timeframe. The intense M&A activity between 2004 and 2008 caused a sharp increase in the number of transactions closed, the financial value of the deals, as well as the (intrinsic) valuation multiples used to fix assets' market value. Just before the blast of the 2008 crisis, terminal assets and port-related companies were evaluated (transaction value or enterprise value – EV) at multiples of operating earnings or EBITDA (Earnings Before Interest, Taxes, Depreciation, and Amortization) higher than 20 times (Rodrigue et al., 2011). After 2008, the generalized credit crunch in the financial markets and the sudden reduction in the number of potential buyers drastically reshaped market conditions for financial transactions related to terminal assets and port companies. In particular, EBITDA multiples in port and shipping industries collapsed to roughly 8x, thus minimizing the number of deals. Focusing on the container port domain, acquisitions were carried out at an average EBITDA multiple of 10.9x during the 2008–2009 period, significantly lower than multiples during the peak. After a couple of depressed years, the market experienced a partial recovery (see, for instance, the acquisition of the Port of Brisbane and the purchase of Fourth Ports PLC). Due to the consolidated nature of the port sector and the diminished risk appetite of investors and lenders, port-related financial transactions, in the future, are expected to be closed in the range of EBITDA multiples of 10–14x (Ward, 2013).

The financial resources in excess not only artificially blew up terminal asset prices but also induced a constant risk underestimation and a reduction of the cost of capital for port firms until 2008. Risk misperception caused a reduction of the sectorial beta parameter and, consequently, other conditions being equal, caused a decrease of the cost of equity, calculated along with the capital asset pricing model (CAPM).

Figure 19.2 reports the beta evolution for investing in the maritime and port sectors, calculated by Damodaran for the USA market in the 2000–2014 timeframe. Empirical evidence shows how during the first half of the last decade, risk underestimation drove to a reduction of the beta parameter in the industry.

Table 19.10 Assets Valuation in Container Port Domain: Implied EV/EBITDA Multiples in Selected Disclosed Deals (2000–2014)

Year	Target	Buyers	Transaction Value (million USD)	EV/EBITDA (x)
2001	Howard Smith Ltd (Towage)	Adsteam Marine Pty Ltd	247.20	7.2
2003	Clydeport PLC	Peel Ports Limited	267.69	10.2
2004	Nedlloyd Container Line Limited	Royal P&O Nedlloyd N.V.	626.97	2.1
2004	PD Ports Group Limited	PD Ports Limited	798.95	9.9
2005	The Mersey Docks and Harbour Company Limited	Peel Holdings (Management) Limited	1,483.91	11.9
2005	CSX world terminals	DP World	1,150.00	14.0
2006	Hutchison Port Holding	PSA International	4,400.00	17.0
2006	PD Ports Limited	Prime Infrastructure Group	616.20	8.4
2006	P&O Ports	DP World	6,800.00	19.0
2006	Patrick Corporation Limited	Toll Holdings Limited	5,303.11	14.3
2006	Associated British Ports Holdings Limited	Goldman Sachs; consortium of financial investors	6,097.87	16.4
2006	P&O Ports (North America)	Ports America (AIG Highstar Capital)	1,100.00	24.0
2006	Shanghai Port Container Co. Ltd	Shanghai International Port (Group) Co.Ltd	1,106.78	13.7
2006	Maher Terminals	RREEF (Deutsche Bank)	2,100.00	25.0
2007	Orient Overseas Container Lines (OOCL)	Ontario Teachers' Pension Fund (OTTP)	2,350.00	23.5
2007	Peel Ports Limited	RREEF (Deutsche Bank)	1,422.31	15.3
2007	Carrix (SSA Marine)	Goldman Sachs	2,800.00	N.A.
2007	Adsteam Marine Pty Ltd	SVITZER (A/S)	767.74	10.2
2007	Drydocks World – Singapore Pte Ltd	Dubai Drydocks World, LLC	425.82	8.5
2009	Tianjin Port Company Limited	Grand Point Investment Limited	2,775.72	12.4
2009	Smit Internationale N.V.	Royal Boskalis Westminster NV (ENXTAM:BOKA)	1,672.24	6.7
2010	DP World's Australian port Assets	Citi Infrastructures	1,500.00	13.0
2010	Port of Brisbane Pty Ltd	QIC Limited; IFM Investors Pty Ltd; Global Infrastructure Partners; Tawreed Investments Ltd	2,837.93	16.3
2011	Forth Ports PLC	Arcus Infrastructure Partners LLP	1,338.37	15.0
2011	Global Ports Investments PLC	N-Trans Group	238.00	10.5
2012	Global Ports Investments PLC	APM Terminals B.V.	952.00	9.2
2013	Shenzhen Chiwan Wharf Holdings Ltd	Shenzhen Malai Storage Company Limited	286.73	11.0
2013	Sehwa Express Co. Ltd	Youngheung Iron & Steel Co. Ltd	165.89	16.4
2013	NCC Group Limited	Global Ports Investments (GPI)	1,650.11	9.8
2014	Veripos Inc.	Hexagon AB	144.82	11.9
2014	EMS Seven Seas ASA	Supreme Group B.V.	104.36	11.7

Source: Authors' own elaboration from S&P Capital I-Q Database and corporate annual reports.

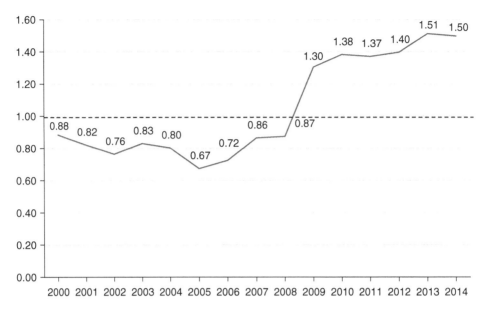

Figure 19.2 Beta parameter for investing in the maritime sector in the USA financial markets (2000–2014).

Source: Authors' own elaboration from Damodaran online data, available at http://pages.stern.nyu.edu/~adamodar/.

The equity remuneration requirement for investing in the maritime domain slowed down during the 2000–2006 period, then slightly increased in 2007 (Table 19.11). In addition, the cost of debt for financing the sector experienced a downturn from 2003 (7.50%) to 2008 (5.45%), additionally supporting the financial profitability of the firms operating in the industry and facilitating the "bankability" of new projects.

After the crisis, investors rediscovered the risky nature of the container port industry: the beta parameter climbed from 0.82 in 2008 to 1.30 in 2009 and continued to grow until today (1.50 in 2014). As a result, the cost of equity sharply raised from 8.99 in 2008 to 10.04 in 2009.

As it happened in the shipping industry (Gavalas and Syriopolos, 2015), also in the port domain the cost of debt initially followed a similar trend, but the monetary policies pursued by the USA government mitigated the effects of the financial shock on the cost of debt for terminal operators and port companies: it decreased from 7.84% in 2010 to 3.26% in 2013. The weighted average cost of capital (WACC) for the firms operating in this sector reached the highest peak in 2010 (8.15%) since they were initially able to counterbalance the increase in the equity remuneration requirement through an increase in financial gearing and the adoption of financial engineering.

19.5 Risk management, financial derivatives, and hedging instruments

The 2008 financial crisis determined a serious breakdown in the ongoing trends and forced industry players to reassess their industry risk perception. The explosion of the financial bubble, in fact, acted as a powerful "wakeup call" due to falling demand and risk rediscovering (Rodrigue et al., 2011). Under new market conditions, the access to finance became much more

Table 19.11 Cost of Equity, Cost of Debt, and Weighted Average Cost of Capital for the Maritime Sector in the USA Financial Markets (2000–2014)

Year	Number of firms included in Damodaran' study	Beta parameter for maritime sector	Cost of Equity	E/(D+E)	Std Dev in Stock	Cost of Debt	Tax Rate	After-tax Cost of Debt	D/(D+E)	Cost of Capital (WACC)	Risk free rate (long-term treasury bond rate)	Market risk premium (risk premium for equity)
2000	22	0.88	10.16%	44.91%	37.75%	6.30%	29.30%	4.45%	55.09%	7.02%	5.30%	5.50%
2001	14	0.82	9.52%	43.32%	53.96%	7.50%	13.90%	6.46%	56.68%	7.78%	5.00%	5.50%
2002	20	0.76	9.20%	45.01%	50.39%	7.50%	15.90%	6.31%	54.99%	7.61%	5.00%	5.50%
2003	20	0.83	7.61%	44.32%	49.29%	5.37%	22.01%	4.19%	55.68%	5.70%	3.87%	4.50%
2004	23	0.80	8.12%	49.67%	47.07%	5.50%	47.84%	2.87%	50.33%	5.48%	4.25%	4.82%
2005	28	0.67	7.48%	61.78%	40.45%	5.47%	11.27%	3.56%	38.22%	5.98%	4.22%	4.84%
2006	39	0.72	7.87%	60.04%	40.79%	5.64%	5.37%	5.34%	39.96%	6.86%	4.39%	4.80%
2007	46	0.86	8.95%	62.47%	36.30%	5.70%	5.91%	5.36%	37.53%	7.60%	4.70%	4.91%
2008	51	0.87	8.99%	66.16%	26.67%	5.45%	5.52%	5.15%	33.84%	7.69%	4.70%	4.91%
2009	55	1.30	10.04%	34.86%	64.67%	6.21%	7.14%	5.77%	65.14%	7.26%	2.21%	6.00%
2010	53	1.38	9.87%	38.53%	76.15%	7.84%	9.70%	7.08%	61.47%	8.15%	3.84%	4.36%
2011	52	1.37	9.79%	41.33%	67.37%	5.29%	6.50%	4.95%	58.67%	6.95%	3.29%	4.74%
2012	52	1.40	10.30%	36.99%	69.19%	3.87%	5.55%	3.66%	63.01%	6.11%	1.87%	6.04%
2013	51	1.51	10.53%	35.56%	62.52%	3.26%	7.92%	3.00%	64.44%	5.68%	1.76%	5.80%
2014	14	1.50	10.52%	60.48%	117.34%	7.04%	4.99%	6.69%	39.52%	9.01%	3.04%	5.00%

Source: Authors' own elaboration from Damodaran online data, available at http://pages.stern.nyu.edu/~adamodar.

stringent, in clear opposition to the easy credit phase characterizing the previous period (Baird, 2013; Mitroussi et al., 2016): consequently, terminal and port operators reacted by moderating risk through various strategies. First, they attempted to adjust terminal capacity by postponing or suspending planned investments. Second, terminal operators started to renegotiate concession agreements and other contracts (e.g., labour, equipment lease, etc.) with public authorities and private parties, to lower fees and mitigate the effects of the drop in demand. Third, in case of severe overcapacity concerns, some players were forced to idle terminals/berths or to sell off non-profitable or non-core assets (Rodrigue et al., 2011). Overall, after the 2008 financial crisis, the sector experienced a sharp devaluation of terminal assets and financial transactions rapidly dropped down, as it became hard to find deep-pocket counterparts.

In order to face such unprecedented risk, the container port industry also started experiencing a greater interest towards financial derivatives for hedging risks. They predominantly include financial derivatives for mitigating real market prices' volatility, foreign currencies' fluctuations, and the exchange risk in market interest rates (World Bank, 2012).

The acceleration in M&A transactions and multiple-site entry strategies experienced before the financial crisis caused a significant enlargement of ITOs' geographic scope in a short timeframe (Parola et al., 2015). After entering a number of new foreign countries, ITOs were forced to face additional financial risks related to capital and currency issues due to fluctuations in foreign exchange rates (Rodrigue et al., 2011). As volatility in major foreign exchange rates is expected to affect both the value of overseas assets and extant liabilities, several operators started scrutinizing innovative financial tools and products for hedging currency risk.

Moreover, the aggressive growth strategies pursued by terminal operators, port companies, and integrated carriers built upon an extensive (ab)use of financial leverage (Rodrigue et al., 2011), not only deteriorated firms' financial exposure (e.g. decayed debt/equity ratios), but also imposed a careful management of companies' interest rate risks, and additional financial instruments for hedging.

In 2014, for example, the proportion of DP World's net operating assets denominated in foreign currencies was approximately 65%. Consequently, the USD consolidated statement of the group's financial position (as well as the amount of shareholder's equity) was exposed to foreign currency fluctuations when retranslated at each year-end rate. To partially mitigate the risk related to foreign currency movements, the firm management relies both on i) natural hedging, by borrowing in the same currencies as those in which the assets are denominated, and ii) financial derivatives by using cross-currency swaps (Table 19.12). Similarly, DP World's revenues and costs are partially generated/incurred outside their main functional currency and the company needs to hedge risks related to short-term currency movement by using forward foreign currency contracts. Finally, DP World tends to enter into or plan capital expenditures and lease commitments in foreign currencies and manages risk using forward contracts and currency swaps.

Next to this, the DP World case brings insights for understanding new viable solutions container port firms may rely on, to mitigate the risk of changes in market interest rates. In 2014, the DP World exposure to interest rate risk primarily originated from its long-term debt obligations with a fixed/floating interest rate and its bank deposits. In particular, DP World manages its interest cost through interest rate swap agreements. Taking into account the effect of interest rate swaps, 93% of the company's borrowings were at a fixed rate of interest at the end of the 2014 fiscal year.

In the same year, the fair value of derivative financial instruments amounted to 343.92 million USD, including 109.91 million USD for interest rate swaps used for hedging and 233.23 million USD related to an embedded derivative option.

Table 19.12 Main Hedging Strategies for Mitigating Currency and Interest Rate Risks

Risk category	*Risk nature and sources*	*Hedging strategies*
Currency risks	Net **operating assets denominated in foreign currencies**: the group's USD consolidated statement of financial position, and shareholder's equity, can be affected by currency movements when it is retranslated at each year-end rate.	**Natural hedging** by borrowing in the same currencies as those in which the assets are denominated and using cross-currency swaps.
	Revenues and costs denominated in foreign currencies: a portion of the group's activities generate part of their revenue and incur some costs outside their main functional currency.	**Natural hedging** as the group operates in several locations. Financial derivatives such as **forward foreign currency contract**s to reduce the short-term effect of currency movements.
	Capital expenditure/lease commitments in foreign currencies: several capital expenditure and lease commitments are entered or planned in currencies other than their main functional currency.	Financial derivatives such as **forward contracts** and **currency swaps** in order to fix the cost when converted to the functional currency.
Interest rate risk	Exposure to the **risk of changes in market interest rates** originating from the long-term debt obligations with a fixed/ floating interest rate and bank deposits.	Financial derivatives such as **interest rate swap agreement**s, in which the group exchanges, at specified intervals, the difference between fixed and variable rate interest amounts calculated by reference to an agreed-upon notional principal amount.

Source: Authors' elaboration on DP World Annual Report (2014).

Some terminal operators and port companies have also started to use financial derivatives for facing real market price volatility and hedging against energy costs, due to the energy-consuming nature of terminal and port activities. Nevertheless, only a few port-related companies are experiencing structured hedging strategies paved on financial derivatives, as they are inclined to mitigate these risks by pursuing more traditional and conservative strategies, which include technical solutions for increasing efficiency (e.g. remotely operated automated stacking cranes), energy assessments at terminals (for identifying energy-saving initiatives), or the adoption of alternative fuels.

19.6 The entry of financial investors in the container port market

Since the early 2000s, given the significant profitability of the container port industry, financial investors were increasingly stimulated to seek new clients and additional investing opportunities in the market (Satta and Parola, 2012). Initially, these players were used to provide a wide range of financial products and services to both shipping lines and port companies. Financial investors, therefore, emerged as key actors orchestrating big financial deals in the sector (Rodrigue et al., 2011). They provided financial resources and technical support for transactions' contractual arrangements (Parola et al., 2015) and supported shipping lines and port companies in the listing process or during bond issuing (Grammenos, 2013).

Institutional investors, i.e. specialized financial institutions, which manage savings collectively on behalf of small investors, heading a defined objective in terms of reasonable risk, return-maximization, and maturity of claims (Davis, 2008; Oyedele, 2014), were among the most active players in the container port market.

In line with other infrastructural assets, container port terminals hold several characteristics attracting financial operators and institutional investors. Port terminals, in fact, impose investments large enough to accommodate the huge amount of capital at their disposal and are long-term assets with significant economic life (Parola et al., 2015). In addition, these assets provide key public services and are interested by a non-elastic demand (Della Croce and Gatti, 2014). Participation of institutional investors in container port domain is also encouraged by the monopolistic or quasi-monopolistic nature of the industry (Turkisch, 2011). The possibility of partially transferring the risk to the host government through public-private partnerships, combined with the low technological risk and the high entry barriers of the sector, increase the attractiveness of this asset class for financial operators and institutional investors (Oyedele, 2014; Della Croce and Gatti, 2014). Container port terminals also naturally hedge investors against inflation and allow investment planning thanks to predictable operating cash flows (Siemiatycki, 2015). Finally, due to low correlation with other traditional asset classes, container port terminals and other infrastructures have acquired increased investment significance for institutional investors seeking exposure to alternative assets and diversification benefits, such as increase in investment performance and reduction of portfolio volatility (Peng and Newell, 2007; Clark et al., 2012; Ottesen, 2011; Oyedele, 2014).

Empirical evidence, indeed, suggests the predominant role of financial operators as investors in this industry. In this perspective, pension funds and insurance companies, sovereign wealth funds, investment banks and private equity funds, investment holding companies, as well as multilateral financial institutions and development banks, emerge as the most common types of players. For each category, Table 19.13 summarizes main strategic objectives, investment strategies, and implementation mechanism, also providing anecdotal evidences.

Container port terminals, in particular, are an attractive asset class to pension funds due to their long-term, predictable, inflation-adjusted returns. These asset characteristics perfectly match pension funds' investment interests, as they are typically long-term investors seeking sustainable returns over a 20/30 year timeframe (Siemiatycki, 2015). Moreover, as pension funds have to face ongoing disbursement obligations to retirees, they need to invest in assets generating cash flows capable to cover promises of monthly payment in line with pension plans subscribed by beneficiaries (Beeferman, 2008). Insurance funds, indeed, share several features with pension funds in terms of size, investment time horizon, as well as return expectations and approach toward risk (Siemiatycki, 2015). Major players include Ontario Teaching Pension Plan (OTPP), Borealis Infrastructure, and AIG Highstar Capital.

As concerns investment strategies, empirical evidence suggests that these players pursue a logic of their own. These institutional investors target brownfield assets that have already been in operation for several years, to overtake construction risks and reduce revenue volatility (Siemiatycki, 2015), while avoiding both greenfield projects and new privatization initiatives. Moreover, when targeting new foreign markets, they unveil a moderate degree of geographic diversification and are prone to invest in Anglo-Saxon countries (UK, Canada, and USA) (Satta and Parola, 2012; Parola et al., 2013).

Pension funds and insurance companies typically operate as equity investors in the infrastructure industry, paving on direct investments in operational private infrastructural assets, or by acquiring a stake in established companies, which hold long-term concessions to operate transportation assets. These institutional investors prefer to rely on single terminal assets or network

Table 19.13 The Major Types of Financial Investors Involved in Container Port industry: Objectives, Investment Strategies, and Implementation Mechanisms

Type	Main objectives	Investment strategies and implementation mechanisms	Major examples
Pension funds and insurance companies	• "buy-and-hold" approach; • long-term sustainable returns over a 20/30 years timeframe; • predictable and inflation-linked returns ensuring that pension plans fulfil their obligations to pay benefits; • portfolio diversification;	• direct investments in operational private terminal assets, or acquisition of stake in established companies with long-term concessions to operate port facilities; • brownfield assets already in operation to overtake construction risks and reduce revenue volatility; • moderate degree of geographic diversification, with assets predominantly held in Anglo-Saxon countries or mature markets; • preference for single terminal assets or network acquisitions compared to long and risky competitive biddings or public awarding procedures; • preference for large equity stakes in each terminal held; • active management of assets in portfolio.	Ontario Teaching Pension Plan (OTPP); Borealis Infrastructure; AIG Highstar Capital (Ports America); ECT Employees Pension Fund; Gestão de Fundos (Angolan pension fund); etc.
Sovereign wealth funds (SWFs) and SOEs	• combination of long-term investment strategies with short-term speculative transactions; • risks related to political or geopolitical motives in investment strategies; • insulate the national budget against commodity price fluctuations (stabilization funds); • create sustainable and diversified portfolio of assets for future generations (savings funds); • increase the return on reserves (reserve investment corporations); • promote socio-economic and industrial policies of a country (development funds); • maximize risk-adjusted returns, subject to tolerable risk.	• diversification of national wealth by investing internationally and in a greater range of assets; • mixed and equilibrated portfolio of secure and more risky business ventures; • significant geographic diversification strategies, focused on developing countries; • high degree of control exerted on subsidiaries through substantial stakes in terminal assets (generally higher than 20%); • partnerships and co-operative strategies to overtake lack of technical/market knowledge; • active management of assets in portfolio.	Temasek Holdings (PSA International); Dubai World (DP World); Government of Singapore Investment Corporation (GIC); Abu Dhabi Investment Authority; China International Trust & Investment Corporation; Oman Investment Fund; etc.

(Continued)

Table 19.13 Continued

Type	Main objectives	Investment strategies and implementation mechanisms	Major examples
Investment banks and private equity (PE) funds	• short- or mid-term perspective toward the business; • speculative perspective; • "hit & run" approach (Independent PE firms); • "multiple expansion" objective; • "value extraction" from acquired firms; • maximize of risk-adjusted returns.	• investments in unlisted port infrastructure in the construction phase (greenfield investments) and during the operational phase (brownfield investments); • aggressive international diversification strategies; • external growth strategies via acquisition; • participation in bidding consortia for getting concessions in new port terminals; • massive resort to financial gearing (and leveraged buyout, LBO); • preservation of existing management teams after the acquisition.	*Investment banks:* Citi Infrastructure Investors; Goldman Sachs; Macquaire; Morgan Stanley; Deutsche Bank (RREEF); Bank of China; JP Morgan Chase (Noatum); etc. *Independent PE firms:* Brookfield Asset Management; Babcock and Brown Infrastructure (BBI) (liquidated in August 2009); Global Infrastructure Partners (IPH); Latin America Infrastructure Fund; etc.
Investment holding companies	• medium- to long-term goal of generating capital appreciation; • capital gains from assets sale and re-investment in new ventures; • portfolio diversification.	• equity interests in both listed and unquoted firms; • diversification strategies with no apparent "core" or "highly strategic" subsidiaries; • periodic rotation of assets; • establishment of broad architecture of ties with overseas capital, either via joint-ventures with foreign companies or via loans from foreign banks; • exploitation of the managerial and business experience of the satellite firms in which they have equity interests; • participation to privatization programs (concession agreements) and complex BOT awarding procedures; • preference for collaborating strategies respect to adoption of wholly-owned subsidiaries; • modest geographic scope due to psychic distance concerns.	China Merchants Holdings International (CMHI); Wharf Holdings (Modern Terminal Limited, MTL); NWS Holdings; Hong Kong Land Infrastructure Ltd; Tumas Group; etc.

(Continued)

Multilateral financial institutions and development banks	• support infrastructures development the inception phase; • long-term commitment; • sustain socio-economic growth and development; • mobilize additional capital for infrastructure projects in developing countries.	• fuel infrastructural projects by offering long-term loans at market rates/ below market rates or grants; • co-investments for funding greenfield and brownfield projects in developing countries; • minority equity interests.	Asian Development Bank; Commonwealth Development Co.; Investment fund for Developing Countries; International Finance Corporation (World Bank Group); etc.

Source: Authors' own elaboration.

acquisitions rather than embarking in long and risky competitive biddings or public awarding procedures (Parola et al., 2015), in order to exploit in-house skills to carry out due diligence on private placements in the port sector (Siemiatycki, 2015).

Sovereign wealth funds (SWF), or state investment funds, are government investment vehicles that hold and administer public funds to acquire and manage a wide range of assets, including national and foreign financial assets aiming to gain higher than risk-free rate of return (Kern, 2007; Drezner, 2008). To some extent, therefore, they are similar to state-owned enterprises (SOEs) (Oyedele, 2014). These operators tend to invest mostly in foreign countries and assume a long-term perspective, but, sometimes, they combine long-term investment strategies with short investment horizons in order to create value for shareholders (Park and Estrada, 2009).

They differ from institutional investors for not being privately owned (Kern, 2007): their state-owned nature, indeed, raises several concerns in terms of political risks, as well as transparency and corporate governance issues (Park and Estrada, 2009; Turkisch, 2011).

In assuming their asset allocation decisions, SWFs pursue both industrial and geographic diversification objectives, aiming at maximizing risk-adjusted returns, subject to tolerable risk (Park and Estrada, 2009). Within the container port industry, SWFs pursue aggressive geographic diversification strategies, in line with their major investment objectives (Parola et al., 2013; Satta and Persico, 2015). Temasek Holdings, through its branch PSA International, holds interests in more than 80 facilities in around 30 nations (in 2013). Analogously, Dubai World, through its port-specialized division (DP World), undertook a spectacular international drive, building a widespread asset portfolio of over 50 terminals in 28 nations.

SWFs prefer foreign direct investments (FDIs) to portfolio management, also because they are prone to operate as active shareholders (Park and Estrada, 2009). Most selected entry mode strategies include M&A activity and greenfield investments, even if they predominantly leverage on multiple-site acquisitions in order to accelerate their international growth (Parola et al., 2015).

Due to their risk-return profile, as well as to their sophisticated valuation skills, some banks and private equity (PE) funds participated by merchant and investment banks have shown some attitude to commit financial resources to unlisted port infrastructures throughout their economic life, including the construction phase (greenfield investments) and also the operational phase (brownfield investments) (Della Croce and Gatti, 2014). Some of these financial operators rapidly expanded their operations overseas, looking for portfolio geographic diversification, network and scale effects, and additional financial margins (Parola et al., 2015; Satta and Persico, 2015). In this vein, investment banks and related PE funds are used to undertake external growth strategies via acquisition and to participate in bidding consortia for getting concessions in new port terminals. For example, Deutsche Bank set up a dedicated branch for asset and wealth management in the infrastructure investment business (RREEF, than re-branded Deutsche Asset & Wealth Management) and has interests in port companies and terminals in Europe and North America, through various ownership structures (Drewry Shipping Consultants, 2014). As concerns the geographic coverage, the bank holds a 100% stake in the Maher Terminals (New York/ New Jersey) and in Prince Rupert Container Terminal (Canada), but it also has interests in Peel Ports (49%).

Analogous considerations can be drawn for other investment banks such as Macquarie, Morgan Stanley, Goldman Sachs, JP Morgan Chase, and Citi Infrastructure Investors.

Conversely, independent PE infrastructure funds, such as Brookfield Asset Management, Babcock and Brown Infrastructure (BBI) (liquidated in August 2009), and Global Infrastructure Partners (IPH), adopt a more speculative approach toward the business, guided by short-term return-driven ambitions (Satta and Parola, 2012). PE funds with equity in port greenfield projects are typically eager to sell their stakes to other investors within 3–10 years from their initial investment, pursuing two-digit (%) returns (Page et al., 2008).

The recent massive port privatization programs undertaken in advanced and emerging economies growingly attracted the interest of investment holding companies looking for new business segments with high-growth potentials. The advent of this category of financial operators experienced a spectacular rise in emerging economies such as the Peoples' Republic of China (PRC), Hong Kong SAR, Vietnam, African countries, etc. (Midoro and Parola, 2003; Olivier, 2005). These complex and multidivisional financial institutions adopt risk-adjusted performance measures in ports and other logistics infrastructures, which are used as a guide for efficient asset allocation, performance evaluation, and capital structure decisions.

In some Far Eastern countries, investment holding companies assume the archetype of ethnic Chinese firms, characterized by a number of key specific features (Kao, 1993, Olivier, 2006). Among them, we find China Merchant Holdings International (CMHI), which owns port terminal facilities predominantly in the Chinese mainland and Hong Kong, the Cheng Yu-tung's New World Developments (under the flagship of NWS Holdings Limited), and the Pao family's Wharf Holdings (through Modern Terminal Limited).

These investment holding companies have emerged from rapid returns on tangible investments not only in the port sectors but also in businesses such as property and logistics infrastructures (Olivier, 2006). Typically, they have minority equity shares (below 20%) in a number of terminal facilities or even relevant shares in port companies (often below 50%), but with a modest engagement in managerial decisions. Wholly owned subsidiaries (WOS) are quite rare.

In expanding the geographic scope of their port network, investment holding companies are quite refractory to invest in far away and unknown market areas (Olivier, 2006).

Multilateral development banks recently emerged also as key co-investors in the container port domain, especially funding greenfield and brownfield projects in developing countries. Among them, Asian Development Bank, Commonwealth Development Corporation, Investment Fund for Developing Countries, and International Finance Corporation (World Bank Group) are famous actors in the sector. For example, Asian Development Bank and International Finance Corporation supported the private sector in the construction and development of the South Asia Gateway Terminal located in the Colombo Port (Sri Lanka), also subscribing minority equity shares.

19.7 Conclusions

This chapter addresses the major drivers of change which affect port investment and financial decisions in the new competitive arena. Empirical evidence, first, suggests that investment decisions are becoming increasingly complex in managerial, financial, and organizational terms, due to the rise of project magnitude. Additional financial resources are requested by the industry to fuel greenfield mega-projects, M&A activity, and the aggressive foreign expansion of ITOs.

Second, new sources of finance emerge as viable options for supporting the corporate finance of leading actors in the business. Not only shipping companies but also terminal operating companies and port authorities holding a stevedoring branch are proved to rely to a larger extent on initial public offering and bond issuing to finance the business. Third, the excessive appetite for profits, experienced during the bubble phase of the market, was shown to have caused a generalized underestimation of industry-related risks, and a consequent mispricing of assets. Then, the unexpected collapse of the market acts as a powerful wakeup call for port investors and lenders. As a result, port managers and financial advisors are expected to rediscover risk, to pay more attention to fundamentals in asset evaluation activity, and to strengthen risk management strategies. In this perspective, some leading operators have started to adopt a wider range of financial derivatives and additional hedging instruments.

Finally, the outcomes show that various categories of financial operators are entering the sector acting as equity investors. By comparing their behaviour and their strategic intent, it is proved that they tend to operate in line with different perspectives in terms of objectives, investment strategies, and implementation mechanisms. Among them, institutional investors such as pension funds and sovereign wealth funds (SWFs) treat container terminals as an investing asset class given the long-term, low-risk, and inflation-adjusted return they are capable to generate. As their goals are aligned with those of their government partners in terms of time horizon and "buy-and-hold" approach toward the business, pension funds and SWFs should hopefully be more involved in financing newly constructed facilities, by reducing project-related risks and creating favourable institutional conditions for making public-private partnerships successful.

Note

1 Notably, the term "financialization" refers to the growing role of financial objectives and motivations, financial markets, models, and institutions (Epstein, 2006) in shaping the evolutionary trajectories of the maritime and port sectors.

References

Baird, A.J. (2013). Acquisition of UK ports by private equity funds. *Research in Transportation Business & Management* 8: 158–165.

Beeferman, L.W. (2008). Pension fund investment in infrastructure: Pensions and capital stewardship project labor and worklife program Harvard Law School. Paper Series No. 3.

Bichou, K., Bell, M.G. (2007). Internationalisation and consolidation of the container port industry: assessment of channel structure and relationships. *Maritime Economics & Logistics* 9(1): 35–51.

Chan, Y.C., Wu, C., Kwok, C.C. (2007). Valuation of global IPOs: a stochastic frontier approach. *Review of Quantitative Finance and Accounting* 29(3): 267–284.

Clark, G.L., Monk, A.H.B., Orr, R., Scott, W. (2012). The new era of infrastructure investing. *Pensions: An International Journal* 17(2): 103–111.

Davis, K.T. (2008). Listed Infrastructure Funds: Funding and Financial Management. http://papers.ssrn.com/sol3/papers.cfm?abstract_id=1337473, accessed March 2009.

De Langen, P.W., Pallis, A.A. (2007). Entry barriers in seaports. *Maritime Policy & Management* 34(5): 427–440.

Della Croce, R., Gatti S. 2014. Financing infrastructure – International trends. *OECD Journal: Financial Market Trends* 1: 123–138.

DP World (2014). DP World Annual Report and Accounts, Jebel Ali Free Zone, Dubai (UAE), Emperor (UK), p. 124.

Drewry Shipping Consultants (2001–2015). *Annual Review of Global Container Terminal Operators*. London, UK.

Drezner, D.W. (2008). Sovereign wealth funds and the (in) security of global finance. *Journal of International Affairs* 62(1): 115 –130.

Epstein, G.A. (2006). Introduction: Financialisation and the world economy. In: G.A. Epstein (ed.), *Financialization and the World Economy*. Edward Elgar: Cheltenham and Northampton, 3–16.

Flinders, M. (2005). The politics of public–private partnerships. *The British Journal of Politics & International Relations* 7(2): 215–239.

Flyvbjerg, B., Bruzelius, N., Rothengatter, W. (2003). *Megaprojects and Risk: An Anatomy of Ambition*. Cambridge University Press, Cambridge.

Gavalas, D., Syriopoulos, T. (2015). An integrated credit rating and loan quality model: application to bank shipping finance. *Maritime Policy & Management* 42(6): 533–554.

Grammenos, C. (2013). *The Handbook of Maritime Economics and Business*. Taylor & Francis: London.

Grammenos, C., Alizadeh, A.H., Papapostolou, N.C. (2007). Factors affecting the dynamics of yield premia on shipping seasoned high yield bonds. *Transportation Research Part E: Logistics and Transportation Review* 43: 549–564.

Grammenos, C., Arkoulis, A. (2003). Determinants of spreads on new high yield bonds of shipping companies. *Transportation Research Part E: Logistics and Transportation Review* 39: 459–471.

Grammenos, C., Nomikos N., Papapostolou, N. (2008). Estimating the probability of default for shipping high yield bond issues. *Transportation Research Part E: Logistics and Transportation Review* 44(6): 1123–1138.

Guasch, J.L. (2004). *Granting and Renegotiating Infrastructure Concessions: Doing it Right.* The World Bank: Washington DC.

Hammami, M., Ruhashyankiko, J.-F., Yehoue, E.B. (2006). Determinants of public private partnerships in infrastructure. *IMF Working Paper* 99: 1–37.

Hoyle, B., Charlier, J. (1995). Inter-port competition in developing countries: An East African case study. *Journal of Transport Geography* 3(2): 87–103.

Inderst, G. (2010). Infrastructure as an asset class. *EIB Papers* 15(1): 70–105.

Kao, J. (1993). The worldwide web of Chinese business. *Harvard Business Review* March/April: 24–36.

Kavussanos, M.G., Tsouknidis, D.A. (2014). The determinants of credit spreads changes in global shipping bonds. *Transportation Research Part E: Logistics and Transportation Review* 70: 55–75.

Kavussanos, M.G., Tsouknidis, D.A. (2016). Default risk drivers in shipping bank loans. *Transportation Research Part E: Logistics and Transportation Review* 94: 71–94.

Kern, S. (2007). *Sovereign Wealth Funds – State Investment on the Rise* (Serie Current Issues). 10 September 2007. Deutsche Bank Research: Frankfurt am Main.

Merikas, A., Gounopoulos, D., Nounis, C. (2009). Global shipping IPOs performance. *Maritime Policy & Management* 36: 481–505.

Midoro R., Parola F. (2003). The role of the global container terminal operators in the China market. Conference proceedings of "Maritime Transport 2003", Barcelona 25–27 November 2003, Universitat Politècnica de Catalunya (UPC) and Museu Maritim, Barcelona/Tarragona – Spain, pp. 41–54.

Mitroussi, K., Abouarghoub, W., Haider, J.J., Pettit, S.J., Tigka, N. (2016). Performance drivers of shipping loans: An empirical investigation. *International Journal of Production Economics* 171(p3): 438–452.

Notteboom, T. (2002). Consolidation and contestability in the European container handling industry. *Maritime Policy & Management* 29(3): 257–269.

Notteboom, T. (2007). Concession agreements as port governance tools. *Research in Transportation Economics* 17: 449–467.

Notteboom, T., Rodrigue, J.P. (2012). The corporate geography of global container terminal operators. *Maritime Policy & Management* 39(3): 249–279.

Olivier, D. (2005). Private entry and emerging partnerships in container terminal operations: evidence from Asia. *Maritime Economics & Logistics* 7(2): 87–115.

Olivier, D. (2006). The globalisation of port business: An Asian perspective. Doctoral dissertation, The University of Hong Kong: Pokfulam, Hong Kong.

Olivier, D., Parola, F., Slack, B., Wang, J.J. (2007). The time scale of internationalisation: The case of the container port industry. *Maritime Economics and Logistics* 9(1): 1–34.

Ottesen, F. (2011). Infrastructure needs and pension investments. *OECD Journal: Financial Market Trends* 2011(1): 97–109.

Oyedele, J.B. (2014). Infrastructure investment and the emerging role of institutional investors: The case of pension funds and sovereign wealth funds. *Academic Journal of Interdisciplinary Studies* 3(1): pp. 43–54.

Page, S., Ankner, W., Jones, C., Fetterman, R. (2008). The risks and rewards of private equity in infrastructure. Public Works Management & Policy 13: 100–113.

Pallis, A.A., Notteboom, T., De Langen, P.W. (2010). Concession agreements and market entry in the container terminal industry. *Maritime Economics & Logistics* 10(3): 209–228.

Pallis, A.A., Syriopoulos, T. (2007). Port governance models: Financial evaluation of Greek port restructuring. *Transport Policy* 14(3): 232–246.

Park, D., Estrada, G. (2009). Developing Asia's sovereign wealth funds and outward foreign direct investment. *ADB Economics Working Paper Series*, No. 169.

Parola, F., Notteboom, T., Satta, G., Rodrigue, J. P. (2013). Analysis of factors underlying foreign entry strategies of terminal operators in container ports. *Journal of Transport Geography* 33, 72–84.

Parola, F., Notteboom, T., Satta, G., Rodrigue, J. P. (2015). The impact of multiple-site acquisitions on corporate growth patterns of international terminal operators. *International Journal of Shipping and Transport Logistics* 7(5), 621–648.

Parola, F., Satta, G., Caschili, S. (2014). Unveiling co-operative networks and 'hidden families' in the container port industry. *Maritime Policy & Management* 41(4), 384–404.

Peng, H.W., Newell, G. (2007). The significance of infrastructure in Australian investment portfolios. *Pacific Rim Property Research Journal* 13(4): 423–450.

Peters, H. (2001). Developments in global seatrade and container shipping markets: Their effects on the port industry and private sector involvement. *International Journal of Maritime Economics* 3: 3–26.

Rodrigue, J. P., Notteboom, T., Pallis, A. A. (2011). The financialization of the port and terminal industry: Revisiting risk and embeddedness. *Maritime Policy & Management* 38(2): 191–213.

Satta, G., Notteboom, T., Parola, F., Persico, L. (2017). Determinants of the long-term performance of initial public offerings (IPOs) in the port industry. *Transportation Research Part A: Policy and Practice* 103: 135–153.

Satta, G., Parola, F. (2012). *I processi di espansione internazionale nella container port industry. Analisi delle determinanti delle scelte di ingresso.* FrancoAngeli: Milano.

Satta, G., Parola, F., Persico, L. (2014). Temporal and spatial constructs in service firms' internationalization patterns: The determinants of the accelerated growth of emerging MNEs. *Journal of International Management* 20(4), 421–435.

Satta, G., Persico, L. (2015). Entry mode choices of rapidly internationalizing terminal operators: The determinants of the degree of control on foreign ventures. *Maritime Economics & Logistics* 17(1): 97–126.

Siemiatycki, M. (2015). Canadian pension fund investors in transport infrastructure: A case study. *Case Studies on Transport Policy* 3: 166–175.

Soppé, M., Parola, F., Frémont, A. (2009). Emerging inter-industry partnerships between shipping lines and stevedores: From rivalry to cooperation? *Journal of Transport Geography* 17 (1):10–20.

Stopford, M. (2009). *Maritime Economics 3rd Edition.* Routledge: London.

Turkisch, E. (2011). Sovereign wealth funds as investors in Africa: opportunities and barriers. *OECD Development Centre Working Paper* 303: 1–39.

van De Voorde, E. (2005). What future the maritime sector? Some considerations on globalization, co-operation and market power. *Research in Transportation Economics* 13: 253–277.

Van Marrewijk, A. (2007). Managing project culture: the case of environ megaproject. *International Journal of Project Management* 25: 290–299.

Ward, H. (2013). Maritime M&A: financial crisis to present day. Why the wild ride for company valuations? *Maritime Professionals* 4Q: 16–17.

World Bank (2012). *Public-Private Partnerships: Reference Guide.* The World Bank: Washington, DC.

20

Private sector participation, port efficiency, and economic development

Jose L. Tongzon

20.1 Introduction

Ports play a key role in a nation's international trade and economic development. Since ports are essential components of logistics chains, they can affect logistics efficiency and responsiveness, and thus a nation's international competitiveness and economic development. Port efficiency or lack of port efficiency has a significant role in affecting the efficiency or lack of efficiency of logistics since port costs account for a large part of maritime transport costs which can be passed to logistics service providers and shippers by way of increased shipping charges. More importantly, delays or longer transit times due to port inefficiency can also lead to higher inventory costs and thus logistics costs and, at worst, could mean a loss of business opportunities.

Maritime transport is the most important mode of transportation, particularly for developing countries which rely heavily on primary exports as their source of foreign exchange and employment opportunities. Since primary exports are bulky and heavy, they are most suitable for maritime transport. Their export performance will thus be negatively affected if their ports and maritime transport are inefficient and unresponsive to their logistics needs.

Furthermore, the port environment is increasingly becoming highly competitive as a result of shipping industry trends, such as continued shipping mergers, strategic alliances, and deployment of VLCs to take advantage of the economies of scale in cargo handling. Ports nowadays operate in an increasingly competitive freight market, with the emergence of a few global players in shipping, to be able to control the allocation of transshipment business to strategically located, well-equipped, and efficiently managed hub ports in hub-and-spoke networks, just-in-time inventory, and the need for quick delivery and a more efficient inland transport system.

Given the importance of port efficiency and its implications for international competitiveness and economic development, several countries across the globe have embarked on promoting private sector participation in various forms in the belief that increased private sector participation can lead to higher port efficiency and thus enhance their countries' international competitiveness and economic development. Ports form a vital link in the overall trading chain and, consequently, port efficiency is a key factor for a nation to achieve internationally competitive advantage and economic development (Tongzon, 1989; Chin and Tongzon, 1998).

On the other hand, many ports, particularly in developing countries of Asia and Africa, continue to adopt the old port governance model under which only governments are directly involved in the ownership and operation of ports, based on the belief that ports are primarily "public goods" and that their primary function is to facilitate and support a country's industrialization strategy and economic development, which cannot be entrusted to the private sector. The role of direct government involvement is therefore essential, especially in certain ports where the private sector is reluctant to invest due to the lack of sufficient business opportunities. For example, in the Philippines, the Philippine Ports Authority (PPA) – a government-owned statutory agency established under a separate charter – has been involved in the ownership, management, and operation of ports, particularly in those regions where the private sector is reluctant to invest while it remains at the same time the regulator of the ports throughout the country. Under the new initiatives to reform their port governance, the Philippine government is classifying various ports in the country into various categories, some of which do not require private sector participation. Although Basilio (2003) asserted that this sheer lack of separation of commercial/operational and regulatory functions is one of the major factors responsible for the high levels of port inefficiency and exorbitant port charges, to the detriment of the port users and the nation's international competitiveness, the country continues to hold unto the old port governance model for certain ports.

There have been several empirical studies on the impact of increased private sector participation on port efficiency. These studies have so far however produced conflicting results. This issue therefore remains unresolved. The role of governments in port development needs also to be further examined in light of the growing emphasis on port efficiency in this era of increasing globalization and inter-port competition. Private sector participation may be an important factor for port development and efficiency improvements. But there are also other issues to consider, based on the criteria of equity and regional development in which the role of governments is critically important.

This chapter aims to revisit the issue of private sector participation, and discusses in detail the pros and cons of increased private sector participation from the perspective of efficiency and economic development. The rest of the chapter is organized as follows. Section 20.2 discusses the concept of private sector participation and its various forms. Section 20.3 reviews the existing literature on the impact of private sector participation on port efficiency and economic development. Section 20.4 discusses the basic principles or best practices for port management, and concludes the chapter with a conclusion and set of policy recommendations.

20.2 The concept and rationale for private sector participation

Traditionally, ports were considered public goods and expected to play the role of facilitating a nation's international trade and economic development. As a result, only governments were directly involved in the construction, maintenance, management, and operation of ports, to ensure that there was sufficient investment in required port infrastructure, that economic benefits from port investments were maximized, and to achieve an equitable distribution of these benefits. Thus, ports in most cases were owned, managed, and operated by their respective governments at the national or local level.

The past decades however have seen an accelerated restructuring of port organizations, giving an enlarged role to the private sector in the ownership, management, and operation of ports. The main motivation of this trend is the widely accepted belief of efficiency enhancement resulting from increasing private sector participation. Associated with this is the trend towards the separation of regulatory and commercial functions of ports to improve further port efficiency and avoid a possible conflict of interest which led in some cases to ports becoming a financial burden on the government and the economy. Other motivations include access to state-of-the-art technology and capital and management, higher flexibility, and attainment of social objectives.

This trend is evidenced by many ports in the developing countries of Asia characterized by shortage of capital and limited access to technology. For these ports (many of which were public-owned) whose resources were limited, more private participation has allowed them to have more access to capital and better technology. In Southeast Asian countries, for example, the major ports of Malaysia, Thailand, and Indonesia can no longer be considered as pure public ports with their respective governments allowing more private sector participation in the operation of port assets. More private participation also allows ports to be more flexible and autonomous in their operations. Public port financing is limited not only by regulations, but also in some cases by the size of the public sector's budget or income. This reliance on public sector income has created some uncertainty on the fate of port infrastructure. This has caused many ports to move towards more private sector participation, and consequently, a reduced dominance of the state over certain ports. Further, a direct involvement of the private sector in the port management can inject more efficient business practices into the system. Due to a clear link between superior performance and financial benefits (Hartley *et al.*, 1991; Parker, 1994), private entrepreneurs arguably have the incentive to perform efficiently, which is not inherent in the public sector, generally relying on state subsidies and protection.

Based on the World Bank's Reform Toolkit (2001), private sector participation in the management and operation of ports or terminals can take on various forms, e.g. lease contracts, build-operate-transfer (BOT), concessions, joint ventures, distinct types of port models (such as service, tool, landlord, and privatized ports), and the separation of commercial and regulatory functions of port authorities, as can be seen in Table 20.1. The major forms of private sector participation are further discussed below to highlight the key features of these port governance models.

20.2.1 Privatization

To allow the privatized ports to operate in a more commercialized way, the port authority may sell its assets to the private sector so that it should be nothing more than a landowner and regulator of port/terminal operations. The sale of port assets, which is a way of transferring ownership of infrastructure, superstructure, and equipment, is normally open to any company or consortia to bid, and the sale is made to one bidder. Such bidders may include a group of management

Table 20.1 Alternative Forms of Private Sector Participation

	Public sector role	Private sector role	Examples
Privatization	None	Owner/Operator	UK ports
Corporatization	Owner and regulator	Operator	Port of Klang
Commercialization	Owner/regulator/operator	None	Port of Trinidad and Tobago
Separation of functions	Owner and regulator	Operator	Port of Singapore
Liberalization	Owner and regulator	Operator	Port of Hong Kong
Concession (BOT)	Owner/Regulator	Operator	Port of Rotterdam
Joint ventures	Owner/Regulator	Operator	Port of Tanjung Pelepas
Management contracts	Owner/Regulator	Operator	Port of Singapore

Source: World Bank, 2001.

staff and employees in a management/employee buy-out (MEBO), typically funded by institutional equity and debt, with a comparatively small amount of equity subscribed by the management team itself. Under this model, the public port authority can provide the infrastructure (quays and terminal paving) while the superstructure (cranes, warehouses, and others) can be owned and managed by private companies.

In countries such as Argentina, France, Italy, New Zealand, and the UK, where a strong central government role has been exercised over the ports, including labour, changes have been significant. The UK had a complex port structure which has changed radically in response to three policy actions: privatization of the British Transport Docks Board which became Associated British Ports in 1983, abolition of the National Dock Labour Scheme in 1989, and subsequent privatization of other ports.

20.2.2 Corporatization

Sometimes referred to as incremental privatization, it occurs where a 100% government-owned company is established to take over the business of providing port services while the port assets are leased to the private sector. In many ways, it represents a half-way house which attempts to gain for the ports many benefits flowing from private sector involvement while at the same time retaining a state interest. It normally sets out to achieve this by establishing a public sector landlord (the port corporation) while at the same time creating greater freedom in port operations by giving the ports full autonomy even though some powers are retained by ministers.

In Malaysia, corporatization was applied when parties for a privatization project were not identified and in the interim period the port was corporatized, and 100% owned by the Ministry of Finance. When the parties had been identified to take over the port, the Ministry of Finance retained the so called "golden share" in the privatized port, the valuation of which had been predetermined by the government. In short, corporatization involves the transformation of the port from its status as a government department to an independent but government-owned entity under a Companies Act or similar national legislation. Examples include Johor port which was corporatized on 1 January 1993 and privatized in September 1995 when it was taken over by Sea Port Terminals at a cost of US$77 million. Then in 1996 Johor was incorporated as the limited company Johor Port Bhd to manage and operate the port for 30 years with an option to extend for a further 30 years. In Singapore, the port of Singapore was corporatized on 1 October 1997.

In Australia, the port of Melbourne under the landlord port model since the early 1990s has retained its management and development of the port estate function; supervision of major civil engineering works, policy-making, planning, and development function; conception and implementation of port policies and development strategies; provision and maintenance of channels/fairways/breakwaters; provision and maintenance of berths/piers/wharves/locks/basins; provision and arrangement of road and rail access to the port facilities; traffic control, regulatory and surveillance function; maintenance of the conservancy function; provision of vessel traffic management; enforcement of applicable laws/regulations and licensing port works; safeguarding port users' interests against the risk of monopoly formation and the controlling of natural monopolies; and marketing, public relations, and promotion function.

20.2.3 Commercialization

There are also other ways by which participation of the private sector in the financing of port facilities and equipment, port management, port operations, and performance of port services can increase.

Ports can embark on commercialization which involves dividing the port authority's principal activities into separate operating units, each functioning as an autonomous commercial company with its own balance sheet. Each company can procure services from any other company according to market needs and at market rates, while paying the port authority a rental for the premises it occupies. In other words, commercialization means that the port entity remains under public sector ownership, management and operation, but commercial management practices are similar to those encountered in the private sector. For example, the Port Authority of Trinidad and Tobago (PATT) was divided into three operating units: (a) PATT Operations Ltd which owns/operates all machinery/equipment for carrying out cargo-handling operations; (b) PATT Marine Ltd which owns/operates all floating craft including the port authority's barges, tugs, floating cranes, and dredger; and (c) PATT Ferry Service Ltd. which is responsible for maintaining the ferry link between Trinidad and Tobago. Its investment and equity in these companies is only in the form of equipment and other fixed assets. PATT owns the port land and retains responsibility for regulatory matters within the port area.

20.2.4 Separation of regulatory and commercial/operational functions

To enhance further port efficiency and international competitiveness in light of increasing interport competition, ports embarked on a separation of these two functions (commercial and regulatory functions). One good example of this trend is Singapore's Maritime and Port Authority (MPA). To separate commercial/operational from regulatory functions, the Maritime and Port Authority of Singapore was established on 2 February 1996 by the MPA Act of 1996 through the merger of the Marine Department (which was under the then Ministry of Communications), the National Maritime Board, and the regulatory departments of the former Port of Singapore Authority (PSA). MPA's main job has since then been to regulate the port and shipping activities in Singapore, while PSA's main job has been to manage and run the port. PSA was subsequently corporatized in order to enhance its flexibility and responsiveness to business opportunities in the fast changing and increasingly competitive port environment. In 2004, to further streamline all maritime-related functions, the industry promotion function for shipping was transferred from IE Singapore to MPA. Before the enactment of the MPA Act of 1996 and subsequent corporatization (a form of port privatization) of PSA, the commercial operations and regulatory functions were under the responsibility of Singapore's PSA. It can be argued that, in addition to other factors, the separation of these two major functions has been a significant factor underlying its prominent level of port efficiency, reliability, and international competitiveness.

20.2.5 Liberalization

Ports can also undertake liberalization, which, as a complement of commercialization, lessens the public port's organizational power by allowing the private sector to provide the same services. It aims to enhance performance through a competitive environment, which normally results in more efficient services. So far there has been only a limited application of this strategy with the broadest application in the UK and a more limited application in Asia, such as in the ports of Busan and Hong Kong. Some terminals at the port of Busan are being leased to particular private companies, although the entire port is still managed by Busan Port Authority. In the port of Hong Kong nine terminals are being operated and managed by five different private operators to foster inter-terminal competition with the port, such as Modern Terminals, Hong Kong International Terminals, COSCO Information and Technology, Dubai Port International Terminals, and Asia Container Terminals.

20.2.6 Concessions

A concession (BOT or lease) is a grant of specific privileges by government. A contract by which the grantor grants to the grantee (the concessionaire) the right to finance, build, and operate a facility for a limited period (usually no less than 21 years), after which the facility and its equipment will be transferred free of charge to the grantor. Concessions (or franchises as they are known in the US) and BOT schemes are a centuries-old system of operation of public utilities, inherited from the Roman Law. They are operated in accordance with the rules on public service: continuity of and equal service to all users. Consequently, they should be awarded (wherever possible) based on public bidding to ensure contestability and transparency, and public interest should be preserved. The concession system has been the backbone of port operations in many countries such as Belgium, France, the Netherlands, and Spain.

Changes in the technology of shipping, cargo handling, and warehousing that required significant investments spurred port authorities not only to modernize and develop infrastructure but also to rent the unequipped bare quays and sites on long-term concessions to private enterprise. For example, Rotterdam Port Authority leases port infrastructure to major private companies such as Europe Combined Terminals (ECT), which in turn provide the necessary terminal superstructure. In Australia, the Sydney Ports Corporation has leased its terminals to P & O and Patrick Stevedores, which also provide labour in addition to superstructure. The port of Melbourne has also leased its terminals to the private sector, which provides rail services, container stevedoring services, and dedicated loading and unloading services. Private companies also provide pilotage and towage services within the port of Melbourne.

A concession provides many advantages. It relieves the grantor of finances. Either the concessionaire pre-finances the whole operation, operates and maintains the facilities, and recovers its investments through tariffs, or it sets aside all reserves necessary for the replacement of facilities and equipment included in the concession. It establishes a strong legal relation between grantor and concessionaire with candidates for concessions being carefully screened and pre-selected. It enables a country (or port authority) to attract capital – especially foreign – without losing long-term control over its vital port facilities.

There are however some disadvantages. They have not always been popular with all governments and all private operators due to complains that concessions lack transparency, that the concessionaire is often subjected to pressure to employ staff designated by the government/ port authority, that it has been a breeding ground for corruption and patronage and an easy means for securing full employment. If the concession operates at a deficit, the concessionaire is reluctant to finance new investments and maintenance. Similarly, when a concession draws to its end, the concessionaire also tends to reduce maintenance/investments to a minimum, if only to inflate the reserve fund to be shared at the end of the concession. The port facility at Westport in Malaysia was built under BOT. Under this scheme, a consortium of developers would have a lease of 30 years during which period they would build 30 berths and develop 1,200 acres of back-up land for port-related activities.

20.2.7 Joint ventures

A joint venture involves the setting up of a jointly owned independent organization. Such ventures in which costs, rewards, technologies, and expertise are shared are generally undertaken for mutual interest. For example, private sector involvement in China's port sector generally takes the form of joint ventures between terminal-operating companies and state organizations. Hongkong International Terminals (HIT) now has several joint ventures in China and its portfolio includes

Shanghai and Yantian and Delta ports of Nanhai, Shantou, Xiamen, Zhuhai, and Jiangmen. The port of Tanjung Pelepas in the southern tip of Malaysia is the product of the joint venture of Maersk and the Malaysian government. The government of Malaysia provides the land and port infrastructure while Maerks provides the superstructure and management expertise.

20.2.8 Management (or technical) contracts

A management (or technical) contract (where the port authority retains ownership of the assets and is responsible for provision of further capital), is one in which a reputable contractor offers the authority a package of expertise to build a profitable business more rapidly than is possible through licensing, consultancy, or other routes. They are very similar in practice to the leases of port premises equipped with port-owned equipment, because they do not imply any major investment up front nor pre-financing by the lessee or contractor. They are usually granted for a period of at least five years and have generally developed in service ports where the performance of the port authority as an operator has not been successful. A certain set of functions that were previously carried out by the public port authority can be contracted out to the private sector to improve port efficiency and performance (World Bank, 2001). The port of Singapore has, for example, opened up its pilotage function, which used to be under the responsibility of more private pilotage operators, to introduce more competition within the port and thus further improve its port efficiency.

20.3 Impact of private sector participation on port efficiency and economic development

There is a continuing debate on whether ownership and management changes accompanying private sector participation lead to performance improvements (Ariff et al., 2009). Existing economic theory fails to provide unequivocal propositions on the issue of the relative efficiency of public vis-à-vis private enterprises (Liu, 1995). Based on the principal-agent theory, private ownership should be more efficient than the public one. It is believed that the transformation from public to private ownership, even without change in the competition, will be associated with improved efficiency (Hartley et al, 1991 and Parker, 1994). However, many economists (for instance, Vickers and Yarrow, 1989, and Estrin and Perotin, 1991) have argued against the opinion in favour of private ownership by suggesting that principal-agent problems may also arise in the private sector as a result of capital market imperfections. Thus, the question of the relative efficiency of alternative forms of ownership is an empirical one (Liu, 1995).

Many empirical studies have provided further empirical support for the link between lower government involvement in the management and operation of ports and higher port efficiency and greater international competitiveness. Relevant examples include the studies by Suykens and Van de Voorde (1998), Estache, Gonzalez, and Trujillo (2002), Cullinane, Song, and Gray (2002), Tongzon and Heng (2005), Pallis et al., (2010) and Pagano et al., (2013). Estache, Gonzalez, and Trujillo (2002) illustrated the efficiency effects of Mexico's 1993 port reform by using a panel data of 44 observations from 11 independent port administrations. The efficiency scores based on the statistical results showed that the reform of decentralization and privatization taken in Mexican ports has generated large short-term improvements in the average performance of the port industry. Cullinane, Song, and Gray (2002) employed both cross-sectional and panel data versions of the stochastic frontier model to assess the relative efficiency of the selected Asian container ports. Based on their purely subjective appraisal of the obtained efficiency levels of selected ports from the above two models, they concluded that there does seem to be some support for the opinion that privatization has some positive relation with port efficiency. Tongzon and Heng (2005) provided an empirical support for the above argument that more private sector participation in the port operation is useful for improving port operational efficiency but that full port privatization is not an effective way to increase port operation efficiency. Their study showed that it is better for port authorities to assume the role of regulator and thus limit the private sector participation within the "landowner and operator" functions. In other words, port authorities should introduce private finance, operation, and management instead of state funds and administration while they remain in place as regulators. In the most recent study on the impact of privatization, Pagano *et al.* (2013) found that privatization for Panama and US ports had a positive impact on their efficiency and effectiveness.

On the other hand, other empirical studies, which investigated the association between port ownership structure and port operational efficiency, seem to provide evidence that there is no clear-cut relationship, or even a negative correlation, between the type of ownership and port efficiency. For example, Liu (1995), based on the stochastic production function to calculate technical efficiency and comparing the influence of public and private ownership on inter-port efficiency differences using the observations of output and inputs for 28 ports in the UK, failed to identify that ownership has a significant effect on port performance. Notteboom, Coeck, and van den Broeck (2000) used the Bayesian stochastic frontier model, developed by van den Broeck *et al.* (1994), to compare the efficiency level of a set of 36 European container terminals, supplemented with four Asian container ports. After comparing the efficiency levels among the studied terminals, no relationship was found between the type of ownership, operations of a terminal, and the efficiency level. Coto, Banos, and Rodriguez (2000) covered the efficiency problem in the port industry by using a stochastic frontier cost function to estimate the economic efficiency of Spanish ports through a panel data of 27 Spanish ports. They found that the type of organization has a significant effect on economic efficiency, but ports with autonomy are less efficient than the rest. Consistent with Liu (1995) and Cullinane and Song (2002), Cullinane *et al.* (2005) by applying DEA analysis to sampled panel data, have found no relationship between privatization and efficiency in the container port industry.

Moreover, Baird (2000) argued that outright sale of port land, combined with a transfer of operation and regulation functions to the private sector, will not definitely increase the operational efficiency, or may even be counter-productive. Due to the specific nature of port investment (long-term payback and high capital cost), an almost total dependence on the private sector to provide both port infrastructure and superstructure will result in significantly delayed investments on crucial operational facilities and equipment, which are obviously contrary to the original objective of port privatization. Thus, full port privatization will impede the improvement in port performance while some extent of private sector participation can increase the efficiency level, which implies that the extent of private sector intervention in the port sector has an inverted U-shaped effect on port operation efficiency. Tongzon and Heng (2005) provided, based on the stochastic frontier approach, some empirical evidence that the impact of port privatization on port efficiency follows an inverted U-shaped curve.

More recently, Cheon *et al.* (2010) undertook research on a similar topic and evaluated the impacts of institutional reforms on port efficiency. By applying the Malmquist Productivity Index (MPI) on 100 global container ports, they concluded that improvement in port efficiency largely came from the reforms of ownership structure and asset management practices, although they rejected any possible roles of decentralization and corporatization in efficiency changes. On the other hand, using a similar approach (the translog distance function), González and Trujillo (2008) investigated the correlations between reforms and infrastructure's technical efficiency (with berth, surface, and labour as input factors) within Spanish container ports.

Their conclusions were in contrast with those of Cheon *et al.* (2009), as they claimed that technical efficiency had changed little after management restructuring and reforms, although significant improvements in technological change were observed after decentralization. They did not, however, proceed further to investigate the possible reasons behind such phenomenon, thus seriously limiting the potential contributions of their work. A more recent and comprehensive review of past studies assessing economic efficiency in the port sector can be found in González and Trujillo (2009).

Although it is not categorically proven that there exists a direct causal link between the degree of private sector involvement and economic efficiency, deregulation policies have been commonly used in many industries and across many countries (especially in the landside transportation sector), and more private sector participation or less government involvement in the running of ports is perceived to be the most important policy for improving the efficiency of the port sector (Cullinane, Song, and Gray, 2002).

In addition, some empirical studies have also examined the effect of port size on port efficiency level. Liu (1995) found that port size is significant when explaining port efficiency, but the effect is small. Martines, Diaz, Navarro, and Ravelo (1999) applied the data envelopment analysis (DEA) to study the relative efficiency of the 26 Spanish port authorities. They showed that larger-size ports are more efficient than the smaller ones. Notteboom, Coeck, and van den Broeck (2000) found that port size has a positive effect on port efficiency. Cullinane, Song, and Gray (2002) argued that ports with larger throughput seem to have certain performance advantages over their smaller competitors. However, Coto, Banos, and Rodriguez (2000) showed that port size is not significant when trying to explain economic efficiency. Tongzon (2001) applied data envelopment analysis (DEA) to make international comparisons in port efficiency among four Australian and 12 other international container ports. The main findings showed that a port's efficiency level has no clear relationship with its size and function (hub or feeder).

Less government involvement in the port management and operation does not guarantee an improvement in port efficiency. Just as governments can fail to allocate resources efficiently, there is also such thing as market failure. Although more private sector participation may be a necessary condition for port efficiency improvement, it is not a sufficient condition. In many countries, the reason for the poor performance of the maritime sector is related to the lack of the capacity to govern on the part of the state and the lack of the capacity to manage on the part of the private sector (Iheduru, 1993). Under these conditions, a change in management of port assets does not necessarily result in efficiency improvements if the change in management from government to the private sector does not lead to an improvement in port management.

Ports can also be considered as a "public good" with substantial positive economic externalities that cannot be left to the profit-oriented private sector. Under this concept, a port does not have to be profitable as long as it provides a vital service and contributes to the economic development of a country by facilitating international trade and providing a vital link between various regions in the country. Several governments in the developing countries of Asia and Africa have adopted this concept and have argued for more direct government intervention in port ownership, management, and operation without private sector participation, particularly in those underdeveloped regions of their countries where the profit-oriented private sector is reluctant to invest in ports due to insufficient port throughputs, low shipping frequencies, and thus uncertain profits.

Moreover, Baird (2000) argued that, due to the specific nature of port investment (long-term payback and high capital cost), an almost total dependence on the private sector to provide both port infrastructure and superstructure will result in significantly delayed investments on crucial operation facilities and equipment, which are obviously contrary to the original objective of port privatization. Thus, full private participation will impede the improvement in port performance while some extent of private sector participation can increase the efficiency level, which implies that the extent of private sector intervention in the port sector has an inverted U-shaped effect on port operational efficiency. Hence, the findings of previous studies on this have provided mixed evidence of the implications of more private sector participation (see for example Martinez-Budria *et al.*, 1999, and Valentine and Gray, 2001).

Wang *et al.* (2004) suggested that port management and operations can also be undertaken by port authorities in a more commercialized way. Rodrigue (2004), in examining the port authority of New York/New Jersey, which dealt with the management of a port's land use, providing support for terminal operators, traffic regulation activities, and for a wide array of infrastructures, concluded that a centralized inclusive port authority – in terms of a diversified portfolio of activities, infrastructures, and terminals within a coterminous geographic and administrative entity – might also provide a successful and stable framework for continuously re-inventing itself and deploying effectively its diversified mandate to serve the needs of port users.

Dasgupta and Sinha (2016) investigated the impact of port privatization on the efficiencies of major Indian ports using DEA and concluded that privatization had a positive impact on port efficiency, but they also found out other factors at work that led to higher efficiency apart from privatization.

Most recently, Tongzon *et al.* (2018) reinvestigated the impact of port privatization on port efficiency based on a sample data drawn from the world's 58 major ports, using the Bayesian approach, and found that ownership *per se* does not affect port efficiency. If pure public ports are excluded from the analysis, the efficiency estimates from both Bayesian and econometric studies are similar to those of Tongzon and Heng (2005), which revealed an inverted U-shaped curve, as can be seen from Table 20.2.

This literature review suggests that there may exist other, more important factors determining port efficiency than privatization. It is therefore possible for a port to improve its efficiency and performance without necessarily resorting to privatization policy. This inference may not be counterfactual since there are examples of pure public ports that are more efficient than privatized ports. For example, the port of Singapore – a fully public port – is well known for its high level of efficiency and is more efficient than some of the more privatized ports.

Table 20.2 Summary Statistics for Port-specific Efficiency by Group

	private score (0/3)	private score (1/3)	private score (2/3)	private score (3/3)
Mean	0.8762	0.84611	0.90555	0.65977
Standard error	0.0081	0.00685	0.00757	0.05325
Q1(25%)	0.8569	0.8254	0.9061	0.5218
Median	0.8862	0.8422	0.91165	0.74255
Q3(75%)	0.8997	0.8608	0.9214	0.7626
Standard deviation	0.0333	0.02987	0.02832	0.150615
Minimum	0.8123	0.7946	0.842	0.4318
Maximum	0.9157	0.904	0.9368	0.8136
N	17	19	14	8

Source: Tongzon *et al.* (2018).

20.4 Basic principles for port management

Irrespective of the diverse types of private sector participation in port management, ports must be managed in accordance with the following principles: self-autonomy and economic development, authority and control over the whole port area and main port functions, financial autonomy and independence, and commercial management methods.

20.4.1 Self-autonomy and contribution to economic development

Ports should be managed by a separate autonomous body (port authority or port trust) under a general supervision by the government. This body should have the following responsibilities:

- be in charge of the current administration and development of the port within the framework of the national economic policy;
- have the right to establish its own rules and regulations, and select and appoint personnel based on their professional abilities, irrespective of political affiliations;
- be responsible for the maintenance of all port works, port improvement, and revision plans and extensions, and for awarding contracts for works and supply of equipment;
- decide the system of port operations to be followed, and carry out the day-to-day operations;
- have the right to establish tariffs of port dues, fix the rates (subject to some form of government's approval), collect the dues, and retain the proceeds;
- be able to lease some property to private firms, buy and sell land adjacent to the port, to incur financial obligations in its own name (with a certain control of the government), and in general to act as a legal entity.

The degree of a port authority's independence and the scope of government's control may vary from case to case. But the government's control should aim at ensuring that the port will be managed and developed to become a net contributor to economic development. In the light of increasing private sector participation in the management and operation of ports, the regulatory function of the government should be effectively exercised to ensure that profitability is not achieved at the cost of economic growth and regional development.

20.4.2 Authority and control over the whole port area and main port functions

The port must be managed as a unit, without being split into parts under different jurisdictions. Daily tasks of processing vessels and cargoes through all phases of port operations, supplying pilots, allocating berths, evacuating imported goods from the port area, and other functions cannot be performed unless the port management is in control of all port waters, all wharves, piers, and land facilities. Planning of future port extension cannot be made properly unless the port can freely dispose of the entire undeveloped water frontage within the port area.

Private ownership of land or port installation can make it difficult to achieve a full unity of control. Highly specialized terminals, which are used by one single customer, as, for example, berths for loading ores and crude oil, can remain in private ownership, under a certain degree of supervision by the port authority. But berths for common use should all be under full control of the port, whenever possible. Unity of command is essential not only from the point of view of the physical area of the port, but also with respect to main port functions, e.g. storage areas and temporary storage of cargoes in the port area should be under port administration and control. Close cooperation between the port management and customs administration is crucial for the efficient management of cargoes passing through the port.

20.4.3 Financial autonomy and independence

No reasonable degree of port autonomy can be achieved unless ports have a considerable degree of financial autonomy and independence. Whoever provides the funds will unavoidably tend to exercise a strict control on expenditure and on management of the ports. If the government is obliged to cover annual operating deficits of a port, in addition to having financed the initial capital investments, it will be reluctant to entrust port management to a separate autonomous body.

Port finances should be entirely separated from the finances of the state. Ports should have their own budgets. Proceeds from port dues and any other port-related activities should be used exclusively for port administration, maintenance, and improvement. Port tariffs should be held on a reasonable level, yet sufficient to cover normal current expenses, including amortization of possible loans. Only funds for major port extension schemes or for access channels to the port should, in case of need, be supplied by the state, either in the form of direct donations or of a guarantee for loans.

When the port revenue is absorbed by the state under direct government management, port officials are often not aware of the level of income and in any event, they are not able to make any use of it. Budgets of such ports usually cover only expenditure and the level of appropriation cannot be changed without government's approval, irrespective how high the actual revenue might be. An important incentive for efficient management is therefore lacking. Hence, under this administration, any net profits should be retained by the port and should not be remitted to the state as practised in some publicly owned ports.

20.4.4 Commercial management methods

Modern business management methods must be applied in a less bureaucratic but more pragmatic and flexible manner. On financial matters, port administration should have full freedom to adjust the level of expenses to the changing requirements of the traffic and to the level of revenue. On personnel matters, ports should have more freedom in promoting and compensating capable officials than it is possible under most civil service systems and not be unduly restricted by seniority and automatic promotion rules. There should be a clear division of responsibilities and an organizational chart for efficient management and effective delegation of authority.

20.5 Conclusion and policy implications

The objective of this chapter is to revisit the literature, particularly on the old but unresolved issue of whether private sector participation is useful in enhancing port efficiency and economic development. The review of the literature showed that both theoretically and empirically, private sector participation does not necessarily enhance port efficiency and economic development.

The literature review implies that there exist other, more important factors determining port efficiency than private sector participation. It is therefore possible for ports to improve their efficiency and performance without necessarily resorting to more private sector participation. These findings are not counterfactual since there are examples of pure public ports that are more efficient than privatized ports. For example, the port of Singapore – a fully public port – is well known for its high level of efficiency and is more efficient than some of the more privatized ports.

In cases where there are no economic incentives for the private sector to be involved in the ownership and management of ports, government intervention is needed to provide much needed port infrastructure for regional development and stimulate regional economic growth. Developing countries usually have dualistic economies and experience uneven and unequal economic development in which there are much neglected peripheral areas co-existing with the core and more developed centres. These peripheral areas have inadequate port infrastructure investments and insufficient cargoes for shipping lines to make a call. On the other hand, shippers and logistics service providers are also less attracted to use these ports due to their lack of shipping service frequencies and of port connectivity. Hence, this vicious cycle can only be broken with the direct involvement from governments.

Ports should therefore focus more on improving their quality of port governance and their political institutions. Good governance is based on the following principles: accountability, transparency, integrity, stewardship, efficiency, and leadership. Accountability means that the port manager should feel responsible and answerable for the port performance and should put in place mechanisms to ensure that the port organization adheres to high standards of performance. Transparency implies that there is a clear delineation of roles and responsibilities, and clear procedures for making decisions and exercising power. Integrity involves acting impartially, ethically, and fairly in the interest of the port and not misusing information acquired through trust. Stewardship is based on the idea that port managers are entrusted guardians of the port assets and should use the port assets for the betterment of the economy it is supposed to serve. Efficiency requires the best use of available port assets and resources to further the aims of the organization, and leadership means strong commitment to good governance starting from the top of the organization.

Moreover, inter-port competition should be achieved and maintained. Achieving and sustaining competition among ports requires co-ordinating competition policies at a regional level to create a level playing field for ports and avoid dominance by single port operators. A broader approach –aimed at encouraging competition in the transport sector as a whole – would need to promote competition by ports with other transport sectors, such as railroad and road transport, and provide incentives for service providers to compete across transport networks by combining transport modes.

References

Ariff M., Cabanda E., and Sathye M. (2009). "Privatization and performances: evidence from telecommunications sector", *Journal of the Operational Research Society* 60 (10): 1315–1321.

Baird, A.J. (2000). Privatisation and deregulation in seaports. In Bradshaw, B. and Lawton, S.H.(eds), *Privatisation and Deregulation in Transport*, pp. 14–19. Wilshire, UK: MacMillan Press.

Basilio, E.L. (2003). *The Philippine Port Sector. PPA: A Case of Regulatory Capture* (mimeo). Manila: Centre for Research and Communication.

Cheon S.H., Dowall D.E., and Song D.W. (2010). "Evaluating impacts of institutional reforms on port efficiency changes: ownership, corporate structure, and total factor productivity changes of world container ports", *Transportation Research* E 46(4): 546–561.

Chin, A. and Tongzon, J. (1998). "Maintaining Singapore as a major shipping and air transport hub". In Toh, T. (ed.), *Competitiveness of the Singapore Economy*. Singapore: Singapore University Press, pp. 83–114.

Coto-Millán P., Banos-Pino J., and Rodríguez-Alvarez A. (2000). "Economic efficiency in Spanish ports: some empirical evidence", *Maritime Policy and Management: An International Journal of Shipping and Port Research* 27(2): 169–174.

Cullinane, K., Song, D.W., and Gray, R. (2002). "A stochastic frontier model of the efficiency of major container terminals in Asia: assessing the influence of administrative and ownership structures", *Transportation Research Part A* 36, 743–762.

Cullinane K., Ping, J., and Wang, T-f (2005). "The relationship between privatization and DEA estimates of efficiency in the container port industry", *Journal of Economics and Business* 57: 433–462.

Dasgupta, M.K. and D. Sinha (2016). "Impact of privatisation of ports on relative efficiency of major ports of India", *Foreign Trade Review* 51(3), 225–247.

Estache A., González M., and Trujillo L. (2002). "Efficiency gains from port reform and the potential for yardstick competition: lessons from Mexico", *World Development* 30(4), 545–560.

Estrin, S. and Perontin, V. (1991). "Does ownership always matter?" *International Journal of Industrial Organization* 9, 55–72.

Gonzalez M.M. and Trujillo L. (2008). "Reforms and infrastructure efficiency in Spain's container ports", *Transportation Research A* 42(1), 243–257.

Gonzalez M.M. and Trujillo L. (2009). "Efficiency measurement in the port industry: a survey of the empirical evidence", *Journal of Transport Economics and Policy* 43(2), 157–192.

Hartley, K., Parker, D., Martin, S. (1991). Organizational status, ownership and productivity, Fiscal Studies 12(2), 46–60.

Iheduru, Okechukwu C. (1993). "Rethinking maritime privatization in Africa", *Maritime Policy and Management* 20 (1): 31–49.

Liu, Z. (1995). "The comparative performance of public and private enterprises", *Journal of Transportation Economics and Policy* September 263–274.

Martinez-Budría, E., Diaz-Armas, R., Navarro-Ibanez, M., and Ravelo-Mesa, T. (1999). "A study of the efficiency of Spanish Port Authorities using Data Envelopment Analysis", *International Journal of Transport Economics* 26(2), 237–253.

Notteboom T., Coeck C., and Van Den Broeck J. (2000). "Measuring and explaining the relative efficiency of container terminals by means of Bayesian Stochastic Frontier Models", *International Journal of Maritime Economics* 2: 83–106.

Pagano, A., Wang, W.Y., Sanchez, O., and Ungo, R. (2013). "Impact of privatization on port efficiency and effectiveness: results from Panama and US ports", *Maritime Policy and Management* 40(2), 100–115.

Pallis A.A., Vitsounis T.K., de Langen P.W. (2010). "Port Economics, policy and management: Review of an emerging research field", *Transport Reviews* 30(1), 115–161.

Parker, D. (1994). "Nationalization, privatization and agency status within government: testing for the importance of ownership". In Jackson, P., Price, C. (eds), *Privatization and Regulation: A Review of the Issues*. Essex: Longman, pp. 149–169.

Rodrigue, J.P. (2004). Appropriate models of port governance: Lessons from the Port Authority of New York and New Jersey. In Pinder, D. and Slack, B. (eds), *Shipping and Ports in the 21st Century*. London: Routledge.

Suykens F., van de Voorde E. (1998). "A quarter of a century of port management in Europe: Objectives and tools", *Maritime Policy and Management* 25(3), 251–261.

Tongzon, J.L. (1989). "The impact of wharfage costs on Victoria's export-oriented industries", *Economic Papers* 8, 58–64.

Tongzon, J. (2001). "Efficiency measurement of selected Australian and other international ports using data envelopment analysis", *Transportation Research Part A: Policy and Practice* 35(2), 113–128.

Tongzon, J.L. and Wu Heng (2005). "Port privatization, efficiency and competitiveness: Some empirical evidence from container ports (terminals)", *Transportation Research A* 39 (5), 383–480.

Tongzon, J.L., Hwang, J., and Chang, Y.T. (2018). "Does privatization really improve port efficiency?" Graduate School of Logistics, Inha University. Submitted to a journal for possible publication.

Valentine, V.F. and Gray, R. (2001). The measurement of port efficiency using Data Envelopment Analysis, *Proceedings of the 9th World Conference on Transport Research*, 22–27 July, Seoul, South Korea.

Van den Broeck J.G., Koop O.J., and Steel M.F.J. (1994). "Stochastic frontier models: A Bayesian perspective", *Journal of Econometrics* 61, 273–303.

Vickers, J. and Yarrow, G. (1989). *Privatization: An Economic Analysis*. Cambridge, Mass.: MIT Press.

Wang, J.J., Ng A.K.Y., and Olivier D. (2004). "Port governance in China: a review of policies in an era of internationalizing port management practices", *Transport Policy* 11(3) 237–250.

World Bank (2001). *The World Bank Port Reform Tool Kit*. Washington D.C: The World Bank Group.

21

The attitudes of port organizations in adapting to climate change impacts

Adolf K.Y. Ng, Yile He, and Yui-yip Lau

21.1 Introduction

Climate change is an important issue due to its significant impacts on human lives and society (Ng, Chen, Cahoon, Brooks, and Yang, 2013; Wu and Ji, 2013). Existing studies show that over the past century, the climate of the Earth has undergone significant changes (Wu and Ji, 2013), this is and arguably the main factor contributing to temperature and sea level rise, as well as more frequent superstorms, all of which cause a significant impact on the natural system and human society (Bierling and Lorented, 2008; Wu and Ji, 2013). Also, such impact causes significant economic loss and even loss of life in many countries, including China (National Development and Reform Commission, 2016; Wu and Ji, 2013). Needless to say, economic loss is also generated due to poor infrastructure replacement or repair, and other operational maintenance (Ng et al., 2013, 2016).

Many works address issues related to climate change, notably on topics such as the impact of climate change (e.g., Intergovernmental Panel on Climate Change, 2014; Lemmen, Warren, Lacroix, and Bush, 2008; Prowse et al., 2009), the nature of the vulnerability in the context of climate change (e.g., Kelly and Adger, 2000; Schneider, Semenov, Patwardhan, Burton et al., 2007), and impacts on the marine system (for instance, Hallegatte et al., 2011; Harley et al., 2006). All these studies point out that climate change has triggered extensive concern by governments around the world and is a major problem that must be addressed effectively. However, one should note that climate mitigation and adaptation are different from each other (Becker et al., 2013; Ng et al., 2016). Mitigation refers to "an anthropogenic intervention to reduce the sources or enhance the sinks of greenhouse gases" (Klein et al., 2007, Section 18.1.2, p.750), while adaptation is, according to the United Nations Framework Convention on Climate Change (UNFCCC), an "Adjustment in natural or human systems in response to actual or expected climatic stimuli or their effects" (Klein et al., 2007, Section 18.1.2, p.750). Most previous research focuses on mitigation, while research on adaptation to climate change impacts remain at the embryonic stage (Ng et al., 2013). This is especially true for transportation, which is crucial to global economic growth (Ng et al., 2016; Gillen, 2001). Ports are critical nodes that connect hinterlands and distant lands along trade paths around the world. Climate change can have a substantial impact on the ports' operation, which can cause considerable economic loss

(Becker et al., 2013; Ng et al., 2013). Although Ng and Liu (2014) point out that maritime transportation occupies most of the world's trade volume, there is still a serious shortage of research investigating adaptation strategies on ports or even transportation in general (Ng et al., 2013). Specifically, the severity of the outcome of climate change impacts still remains uncertain, but actions need to be implemented so as to respond to such impacts.

To adapt to climate change impacts effectively, sharp awareness of this issue is pivotal for port organizations . However, we cannot confirm whether port organizations are aware of the situation until there is a thorough understanding of their attitudes on adaptation to climate change. However, such understanding is currently inadequate due to the traditional emphasis of climate change adaptation on the physical/engineering components (Becker et al., 2012; Ng et al., 2013). Thus, improving our understanding of port organization attitudes (from the organizational decision-making perspective) can offer useful insight on a major research gap.

By focusing on nine port organizations in China, this chapter investigates the attitude and perception of port organizations on the development and implementation of climate change plans and strategies. The research question of this study is as follows:

How do port organizations in China think about adaptation strategies for their ports to address the impacts posed by climate change?

The objectives include (1) to review the attitudes of port organizations towards climate adaptation plans and strategies; (2) to identify factors that influence such attitude and perception; and (3) to compare adaptation strategies with mitigation strategies. On the other hand, port organization is defined as an organization that corporates with ports or is in charge of the regulation of ports. These include non-profit organizations and marine organizations from different hierarchies of the government.

Also, we believe that the focus on China is relevant due to the following reasons. First, the study on Chinese ports' adaptation to climate change impacts is extremely limited Wu and Ji, 2013). Second, previous research indicates that the attitude and perception of port organizations on climate change diversify between different continents (Becker et al., 2012; Ng et al., 2018). With the growing significance of China along global supply chains, whether Chinese ports adapt to climate change impacts effectively poses huge impacts on the global economy and social welfare. There is an urgent need to investigate whether the conventional "western wisdom" in climate change adaptation can be implemented in the Chinese context and, if not, what should be done. Some more detailed justifications can be found in Section 21.3.

The rest of the chapter is structured as follows. In Section 21.2, the research methodology is explained, while Section 21.3 presents an overview on how climate change impacts on Chinese port organizations. Section 21.4 illustrates the research findings, followed by the discussion and conclusion in Section 21.5. Finally, major contributions, limitation, and future research direction can be found in Section 21.6.

21.2 Research methodology

Understanding the nature of the study, we collected relevant information through conducting ten semi-structured, in-depth interviews with relevant industrial professionals from nine Chinese port organizations (these included one private wharf and six ports located in different regions along the Chinese coastline). They included Hongkong International Terminals, Jiuzhou Port, Jiangmen Port, Guangzhou Shipping Co., Fuzhou Port, Zhoushan Port, Shanghai Port, Guangzhou Port, and Zhuhai Port Office. We strive to investigate how these port organizations understand, forecast, plan, and implement strategies that address the impacts posed by climate change on their operation and other activities. These port organizations were chosen because it was perceived that the preparation and implementation of adaptation plans and strategies, respectively, would significantly affect their operation and interests. Each interview lasted for 1–2 hour(s) and during these interviews, the following major issues were discussed:

1 the historical and current impact posed by climate change on ports and in their districts;
2 the impact posed by climate change on supply chain;
3 the adaptation to response to impact posed by climate change;
4 comparison between mitigation and adaptation strategies;
5 forecast on climate change impacts;
6 factors or barriers when implementing the adaptation strategies.

All collected information was transcribed into interview scripts for further analysis.

21.3 Climate change and Chinese ports or terminals

Since 1978, China has transformed itself from a planned and closed economy to an open economy in which international trade and finance can take place (Wang and Ng, 2011). The outcomes of the "open door policy" were far reaching, including the port sector. Prior the open door policy, only Shanghai Port was permitted to have trade relations with the world and thus the volume of port traffic was limited due to the trading environment (Lau et al., 2015). However, nowadays, China has opened 31 ports to foreign ships and attracted 2,000–8,000 foreign vessels calling per year. In addition, joint venture activities were formed with foreign companies (Tang et al., 2014). Since then, a variety of shipping service portfolios have emerged, for instance, shipping and chartering, ship registration, shipping agencies, arbitration, training and education, to name but a few. Over 80% of such trade has been accomplished with the involvement of ports under the subsequent expansion of open cities in China. Clearly, China's port industry has the potential to absorb foreign investment and encourage local economies (Wang et al., 2017). By now, China is one of the few countries that have a large number of ports with a long coastline (Wang and Ng, 2011).

In this case, Tang et al. (2014, p.2) described China's maritime wealth as follows: "situated in the east of Asia, China is surrounded by the Bohai, the Yellow Sea, the East China Sea and South China Sea. It has a coastline stretching over 18,400 km, which added to those of outlying islands, amounts to a length of 32,000 km in total. China has more than 700 ports and harbors of which there are 70 seaports handling over 100,000 tons of cargo a year". As such, ports in China play an important role in promoting the development of both domestic and foreign trade. In addition, they facilitate transport networks integration (Meng, 2014). The re-establishment of direct links across the Taiwan Strait has created rapid development of the Chinese port industry (Lau et al., 2012). The significant growth of China's port generates substantial transformation of the Chinese port system, especially in the ports' interrelationships. These foster the hinterland development and enlarge the shipping network coverage (Wang et al., 2017). At present, more than 90% of the foreign trade of goods transport volume is undertaken by Chinese ports (Wu and Ji, 2013). Chinese ports undertake most domestic bulk cargo shipment (Meng, 2014; Wu and Ji, 2013), unload 95% of the imported crude oil, and 99% of imported iron ore (Wu and Ji, 2013). Meanwhile, the development of Chinese ports needs nearly $15 million in the construction, renovation, expansion, and maintenance of port infrastructures (Wu and Ji, 2013). In this case, climate change influences many countries and regions around the world, including China. There is relevant data suggesting that in forthcoming decades, climate change will lead to a rise in the sea level, a fall in the water level of rivers and lakes, more frequent and serious storms, and an increase in extreme temperatures and weather in China (Chen and Yao, 2010; National Development and Reform Commission, 2016; Wu and Ji, 2013). Thus, climate change is likely to pose huge impacts on Chinese port facilities and operations. In China, extreme weather caused by climate change could generate considerable economic loss (Wu and Ji, 2013) and produce direct impacts on resources and ecological environment (Wang et al., 2017). However, as mentioned, research about climate impact and adaptation strategies among Chinese ports is currently rather scarce.

21.4 Research findings

As mentioned in the introduction, many recent studies have investigated the potential impact posed by climate change on port stakeholders in China. However, some questions still need further study. For example, do port stakeholders in China recognize the impacts posed by climate change on respective port and terminals operations and other activities? In addition, what plans and actions are being implemented in respective ports or terminals so as to assure effective mitigation and adaptation strategies? How do port stakeholders balance between mitigation and adaptation strategies? The findings from the case studies and interviews are structured in terms of the following issues:

- major climate change variables that affect the port stakeholders;
- climate impacts on supply chains;
- impact posed by climate change on operation or business activities of port stakeholders;
- climate change adaptation plans;
- comparison between adaptation and mitigation strategies.

21.4.1 Major climate change variables that affect the port region

The climate variables faced by different port stakeholders are slightly different from each other. In general, the most significant climate variables are rainfall and storms, dry seasons, and high temperatures. Heavy rainfalls and storm surge create typhoons and flooding, while dry seasons can lower water levels. Finally, high temperature can cause difficulties in operating activities. In this case, dry seasons will only impact ports or terminals that are not "deep-water" ports. The ports and terminals that are located in some heavily polluted cities (e.g., Shanghai) are also concerned about the increasing intensity of haze. Heavy rainfalls and storm surge can lead to land inundation. The views of policymakers, industrial practitioners, and port planners about these variables correspond to the report of the Intergovernmental Panel on Climate Change by Yasuaki et al. (2013), who note that the numbers of warm days and nights have increased in the past decades and are expected to continue to increase in the foreseeable future, as is the heat wave frequency. Their views are also consistent with the climate change assessment report of China that the annual average temperature has increased by ~0.5–0.8°C and the coastal sea level annual average has had an increase rate of 2.5mm in the past five decades. In terms of future impacts from climate change, most port stakeholders tend to focus on these impacts with anecdotal concerns, as well as reports or instructions from the Chinese Meteorological Administration on increased intensity and frequency of rainfalls or typhoons creating storm surge or inundation which might lead to the damage of goods in containers, port infrastructures, and other facilities. On the contrary, lower water levels or changes in tide are not treated as real concern for deep-water ports and terminals (e.g., Hongkong International Terminals).

Overall, port stakeholders in China expect hotter climates in most coastal regions with storm surges with higher extremes and frequencies. Still, the actual impacts remain largely uncertain. In addition, most of them believe that studies of predictions or forecasting about climate change and impacts are necessary and would be helpful for their operation and business activities.

21.4.2 Climate impacts on supply chains of freight

Climate change does not only impact ports or terminals, but also related business stakeholders, and other nodes along the supply chains. The interview questions in this section are separated into two aspects (ports and supply chains). Also, answers are divided into two groups based on the stakeholders that interviewees came from: 1) ports and terminals; 2) other port stakeholders. Understanding this, the questions can be analyzed through a comprehensive aspect.

The impacts posed by climate change on supply chains that flow through respective ports and other port stakeholders have been investigated. First, all interviewees agree that ports and terminals are important nodes of global supply chains. In terms of shipping lines and supply chain, interviewees include both the operators from the ports or terminals and the stakeholders which relate to ports or terminals, so questions were asked on how climate change might impact their business, while further questions were posed on whether there would be any implication for how cargoes would move along transportation systems considering the potential impacts of climate change.

Among their responses, we found that flooding, storm surge, and server heat are common impacts. Interviewees from port and terminals point out that the roads and railways which connect to ports can be easily damaged because of storm surge. In addition, extreme heat and cold (e.g., snow storms in China in 2008) can lead to the delay of the shipping of cargoes that in turn can lead to significant economic loss and depreciation of value of time-sensitive goods. Furthermore, the impacts on major roads and rail tracks can cause a loss of connection with very important partners, as many original routes would become impassable. In terms of cargo shipping between ports and terminals, many interviewees raised their concern on the consequential congestion of vessels which can affect planned throughputs via their ports and terminals. The major concerns for the interviewees which corporate with the port or terminals were fines due to congestion and delays in cargo shipping.

21.4.3 Impact posed by climate change on port operation

Interviewees were also asked to consider how climate change has already impacted or might impact on their ports and terminals or, for the stakeholders who have related business with ports and terminals, operations or other business activities.

The general impacts of climate change on the ports or terminals based on the climate variables discussed above are damage to facilities, notably containers, cranes, and warehouse. Sometimes, these impacts can also lead to human casualties (due to accidents). Moreover, economic loss can be tremendous when the extreme impacts posed by climate change happen to these terminals and ports. Quoting one interviewee who was the vice-president of a private terminal company:

> Last year, we experienced an unexpected typhoon which is so strong that nearly no one can stand outside. The sky suddenly became dark without an omen. Many containers were damaged and even some of the crane scrapped. More than millions of dollars of economic loss because of this unexpected typhoon. We are small business compared with other port stakeholders, so this economic loss resulted in a long time for us to recover.

Besides the damage caused by the extreme climate variables, several interviewees proposed that more proactive changes in the maintenance are expected. Facilities in ports and terminals located in salt water zones where the wind and water contain corrosive elements are especially vulnerable. Also, interviewees point out that there is a need for additional maintenance routines, including anti-corrosive measures to protect the facilities in these ports and terminals. Moreover, port stakeholders located in the south of China report that they are seasonally affected by typhoons. As mentioned above, the delay in shipping, congestion of vessels in ports and terminals, and stoppages are anticipated as the major outcomes of increasing intensity and frequency of typhoons. In addition, the number of days that ports along the southern Chinese coastline need to close and suspend operations due to typhoons is significantly higher than in the past.

Extreme heat also impacts on the daily operation of ports and terminals. In China, many port operations are generally supplemented by human labour, and usually for 24 hours of three consecutive operations and cargo space displacement. Interviewees mention that this does not only increase the maintenance practices of the facilities but also the safety risks for dock workers. Extreme heat can cause heatstroke. Other issues are related to lower water levels caused by dry seasons, which affect the passage of ships, thus increasing maintenance and operating costs of ports and waterways dramatically.

To understand the perception of the impact posed by climate change in a more comprehensive way, interviewees were asked about how they forecast and prepare for extreme weather and climate. Most respond to us that they rely on the notification and forecasting from the China Meteorological Administration. None of the port stakeholders that have been interviewed have a dedicated group/department for the same purpose. In addition, some participants highlight that, hitherto, little has been done on the impact assessment and adaptation of the transportation and port areas.

21.4.4 Climate change adaptation plans and perception

Based on interviewees' responses, there is no doubt that they believe that climate change has a significant impact on Chinese ports. Despite different levels of commitment, more or less each port and terminal has applied at least some adaptation strategies or has corporate plans with the aim to reduce the vulnerability of their ports or terminals to climate change impacts.

In a recently published government report on climate change, it was found that ports and terminals in China are actively involved in climate change issues and some adaptive measures are proposed and implemented (Government of the PRC, 2017). In addition, related policies are highlighted in this report (National Development and Reform Commission, 2016). This illustrates social awareness on strategies coping with impacts posed by climate change and problems in accordance with climate change in the marine environment.

Indeed, all interviewees appear to be aware of potential climate change impacts on ports and terminals and their surrounding regions. However, we need to know whether such awareness has actually been transformed into real actions, as reflected by adaptation plans and strategies. Hence, we further asked interviewees about the necessity and knowledge on adaptation strategies. Interviewees agree that adaptation strategies are necessary for ports and terminals to reduce vulnerability to climate change impacts. However, most of them do not understand or possess the knowledge to implement the adaptation strategies that have been used in other western countries (e.g., the best practice guidance proposed by the United Nations Conference on Trade and Development introduced in 2012). Despite such lack of knowledge, still, most ports and terminals have implemented some adaptation strategies. With this premise, interviewees were asked about existing adaptation strategies.

Enhancing transportation infra- and superstructures was reported as being undertaken by the interviewees to respond to typhoon and flood inundation caused by cyclones and the rise in the sea level. In addition, the elevation of port land is another strategy undertaken by ports and terminals. In some ports and terminals in South China, the first strategy is used to ensure that port and terminal facilities can withstand strong wind caused by typhoons. Increasing the weight of cranes and reinforcing the ability to withstand wind are included in this strategy. The second strategy is used to keep cargoes inside containers dry during inundations and to ensure that the containers are positioned above the highest predicted tidal surge areas and thus cannot be washed to harbours or elsewhere. However, as the Chinese government has policies on the height of port land in certain regions, in most cases the elevation of port land does not elevate the entire port. More specifically, parts of the land are higher than the rest and the containers would stand on higher grounds. This process relocates containers that are carrying critical cargoes (e.g., dangerous goods) to areas above the tidal surge zone. On the other hand, there are no certain answers for the question on whether port and terminal infrastructures, such as wharfs and cranes, should be built even higher so as to adjust to floods in the future. In general, interviewees believe that they would not change existing land height unless related policies implemented by the Chinese government or authentic data prove that it is necessary to do so. Finally, some emergency response plans are adopted to prevent the vessels or containers losing their moorings and becoming adrift in the harbours due to the increase in storm intensity.

Responding to the impact of the increasing number and intensity of hot days, which would lead to the damage of facilities and road surface and to health and safety issues, policies related to hot days are formulated by the Chinese government and each port stakeholder has agreements with hot weather policies. To be more specific, the governments have policies related to hot weather and the ports or terminals' behaviour is based on these policies; they also adopted their own strategies to cope with hot weather depending on each port's situation. In addition, suspension or a longer break time is included in the ports' policy to reduce the extent of potential safety hazard. Quoting an interviewee:

> In summer, this year we give the workers a two- hour break or longer depend on the intensity of the heat at noon to prevent the workers from getting heatstroke.

Another approach adopted by some ports is using an air blower to increase the extent of cross-ventilation. These measures are existing adaptation strategies used by ports and terminals in China. However, more adaptation approaches are proposed by some marine stakeholders or ports in other countries. For example, ports in Australia use cyclone tidal surge and sea level rise flood inundation mapping to protect infrastructures from damage or from being washed away by the high tidal surge (Ng et al., 2013). As mentioned, knowledge and education about climate adaptation strategies is lacking in China. Some respondents point out that improvements are needed because ports and terminals are still in the process of remedial actions after incidents. Thus, we further ask interviewees about the evaluation of existing adaptation strategies and whether more adaptation strategies are required in ports and terminals. Their responses indicate that existing adaptation strategies are necessary and effective, but more adaptation strategies would need more manpower and financial support. In addition, their behaviours are regulated by Chinese government policies, and thus some of the strategies would only be implemented when policies are required. There are some specific reasons that explain this situation. Quoting one interviewee:

> We are under the supervision of the port's office and local government, nearly every action needs to be approved by these departments, especially the approach related to construction.

In addition, whether the reduction of the economic loss due to the impact of climate change is more than the extra financial expenditure for additional adaptation strategies is unknown. Some of the interviewees are also concerned that the existing port facilities are restricted by the design standard and may not be adapted to the impact of sea level rise.

Other port stakeholders that have business or other connections related to ports and terminals agree that the benefits they can gain from the implementation of the adaptation strategies will be a priority when they consider whether they are going to implement adaptation strategies or not. Overall, it appears that while climate change impacts are considered by all the studied port stakeholders, only some adaptation strategies are being implemented. Here one should note that, in certain cases, adaptation plans and strategies (e.g., emergency plans), and their implementation, are not specifically formulated in corporate development or strategic planning. More knowledge and education are required for port stakeholders to better understand climate change impacts and adaptation strategies. Finally, the pursuit of co-benefits is an important driving factor for the adoption of climate change adaptation policies among Chinese ports and terminals.

21.4.5 Comparing the attitude towards mitigation and adaptation measures and strategies

In addition to adaptation, mitigation strategies are also adopted by port stakeholders to reduce global warming and greenhouse gas emission. It is evident from interviewees that mitigation strategies and corporate policies (for instance, the regulations of the People's Republic of China on the prevention and control of marine environmental pollution by the ships of the People's Republic of China and their related activities, and the law on the prevention and control of air pollution in the People's Republic of China)dedicated to reduce the emissions of greenhouse gas have been considered in port and terminal planning. In this study, the interview questions only probed the attitude towards mitigation strategies and the comparison between mitigation and adaptation strategies.

First, all interviewees were asked about the overview of mitigation strategies. All of them agree that mitigation strategies are critical to protect the environment and alleviate global warming. Also, they cite the desire to reduce energy costs and improve environmental conditions. They indicate that the notion of green gas emission reduction is considered as a responsibility. In fact, government policies and international environmental stakeholders require port stakeholders to implement mitigation strategies, otherwise the government would impose punitive actions against them. Quoting one interviewee:

> Energy conservation and emission reduction is the measures that China encourages to take. There are also mandatory requirements for the implementation of energy conservation and emission reduction measures in the construction and approval of construction projects.

A follow-up question was asked about the effectiveness of the mitigation strategies. Both the interviewees from ports and terminals and other port stakeholders say that the outcome of mitigation strategies is difficult to be evaluated because they are mostly long-term strategies. In addition, they indicate that mitigation strategies will be useless if there are only a few stakeholders that are committed to implement them. In spite of the unpredictable results, most interviewees argue that it is the obligation of every individual to reduce greenhouse gas emission so as to protect the environment.

When asked about the comparison between mitigation and adaptation strategies, most interviewees argue that they are of similar importance and do not necessarily conflict with each other. Some port stakeholders also point out that mitigation strategies can help them to gain better reputation, which can result in expanded market share and more financial gains. At the same time, they also believe that adaptation strategies can help port stakeholders to minimize economic loss in the future. In terms of financial concern, questions were asked about the balance of the financial expenditure of these two strategies. In this case, interviewees answer that most adaptation or mitigation strategies are implemented because 1) they believe that it is necessary to do so, and 2) they are required by government policies. They also point out that the implementation of these two strategies would not affect each other because of the financial budget. Because the financial budget is limited, the interview questions asked about the financial balance of these two strategies.

Also, interviewees highlight government regulations in their responses. Interviewees mentioned that the management and governance of most Chinese ports is centrally managed. To be more specific, local authorities are mostly responsible for the management of leading cadres within the ports (Gao and Sun, 2002) and other areas are largely managed by the Chinese national government (Gao and Sun, 2002). Under such circumstances, it was not surprising for local authorities to remain enthusiastic in managing ports (Gao and Sun, 2002). However, many ports in other nations are decentralized or under district management. The policies formulated by the Chinese national government have largely influenced the implementation of climate mitigation and adaptation strategies. For example, they have set the height of port land, protecting the ports from flooding. Local ports or terminals follow the standard height and they would not have reason to further consider the height of the port land. Quoting one interviewee:

> At present, we mainly organize the port design construction according to the national standard. We will keep track of relevant national policies and regulations.

Many interviewees point out that the current implementation of adaptation and mitigation strategies still lacks adequate support from policies and norms, and financial support. In general, it appears that both mitigation and adaptation strategies are considered by all the studied port stakeholders. Moreover, both adaptation and mitigation strategies are considered as equally important and necessary for ports or terminals to implement.

21.5 Discussion and conclusion

This chapter investigates climate adaptation and mitigation strategies and their implementation. The Chinese cases offer a deep insight on how port stakeholders view adaptation and mitigation measures. The findings indicate that port stakeholders are aware of the impacts posed by climate change and most have at least developed some forms of adaptation plans and strategies. However, they do not possess adequate knowledge and education on climate adaptation planning and on the development of related strategies. For instance, none of the studied ports have established a dedicated department, team, or group of employees to deal with climate change-related issues. Having said so, while inadequate knowledge on climate change adaptation might be an issue, their positive attitude and perception towards adaptation to climate change impacts are not in any serious doubt.

Participants disclose similar cognition about climate variables and concerns and prediction about extreme weather events. In this case, interviewees from different ports have slightly different views on climate variables. For instance, ports and terminals in Shanghai have experienced the impacts of haze, which have not been experienced by ports and terminals in southern

China (e.g., those along the Pearl River Delta). For mitigation strategies, the results contrast with Becker et al. (2012). However, they share the view that climate mitigation and adaptation are equally important. In addition, they believe that there are no conflicts existing between them. This aspect is consistent with the view from the literature review that both mitigation and adaptation strategies are needed for port stakeholders to deal with climate change. Thus, further research would certainly benefit port planning and development. One of the barriers for port stakeholders is the lack of reliable prediction about climate change and the evaluation of adaptation strategies. All studied port stakeholders consider budgetary constraints when making development or daily plans. In addition, each port stakeholder can only make plans for the foreseeable future.

A major feature of Chinese port management is that most of its ports are centrally managed, whereas many ports in other nations are decentralized or under district management (Gao and Sun, 2002; Zhang, 2000). Most large ports in China are solely state-owned or Sino-foreign joint ventures, and the latter are only a small number. For example, the Port of Shanghai is operated by 11 solely state-owned companies and three Sino-foreign joint venture companies. This also means that the policies and guidelines from the national government play a crucial role in the ports' operation. To be more specific, every port stakeholder's strategic plan or development plan is designed based on the policy enacted by the government. Most interviewees put forward the notion that regulations and policies implemented by the Chinese government are considered as guidelines when they design their strategies and development plans. Hence, the Chinese government plays a pivotal role in developing adaptation strategies in ports and can be considered as a key criterion when analyzing the attitude and perception of port stakeholders toward adaptation strategies.

Smith et al. (2009) highlighted the neglect of previous literature that mainly focuses on the identification of climate change impact, evaluate both risk and vulnerability, and assessment of adaptation strategies, while only a few research papers pay attention to the impact of adaptation policies formulated by the government, which address problems related to the supporting policy to facilitate the implementation of adaptation strategies and education to encourage managers to learn more about these strategies. The results from this study confirm the importance of the role that the government plays in adaptation decision-making, planning, and implementation. Especially in China, where most major ports or terminals are owned by the state and operated by the national government.

A brief comparison between Hongkong International Terminal and the Port of Zhuhai helps to better understand the difference between a representative of large ports in mainland China and a representative of other private owned ports. The Port of Zhuhai is operated by Zhuhai Port Holdings, which is a wholly state-owned enterprise, whereas HIT is operated by Hutchison Port Holdings, a private holding company incorporated in the British Virgin Islands. Port Law of The People's Republic of China is considered as a guideline for the Port of Zhuhai when the operation managers formulate the developing plan. In this policy, it is clarified that the department of transportation under the state council is in charge of the management of ports throughout the country. In addition to this, the local governments shall, in accordance with the provisions of the state council on the port administration system, determine the management of the ports in the administrative region. All the management decisions and construction should be consistent with standards in the policy and any changes need be reported to the related department in the upper level government to get a permit. The operation managers in the Port of Zhuhai explained as follows:

"Any construction changes and major strategies and plan modifications of the ports operation or developing plan need to reported to the related government department or port authorities to get approved. Financial support from the government is also necessary for us to adapt to the impact posed by climate change."

Based on the Maslow theory, the Chinese port stakeholders still mainly focus on the basic needs of the ports. To be more specific, the benefit of implementation of adaptation is still one of the major concerns for them. On the other hand, government policy and guidelines can help to encourage the stakeholders to learn more about climate change adaptation. In addition to this, the uncertainty about adaptation for ports or terminals could also be reduced by the decision-making techniques provided by the policymakers, which help the managers identify appropriate choices in the face of uncertainties. In this case, we argue that regulations and policies should encourage knowledge creation and better education on climate change impacts. Also, they should effectively help port stakeholders to balance resources and efforts between mitigation and adaptation plans and strategies. Further incentives should be created to facilitate the development of adaptation strategies in port regions. As stated earlier, the implementation of adaptation strategies is still at its embryonic stage. The scarcity of policies as guidelines and adequate incentives, and the lack of education about adaptation and related research studies, are the main barriers for port stakeholders. Support from both the government and related organizations are necessary for the development of effective adaptation strategies.

Based on previous findings, the role of government can be considered as a dominant factor of port adaptation planning. Becker (2016) put forward a collaborative approach which would benefit the adaptation development on ports. He highlighted the importance to take all the stakeholders' perspectives into consideration throughout the whole adaptation process. These stakeholders include every organization from specific ports management companies to nations. He also emphasized that an engagement from every organization, including both internal and external stakeholders, is necessary for the adaptation strategies to ensure success, because adaptation is affected by various factors, including policies, communications with organizations from different sectors and countries, and public engagement (Becker, 2016). Based on the result from the survey and interviews, indeed, adaptation requires support from researches of academic organizations, policymakers, industrial practitioners, interest groups, and other port stakeholders. In the collaborative approach perspective, this concept highlighted the partnership and mutual trust between different stakeholders at a global level from different sectors, countries, and regions to benefit the knowledge transfer and communication within the network.

However, is this collaborative approach also applicable in the situation of the adaptation in the ports of China? The answer is worth discussing. The short cases comparison between the Hongkong International Terminals and the Port of Zhuhai indicated the crucial role that national government plays in the Port of Zhuhai, which is quite different from the circumstances in HIT. In HIT, the government role is the same as or less important than that of the other port stakeholders, while in the Port of Zhuhai, the government is the dominant factor affecting port operation and developing plans. Ports operated by privately held companies (e.g., Hongkong International Terminals) have more autonomous rights. However, in China, the administration authority of the ports' investment management is divided according to subordinate relations and investment volume (Zhang, 2000). The construction projects and operations under the direct and dual leadership ports are directly managed by the central government, and those of local ports and freight terminals are managed according to the different scales of construction. In addition, port investment structures and investment subjects are under the general port management policy in China (Zhang, 2000). The amount of the funds needed for port construction and operation is substantial. Although the Chinese government encourages various sources of investments, the fact is that the investment is government's monopoly and the operation of ports is port authority's monopoly due to strict planning management and conditions.

More specifically, the part of investment and operation of other private organizations or companies is still limited (Zhang, 2000). As we can see, due to different governance systems, when applying the collaborative approach to the Chinese ports, government intervention and policy regulation should be considered as the priority to facilitate adaptation implementation.

The chapter provides an overview of the attitude of port stakeholders towards climate change and analyzes some possible explanations. At the same time, recognition of impacts posed by climate change calls for port stakeholders to pay attention to the knowledge and assessment of climate change impacts. Based on the research findings, we believe that all the factors included in this study can partly impact the attitudes of port stakeholders. Some of the advantages to calling port stakeholders to highlight the impacts posed by climate change can be based on these factors. For example, policymakers can formulate climate change-related policy to inform port stakeholders of the importance of responding to the impact posed by climate change. The results showing that port stakeholders do not believe that adaptation strategies are effective indicate that more efforts are required to encourage port stakeholders to implement climate adaptation strategies. In addition, current management and planning need to be transformed to respond to climate change. Practical suggestions are provided in the paper that can be considered as reference for the decision-makers in port stakeholders and related organizations when they analyze the climate change impact. This study applies two theories – ambiguity effect and hyperbolic discounting – and these two theories are partially confirmed. Indeed, to the best of our knowledge, this study is a pioneer in using these two theories to explain the attitudes of port stakeholders.

Based on this study, further research can apply these theories more frequently in analyzing organizations' attitudes towards climate change or strategies in the context of climate change. In addition, this study investigates the general attitude of port stakeholders towards climate change and some possible impact factors are verified. Further study can consider this thesis as a platform to further investigate the reasons that port stakeholders hold this attitude.

This study is as an attempt to systematically investigate the attitude and perception of stakeholders on climate change adaptation. It highlights the importance of government policies towards the development of adaptation strategies in ports in the Chinese context. One should remind policymakers and managers in port stakeholders of the necessity of implementing adaptation strategies and the risk posed by climate change that they may face in the future. The limitations include the small sample size and that some investigations are undertaken at a relatively preliminary stage. A larger sample size should be used in future research. Moreover, more detailed comparisons between mitigation and adaptation strategies can be undertaken. Having said so, we believe that this chapter offers a decent platform for further research.

Acknowledgements

This study is supported by the Social Science and Humanities Research Council of Canada (SSHRC)'s Insight Grant (no. 435-2017-0735).

References

Becker, A. (2016). The state of climate adaptation for ports and the way forward. In: Ng, A.K.Y., Becker, A., Cahoon, S., Chen, S.L., Earl, P., & Yang, Z. (Eds.) *Climate Change and Adaptation Planning for Ports*. New York, NY: Routledge, pp. 265–274.

Becker, A.H., Acciaro, M., Asariotis, R., Cabrera, E., Cretegny, L., Crist, P., ... & Velegrakis, A.F. (2013). A note on climate change adaptation for seaports: A challenge for global ports, a challenge for global society. *Climatic Change, 120*(4), 683–695. https://doi.org/10.1007/s10584-013-0843-z

Becker, A., Inoue, S., Fischer, M., & Schwegler, B. (2012). Climate change impacts on international seaports: Knowledge, perceptions, and planning efforts among port administrators citation/publisher attribution. *Journal of Environmental Law and Policy, 110*, 5–29. https://doi.org/10.1007/s10584-011-0043-7

Bierling, D. & Lorented, P. (2008). Ports and climate change: perceptions and planning practice. In: *2008 Texas Ports and Waterways Conference*, Galveston, TX: Texas Transportation Institute.

Chen, Y. & Yao, T. (2010). Global warming and a new stage of world ports. *Modern Business, 35*.

Gao, H. & Sun, J. (2002). The reference unction of the typical port management system in the world to China's port system reform. *Journal of Waterborne Transportation Institute, 12*(4).

Gillen, D. (2001). Public Capital, productivity, and the linkages to the economy: Transportation infrastructure. *Building the Future: Issues in Public Infrastructure in Canada*, 36–72.

Government of the PRC (2017). *2017 China's Policies and Actions for Addressing Climate Change*. Beijing, China PR: Government of the PRC.

Hallegatte, S., Ranger, N., Mestre, O., Dumas, P., Corfee-Morlot, J., Herweijer, C., & Wood, R.M. (2011). Assessing climate change impacts, sea level rise and storm surge risk in port cities: A case study on Copenhagen. *Climatic Change, 104*(1), 113–137. https://doi.org/10.1007/s10584-010-9978-3

Harley, C.D.G., Randall Hughes, A., Hultgren, K.M., Miner, B.G., Sorte, C.J.B., Thornber, C.S., ... & Williams, S.L. (2006). The impacts of climate change in coastal marine systems: Climate change in coastal marine systems. *Ecology Letters, 9*(2), 228–241. https://doi.org/10.1111/j.1461-0248.2005.00871.x

Intergovernmental Panel on Climate Change. (2014). Summary for policymakers. In: McCarthy, J.J., Canziani, Leary, N.A., & D.J. Dokke, D.J. (Eds.) *Climate Change Impacts, Adaptation and Vulnerability (contribution of working group II to the Fourth Assessment Report of the Intergovernmental Panel on Climate Change)*. Cambridge, United Kingdom and New York, New York: Cambridge University Press.

Kelly, P.M. & Adger, W.N. (2000). Theory and practice in assessing vulnerability to climate change and facilitating adaptation. *Climatic Change, 47*(4), 325–352. https://doi.org/10.1023/A:1005627828199

Klein, R.J., Huq, S., Denton, F., Downing, T.E., Richels, R.G., Robinson, J.B., & Toth, F.L. (2007). Inter-relationships between adaptation and mitigation. In C. Parry, M.L., Canziani, O.F., Palutikof, J.P., van der, Linden P.J., Hanson C.E (Eds.), *Climate Change 2007: Impacts, Adaptation Assessment Report of the Intergovernmental Panel on Climate Change*, pp. 745–777. https://doi.org/10.1007/BF00379720

Lau, Y.Y., Lei, Z., Fu, X., & Ng, A.K.Y. (2012). The implications of the re-establishment of direct links across the Taiwan Strait on the aviation industries in Greater China. *Research in Transportation Economics, 35*, 3–12.

Lau, Y.Y., Rodrigue, J.P., & Ng, A.K.Y. (2015). Villes et logistique en Chine. In: Dablanc, L. & Fremont, A. (Eds) *La métropole logistique: le transport de marchandises et le territoire des grandes villes*. Paris: Armand Colin, pp. 235–250.

Lemmen, D.S., Warren, F.J., Lacroix, J., & Bush, E. (2008). *From Impacts to Adaptation: Canada in a Changing Climate*. Ottawa: Government of Canada. https://doi.org/10.1029/2005GL024234

Meng Yan. (2014). Chinese port: development in transformation of thought. *Chinese Ports*, (2), 4–4.

National Development and Reform Commission. (2016). *Chinese Policies and Actions for Addressing Climate Change*. Beijing.

Ng, A.K.Y. and John, L. (2014), *Port-focal Logistics and Global Supply Chains*. Basington: Palgrave Macmillan.

Ng, A.K.Y., Becker, A., Cahoon, S., Chen, S.-L., Earl, P., & Yang, Z. (2016). Time to act: The criticality of ports in adapting to the impacts posed by climate change. In: *Climate Change and Adaptation Planning for Ports*, 1st ed., New York: Routledge. pp. 1–23.

Ng, A.K.Y., Chen, S.L., Cahoon, S., Brooks, B., & Yang, Z. (2013). Climate change and the adaptation strategies of ports: The Australian experiences. *Research in Transportation Business and Management, 8*, 186–194. https://doi.org/10.1016/j.rtbm.2013.05.005

Ng, A.K.Y., Zhang, H., Afenyo, M., Becker, A., Cahoon, S., Chen, S.L., Esteben, M., Ferrari, C., Lau, Y.Y., Lee, P.T.W., Monios, J., Tei, A., Yang, Z., & Acciaro, M. (2018). Port decision-maker perceptions on the effectiveness of climate adaptation actions. *Coastal Management 46*(3), 148–175.

Prowse, T.D., Furgal, C., Chouinard, R., Melling, H., Milburn, D., & Smith, S. (2009). Implications of climate change for economic development in northern Canada: Energy, resource, and transportation sectors. *A Journal of the Human Environment, 38*(5), 272–281.

Schneider, S.H., S. Semenov, A. Patwardhan, I. Burton, C. H. D., Magaza, M., Oppenheimer, A. B., Pittock, A., Rahman, J. B., Smith, A., ... & F. Yamin. (2007). Chapter 19: Assessing key vulnerabilities and the risk from climate change. In: Parry, M.L., Canziani, O.F., Palutikof, J.P., van der Linden P.J., & Hanson, C.E. (Eds.) *Climate Change 2007: Impacts, Adaptation and Vulnerability. Contribution of Working Group II to* the Fourth Assessment Report of the Intergovernmental Panel on Climate Change (p. 976). Cambridge, UK: Cambridge University Press.

Smith, J. B., Vogel, J. M., & Cromwell III, J. E. (2009). An architecture for government action on adaptation to climate change. An editorial comment. Climatic Change, 95(1–2), 53–61.

Tang, O., Lau, Y.Y., Tam, K.C., & Ng, A.K.Y. (2014). A critical review of the evolution of the maritime code in the People's Republic of China. Asian Geographer, 31(2), 115–127.

Wang, J.J., & Ng, A.K.Y. (2011). The geographical connectedness of Chinese seaports with foreland markets: A new trend? Tijdschrift voor Economische en Sociale Geografie, 102(2), 188–204.

Wang, L., Notteboom, T., Lau, Y.Y., & Ng, A.K.Y. (2017). Functional differentiation and sustainability: A new stage of development in the Chinese container port system. Sustainability, 9, 328–345.

Wu, X. D., & Ji, L. (2013). Research on the impact of climate change on the port of China and the countermeasures. China Water Transport, 10, 116–118.

Yasuaki Hijioka, Lin, E., & Pereira, J.J. (2013). Asia. In: Perez R. & Takeuchi K. (Eds.) Climate change 2013: the physical science basis: Working Group I contribution to the Fifth assessment report of the Intergovernmental Panel on Climate Change. New York, NY: Cambridge University Press, pp. 1327–1370. https://doi.org/10.1017/CBO9781107415386.004

Zhang, J. (2000). Comparison and reference – World and China port management system. World Shipping, (3), 10–13.

Index

For Product Safety Concerns and Information please contact our EU
representative GPSR@taylorandfrancis.com
Taylor & Francis Verlag GmbH, Kaufingerstraße 24, 80331 München, Germany

www.ingramcontent.com/pod-product-compliance
Ingram Content Group UK Ltd.
Pitfield, Milton Keynes, MK11 3LW, UK
UKHW011456240425
457818UK00022B/866